£25
£19

CW01429689

SOCIAL LIFE

AT THE

ENGLISH UNIVERSITIES

IN THE

EIGHTEENTH CENTURY.

Cambridge:
PRINTED BY C. J. CLAY, M.A.
AT THE UNIVERSITY PRESS.

SOCIAL LIFE

AT THE

GLISH UNIVERSITIES

IN THE

EIGHTEENTH CENTURY.

'*Celebrare domestica facta.*'—Hor.

COMPILED BY

RISTOPHER WORDSWORTH, M.A.,

FELLOW OF PETER-HOUSE,
AND SOMETIME A SCHOLAR OF TRINITY COLLEGE,
IN CAMBRIDGE.

CAMBRIDGE:
DEIGHTON, BELL, AND CO.
LONDON: GEORGE BELL AND SONS.
1874.

PREFACE.

THE following pages are the result of several months' miscellaneous reading of the ephemeral literature and of the biographies which bear upon Social Life in the English Universities during the eighteenth century.

That so portly a volume is now sent out into the world, is due partly to the inexperience of the compiler, in part to the interest which he could not fail to feel even in the minute and comparatively trivial particulars of the life of those who, in earlier generations and very different times, had passed through the same stages through which he was passing; in a measure also to the circumstances under which the first instalment of the work was written, as a prize competition to be completed by a fixed date; and in no slight degree to the abundance of material which the libraries poured forth.

It was hoped that the end proposed by the authorities of our University in their choice of a subject for the   e Bas Essay in 1871, viz. *University*

L. B...   *b*

Life and Studies in England during the Eighteenth Century, would be more easily attained through the existence of such a collection as the present, and of the materials gathered for the two remaining sub-divisions of the subject which are mentioned on page 4:—for where the supply of information is so great, and at the same time lies so much in the dust of pamphlets and books of little general interest, it would seem to require the familiar study of many years to justify even an expert historian in undertaking to give an intelligent and trustworthy view of the times: a view, that is, in which ideas and theories should be presented to the reader with that assumption of a right of judgment which only long experience can claim.

In the present instance the old materials have been, as it were, carted to a clear spot, and the reader may re-construct for the home of his academic ancestors prison or nursery, hut or palace, as each loose stone tells its own history to him: or else he must look for some skilled architect, or be content to wait till the carter has learnt mason's work.

In order that the pile of materials may not utterly appal or deter from the work of construction, a TABLE OF CONTENTS has been furnished for the purpose of indicating the nature of the materials which make up the heap, and shewing the method in which they are arranged; where it may be seen that they have not been shot as mere rubbish in disregard of future usefulness.

It remains for the compiler to express his thanks to the following gentlemen, without whose help the work would have been more imperfect than it is. The Reverend Henry Wilkinson Cookson, D.D., Master of Peterhouse or Saint Peter's College, and Vice-Chancellor of the University of Cambridge; Henry Bradshaw, Esquire, M.A., Fellow of King's College and University Librarian; The Reverend Henry Octavius Coxe, M.A., of Corpus Christi College, Oxford, and Bodley's Librarian; The Reverend William Magan Campion, D.D., Tutor of Queens' College; The Reverend Henry Richards Luard, M.A., Fellow of Trinity College and Registrary of the University; The Reverend John Eyton Bickersteth Mayor, M.A., senior Fellow of Saint John's College and Professor of Latin, who has kindly assisted while the sheets have been passing through the press; J. Bass Mullinger, Esquire, M.A., of Saint John's College (who in his recent work on the *Early History of the University of Cambridge* and of European education, has already restored the more ancient portion of the structure, whose *débris* of later workmanship still need a master-hand to call them up before the sight of this our generation); The Reverend John William Nutt, M.A., Fellow of All Souls' College, Sublibrarian of the Bodleian; The Reverend

b 2

Richard Shilleto, M.A., Fellow of Peterhouse; and the Compiler's brother, with other friends. All of whom, though in no way responsible for the errors of this volume, have by different acts of kindness contributed to its completion.

From the nature of the work the debt due to authors of books is very great: such authorities as Mr Cooper's *Annals of Cambridge*, Dr Bliss' *Reliquiae Hearnianae*, and Professor Mayor's additions to *Baker's History of St John's College Cambridge*, have been used unsparingly. The Compiler hopes that the references given by him in the text and notes may be accepted as a grateful acknowledgment of the assistance which he has received from these and many other writers.

TABLE OF CONTENTS.

[1] The arabic numerals inclosed in marks of parenthesis, (545) and upwards, refer
to additional illustrations or comments contained in the pages of Appendices and
Notes at the end of this Volume.

* In the last paragraph on p. 59, *for the words* 'two months earlier,' *read* 'in March, 1729.'

(1) The TRIPOS[1], called

(2) The PRAEVARICATOR, or Varier, called

---

[1] The history of our Cambridge term TRIPOS, as equivalent to 'honour examination,' is curious and interesting.

   (1) The B.A., who sat on a *three-legged stool* (pp. 211, 227) to dispute with the 'Father' in the philosophy schools on Ash-Wednesday, was called Mr Tripos, from that on which he sat.

   (2) The satirical speech made by him (pp. 219, 220) was called the *Tripos-speech:* and

   (3) His humorous verses distributed by the bedels were called *Tripos-verses*.

   (4) His office became obsolete in the last century; and similar verses being still circulated by authority each *sheet of verses* was called 'a *Tripos*,' or 'Tripos Paper' (*Gradus ad Cantab.* ed. 1803).

   (5) On the back of each sheet after the year 1748 a *list* of 'Wranglers' and 'Senior Optimes,' or of 'Junior Optimes' (*Gradus ad Cantab.* ed. 1824). These lists were called the 'Triposes,' or first and second 'Tripos lists' (pp. 210, 255).

   (6) The mathematical *examination*, whose interest centered in this list, was called the Tripos.

   (7) When other 'honour examinations' were instituted they were distinguished as the 'classical tripos,' &c. from the 'mathematical tripos.'

INTRODUCTORY.

AFTER laying down such a book as Izaak Walton's *Memoirs of George Herbert* or Bishop Monk's *Life of Bentley*, we naturally put to ourselves the question: whether, if we had our choice, we should prefer the times in which either of them lived to our own days.

Such a comparison is not unprofitable as an exercise of the Affections or the Imagination; but it has a distinct value with reference to our own Conduct and Opinions at the present time.

It is true, no doubt, that most of us are inclined to dwell with pleasure upon the lively Chronicles of the post-Elizabethan Age; and to recoil from the deathlike Effigies of the Eighteenth Century, when the Spirit of Chivalry seems dead, and the Christian Life paralysed and obscured. And in our days, when men's minds are fixed upon the Present almost to the exclusion of what is Past or Future from the range of their view, we can hardly do wrong in encouraging in ourselves and others the Contemplation of the Seventeenth Century, and of still remoter times.

Nevertheless the student of history must not neglect those periods which *seem* to him uninteresting. *Without interest* no period of history can ever be in its relation to that which has followed it or is to follow; since the darkest and even the blankest pages of history can never be blotted out or removed without destroying the Unity and Continuity of the whole. The sons cannot wholly do the fathers' work : much less can they undo it ;—even though that work be Idleness.

And if this be true of the study of Ecclesiastical History (as Professor *Westcott* teaches us), it is a principle no less to be observed in reviewing that most important section of the great educational question of the day; the Condition and Proper Destiny of our Universities.

In examining the pile of different parts which compose the architectural whole of the University Structure, we must not be content with fixing our eyes upon the point towards which the lines converge (a point still enveloped in the dim mysterious distance), nor yet with taking a bird's-eye view from the high places of Philosophy.

> despicere unde queas alios, passimque uidere
> errare atque uiam palantis quaerere uitae,
> certare ingenio, contendere nobilitate,
> noctis atque dies niti praestante labore
> ad summas emergere opes rerumque potiri.

In addition to these, and in order to complete our fore-shortened sketch of past and present, there is need to make, at intervals in the length, Transverse Sections from which to gather the general condition of the Societies in each stage of their development. In a word, we must contemplate the parts in their Solidarity as well as in their Continuity.

Any attempt to take such a view of the condition of our Universities in the Eighteenth Century, must, except in the hands of the practised Historian, be at present partial and of doubtful success. The Life of that Age is not as yet consolidated into History; and for that reason there will be gaps and doubtful tints in our Chart of the Section.

At present we must content ourselves with hoping that the day will soon come when some diligent Lover of Truth will piece together the later history of our Universities from the Pamphlets of a Pamphleteering Age.

Such a work would be unquestionably a most important assistance in grappling with difficulties which now beset us. It would, I believe, enable us to see in many cases the causes of neglect from which Disease moral, religious, and political has spread in our great educational bodies, and so, since the importance of the Universities has increased,

in patriam populumque fluxit.

At the same time we should, I believe, learn to our profit that, whereas we are apt to boast of our Advancement and to despise our forefathers in the last century, many (if not most) of those Educational and Constitutional Movements in which the Party of Progress in our Universities are now most interested, had been suggested or elaborated by persons or by important minorities long before we ourselves were born.

Such a *history* is however beyond the scope of the following compilation.

The Method proposed is to take the different topics severally which relate to the *University Life and Studies in* England *during the Eighteenth Century* under these three heads:

1. SOCIAL LIFE. This division contains remarks upon the Political and Moral Condition of the Universities; the Mutual Relations of different classes of their members; the Amusements, the Discipline; with some account of Proposals for Reform put forward at the time.

This part only has been completed in the present volume. The Elements of the two following are already *in solution* in my Note Books, but are not as yet *precipitated* upon Paper as Copy for the Press.

2. The INDIVIDUAL STUDIES pursued in the University Curriculum, or advanced by the efforts of private Students: the Tools and Helps afforded them, or needed by them, as Libraries, Editions, Scientific Apparatus, and Laboratories. This division of the sketch should treat of some of that second class of Instruments to the advancement of learning mentioned by Bacon at the commencement of the second book '*de augmentis scientiarum;*' while the first division is devoted to the Workshop and the Men ('*litterarum sedes*'—'*personae eruditorum*') in their relation to the common weal.

As an appendage to the Studies, should follow some account of the proceeding to Degrees, and of the early University Calendars.

3. The RELIGIOUS LIFE in its personal and social aspects.

PART I.

SOCIAL LIFE.

King George observing with judicious eyes
The state of both his Universities,
To Oxford sent a troop of horse; and why?
That learned body wanted loyalty.
To Cambridge books he sent, as well discerning
How much that loyal body wanted learning.

The King to Oxford sent a troop of horse,
For Tories own no argument but force;
With equal skill to Cambridge books he sent,
For Whigs admit no force but argument.

'EVERYTHING'—says Hartley Coleridge[1], in his Life
of Dr Richard Bentley—'everything in England
takes the shape and hue of politics.' If this was
true of the country in the earlier half of the present
century, it was so pre-eminently at the Universities in
the Eighteenth.

The Civil War in the days of King Charles I. had
spread so widely over the country that it was almost
impossible for any man, much more for any woman,
to abstain from espousing earnestly that cause which
appeared to have the better claim to advantage or to
right. And if the horrors of civil broils and the sour
tyranny of a body more imperious than one man
could be, made many no longer unwilling to welcome

[1] *Northern Worthies*, p. 151.

back the exiled Prince ; yet, after the disturbing influences of a luxurious reign, the infatuation of King James roused the dormant indignation of his subjects; the succession, which by a prudent and a sober king might have been established to the welfare of the nation, was violently interrupted, and England was once more the scene of faction and distress.

It would perhaps have been difficult to augur on which side the sister Universities would place themselves. Many Colleges in each had given their plate and their men to further the good cause. The words of Dr Bliss[1] will apply to Cambridge, as well as to Oxford, of which he is writing; witness the pages of Mercurius Rusticus, and the acts of the Earl of Manchester.

'They had been despoiled of their property, ejected from their livings and subjected to every injury and insult at the hands of a rabble who thought themselves reformers, but had no other aim than their own advancement and the plunder of those which had anything to lose. Can we wonder at the popularity with which Charles II. ascended his father's throne, or be surprised that Hearne and those who thought with him still adhered in the following reign to the race of the Stuarts?' They had suffered for the king and they had suffered with him. Was not that enough to make them faithful? For the loyalty of benefactors is most loyal; they engender affection, the offspring of adoptive parents. But the second Charles in the gaiety of the court often played the

---

[1] *Reliquiae Hearnianae*, III. Appendix I. pp. 188, 189.

part of Pharaoh's chief butler to those who had restored him to his liberty, and to his office. Such conduct would make some bitter enemies:—others (like the dog who does not hate his master for the blow or cruel word) would increase in loyalty; their sense of duty and of chivalry becoming stronger with their sense of the difficulty of maintaining them.

Then came the trial of conscience. King James in his ardour for Romanism, and urged on perhaps by a suspicion that he had but little time wherein to advance his cause, by attempts to an exertion of arbitrary power in either University struck with his own hand two fatal blows to the security of his throne[1].

At Oxford upon the death of Dr Clarke in 1687 a mandamus was received from the king by the Fellows of Magdalene College to elect Mr Anthony Farmer, a man of no good character and a Papist, to the vacant Presidency. But the Fellows of Magdalene stood firm. They proceeded statutably to elect Dr Hough—who (as we learn from Hearne's diary[2]) only agreed to hold the Presidency against the king's mandamus when Dr Baptiste Levinz, bishop of Man, withdrew. The Fellows were summoned to Whitehall. James could no longer insist upon the election of one of such notoriety as his nominee; he therefore issued

---

[1] Burnet's *Own Time*, III. 139, ed. Oxon. 1823 (= I. 697, *sqq.* folio ed.). On the great influence of the Universities in the country, at the end of the 17th cent., see Macaulay's *Hist.* ch. viii.

[2] *Reliquiae Hearnianae*, III. 167.

another mandamus for the election of Dr Parker. But the king had shewn his weakness, and the Fellows knew their strength lay in doing their duty.

They bore the unkingly conduct of their sovereign, who came to Christ Church Hall and rated them in person. Dr Hough was deprived, and the door of his presidential lodgings broken open by the servants of the Commission: for no Oxford blacksmith could be induced to do the deed. Twenty-five Fellows were expelled and most of the Demies followed their example. The college servants also suffered and acted boldly for their masters.

'Already' (writes Lord Macaulay of the year 1687) 'had University College been turned by Obadiah Walker into a Roman Catholic seminary. Already Christ Church was governed by a Roman Catholic Dean. Mass was already said in both those Colleges. The tranquil and majestic city, so long the stronghold of monarchical principles, was agitated by passions which it had never before known. The undergraduates, with the connivance of those who were in authority over them, hooted the members of Walker's[1] congregation and chanted satirical ditties under his windows. Some fragments of the serenades which then disturbed the High Street have been preserved. The burden of one ballad ran thus:—

"Old Obadiah sings Ave Maria."

[1] For an anecdote relating to Obadiah Walker, see the quotation from Cibber's *Life* given below. His name is still commemorated in an

'So mutinous indeed was the temper of the University that one of the newly-raised regiments—the same which is now called the Second Dragoon Guards, was quartered at Oxford for the purpose of preventing an outbreak. As a necessary consequence of James's arbitrary proceedings, when in 1688 the insurgents under Lovelace appeared before Oxford, they were received with a hearty welcome. Already some of the heads of the University had dispatched one of their number to assure the Prince of Orange that they espoused his cause, and would willingly coin their plate for his service. The Whig chief therefore rode through the capital of Toryism amidst general acclamation, and at the head of a long procession of horse and foot[1].'

Yet the Jesuits had made some way at Oxford, whether by deluding the conscience of the famous Quaker William Penn, or through the pervert Master of University, Obadiah Walker, who had a press in the College for printing unlicensed books[2].

Oxford had at this critical time a Vice-Chancellor (Dr Gilbert Ironside of Wadham) worthy of the men of

'Maudlin, Magdalen, or Magdalene.'

He could answer the king with dignity, yet without for-

admonition to pass the wine, which is, I am told, traditional in *the Club* at Oxford—a Society founded in the 18th century.
'Obadiah Walker us'd to say,
"If *you* don't drink, your neighbour *may*."'

[1] Macaulay's *Hist.*, compare Burnet's *Own Time*, III. 321, 331 = folio ed. I. 793, 798.

[2] Cp. the passage from Cibber's *Life* quoted below. Dr Sykes' *Letters to Dr Charlett of Univ. Coll. in* 1687. *Letters from the Bodleian* (1813), Vol. I. No. xvi. foll.

---

getting the obedience which he owed to the royal command in all things lawful[1]. It was he who prudently answered a captious question put to him by one who was sent to test the willingness of the University to confer the degrees of D.D. and LL.B. on persons nominated by the king[2].

Our Cambridge also had brooked the royal displeasure by withstanding an attempt to set aside her laws, when the king would have forced her to admit Alban Francis, a Benedictine monk, to the Degree of M.A. without his taking the oaths[3]. The Vice-Chancellor (Dr Peachell) was deposed, but still the University persisted, and Father Francis was rejected. And for king James himself, 'it is not too much' (says the now Master of Jesus College Cambridge) 'to say that the following out of those designs cost him his throne[4].'

[1] *Letters from the Bodleian*, I. pp. 35, 36.

[2] In 1711 (Nov. 19) there came a mandate from Queen Anne 'to make Mr Nicholas Sanderson (a blind man from his infancy, but who had taught Mathematicks in Christ's College about 4 years) Master of Arts. It did not command, but only recommended him; and yet he was immediately admitted and created without reading any grace for it. 20. He was chosen Mathematick Professor in the room of Mr Whiston, who was expell'd for Heresy.' *Diary of Edw. Rud*, p. 7. Camb. 1860, ed. Rev. H. R. Luard.

[3] See a Pamphlet in the Bodleian Library (Gough, Cambr. 103). 'The *Cambridge* Case, being an exact narrative of all the Proceedings against the Vice-Chancellour and Delegates of that University, for refusing to admit *Alban Francis* a Benedictine Monk to the Degree of Master of Arts, without taking the Oaths. London, Printed and are to be Sold by *Randal Taylor* near *Stationers' Hall*. 1689.' (pp. 16.)

[4] *Brief Historical notices of the interference of the Crown with the affairs of the English Universities*, by G. Elwes Corrie, B.D., Fellow and Tutor of St Catharine's Hall, and Norrisian Professor, Cambridge, 1839. p. 85.

Then stood forth the seven Bishops and spoke the mind of the country, seeing how dangerous were the encroachments of the papal court to the stability of the English Church and State. Here be nine Worthies, viz. *William Sancroft, Abp Cant., of Emman. Coll. *Camb.*, William Lloyde of St Asaph, of Oriel and Jesus Coll. *Oxon.*, *Thomas Ken of Bath and Wells, of New Coll. *Oxon.*, *Francis Turner of Ely, of New Coll. *Oxon.*, *John Lake of Chichester [S. T. P. per regias literas, *Camb.* 1661], *Thomas White of Peterborough, †William Thomas of Worcester, St John's and Jesus *Oxon.*, *Robert Frampton of Gloucester, C. C. Coll. and Ch. Ch. *Oxon.*, Sir Jonathan Trelawney of Bristol, of Christ Church, *Oxon.* Seven of them were committed to the Tower,[1] and we know with what acclamations their acquittal was welcomed in London—so loud that they forced themselves upon the ear of James. Bishops Thomas and White died in the year 1689 before they had incurred suspension for their refusal to take the Oaths to William. Their colleague Lake lived long enough to be suspended, but anticipated the sentence of deprivation by his death. Ken, whose honest refusal to receive the

* Those marked with an asterisk were deprived as non-jurors after the Revolution. † Bishop Thomas was suspended, but did not live to be deprived, see Wood's *Fasti*, Bliss, IV. 264. Trelawney alone, the darling of Cornwall, joined the Bishop of London in inviting over the Prince of Orange. He had opposed James almost as soon as he took his seat in the House of Lords. (Wood, Bliss.) That king advanced him to Exeter in the following September, and King William confirmed the appointment. Mr Palin's *History of the Church of England*, 1851, p. 65.

[1] The first six and Trelawney.

mistress of Charles the Second had won from the
merry monarch his important charge[1], was now left
with his dear friend and old fellow-student Turner to
head those disinterested and conscientious men who
could not transfer their allegiance.

It was not till after an unsuccessful attempt towards
the comprehension of Protestant Dissenters[2] (which
was rendered abortive by the change of Government),
that Archbishop Sancroft with his brethren were
brought into conflict with the new king.

We may *now* perhaps, in commenting upon the
history of those who refused to take the oaths, be
inclined to the opinion that after the breathing-time
of the interregnum and the vote of the two houses of
Parliament, the clergy might have all united (as indeed
by far the most of them did) to welcome the Prince of
Orange as their king. If they had done so, much
might have been done towards the harmony of the
Church and of the State, which in a few years became
impossible; when parties had become crystallized,
and party cries familiar to men's tongues, when Dissenters were suspicious of High Churchmen, and
when High Churchmen would not trust the Whigs, nor
even William himself, whose own proposals were a
thousand times more tolerant than the measures of
the Whigs with all their boasted love of toleration.
But whatever may be our regrets, we cannot help

[1] See Introduction to Ken's *Manual of Prayers for Winchester
Scholars*, by the present Bishop of Salisbury, p. vi. Parker, 1860.

[2] See the statements of Dr Wake, delivered at Sacheverell's trial
(when he was Bishop of Lincoln), quoted by Mr Palin, *History of the
Church of England*, p. 34.

admiring the noble firmness of those men who could be loyal and obedient to that other king whom they were not afraid to withstand to the face when he was worthy to be blamed. But which side did the Universities take at the Revolution?

At Cambridge the Thanksgiving Day[1] 'for the deliverance of the nation from Popery and arbitrary power was observed' on Valentine's Day 1688—89, and a sermon preached in St Mary's by Mr [Jo.] Laughton of Trinity. The King William and Queen Mary were proclaimed in Cambridge, the bells rang all the afternoon, and at night there were bonfires. The Vice-Chancellor John Montague, Master of Trinity, entertained the officers at dinner, and afterwards manifested his allegiance, with the Provost of King's and the Masters of Peterhouse and Trinity Hall and other members of the University, in loyal effusions of congratulatory verse.

Yet even a week later[2] so little had parties become consolidated that the University still expected that Archbishop Sancroft would consent to be their Chancellor. On his refusal Charles Seymour, Duke of Somerset, K.G., was elected and held the office until his death in 1748, sixty years later, when he was succeeded by the Duke of Newcastle, who was then High Steward of the University, and of whom we shall have more to say anon.

Oxford too (as we learn from Bishop Burnet[3]) had

---

[1] Cooper's *Annals of Cambridge*, IV. 2. (William and Mary, 1688.)
[2] *Ibid.* 1688—89.
[3] Burnet's *Own Time*, III. 321, 331 (=I. 793. 798, folio ed.).

welcomed the new king. Her indignation against James was justly great, and it was not wonderful that a considerable number of men in the University should be glad to be rid of attempts at tyranny.

Among the clergy, those who maintained their strict adherence to the doctrine that a king could not abdicate, much less be constrained to resign his functions, and that no wrong suffered could compensate an act which they believed not right, 363 were firm even to the losing of their benefices. Of this number the non-jurors residing in the Universities[1] were as follows :

Cambridge.	Oxford.
2 Fellows of Trinity	2 Fellows of Magdalen
1 Scholar ,, ,,	1 Fellow of Queen's
1 Fellow of Queens'	1 ,, ,, All Souls'
3 Fellows of Peterhouse	1 ,, ,, Lincoln
1 Fellow of Magdalen	2 Fellows of Oriel
1 ,, ,, Caius	5 ,, ,, Balliol
28 Fellows of St John's	1 Fellow of Brazennose
2 ,, ,, Catherine Hall	*H. Dodwell*, Professor of History
2 ,, ,, Pembroke Hall	
1 Fellow of Trinity College Hall	

According to the above list the number of non-jurors in the Universities in the reign of William III. was at Cambridge 42, at Oxford only 14. It would be interesting to enquire whether this was the complete case; or whether there were not Colleges where loyalty to James was so strong as to baffle the efforts of intolerance of which King William did not in his own heart approve. The reader will observe

[1] Appendix to Palin's *History of the Church of England.*

the mention of two Fellows of Magdalen College Oxford among the non-jurors, like the bishops merging the sense of personal wrongs in the deep feeling of loyalty to the 'vacating' king. We must not pass over the two Fellows of Trinity College Cambridge and the 'one Scholar of the same,' a brave trio to stand aloof from their many comrades in the royal College whose master as Vice-Chancellor had proclaimed King William. But more noticeable perhaps than all is the fact that a single College (St John the Evangelist's) sent forth a number of non-jurors equal to that produced by all the Colleges of Oxford and the rest of those of Cambridge combined. Thomas Baker was then at his Rectory of Long Newton in the diocese of Durham ; and it was not until the reign of George I. that he was deprived of his fellowship with one-and-twenty others of his College. The list given above therefore does not give a complete catalogue of the members of the Universities who suffered as non-jurors in William's reign[1]. In addition to Baker, there were probably several in the country who, like the elder Bonwicke,

---

[1] *E.g.* We might enquire 'what was the state of the case at St John's College Oxford?' Were there no Jacobites there in May, 1701? Or was the elder Ambrose Bonwicke the only *honest* member of that foundation in the two senses in which that word is used, by Tho. Hearne and less violent partizans? (See *Life of Bonwicke*, ed. 1870, p. 116, l. 32.) It appears that while Dr Gower was Master of St John's, Cambridge (till March, 1710—11), it was possible for a few non-jurors to keep their fellowships by his connivance. (Baker—Mayor, 998.) At Oxford, Nic. Amherst says of the year 1715 or 1716, that 'the oath of allegiance to King *George* is often evaded.' *Terrae Filius*, No. XVII. p. 93.

were deprived as clergymen or schoolmasters rather than as Fellows of Colleges.

The history of Ambrose Bonwicke has become familiar to some of us through the works of his grateful pupil, William Bowyer Esquire, printer, a sizar of St John's College, and of his partner John Nichols, and through his own anonymous account of the martyr, his son Ambrose Bonwicke, which has lately been made accessible and most valuable to us by the labours of Mr John E. B. Mayor of St John's.

The elder Bonwicke had been librarian and was Fellow of St John's College *Oxford*, and Master of the associate School of the Merchant Taylors (elected in 1686). He was at first (June, 1690) allowed to hold the mastership[1] on condition that he resigned his fellowship. A month had not passed before he was molested, and, in spite of the innocency and usefulness of his conduct and the representation of the College in his favour, he was asked whether he had taken the oaths of allegiance; and in thirteen months' time was dismissed from the head-mastership, having 'time till *Michaelmas* next to provide for himselfe[2].' After his ejection he established a private school at Headley[3]. It was in the interval between his

---

[1] In the list of non-jurors given in Palin's *Appendix*, dio. London —'Bonwick, Master of Merchant Taylors' School' fellows 'Jeremy Collyer, some time Lecturer of Grays'-inn.'

I have seen a book (an edition of Macrobius, if I remember right) belonging to the library of St John's Coll. Oxon., and apparently presented by A. Bonwicke.

[2] *Life of A. Bonwicke* (1870), p 116.

[3] *Hist. Reg.*, Wilson 392, quoted by Mr Mayor, *Life of A. Bonwicke*, p. 116.

father's notice of ejection[1] and the time that he and his wife quitted Merchant Taylors, that young Ambrose Bonwicke was born (Sep. 30. 1691), and being removed with the family to Headley he made there great progress in piety and in his studies till he was eleven years old: and after studying in the Merchant Taylors' School, where his father had before been master, for seven years and a half, 'and above six of them in the head form;' he had good hopes to succeed to one of the two vacancies at St John's College in Oxford where his father had been till he declined to take the oaths. Young Ambrose passed the scholarship examination with more than ordinary credit—he was proved to be *facile princeps*, and was complimented by the examiners. But through the malice of some informer it was remembered that when it was his course to read the prayers in school Bonwicke had omitted that for the king, 'a governor whom he thought was not so *de iure* as well as *de facto*[2].' He was questioned on the subject, and when a word might have gained the honour which his family so much desired for him, he would not sacrifice to dishonesty and to ambition, but 'in short answered: "Sir, I could not do it." Upon which the master and several other persons there present, said, It was a very honest answer, the best answer he could give; and one, that he was very sorry for him.'

This happened on Sunday, St Barnabas Day, 1710. The result was that Ambrose was supplanted by two

[1] *Life of A. Bonwicke*, p. 8.   [2] *Life*, p. 14.

2

of his fellow scholars who were less proficient in scholarship than himself, and who could not have been more distinguished for piety and virtue.

His father, an old Oxonian, appears to have thought that his son might not like to go to the College of St John the Evangelist[1] at the sister University. But the youth went home to Headley, and followed the example of his Lord at Nazareth; until the 'Bartholomew Vacation' gave parents and son leisure to travel together to Cambridge, where he was admitted (Aug. 25) to St John's College[2].

There they were not afraid to elect him to an exhibition and afterwards to a scholarship (Nov. 6. 1710), his duty being to wind up the clock. The performance of this office when he was in a weak state of health hastened his early death. Every line of his short biography is full of interest, and we must leave the reader to study it for himself; reserving however some notices of his life for other sections of this Essay, while we now only remark, that we may conclude, from information gleaned from the book (if we might not conjecture it from the existence of such a life), that there were others residing at Cambridge whose conscience (whether right or wrong) led them to adhere to their old allegiance to king James. Such were Ambrose's brother Philip, and their chum who shared the college chamber in common with

---

[1] See a letter from him, Feb. 22, 1709—10. Nichols' *Lit. Anecd.* v. p. 121, n.

[2] *Life*, p. 22, ed. 1870, and notes.

them. Among the elder members of the University were Francis Roper, late a Fellow of St John's[1], who in 1690 was deprived of his stall at Ely and of the rectory of Northwold, Norfolk[2]. He was residing in St John's and reading with pupils in 1711 when he received the news of the death of holy Bishop Ken[3]. This was in the vacancy of the mastership of the College and of the Margaret Professorship of Divinity by the death of Dr Gower, who was succeeded in both offices by Dr R. Jenkin[4]. The new master, though he had resigned his preferment with other non-jurors in 1690, changed his political opinions and took the oaths to Queen Anne in 1711—having been admitted to proceed in Divinity two years before (see *Mayor on Baker*, p. 1006)—feeling perhaps with Sir Matthew Hale, according to the principle of R. Sanderson, that allegiance was not due to a disputed dynasty when the representative of it was no longer in the field. His conduct, however, caused much distress to his old friends[5], and this was heightened by the enforcement of the oaths in virtue of an Act of Parliament passed in his mastership, when 22 Fellows of St John's were ejected 'on the fatal Jan. 21, 1716—17, when the ejected had sinned not by denying,

---

[1] [And his pupil Tho. Browne, a kind friend of the Bonwicke family. *Life of A. B.*, pp. 22, 135, 175, 176.] *Life of A. Bonwicke*, (1870), p. 175.

[2] Palin, *Hist. Ch. England*, Appendix, dio. Norfolk.

[3] *Life of A. Bonwicke*, p. 28, ed. 1870.

[4] *Jenkin* did good work as Margaret Professor by his *Reasonableness of Christianity*. Like *Lardner* he was a forerunner of *Paley*.

[5] Masters' *Life of T. Baker*, p. 34. Camb. 1784.

but merely by declining to affirm the omnipotence
of Parliament to dispense with oaths[1].'

It was on this occasion that gentle Thomas Baker,
author of the MSS. so valuable to the history of the
country and the University, was deprived of his
fellowship.

He was a quiet harmless man, a friend of the whig
Bishop Gilbert Burnet as well as of Tom Hearne
and Dr R. Rawlinson (brother of 'Tom Folio'),
the antiquaries, and one of Ambrose Bonwicke's
'special benefactors[2].' More than this, he was a
religious bible-loving man, as may be seen from his
anonymous pamphlet *'Reflections upon Learning*[3],'
which was published sometime before he could claim
his title *'socius eiectus.'* His diligence and consci-
entiousness in study was unbounded, witness the
fact that he was set upon compiling a laborious

---

[1] Mr Mayor, *Preface to the life of A. Bonwicke*, 1870, p. IX. Cooper
in his *Annals of Camb.* gives the date as Jan. 20. (Following Masters'
Life of Baker, p. 34, who tells us that the ejected were 'to the number
of twenty-two in that College only, whose names are mentioned in App.
to the Life of Kettlewell, p. 33.') Cp. *Mayor's Baker*, p. 1008.

[2] Letter of A. Bonwicke senior to his wife on the publication of the
Pattern for young Students (the life of his son), quoted in Mayor's
notes to the *Life*, p. 136.

[3] See Travels of Z. C. Von Uffenbach, III. 20, 24, who enjoyed
Baker's kindness, Aug. 1, 1710, and says of him, 'He is a very quiet,
modest and affable man, and could have held high offices if he were not
a *Jacobite* and *non-jurer.'*
The scope of the book is to show, from a consideration of the unsatisfactory and variable character of all branches of human knowledge,
the value and necessity of religion. Editions noted in the new catalogue
of the Bodleian, are, 1699; ed. 3, 1700; ed. 7, 1738. 'Reflections upon
learning, Wherein is shewn the Insufficiency Thereof in its several Particulars: in order to evince the *Usefulness* and *Necessity* of Revelation.

history of his College by the request of a friend who wanted notices of the lives of northern worthies from the records of St John's; and that he could cast it aside because through no fault of his own it could not be made complete. Well might Hearne say[1], 'A Mr Baker is not to be met with but in a few places.'

As for Tom Hearne himself, he was of a more petty and of a hotter temper than Baker; but he was like him in his diligence and in his sufferings as a non-juror. He performed his duty as Under-Librarian of the Bodleian[2] so long as he was permitted to do so. He had a high opinion of the duties of the University with respect to the use of Bodley's magnificent storehouse of precious materials, and he exerted all his influence and energies in making those treasures accessible to the country. But in December 1716 he was in danger of having his papers seized[3] by the Vice-Chancellor of Oxford;

The seventh edition, by a Gentleman, London: printed for *John* and *Paul Knapton*, at the Crown, in Ludgate Street, 1737' (pp. 275). A copy in the Camb. Univ. Lib. is 'Printed for A. Bosvile at the Dial against St *Dunstan's* Church in *Fleet Street*, 1700.'

[1] *Reliquiae Hearnianae*, Bliss, III. 161.

[2] There is a curious mention of our friend in the travels of Zach. Conrad von Uffenbach (1754), III. 158. In his *Itinerary*, Sept. 17, 1710, Uffenbach, in one of his visits to the Bodleian while at Oxford, relates that the Protobibliothecarius, 'Bookseller' *Hudson*, left the work of making the new Catalogue to the Hypobibliothecarii Master *Crab* and Master Hearne. 'This *Hearne* is a man of 30 year, a poor starveling mean little creature, yet diligent withal and of good scholarship. He is only keeper (*Beschleisser*) of the Library, and shows the Anatomy Camera, wherefore he is very eager for the fee. He has not much from the Library, and, as he assured me, only £10.'

[3] *Reliquiae Hearnianae*, Bliss, II. 43.

and rather more than a year earlier he had been
debarred from the use of the Library; and as he had
the keys, being Hypobliothecarius, the locks were
altered to keep him out[1]. Hearne lived on at Edmund Hall in Oxford till 1735, solacing himself
in the company of 'honest antiquarians,' in listening
to the Oxford bells, and in complaining to those
diaries his 'collectanea,' which, as far as they are
accessible to us, are of no less interest than the MSS.
of Baker.

Here the reader may find interest in reading the
following character of the non-jurors drawn by one
who seceded from their number (*Abraham Dela
Pryme*, His Diary, *Surtees Society*, 54. p. 70). 1695,
'October 3. Some may be asking in future times
how the Jacobites behaved themselves under this
government, which they were so much against. I
answer, that when anything went of their side, they
were very merry and joyfull; and, on the contrary,
were as much cast down when anything went against
them. They were frequently exceeding bold, and
would talk openly against the government, which the
government connived a little at, for fear of raising
any bustle, knowing that they were inconsiderable
by reason of their paucity. They set up separate
meetings all over, where there was any number of
them, at which meetings I myself have once or twice
been in Cambridge, for we had above twenty fellows
in our Coll[ege] that were non-jurors. The service

---

[1] *Reliqu. Hearn.* II. p. 82; III. 96, 104, 109, 121, 133, 145,
154, 180.

they used was the Common Prayer, and always pray'd heartily for king James, nameing him most commonly; but in some meetings, they onely prayed for the king, not nameing who.

'About three years ago, they held a great consultation at the nonjuring arch-bish[op] of Canterbury's house, where about all the chief nonjurors were present in all England, in which the arch-bish[op] gave them rules how to behave themselves, and how they should pray for the king, and such like.

'Their meetings in Cambridge were oftentimes broken up by order of the vice-chancellor, but then they always met again in some private house or other.

'They had a custom in our college, [St John's] while I was there, which I did not like, and that was always on publick fast days, which was every first Wednesday in every month, they always made a great feast then, and drunk and was merry; the like they did at London.'

The oaths prescribed at the Universities at the end of the Revolution were

1. The Oath of Allegiance to the Sovereign.

2. The Oath of the King or Queen's Supremacy, and against the power and authority of all foreign Potentates, *i. e.* 'The Oath of the Queen's Sovereignty' in the Ordinal.

3. The Declaration against Transubstantiation, Invocation and Adoration of the B. V. Mary or any other Saint, and the Romish doctrine of the Mass.

These Oaths were first taken at Peterhouse, June 22,

1689, and continued till 1719, by persons retaining or entering upon their fellowships. One memorandum in the Register of the House states that 'Mr Worthington having in his Letter to yᵉ Master, dated at London, November 5, 1691, acknowledged that he hath not taken yᵉ Oathes to their Majesties, injoined by yᵉ last Act of Parl. his Fellowship was ordered (this present 9th of Novemb. 1691) in scrutiny, to be vacant according to the said Act.'

A few extracts from the Register of the Oaths of Qualification at St John's are given by Mr Mayor in his addition to Baker's *History*, pp. 552—554.

We have seen that the consolidation of parties had led in the reign of George I. to the persecution of inoffensive members of either University; and that friends had learnt to transfer to friends that resentment which was due not to the persons but to the principles which they held.

We may now proceed to take a more general view of the political tendencies in the two seats of Learning.

It might at first sight appear that Politics could have very little to do with the *Life and Studies* of a University. But this is far from being the real state of the case. After three such revolutions as the country had experienced within half a century, it was impossible that the interest of the country should not be fixed upon public affairs. The taste for Pamphlets which had arisen in the days of Charles I. had now increased a thousand fold. It was no uncommon thing to inform the reader upon the title-page, with that happy disregard for grammar which convenience had sanctioned, that the work in his hand was 'Printed: and are to be Sold at all the Pamphlett-Shops in *London* and *Westminster*'.

This ephemeral literature supplied the place which newspapers and magazines occupy in our time, as well as in some measure the need for books. Pamphlets were one of the important commodities with which the master of the coffee-houses supplied his guests, and these establishments we know were the stronghold of politicians, as early as the time of Charles II., who had it in his mind to shut them up, within twenty years of the first opening of a house for the retail of the 'coffee-drink[1]' by an enterprising Turkish merchant of England. People in those days had more time to read if only they had the books; still when we count volumes of pamphlets in our libraries by hundreds,—pamphlets which have escaped the fire and the housemaid's hands, and pamphlets which some one has thought worth the binding,— the demand for such numbers would seem incredible if we were not witnesses of the supply.

If we take up a chance volume ·containing 18th century tracts relating to either of the Universities, it will be no extraordinary thing if there are one or more bearing directly upon the politics of the day: very few we shall find, if we have the time or the patience to read them through, are totally un- connected with party dissensions. And in this

---

[1] D'Israeli, *Curiosities of Lit.*

respect, a volume of pamphlets of miscellaneous design and authorship gives a true counterfeit of the condition of the Universities of that time. Each writer wears the badge of party, some openly, some half concealed, in the motto on the forefront of his title-page.

Can we think of any subject more widely removed from politics than regulations for the gowns of fellow-commoners and for the closing of taverns at eleven o'clock at night. But a whig Chancellor (the Duke of Newcastle, 1750) had commended them to the University, a whig Proctor had tried to enforce them on an unfortunate occasion (as will be seen hereafter), and all the University was divided. Pamphlet followed pamphlet, fragment supplemented fragment, squib sputtered after squib, appeal succeeded trial.

Then opened the vexed question of the right of application to another court from the decision of Chancellor or Commissary, in matters of discipline. Nor was this, or the earlier case of Dr Bentley, which had amused or enraged our University some thirty years, a single though an extraordinary case.

Politics usurped the place of Christian doctrine in the pulpit; politics lurked in the coffee-houses and in the taverns—her spirit was not expelled even from the 'Triposes' (or Tripos verses) and Tripos-speeches. At Oxford the Act (or Commemoration) was full of it; it was the mainspring which set agoing the more decent compositions of that official merry-andrew the *terrae filius*.

Party feeling had (as we shall see) a great power in

producing and in fostering the nightly demonstrations which disturbed the more peaceful students and inhabitants of Cambridge and Oxford, at the beginning of the last century, and early in our own.

It led to expulsions and trials, to persecution and intolerance. The attention of men became fixed upon the badges which their neighbours wore,—and many regarded them alone, to the neglect of 'Justice and the love of God'—and consequently of the love of man.

It has been a custom sanctioned by convenience to say that in the last century Cambridge was whig and Oxford tory; and this is perhaps the only short form in which the truth can be given approximately.

But this, like most brief classifying formulae, requires explanation, and, it may be, correction. That this is true, will have been observed by any one who has read lives of persons in the Universities, or annals of the two great English seats of learning. More than forty years ago bp. Monk[1] protested against this generalization with respect to Cambridge. And just four years since a writer in the Oxford *Undergraduates' Journal* made a corresponding protest in behalf of the sister University.

[Mr Richard Robinson of Worcester Coll. Fellow of Queen's Coll. Oxon. who wrote *Five Letters on Oxford* from 1688 to 1750, under the signature of 'A Templar,' which appeared in May and June 1867, in Nos. 18—22 of the Oxford *Undergraduates' Journal.* Mr Robinson has left a high repute for knowledge of the history of

---

[1] *Life of Bentley,* I. 375, ed. 1833.

Oxford among eminent members of that University. But for his early death 2 years ago we might already be reaping the fruits of his labours in a rich but almost untouched field. It is a great misfortune that his notes (as we are informed) are illegible, and the *Five Letters* contain no references.]

We have already referred to bp. Burnet's statement that Oxford had declared for William; and it is certain that the compulsatory measures of government[1] had produced at least a seeming loyalty to the new king among its governing body. In 1705, as we learn from notices in Hearne's *Diary*[2], the Jacobites were hardly used by some chief members of the University, who presented them to the Bishop: and the non-jurors were forced to receive the Holy Communion secretly in Christ Church[3] at the chamber of Mr Seldon the Archbishop's nephew. It was in that House that Dr John Massey[4], a roman Catholic, had been made Dean by James II., and thither Francis Atterbury was to be promoted in the reign of queen Anne. But now Massey had been supplanted by Henry Aldrich[5] the learned opponent of Obadiah Walker, and one whom William had advanced.

---

[1] By an Act which received the royal assent March 2, 1702, all members of the foundations of any College or Hall in the Universities being of the age of 18 years, and all persons teaching pupils, were obliged to take and subscribe the oath of abjuration in the court at Westminster or at the quarter sessions.—Cooper's *Annals*.

[2] *Reliqu. Hearn.* Bliss, I. p. 6.   [3] *Ibid.* p. 32.

[4] Mr Middleton Massey of whom in 1710, Hearne says, *Reliqu. H.* Bliss, I. 227, that he took no degree, being a non-juror, was perhaps a relation of this man.

[5] *Biog. Brit.* Kippis, art. *Aldrich.*

Some were open to base arguments like the cha-racter described by Law[1]: '*Succus* is very loyal, and as soon as ever he likes any wine he drinks the king's health with all his heart. Nothing could put rebellious thoughts into his head unless he should live to see a proclamation against eating of *pheasants' eggs*[2].'

In queen Anne's reign we find the duchess of Marlborough sending Mr Evans a good fat doe to treat the warden of Wadham and others well affected to the memory of William. This party apparently was not very strong at Oxford, for we find Burnet[3] complaining that in 1704 'the Universities, Oxford especially, have been very unhappily successful in corrupting the principles of those who were sent to be bred among them: so that few of them escaped the taint of it, and the generality of the clergy were not only ill-principled but ill-tempered '—*i. e.* they opposed the toleration which king William and Burnet himself advocated.

The family of James I. had always been popular

---

[1] *Serious Call*, ch. XII.

[2] *Reliqu. Hearn.* Bliss, I. 73. So in Sept. 1732 (*Ibid.* III. 90) the Bishop of Winchester sends the Fellows of Magdalen half a buck in the absence of the President; and Queen Caroline sends them a whole one, on which occasion they dine at the unusually late hour of 1 o'clock.

> Cp. 'As to the eating part, of that
>   Good plenty was at hand ;
>   Twelve bucks in larder firm and fat,
>   From good Lord Westmoreland.'

Dr Mansel's account of the Emmanuel jubilee sent to Mathias, Oct. 12, 1781.—*N. and Q.* 2nd s. X. 41.

[3] *Burnet's Own Time*, V. 137, ed. 1823 (=II. 380, folio).

at Oxford. Although he favoured Cambridge by a second visit to the performance of *Ruggle's Igno-ramus*[1], yet that monarch found the spirit of Oxford more congenial to his own tastes. He considered the condition of subscription required by that University to be worthy to be imitated in the other. He was graciously pleased to guide her studies in divinity; and it was in accordance with his second advice that Oxford went to the well-springs for her theology instead of contenting herself as theretofore with the 'green mantle of the standing pools' of dry com-pendiums and Calvin's *Institutes*.

Beside this, 'the pedantry of king James I.' (says Dr Bliss[2]) 'was in accordance with the literary taste of his times; and Oxford of course delighted in scholastic exercises, religious conferences and quaint disputations. Charles was a peculiar favourite; Ox-ford had welcomed him in his prosperity, nobly supported him in time of trouble and defeat. The king's love of literature, his fondness for the arts, his generous patronage of the University, his court-eous affability towards her members, and, above all, his maintaining what he considered to be the right cause, had endeared him to all the old members of Oxford, where he was both respected and beloved; and these feelings had descended from father to son, even to the days of Hearne.

The Restoration was hailed with delight through the whole of England; but nowhere more heartily

[1] [Bp.] R. Corbet's Poems, Nichols' *Royal Progresses*.
[2] *Reliqu. Hearn.* Bliss, Appendix 1. vol. III. p. 188.

than in Oxford. About the year 1637—we learn
from one who was then in his seventeenth year
a 'Fellow Com'uner in Baliol,' for, so John Evelyn[1]
calls himself—'was the University exceedingly
regular under the exact discipline of William Lawd
Archbishop of Canterbury, then Chancellor[2].' But
alas the good efforts òf the pious but ungenial lover
of Oxford were frustrated upon the accession of the
prince and 'the little Duke of York,' whose boyish
fancy had been pleased by the pretty book brought
from little Gidding by young Nicholas Ferrar at
the command of my Lord of Canterbury[3]—ah, *'si sic
omnia!'* In the reign of Charles and James II. were
sown the seeds of idleness and licentiousness in
morals and in religion which brought forth such a
crop of drowsiness and debauchery in all classes of
society, from the highest to the lowest, as we see
portrayed in the works of Fielding and of Hogarth,
and no less in the biographies of the eighteenth
century.

The severity of puritanism was still fresh enough
in the minds of Englishmen to tempt them to
protract the rejoicing at the Restoration; and they
did not withstand the temptation till the celebration
of their freedom became not an annual but a perennial
jollity.

It was not until[4] personal holiness was well nigh

---

[1] *Evelyn's Diary*, anno 1637.
[2] *Evelyn's Diary*, sub anno 1637.
[3] *Life*, by John Ferrar, p. 136. Camb. 1855.
[4] Whiston's *Autobiography*, I. p. 10 (ed. 1749).

dead, and public religion was almost forgotten, that the death of the merry monarch brought his less genial brother to the throne. The house of Stuart was still popular at Oxford, and even the wrongs done them by James II. could not efface from their hearts the loyal feeling impressed there by the other wrongs voluntarily suffered for his father.

Those who had not forgotten their reverence for God's worship,—what sympathy could they feel with a king who wore his hat in church[1]? King James at least did not err upon *that* side. Where again was William's learning? what encouragement did he give to literature? As to taste—*that* in a Dutchman was out of the question. Above all, what right has he to rule over us? Let us not do evil, even if we are quite sure that good will come.

Such perhaps were the arguments of those who became known as the high-church party, and, as Hickesites, some of whom suffered as non-jurors, and who stood up boldly in the lower house of the Southern Convocation against the new low-church Bishops and Hoadleians, to be silenced only by the unconstitutional measure of suppressing Convocation.

While that body was permitted to represent the Church of England, as it did by the mandate of William, upon the most important question of a comprehensive scheme, the strength of the high-churchmen, may be estimated by the fact that Dr Jane[2], the King's Professor of Divinity at Oxford,

---

[1] See Palin, *Hist. Engl. Ch.* p. 118.
[2] Macaulay's *Hist.* ch. xiv. See my notes.

was elected Prolocutor, by a majority of 55 to 28; while Tillotson, whom the King intended to succeed archbishop Sancroft, did not secure one-third of the votes. And this was a few months after sentence of suspension had gone out against the non-juring bishops.

Many, if not most of the non-jurors were opposed to popery, even George Hickes himself (of St John's and Magdalen Colleges, and afterwards of Magdalen Hall, and Fellow of Lincoln, rector of St Ebbe's Oxford, and D.D.), one of the most ardent and reckless of the non-jurors and high-churchmen, had, on the accession of James II., lost his expected appointment to the bishopric of Bristol, because he was a foe to romanism. This could not be said of all the jacobites: and many, who sided with them, incurred the odium which often attaches to those who religiously adhere to their principles, from their companionship with some who do not in all points agree with them.

While Oxford, though outwardly acquiescing in the Revolution, was still jacobite at heart,—so much so as even in the middle of the century to be accused of wholesale dishonesty and unconscientiousness,—there was within her a party of young men who manifested their detestation of the Stuarts. On January the 30th, 1706-7[1], which the non-jurors would be observing as a day of humiliation, the anniversary of the martyrdom of their king, there was, in the words of Hearne, no favourable historian, 'an abomin-

[1] *Reliqu. Hearn.* Bliss, I. 127.

able riot at All Souls.' Mr Dalton A.M., and Mr Talbot, son to the bp. of Oxon. A.B., both Fellows, had a dinner drest at 12 o'clock (a late hour for those days). Two of the pro-proctors, Oriel men, Ibbetson and Rogers, were present. They beheaded woodcocks in mockery, and Dalton (a nominee of abp. Tennison) 'was for having calves' heads[1], but the cook refused to dress them.'

It was a few years later, in the days of queen Anne, whose heart may still have inclined towards her father and her brother even before the fall of Marlborough, that there were signs of political trimming in each direction[2]; among others, John Johnson (author of the once popular *Clergyman's Vade-Mecum*, 1705 and other years) who had been a staunch Hanoverian, became a high churchman and anti-dissenter; —nor was his a singular case[3].

> 'Among the high-churchmen I find there are several
> That stick to the doctrine of Henry Sacheverell,
> Among the low-church too I find that as oddly
> Some pin all their faith upon Benjamin Hoadly.
> But we moderate men do our judgment suspend,
> For God only knows where these matters will end.
> For Sal'sbury, Burnett, and Kennet White shew,
> That as the times vary so principles go:
> And twenty years hence, for aught you or I know,
> 'Twill be Hoadly the high, and Sacheverell the low.'

The reader will remember the attitude which the two clergymen last mentioned in the doggerel just

---

[1] See the account of the *Calves'-head Club*, Jan. 30, 1734-5. Hone's *Every-Day Book*, II. 158, 159, quoted below. Cp. also Cooper, *Annals*, IV. 4:0 (1794), and Report 2 of *Hist. MSS. Commission* (1872), p. 112. App.

[2] See the sneers of Amherst, *Terrae Filius*, VI.

[3] 1709, 10. 'The Thanksgiving,' quoted by *Hearne*, Bliss, I. p. 189.

quoted took upon the question of passive obedience. It is significant of the altered face which political affairs bore at this period in Oxford and in the country generally, that Francis Atterbury was elected dean of Christ Church by queen Anne in 1712, when some two years before he had opposed Hoadly upon the question of passive obedience and was believed[1] to have penned the defence of Sacheverell, assisted perhaps by his neighbour the young Christ Church wit and Westminster usher, the jacobite Samuel, the eldest of the Wesleys[2]. It is a fact indicative of the strange effect of party spirit that the hero of the great demonstration which overthrew the ministry should have been a worthless noisy incendiary (for such a character is attributed to Sacheverell), the spokesman at once of honest men, of deep and audacious plotters, and of a rabble of dissolute and discontented subjects. Be this as it may, Sacheverell, when, in the course of his triumphal tour in 1710 he arrived at Oxford, was enthusiastically received there as in other places; he 'was met and magnificently entertained by the Vice-Chancellor [Dr Braithwait] and the heads of that University as well as by most persons of distinction in the neighbourhood of that city[3].' It was by a similar expression of anti-*constitutional* principles that the senior members of the same University[4], 'upon their Chan-

[1] *Reliqu. Hearn.* Bliss, II. 203.
[2] Southey's *Life of Wesley*, edited by his son, I. p. 19.
[3] *Life and reign of Queen Anne*, p. 541.
[4] Monk's *Life of Bentley*, I. 375.

cellor, the duke of Ormond, openly embarking in the service of the Pretender, testified their unaltered attachment to him by choosing his brother, the earl of Arran, to hold his station.'

Let us now turn to our own University.

While we meet with fewer expressions of Oxford allegiance to the dynasty of the Revolution, we cannot but be struck by the pains which the majority at Cambridge took to assure the Sovereigns of their loyalty. It is almost impossible to open a page of the fourth volume of Mr C. H. Cooper's *Annals* of that University and Town, without finding the notice of at least one address to the Crown or Royal family.

These were generally presented at St James' by the Chancellor and Vice-Chancellor and other members of the University in their academical robes:—a strange sight in London, where, as Hearne informs us (*Reliqu. Hearn.* Bliss II. p. 107, Feb. 1719-20), the tory clergy only wore the M.A. gown, while 'the whigs and enemies of the Universities go in pudding-sleeve gowns.' I shall give in the notes a chronological list of the addresses to the Crown from Cambridge in the last century.

It does not appear that King William had much sympathy with either of the Universities. He had on one occasion thought of making a royal visitation (whether in person or through commissioners as his predecessors had done I do not know), but he was dissuaded from it by the legal advisers of the Crown.

It may have been owing to her womanly tact that

his successor and the sister of his good queen Mary was pleased to visit our University in 1705. She was received by lines of students with acclamations of *Vivat Regina.* 'The ways were all along strowed with flowers; the bells rung and the conduits run with wine.' After the conferring of honorary degrees, Dr Bentley received her Majesty at Trinity College, where I. Newton and the Vice-Chancellor and the Council for the University were knighted. She was entertained in the Hall of that Royal College 'at the expence of the University, upon a Throne erected five foot high for that purpose.' She afterwards visited the college Library, and after being received at St John's she went to Prayers in King's college Chapel, and thence to visit Queens', and so to Newmarket. So great was the loyalty then felt by Cambridge for queen Anne, that the vice-chancellor Dr Bardsay Fisher, *Sid.*, and eight heads, deprived Dr Tho. Tudway, music professor of his degrees and Organist's office in S. Mary's church and King's and Pembroke, for reflecting in a bad pun upon the conduct of the Queen. The poor wretch made a most humble apology, and was by her Majesty's command restored. (July 20, 1706, March 10, 1706-7.)

Although, as we are informed by bishop Monk (*Life of Bentley*, I. 276), only a small proportion of the High Church party at Cambridge were jacobites—while such was not the case at Oxford—the change in parties which was going on throughout the reign of Q. Anne appears to have produced a considerable increase in the ranks of the tories at our University. The sympathies of Cambridge in the following reign were with Sherlock and the inferior clergy against Hoadly in the Bangorian controversy (1717). 'At the general election in 1715 the tory representatives were re-elected ; and in all subsequent struggles, by which the strength of the parties can be estimated, that interest maintained a majority of at least two to one.' (Monk's *Life of Bentley*, I. 376.) The dynasty of the Revolution was already taking firm root ; and many who held high views of royalty were already transferring their allegiance to the now established descent, and swelling the ranks of the party which favoured personal government and the religious spirit which yet lay between the leaves of the Book of Common Prayer. Or (shall we not rather say it?) many were compelling the Hanoverian line to wear in their crown the badge of the white tory rose. But the political utterances of Cambridge could be enunciated by a very small but all-powerful minority.

In the University the *Caput* was autocratic. It consisted of the Vice-Chancellor (or Chancellor's Commissary) and five other members. Three of them were Heads of Colleges, or Professors representing the faculties of Divinity, Law and Physic; the remaining two were the senior members of the two 'houses' which composed the Senate: the Non-Regent House, who wore *black hoods*, and the Regent House, which was composed entirely of Masters of Arts under five years' standing, whose duty was to preside at the Acts or Disputations (*regere in schola*). These last alone wore white linings to their M.A. hoods.

Any individual member of the *Caput* had an absolute veto upon any university question whatever, and the Vice-Chancellor was absolute among them, for he could refuse to call a *Caput*, as was done by Dr Wilcox, master of Clare Hall, when the University was distracted upon the question of Appeal in 1751-2.

A few months before, a grace on the same question had been stopped in the *Caput*, and the disappointed *Associators* (for so the supporters of the Right of Appeal were called) in their exasperation stopped a Degree in their stronghold, the non-regent house, the same afternoon. (Compare Cooper's *Annals*, p. 285, with the remarks of the late Mr R. Robinson of *Queen's*, in the Oxford *Undergraduates' Journal*, p. 149 *a*.)

The above statement gives a clear instance of the conservative capabilities of the university constitution: but it is premature in our sketch of the politics of Cambridge. We may nevertheless conclude that the power of a Vice-Chancellor would enable him, if he were so inclined, to defy the principles of a constitutional Senate, provided he had only got his election safe.

There had already been signs of disorder among the young men of England. Hearne[1] speaks of the band of Mohocks in London (March 30, 1712). His

[1] *Reliqu. Hearn.* Bliss, I. 247, 248. Cf. *Spectator*, Nos. 324, 347, &c.

statement that they were 'all of the whiggish gang' may be questioned; but it is noteworthy that the whigs tried to prove that they were no such persons. Bishop Burnet's son (late of Merton) was said to be the ringleader.

At Oxford much disappointment must have been felt upon the accession of George I. The rejoicings there on the night of his coronation, Oct. 20, 1714, were, according to Hearne[1], 'very little; nor did any person that I know of drink king George's health but mentioned him with ridicule. The illuminations and bonfires were very poor and mean.'

At Cambridge, on the other hand, he was proclaimed immediately upon the news of the Queen's death by Dr Lang of Pembroke Hall, in the absence of Thomas Greene (Bene't Coll.) the vice-chancellor, who however contributed to the collection of poems of condolence and congratulation produced on this as on other similar occasions by the University.

There were however some evidences of jacobite feeling, at least among the junior members of our society. 'One Mr Lawes, A.M. of Cambridge, was lately degraded by the means of Dr Adams, head of King's College' and vice-chancellor, 'who complained to the present lord-treasurer (who was zealous for his degradation) upon account of some queries in his speech called tripos speech, such as Whether the sun shines when it is in an eclipse? Whether a controverted son be not better than a controverted successor? Whether a dubious successor be not in

[1] *Reliqu. Hearn.* Bliss, I. p. 311.

danger of being set aside ? With other things of the same nature[1].'

Upon the accession of king George I., when the old non-jurors had either left the University or were living a harmless and generally a useful life, it was plain to see that in the late queen's reign there had grown at Cambridge as well as at Oxford a generation of undergraduates who were strong anti-Hanoverians. It was an unfortunate thing for the quiet of the king's subjects that his birthday was also the eve of the anniversary both of the birth and restoration of king Charles II.; a day which the whole nation had once been used to celebrate with a general thanksgiving and rejoicing.

On May the 28th, 1715, the first anniversary of George's birthday since his accession, some bells in Oxford (we are told by Hearne[2], who would think his favourite music desecrated by such an occasion) were 'jambled' by the whigs, but not much observed. The mob, who stopped all signs of rejoicing, were so far infuriated at the slight show of loyalty to the Hanoverian, that they pulled down 'a good part of a presbyterian meeting-house.'

On the 29th, which was a Sunday, there were

[1] This extract is from *Hearne's Diary* (Bliss, I. 282) of the date July 30, 1713. The first Tripos speech in the century which we know (Sam. Cobb's) was delivered Feb. 19 (1701-2), i.e. at the time of the *comitia priora* in later years. Was there ever a *Tripos* speech at the 'commencement' in July? Or did University proceedings and news travel slow? The second query mentioned by Hearne would be more pointed than ever when the decease of Q. Anne was daily expected.

[2] *Reliqu. Hearn.* Bliss, II. pp. 2-4, and for the whig account of the transaction see [Amherst] *Terrae Filius*, No. L.

great demonstrations for 'King James III.' which contrasted strongly with the disaffection manifested to the reigning Sovereign on the morning of the preceding day. The mob disgraced themselves so far as to repeat their act of violence and intolerance by demolishing the meeting-houses of quakers and anabaptists. Several members of the University were concerned in these disturbances. During the two preceding reigns there had been little manifestation of extreme whiggery at Oxford, but no sooner was king George safely on the throne than a society of advanced whigs came upon the scene.

The *Constitution Club*, as they called themselves, held their meetings at the King's Head Tavern in the High Street[1]. Among their members we have mention of five Fellows, a chaplain, and four gentlemen commoners of New College, one gentleman commoner and seven others of Oriel, three of Christ Church: Hart Hall, Worcester, All Souls, Merton, St John's, Trinity, and Wadham contributed at least one member each,—usually a gentleman commoner.

On the king's birthday, the 28th of May aforesaid, the whole body of the *Constitution Club* met together at a tavern, and ordered the windows of the house to be illuminated and some faggots to be prepared for a bonfire. But before the bonfire could be lighted, a very numerous mob, which was hired for that purpose, tore to pieces the faggots and then assaulted the room where the club was sitting, with brickbats

[1] Mr Jeaffreson's *Annals of Oxford*.

and stones. All the time that the mob was thus employed, the disaffected scholars, who had crowded the houses and streets near the tavern, continued throwing up their caps and scattering money amongst the rabble and crying out, 'Down with the *Constitutioners;* down with the *Whigs;* no *G——e; Ja——s* for ever, *Ormond, Bolingbroke,'* &c. It is perhaps hardly possible to tell how much of the above account and of that which follows is true, and how much is to be attributed to the malice of Nicholas Amherst. Our other authority, Thomas Hearne, though no less prejudiced in the other direction, yet bears a more respectable character, and was writing for his own satisfaction, not with a view to produce any immediate effect upon public opinion. The following statements, at least, there seems no cause to doubt:—The 'Constitutioners' thought it prudent to make the best of their way to their colleges for the night. On the Sunday the club met again, at Oriel, and were the objects of the indignation of the mob ('scholars and others,' according to Amherst), who thronged the streets at six o'clock. A Brasenose man was wounded by a gunshot fired by óne of the Constitutioners, or their friends in Oriel, after which the crowd retired to pull down the conventicles.

Such a disturbance could not be overlooked: the Heads of the Houses, or 'Sculls' as they were vulgarly called, met in Golgotha[1] beneath the portrait of the late Queen and laid the blame upon

[1] A room in the Old Clarendon described in *Terrae Filius*, No. XI.

the Constitution Club, who naturally appeared to them to have been the aggressors. But king George was not well pleased: so that 'rattling letters' were sent early in June to Dr Arthur Charlett, the Vice-Chancellor and Master of University. The Heads therefore were forced to draw up a 'programma' and to send 'old Sherwin the Yeoman beadle' to London to represent the truth of the matter[1].

At Cambridge also there had been jacobite demonstrations on the 28th and 29th of May, but there was little harm done; a few windows were broken and there were shouts of 'no Hanover,' but by the prudence of the vice-chancellor, Dr Thomas Sherlock[2], 'warden' of Catharine Hall, who was a moderate tory for those days, and the son of a 'Complier,' the offenders were treated as having committed an ordinary breach of good manners, without reference to their political expressions. He was however thought to have connived at jacobitism, as was Dr T. Gooch of Caius when Vice-Chancellor in 1718 (Monk's *Bentley*, II. 45), and it required

---

[1] *Hearne*, Bliss, II. 5.

[2] Dr Tho. Sherlock was son of Dr Will. Sherlock—[of Eton and Peterhouse, master of the Temple, a non-juror, afterwards a 'Complyer,' Dean of St. Paul's, opposes Dr South]—Eton and Catharine Hall, 1704, succeeded his father as Master of the Temple; 1714, Master of Catharine Hall; 1716, Dean of Chichester. Sherlock succeeded his antagonist Benjamin Hoadly in the bishopric of Bangor 1728, and of Salisbury 1734. Their portraits now hang near together in the hall of St. Catharine, where they were Fellows together. Sherlock, having refused the primacy, was afterwards translated to the see of London, 1748. Died July 18, 1761.—Gorton, *Dict. Biogr.*

the influence of Daniel Waterland, who was a Hanoverian, to quell the animosities.

Some apprehensions may have arisen from the more serious disorders at Oxford. True at least it is that our University presented an address to king George[1]; with which expression of loyalty his Majesty was so well pleased that at the suggestion of Charles viscount Townshend he purchased for £6000 the most valuable library of the late bishop Moore of Ely, containing upwards of 30,000 volumes, and with royal munificence presented the collection to the University of Cambridge.

It was on this occasion that the well-known epigrams prefixed to the first portion of this essay were composed. The former is variously ascribed to two Oxford professors of poetry, Dr Joseph Trapp and Tom Warton the elder. The retort was the composition of sir William Browne (founder of the prizes for verse), who, if we may trust the statement of Mrs Thrale (*Johnsoniana*, § 11.), *improvised* the lines in reply to Dr Johnson, who in one of his fits of rude oxonianism had repeated Dr Trapp's epigram.

Scarcely had Cambridge returned her thanks in an address[2] presented, and it is thought composed, by Sherlock, when 'the ministry were obliged to send to Oxford a squadron of horse[3] under Major-

---

[1] Van Mildert's *Life of Waterland*, p. 18 (for an account of Daniel Waterland, see below). Compare Cooper's *Annals*, IV. p. 137 ; Monk's *Life of Bentley*, I. 376.

[2] Monk's *Life of Bentley*, I. 377.   [3] Cooper's *Annals*, IV. 141.

General Pepper to seize Colonel Owen and other jacobite officers who had been turned out of the army¹.'

The report which had reached Oxford a few weeks before, that 'King James' had landed in Scotland, did not tend to the quiet of that University. In spite of the loyal 'programma put forth by Dr Gardiner, our present pharisaical Vice-Chancellor' (as Hearne calls him), the memorable kalends of August², the anniversary of king George's accession, were 'very little observed³.' Soon after there was a demonstration of Balliol men and others against a recruiting officer of volunteer dragoons, and they whipt 'a noted roundhead, commonly called my Lord Shaftesbury⁴,' a deformed tailor.

In this same month of August, 1715, we have a curious instance of the irregular way in which some men unpopular with the authorities retired from the University. Dr John Ayliffe had written a valuable work entitled the *Antient and Present State of Oxford* (1714)⁵, which had given offence to the Vice-Chancellor (Dr Gardiner of All Souls) by 'disclosing... facts which did not consist with the favorite dogma of its Trojan foundation, and which told the outer

---

¹ *Reliqu. Hearn.* II. p. 6.

² The memory of the first of August was perpetuated for ever by the legacy of the whig Dogget, Cibber's fellow-comedian—the Thames watermen's coat and badge.

³ *Hearne*, II. pp. 11, 12.   ⁴ *Hearne*, Bliss, II. pp. 11, 12.

⁵ Printed for *E. Curll*, at the *Dial and Bible*, against St. *Dunstan's* Church in *Fleet* Street, 1714. Nichols' *Lit. Anecd.* I. 456. Offered in 173°, by Henry Curll, at lowest selling-off price for 10s.

world too much[1].' The book had been burnt ('by the common hangman,' a MS. note in our copy says) and himself degraded and expelled from the University but not from the College. In the following year we are told he and three other Fellows of New College 'have sold their fellowships, which is a custom here, under pretence of resignation and so will go off[2].'

The loyalty of Cambridge did not exempt her from the imposition of the oaths,—nor was this to be expected while the 'pretended Prince of Wales[3]' was 'takeing upon himself the style and title of King of Great Brittaine, by the name of James the third[4].'

Daniel Waterland, master and tutor of Magdalene, a Hanoverian, had succeeded the tory Sherlock, as Vice-Chancellor, and the day after his election Bentley (who had now thought good to become a whig) his coadjutor preached his famous Fifth of November sermon in the University Church against Popery.

In the preceding year Bentley had been eulogized by *Philo-Georgius et Philo-Bentleius*, an ardent whig, in a pamphlet entitled 'University Loyalty considered; in a Letter to a Gentleman at *Cambridge*[5]' (London, 1715). We gather from the tract

[1] Mr R. Robinson of Queen's, *O. Undergrad. Journal*, p. 149 *a*. *Oxoniana*, IV. 225, 227. Dr Rawlinson's MSS.

[2] *Hearne*, Bliss, II. p. 13.

[3] See the extracts from the *Book of Oaths of Qualification* to be subscribed by Masters of the College, in Mr Mayor's notes to Baker's *Hist. of St John's*, p. 552.

[4] *Ibid.* p. 553.

[5] Monk's *Life of Bentley*, I. 378, on whose authority this notice has been taken, p. 22.

that there had been hisses heard when the Public Orator expatiated on the virtues of King George, and that certain speakers in the University of Cambridge had dwelt unnecessarily long upon the loss sustained by the death of good queen Anne.

'Philo-Bentleius,' though he has no idea of tolerance for the tories, advocates the restoration of William Whiston, who had been deprived for heresy five years before. Herein we may observe the presence of the High-Church element in the tory party, which was by no means co-extensive with jacobitism at Cambridge or elsewhere.

The new vice-chancellor, Mr Waterland, had done wisely in publishing early in May, 1716, a notice that the statutes of the University would be enforced against scholars under the degree of M.A., who dined or supped in taverns or public-houses (Cooper's *Annals*, referring to Baker MS. xxv). But in spite of these precautions, there was a great disturbance in Cambridge, on the 29th of May, 1716, 'and the scholars of Clare Hall were miserably insulted for their loyalty to the Government, together with those of Trinity College.' Calamy (*Historical Account of his own Life*, ed. Rutt. II. 252 ap. Cooper, III. 556 n.) goes on to tell how 'Mr Hussey's meeting-house was pillaged and plundered, and almost demolished.' It is too probable that some members of our University followed on this occasion the bad example of the Oxford riot a year before, and joined in the attack upon the conventicles, for the impartial vice-chancellor Waterland, in a notice published six weeks later, prohibits the carrying of 'any stick, club, or any manner of arms,' and the using 'any opprobrious words, or invidious names[1]'—together with hissing, pointing, or making 'any loud shoutings, or outcries, tending to incite, or raise any mob within the limits of the University.'—The preamble states that 'there hath been of late divers disorders, among several scholars of the University tumultuously meeting together, provoking, and exasperating one another by...throwing of stones and other great irregularities.'

It was, perhaps, as well for the credit of the University with the Court, that the address[2] which was presented in Waterland's Vice-Chancellorship had met with opposition :—a fate which every composition of Bentley's must have learnt to take as a matter of course. Like everything else of Bentley's it was carried by a *coup*[3]: when he and two of his friends acted on the Caput, as deputies of the Pembroke men, who had once put their veto on it. The address thus came very opportunely, as the expression of the loyalty of the University, after, instead of before, the disturbance on the 29th of May[4]. The fact of its opposition however, (for after it had passed the Caput, the voting in the Senate in its favour was 36 to 15 in the Non-Regent, and 34 to 14 in the Regent House,) no less than the disturbances among

[1] Cooper's *Annals*, IV. 143.
[2] Cp. Bentley to Sam. Clarke, quoted by Van Mildert, *Waterland*, I. 20.
[3] Van Mildert's *Life of Waterland*, p. 18.
[4] Cooper's *Annals*, anno 1716.

the Scholars, is a clear evidence of jacobite feeling, existing at this time in Cambridge.

Meanwhile at the tory University, there had been a similar address proposed, to congratulate the King upon the suppression of a rebellion 'which' (writes Mr Robinson, addressing the Undergraduates of Oxford, in their *Gazette*, for May 4, 1867) 'you were known to have fomented, and on his return from a country more suitable to him, and where you only wished he had stayed, and to thank him for the favour of omitting at your asking to burn, in company with the figures of the Pope and the Devil, effigies of the son of your King, and of Ormond and Mar. You reasonably demurred, nor was the unnecessary insult of the presence of soldiery among you against whose outrage you in vain remonstrated, calculated to sooth your feelings, your expression of indignation was received by the House of Lords in a way which was probably unparliamentary, and assuredly ill-advised and cruel.' The Hanoverian Club of 'Constitutioners' had repeated their noisy meeting on the 29th of May 1716.

We will take the account of their advocate Nicholas Amherst: 'In the evening, the *Constitution Club*, and several officers in Colonel *Handyside's* regiment, met together at the tavern. Whilst they were drinking the king's and other loyal healths, several squibs were thrown in at the window, which burnt some of their cloaths, and filled the room with fire and smoak. Besides this, they were continually insulted with loud peals of hisses and conclamations of *Down with the*

Roundheads, from the gownmen, and other disorderly people in the street; of which they took no notice. They continued together till about eleven of clock, or not quite so late, when Mr *Holt* of *Maudlin* College, *Sub-Proctor* at that time came, and making up to Mr *Meadowcourt* (who happened to be steward of the *Club* that night,) demanded of him the reason of their being at the tavern. Mr *Meadowcourt* rose up and told him, that they were met together to commemorate the *Restoration* of king *Charles* II. and to drink king *George's* health; *and that they should be obliged to* HIM *if he would be pleased to drink king* George's *health with them;* which the *Proctor*, after some entreaties, comply'd with. After which, one of the captains went to him, and desired him to excuse the scholars that were there, promising him that he would take care that no harm or disorder should be committed, and then waited upon the *Proctor* down stairs.'

The reader will observe that Amherst is anxious to make out a good case for his companions in disgrace; for the chief members of the Club were kept long waiting for their next degrees. Mr Meadowcourt, a young Fellow of Merton, three years later gave the Vice-Chancellor some trouble[1] by accusing the University governors of disaffection. In spite of these proceedings against members of the Constitution Club in Oxford, they held a meeting at the Three Tun Tavern on the King's Accession in the

[1] *Terrœ-filius*, Nos. XXII, XXIII, XXIV.

4—2

following year (Aug. 1, 1717) with a bonfire and illumination.

It will be remembered that it was in January 1716–7, in the Vice-Chancellorship of Mr Grigg, master of Clare Hall, that Thomas Baker, and one and twenty other members of St John's, had been ejected from their fellowships at Cambridge, for refusing 'to affirm the omnipotence of parliament to dispense with oaths.' It was in the preceding month (Dec. 1716: see *Hearne*, Bliss, II. 43) that Tom Hearne was in great danger of having his papers searched for jacobite sentiments by the Vice-Chancellor (Dr Baron, of Balliol). This was rather more than a year since he had been debarred the use of Bodley, of which he was Hypobibliothecarius. Nevertheless we find him doing useful work, in this and the next reign[1],—interested in the literary activity of Oxford, and in 1734 speaking to Vice-Chancellor Holmes about a committee for publishing MSS.[2] belonging to the University. He still lived in Edmund Hall and walked frequently to 'the third house on the left hand after you have passed High Bridge, going from Worcester College[3]'—a tavern, known as 'Antiquity Hall,' where he met many young gentlemen of Christ Church and other 'honest' antiquaries, to chat over pot and pipe.

In 1716–7, 'the Government contemplated intro-

---

[1] *Hearne*, Bliss, III. 102, 165.   [2] *Ibid.* III. 165.

[3] *Ibid.* II 82, cf. III. 164, where Hearne complains that he has been ridiculed in a print of that house in 1723, by two 'very conceited fellows of little understanding, tho' both are Masters of Arts.'

ducing into Parliament, a bill for regulating the two Universities[1].' Soon after the Parliament met, Edmund Miller, Sergeant at Law, and Deputy High Steward of the University, published a tract purporting to be, 'An account of the University of Cambridge, and the Colleges thereof[2],' addressed to the Houses of Parliament. It is in fact an attack upon Bentley who had declared his fellowship vacant, because he opposed his scheme, six years before. Miller's position was that the statutes required changing because they were not kept; he takes Trinity College as a specimen, and thus has a splendid opportunity for abusing his adversary the Master. The pamphlet was considered a 'famosus libellus', and proceedings were instituted thereupon; but Miller was a cunning lawyer, and the affair was dropped.

On the 6th of October 1717 K. George I. paid Cambridge a visit, chiefly memorable because Bentley, as Master of Trinity, and Regius Professor, was prominent upon the occasion, and for the dispute about fees between 'fiddling' Conyers Middleton and himself which arose out of it.

In the next year we find the result of the agitation for University reform in a careful scheme[3] drawn up by Lord Macclesfield (but not adopted). For the

---

[1] Cooper's *Annals*, IV. 145.

[2] The title of the tract is given in full with an extract from it relating to *Bentley*, in an Appendix (A. I.) to this part of the Essay, before the Analysis of Ld. *Macclesfield's* Scheme. (Appendix A. II.)

[3] A digest of Lord *Macclesfield's* Scheme, taken from *Gutch Collectanea Curiosa*, No. ix, will be given in an Appendix (A. II.) to this 1st Part of the present Compilation.

present it is enough to state that two questions are discussed in it:—*firstly* the promotion of Learning and Industry, irrespective of party considerations; *secondly* a remedy for the present disaffection of the Universities. Some of the details will be found elsewhere.

We have already referred to the dispute between Middleton and Bentley, but for an account of the numberless litigations in which the great Master of Trinity baffled his opponents, we must refer the reader to one or all of the interesting publications which have become a part of English literature.

The two volumes of the Life by bishop Monk of Gloucester, are impartial and most full of interesting and entertaining matter.

The Biography of Dr Ri. Bentley in the *Worthies of Yorkshire and Lancashire* (pp. 65—174) is founded upon Monk's Life 'and other sources of information' (p. 68). In addition to the advantage of conciseness, this has the recommendation (in itself sufficient) of proceeding from the pen of Hartley Coleridge (1836) whose comments cannot fail to charm us even where we dissent from them.

Readers of Tom De Quincey will not need to be reminded of the amusing Essay wherein he leads us (*ut solet*) like Will o' the Wisp, through the marisch ground of plausibilities until we find ourselves awakened by a sudden gurgling of the cold water of paradox in our ears; yet can hardly resist joining in the laugh with Puck and Ariel at the pretty pickle we are in.

Although (in spite of the enticing lanthorn of

utility which De Quincey holds out to us—as in spite of all the piping and taboring of Ariel) we cannot consent to 'hang the little dog' (poor Colbatch, who at least could go out of his way to oblige a stranger)[1] rather than give the great dog a bad name; yet we can find great pleasure in thinking on the good which Bentley did. His improvement in the election of Scholars and Fellows at Trinity, from which none but himself has ever departed: the impulse which he gave to that accurate criticism which has since become the aim, though not the method always, of European Thought: the power that was given him, in spite of his pugnacious propensities, and in spite of his *hauteur*, of concentrating the interests of the learned men of continental countries[2] and our own— these things alone would give Bentley a claim to stand among the foremost of the heroes of the 18th century.

But while we reflect how great he was, and how much was done by him with all his faults, we cannot help adding, What might he not have done without them! If he had devoted to the critical study of the Scriptures that time which he did worse than waste in litigation, the cause of Truth might have been advanced beyond its present stage, and Bentley might have made what Kipling was allowed to mar and what Mr Scrivener has been forced to undo and do again. But the Doctor was like the *Lemuel Gulliver* of his opponent Swift, and he was conscious that his contemporaries (How the very words conspire to

[1] See Thoresby's *Diary*, quoted below.
[2] See the Preface to Wordsworth's Edition of *Bentley's Correspondence.*

attest this statement !)[1] were but as Lilliputians by his side. Like Gulliver he could not resist the temptation of amusing himself with the littlenesses of the little men. He appropriated their household stuff and had a fine lodging built and furnished at the expense of the community; he dabbled in the politics of Lilliput and Blefuscu as seemed most to his advantage at the moment. Each party was glad of his assistance but each party was thankful to be rid of him. They might take away his title of *nardac*, but they could not send him bound. And after all, when either side had done their best and their worst to punish him ; this Quinbus Flestrin, *the great man mountain*, comes off scot free with their cows and sheep in his coat pocket.

The State of Trinity College under Bentley, as it represents the most remarkable and the most important college quarrel of the time, so it was but too truly typical of the dissensions which prevailed in the university societies in the former half of the last century.

In addition to this, it contained, owing to its extent, the germs of every species of dispute which destroyed the harmony and impaired the usefulness of those places of education.

The dissension between High Church and Low was exemplified in the antagonism of Bentley and Middleton. Bentley took some pains to ingratiate himself with the reigning sovereign, Sergt. Miller was

---

[1] See Bentley's *Phalaris*, where he *co*gratulates 'Mr B.' on his *co*position of the word 'cotemporary.'

a staunch supporter of the ministry; the Master was an Absolutist, the recalcitrant Fellows were for limited authority: the appeal to the Visitor and the visitatorial sanctions, which are such important elements in the university quarrels of the time, were debated in the case of the Master and Fellows of Trinity College with as great eagerness and with as strange results as in any of the later controversies.

Turning again to the other university: of the uncomfortable condition in which the Colleges at Oxford were with respect to the attitude which the members of any college bore to one another, we have evidence more than enough in the Diary of Hearne[1]. In June 1726 he writes, 'There are such differences now in the university of Oxford (hardly one college but where all the members are busied in law business and quarrels, not at all relating to the promoting of learning) that good letters miserably decay every day insomuch that this ordination on Trinity Sunday at Oxford there were no fewer (as I am informed) than fifteen denied orders for insufficiency which is the more to be noted because our bishops and those employed by them are themselves generally illiterate men.' This was the year after John Wesley was ordained.

It must be borne in mind that Hearne had no sympathy with the 'Low Church' Bishops, and considered the popularity of 'Burnetts romance or libel called by him *The History of his own Times*' as an instance of the low depths to which learning had sunk in 1734. *Hearne*, Bliss, III. 125, 129.

---

[1] *Reliqu. Hearn.* Bliss, II. 247.

In this same year (1726) John Wesley writes of Lincoln college to his brother Samuel whom he had lately joined as fellow of that society;—' I never knew a College besides ours whereof the members were so perfectly satisfied with one another and so inoffensive to the other part of the university. All I have yet seen of the fellows are both well-natured and well-bred men, admirably disposed as well to preserve peace and good neighbourhood among themselves as to promote it wherever else they have any acquaintance[1].'

In 1727–28 there was at Oriel one of the disputes to which allusion has been made. Mr Wicksey (or Weeksy) having done all he could to hinder the peace of the college and annoy his rival the new Provost, was deprived of his fellowship as being incapacitated from holding it by his possession of *uberius beneficium*[2].

In September 1729 Ld. chancellor sir Peter King, being ignorant of college affairs, as Visitor restores Weeksey and confirms Dr Hodges in the office of 'Warden.' A little earlier, in the last months of the reign of George I., it was discovered that the king, and not the Vice-Chancellor, proctors and Doctors of Divinity, was Visitor of University Coll. Oxon. Accordingly Mr Cockman was elected as master instead of Denison, the nominee of the university officers. Scenes of disorder thereupon ensued. ' Jolly'

---

[1] Southey, Coleridge, and C. C. Southey's *Life of Wesley*, 1846, I. 34 *n.*

[2] *Reliqu. Hearn.*, III. 4, 13, 29.

Geo. Ward, senior resident fellow, goes early into the chapel, usurps the Master's place, and strikes Cockman's name out of the buttery-book[1]. He also removed his chair from the College Hall. In May 1729 a Commission restored Cockman and declared five fellowships vacant, Denison's among them[2].

Nichols, *Lit. Anecd.* v. 339, tells how about the year 1725, when Dr Snape (son of the serjeant-farrier to K. Charles II.) was provost of King's, a Mr Bushe was expelled for some whiggish reflections in a college exercise ; he too was reinstated by the Visitor (the bishop of Lincoln) and though this judgment was litigated, 'in the end the whigs prevailed and gave a turn to the political sentiments of the whole University.'

At Cambridge two months earlier the bishop of Lincoln, Dr Ri. Reynolds, had restored Mr Dale to his fellowship at King's, whence he had been deprived for reflecting in a set speech upon K. Charles I. (Dr Andrew Snape, provost). Later too in the same year there was a memorable party struggle at Cambridge, which almost proves how hot men must have waxed in politics, so near was the division. The election to the office of Vice-Chancellor fell upon Dr Rob. Lambert a tory (Master of S. John's[3]) who polled 84 votes against Matthias Mawson of Bene't Coll. (afterwards bishop of Ely), who in spite of Waterland's canvassing wanted one vote to equal

---

[1] *Reliqu. Hearn.* Bliss, II. 316-318, III. 22.
[2] *Ibid.* III. 18 (Mar. 1729).
[3] Mr Mayor on *Baker's Hist. of S. John's*, p. 1017.

Lambert. Nevertheless he held the office in the two subsequent years.

Meanwhile there was not wanting time to those who chose it for disputes between college and college. The occasion for the most frequent class of these quarrels was the jealousy felt by one society against another who lured away her pupils.

The most famous case was that of *Hart Hall* (or Hertford College as Dr Newton loved to have it called).

The following is the account given by Hearne—

'Dr Carter provost of Oriel Coll. having entered a young gentleman some time ago from *Hart Hall*, the principal of Hart Hall, Dr Newton, hath made a great stir in the matter because the young gentleman had no *discessit* from the hall as the statutes require; tho' after all Dr Carter forfeits only 40 shillings for such entrance by the statutes, which Newton would have raised to 40 libs. Newton is famous for talking much, Carter for saying nothing [1]'—and it seemed a question which would hold out longest. This was expressed in an epigram [2].

Mr Sayman the student in dispute died of the small-pox (May 11, 1735), fellow of Oriel [3].

Dr Carter paid the 40 shillings: the smallness of which recompense Ri. Newton resenting, he published in folio in six sheets 'A Letter to the rev. Dr *Holmes*

---

[1] *Hearne*, Bliss, II. 209, 210.
[2] See Amherst's *Appendix to Terrae-filius*, 1726, or Dr Newton's book entitled *University Education, &c.*
[3] *Hearne*, Bliss, III. 158.

Vice-Chancellor of the University of *Oxford* and Visitor of *Hart Hall* within the said University. By *R. Newton* D.D. Principal of *Hart Hall. London.* Printed in the year 1734.' In it he advocated his favourite project of getting a collegiate charter for Hart Hall. In this he was opposed by Exeter College, one of the late Fellows of which Dr John Conybeare[1] then famous as Dean of Christ Church he attacked : but Hearne says that no one commended his conduct (III. 184).

In addition to these personal feuds the political struggle was as violent as ever in the universities.

We are able at present only to allude to the case of Exeter College, an election dispute which evoked a letter from 'a Cambridge Soph' with several other pamphlets and squibs which are to be found in the Libraries of our Universities. Even after the battle of Culloden in 1746, and the Peace of Aix-la-Chapelle two years later, Oxford was open to the imputation of jacobitism. The title of one single Pamphlet will sufficiently illustrate this statement. It is 'Oxford Honesty[2]: or a Case of Conscience Humbly put to the Worshipful and Reverend The Vice-Chancellor, The Heads of Houses, The Fellows &c. of the University of Oxford. Whether one may take the oaths to King George; and yet consistently with *Honour* and *Conscience* and the *Fear* of *God* may do

---

[1] Had been Rector of Exeter, afterwards bp of Bristol—*Hearne,* Bliss, III. 92. See *Calumny Refuted,* by J. Conybeare, D.D., Ed. 2, 1735.

[2] In the Bodleian, *Godwin Pamph.* 1081.

all one can *in Favour* of the *Pretender?* Occasioned by the *Oxford* Speech and *Oxford* Behaviour, at the opening of *Radcliff's* Library April 13, 1749. The second edition with additions. Ezek. xxii. 25... London: Sold by *M. Cooper* at the *Globe* in *Paternoster Row*, and at the Pamphlet shops in *London* and *Westminster.* [price sixpence.]' pp. 39.

On page 5 the anonymous writer asks 'Who is it that is ignorant that *you* take the *Oaths* to *King George* and *abjure* the *Pretender* not *a man* of you *excepted?* It is likewise, I believe, well known even at *Paris* and *Rome* what *sort* of *People* are *most caressed* at *all publick Meetings*, your *Races*, your *High Borlace* &c. [for the *High Borlace*, see the notice below among the Oxford Clubs] and how you dispose of your Places of *Honour, Trust* and *Profit.* Your *members* of *Parliament* too! How warmly have these *always* spoken of the *Revolution?* Their Respect how singular to the *present Government?* How *zealous* in *its Defence* in the late *Rebellion?*'

Nevertheless the authorities at Oxford published a programma against seditious practices: but whether they were considered partial, or for some other reason, the jurisdiction was taken out of their hands in 1748, when two or three young men were convicted of drinking the Pretender's health. Two of the offenders were tried in the Court of King's Bench and 'sentenced to walk through the courts of Westminster with a specification of their crime fixed to their foreheads; to pay a fine of five nobles each;

to be imprisoned for two years, and find security of their good behaviour for the term of seven years after their enlargement.'[1]

It was in 1748 while the matter was before society[2] that William Mason (1725–1797, who, having spent part of his Cambridge career at St John's, was elected fellow of Pembroke Hall in 1747[3], where nine years later he was joined by his friend Gray) wrote his 'Isis.' In that poem he taunts Oxford's degenerate sons who

'madly bold
To Freedom's foes infernal orgies hold.'

Tom Warton of Trinity College Oxford retorted in 'The Triumph of Isis,' upon 'the venal sons of slavish Cam' whom he taunts with being 'still of preferment ...... queen.' He openly boasts of the company which tory Oxford delighted to honour in the Radcliffe and the Theatre. 'It is remarkable (says Dr Anderson in the notice prefixed to Warton's poems) that though neither Mason nor Warton ever excelled these performances, each of them, as by consent, when he first collected his poems into a volume omitted his own party production.' It was a good example of gentleness. In later days Mason's republican feelings like those of some other poets received a shock from the french Revolution, so violent as to wrench out a recantation.

At this time Cambridge and the Government were upon the best of terms.

---

[1] Smollett's *Hist.* Bk. III, ch. i, § 16. Cp. the *Gent. Mag.* XXV. 168—170, also the vol. for 1748, pp. 214—234, 521.

[2] Cooper's *Annals*, IV. 236.   [3] *Ibid.* p. 255.

On the death of the E. of Anglesey in 1737, Thomas Holles Pelham, duke of Newcastle, then Secretary of State, was elected High Steward of the University. From that time till his resignation of the office of First Lord of the Treasury in 1756, and later, he was most constant in attendance upon the desires of the governing body at Cambridge. The duke of Newcastle accompanied an Address to the Crown from the University a few weeks after his appointment by that body, and nine years later when Dr Rooke of Christ's was vice-chancellor we find him engaged in a similar way. In 1748 he succeeded the D. of Somerset as Chancellor, being elected by the University in accordance with the desire of the king, who did not choose that Frederick prince of Wales should have the office[1].

The Installation of the Chancellor was celebrated with all honours and dishonours. 'Every one while it lasted was very gay and very busy in the morning, and very owlish and very tipsy at night: I make no exception from the chancellor to blue-coat[2].' So writes Gray to Dr Wharton in giving an account of the festivities at the request of Dr Keene. The poet was not likely to appreciate such merry-making, especially in honour of one whose politics he despised, and from whom if he expected no favour he was not

---

[1] See the letter quoted by Mr Cooper (*Annals* IV. 263, 264). Compare *A Fragment*, p. 2.

[2] *Blue-coat*, a servant of the Vice-Chancellor's, whose business was to attend acts, degrees, etc., see Gray's *Letter* No. 59. Gray's *Letters* (ed. 1819) No. 71.

destined to be disappointed[1]. Indeed he confesses in the same letter that the only thing which gave him pleasure at the time, was the performance (to Boyce's Music) of the Installation Ode[2], which had been composed by his friend and fellow-poet Will. Mason, once of St John's, then Fellow of Pembroke Hall, who was afterwards to be the editor of his life and works. Very different were Gray's feelings when, exactly twenty years later, he himself composed the Ode for the Installation of the duke of Grafton.

It was not intended that the new Chancellor should be useless and merely an ornament to the University. There were frequent meetings at Christ's Lodge, and packets with the signature of the Secretary of State (D. of Newcastle) were doubtless observed to come by the evening mail to the Blue Boar or to the Red Lion, addressed to Drs Rooke and Keene and Chapman. The bishops of Ely, Lincoln, Chichester and Peterboro' were sometimes noticed driving into Cambridge, and their faces had become familiar to the residents since the late Installation.

At last the secret of all this mystery was known. The Chancellor had sent a code of *Orders and Regulations* for the approval of the Senate. On May 11, 1750, they were first brought before that body; when some of them were rejected by a small majority. But on the 26th of June, the whole eighteen were passed: a nineteenth not having been permitted by the Heads to come before the Senate on account of

---

[1] Cf. *Letter on a Late Resignation*, 1756, p. 14 *n.*
[2] See Cooper's *Annals*, IV. 269.

its absurdity. It required an annual account of the character and behaviour of every person in the University to be transmitted to the Chancellor.

In the *Occasional Letter to Dr Keen*, however, it is stated that ' the work contain'd one-and-twenty distinct Orders most of them Copies from our public Statutes, some such as could never be put in execution, and the last so insufferably ridiculous that you was ashamed to offer it to the Senate.' Perhaps the first Order originally stood as two or three. Yet it may be that the objection to the discarded Order was in those days made rather on the score of impracticability than impertinence; for in the present century we find that the tutors of Colleges used to furnish the proctors and moderators with a list of questionists, with 'appropriate marks' against the name of each, as '*reading*' '*non-reading*,' '*hard-reading* man,' and the like. See Camb. Univ. Calendar for the year 1802.

The Allegorical 'Fragment' represents the number of Orders as 20, one being foisted in by Dr Sam. Squire of St John's, the chancellor's chaplain (who preached at St Mary's on the Sunday afternoon before the Inauguration): though Dr Chapman subsequently got rid of it.

The xviii. Regulations may be seen in full in Mr C. H. Cooper's *Annals of Cambridge*, IV. 278-280, and in 'Excerpta e Statutis...ad officia Scholarium pertinentia,' Camb. Univ. Press (issued frequently at least since 1714). They may be summed up as follows:

1. 'Every person *in statu pupillari* shall wear

cloaths of a grave colour in the judgment of the officers of the University, without lace fringe or embroidery, without cuffs or capes of a different colour from their coats.'

Fellow-commoner graduates to wear the proper habit of their degree.

B. A. to wear gowns 'of prunello or of princes stuff.'

2. Fellow-commoners to wear their 'proper gown, cap and band.'

3, 4. No one *in statu pupillari* to keep a servant or a horse, without the consent of parents or guardians and the head of his college.

5. No person *in statu pupillari* to go to a coffee-house, tennis-court, cricket-ground, &c. between 9 and 12 A.M.

6. A fine of sixpence for not attending the Univ. Sermon. A distribution of seats in the galleries of S. Mary's. Sizars to mark the absentees.

7, 8. Tavern-keepers and coffee-house-keepers not to allow bills above 20*s*. Nor to serve wine, punch, or any other strong liquor, after 11 P.M.

9, 10. No one to ride or drive out of Cambridge without leave of his tutor or master of the College. Nor to be out of his College after 11 P.M.

11. Respect to be shown to superiors. Any M.A. may demand a man's name and College.

12. Dining in a coffee-house forbidden except as under Stat. XLVII.

13. Guns and sporting-dogs forbidden.

14. Noblemen and fellow-commoners to be amenable to discipline upon a Declaration.

5—2

15, 16. Keeping evil company, 'breaking windows, making and fomenting riots and disturbances' are to be punished.

17. Dice forbidden; also cards, except for small sums and at statutable times.

18. Fines to be collected and applied by Stat. Univ. 50.

It will easily be imagined that these New Regulations were not popular upon the whole.

A squib, in which allusion is made to most of the Orders and Regulations, is printed in the *Student, or Oxford and Camb. Monthly Miscellany*, vol. I. pp. 311, 312, and signed *Cambridge*, August 1, 1750, *Sophista.* It is entitled 'The Happiness of a good Assurance. Horace, Book I. Ode 22. Imitated and modernized.'

'Whoe'er with frontless *phyz* is blest,
  Still in a blue or scarlet vest
    May saunter thro' the town,
  Or strut, regardless of the *rules*,
  Ev'n to St *Mary*'s or the *Schools*
    In hat or poplin gown.   [*Orders and Regulations*, I. II.]

A dog he unconcern'd maintains,   [*O. and R.* XIII.]
And seeks with gun the sportive plains
  Which ancient *Cam* divides;
Or to the hills on horse-back strays   [*O. and R.* IV. IX.]
(Unask'd his Tutor) or his chaise
  To fam'd *New-market* guides.

For in his sight (whose brow severe
Each morn the coffee-houses fear,   [*O. and R.* V.]
  Each night the taverns dread;   [*O. and R.* VII.]
To whom the tatter'd Sophs bend low,
To whom the gilded tossils bow
  And Graduates nod the head;)   [*O. and R.* XI.]

Ev'n in the Proctor's awful sight
On *Regent-walk* at twelve last night   [*O. and R.* x.]
   Unheedingly I came;
And tho', with WHISH's claret fir'd,   [*O. and R.* VIII. XII.]
I brush'd his side, he ne'er enquir'd   [*O. and R.* XI.]
   My college or my name.

Were I oblig'd whole terms to keep
And haste to Chapel, rouz'd from sleep,
   At five each frosty morning;
Or for a riot should my ear   [*O. and R.* XVI.]
Of hated rustication hear
   The first or second warning:' &c. &c.

The Senate did not approve of the intervention of the Chancellor and the Bishops; and they were jealous of the power of the *Caput*, and smarted under the indignity of having been forced to adopt their measures. These two sections of the governing body of the University corresponded, to a considerable extent, with other pairs of parties in the commonwealth.

The *Caput* as a general rule were constitutionalists and supporters of the Bishops[1]; while a large proportion of the *Senate* was tory, if not jacobite, friendly to high-churchmen and the remnant of the Lower-House of Convocation. Nevertheless in November the Public Orator was directed to thank the Chancellor for his condescension and to assure him that his orders would be carried out. The non-placets were but few[2].

And they were as good as their word. A few days before this grace had passed, the Senior Proctor,

---

[1] Cf. *The Academic*, pp. 47, 48.   [2] Cooper's *Annals*, IV. 281.

James Brown M.A. fellow (and afterwards master
1770-1784) of Pembroke Hall, in his zeal to carry out
the 8th and 10th Regulations, visited the *Tuns*
Tavern punctually at 11 o'clock on the evening of
Nov. 17th.

Forty-six members of the *Westminster Club* were
keeping, as 'Old Westminsters' use, the Anniversary
of the Accession of their Foundress Q. Elizabeth—
the regius professor of greek, Thomas Francklyn,
Fellow of Trinity (translator of Sophocles), was in
the chair, and other senior members of the University
were present; the bill had been called for; some
slight matter it was said detained them, and while a
subscription was being levied for the waiters, the
health of Dr Nichols the head master was being
drunk. It is probable that some at least of the party
were in high boisterous spirits, and the presence of
the Proctor was not received with respect by all. It
was (we may be inclined to think) not very wise in
that Gentleman to exercise his power in a company
where there were several Masters of Arts and a
Professor who could see good order observed; and
such an act was considered an infringement on
etiquette[1]. The Professor remonstrated with him
upon what he considered an intrusion; his remonstrance was cheer'd by the company, as also was a
speech from Thomas Ansell, LL.B. fellow of Trinity

[1] Compare Gunning's *Reminiscences*, I. p. 60 (ed. 1854), with Camb.
Univ. Stat. 47, referred to in the 12th of the New Regulations. Also
Key to the Fragment, pp. 26, 27. *Authentic Narrative of the late Extra-
ordinary Proceedings at Camb. against the W——r Club*, p. 17.

Hall, who drew the Proctor's attention, not very respectfully, to the sobriety of the party. A burst of applause also followed when Samuel Crew, M.A., Fellow of Trinity, protested against the encroachment upon the rights of Masters of Arts. After drinking the toast, which had been proposed before their interruption, the Club dispersed. It was clear that, however unwisely Mr Brown the Proctor may have acted, the learned grecian and the other senior men who were of the party at Mr *Wish's* Tavern[1] acted wrongly, and set a fatal example in questioning his authority before an excited audience. The affair was most unfortunate and the sequel most disastrous.

The University had already been much agitated while the question of the New Regulations was being moved. The following extract from a Letter dated Cambridge, November 16, 1750 (from a page of MS. (qu. a copy), is bound in a volume in the Bodleian Library[1] [*Gough, Camb.* 47]. *It was written* [apparently to an Oxford friend: there is no signature. Ri. Gough himself was at Corpus Coll. Cambridge, and did not come into residence till 1752, and took no degree (Gorton, *Dict. Biog.*). His books were bequeathed to 'Bodley' on his death in 1809.] *the very day before the meeting of the Westminster Club,* and will give a fair account of the state of feeling at the time: 'Our conversation in the University has been of

---

[1] '*Wish* calls—the Midnight Revels must be done.' *Epistle to a Fellow-Commoner* (1750).

'Thro' his (Keene's) direction Vice shall be no more,
Poor Wish for want of trade shut up the Tuns.'

The Capitade, 1750.

late very much in the disputatious way, and I am satisfied we are both equally grieved to find that Party dissensions have at last found their way into *this* university as well as that of Oxford. Nothing now to be heard but party squabbles and literary scandal. Since the letter to Lord Egmont there has appeared another to Dr Keene equally scurrilous and abusive: and what has made more noise than any of the letters; an infamous Libel on the Heads of Houses called the Capitade which was printed in the London evening Post of thursday, Novem^r. 1st. The other day came out a pamphlet called " The Academic, or a Disputation on the propriety of the late Regulations and the State of the University:" with a great profession of candour, it is one of the most unfair and disingenuous Pieces I ever read, and plainly wrote as an abuse of the Vice-Chancellor. The authors by repute are Powel of St John's, with Balguy and Allen and Mason of Pembrook. But I believe they have made a rod for their own backs.'

There had lately been cases of disorderly conduct which had come before the Vice-Chancellor, and which had probably been the occasion of the new Regulations[1]. In the pamphlets of the time were frequent references[2] to the disorders in '49, in which window-breaking was a prominent offence. In the first year of his vice-chancellorship, Dr Keene had 'publickly admonished twelve young Gentlemen of

[1] *The Academic*, pp. 10, 19, 40.
[2] *Ibid.* p. 26. *Another Fragment*, p. 5, compared with Regulation XVI.

the first Character in the University[1],' who had
behaved rudely in the round of visits which it was
then customary for some 'men.' in the first class on
the first day of the degree examination, as it then
was, to make in order to receive congratulations from
the 'Toasts' of their acquaintance. On this occasion, as well as on another[2] soon afterwards, the
Vice-Chancellor was thought by some to have acted
without due enquiry and examination. 'Upwards
of twenty Persons, many of good Families and Fortune,' as Dr Green informs us (*Observations on Regulations*, pp. 17, 18), had been expelled or rusticated
'for very heinous violations of our Laws and Discipline.'

It was therefore extremely unlucky that a personal affront to the Proctor was made the cause of
summoning before the Vice-Chancellor's court, the
greek Professor (Francklin), a Fellow of Trinity
Hall (Ansell), a Fellow of Trinity (Crew—besides
Francklin), and two Fellow-commoners (Vernon
Trinity, Vane *Peter House*).

The Court was held[3] in the Law Schools on
Saturday, Nov. 24, and at dusk adjourned to 'the
Theatre', where the Undergraduates in the gallery
took the opportunity of expressing their sympathy
with the accused. Ansell made matters worse, by
appealing to them to be quiet 'for our sake,' and

---

[1] *Friendly and Honest Advice of an old Tory*, 1751, pp. 26, 27.
[2] *Honest and Friendly Advice*, pp. 29, 30.
[3] The following account is taken chiefly from [Ansell's] *Authentic Narrative*, (see the Notes at the end).

behaved in an unseemly and contemptuous manner[1]. After another sitting in the Law School[2], where sixteen proproctors· were provided to prevent a recurrence of the disturbances, Franklin, Ansell, Crew, Vernon and Vane, were found guilty of insulting and interrupting the Proctor in the execution of his office, and were reprimanded.

Ansell alone[3] was suspended (on account of his behaviour in his defence), 'ab omni gradu suscepto et suscipiendo.' The defendants had to pay the costs, and such members of the Club as were in statu pupillari were fined 6s. 8d. for being out of College after Eleven P.M.

Whatever may have been the indiscretion of the Proctor (and of this we can hardly judge from violent pamphlets[4]), there seems no reason to suppose that the sentence was unjust, or that it could have been reversed.

Ansell, however, who had manifested when under examination the same impudent conduct which had betrayed itself under excitement at the Westminster Club, declared his intention of appealing from the

[1] *Appendix to Inquiry into Right of Appeal*, compared with Ansell's own account, *Authentic Narrative*, p. 32 n., and *Another Fragment*, p. 26, *Fragmentum est pars*, p. 31. (Tuesday, Nov. 27.)
'Their Harangues seem'd to make no more Impression upon *Mun* and the *Gentlemen* of the *Jury* than if they had read to them *The* FRANKLEIN's *Tale out of Chaucer.' Fragmentum est pars*, p. 32.
[2] (Thursday, Nov. 29.)
[3] See *Appendix* to *Inquiry, Authentic Narrative*, p. 32 n. *Another Fragment*, p. 26, *Fragmentum est pars*, p. 31, and the notice of Dr Will. *George* of King's, which will be found in the Notes.
[4] (The *Authentic Narrative* was drawn up by Ansell himself.)

Vice-Chancellor's sentence [1]. Dr Keene, after some delay caused by waiting for legal opinions, decided that no appeal lay from his sentence in cases of discipline [2].

Although we find that Ansell did not think fit to prosecute his intention, the question of appeal absorbed the attention and the animosities of the University for some time, and produced almost as plentiful a crop of pamphlets, as the earlier grounds of the dispute on the Regulations and the Club.

At a congregation about a fortnight later the Vice-Chancellor, on the strength of legal opinions, refused an application from a future regius professor of civil law (Will. Ridlington of Trinity Hall) to appoint delegates upon Mr Ansell's appeal; and though he informed them of his intention of bringing in a grace to appoint syndics to inquire into the question, the Associators (as they were called) [3] not only rejected the grace when it was brought forward a month later (by 52 against 11 placets in the Non-Regent House), but gave an immediate evidence of their discontent by stopping a supplicat for a B.A.'s degree.

In November 1751, Edmund Keene retired from the office of Vice-Chancellor, which he had held for two unquiet years. He was succeeded by Dr John

---

[1] *Appendix* to *Inquiry into Right of Appeal.*

[2] *Honest and Friendly Advice*, passim.

[3] The *Associators* were a body of about 36 MM.A., who asserted the right of appeal. They used to meet at the Tuns Tavern (the scene of the Westminster Club meeting). At their head (Cooper's *Annals*, IV. 283) was John Banson, LL.D., Fellow of Trinity Hall.

Wilcox of Clare Hall[1]—Dr Will. George, provost of King's, being the other candidate.

Wilcox was scarcely more a favourite with the Associators than the Master of Peter House had been, and when the grace offered by James Bickham of Emmanuel was rejected in the caput, a degree was stopped by the Non-Regents as before. In the following month, however, a similar attempt at obstruction was frustrated in each House of the Senate. A more constitutional attempt to gain their object was frustrated by the Vice-Chancellor refusing to call a caput;—a prudent use in this instance of a strangely autocratic power: for it is hardly likely that the Caput would have accepted Mr Bickham's grace without inquiring into the question on its merits. A proposition, which seemed likely to determine the difficulty by impartial search into the legal aspect of the alleged right, was quashed by the reasonable refusal of the D. of Newcastle (the chancellor of Cambridge) to act as referee[2]: and the question it seems was never settled.

The disturbances appear to have been kept up[3] by the Undergraduates almost till the close of the controversy: the latest phase of their fury was a bacchanalian impulse to rush through the streets with lighted links and torches.

[1] In *The Capitade* he figures as 'good though gloomy W—c—x,' which is rather high praise.

[2] Cooper's *Annals*, IV. 286.

[3] *Ibid.* 285. See Decree of Vice-C. and Heads, Dec. 5, 1751, there quoted.

After a while the University seems to have sobered down to the more peaceful arts of receiving visits from the Chancellor, opening the New Library, presenting addresses to the King, and writing for the new prizes for composition &c., which inaugurated the second half of the century.

Of the character of the D. of Newcastle I am not competent to speak: but in his capacity as Chancellor of our University his conduct was apparently upright and considerate. He visited Cambridge in June, 1766, the year when he retired from all state employments. Within eighteen months he had died; and the D. of Grafton was installed in his room[1], having, like his predecessor, retired from being the First Lord of the Treasury.

Whatever we may think of the wisdom of the 'Regulations,' the impression which will probably be left upon our minds is, that the condition of the University can hardly be called satisfactory when Caput and Senate were not ashamed[2] to charge one another with bidding for royal and ducal favour by no honest means.

In 1764, Cambridge was again disturbed by a warm political contest for the office of High-Steward or Seneschal of the University, in the room of the late lord chancellor Hardwicke[3]. His son Philip, the second earl, was elected after a most remarkable conflict[4], which involved some nice questions on the

---

[1] Cooper's *Annals,* IV. 353—356.
[2] *The Academic,* 32, 49 foll. with passages in the other pamphlets.
[3] Cooper's *Annals,* IV. 297, 334, 399; his death, IV. 437.
[4] See at length Cooper's *Annals,* IV. 334, 335.

order of voting, and very nearly ended in a tie. The unsuccessful candidate was John, Earl of Sandwich[1] (three times first lord of the admiralty, twice a secretary of state, postmaster-general in 1770, took part in the conference at Aix-la-Chapelle in 1748, and died 1792). Although his private character was far from respectable, the clergy preferred his political principles to those of lord Hardwicke, who was supported by the faculties of Law and Medicine. The reader will remember the bitter election squib wherein Gray satirized him as '*Sly Jemmy Twitcher*[2].'

He also figures as 'Lord *Sandtown*,' a gay nobleman, who is represented as having stood for the office of High-Steward '*a long time ago*,' in a pamphlet[3] which preserves a similar strain of earnest banter throughout.

[1] Cooper's *Annals*, IV. 334 *n.*

[2] '*The Candidate, or the* Cambridge *Courtship*,' Gray's Works. See also ' *The Candidate*,' by C. Churchill (where *Lothario*, lord Bute, is mentioned), ' Black Smith of Trinity,' Sumner, then V.-C., and Roger Long, of Pembroke, are mentioned as supporters of Sandwich.

[3] ' An Address to the Members of the Senate of the University of Cambridge on The Attention due to *Worth* of *Character* from a *Religious* Society: with a View to the ensuing *Election* of a High Steward. To which is added a Letter of Mr Jos. Mede formerly of Christ's College, copied from a MS. in the *Harleian* Collection [if it is a genuine Letter to Sir Martin Stukeville, Kt. at Dalham, Suffolk, Christ Coll. June 3, [1626], it will be found probably in *MS. Harl.* 390] giving a very particular Account of the Circumstances attending the Duke of *Buckingham's* Election in King *Charles* the First's Time. By a Master of Arts. Prov. xxiv. 24, 25. Printed for the Editor in the Year 1764.' (8vo. pp. 60.—Bodl. *Gough, Camb.* 36). Mr Cooper, *Annals*, IV. 334 (as well as a MS. note in a copy I have seen in an old hand), attributes it to 'John Gorden, fellow of Emmanuel College, afterwards fellow of Peterhouse, D.D., and Archdeacon of Lincoln.' (J. Gordon was also Chancellor of Lincoln. See Nichols, *Lit. Anecd.*)

By this time, in the reign of George III., there had been working a radical change in the meaning of party names. 'When the possibility of the restoration of the Stuarts became extinct, the minds of the tories were set free; and so the strong feeling of personal loyalty began to concentrate itself round George III., who was an englishman born, and a monarch by hereditary right, though derived from usurpation. The king was a man of great force of character and fair abilities, and one who could command respect. It was not surprising therefore that he was enabled to enlist the sympathies of the party of prerogative whose toryism was now a *habit* rather than a *sentiment*[1]. Instead of attempting to suspend the laws which were affecting prerogative, the king made free use of patronage,—a powerful engine with all parties when the House of Commons was nominated by lords of boroughs headed by the king. The tories as yet had with them, as they had had all along, the sympathies of the people. In the eighteenth century whiggism was by no means popular, and it was not till the present century that the whigs bethought them, as a last resort, of attempting to enlist the power of public opinion on their side.'

At no time perhaps was a shuffling and a changing of the suits of party more easy than in the years which followed 1760. In the reigns of the first two Georges the most consistent tories had found themselves doing the same work of opposition to the

[1] Notes of a lecture delivered by the Professor of Modern History; (the office was instituted in Cambridge in 1724 by George I.).

Crown as the more thorough and the less conservative of the whigs. But as soon as George III. was
come to revive the flame of loyalty which was lan-
guishing for want of one to feed it, the ardour of the
tories was satisfied in him, and they became attached
to him and his successors, yet not with all the devotion of a first love, but rather in the more cautious
and unabandoned spirit which had characterized the
allegiance of the more moderate whigs.

For the remainder of the century both Universities became assimilated to the new tory party[1], the
one from High Church Whiggism, the other from
High Church Toryism. So that even at Cambridge
by 1793, the friends of the first french Revolution
were in such discredit that even a whig was scarcely
to be found. It was not till the present century that
the 'evangelical' movement gained any strength at
Cambridge—and then many of its members held
High Church Doctrine in the 18th century use of the
term,—or that the 'tractarian' school developed itself
in Oxford.

Of the prognostications of those great revolutions
in the religious life of the Universities we shall have
occasion to speak in the last division of this work.

Yet at Cambridge (if not at Oxford) there remained some portion of the bitter root, some seeds
of the inveterate mischief of dissension. In 1772
there was an attempt made by the Senate[2] to choose

---

[1] Gunning, *Reminisc.* I. 189.

[2] Monk's *Life of Bentley*, I. 335, 336 *n.*　Cooper's *Annals*, IV. 110.
366.

a Fellow of Trinity as Vice-Chancellor, but it was frustrated by the refusal of their nominee, Stephen Whisson; and Dr Cooke, the provost of King's, was duly elected. There had only been one other attempt of the kind (since 1586, when Dr Copcot, fellow of Trinity, held the office), and that at the time when the Senate was beginning to manifest a hostile spirit, when, in 1712, some members of that body took advantage of the small attendance of the Heads, at the preliminary nomination, to propose Mr Hawkins, fellow of Pembroke; but the design was defeated by the entry of two voters who were not in the plot.

It is, perhaps, not the least of the improvements introduced into our University constitution, that the Council has been substituted for the Caput. The Senate take pains to select the best men; and the employment of Tutors and others in that body is beneficial to the University no less than to themselves.

Meantime, an ex-Vice-Chancellor of Cambridge had given a prophetic account of the results which should follow the dissensions of which he had seen but the beginning. There is the following striking passage in Daniel Waterland's Thanksgiving Sermon, preached in 1716.

'As divisions increase, Christian Charity will decline daily, till it becomes an empty name or an *idea* only. Discipline will of course slacken and hang loose; and the consequence of that must be a general dissoluteness and corruption of manners. Nor will the enemy be wanting to sow tares to corrupt our faith as well as practice, and to introduce a general latitude of opinions. *Arianism, Deism, Atheism*, will insensibly steal upon us, while our heads and hearts run after politics and parties.'

We have already seen enough of the distractions of the times, and we can easily understand that, amid so much wrangling and disputing, there was little room for piety or Christian love. And where there was not the fulfilling of the law and will of God, how could men hope to know of the doctrine?

Since the preceding century there had been a great falling off from the search for truth in the Science of Religion. The great civil conflict had unsettled the habit of quiet search, of sober life, and religious communion; of the formation of which there had at one time been promise in this country. And when the struggle was over for a while, the selfish worship of the puritan, and the more selfish ungodliness of the cavalier, conspired towards the debasement of the land. A thousand pities that the one could not lend the other his good qualities, and fling the bad away; that serious purpose and an inclination for religion could not have been graced with geniality, and exalted into the communion of the manifold Christian Life. As it was the two combined (the one by deficiency, the other by extravagance,) to bring into being the classes whose characteristics retarded the progress of Christian Unity.

Although there were not wanting men of learning and of purity in either body, the few great divines of the Eighteenth Century did not communicate their knowledge and enthusiasm to the younger men. For a Professor at the University to lecture was almost the exception. In 1766, indeed, we find Dr Edward Bentham, of Christ Church, delivering a course, as King's Professor of Divinity; and, in 1780, Dr John Hey, late fellow of Sidney Sussex College, did the same, as the first Norrisian Professor; and his successor, Fawcett of St John's, followed his example. Still, according to the Cambridge University Calendar for 1802, there were public lectures delivered only by the following Professors:—Jowett, on *Civil Law;* Vince, on *Experimental Philosophy;* Farish, on *Chemistry;* Martyn, on *Botany;* Harwood, on *Anatomy;* Symonds, on *Modern History;* Fawcett, Norrisian Prof. of *Divinity;* Wollaston, on *Natural* and *Experimental Philosophy;* Edw. Christian, on the *Laws of England;* nine Sadlerian *Algebra* Lecturers, and four *Barnaby Lecturers.* Meanwhile, the list of Professors delivering no lectures (though some of these presided at the 'Acts') seems to us of a disgraceful length. Dr Sam. Parr, however, did not think so, when two years earlier he wrote: 'In regard to Cambridge, the persons there appointed to Professorships, have, in few instances, disgraced them by notorious incapacity or criminal negligence. A late work of Dr Hey furnishes us with a decisive proof of his abilities and his activity. Dr Waring and Mr Vince, in their writings, have done honour to the science, not only of their University, but of their age. The profound researches of Dr Waring, I suppose, were not adapted to any form of communication by lectures. But Mr Vince has, by private instructions, been very useful both to those who were novitiates[1], and to those who were proficients, in mathematics. Dr Hallifax, Dr Rutherforth, and Dr Watson, very abundantly conveyed the information which belonged to their departments, sometimes in the disputes of the schools, and sometimes by the publication of their writings. Chemistry has been adorned, not by their labour only, but by the sagacity of Dr Watson, and Dr Milner. Mr Porson, the Greek Professor, has not read more than one lecture, but that one was πίδακος ἐξ ἱερῆς ὀλίγη λιβάς. He has written, however, books of utility far more extensive than lectures could be; and I speak from my own actual observation when I state, that the Greek Plays edited by this wonderful man have turned the attention of several academics towards philological learning, which, it must be confessed, has few and feeble attractions to the eagerness of curiosity, or the sprightliness of youth.' (Parr's *Spital Sermon*, published August, 1800, note 84.)

To return to the list of professors who delivered no lectures at Cambridge in 1802. It is headed, in spite of his boasted enlightenment and ardour in University educational reform, by Ri. Watson, King's Professor of *Divinity;* then follow *Physic, Hebrew* (because he met not 'with suitable encouragement,' p. 20), *Greek* (Ri. Porson), Lady Margaret *Divinity, Casuistry, Arabic*, Lucasian *Mathematics*, (but Is. Milner[2] 'is at all times accessible to Students of any College, by whom

---

[1] noviciate = novice, Addison, *Spect.* No. 164. 'improperly,' says Todd on Johnson.

[2] For *Is. Milner's* neglect of lectures, Mr *Mayor* refers me to his *Hist. of St. John's*, p. 849 l. 45, and to a tract by *Frend*.

he is frequently consulted,' p. 22), *Music, Mineralogy* (but Prof. Hailstone attends at the Museum three days a week, 9—11 A.M., 2—4 P.M.), *Astronomy.*

As to the industry of the Professors at *Oxford* Dr Parr writes: 'what I know I will relate. Dr Trapp, Mr Hawkins, and Dr Lowth, have published their lectures as *Poetry* professors. Mr Wharton has inserted one lecture into his edition of Theocritus. The gentleman who is now professor [James Hurdis] reads lectures, and has published a part of them I believe in English. That the lectures of Sir William Scott upon *History*, if given to the world, "would form a most valuable treatise," Mr Gibbon himself has been assured. In addition to this respectable testimony I would beg leave to say, that many years ago Sir William read to me a part of one lecture which contained some curious matter on the revenues of the Grecian States, and which seemed to me perfectly worthy of the writer, from variety of learning, acuteness of observation, and elegance of style. The Commentaries of Dr Blackstone, and a very excellent work of Professor Woodison, are proofs that the institution of the *Vinerian* Professorship is not wholly useless. Dr Bentham formerly read lectures in the *Divinity* School, and the same office is now performed with great ability by Dr Randolph, whose cares as a prelate have not made him inattentive to his duties as a Professor. In *Chemistry* and in *Anatomy*, lectures I know were, for some years, regularly given; and I believe they were largely attended. The lectures of the *Saxon* Professor [Charles Mayo] were much applauded, and his successor [James Ingram] I am persuaded will justify the choice of the University by his knowledge, his activity, and his judgment. I have not heard whether Dr Hunt or Dr White, read lectures in the *Oriental* languages, nor am I sure that such lectures would have been of great use according to the method in which those languages are now learned. But I know that both the Professors just now mentioned hold a very high rank in the estimation of foreign scholars. Dr Hunt supplied many valuable notes to the *Praelectiones Hebraicae* of Dr Lowth; he read in the schools, and then printed, one Oration *de Antiquitate elegantiâ et utilitate linguae Arabicae*, 1738; and another *De usu Dialectorum Orientalium et praecipue Arabicae in Hebraico Codice interpretando* in 1748. He, in 1744, addressed to Oxford Students, "A Dissertation on Proverbs vii. 22, 23," and this Dissertation, in 1755, was republished by Dr Kennicott, who added to it critical observations of Dr Hunt on other passages in Proverbs, and two very learned Sermons on two very difficult subjects. Dr White was always ready to assist young men who applied to him for instruction. He is author of a very judicious Sermon upon the Septuagint. He published an inaugural speech.... He translated and edited in two vols. 4to., the Syriac Version 'of part of the New Testament, which belonged to Dr Gloucester Ridley. He is said to be now engaged in preparing the Epistles. He long ago completed...what Pocock, junior, left unfinished in the translation of *Abollatiph's Egyptian History*. He has lately done signal service to young clergymen by an edition of the received Text of the New Testament, with the most important variations in Griesbach, and by a *Diatessaron*, drawn up in conformity to the Chronology applied by Archbishop Newcome; and to his professorial studies, he in his Bampton Lectures was much indebted for the happy choice of a subject, and for the very masterly manner in which it has been treated.'

It will be observed that Dr Parr makes no mention of the Oxford Professors of *Civil Law* (French Laurence), *Medicine* (Will. Vivian), *Greek* (Will. Jackson), *Margaret Prof. of Divinity* (Septimus Collinson), *Natural Philos.* and of *Anatomy* (Tho. Hornsby), *Geometry* (Abram Robertson), *Music* (Will. Crotch), *Botany* (Geo. Williams), *Modern Hist. and Mod. Languages* (Tho. Nowell), and the *Clinical* Professor (Martin Wall),—(an Oxonian perhaps could have given a better account of them) ;—and while he plainly shows that the Universities were by no means altogether dens of idleness, there was then, as now, a great part of the instruction of younger men which was not covered by the efforts of the *University* Professors. This deficiency was supplied in part by the work of *College* tutors, or of 'pupil-mongers,' of whom we shall have occasion to speak by and by. But whether they did their work conscientiously or no, there was not that intercourse between the senior and junior members of the Universities that once had been.

In the earliest stage of the University community poor students, who were not inmates of halls, clubbed together, two or three or more in a party, to hire a common room ('camera')[1]. Hence they were distinguished from the regular inmates by the names 'camerâ degentes,' 'chamber-dekyns,' or 'chums.' The last name lost its opprobrious signification in Elizabethan times, and was then applied to those companions who shared a common room *in College.* For in those days, when it was the custom to enter at the University at the age when boys now go to a public school, it was no longer lawful for a student to lodge without the college walls: and since that time most of those societies have enlarged their buildings, and are yet enlarging. In those days scholars were content to '*lodge*' in College, not to 'keep[2];' they were content to share a single chamber; no one dreamt of the luxury of rooms: *commorabantur non habitabant.*

By the Elizabethan statutes of Trinity College, Cambridge (cap. 26, *de cubiculorum distributione,* a chapter important in the case of Dr Bentley), a Doctor of Divinity is to have a whole chamber to himself; the share of a Fellow below a Doctor's degree is half a Doctor's; the Scholar's or Sizar's share is half that of a Fellow; the Pensioner's and Subsizar's half a Scholar's or Sizar's. So that a

---

[1] See Mr Jeaffreson's *Annals of Oxford*, 1870, I. ch. iii. Prof. Malden's *Origin of Universities*, 1835, pp. 32, 85.

[2] '*habere*' in the old College Statutes of Trinity College, Camb. (*Elis.*) cap. xxvi. (See also Stat. Coll. Diui Joh. Euang. *Cant.* cap. xxxii.) The Cambridge local use of the word to *keep*, however, will be found in the letter from Mede quoted below in the text. Compare also *Gradus ad Cantabrigiam*, 1802, quoted in the notes.

B.A. Fellow designate should have for his chamber-fellows either a B.A. Fellow, or two Scholars, or a Scholar and a Sizar, with two Pensioners or Sub-sizars. Where a chamber contained undergraduates there should be four of them if possible, one being a scholar or sizar. Bentley says (*Corresp.* II. 682) that this 'has been obsolete time out of mind, since the College has enlarged itself with a second large Court.' It appears that the graduates had the use of a key. At St John's (Statut. cap. xxxii.) every Doctor, preacher, and member of the Seniority, was to have one chamber to himself with two scholars if he pleased. Two Fellows at most were to be in one room, or four scholars. The Fellows, scholars, and students who were above fourteen years of age were to sleep alone, or two in a bed, according to the judgment of the Master and Seniors. The elder students were to superintend the conduct of their junior 'chums' (*concubicularii*). And if a Fellow were at any time introduced into the chamber of which they had been head, they were to surrender to him the library or study ('*musaeum.*' This is the word which Z. C. von Uffenbach applies to T. Baker's 'keeping room' in 1710), and other furniture of the room. Three chambers might be set apart to the use of Fellow-Commoners. According to the original Statutes of Corpus Christi Coll. Oxon. a scholar slept in a truckle-bed below each Fellow. *Hist. MSS. Commission* 2, p. 126, 1871. See *notes.*

The following extract from a letter from *Mede* to sir Martin Stuteville (*Mar.* 26, 1625) will illustrate the arrangement which had to be gone through. 'I have no way left but to get one of my Bachelors (March), who keeps in the same building, to keep with the Master of Arts, and let yours have the use of his study, though it be not in so good a chamber.'

In 1662 the famous John Strype[1], then a scholar of Jesus College, Camb., writes to his mother; 'as yet I am in a Chamber that doth not at all please me. I have thoughts of one, which is a very handsome one, and one pair of stairs high, and that looketh into the Master's garden. The price is but 20*s.* per annum, ten whereof a knight's son, and lately admitted into this College, doth pay: though he did not come till about Midsummer, so that I shall have but 10*s.* to pay a year: besides my income which may be about 40*s.* or thereabouts...At my first coming I laid alone: but since my Tutor desired me to let a very clear lad lay with me and an Alderman's son of Colchester, which I could not deny, being newly come: he hath laid with me now for almost a fortnight, and will do till he can provide himself with a Chamber.'

It appears from Abraham de la Pryme's account of the suicide of his friend, Mr Bohun, 'of the year above me,' in 1692, that he and another student shared a 'chamber,' or sleeping-room, of which the bedmaker had a key, and a 'study.' His 'chum... say'd that he went to bed and slept very well till the morning, and arising then he put on his studdy-

---

[1] Cooper's *Annals*, III. 505. Ellis's *Letters of Eminent Literary Men*, 177.

ing gown and cap and his stockings and shoos, and going into his studdy lock'd the dore after him.' *Surtees Society*, 54, p. 26.

Necessity thus often made strange chamber-fellows. Henry Sacheverell shared a room with Addison at Magdalen College, Oxford. Archbishop Tillotson was chum of Francis Holcroft, who was afterwards ejected from his Fellowship at Clare, and having been imprisoned several times, joined with Joseph Oddie[1] (ejected Fellow of Trinity) in founding independent congregations in Cambridge.

Evelyn[2], who was a Fellow-Commoner in Balliol, when in his 19th year had his brother Richard to be his chamber-fellow. The custom was not extinct in 1711, when Ambrose Bonwicke[3] arranged for his brother *Phil.* and another chum to share his room; but it was not universal, nor (what is most important for our present point) do we hear of any senior member of a College sharing a chamber with an undergraduate. This was owing in a great measure to the change which was passing over University society. The social aristocracy, which had prevailed in the Universities in the days of George Herbert and Francis Bacon, of sir Henry Wotton and the Norths, had grown well-nigh extinct there at the end of the XVIIIth century, and the remnant which remained no longer coalesced with the bulk of the

[1] See Robinson's Church-book ap. Dyer's *Life of Rob. Robinson*, p. 37.

[2] Evelyn's *Diary*, Jan. 21, 1640.

[3] *Life of Ambrose Bonwicke*, (ed. 1870) pp. 34—38, 44, 64; and 182, Mr Mayor's *note*.

community. The unhappy divisions in the country and in the University made it no longer possible for that intimacy to exist between tutor and pupil which had been so admirably exemplified in the martyr, Nicholas Ridley, when he had been tutor in Pembroke Hall, and of whom his pupil bears witness that 'his behaviour was very obliging, and very pious, without hypocrisy or monkish austerity: for very often he would shoot in the Bow or play Tennis with me'[1]. It will be remembered also how later in the xvith century Roger Ascham loved to practise Archery in St John's at Cambridge, in accordance with the Statutes of his College, and how well he preached what he practised, in his Book of Shooting.

In earlier times the relation between tutor and pupil at the Universities, had been similar to that which has of late so happily grown up in higher schools between boy and Master. And indeed the '*children*' of the 16th, the '*boys*'[2] and the '*schollers*' of the 17th, and the '*lads*' of the 18th century, differed little in age or discipline from the public school-boys of the present day. While they had been under their Udalls and Busbies they had learnt not less of latin and hebrew and of greek (as they were then known) than the upper-school boy of our public schools: or if any young Paston or

---

[1] Letter from *W. Turner*, Physician to Protector Somerset, and Dean of Wells, to *Foxe* the Martyrologist—translated by Strype, *Memorials*, III. 229.

[2] 'Boys,' circa 1660, Life of *Matt. Robinson* (Mayor) 1856. 32, 107.

William Page would make no progress in the world
with his book, he was sure to be 'trewly belasschyd'[1]
(or 'preeches' as Sir Hugh Evans would say) for his
lack of pains: the same boys when they arrived
at Oxford or Cambridge in the 16th or 17th century, still found the birch at the buttery-hatch : but
they also found more liberty than they had enjoyed at Winchester or Westminster, at the Charterhouse or Merchant Taylors. They found, that is,
at the University, much the same amount of liberty
as those who are now Bachelors of Arts found
when they went from a private to a public school.
There was still the same regularity of hours ; morning and evening prayer in the Chapel, early dinner
and supper in a common room,—dormitories neither
with complete privacy, not yet entirely open to
all comers, but arranged with some view to pleasant
or profitable neighbourhood of sleepers. They found
among the less respectable of their comrades a craving
for ale, and for tobacco smoke, as soon as it was
to be had. They found also, in earlier times, those
'menne not werye of theyr paynes, but very sorye
to leue theyr studye,' who being without fire were
'fayne to walk or runne vp and downe half an
houre to gette a heate on their feete whan they
go to bed.'

These assuredly had chosen the better part; but
we cannot suppose that in the middle of the 16th

[1] See Errands to London of *Agnes Paston*, 28 Jan. 1457: 'and so
ded the last mastyr and yᵉ best that euᵉʳ he had att Caumbrege '—Fenn's
Paston Letters, I. 144, ed. 1787. No. XXXV.

century, there were none who (like Ascham a few years earlier) fitted themselves for a better attention unto their 'reasonyng in problemes or vnto some other studye,' by some more healthful and refreshing bodily exercise, than walking or running up and down 'to gette a heate on their feete whan they go to bed.'

Of the relaxations we will speak again hereafter. At present enough has been said to show that the condition of the undergraduates in earlier times was very different from what the last century has made for ourselves.

Although such cases as that of William Wotton[1] (who went to Catharine-Hall in 1676), or George Grenville (ld. Lansdowne) who in 1667 entered as a nobleman at Trinity, before they were ten years old, must not be taken as anything but exceptions; yet they prove at least that a precocious boy *could* enter at an age at which now-a-days he would be not only discouraged, but practically inadmissible. Yet as late as 1806 we find Keble admitted scholar of C. C. C., Oxon, when he had just turned fourteen years and a half. Swift went to Dublin at fourteen. Gibbon entered at Magdalen, Oxford, as a gentleman commoner (April 1752) before he had completed his 15th year. And, that entries at that early age were contemplated as possible, is evident from the fact that there was a regulation at Oxford, which provided that students who entered at an

---

[1] Hearne Bliss, 1. 6: (and so took his M.A. degree at *thirteen*) *Johnson's Life of Granville.*

earlier age should not subscribe the xxxix Articles on their matriculation, but should wait till they had completed their 15th year. Out of a dozen cases taken at random, of men who studied at the Universities in the last century (not including Gibbon) I find three who entered at 15 years of age, two at seventeen, three at eighteen, and four at nineteen.

If this be a fair average of the age at which matriculations took place, it would seem that students were admitted, on the whole, at a later age than they had been in earlier time. In which case, this will be one of the causes which led to the discontinuance of the intimacy which had existed between tutors and pupils. Be this as it may, there can be little doubt but that the violence and suspicion which prevailed, the offspring of those party struggles which, as we have seen, were very rife in the early part of the last century,—together with the spirit of self-indulgence, which was let loose after the Restoration, and fell down in the stupor of repletion to doze and glut itself and doze again after the Revolution, (and intensified, perhaps, by the very intimacy of the orders which, when ill-directed, had brought on at Cambridge the laxity of discipline resulting in the 'New Regulations' strife in 1750)—were thoroughly successful towards the end of the last century in bringing about an estrangement between the older and the younger men[1]: dons

[1] A Plain and Friendly Address to the Undergraduates of the University of *Cambridge*, particularly to those of *Trinity*-College, on the following important Topics: *Associates*,... By a late Undergraduate, *London*: Printed for *J. Dodsley, Pall-mall*, 1786. (pp. 40. Gough. Camb. 65 in Bodleian) p. 11.

not caring for the society of undergraduates, and undergraduates avoiding dons. The writer of ' *Considerations on the expediency of making*, &c. *the late Regulations at* Cambridge,' p. 47 (1751), states his opinion, that the intimate connexions and friendships between Tutors and the young students led to laxity of Discipline. See, however, a writer in 'the *Student, or* Oxford *and* Cambridge *Monthly Miscellany*' of the same year, II. 301.

If we have found the word *donnishness* in the 19th century, the *thing* was the invention of the last. Not that there were none in the latter part of the 18th century that were free from it (such, for instance, as Thomas Baker, the gentle antiquary and *socius eiectus* of S. John's, who hastened his death in 1740 by the unselfish spirit in which he welcomed his grand-nephew when he came up as a freshman from Eton¹), nor yet that there was ever a time, since the universities were founded, when the world has been without the hardness, pride, and selfishness, in a man, that makes him 'farther off from heaven than when he was a boy.' Most men, it seems, are liable to this disease; but none more so than the Resident at the university. Being constantly in the position of a critic, he is, like all students, tempted to forget that there are matters in which he ought always to be a learner; and then he is apt to become proud, self-sufficient, and supercilious.

We have lately seen some bright examples to the contrary at Cambridge among eldest members of the

¹ Masters' *Memoirs of T. Baker*, 1784, p. 90.

University; and, I believe, at Oxford there is no want of pleasant intercourse between 'don' and undergraduate.

In the last century at Cambridge (and, I believe, at Oxford,) there were great difficulties arising from the social condition of the members of the Universities. It is well known that the number of Fellow-Commoners or Gentlemen-Commoners was far greater in proportion to the total number of residents than it is at present, or than it was five years ago. There were two main divisions of the undergraduates at Cambridge in the last century; gentlemen of fortune, and poor scholars. The former class included the '*generosorum, nobilium, et magnatum liberi;*' noblemen, that is, and fellow-commoners (*pensionarii maiores*, Ashton's *Collectanea*, fol. 70, or even '*pensionarii;*' ibid fol. 62, on Univ. Stat. 50 § 5, *pensionarii in commeatum sociorum admissi*. Stat. Coll. SS. et Indiv. Trin. cap. XIV. *de pensionariis*). The latter comprised scholars proper on the foundation (*discipuli scholares*); sizars (*sizatores, quadrantarii*, Dr Ashton's *Collectanea*), who were then in a much better condition than the servitors at Oxford, who continued to perform many menial offices until late times; lastly, the Pensioners, in our modern sense of the term (i.e. 'Commoners' at Oxford;—*pensionarii minores*, Ashton's *Collectanea;—pensionarii in commeatu discipulorum*, included in the term *discipuli* in Statut. Trin. Coll. Cant.). These last were generally exhibitioners either in connection with their college, or with some school or corporation (see *Gradus ad Cantabrigiam*, 1803, s. v. 'Pensioners').

It appears from statistics, which are given in the notes, that at the opening of the 19th century, the numbers of Fellow-Commoners, foundation Scholars, and Sizars, at Cambridge, were equal to one another; while the Pensioners proper equalled in numbers the other three combined.

Though this is a larger proportion of Fellow-Commoners than we have now, the Lesser Pensioners had increased in strength to an extent that would probably have astonished the framers of the early statutes if, when they provided for the admission of '*socii studiorum*' and pupils in the Master's Lodgings, they had known to what a goodly body they would grow.

In the eighteenth century, as with us at present, the Pensioners were scarcely distinguishable from the Scholars; but in the eighteenth century both Pensioners and Scholars were, *to a great extent*, taken from a lower social grade than they are at present.

The Fellows were elected from the Scholars; more, apparently, from the Sizars. Any one who glances at the pages of a dictionary of Biography will see in how great a degree we are indebted to this class for our great men in Church and State. At the same time we cannot wonder if some cases were found of young men whose heads were turned by a sudden revulsion from poverty into a 'comfortable independence.' What wonder if some of them were tempted to become vain and silly[1], while some others (like Sir

[1] *The Student*, 1751, Vol. II. p. 189.

Pertinax Macsycophant in Macklin's *Man of the World*) were unable to 'stond straight i' th' presence of a great mon, but always boowed and boowed and boowed as it were by instinct.'

Certain it is that we constantly find complaints of undue indulgence and deference paid to Fellow-commoners.

'Fellows and Tutors of almost every College,' says a writer in 1792, 'join frequently without scruple' in the extravagant parties, and occasionally in the excesses, of their richer pupils. (*Strictures upon Discipline*, p. 11.)

So too the great Wilberforce, when, as a good-natured Undergraduate at St John's, Camb. (1776-1779), he was at any moment ready to receive visitors, who found the great Yorkshire pie always inviting their attack; was foolishly encouraged in idleness by some of the Fellows of his College, because forsooth he was a talented young man of fortune and did not need to work to earn his bread! But this was not universally the case.

Just as in Evelyn's time the 'Fellow com'uners' in Balliol were no more exempted from exercise than the meanest Scholars there, (*Diary*, anno 1637); and as in *Nov.* 1721, Erasmus Phillips 'Fellow Commoner' of Pembroke, Oxon. took his Essay *on Pride* to the Master, and had to declaim publickly in the hall on 'Virtutem amplectimur Ipsam Praemia si tollas' (*N. and Q.*, 2nd S., x. 443), so towards the close of the 18th century in the first *College* examinations which were held in Cambridge;—the first, that is,

7—2

which required the attendance of all the members of the society, and which employed them all at once in a way in which the old College disputations could not do:—we find that Fellow-Commoners were obliged to be present[1], and some of them (e.g. Lord Powis in *Sophocles*) acquitted themselves creditably.

This will be seen in the extracts which we purpose to give in the next part of this Essay from a MS. *Report*, in the Bodleian, *of the Examinations* at St John's College, Cambridge, in Dr W. S. Powell's time, 1773—5.

Nevertheless there was, even at that time, in some quarters, a decided feeling against Fellow-Commoners; so that in 1788, we find a scheme for the abolition of their order published by the writer of 'Remarks on the Enormous Expense in the Education of Young Men' in *Cambridge*, which will be noticed at length in an Appendix to Part I. of the present Essay[2].

Such protests were not without their fruit; for, *Philalethes*, answering Vicesimus Knox, in behalf of Oxford, in 1790, writes: 'that in *all* the Colleges, a more rigorous discipline is enforced upon Noblemen and Gentlemen Commoners, than what even your amendments propose: and that in *several* Colleges, the heirs of the first families in the kingdom submit to the same exercises, and to the same severity of discipline with the lowest member of the society.'

[1] Cp. *Cambridge in the 17th Century.* Mayor, 1855. pt. I. p. 7. (*Life of N. Ferrar*). N.B. Strype. ap. Cooper, *Annals*, III. p. 505.

[2] See also the 5th query proposed by the Chancellor in 1675, and the answer of the V. C. and Heads of Cambridge. Cooper, *Annals*, III. 568.

When Simonds D'Ewes[1] came up as a fellow-commoner to St John's in 1618, his subsizar, one Thomas Manning (the son of a clergyman who had been silenced by Whitgift's Three Articles), entered with him. He used to call him in the morning and to carry letters and messages for him into the town.

It appears from an entry in the Trinity College Conclusion Book, *Jan.*, 1660—1, (quoted by Dr Edleston '*Correspondence of* Newton *and* Cotes,' 1850, p. xli., and transcribed in a note on p. 18, of Brewster's 1st Vol., of the *Life of Newton*, 1860) ; that Sizars then waited upon their Tutors, and even fetched their quantum from the Butteries.

In Baker's Comedy, 'an Act at *Oxford*,' 1704, one of the characters is '*Chum* ('whose Father's a chimney-sweeper, and his mother a poor ginger-bread woman at *Cow-Cross*'), a gentleman-serviter at *Brazen-Nose* College,' whose business is to wait upon Gentlemen-Commoners, to dress and clean their shoes and make their exercises. In the drama he takes the place of the faithful slave in the old heathen comedy; and, by personating a rich lover, wins *Berynthia* for his master *Smart*. The poor fellow, whose Fortune was 'soon told—the reversion of old shoes which Gentlemen-commoners leave off, two Raggs call'd shirts, a dog's eard *Grammar*, and a piece of an *Ovid de Tristibus*,' —is rewarded by a present of 500 guineas.

The descriptions in the '*Servitour:* a poem, written by a *Servitour* of the University of *Oxford*, and faithfully taken from his own *Original Copy*, &c., *London*,

[1] *Diary*, p. 4.

printed and sold by *H. Hills* in *Black-Fryars*, near the
water-side, 1709,' is yet more dismal.   He is depicted
as 'Emerging from a Skittle-Yard' in his rusty round
cap,

> Like *Cheesy-Pouch* of *Shon-ap-Shenkin*,
> His Sandy Locks, with wide *Hiatus*,
> Like Bristles seem'd Erected at us.
> Clotted with Sweat, the Ends hung down;
> And made Resplendant Cape of Gown;
> Whose Cape was thin, and so Transparent,
> Hold it t' th' Light, you'd scarce beware on't.
> 'Twixt Chin and Breast contiguous Band,
> Hung in an Obtuse Angle, and—
> It had a Latitude Canonick,
> And was as short as Stile Laconick.
> His Coat so greasy was, and torn   ⎫
> That had you seen it, you'd ha' sworn ⎬
> 'Twas Ten Years old when he was born. ⎭
> His Buttons fring'd, as is the Fashion,
> In Gallick and Britannick Nation:
> Or, to speak like more Modern fellows,
> Their Moulds dropt out like ripe Brown-shellers.
> His Leather Galligaskins rent,
> Made Artless Music as he went;
>
> .   .   .   .   .
>
> His Holey Stockins were ty'd up,
> One with a Band, one with a Rope.

He is described as the son of an aspiring husband-
man who hopes

> If he can get Prevarment here,
> Of Zeven or Eight—Pounds a Year,
> To preach and zell a Cup of Beer
> To help it out, he'll get good Profit
> And make a pratty Bus'ness of it.

When he first comes up;

> He struts, pulls off his Cap to no-Man;
> And to conceal, betrays the Plow-man:

But checkt for 's Insolent Behaviour,
And fearing to be out of Favour,

. . . . .

His Duty h'as so much Regard of
He'll Cap a Master twenty Yard off :
To whom such Fear is him upon, Sir ;
When spoken to, he dares not Answer.
I' th' Morn when call'd to Prayer-Bell,
Doleful to him as Passing-Knell ;
From Garret lofty he descends
By Ladder, which dire Fate portends.

. . . . .

'Bout Dinner-time down comes the Lubber,
When 's Belly (hungry Dog) cries Cubbord,
To get a Mess of Broth i' th' Kitchen,
Where he sees Dainties so bewitching,
As Turkies, Capons, Ribs of Beef,
No wonder if he plays the Thief ;
And, like a Fox to Fowl Insidious,
When Cook has turn'd his Back, perfidious-
ly—whips off Liver, or a Gizzard,
From pinion'd Wing of Bird ; for 'tis hard
To suffer *Tantalus* his Fate—
To see, and smell, and yet not eat..
Poor Scraps, and Cold, as I'm a Sinner,
Being all that he can get for Dinner.
Once out of Curiosity——
What Lodging th' had, I needs must see ;
A Room with Dirt, and Cobwebs lin'd,
Which here and there with Spittle shin'd ;
Inhabited, let's see—by Four ;
If I mistake not, 'twas no more.
Two Buggy-beds . . .
Their Dormer Windows with Brown-paper,
Was patch'd to keep out Northern Vapour.
The Tables broken Foot stood on,
An Old *Schrevelious* Lexicon,
Here lay together, Authors various,
From *Homer's* Iliad, to *Cordelius* :
And so abus'd was *Aristotle*,
He only serv'd to stop a Bottle,
Or light a Pipe, of which were many,
On Chimney-piece, instead of Cheney ;

> Where eke stood Glass, Dark-Lanthorns ancient ⎫
> Fragment of Mirrer, Penknife, Trencher, [sic] ⎬
> And forty things which I can't mention. ⎭
> Old Chairs and Stools, and such-like Lumber,
> Compleatly furnisht out the Chamber.

Some forty years earlier John Eachard, Master of Catharine Hall, had remarked in his sprightly '*Grounds and Occasions of the Contempt of the Clergy and Religion Enquired into*,' 1670, pp. 15—17.

'All this may seem at first sight to be easily avoided by a strict examination at the Universities, and so returning by the next carrier all that was sent up not fit for their purpose. But because many of their relations are oft-times persons of an inferiour condition, and who either by imprudent counsellours, or else out of a tickling conceit of their son's being, forsooth, an University scholar, have purposely omitted all other opportunities of a livelihood, to return such would seem a very sharp and severe disappointment. Possibly it might be much better, if parents themselves, or their friends, would be much more wary of determining their children to the trade of learning. And if some of undoubted knowledge and judgment would offer their advice: and speak their hopes of a lad about thirteen or fourteen years of age: (which I'll assure you, Sir, may be done without conjuring): and never omit to enquire whether his relations are able and willing to maintain him seven years at the University, or see some certain way of being continued there so long, by the help of friends, or others; as also upon no such condition as shall in likelihood deprive him of the greatest part of his studies.

'For it is a common fashion of a great many to complement and invite inferiour people's children to the University, and then pretend to make such an all-bountiful provision for them, as they shall not fail of coming to a very eminent degree of learning. But when they come there, they shall save a servant's wages. They took, therefore, heretofore a very good method to prevent sizars over-heating their brains: bed-making, chamber-sweeping, and water-fetching were doubtless great preservatives against too much vain philosophy. Now certainly such pretended favours and kindnesses as these are the most right down discourtesies in the world. For it is ten times more happy both for a lad and the Church, to be a corn-cutter, or tooth-drawer, to make or mend shoes, or to be of any inferiour profession, than to be invited to, and promised the conveniences of a learned education, and to have his name only stand airing upon the college tables, and his chief business shall be to buy eggs and butter.'

When Erasmus was at Queens' his servitor's rooms were close above his own. He was wholly at his master's command, and sometimes at his mistress's. We are further reminded, by one of the papers on 'Oxford during the Last Century,' which appeared in the *Oxford Chronicle* in 1859, of Aubrey's description of Willis (the discoverer of the chalybeate properties of Astrop Wells), who, when servitor to Dr. Iles, Canon of Christ Church, studied in his blue livery cloak at the lower end of the hall by the door, and assisted his master's wife in mixing drugs.   In 1728, George Whitefield[1], as a servitor at Pembroke, Oxon., was winning popularity in that office by reason of the experience which he had previously gained as drawer, at his home, the Bell Inn, Gloucester.   Nor was this a single instance: Hearne tells of one Lyne, son of a clergyman, and grandson of the Town Clerk of Oxford, who was drawer at the King's Head Tavern, in that city, in 1735 ; his elder brother being Fellow of Emmanuel, and his younger an eminent scholar of King's.

Dr Johnson, writing to Tom Warton, *Nov.* 28, 1754, alluding to the delay in a work on Spenser caused by the number of his correspondents, and pupils at Oxford, says : 'Three hours a day stolen from sleep and amusement will produce it.   Let a servitor transcribe the quotations, and interleave them with references, to save time.'   And at the beginning of this century[2] Dr Hyde complains that 'some in the University have been very troublesome in pressing that their servitors may transcribe manuscripts for them, though not capable of being sworn to the Library.'

At Oxford in 1733, Shenstone (as we learn from his friend and biographer Ri. Graves, author of *the Spiritual Quixote*) could only visit Richard Jago (author of *Edge Hill*, a poem in four Books) in

---

[1] Southey, Coleridge, and Southey's *Life of Wesley*, I. 47, ed. 3. Philip's *Life of Whitefield*, p. 27.

[2] *Oxford during the Last Century*.   Reprint, 1859, p. 52.

private, as he wore a servitor's gown; it being then deemed 'a great disparagement for a commoner to appear in public with one in that situation.'

At Cambridge the position of the Sizar was, perhaps, preferable to that of the Oxford servitor. In 1687 we find William Whiston in intimate connection with the Senior Fellow, Dr Nat. Vincent, who kindly took the lad into Norfolk on account of his health. There the Doctor preached a 'Court-Sermon.' After their return, 'it soon happened that the Prince of *Orange* came to our deliverance, and the *Cambridge* mob got up, and seized Dr *Watson*, the Bishop of St *David's*, of much the same character with Dr *Vincent*, and threatened Dr *Vincent* himself, who thereupon thought of saving himself by going out of the College for awhile[1]. Accordingly he called for me, as then his Sizar, to assist him in preparing for his removal.' Zachary Conrad von Uffenbach, in his Travels[2], says that he learnt that at Cambridge (28 July, 1710) 'the Lords' sons of quality, and others, are so wealthy, and are called Fellow-Commoners, take the poor men who wait on them as servants.' He got his information from his cicerone Ferrari, an Italian, and his visit was paid in the long Vacation, when students and professors had gone off to the country or to London. It is noteworthy that the writer of '*Considerations* on the *Oaths* required by the University of *Cambridge* at the Time of Taking Degrees and on other subjects which relate to the

---

[1] Whiston's *Autobiog.* 1749, I. pp. 21, 23.
[2] *Ulm*, 1754, Vol. III. p. 2.

Discipline of that Seminary. by a Member of the Senate. *London*: printed for and sold by *J. Deighton*, Holborn. Sold also by *F. Hodson*, Cambridge, 1788. price eighteen pence' (8vo. pp. 56. Bodl. *Gough, Camb.* 65.) p. 11. remarks that the distinctions of Fellow-commoner and Sizar were a matter of great offence 'to many, *especially to foreigners.*'

The concluding lines of Kit Smart's Tripos on *Yawning* shew that in 1742 the custom of Sizars waiting at the high table had not yet gone out of the University of Cambridge:

> Haud aliter Socium esuriens Sizator edacem
> Dum videt, appositusque cibus frustratur hiantem ;
> Dentibus infrendens nequicquam lumine torvo
> Saepius exprobrat ; nequicquam brachia tendit
> Sedulus officiosa dapes removere paratus,
> Olli nunquam exempta fames, quin frusta suprema
> Devoret et peritura immani ingurgitet ore ;
> Tum demum jubet auferri ; nudata capaci
> Ossa sonant, lugubre sonant, allisa catino.

Bishop Ri. Watson of Llandaff in the *Anecdotes of his Life*, written before 1814[1], says that in his own time (at Trinity, in 1755) 'the sizars were not so respectfully looked upon by the pensioners and scholars of the house as they ought to have been, inasmuch as the most learned and leading men in the University have ever arisen from that order.' We may instance at once, Newton, *Trin.*; Bentley, *St John's*; Ri. Dawes and Joshua Barnes, *Emman.*

By a College Order in the St John's Conclusion Book[2], 18 Mar. 1765, it was 'agreed that 9 of the

---

[1] Edit. 2, 1818, I. p. 13.   [2] Baker-Mayor, p. 1071, l. 19.

Sizars be appointed to wait at the president's table,' etc.

I am unable to say when the great change in the social position of Sizars was wrought at Cambridge. The Article on that word in the *Gradus ad Cantabrigiam*, published in 1803, contains a protest against the vulgar opinion, that Sizars were as badly off as Oxford Servitors. It is then stated that 'whoever has resided any little time at Cambridge must know that, in point of rank, the distinction between *Pensioners* and *Sizars* is by no means considerable. Between *Commoners* and *Servitors* there is a great gulph. Nothing is more common than to see *Pensioners* and *Sizars* taking sweet counsel together and walking arm in arm to St Mary's...In respect to their academical habit : At Trinity College, the *Sizars* wear precisely the same dress with the Pensioners. At other Colleges, the only difference is that their gowns are not bordered with velvet. At Peterhouse, the *Pensioner's* gown is the same as is worn by the Bachelors of Arts; and the *Sizar's* is the same as is worn by the *Pensioners* of St John's, Emmanuel, &c. In every College, the *Sizars* invite, and are invited by, the *Pensioners* to wine parties ; and some of them (the former) endeavour to vie with the latter in fashionable frivolity.'

In 1807 Southey puts into the letters of Espriella (no. XXXII. ii. p. 73) complaints of the Oxford system of servitors 'tolling the bell, waiting at table, and performing other menial offices.' While in the *Life of Wesley* (1820), he holds up to Oxford the example of Cambridge, where the distinction of dress and service had been done away.

As I have spoken of the change in the connection between tutor and pupil; and have also been drawn on to speak of the Professors' Lectures, it may be as well to treat the subject of Lectures as part of the social life of the Universities instead of considering them in the next part of this compilation.

In the early days of the Universities, the tutorial system was unknown. It was not (says Professor Henry Malden in his essay *on the Origin of Universities*[1]) till the time when Leicester was chancellor [at Oxford, in 1564] that the University undertook to regulate who might be tutors; and it was not till the chancellorship of Laud [in 1630], that it was made necessary to enter under a tutor resident in the same College or Hall with the pupil[2]. Laud therefore may be regarded as the author of the system of College tuition. The duty of these College Tutors was to superintend the moral and religious discipline of their pupils, rather than to instruct them in their studies. But when stricter attention was paid to the performance of Exercises for degrees, and above all when the Examinations were enforced, there grew up a class of private Tutors; the offspring in the main of the system of

[1] 1835, *p.* 86.

[2] *Edin. Rev.* cvi. p. 391, comparing Wood, A.D. 1581, and Corp. Statut. *t.* iii. *s.* 2.

competitive Examination. Their use, as Dr Whewell shews, has a tendency to become abused when the same persons may exchange the office of private tutor for that of examiner, within a very brief period[1]. We shall presently have occasion to speak of an abuse of this kind at Oxford, which survived till the first years of this century. It was usual in Dr Johnson's time[2] for College Tutors to lecture both in the Hall and in their own rooms, as well as to set weekly themes for composition. When he was at Pembroke, Oxford, in 1728, Undergraduates generally depended entirely upon the Tutor to guide all their reading. His first tutor Jordan was like a father to his pupils, but he was intellectually incompetent for his important position. For this reason Johnson recommended his old schoolfellow Taylor to go to Christ Church on account of the excellent lectures of Bateman then tutor there. Just when Johnson quitted Pembroke through penury in 1731, Jordan was succeeded by Adams (afterwards Master), a man of considerable ability. Thus we see how cautiously we must form a general opinion of the efficiency of a College from its character at any particular moment. Gibbon's experience in the matter of Tutors at Magdalen was similar to that of the other at Pembroke. The idea which Uffenbach formed of our lectures in his visit at the Vacation-

---

[1] 'Of a Liberal Education...with particular reference to...Cambridge,' 1845, p. 217, ¶ 268. See also Dean *Peacock* on the Statutes, 1841, pp. 153, foll.

[2] Boswell's *Johnson*, Philip's *Whitefield*, p. 20.

time in 1710 is amusing. 'We were surprised that there are no lectures (*Collegia*) given : and only in winter three or four lectures given by professors to the bare walls, for no one comes in. On the other hand the "Scolars" or Students have some of them a professor or old *Socium Collegii*, whom they call *Tutorem*, who instructs them, as then the noblemen and others are so rich, and are called " Fellow-commoners," as to take to them the poor men who wait on them as servants. In summer, however, hardly anything is done, both Students and Professors being in the country or in London ¹.'

That Tutors at Cambridge used to direct their pupils' studies, will be seen from the scheme drawn up by Waterland, which will be printed in analysis in an appendix to the second part of this work. We may gather also from a letter written by Ambrose Bonwicke to his father² six weeks after Uffenbach's visit, that it was unusual for the Tutor at St John's to omit to speak to his pupils 'about a method, &c.'

Before the century with which we have to do, there had grown up a natural practice of flocking to certain favourite Tutors, or '*pupil-mongers*' as they were called. Indeed when a Student found, like John Evelyn 'Fellow-com'uner in Balliol' in 1637, that the Tutor to whom his father had sent him was too much occupied with college animosities, it was high time for him to 'associate' him-

---

¹ *Reise*, III. p. 2.
² *A. Bonwicke*, by Mayor, 1870, p. 21.

self with 'a young man of the Foundation, afterwards a Fellow of the House, by whose learned and friendly conversation I received great advantage.'

Several persons are mentioned as regular 'pupil-mongers.' James Tunstal in Baker's time[1]; in 1715 Dr Chr. Anstey the elder[2]: at St John's. Another famous diarist, Ralph Thoresby of Leeds, came up to Cambridge in 1714 (July 8th) to see for a Tutor for his son. He 'visited Dr Bentley, Master of Trinity; then at Clare-hall, to visit and consult the famous pupil-monger Mr Laughton [Dr *Ri.* Laughton one of the first teachers of the Newtonian philosophy. Dr *John* Laughton of Trinity was University Librarian], to whom I was recommended by the bishop of Ely; and after at Queens' College with the ingenious Mr Langwith (a native of York) recommended by Mr Baker of St John's, and preferred rather than any of his own College. The Lord direct me in this matter of so great concern to the temporal and eternal interest of my son Ralph. Whether Clare Hall or Queens' College I cannot determine,' &c.

On the 27th of Feb. 1721–2, upon a petition[3] of forty-two Tutors, it was agreed that each Pensioner should pay a fee of 30s. a quarter, and others in proportion. Other regulations were made as to 'caution money' for security in case of debts. The insuffi-

[1] *Life of Baker*, 1784, p. 114.
[2] *Life of Bonwicke*, 1870, p. 172.
[3] Cooper's *Annals*, IV. 167.

Pryme[1] says, that it was repealed after he ceased to be Fellow. He says also that in 1799, owing to that regulation, the system of private tuition had not become common, and the lectures of the tutors during term-time were by many of the students (himself included) deemed sufficient.

Since then, however, the employment of private tutors or 'coaches' at Cambridge has become more common, though it has at times received checks by such events as the establishment of 'composition' or of 'inter-collegiate' lectures. But with candidates for the Mathematical Tripos, the tutor is often as important an agent as themselves; so that William Hopkins, of Peterhouse[2], could boast in 1849, that 'from January 1828 to January 1849, inclusive, i. e. in twenty-two years, I have had among my pupils 175 Wranglers. Of these 108 have been in the *first ten*, 44 in the *first three*, and 17 have been *Senior Wranglers.*'

As to the effect upon young tutors themselves, William Wordsworth wrote in 1833 to a young graduate of Cambridge, 'I have only one observation to make, to which I should attach importance, if I thought it called for in your case, which I do not, I mean the moral duty of avoiding to encumber yourself with private pupils in any number[3]. You are at an age when the blossoms of the mind are setting to make fruit; and the practice of *pupil-mongering* is an absolute blight for this process.'

<hr />

[1] *Autobiog. Recoll.* 1870, pp. 48, 49.
[2] Gunning, *Reminisc.* 1854, II. p. 359.   [3] *Memoirs* 1851, ch. XLIX.

Of the college lectures in 1755, bishop Watson[1] says: 'It was then the custom in Trinity College (I am sorry it is not the custom still) for all undergraduates to attend immediately after morning prayers the college-lectures at different tables in the hall during term-time. The lecturers explained to their respective classes certain books, such as Puffendorf *de Officio Hominis et Civis*, Clarke *on the Attributes*, Locke's *Essay*, Duncan's *Logic*, &c., and once a week the head-lecturer examined all the students.'

So we find young Ambrose Bonwicke[2], in the October term 1711, receiving 'more than ordinary satisfaction in being returned to this pleasant seat of the muses, when I find my books and all things in a very good condition, and myself happy at the ethic-table at morning lectures in the hall.' In the St John's College Conclusion Book[3] is the entry 21 Jan. 1737 -8: 'Agreed that the two logick tables be join'd.'

As to the staff of lecturers: there was at Peterhouse elected yearly a Prælector, a Rhetoric, Greek, Ethics, and Logic Lecturer: the Hebrew lectureship being vacant. But in some colleges from time to time (and this was the real occasion for private tuition), the tutors were not up to their work. Thus in 1752 Gibbon, at Magdalen College, Oxford, was tacitly allowed to abstain from attending any lectures; while, in 1764, Sir William Jones, the Oriental Scholar, complaining of the dulness of lectures, and

[1] Watson's *Anecdotes*, I. p. 12. Ed. 1818.
[2] *Life* (Mayor), 1870, p. 33.
[3] Baker-Mayor, p. 1035, l. 32.

of the barbarous Latin in which they were read, was formally excused attendance[1], and set to work by himself to read 'all the Greek poets and historians of note, besides the entire works of Plato and Lucian,' as well as Arabic.

Besides these early lectures, and those after breakfast, which, as now, were common at least towards the close of last century[2], there were afternoon lectures after the early dinner. *Hierocles*, for instance, and other greek prose authors were read in lecture at St John's on Monday afternoons in 1710. So too, later in the century, Professor Busick Harwood delivered his Anatomical lectures in the afternoon. In the evening, as we shall see, there were even papers set for the mathematical tripos.

But the college halls had other uses. It was not a very uncommon thing for some refractory Scholar (or even Fellow) to have to make recantation or confession of faults therein.

It was agreed at a College meeting in St John's, 19 Dec. 1764, 'that if any undergraduate make any disturbance in the hall at the time when any other undergraduate is reading an acknowledgment of his offences by order of the deans or a superior officer, he who makes such disturbance shall be rusticated.' In the preceding century at Peterhouse, *Novem.* 7, 1663, Sir Gosnal was to make a recantation in Hall for his former great extravagances; and about a year later, his time of probation being finished, he was

---

[1] Life by Ld. Teignmouth, 1815, pp. 39—41.
[2] Bonwicke-Mayor, 1870, p. 21.

judged by the Master unfit to be admitted to his Fellowship. In 1698 Charles Squire, of the same House, had to confess in Hall his 'madness and profligacy, and to beg pardon of God Almighty, of the Visitor ye Master, y Society and Students, wch I hope will not be deny'd to a serious convert.' Two years later he was expelled, and took with him some of the College plate.

In that century it was not uncommon for scholars on certain foundations to put in the hands of the President at Hall-time some epigram or set of verses in Greek or Latin. So in 1792 there was a classical recitation from Homer, Virgil, &c., called a *narrare*, made at Trinity College, Oxon. by some undergraduate standing by the 'Griffin's head' while the dons were finishing dinner. Among Dr Ri. Newton's *Rules for Hertford College*, 1747, p. 27, there is one providing that two undergraduates a week should deliver *Narrations* (recitations of Elegant Extracts) instead of their Theme or Translation.

The College fare was simple, *i.e.* it consisted of less variety of viands than at present. In his sermon at Paules crosse in 1550, Thomas Lever, Fellow and Preacher of St John's, told of those 'menne not werye of theyr paynes' at Cambridge, whose first meal was when 'at ten of the clocke they go to dynner, whereas they be contente wy^th a penye pyece of byefe amongest iiii., hauyng a fewe porage made of the brothe of the same byefe, wy^th salte and otemell, and nothynge els.' Their only other food was taken at 'v. of the clocke in the euenyng, when as they haue a supper

not much better then theyr dyner.' It was one of
sir Tho. More's humorous proposals to his children
when he resigned the Chancellorship to retrench
their expenses by degrees from Lincoln's Inn diet
to the new Inn fare, and so on at last to the Oxford
fare, 'which if our power stretch not to maintaine,
then may we like poore schollers of Oxforde goe
a begging with our bags and wallets and sing *salve
regina* at rich mens doores, where for pitie some
goode folkes will give us their mercifull charitie; and
so keep companie and be merrie togeather[1].'

The 16th of *Sundry Queries concerning the University of* Oxon., &c. London, *Printed by* Thomas Creeke,
1659, asks[2], 'Whether the Canons of Christ Church
ought not to eat the bread of affliction and drink
the water of affliction; since they refuse to eat the
same bread and drink the same drink with the rest
of the college, which indeed is so bad as never was
worse eaten or drunk but by the same canons before
they came to be canons.' A similar question was
asked with no less vehemence in 1865.

In his thoughtful letter, written to his mother in
1662, John Strype, the ecclesiastical historian, whilst
a student of Jesus College, gives a curious account
of Cambridge fare[3]:

'Do not wonder so much at our Commons: they
are more than many Colleges have. Trinity itself

---

[1] Life of More by Ro. Ba.; Wordsworth, *Eccl. Biog.* II. pp. 81,
82. Ed. 3.

[2] *Misc. Harleian*, VI. p. 91.

[3] Cooper's *Annals*, III. pp. 504, 505. Sir H. Ellis, *Letters of Eminent Literary Men*, p. 177.

(where Herring and Davies are), which is the famous-
est College in the University, have but three half-
pence. We have roast meat, dinner and supper
throughout the weeke; and such meate as you know
I had not use to care for; and that is Veal: but
now I have learnt to eat it. Sometimes neverthelesse, we have boiled meat, with pottage; and beef
and mutton, which I am glad of: except Fridays
and Saturdays, and sometimes Wednesdays; which
days we have Fish at dinner, and tansy or pudding
for supper. Our parts then are slender enough. But
there is this remedy; we may retire into the Butteries, and there take a half-penny loafe and butter
or cheese; or else to the Kitchen and take there
what the Cook hath. But, for my part, I am sure,
I never visited the Kitchen yet, since I have been
here, and the Butteries but seldom after meals; unlesse for a Ciza [or *Size*, or *Sice*] that is for a Farthing-
worth of Small-Beer: so that lesse than a Peny in
Beer doth serve me a whole day. Neverthelesse
sometimes we have Exceedings: then we have two
or three Dishes (but that is very rare): otherwise
never but one: so that a Cake and a Cheese would
be very welcome to me: and a Neat's tongue, or
some such thing; if it would not require too much
money...Mother I kindly thank you for your Orange
pills you sent me. If you are not too straight of
money send me some such thing by the Woman, and
a pound or two of Almonds and Raisons...We go
twice a day to Chapel; in the morning about 7, and
in the evening about 5. After we come from Chapel

in the morning, which is towards 8, we go to the Butteries for our breakfast, which is usually five Farthings; an halfepenny loafe and butter and a cize of beer. But sometimes I go to an honest House near the College, and have a pint of milk boiled for breakfast.'

Of the monotony of Cambridge dinners in 1710 Uffenbach[1] complained; as well as of the closeness of Trinity College Hall, which smelt so of bread and meat that he was sure he could not eat a morsel in it. Francis Burman, who was there in 1702, mentions that at a grand dinner the dishes with few exceptions were square wooden platters: (still partially used at Winchester).

The Hon. Roger North, writing, I suppose, between 1720 and 1730, compares the state of the University in his own days with that when his elder brother, the Hon. and Rev. Dr John North, was Fellow of Jesus Coll., Cambridge, before he succeeded Dr Barrow as Master of Trinity:

'The Doctor conformed to all the orders of the college, seldom ate out of hall, and then upon a fish-day only, being told it was for his health. He was constantly at the chapel prayers, so much as one may say that, being in town [Cambridge] he never failed. This, in the morning, secured his time; for he went from thence directly to his study without any sizing or breakfast at all.'

I gather from the Cook's accounts at Peterhouse that in the 17th century rarely more than one joint

[1] *Reise*, 1754, p. 85. *Ibid.* p. 3.

appeared at the Fellows' table, and on Fridays fish only. It was, perhaps, the Master of that House, Dr Cosin, or Dr Sterne of Jesus, who represented to Abp Laud in 1636 that 'upon Frydays and all Fasting days, the victualling houses prepare Flesh good store for all Schollers and others that will come or send unto them,' and the Tutors allow double money for suppers on those days. At Peterhouse, after the Revolution, the custom of eating fish on Fridays remained, but it was in addition to the ordinary provision of meat. As Johnson's *Idler* (No. 33[1], in 1758) has commemorated the dinners of this College, it may be as well to give in a note the ordinary bill of fare for a day when Gray and Cavendish dined in Hall; also another of a grand feast on Bp Cosin's Commemoration Day (St Andrew's, Nov. 30) in 1779.

'It was the custom for colleges, and indeed for most other people, till towards the middle of the 17th century, to dine at ten or eleven o'clock in the forenoon. "With us (says the preface to Holingshed) the nobilitie, gentrie, and students, do ordinarilie go to dinner at eleven before noone, and to supper at five, or between five and six, at afternoone. The merchants dine and sup seldome before twelve at noone and six at night, especiallie in London. The husbandmen dine also at high-noone, as they call it, and sup at seven or eight; but out of the terme in our universities, the scholers dine at ten[2]."'

---

[1] By *T. Warton.*
[2] *Oxoniana,* I. 231.

The gradual change in the dinner hour was a matter of great groaning to the conservatives.

On *Feb.* 10, 1721–2, Hearne wrote in his diary 'Whereas the university disputations on Ash-Wednesday should begin at 1 o'clock, they did not begin this year 'till two or after, which is owing to several colleges having altered their hours of dining from 11 to 12, occasioned from people's lying in bed longer than they used to do.' So a year later he laments that whereas Oxford Scholars were summoned to meals at 10 o'clock on Shrove Tuesday by the pancake-bell at S. Mary's, and at 4 o'clock; at Edmund-hall dinner was now at 12 and supper at 6, and no fritters, 'When laudable old customs alter 'tis a sign learning dwindles.' So on Christmas Day, 1732, the University Sermon was, by order of the Vice-Chancellor, advertised not to begin till 11 o'clock, 'the reason given was sermons in coll. chapels. This reason might also have been given formerly. But the true reason is that people might lye in bed the longer. They used formerly to begin in chapels an hour sooner, and then they were ready for the university sermon. The same reason, viz. lying a-bed the longer hath made them in almost all places in the university alter the hours of prayers on other days, and the hour of dinner (which used to be 11 o'clock) in almost every place (Christ Church must be excepted) in the university where ancient discipline, and learning, and piety, strangely decay.'

In 1747, Dr Ri. Newton's Rule for Hertford College (p. 70) was dinner at 1, supper at 7. He proposed to provide 1lb. of meat per man, value not exceeding threepence (which was double the existing price, pp. 67, 115). He attempted also to obviate an abuse such as he had witnessed where the ten seniors would eat all, and leave the ten juniors to dine 'abroad in Public-Houses at four times the *Expence* attended with *Other* Inconveniences' (p. 114).

At Cambridge in 1755, and for many years after[1], every College dined at 12 o'clock, and the students after dinner flocked to the philosophical disputations which began at 2. At St John's, in 1799, it was 'agreed that the hour for dinner be 2 o'clock during non-term.' In D'Ewes' time, 1620, during Sturbridge fair they swallowed down their dinner at 9 o'clock 'and having quickly ended by reason of short commons, the greater part of the undergraduates did run presently to the fair.' At Emmanuel[2] the hour was changed from 1 to 3 about the year 1785. This arrangement tended to thin the attendance in the divinity schools when Dr Watson was moderating. At Trinity, in 1800, it was at 2h. 15m. On Sundays it was at a quarter past 1, and the sermon at St Mary's, which was well attended by students, was at 3 o'clock. The Vice-Chancellor's weekly dinner parties were at 1.30, and all his company accompanied him to St Mary's[3]. At Oxford[4], in 1804, 1805, those colleges which had dined at 3 advanced to 4, those

[1] Bp. Watson's *Anecdotes*, 1818, I. p. 35.
[2] Gunning, *Reminisc.*, 1854, II. p. 48.
[3] *Autobiog. Recoll. of G. Pryme*, p. 42.
[4] Oxford in the Last Century (from the *Oxford Chronicle*, 1859, p. 49 *reprint.*).

which had dined at 4 to 5. In 1807, Southey's Espriella (letter xxxii.) speaks of dining with a friend in hall: 'instead of assembling there at the grace, we went into the kitchen, where each person ordered his own mess from what the cook provided, everything having its specific price. The students order their messes according to seniority; but this custom was waived in our friend's favour, in courtesy to us strangers.' This was at Balliol.

Breakfast was a meal which saw strange revolutions: it became a more serious meal as the dinner-hour waxed later. 'Whilst Dr John North was at Jesus College, Cambridge[1], coffee was not of such common use as afterwards, and the coffee-houses but young. At that time, and long after, there was but one, kept by one Kirk. The trade of news also was scarce set up; for they had only the public gazette till Kirk got a written news-letter circulated by one Muddiman. But now [cir. 1725], the case is much altered; for it is become a custom, after chapel, to repair to one or other of the coffee-houses (for there are divers) where hours are spent in talking; and less profitable reading of newspapers, of which swarms are continually supplied from London. And the scholars are so greedy after news (which is none of their business), that they neglect all for it; and it is become very rare for any of them to go directly to his chambers after prayers, without doing his suit at the coffee-house; which is a vast loss of time grown out of a pure novelty, for who can apply close to a subject

[1] B.A. in 1663.

with his head full of the din of a coffee-house? I cannot but think [continues John North's brother and biographer Roger—*Lives of the Norths*, ed. 1826, iii., *pp.* 309, 310], that since coffee with most is become a morning refreshment, the order, which I once knew established at Lambeth House, or somewhat like it, might be introduced into the Colleges; which was for the chaplains and gentlemen officers to meet every morning in a sort of still-house, where a good woman provided them their liquors as they liked best; and this they called their coffee-house.'

In 1737, Thomas Gray, of Peterhouse, and Walpole, of King's, who drank nothing but *tea*,—were out of the fashion of the day.

The breakfast of the old stagers was simple. In the earlier editions of the *Oxford Sausage* (1764) is a picture of a student, whose square cap lies on the floor, sitting in his garret with his hand upon a tankard, while duns flock around him (one of them being a barber with his chafing-dish). Below the cut is Tom Warton's '*Panegyric on Oxford Ale.*'

> Nor Proctor thrice with vocal Heel alarms
> Our Joys secure, nor deigns the lowly Roof
> Of Pot-house snug to visit : wiser he
> The splendid Tavern haunts, or Coffee-house
> Of JAMES or JUGGINS, where the grateful Breath
> Of loath'd Tobacco, ne'er diffus'd its Balm...
>   Let the tender Swain
> Each morn regale on nerve-relaxing Tea,
> Companion meet of languor-loving Nymph :
> Be mine each Morn with eager Appetite
> And Hunger undissembled, to repair
> To friendly Buttery; there on smoking Crust

And foaming ALE to banquet unrestrained,
Material Breakfast! Thus in ancient Days
Our Ancestors robust, with liberal Cups
Usher'd the Morn, unlike the squeamish Sons
Of modern Times.

The ladies also considered a man who breakfasted on Toasts and Ale a very vulgar fellow[1].

Tea was a luxury. I have seen the bill of a Cambridge man who, in 1772, paid 3s. for 4 oz. of Souchong. In 1650 it cost eight times as much.

A letter from an undergraduate of Trin. Coll., Oxon. in 1792, who used to breakfast at 8.30 with his neighbour,—

Friend Warren takes accustomed seat
Pours tea on sugar very sweet
      And cream not over rich;
And rolls he cleverly does spread
Or from brown George toasts slice of bread,—

speaks of a change in habit. 'Brown George' is the name for a loaf in a poem of Sam. Wesley the elder. In *Espriella*, no. xxxiii., it appears as 'George Brown. [*George Bruno*, probably some kind of roll, so called from its first maker, like the *Sally Lunn* of Bath.—TR.]'

Suppers in Hall have always met with varying popularity. In his *Rules for Hertford College* (p. 126), Dr Newton says, 'The general hour of *supper* throughout the University [of Oxford] is *six*. This meal, if it be *at all* regarded (for it is much grown into disuse [1747]), is over in less than half an hour. The members of societies then dispose of themselves for the remainder of the evening. I would hope by

[1] *The Guardian* (1713), No. 34.

far the greatest part of them would spend their evenings chiefly with one another of the same society; the *summer* evenings, if the weather invite, in walking abroad; the winter in each other's rooms, as they should choose to sort themselves together.' He had mentioned seven as the hour for supper (p. 70).

At the close of the last century it was usual at Cambridge to take some relaxation after dinner, to go to Chapel at half-past five, then to retire to their rooms, shut the outer door, take tea, and read till 10 or 11 o'clock.

At Trinity there was Supper in Hall at a quarter before 9 o'clock, but very few partook of it[1]. There was always Supper on Sunday evening at Cambridge (often in the Combination-room) for the benefit of those clerical Fellows who had been 'taking duty' in the country. This is still kept up at King's as the '*Samaritan Supper.*' It was also called, from the only dish (of mutton) which was provided, '*Neck or Nothing.*' At St John's it was known as '*the Curates' Club:*' at Christ's the meeting was designated '*the Apostolic:*' there the Supper was always tripe dressed in various ways[2].

With undergraduates, Supper was the favourite meal of sociality.

At 8 P.M. the 'Sizing Bell' was rung to shew that the 'Sizing Bill' was ready. This was a bill of fare for the evening, with the prices marked. Each guest of the 'Sizing-party' ordered, at his own expense,

---

[1] *Autobiog. Recoll. of G. Pryme,* p. 42.
[2] Gunning's *Reminisc.* I. 181.

whatever he fancied, to be carried to the entertainer's rooms;—'a *part* of fowl' or duck; a roasted pigeon; 'a *part* of apple pie,' &c. The host supplied bread, butter, cheese, and beer, a 'beaker,' or a large tea-pot full of punch, which was kept upon the hob. 'These tea-pots were of various sizes (some of them enormous), and supplied by the bed-makers, who charged according to size. Nothing could be more unexceptionable than these meetings.' Wine was not allowed[1].

A supper at Trinity, Oxon., in 1792, is described as commencing at 9 o'clock (after tea at 6) with

> Boiled fowl, salt herrings, sausages,
> Cold beef and brawn and bread and cheese
> With Tankards full of Ale.

There it was the custom for men, of the same college as the host, to pay for his own share of the dessert at a wine party.

One custom prevailed at both Universities,—a cus- which has become obsolete,—that of regularly dressing for dinner. Everyone arrayed himself in white waistcoat, and white stockings, and low shoes; (for boots or gaiters were not allowed to be worn at dinner-time at Trinity, or at St John's, even in the early part of the present century); and his wig—or, latterly, his own hair—was combed, curled, and powdered.

The University Barber in old days was no mean practitioner. At Oxford, theirs was the only trade which might be followed by matriculated persons;

---

[1] Gunning's *Reminisc.* 1854, II. pp. 44, 45. *Gradus ad Cantab.*, 1803, s.v. *Sizing-bell, Sizing-party.*

and the Members of the Company of Barbers[1], which existed till 1859, dined once a year with the Vice-Chancellor, and supped annually with the Proctors. They had been incorporated by the Chancellor in 1348[2]: one stipulation being that they should maintain a light before the image in our Lady's Chapel in St Frideswyde's; another, that they should not work on Sundays, only on the market Sundays in harvest-time, nor shave any, but such as were to preach or do a religious act, on the Sundays in any part of the year. In the Bodleian (*Gough, Oxford*, 90) is a copy of an "Address to the Worshipful Company of Barbers in *Oxford*, occasioned by a late infamous Libel intitled 'Tu *Barber* ad Fireworks, a Fable, highly reflecting on one of the Honourable Members.' By a Barber. Psalm lii. 3. The third edition. *Oxford*, printed in the year 1749," pp. 12. It is signed by

> John Tubb, *Master*
>
> John C—lc—t⎱
> Joseph M—ss⎰ , Wardens

of the Worshipful Company of Barbers at the *George* Inn assembled.

We learn (p. 8) that the Barbers of Magd. Hall (K—ne), and of Exeter (H—rn—r), were also college Butlers. Others were Lay Clerks and Manciples of colleges.

> To painted Peruke and long Pole
> Jo. F—wl—r joins a gilded Scroll;

---

[1] *Recollections of Oxford*, by G. V. Cox, 1868, pp. 16, 17.
[2] *Oxoniana*, IV. pp. 156, 157.

Whose Lines declare his House is handy
For Coffee Chocolate Wine Rum Brandy:
And *Scholars* say he's not a worse Man
Than F—rtn—m, or the smart James H—rsem—n.

We find that they were also Phlebotomists and Dentists.

In the Peterhouse Order-book is the following conclusion: '*March* 24, 1739. The Barber's place being void by the death of John Elbonne; his widow, Anne Elbonne, was nominated to the said place by the Master; *cum Consilio Decanorum.*' Other notices of female barbers are given by Hone (*Every-Day Book* i., col. 1272).

It was the duty of the College Barber, who was a regular servant of the society, to attend to the tonsure of the clerks of the foundation. In the Elizabethan Statutes of St John's College in Cambridge, in the chapter '*Of College Servants*' (cap. 19) it is said

'Est et pernecessarius Collegio tonsor; qui magistro, sociis, scholaribus, et discipulis prout cuiq: fuerit opus caput et barbam hebdomadatim radat vel tondeat. Neq: minus necessariū est, ut vestes omnes lineae tam illae quibus in mensā quam aliae quibus utuntur alias hebdomadatim abluantur.'

In post-reformational times, this functionary appeared daily before Hall-time to powder the Fellows' wigs. As lately as 1775 there was a barber's shop just within Trinity gate near the Bishop's Hostel, where their wigs were dressed; whence a wag abstracted them one Saturday night and placed them upon the heads of the statues on the roof of the Library. This must have been especially mortifying to their owners, because Sunday was a great occasion for the display of capillary attraction[1]: so much so that in 1728 the Vice-chancellor had issued a *programma* 'to All and Singular Barbers,' forbidding them to ply their trade upon that day: just as 'His Highness the Lord Protector' had done some 85 years earlier; when by a Proclamation he also forbade 'vainly and profanely walking' on the Sabbath.

Mr Donagan of Trinity Street still designates himself as 'Hairdresser by Appointment to Trinity College:' and the Peterhouse barber, Bendall, is still alive. He used to come round the College in the morning till within three or four years ago, to wake the men for Chapel, and to shave them, —the lazy ones as they lay in bed. Every Fellow of the society on admission still pays a fee of 7s. 9d. to this officer.

When Shenstone the poet was at Pembroke Coll. Oxon. it was with some personal inconvenience that he transgressed the reigning fashion of wigs, by wearing his own long hair[2] in the way which was afterwards practised at Cambridge by prince William of Glo'ster to whom, as to others who did the same, was applied the nickname *Apollo*[3]. But in Shenstone's time few at Oxford would visit him;

[1] *Autobiog. Recoll. of G. Pryme*, 1870, p. 44.
[2] Cp. *The Student*, or *Oxf. and Camb. Monthly Misc.* II. 189, in 1751.
[3] *Gradus ad Cantab.*, 1803, s.v. *Apollo*.

and it was therefore perhaps with some personal bitterness of feeling that he wrote the 'Extent of Cookery,' *Aliusque et idem,*

> When *Tom* to *Cambridge* first was sent
> A plain brown Bob he wore, &c.

or the 'Many ways of dressing a Calf's Head.'

A year or two before he and Johnson had lain in the 'perfect nest of singing-birds,' another eminent man at the same college, George Whitefield[1] the servitor, had gone with unkempt hair from a very different motive,—because he 'thought it unbecoming a penitent to have it powder'd.' So too his exemplar, John Wesley of Christ Church, had saved barber's fees to give to the poor; and it is recorded[2] that the only instance of his deferring to the advice of another was when his brother Sam persuaded him to have the ends off. But until the fashion of crops grew up in 1795, the college barber had his hands full. It was well for all parties that Rob. Foster could 'fly' with foot and hand, as well as tongue: for in those days, when the decorous custom of dressing for 2 o'clock Hall prevailed, each undergraduate was impatient to have his head powdered: and Erskine, when 'ruthless Coe' failed him, preferred to 'cut Hall,' rather than that his upper extremity should disaccord with the regular white stockings and shoes: he therefore spent his time in reviling the faithless barber in a parody on Gray's *Bard*.

[1] Philip's *Whitefield*, p. 34.
[2] Southey's *Wesley*, I. 117.

The following description is from an unpublished letter by an Oxonian in 1792 :

> A quarter wanting now of three
> On entering gates of Trinity
> For dressing will suffice;
> As Highland Barber, far-famed Duff,
> Within that time will plenty puff
> Of lime in both my eyes.
>
> Speaking of skating, I declare,
> *His* motions far more rapid are,
> Whilst up and down he runs :
> At least he thirty has to dress,
> Who all at the same instant press,
> As clamorous as duns.

The following is the barber's bill of Francis Dawes, Fellow of Peterhouse and Esquire Bedel in 1771.

	£	s.	d.
'Mr Daws, Dr Tho. Randall. To a Quarter Dressing, due Lady-day. Pins and Sope...	0	11	2
A Quarter Dressing due Midsummer. A Fillet	0	15	6
A Quarter Dressing due at Michaelmas	0	10	6
Received the contents in full by me Thos. Randall...............................	1	17	2'

Again in 1772,

	£	s.	d.
'A Quarter dressin March 25th	0	10	6
Powder...................................	0	0	4'

I have mentioned Rob. Foster: he was quite a character in Cambridge, where he was known as *the Flying Barber*. Hone gave him a paragraph in the *Year-Book* (columns 1507, 1508) as he did to Nicholson (*Maps*) and Jemmy Gordon. ' Forster', he says, ' died at the end of 1799. During many years he was hair-dresser to Clare Hall, and an eccentric

but honest fellow. He was allowed to be so dexterous in his profession, and trimmed his friends
so well that, some years before his death, the
gentlemen of the University, by subscription, bought
him a silver bason ; and he was so famous, that
it was no light honor which enabled a stranger to
say, he had been shaved out of " Forster's bason."
A striking likeness was etched of him in full trim
without his hat ; for, having lost the only one he
possessed, many years before he died, he never
wore one afterwards. The etchings have become
scarce, or one would have accompanied the likeness
of " The Major." *Nemo.'*

Mr Elijah Johnson of Trinity Street has two engravings of this worthy. The first with the motto

> saepe velut qui
> Currebat fugiens hostem

represents him as a thin elderly man with bason
and towel under his arm, and running, chafer (for
hot water) in hand. 'Pub. Jan. 1, 1787, by J. K.
Baldrey, *Cambridge.'*

The other is inscribed

> 'Tonsor ego—Tonsoris opem si forte requiras
> Mappa subest—ardet Culter—et Unda tepet,
> Des nummos—uno tibi Barba evanuit ictu,
> Si male tolle obolum ; si bene plura refer.

'Pub. Feb. 23, 1785, by J. K. Baldrey, *Cambridge.'*
Drawn by Bearblock, a Fellow of King's. It represents a young Student in tye-wig and brown stockings, sitting in a chair covered with the barber's
involucrum. Foster strides across one of the knees

of his victim; slightly raises the lathered chin with his left hand; leans back at his long arm's-length and contemplates the field on which his open rasor, which he holds above his head, will flash down and perform its office instantaneously.

Dyer gives a different version of the epigram, which he ascribes to Gilbert Wakefield (*Dyer's Privil. of C.* ii. supplement 2 to *Hist. Camb.* p. 91):

> Tonsor ego: vultus radendo spumeus albet,
>   Mappa subest, ardet culter, et unda tepet.
> Quam versat gladium cito dextra, novacula laevis
>   Mox tua tam celeri strinxerit ora manu.
> Cedite, Romani Tonsores, cedite Graii;
>   Tonsorem regio non habet ulla parem.
> Imberbes Grantam, barbati accedite Grantam;
>   Illa polit mentes; et polit illa genas.

The Flying Barber is evidently celebrated in the second of the Tripos verses *Comitiis prioribus*, Feb. 10, 1785. The motto is

> Ille vel intactae segetis per summa volaret
> Gramina; nec teneras cursu laesisset aristas.

It appears from a characteristic story told by Gunning (*Reminisc.* i. p. 179, 1854) that Bob Foster was barber to Dr Farmer, of Emmanuel, among others. Charles Lamb writes to Manning, a Cambridge Mathematical tutor, whom he tries to bring home from China by a fictitious narrative of the changes which have taken place in his absence: 'We will shake withered hands together, and talk of old things, of St Mary's Church, and the barber's opposite where the young students in mathematics used to assemble. Poor Crips, that kept it afterwards, set up a fruiterer's shop in Trumpington-street, and for aught I know resides there still, for I saw the name up in the last journey I took there with my sister just before she died.' The barber's shop, probably, was in reality no more extinct than Mary Lamb. The whole letter is as fabulous as that mischievous one which he wrote to H. C. Robinson in 1829 (*April* 10) when he pretended that he had the rheumatism. He mentions Crips in another humorous letter relating to a present of brawn which he had received from a college servant.

Another Cambridge barber has been celebrated by Hone (*Year-Book*, columns 1507, 1508): he calls him Jacklin; but I am assured by Mr. Smith, the verger of St Mary's, that his name was Tomlinson. He was known as 'the Major,' in a club called the 'sweet Sixteen.' He died in 1824, and as his history belongs to the present rather than to the preceeding century I will simply refer the curious to the passage and caricature in Hone.

The barber's was not the lounger's only refuge: he had another rendezvous, no less a favourite then, and no less obsolete at the present time.

A hundred years earlier Sam. Purchas 'knew well what was *Coffee*, which they drink as hot as they can endure it; it is as black as soot (says he), and tastes not much unlike it; good, they say, for digestion and mirth :'

> Coffee which makes the politician wise
> And see through all things with his half-shut eyes.

Then in the middle of the 17th century an enterprising Turkish merchant of England opened a house for the retail of the 'coffee-drink :' and by the opening of the 18th century such establishments were more numerous and flourishing than ever, in spite of the suspicion in which they were held in some high political circles.

Already each class of society had its peculiar haunt. The *Grecian* for the literary man ; for the clergy, *Child's* in Paul's Churchyard ; *Lloyd's* for the auctions; *St James'*, the *Cocoa-tree* and *Will's* for the man of fashion, the poet, and the politician. Further than this ; the company changed almost every hour. At 6 in the morning *Beaver*, the haberdasher, would hold his own; at 8 the young lawyers would come dropping in ;—some, who lodged near, in dressing-gown and slippers;—at noon the business-man and the idler were brought into contact by different influences : later in the day the wit and the politician would drop in to dispute and discuss, each in the measure of his natural vivacity, the news, the politics, the business, and *the Spectator* of the morning. These coffee-house debates were, as might be supposed, irregular and un-systematic ; the disputant often in the heat of argu-ment omitting the more forcible reasons which cooler moments would suggest. 'There is not one dispute in ten' (says Addison) 'which is managed in these schools of politics, where after the three first sentences the question is not entirely lost. Our disputants put me in mind of the scuttle-fish that, when he is unable to extricate himself, blackens all the water about him until he becomes invisible.'

Some years after the first establishment of coffee-houses, there was provided another place of refuge for the homeless. The *Chocolate-house*, though of the same nature as the earlier establishment, was restricted to more elegant and refined society; and here it was that the gamester found a place. Of this class was *White's*, from which house the fashionable intelligence of the *Tatler* was dated, and here 'Sir Thomas,' the despotic head-waiter, reigned supreme. (*Tatler*, 16, 17, &c., *Spectator*, 49.)

Dryden had had his winter and his summer seat at *Will's* coffee-house: Addison had frequented *Button's*, 'on the south side of Russell-street, about two doors from Covent-garden,' which was named after the owner, who had been in the family of his spouse the countess of Warwick. *Tom's* coffee-house in Cornhill was noted for 'the best Bohea Green Tea and Coffee:' and there were others of the same name. Johnson himself paid frequent visits to the *Turk's Head*. And the Wits and their successors were not the only favoured persons: the Templar had his place of fashionable resort, and even the Universities were not without their coffee-houses.

In 1675, the Cambridge Heads had made answer to a Quaere proposed in his Ma^{tie's} name, that 'the Coffea-houses are daily frequented, and in great numbers of all sorts (the Heads of houses and other Doctors excepted) at all hours, especially morning and evening:' and the account of Roger North, already quoted, testifies no less to the popularity of these places of entertainment. (P. 126.)

In 1710, there was the house where Uffenbach met Whiston and read the *Athenian Oracle*. It was called 'the *Greek's*' from the nationality of its proprietor. He appears from Rud's diary (ed. Luard, 1860, *Camb. Antiq. Soc.*, p. 2), to have set up a 'coffee-booth' at Sturbridge-fair in 1709. Mr Laughton, the senior proctor, visited it, and was abused by 'the Grecian.' In like manner another was set up at the fair about 1770, by *Dockrell* (Hone's *Year-Book*, col. 1543), where there was first-rate milk-punch to be had. At the regular establishment in Trumpington-street, Paley used to spend his evenings when an undergraduate. The Masters of Arts used to occupy the upper, the Bachelors and Undergraduates the lower parts of the room. And later, when he was tutor[1], he went at 9 o'clock 'to supper at *Dockerell's* coffee-house, or elsewhere.' In the *Gradus ad Cantabrigiam*, 1803, is the following article, '*Master of Arts' Coffee-house*. It is sufficient to announce, that there is such a place, where M.A.'s meet together to take their coffee *like other men!*—read the papers, and relate anecdotes of "the men of *our* College."'

A good idea of the appearance of the interior of a coffee-house may be gathered from the frontispiece to 'the Coffee-house,' a Play, 1737, (*Camb. Univ. Lib.* xxiii. 17, 22). From a set of Tripos verses (*Comitiis posterioribus*, Mar. 9, 1780), it seems that the game of chess was sometimes played therein. Another set (*Com. posterior.*, Mar. 6, 1788) gives a description of the *Union* Coffee-house, under the motto *Concordia*

---

[1] Meadley's *Memoirs of Wm. Paley*, pp. 16, 17, 70.

discors. It depicts the rednosed-keeper, half barber, half landlord, looking with his keen eyes from his den among the jugs. The company consists of a parson hunting in the papers for vacant preferment: but the 'fast' riding-man, who can scarce speak of anything but horses, tells him some one else has been before-hand with him. There are, besides, two sportsmen, who boast of nights spent alone in the fens in otter hunting. There too in a corner sits the 'questionist,' who is anxiously awaiting the 'act' which he must 'keep' to-morrow. He spends the time in drawing mathematical diagrams on the table with a wet spill or match, till he jumps up and runs off to read Locke and Newton in his rooms. In front of the fire stands a Nugax or Lounger with his arm beneath his coat-skirt, the other hand dallying with his toothpick. You would know him anywhere by his huge pow-dered wig: he affects the spleen, and has most tender nerves. After a sufficient amount of noise and drink-ing, the less reputable part of the company adjourn to a still noisier reunion at the *Bear*[1] (which stood where the Master's Hostel of Trinity now stands, but which, in 1788, was known as *Adkin College*[2], from a noisy fellow-commoner of Corpus who lodged and gave dinners there, and who, in 1788, assaulted James Wood, of St John's, at the *Union* Coffee-house).

[1] Hi gaudent vino et strepitu risuque jocoque
Lascivo, inter quos heros princepsque tumultûs
Extat pacatis sedibus [sic] qui pulsus *ad Vrsum*
Collegos sociare novos, dicique *Magister*
Jura negans sibi nata, suis circumdatus audet.

[2] Gunning, *Reminisc.* 1854, I. p. 59. Cooper's *Annals*, IV. 432.

There is, however, a reading-man's club or coffee-house designated 'Caryophylli' (perhaps the *Cocoa Tree*).

'A Plain and Friendly Address to the Undergraduates' &c. 1786, complains (p. 17) that 'we shall be called upon to walk, to dress for dinner, or —*to take a dish of coffee at the Union.*' At the end of the list of College Servants in the *Cambridge University Calendar* for 1802, comes '*Master of the Union Coffee-House*, Frank Smith.'

Mention is sometimes found of other Coffee-houses in Cambridge, *e.g.* 'The Johnian Coffee-house in All Saints' Yard,' in 1740. Professor Pryme says (*Autobiog. Recoll.* 1870, p. 43), 'there were two Coffee-houses in the town, where men used to take tea or coffee on summer evenings when there was no fire in their rooms. Frank Smith kept one in Bridge Street, opposite the Round Church. The other was at a room in the *Rose* Inn, set apart for that purpose, facing the Market Place.' This was in 1799.

In 1763, a Coffee-Room was 'opened next to Emmanuel College, in a pleasant garden, where different Languages (French in particular) will be one of the principal Studies, and made easy and familiar by conversation.' Harangues were occasionally to be delivered against the follies of mankind. 'None but the free, generous, debonnaire, and gay, are desired to attend.' Morality was to be enforced by Prints and Diagrams. 'In order to prevent Intemperance, no Spirituous Liquor will be admitted, unless meliorated and duly authorized according to Law; but harmless Tea, Lacedemonian Broth, and invigorating Chocolate, comforting Cakes, with cooking Tarts and Jellies, &c.' John Delaport, the proprietor, offered also advice to persons in legal difficulties from the hour of 10 to noon. 'The best of Tea, with Rolls and Butter, at Sixpence per Head.

'A Library of Books is now in the Coffee-room, which will be increased; and for the entertainment of such Gentlemen who are musically inclined, Instruments will shortly be provided.'

Mr *Delaport* found that Emmanuel Coffee-house was made a public promenade: he therefore instituted admission by ticket, and held out additional attractions.

'A person will attend, to gather the Fruit, Pease or Beans, for such as choose to take a Dinner or Supper.' There was to be a musical performance on Monday afternoons, weather permitting. French lessons, fishing, and perukes were also to be had on the premises.[1]

Though coffee was introduced at Oxford very early, I know little of the Coffee-houses there in the 18th century.

Anthony Wood relates how in 1650 'Jacob, a Jew, opened a Coffey-house at the *Angel*, in the parish of S. Peter in the East, Oxon. and there it was by some, who delighted in noveltie, drank. When he left Oxon. he sold it in Old Southampton buildings in Holborne, near London, and was living there 1671.'

[1] Cooper's *Annals*, IV. 328, 329.

'1654, Cirques Jobson, a Jew and Jacobite, borne neare Mount-Libanus, sold coffy in Oxon. in an house between Edmund-hall, and Queen's Coll. corner.' In commenting on the former passage from Wood's autobiography, Dr Bliss writes : 'The fashion of drinking coffee in public, prevailed in Oxford immediately upon its introduction into England, and continued to a late period. I am told by a venerable friend, now (Feb. 1848) in his 93rd year, that he well remembers the time when every academic of any fashion resorted to the coffee-house during the afternoon : *Tom's*, nearly opposite the present market, being frequented by the most gay and expensive ; *Horseman's*, also in the High-Street, nearly opposite the house of the principal of Brasenose, received the members of Merton, All Souls, Corpus, and Oriel ; *Harper's*, the corner house of the lane leading to Edmund Hall, those of Queen's and Magdalen ; *Bagg's*, the stone-house (built, by the way, out of the surplus materials from Blenheim by Sir John Vanburgh, who built also a similar house in New Inn Hall Lane, now occupied by Mr Walsh, and another in St Aldates, near Folly bridge, pulled down some twenty years since) at the corner of Holywell, facing the King's Arms, used by New College, Hertford, and Wadham ; and *Malbon's*, a diminutive tenement some feet below the present street at the north-east corner of the Turl, was filled from Trinity, and by the members of the neighbouring colleges.'

The line from 'the Lounger' in the *Oxford Sausage*, 1764,

Dinner over to *Tom*'s or to *James*'s I go :

stood in the *Student*, II. 279, 1751,

Dinner over to *Tom*'s or to *Clapham*'s I go,

and a note describes them as '*Noted coffee-houses in* Cambridge.' *James'* is mentioned in Warton's Panegyric on Oxford Ale, in the *Oxford Sausage*, as an *Oxford* house.

We see that the coffee-houses frequently took some political connexion. Thus K. Charles II. once made the experiment of closing them by Proclamation in 1675 (I. D'Israeli, *Curios. of Lit.*); and they were often looked upon with suspicion, as likely to harbour sedition. In the Bodleian (Godwin, *Pamph.*, No. 1686) is a copy of a notice by the Vice-Chancellor of Oxon., Tho. Brathwaite, dated Oxon. the 27th day of July, 1711, prohibiting all Stationers, Booksellers, Hawkers, Keepers of Coffee-houses, other Publick Houses, &c., from publishing, &c., 'the *Medley*,' number 41, which was a libel upon the Lower Houses of Commons and of Convocation, or 'the *Laity's Remonstrance*,' in obedience to the Charge, given by Mr Justice Powell, at Assize. But we must pass on.

Of earlier Oxford coffee-houses, Wood mentions also that, in 1655, 'Arth. Tillyard, apothecary and great royallist, sold coffey publickly in his house against All-soules Coll. He was encouraged to do so by som royallists, now living in Oxon. and by others, who esteem'd themselves either virtuosi or wits; of which the chiefest number were of Alls. Coll., as Peter Pett, Thom. Millington, Tim. Baldwin, Christop. Wren [Sir Chr. Wren], Georg. Castle, Will. Bull.

&c. There were others also, as Joh. Lamphire, a physician, lately ejected from New Coll., who was sometimes the natural droll of the company, the two Wrens, sojournours in Oxon, Matthew and Thomas, sons of Dr Wren, bishop of Ely, &c. This coffey-house continued till his majestie's returne and after, and they became more frequent, and had an excise set upon coffey.' In 1677 he asks, 'Why doth solid and serious learning decline, and few or none follow it now in the University? Answer, because of coffea-houses, where they spend all their time; and in entertainments at their chambers, where their studies and coffea-houses are become places for victuallers; also great drinking at taverns and ale-houses, spending their time in common chambers whole afternoons, and thence to the coffea-house.'

This disease spread in the Universities no less than in the country at large. Whereas Mr Harris (afterwards the first Ld. Malmesbury) says of his career at Merton in 1762, 'Our life was an imitation of High Life in London. Luckily, drinking was not the fashion; but what we did drink was claret; and we had our regular round of evening card parties to the great derangement of our finances. It has often been a matter of surprise to me that so many of us made our way so well in the world, and so creditably:' in 1785 (Mr Gunning says, *Reminisc.* I. xx. 24, 50), drinking was almost universal. Professor Pryme recollected (pp. 49—51) a similar state of affairs in 1799. 'It was usual to invite a large party to partake of wine and a moderate dessert after hall. The host named a Vice-President, and toasts were given. First, a lady by each of the party, then a gentleman, and then a sentiment. I remember one of these latter: "the single married, and the married happy." Some of them were puns. Every one was required to fill a bumper to the toasts of the President, the Vice-President, and his own...."Buzzing," unknown in the present day, was then universal [see *Gent. Magazine*, Vol. 64]....If any one wished to go to chapel, he was pressed to return afterwards.'

The vice was of old standing. Hearne relates (*Diary*, Bliss, ed. 2. II. 269) that about the year 1704 a commoner of Magdalen Hall Oxon., a son of Dr Inett, was found dead from drinking ale and brandy in company with three others, all of whom had fallen asleep.

The writer of '*Advice to a Son in the University* (London; printed by *Edm. Powell* in *Blackfryars*, near *Ludgate*, and are to be sold by *John Morphew*, near *Stationers'-Hall*, 1708.') [Bodl. *Gough, Camb.* 66.] warns him against drinking, as against a fashionable vice. (See Swift's '*Project for the Advancement of Religion*.')

We read of disgraceful scenes of debauchery even in the common and combination-rooms. In the days of early dinners, the effect of such orgies must have been more than ever degrading. In some colleges there seem, even at that time, to have been common-rooms for Bachelors of Arts, as at Exeter, Oxon., in 1754. (*The Conduct of...College Consider'd*, &c. 1754; Bodl. *Gough, Add'. Oxfordshire*, 4to, 31.)

Against the habit of students giving private dinners, there was a loud outcry[1]: and it was complained
that non-attendance at Hall was frequent.

Another abuse was the custom of turning Fast-
days into feasts : the dinner hour being simply postponed till after chapel. (Pryme, *Autobiog. Recoll.*, p. 93.)

I have observed that while Peterhouse was stricter
than most Colleges in adhering to the fish dinner on
Fast-days in the 17th century; after the Restoration
the custom was there dropped, the intermediate stage
being to have meat, *in addition* to fish ; and latterly,
flesh *instead* of fish.

The taverns were frequently the scenes of great
disorder, inflamed sometimes, as we have seen, by
party quarrels. At Cambridge, the *Tuns*, kept by
Wish, had a noisy reputation. It bore a name famous in the University, from the days of Nevile's
Poor Scholar, a play in 1662 (Act II. sc. 6).

Its namesake at Oxford was the rendezvous of the
'*Poetical Club*,' which is ridiculed by Nicholas Amherst in April, 1721 (*Terrae Filius*, Nos. 25, 26). The
meetings there are thus described by one more favourable to them. '1721, *July* 13. Went to the
Tuns with Tho. Beale, Esq. (Gent. Comoner), Mr
Hume, and Mr Sylvester, Pembrokians, where motto'd, epigrammatiz'd, &c.' '*Aug.* 17. Went with Mr

---

[1] *The Expence of the Univ. Education Reduced*, p. 23, ed. 4,
1741, written in 1727 by Dr R. Newton ; also his *Statutes of Hertford Coll.* p. 68. *Remarks on the Enormous Expence...in the Univ.
of Cambridge*, &c. 1788, pp. 6, 36. *Strictures upon the Discipline of
the Univ. of Camb.* 1792, p. 14. *Advice to a Young Man of
Quality*, &c. 1760, p. 29.

Tristram to the Poetical Club (whereof he is a member) at the Tuns (kept by Mr Broadgate), where met Dr Evans, Fellow of St John's, and Mr Jno. Jones, Fellow of Baliol, members of the Club. Subscribed 5*s*. to Dr Evans's *Hymen and Juno* (which one merrily call'd Evans's Bubble, it being now South Sea Time). Drank Gallicia wine, and was entertained with two Fables of the Doctor's Composition, which were indeed masterly in their kind: but the Dr. is allowed to have a peculiar knack, and to excell all mankind at a Fable.' (Diary of *Erasmus Phillips*, 'Fellow-Commoner' of Pembroke, Oxon., *N. and Q.*, 2nd S., x. 366, 443.)

There was the '*Nonsense Club*[1],' which Geo. Colman, Bonnel Thornton, and Lloyd founded about 1750: there was the '*Jelly-bag Club*[2],' so called from the famous *Epigram on an Epigram* ascribed to Ralph Bathurst,

> 'Make it at Top both wide and fit
> To hold a Budget-full of Wit,
> And point it at the End.'

The *Terrae Filius* of 1733, in his speech, which was prohibited, proposed thus to satirize the Fellows of All Souls. 'I would next willingly pay a visit to their college, if I could find it out;·it used to stand on the right hand above Queen's, but if we may judge from the resort of its members we should judge it to be translated over the way, and that the *Three Tuns*

---

[1] *Oxford during the Last Century*, p. 64 (from the *Oxford Chronicle*, 1859).

[2] *Oxford Sausage*, 1764.

Tavern was All Souls' College; did not the effigies of the good Archbishop over the door convince us to the contrary.' The Fellows of St John's Oxon., we are told by Amherst in his *Terrae Filius* essays (No. 34), 'valu'd themselves for having the best *single* and double COLL. (*i.e.* College ale) in the University.'

There was another class of houses common about Oxford, which are thus described in a paper in *The Student,* or Oxf. and Camb. Monthly Miscellany, 1751, II. 373 (anticipating Tom Warton's facetious '*Companion to the Guide, and Guide to the Companion*, being a Supplement to all the Accounts of *Oxford*, hitherto published. 12mo. 1762').

'It is well known that before *colleges* were establish'd, our members were scattered about and lodg'd at private houses: at length, places were set apart for their reception, and dignified by the names of *hospitia*, or *halls*, or (in the modern dialect) *inns* or *tippling-houses*. We must not therefore be surpriz'd to find several remaining which retain their ancient occupation, not only in the body but in the skirts of the town; such as *Fox-hall, Lemon-hall, Feather-hall, Stump-hall, Cabbage-hall, Caterpillar-hall,* &c., &c. But there is one that deserves particular notice, situated N.N.E, a little way out of town, known by the name of *Kidney-hall;* which has long been a very noted *seminary*[1].' Hearne used to solace himself with his antiquarian researches, 'sometimes at Heddington, sometimes at Iffley, sometimes at *Blind Pinnocks* [at Cumnor], sometimes at *Antiquity Hall*' (1718-19).

[1] *Oxoniana,* III. 107.

The last, which bore the sign of *Whittington and his Cat*, was near Rewley, and was known in earlier times as the *Hole in the Wall*. It was a favourite haunt of 'honest' antiquaries.

A no less famous hostel was *Louse Hall*, which was kept by a venerable matron, *Mother Louse*, 'at the further end of a row of tenements, at the bottom of *Headington* Hill, near the lane leading to *Marston*, now, not unaptly, called *Harpsichord Row*. Granger, in his *Biographical History of England* [describing a print by Loggan], informs us that she was probably the last woman in England that wore a ruff. *Mother George* [whose name is associated with hers in Wood's Life, *anno* 1673] lived in Black Boy Lane, and afterwards in the parish of St Peter's in the Bailey, where she died [in her 119th year, July 12, 1691] by an accidental fall which injured her back... She used to thread a very fine needle, without the help of spectacles, and to present it to her guests, who in return gave her some gratuity towards her support[1].' Granger states that *Cabbage-hall* (situated directly opposite the London road on Heddington hill) was founded by a tailor. '*Caterpillar-hall*, the name of the house higher up the hill, was no doubt a complimentary appellation, intimating to posterity that, on account of its better commons, it had drawn away a great number of students from its inferior society, or, in other words, that the caterpillar had eat up the cabbage[2].'

[1] *Oxoniana*, I. 111.
[2] *Life of Wood*, Bliss, s. a. 1673.

Having mentioned two good ladies of the 17th century, it is but fair to refer to the portrait of one of the 18th. There is a caricature of 'Mother *Goose* of Oxford, *Dighton* ad vivam delt.: pubd. July, 1807, by Dighton, Charing Cross.' The worthy lady is represented in a slate-coloured hat and gown, a white kerchief, stockings and apron, long white mittens, tye shoes and roses; and is carrying a cloth in a large gardener's basket.

Of Clubs at Oxford (in addition to the *Constitution*, and *the* Club, with others which I have already mentioned), there were the following: the *Banterers*, whom A. Wood describes (1678) as 'a set of scholars so-called, some M.A., who make it their employment to talk at a venture, lye, and prate what nonsense they please, if they see a man talk seriously they talk floridly nonsense, and care not what he says; this is like throwing a cushion at a man's head, that pretends to be grave and wise.' There were the *Freecynics* in 1737, 'a kind of Philosophical Club...who...have a set of symbolical words and grimaces, unintelligible to any but those of their own society[1].' There was also the *High Borlace*, a tory club which had a convivial meeting held annually at the King's Head tavern in Oxford, on the 18th of August (or, if that fell on a Sunday, on the 19th, as in 1734), on which occasion Dr Leigh, Master of Balliol, was 'of the High Borlace,' and the first clergyman who had attended. It seems to have been patronized by the county families, and it is not improbable that

[1] From Dr Rawlinson's MSS. *Oxoniana*, IV. 246.

there was a ball connected with it. The members chose a Lady Patroness: in 1732, Miss *Stonhouse;* 1733, Miss Molly *Wickham*, of Garsington; 1734, Miss Anne *Cope*, daughter of Sir Jonathan Cope of Bruern. On that occasion, Mr Moseley[1], of Merton, was proposed as a member of the said Borlace, but rejected, probably because he was a member of a whig college.

1749. I have already quoted the remonstrance against Oxford jacobitism as manifested, among other things, in the 'sort of People...most caressed at... your *High Borlace,*' in the pamphlet entitled '*Oxford Honesty.*'

1751. This date is engraved with the motto HIGHBOR LACE on the gold back of 'an ancient brooch richly enamelled, and jewelled with about fifty rubies; [which] has a St Andrew's cross worked in white and blue enamel, with a sort of love-knot encircling it; and underneath this cross is a motto worked in white enamel.' It bears 'the names of two persons, one of whom is designated "Lady Patroness."' This notice in *Notes and Queries*, 2nd S., IV. 248, col. *b*, was answered by various conjectures. 'D. B.' suggested that it might be 'a Cornish motto composed of the name of the person who adopted it.' 'F. C. H.' thought it might be 'merely intended for *Highborn Lass:*' on p. 317 the quotations from Hearne were given.

1763. Letter from the *North Briton* to the *Cocoa-Tree.*

'The Earl of *Westmoreland* was succeeded by Lord

---

[1] *Hearne*, Bliss, III. 103, 150.

Litchfield, and your party [the tories] gentlemen grew so greatly in favour that Oxford now gave us chancellors for courtiers, and of her doctors we made chancellors; for the remarkable year teemed with the dire omen of the same doctor made Chancellor of the Exchequer and comptroller of the high borlace club.' (*Gent. Mag.* XXXIII. 66).

1765. Monday, Aug. 19, 'was held at the *Angel* inn, at Oxford, the High-Borlase, when Lady *Harriot Somerset* was chosen Lady Patroness for the year ensuing.' (*Gent. Mag.*, 1765.)

The import of the name is still open to conjecture. In addition to the suggestions already recounted we may propose,

'*Hebolace.* A dish in cookery, composed of onions, herbs, and strong broth' (Halliwell's *Archaic and Provincial Dictionary*).

'Hispanis *Burlar* est jocari, ludere, Vasconibus *Burlaze*, Occitanis *Bourlos* ludus, jocus, illusio.'

(*Du Cange,* gloss. s.v. *Burlare,* cp. 'Burlesque.')

But I should be inclined to content myself with supposing that some member of the old Cornish family of *Borlace, Borlase,* or *Borlass,* several of whom were Oxonians and staunch jacobites, gave his name originally to the meetings. My friend, Mr William Copeland Borlase, of Castle Horneck, informs me that a member of a wealthy branch of the family situated at Great Marlowe *com.* Bucks was at Oxford in the latter part of the XVIIth century: he seems to have been a person of genial temper and a firm adherent to the Stuarts.

At *Cambridge* also there were several Clubs. The *Old Maids*[1] who met at a coffee-house after evening chapel for the benefit of literary conversation. Of this party was Dr Middleton, Mr Baker the antiquary, Dr Dickens the celebrated Professor of Civil Law, Dr Tonstal and others.

Of a different nature were the meetings of such clubs as the *Westminster* and the *Charterhouse*. Of a disturbance connected with the former in 1750, I have spoken above. Richard Laughton, of Clare[2], when proctor in 1709, had laboured to suppress several clubs of a noisy character. We have also caught a glimpse of a society of university-politicians, the *Associators*, who asserted the right of Appeal from the Vice-chancellor's Court, and who met (like the Westminster Club) at the *Tuns* tavern in 1751.

Gunning (*Reminisc.* II. 153) mentions a very expensive club, to which several King's men belonged, about the year 1790, and 'Turk' Taylor of Trinity, who was supposed to have killed a drayman in a 'Town and Gown row' in 1788. There were 12 members of the club, who wore 'coats of bright green, lined and bound with buff silk, with buttons made expressly, and upon which *Sans Souci* was elegantly engraved; the waistcoat, curiously adorned with frogs, was buff, with knee-breeches of the same colour. The members met at each others' rooms one evening in the week, when they played for

[1] Dyer's *Priv. of Camb.* II.; *Supplement to Hist.* II. pp. 135, 136.
[2] Monk's *Bentley*, I. 286. Mr Mayor's account of R. Laughton in his *Cambridge under Queen Anne* will contain some curious information on this matter.

very high stakes ; also they dined together once a month, when each member was allowed to invite a friend ; and in conclusion, they had a grand anniversary.'

Professor Pryme speaking of his early days (*Autobiog. Recoll.*, 117), about 1799, says : ' The " Cambridge Union " did not exist. The only clubs that I can recollect were " The *True Blue*," said traditionally to have existed from the time of the revolution of 1688, and to have taken its colour in opposition to the Orange of King William. An especial dress, including a blue coat, was worn by the members, who were few in number, and it was confined tó Trinity College. It was reputed to be a hard-drinking club. The other called "The *Speculative*," after a great debating society at Edinburgh, met once a week in term time, and consisted of twenty members ; Pattison (afterwards Judge), Sumner (Bp. of Winchester), and Pearson (afterwards Archdeacon, and son of the eminent surgeon of that name), and I, belonged to it. The present " *Union* " was formed in 1815, as its name implies, by the junction of two rival societies. It first met in a small room at the back of the Red Lion Inn, and afterwards removed to premises which had been formerly used as a dissenting chapel.'

On the 10th of December, 1725, was established at Cambridge a literary society called the *Zodiack* club[1], consisting of 12 members denominated from

[1] Cooper's *Annals*, IV. 187; Nichols' *Lit. Anecd.* VI. 228; *Oxford Undergraduates' Journal*, 1867, p. 158.

the 12 signs.   In 1728, 6 planets were added.   The members were pledged to present, recommend, and elect to all offices none but such as belonged to the Society [1].

The *Hyson* club was established by the Wranglers of 1758.   (*Milner's* Life of *Milner.*)   Among the extracts from a diary which will be printed in an Appendix to this compilation will be found notices of a Literary Society to which S. T. Coleridge and Chr. Wordsworth (afterwards Master of Trinity) &c. belonged in 1795.

The *Progress of Discontent* by T. Warton (written in 1746, printed in the *Student*, 1750, and the *Oxford Sausage*, 1764, &c.) gives the following summary of the life of a don without worthy aspirations :

> What endless pleasure
> I found in Reading or in Leisure !
> When calm around the Common Room
> I puff'd my daily Pipe's Perfume !
> Rode for a Stomach, and inspected,
> At annual Bottlings, Corks selected :
> And din'd untaxed, untroubled, under
> The Portrait of our pious Founder !
> [When, for Amusement, my tyrannic
> Sway could put Freshmen in a Panic;]
> When *Impositions* were supply'd
> To light my Pipe—or sooth my Pride !
>
> Too fond of Liberty and Ease
> A Patron's Vanity to please,
> Long Time he watches, and by Stealth,
> Each frail Incumbent's doubtful Health ;
> At length—and in his fortieth Year,
> A Living drops—two hundred clear !

[1] Cooper's *Annals*, IV. 298.

To the diary of the 'genuine *Idler*' (*Idler* No. 33, said to have been written by Tom Warton, as also Nos. 93, 96), in 1758, reference has been made already. Another sketch is given in a Parody on *Gray's Elegy* which appeared in the *Oxford Sausage*, 1764, under the title 'An *Evening Contemplation* in a *College.*' A portion of it is subjoined:

> Within these Walls, where thro' the glimm'ring Shade
> Appear the Pamphlets in a mould'ring Heap,
> Each in his narrow Bed till Morning laid,
> The peaceful Fellows of the College sleep.
> The tinkling Bell proclaiming early Prayers,
> The noisy Servants rattling o'er their Head,
> The calls of Business and domestic Cares,
> Ne'er rouze these Sleepers from their downy Bed.
>
> .   .   .   .
>
> E'en now their Books from Cobwebs to protect,
> Inclos'd by Doors of Glass in Doric Style,
> On fluted Pillars rais'd, with Bronzes deck'd,
> They claim the passing Tribute of a Smile.
> Oft are the Authors' Names, tho' richly bound,
> Mis-spelt by blund'ring Binders' Want of Care ;
> And many a Catalogue is strew'd around,
> To tell th' admiring Guest what Books are there.
>
> .   .   .   .
>
> *Reports* attract the Lawyer's parting Eyes,
> Novels Lord Fopling and Sir Plume require;
> For Songs and Plays the Voice of Beauty cries,
> And Sense and Nature *Grandison* desire.
> For thee, who mindful of thy lov'd Compeers
> Dost in their Lines their artless Tales relate,
> If Chance, with prying Search in future Years,
> Some Antiquarian shall enquire thy Fate,
> Haply some Friend may shake his hoary Head,
> And say, 'Each Morn unchill'd by Frost, he ran
> With Hose ungarter'd, o'er yon turfy Bed,
> To reach the Chapel ere the Psalms began.
> There in the Arms of that lethargic Chair,
> Which rears its moth-devoured Back so high,

At Noon he quaffed three Glasses to the Fair,
And por'd upon the News with curious Eye.
Now by the Fire, engag'd in serious Talk
Or mirthful Converse, would he loit'ring stand;
Then in the Garden chuse a sunny Walk,
Or launch the polish'd Bowl with steady Hand.
One Morn we miss'd him at the Hour of Pray'r,
Beside the Fire, and on his fav'rite Green;
Another came, nor yet within the Chair,
Nor yet at Bowls, nor Chapel was he seen.
The next we heard that in a neighbouring Shire,
That Day to Church he led a blushing Bride.'

Tobacco seems to have been taken at Cambridge as early as 1614—15; for the 10th order for preparations against King James' coming at that time provided

'That no Graduate, Scholler, or Student of this Universitie, presume to resorte to any Inn, Taverne, Ale-howse, or Tobacco-shop, at any tyme dureing the abode of his Majestie here; nor doe presume to take tobacco in St Marie's Church [at the Act] or in Trinity Colledge Hall [at the performance of *Aemilia, Ignoramus, Albumazar,* and *Melanthe*], upon payne of finall expellinge the Universitie.'

At Oxford, dean Aldrich of Ch. Ch. was a habitual smoker. It is well known that he wrote '*a Catch to be sung by four Men smoking their Pipes, not more difficult to sing than diverting to hear.*' A student once visited the dean at 10 A.M., having laid a wager that he would find him in the act of smoking. The dean said good-humouredly, 'You see sir, you've lost your wager, for I'm not smoking, I'm filling my pipe.'

Tho. Baker, of St John's, Cambridge, 'used generally to fetch a clean Pipe about 3 o'clock' in the afternoon. He was found dead with one lying broken at his side in 1740.

In 1786, Gunning says (*Reminisc.* i. 44), smoking was 'going out of fashion amongst the junior members of our combination-rooms, except on the river in the evening, when every man put a short pipe in his mouth.'

Prof. Pryme states (*Autobiog. Reminisc.*, p. 51) that in 1800 ' Smoking was allowed [as now] in the Trinity combination-room after supper in the twelve days of Christmas, when a few old men availed themselves of it ['with the wine, pipes and tobacco-box were laid on the table. Porson was asked for an inscription for the latter (a large silver one), and he said "τῷ Βάκχῳ,"' *ibid.* p. 86, s.a. 1808]. Among *us* undergraduates it had no favour, and an attempt of Mr Ginkell, son of Lord Athlone (a Dutch family mentioned in Macaulay's *History of England*), to introduce smoking at his own wine-parties failed, although he had the prestige of being a hat-fellow-commoner.'

Gunning[1] relates how Busick Harwood used to spend his evenings in Emmanuel parlour, which, under the presidency of Dr Farmer, was always open to those who loved pipes and tobacco and cheerful conversation.

At Peterhouse, it was by a College Order, '*April* 3rd, 1735, agreed at a Meeting of the Mʳ. and Fellows, that the person attending the Parlour be allow'd forty shillings, ꝑ an. to be placed under the Head of Expensae Mri. et Soc.:' '*Oct.* 31, 1749, a fire to be

---

[1] *Reminisc.* I. 54.

L. B. E.   II

made in the Combination at noon, to continue till two o'clock in the afternoon from the Audit till lady-day.'

It is called 'the *Common-room*' (as at Oxford), in an Order made *March* 1st, 1749—50.

The ordinary name for the college parlours at Cambridge, '*Combination*-room,' is said by a good authority to be derived, not from the convivial meetings held there, but from their sterner use for business, not for pleasure: inasmuch as *there* were drawn up the 'First Combination Paper,' a list of the Preachers of the Sunday morning university Sermons, a certain number of whom were appointed (as the Proctors and Moderators are) by each college in turn (excepting Trinity Hall), according to the *Prior Combinatio;* and of the preachers on Saints' days and Sunday afternoons, according to the order of names in the Registrary's book,—the *Posterior Combinatio:* a substitute for one of the latter set received two guineas.

In the Combination-room there was always a seed cake ready, and a bottle of sherry sack (or dry sherry) for those engaged in Acts for the higher degrees, and thither came the maces to conduct the disputants to the Schools.

The frequenting of taverns and the lounging at coffee-houses was at once an effect and a cause of a lack of healthy exercise. If some of us are too strenuous in our diversions now-a-days; in the preceding century there was a want of vigour and falling-off from the days of the Book of Sports, from the trials of strength in the merry England of good queen Bess, and from the long-bow of our more distant ancestry. The Hanoverian dynasty seems to have brought in, along with certain good things, a sort of triumph of Pudding, Turnips, and muddy Ale, over the Lace, Maypoles, Champagne and Burgundy of the preceding period. For riding the Great Horse, we have *schemes* in phaetons to Blenheim or Madingley: instead of bell-ringing there is beer, and billiards played lazily at Chesterton.

The following account of amusements at Oxford, in 1667, is taken from *Oxonium poema*, some Latin verses [Bodl. *Gough, Oxford*, 90], 'authore F. V. [ernon], Ex Aede Christi, Oxon.: Typis W. Hall. Impensis Ric.: Davis, 1667,' pp. 26. In 'the margent' is a running argument indicating the different topics of the descriptions; among them are 'Schollars that dispute as they walk,' 'Authors quoted in dispute' [Burgersdicius, Brerewood, Aristotle Organon, Smiglecius, Scotus, Aquinas, Suarez, Vasquez, Scheiblerus, Herebordus, Combachius, Magirus, Isendornus, &c.].

Then comes a description of Oxford in spring, 'Swimming in Merton Pool and Schollars Pool, Tumbling in the Hay.' Another watches 'Frogs swimming;' while a third tells 'Stories under a Hay-mow.' But the more sad student on his way to the river 'will repeat Virgil or the lines of the great Horace.' There is also 'Leaping, Wrestling, Playing at Quoits,' as well as the more pastoral occupation of 'making Trimtrams with Rushes and Flowers.' Another party sits on the bank and 'non regressuros educit arundine pisces;' while a stray Piscator looks out for the lurking den of the ravenous Luce or Pikerel.   Others search in the mud for 'Chubs and Craw-fish:' but they will be startled by shrew mice, 'Water-ratts, toads, snakes,' or owls.   The poem concludes with prayers for a blessing on Oxford:

'Surplices] *Nempe tuae niveo memorantur ab agmine laudes.*'

It must be remembered that this is a description of the pastime of *boys*.   The recreations of youth are recounted in '*The Compleat Gentleman: Fashioning Him absolute in the most Necessary and Commendable Qualities concerning Mind, or Body, that may be required in a person of Honor.   By Henry Peacham, Mr of Arts, Sometime of Trinity Colledge in Cambridge...1661*' [ed. 1. 1622].   Chapter XVII., 'Of Exercise of the Body, Horsmanship, Tilting and Torneaments, throwing, leaping, and wrestling (not so well beseeming Nobility), running, leaping, swimming, shooting, as in that excellent Book of Mr *Aschams* intituled *Toxophilus*, wherein you shall finde whatsoever is requisite to be know of a compleat Archer.'

Bell-ringing was an amusement which had not been unknown in the earlier days.   Thus, Sir Symonds D'Ewes in 1618, on the morning of St Thomas' day, amused himself by taking the rope from the hands of the subsizar at St John's, whose duty it was to ring, and pulled till he fell down the stairs exhausted, and was stunned.   This amusement received a great impetus at the time of the rejoicings at the Restoration in 1660. It bears a curious part in Bunyan's Life and writings (*Grace Abounding*, §§ 33, 34. *Life and Death of Mr Badman*, ch. VII. [Offor, III. p. 625]; *Holy War*, passim; also Clark's *Looking Glass for Saints and Sinners*, 1657, 568—9). Uffenbach, when at Cambridge in 1710 (*Reise*, III. 63), says that the English performed poorly on all instruments but the organ, yet they pride themselves on their chimes, and 'aim at an artistic style of ringing; but we could not fancy the clatter, rather were annoyed to hear it so often : for the *scholars* or young students mount the towers and ring when they please, often for hours together. Accidents often happen in bell-ringing, some students being struck, or falling down and breaking leg and arm.' [Mr *Mayor's* translation.] In his sober years, R. Dawes, the critic, took to bell-ringing at Cambridge about 1733, as he did to boating at Heworth in 1750. He was a member of the 'Cambridge Youths' in 1731. On the 3rd of August, 1724, 'was established the Society denominated the *Cambridge Youths*, instituted for the purpose of change-ringing on Great St Mary's Bells (a new peal of ten being put up this year). Several distinguished members of the University [10 are enumerated, 1725 —73] have belonged to this Society, which still exists' (Cooper's *Annals*, IV. 185, published 1852).

At Oxford, Hearne took great interest in the ringing matches[1] 1733—5 (as Ant. Wood had done in 1656, when he, with his mother and brothers, sub-

---

[1] Bliss, *Hearne*, ed. 2. III. 96, 104, 109, 121, 133, 145, 154, 180.

scribed towards the founding of Merton bells: and though they were not satisfactory to 'the curious and critical hearer,' he plucked at them often with some of his fellow-collegians for recreation sake).

Mr G. V. Cox (in his *Recollections*, 1868, p. 30) says, that at Oxford 'bell-ringing, a fashionable exercise some twenty years before, was, in 1797, voted vulgar.' It gave place to the more aristocratic door-bell and knocker wringing. The following account of amusements in Oxford in 1751 is taken from the *Student* (II. 374), where the burlesque account of 'Several *Public Buildings* in *Oxford*, never before described,' is given. 'The several *gymnasia* constructed for the exercise of our youth, and a relaxation from their severer studies, are not so much frequented as formerly, especially in the summer: our ingenious gownsmen having found out several *sports* which conduce to the same end, such as *battledoor and shuttlecock, swinging on the rope*, &c., in their own apartments; or, in the fields, *leap-frog, tag, hop-step-and-jump*, and among the rest, *skittles;* which last is a truly *academical* exercise, as it is founded on arithmetical and geometrical principles.' The introduction of gymnasiums into England seems to have taken place at a comparatively recent date. Hone, in his *Every-Day Book* (I. 19, 1315, II. 653—8), 1826—7, records the rise of the exercise under the advocacy of Mr Clias, and the superintendence of Herr Voelker, in New Inn Road, and in Finsbury Square; and by the formation of a 'London Gymnastic Society.'

But 'the Great Horse' of the 17th and 18th centuries was a very different creature from that of the present gymnasts. In an appendix to this compilation will be found an account, abridged from Gutch's *Collectanea Curiosa*, of· a Letter from a Friend of the *Universities*, in reference to the new *Project* for riding 'the *Great* Horse,' written probably by Dr Wallis in the year 1700. The proposal was for a riding-school, which was to serve almost as many purposes of education as *Emmanuel Coffee-house* mentioned above. It was intended[1] 'to devote the profits of Clarendon's *History* to supporting a riding-school.' Hearne (*Reliquiae*, III. 90, Bliss) tells us that when Mr Lewis Maidwell had his proposal for supporting a publick school (designed, amongst other things, for the sea-service of the nation), his petition delivered into the House of Commons, Feb. 3, 1699, upon mature deliberation was thrown out chiefly by Wallis, whose MS. was offered to Hearne for publication. He adds, 'The project then on foot was for an academy of exercises in the University, such as riding the great horse, fencing, &c. I well remember the thing to have been much talked of in the University: I think it was wisely stopped, because, without doubt, 'twould have utterly obstructed all true learning.'

In his *Cheape and Good Husbandry*, Book I. pp. 8—31, (in his *Way to get Wealth*, ed. 10, 1660) G[ervase] M[arkham] gives a treatise '*of the great Horse*,' with full directions for Cherishings ('as crying *holla so boy, there boy there*') for performing the

---

[1] *N. and Q.* 1st S., x. 185, XI. 32; 2nd S., x. 74.

Corvet, Capriole, Terra Terra, Caragolo, Serpeigiare, Incavellare, Chambetta, the *Carere,* the *Gallop Galliard,* as well as instructions for 'Riding before a Prince.'

This had been a fashionable amusement. Ben Jonson's *Hedon* 'courts ladies with how many great horse he hath rid that morning' (*Cynthia's Revels,* II. I.). Riding, though discouraged by the University authorities, was a favourite, but expensive amusement. We have indeed, in Cobb's Tripos speech (described below), as early as 1701—2, an instance of a don (Awbery, the junior proctor) distinguishing himself by his unskilful riding on the Hills Road. So too 'the Female Student' (in the *Student,* II. 302, 1751) describes the life of a Master of Arts as 'confin'd to those of his own standing: and the college-hall, the common-room, the coffee-house, and now and then a ride on the Gog-magog-hills, is all the variety he has a taste for enjoying.' We may compare also [Warton's] 'Diary of a genuine Idler' in 1758 (*Idler,* No. 33). It is recorded in *Remarks on the Enormous Expence in the Education of many young men in the University of Cambridge...&c.* 1788 [p. 39, Bodl. *Gough, Camb.* 65] that 'a Horsekeeper, one James Barrow, who in 1773 was not worth £10, died in 1786 worth £3000, which he had acquired by letting and selling horses to the young men of the University. The charges at present [1788] are I think as follows:

	£	s.	d.
Fox and Stag hunting	1	5	0
Hare ditto		15	0
New Market meeting per day	1	1	0
The Amusement of most mornings' Racing at the Hills		10	6
A common Ride		4	6

The price given for Horses is from £18 to £120.

Another man, one Fordham a butcher, who within four years has raised a fortune by horses, has lately built a prodigious range of Stables near the County Hall.'

In the *Pleasure of being out of Debt* (which appeared in the *Student*, I. 114, 1750, and afterwards in the *Oxford Sausage*, 1764) is noted as a piece of liberty, that a man

> on a spurgall'd Hackney runs
> To *London* masquerading.

As late as 1797, according to Mr G. V. Cox (*Recollections*, p. 30), it was no uncommon thing 'for a "gentleman" (the Oxford tradesman's designation of a member of the University) to ride *a match against time* from Oxford to London and back again to Oxford (108 miles) in twelve hours or less with, of course, relays of horses at regular intervals. In one instance this was done in 8 hours and 45 minutes... Betting was, no doubt, the first and chief motive; a foolish vanity the second; the third cause was the absence at that time in the University of a better mode of proving pluck and taming down the animal spirits of non-reading youngsters...Hunting then, as now, was an expensive amusement, only to be enjoyed by a few, and by them only for a part of the year ; racing had not *then* been thought of...To ride well is indeed an accomplishment be-fitting a gentleman, but a gentleman need not learn to ride like a jockey.'

Fox-hunting is the theme of one of the sets of Tripos verses for 1791.

By the 9th of the celebrated 'Orders and Regula-tions' of 1750, riding on horseback was forbidden to persons *in statu pupillari* at Cambridge, unless they had special leave.   But in 1807 the decree which forbade 'driving out in carriages drawn by two or more horses,' prohibited *riding* only on Sundays. In 1798 there had been a decree against driving, especially in the streets.

Walking regularly for the sake of exercise is a modern refinement.

It is mentioned in W. Gilpin's *Posthumous Dia-logues on various subjects*, 1807, p. 310.   In 1799, Daniel Wilson writes to his father, that very few days passed when he did not walk for about an hour.

The practice of making short tours was earlier.

Dr Tho. Blackwell, Professor of Greek at Aber-deen, and principal of Marischal College, writes on June 25, 1736, to beg Warburton to accompany Middleton and their 'common friend, Mr Gale,' in a tour in Scotland for two months in the summer during the long Vacation.   At the same time it was not very uncommon for Fellows and Students (especi-ally Sizars, as Sam. Jebb at Peterhouse, and Bp.

Watson at Trinity) to live for several years together without sleeping a night out of Cambridge. The writer of '*Advice to a young man of Quality upon his coming to the University :* London, printed for C. Gay in Newgate Street, 1760,' advises him to travel in the neighbourhood of the University instead of hunting; and to spend the vacations in tours in Britain, visiting manufactories, interesting buildings, and antiquities. R. Gough, when a Fellow-Commoner of Bene't College (now Corpus Chr'sti, Camb.), in July 1756 visited Peterborough, Croyland and Stamford. (Nichols, *L. A.* VI. 268.)

In 1742, Tho. Townson started for a 3 years' tour in France, Italy, Germany and Holland, with Dawkins, Drake, and Holdsworth[1]. 'On his return from the Continent he resumed in College [Magd. Oxon.] the arduous and respectable employment of tuition, in which he had been engaged before he went abroad.'

William Wordsworth took walking tours in France in 1790—91 (at a time no less awfully interesting than that which the country has been now passing through) before and after taking his degree. In the first instance he was accompanied by his college friend Rob. Jones, with about £20 apiece in their pockets. 'Our coats which we had made light on purpose for the journey are of the same piece' (he writes); 'and our manner of carrying our bundles, which is upon our heads, with each an oak stick in our hands, contributes not a little to the general curiosity which we seem to excite.' He speaks of the Swiss innkeepers

[1] Churton's *Townson*, I. pp. xii. xiii.

even then, as 'corrupted by perpetual intercourse with strangers.'

In Hone's *Table Book* (I. 138) are quoted some lines which show that as early as 1826 visitors wrote 'in the book at Rigi, in Switzerland;' and stayed there for the sunset and sunrise, and were disappointed.

Wordsworth's tour was pedestrian, excepting that they bought a boat at Bâle and floated down the Rhine to Cologne (*Memoirs*, ch. VII., where there is given their Itinerary from July 13 to Sept. 29).

'Reading-parties' belong to the 19th century. In 1805, bp. Watson complained of the constant flux of *Lakers* (or tourists) in Westmoreland. University men did not begin to go there in parties till later: our university leading the way, so that when the first Oxford party settled in those regions (about 1830) they were called by the natives 'the Oxford Cantabs.' Wordsworth's *Guide through the District of the Lakes* was enlarged from an essay published by him as an Introduction to Wilkinson's Views, and printed in 1820 with 'Sonnets on the River Duddon, &c.'

The amusements of sir Erasmus Philipps, when a 'Fellow-Commoner' of Pembroke, Oxon., in 1720, seem to have been fox-hunting, attending cock-fighting and horse-races, giving and frequenting balls, riding to Woodstock, Godstow, Nuneham, &c., occasionally attending meetings of the *Poetical* club at the Three Tuns, learning the violin, listening to declamations in hall or speeches in the schools, or conversing with the 'Arabick criticks,' Mr Solomon Negri of Damascus, and others. He seems to have stayed in

Oxford through what is now the long Vacation, and to have gone down at Christmas for about the same period as we do now.

The following extracts from his Diary (given in *N. and Q.*, 2nd S., x. 366) may be found interesting:—

'1721. *July* 4. Went up the river a fishing with Mr Wilder, Mr Eaton, Mr Clerk, Mr Clayton (Gent. Commoner), Mr Sylvester, and Mr Bois, all Pembrokians, as far as Burnt Island. Whereon we landed and dressed a leg of mutton, which afterwards we dispatched in the wherry. The passage to this diminutive Island is wonderfully sweet and pleasant.'

'1721. *April* 14. Rode with Mr Wilder, Fellow and Vicegerent of Pembroke, and Mr Le Merchant to Newnam, where dined upon Fish at the pleasant place mentioned, page 107. Coming home a dispute arose between these two gentlemen, whom, with great difficulty, I kept from blows.'

Swimming (though forbidden[1] in ancient times) was common in the 18th century. Rowland Hill, in 1768, swam against the stream from Cambridge to Grantchester. In Charles Simeon's diary occurs the following entry: 1784, '*May* 28th, went into the water, and shall continue it at 5.' It would seem as if he bathed early in the Cam in King's College grounds.

Fishing was not a very common recreation, though sometimes it formed a pleasant amusement in the water-parties of the time.

Will. Pattison, the poet of Sidney Sussex Coll., used

· [1] See Cooper's *Annals*, anno 1571.

to fish at Cambridge in 1724. He was compelled to
retire from the University.

Gunning says that in 1788 he does not think there
were ten men in the University who were regular
anglers, although the Rev. Mr Pemberton gave every
encouragement to fishermen. He mentions fishing
parties at Upware, and pond-netting at Dimmock's
Court (*Reminisc.* I. 43, 116).

The Thames had been made navigable to Oxford
in the reign of James I., when dean King of Christ
Church was Vice-chancellor (1608—10): and there
had been an 'Act for making the River *Cham* alias
Grant, in the County of *Cambridge*, more navigable
from *Clay-Hithe-Ferry* to the *Queen's Mill*,' &c., in
the year 1702 (it was extended in 1813); yet rowing
was not made a regular exercise till the present century. Southey, who used to say that he 'learnt but
two things at Oxford, to row and to swim,' gives the
following picture of a scene on the Isis, in his *Espriella*,
1807, Letter XXXII.: 'A number of pleasure-boats
were gliding in all directions upon this clear and rapid
stream; some with spread sails; in others the caps and
tassels of the students formed a curious contrast with
their employment at the oar. Many of the smaller
boats had only a single person in each; and in some of
these he sat face forward, leaning back as in a chair,
and plying with both hands a double-bladed oar in
alternate strokes, so that his motion was like the path
of a serpent. One of these canoes is, I am assured,
so exceedingly light, that a man can carry it; but
few persons are skilful or venturous enough to use it.'

Speaking of 1799, Prof. Pryme says (p. 43), 'Rowing on the river was not then the custom, but we took a boat one day, rowed down to Clayhithe, hired a net to fish with, and rowed back in the evening. This was my only excursion during my first term.'

Boat races were unheard of in Mr G. V. Cox's day (about 1790); 'boating had not yet become a systematic pursuit in Oxford. Men went indeed to Nuneham for occasional parties in six-oared boats (eight-oar'd boats were then unknown), but these boats (such as would now be laughed at as "tubs") belonged to the boat-people; the crew was a mixed crew got up for the day, and the dresses worn anything but uniform. I belonged to a crew of five, who were, I think, the first distinguished by a peculiar (and what would now be thought a ridiculous) dress; viz. a green leather cap, with a jacket and trowsers of nankeen!'

At Cambridge about the year 1810 a few men would take a boat from the locks, or at Chesterton; and sometimes two rival boats would sally forth together; not so much for a race as for a *splashing match!*

In the *Classical Journal*, v., 412–414, is printed, at the request of Sir Walter Scott, a set of Tripos verses signed V. L.[1], '*in Comitiis posterioribus*, March 12, 1812.' They contain an account of the students working, and of the manner of spending the day among the undergraduates:

'comites vocat, et rogat adsint
Aut ad equos, aut si placeat ad flumina cymbae.'

[1] *Chas. Val. Le Grice.*

In the 6th number of the *Tatler in Cambridge*, 1871, is an amusing account of early boating from the year 1822, seven years before the earliest inter-university race.

Shooting was a favourite sport in the days before the fens near Cambridge were drained.

In Cooper's *Annals* (IV. 423) is given a facetious notice to trespassers, which was printed by the tenant-farmers of Grantchester in 1787. Mr Gunning writes (*Reminisc.* I. 40) that about the same period 'in going over the land now occupied by Downing Terrace, you generally got five or six snipes. Crossing the Leys, you entered on Cow-fen; this abounded with snipes. Walking through the osier-bed on the Trumpington side of the brook, you frequently met with a partridge, and now and then a pheasant. From thence to the lower end of Pemberton's garden was one continued marsh, which afforded plenty of snipes, and in the month of March a hare or two. If you chose to keep by the side of the river, you came to Harston-Ham, well known to sportsmen; and at no great distance from this you arrived at Foulmire Mere, which produced a great variety of wild fowl. The heavy coach changed horses at the Swan, and would set you down, between seven and eight o'clock, at the Blue Boar. If you started from the other corner of Parker's Piece, you came to Cherryhinton Fen; and thence to Teversham, Quy, Bottisham, and Swaffham Fens. In taking this beat, you met with great varieties of wild fowl, bitterns, plovers of every description, ruffs and reeves, and not unfrequently pheasants. If you did not go very near the mansions of the few country gentlemen who resided in the neighbourhood, you met with no interruption. You scarcely ever saw the gamekeeper, but met with a great number of young lads, who were on the look-out for sportsmen from the University, whose game they carried, and to whom they furnished long poles, to enable them to leap the very wide ditches which intersected the Fens in every direction.'

This seems almost as strange to us now, as the account of London given in Macaulay's History, when a woodcock might be found where Regent-street is now.

The Tripos verses for 1788, and 1795, bear witness to the taste for shooting in Cambridge at the time.

In the Oxford University Statutes among pro-hibited games are mentioned 'every kind of game in which money is concerned, such as dibs, dice, cards, cricketing in private grounds or gardens of the towns-people:' and then 'every kind of game or exercise from which danger, injury, or inconvenience might arise to other people, such as hunting of beasts with any sort of dogs, ferrets, nets, or toils; also any use or carrying of muskets, cross-bows, or falcolns: neither rope-dancers, nor actors, nor shows of gladiators are to be permitted without especial sanction; moreover the scholars are not to play at football, nor with cudgels, either among themselves or with the towns-folk, a practice from which the most perilous con-tentions have often arisen[1].'

[1] *Huber*, ed. Newman, ii. 11. 427.

At Cambridge the Elizabethan Statutes (cap. 47) forbade dice, and (except at Christmas) cards : daily resorting to the town : vain clubbing of money : sword-playing, fencing, and dancing-schools : gaming-houses : cockfighting, bear or bull-baiting : quoits : or looking on at any of these.

The 5th of the Orders and Regulations of 1750 provided that 'every person *in statu pupillari* who shall be found at any coffee-house, tennis-court, cricket-ground, or other place of publick diversion and entertainment, betwixt the hours of nine and twelve in the morning, shall forfeit the sum of 10*s.* for every offence.'

D'Ewes, in 1620, played at *tennis* at Christ's coll. He also mentions the Tennis-court in St John's. (*Halliwell* I. 109.) There is a Tennis-court marked in a map (dated 1688, in Loggan's *Cantab. Depicta*), as standing to the west of Peterhouse Grove. Racquets is mentioned in *an Epistle to a Fellow-Commoner* (Pelham) in 1750.

Fives is mentioned by Amherst in his *Terrae Filius*, No. 34, 1721 (or *Fifes*, as it is printed, ed. 1726), when he complains that the old Ball-court has been improved away.

Of a later time Mr G. V. Cox remembered (*Recoll* p. 53, 54), that 'the game of *cricket* was kept up chiefly by the young men from Winchester and Eton, and was confined to the old Bullingdon Club which was expensive and exclusive. The members of it, however, with the exception of a few who kept horses, did not mind walking to and fro.' *Football* was not,

I think, played much in the last century; though it had once been carried on with vigour. Symonds D'Ewes speaks of a match which ought to have come off on Sheep's Green, on March 29, 1620 (?) between the *Trinitician* and the *Johnian* 'faction.' The former did not appear. They played also sometimes on 'Trinity Green,' near the Nevile Court.

Though Sir P. Sidney speaks of women playing at the game, it was not a gentle one. About 1632, John Barwick[1] at St John's, 'would frequently recreate himself with bodily exercises and those violent enough, such as pitching the Bar, and playing at Football, at which latter game, having the misfortune to break a player's collar-bone, he would never play again.'

'There was a decree[2]' Perne Procan. [1574] 'that scholars should only play at football upon their own coll' ground, &c., and not admit Strangers or other Scholars under Penalty of 5s. the first offence.'

In 1579, the scholars, when playing, were assaulted by the men of Chesterton, and Dr Perry, of Peterhouse, made another order as Justice of the Peace.

At Oxford[3], it was ordered by the Chancellor in 1584, that 'no minister or deacon shall go into the fields to playe at foot-ball, or beare any weapon to make any fraye or maintain any quarrel.'

Sir T. Overbury, in his character of 'a meere Scholar,' 1616, notes as a characteristic, that 'the antiquity of his University is his creed, and the ex-

[1] Barwick's *Life of Barwick*, ed. 1724, pp. 9, 10.
[2] Ashton's *Collectanea*, fol. 56, in *Stat. Acad.* cap. 46. Cooper's *Annals*, II. 321, 371, 382.
[3] *Oxoniana*, IV. 176.

cellency of his Colledge (though but for a match at foot-ball) an article of his faith.'

The writer of *Advice to a Young Man of Quality, &c.*, 1760, recommends him to strike out of his accounts all his 'expenses for servant, for horses, for tennis and billiards, for coffee-houses and taverns, and for entertainments of dinners and suppers at your private chambers' (p. 29).

Gunning says (*Reminisc.* I. 44), of their evening water-parties in 1786, 'when we arrived at Chesterton, two or three of our party would sometimes leave the boat and stop to play at *billiards;* but this was generally disapproved of, and the billiard-players were seldom admitted into our future parties.'

Chesterton continued to be the resort of billiard-players far on into the present century; and it is a good thing that the game is now tacitly admitted to be played in Cambridge, where, at least, the *moral* atmosphere is less stifling.

The bowling-greens of the Colleges were favourite places of resort. D'Ewes, in 1620, amused himself with running, jumping, pitching the bar, and bowls on the green. The 'Evening Contemplation in a College' has been quoted already; and it will be remembered that Addison wrote some elegant latin verses, entitled *Sphaeristerium.*

Though cardplaying was forbidden by the Statutes of the University and of some of the Colleges, except at Christmas, and then only in the College-hall, and with moderation: it was complained in 1792, that cards were played in private rooms, and even in the

Combination-room[1]. In 1760, the *Advice to a young man of Quality* is (p. 29), not to refuse to play cards occasionally, if invited. We learn[2] that *whist* was played at Caius in 1730, from Taylor's Musick Speech. In 1620, D'Ewes played *shovel-groat* and cards at St John's, and the shovel-board was in use at Corpus, Oxon., till the beginning of the present century.

D'Ewes also played *chess* sometimes, and the game is mentioned in the Tripos verses for 1780, as being played in a coffee-house at Cambridge.

In 1727, Dr Rawlinson[3] notes 'Apr. 4. A great disturbance between the scholars of the University and the townsmen of Heddington at a *bull-baiting*, at which some scholars were beaten.'

This was a fashionable sport. Uffenbach mentions, while in London, in June, 1710, that he went in the evening to a bull-baiting: and that almost every Monday, baiting went on at two places; a bear was also baited, and an ass ridden by a monkey.

In 1620 an intended bull-baiting and 'Olympic games' was put down at Commencement-tide (as D'Ewes relates), by order of the Vice-Chancellor. It was to have taken place on the 'Hogmagog hills.' There is in the Bodleian [*Gough, Cambr.* 103.] a Cambridge programma;

'Dec. 27, 1763. *Whereas*, there have been several Bull-baitings lately in the Town of *Cambridge*, to the great annoyance of the University and Inhabitants of

---

[1] *Strictures on the Discipline of the University of Cambridge,* &c. p. 22.

[2] Nichols' *Lit. Anecd.* IV. 529.

[3] *Oxoniana,* IV. 240, 241.

the said Town; and Information has been given to
the Vice-Chancellor that many Scholars of the University have been present at, and given encouragement to the same, contrary to the Rules and Statutes
of the said University: We, the Vice-Chancellor and
Heads of Colleges, whose Names are hereunto subscribed, do hereby strictly require that no Scholar of
what Rank soever, be for the future present at any
such Bull-baitings, upon pain of being proceeded
against with the utmost severity.

'*And whereas* great Confusion and Disorder in this
University have been introduced by Scholars appearing in Coffee-Houses and in the Streets without their
Academical Habits, and great Offence has been occasioned thereby: We do further strictly charge all
Scholars under the Degree of Master of Arts, that
for the future they presume not to appear anywhere
in the precincts of the University without their respective Statutable Habits, as they will answer the
contrary at their peril.

'W. ELLISTON, *Vice-C., &c. &c.*'

Uffenbach, in 1710, mentioned *Cockfighting* also as
an English sport, 'though to a stranger it seems very
childish.' On the 18th of June he bought some silver
cock-spurs as a curiosity. Gunning tells (*Reminisc.* II.
65, n.) that about 1795 matches between the gentlemen of Cambridge and Suffolk were frequently announced. This reminds us of Miss *Neville's* reading
of *Tony Lumpkin's* letter. The 'basket,' mentioned
by Gunning as the pillory of the insolvent gamester

(and noticed in Grose's *Dict. of the Vulgar Tongue*), is indicated by its shadow on the floor of the cock-pit engraved on Hogarth's Pit-ticket. There also is represented a foreigner turning up his nose at the sport. Cooper mentions (*Annals*, IV. 188) that, in 1726—7, the Vice-Chancellor (Joseph Craven) gave orders to prevent Students from frequenting the cock-fighting (qy. cock-shying) at Market-hill on Shrove Tuesday. In 1721—2, Erasmus Philipps of Pembroke, Oxon., went to the great Cock-match in Holywell.

Gambling, says Gunning (*Reminisc.* I. 22), was not the vice of Cambridge in 1785, with a very few exceptions. But, in 1721, Amherst asserted (*Terrae Filius*, No. 47) that 'of late years the spirit of *gaming* has nowhere prevailed more than at *Oxford*, and (what is more remarkable) amongst the *seniors* of the University.'

In 1782, the Act for licensing *lotteries* especially excepted Oxford and Cambridge, where it could not be applied. However, the private accounts of Dr Fras. Barnes, Master of Peterhouse (written in some spare pages of a 17th century Fellows' Exit Book), shew that he dabbled in lotteries between the years 1795 and 1803. In 1783—5, three prizes of 50 guineas each were gained by Dr Ri. Hey, of Magdalene, for his Essays on *Gambling*, *Duelling*, and *Suicide*.

In 1790, C. Moore published a treatise on Gaming, deploring the vicinity of Newmarket to Cambridge. For notices of Horse-racing at Oxford on Portmead, see the Diary of Erasmus Phillips, 'Fellow-Commoner' of Pembroke [*N. and Q.* 2nd S., X. 365, 443, *passim*] circa 1720; also, Uffenbach (*Reise*, III. 158) in 1710.

Nov. 23, 1791. Mr Rycroft was mortally wounded in a *duel* near Newmarket by another undergraduate of Pembroke. The Vice-Chancellor (Postlethwaite) published an edict against duelling, under the 42nd Statute, and T. Jones, tutor of Trinity, preached a University Sermon in December (*Exod.* xx. 13) on the subject. Nevertheless, though prevalent in 'higher circles,' duelling met with no encouragement in Cambridge[1].

In December, 1729, the Vice-Chancellor of Oxford[2] stopped a *prize-fight* which the Mayor had licensed. No doubt some of the English students took lessons in boxing from Broughton[3] and Figg in town; but, at Dublin, self-defence may be called almost a part of the regular course: for not only was Phil. Skelton[4], when sizar there in 1725, an excellent boxer and 'very dexterous in the small sword, and a complete master in the back sword. He could come up to a St George, throw an out and cut an in, save himself, and strike his antagonist:' not only did he win the hat for cudgel-play at Donybrook fair while still at college (where he rejoiced in 'throwing the stone, the sledge, long-bullets,' &c., and in dancing): but even old Baldwin, the *Provost* of *Trinity, Dublin*, and Skelton's enemy, thought it his duty to lead the van in one of the *skirmishes* between the students and the

[1] Gunning, *Reminisc.* I. 249—51.
[2] *Hearne*, Bliss, III. 45.
[3] 1747, *Tom Jones*, XI. 5, n. Paul Whitehead's *Gymnasiad*, 1744.
[4] *Lives*, edited by Chalmers, II. 267—281. Rivingtons, 1816.

butchers in Patrick's market on one of the *Sundays* in Lent.

In *Advice to a Young Man of Quality*, 1760 (p. 31), *dancing* is enumerated among the 'occasional expenses' which may reasonably be incurred in moderation.

In 1637 Evelyn says in his *Diary*, when at Oxford, 'I was admitted into the dauncing and vaulting Schole, of which late activity one Stokes the master, set forth a pretty book, which was publish'd with many witty elogies before it.' ['*The Vaulting Master, or the Art of Vaulting, reduced to a method comprised under certain Rules.* Illustrated by examples and now primarily set forth by *Will. Stokes.* Printed for *Richard Davis* in *Oxon.* 1655.'] In the next century the vaulting had given place to the dancing. '*The Art of Dancing explained by Reading and Figures;* whereby the manner of performing the Steps is made easy by a new and familiar method; being the original Work first designed in the year 1724. And now published by *Kellom Tomlinson,* Dancing-master. In Two Books. *Tulit alter Honores.*' [Printed by Bowyer 1735.]

Sir Will. Jones (who had played little as a schoolboy) in his vacation (circa 1765) daily attended Angelo's riding and fencing schools in London. [*Life,* p. 42.]

At Oxford in 1798 the University Volunteer corps or 'Armed Association' was much stronger than that of the City: there were enrolled 'about 500, commanded by Mr Coker of Bicester, formerly fellow of

New College. Such indeed was the zeal and spirit called forth in those stirring times by the threat of invasion that even clerical members did not hesitate to join the ranks...Some also of the most respectable college servants were enrolled with their masters... The dress or uniform was of a very heavy character but also very imposing: a blue coat (rather short but somewhat more than a jacket) faced with white; white duck pantaloons, with a black leathern strap or garter below the knee, and short black cloth gaiters. The head-dress was also heavy; a beaver round-headed hat surmounted by a formidable roll of bear-skin or fur of some kind[1]!'

There was one institution which kept Cambridge in amusement in the month of September. This was *Stirbridge Fair*, which before the days of goods trains and sample posts was most important, not only to the Eastern Counties, but to a great part of England. In early days it had even been used as the spot for feeling the political pulse of the nation. I have neither time, nor space, to enter at length into the delights and the curiosities of the gathering: the pomp and feasting in the *Tiled Booth*, with which the Vice-Chancellor and Proctors opened it: the topography of the booths: 'Garlic row,' 'Cook's row,' 'the Duddery;' and other rows as numerous as those of Vanity Fair:—the Book auction (where Newton bought a book of Judicial Astrology, 1662): the drinking-booths, classically inscribed *Quod petis hic est*, where geese were as plentiful and as savoury as

---

[1] G. V. Cox, *Recollections*, 33, 34.

sucking-pigs at Bartlemy. For an account even of
the admission of greenhorns to the freedom of the
fair, of their mock-solemn nicknaming by 'Lord
Tap,' the ancient functionary 'arm'd all over with
spiggots and fossets, like a porcupine with his quills,
or looking rather like a fowl wrapt up in a pound of
sausages ;'—for these, and for the rest, I must refer
the curious reader to the account in Hone's *Year
Book* (pp. 1538—1548) relating to the year 1762, to
Gunning's *Reminiscences* (1st ed. I. 162—173), and to
Mr J. E. B. Mayor's full account of the bibliography
of the Fair in his *Notes to the Life of Ambrose Bonwicke* (1870, pp. 153—165). Suffice it to say that
lectures and everything gave way for it, and everyone
gulped down his dinner to hurry to it, save a very few,
like Bonwicke, in 1710, who preferred his studies, or
like Gray of Peterhouse, in 1738, who wrote to his
friend West:

'I am coming away all so fast, and leaving behind
me, without the least remorse, all the beauties of
Sturbridge Fair. Its white bears may roar, its apes
may wring their hands, and crocodiles cry their eyes
out, all's one for that ; I shall not once visit them nor
so much as take my leave. The University has published a severe edict against schismatical congregations, and created half-a-dozen new little procterlings
to see its orders executed, being under mighty apprehensions lest [Orator] Henley and his gilt tub should
come to the fair and seduce their young ones: but
their pains are to small purpose, for lo, after all, he
is not coming.'

But there is one point which I do not wish to pass over : the dramatic entertainments there.

In 1533, there were bonfires and music at the fair ; in 1555 'the vagabonds naughtie and jolly persons...are farr. more in numbre...then hath been sene in tymes past:' in 1592 the University complains of the distraction caused to study by players at *Chesterton* during the fair. Sir John Harrington writing (about 1597) in *a Treatise on Playe* (*Nugæ antiquæ Harrington* : ed. 1804, I. 191), says 'for my part I commend not such sowere conjurers, but I thinke in stage-playes may bee much good, in well-penned comedies, and specially tragedies ; and I remember in Cambridge, howsoever the presyser sort have banisht them, the wyser sort did, and still doe mayntayn them.'

About 1536 Aristophanes' *Plutus* was acted in St John's College, with Smith and Cheeke's pronunciation.

The Elizabethan Statutes of Trinity College, Cambridge, in 1535, lay down (*cap.* 24) that the nine lecturers of the house shall, for the edification of the Scholars, act tragedies and comedies at Christmas, two and two together: except the chief lecturer, who shall act one comedy or tragedy by himself. These they shall exhibit on the 12 days of Christmas, or shortly after, at the discretion of the Master and 8 seniors, privately in the Hall, or in public, or in case of default shall pay 10*s. totiens quotiens.*

There was of course no such provision in the Statutes of ' the pure house of Emmanuel.'

In 1544 *Pammachius* was acted at Christ's College.

At Cambridge in 1557, on Sunday, May 23, 'my lord of Norfolkes players played in the hall and at the folkon.'

On the evening of *Sunday*, Aug. 6, 1564, the *Aulularia* of Plautus was performed before Queen Elizabeth in King's College *Chapel. Dido*, and *Hezekiah* by Nic. Udall, were acted in King's Chapel on this visit.

In 1580, the Vice-Chancellor declined on account of the plague to accede to the recommendation, from Lord Burleigh and others, of the Earl of Oxford's players.

In 1586—7 *Richard the Third* (by Legge) was performed in Trinity. (See C. H. Cooper, *Camb. Ant. S.* XL.)

In 1590 the tragedy *Roxana* was acted in the hall of Trinity College with such life-like passion, that a gentlewoman 'fell distracted and never after recovered her senses.' A play called *Lelia* was acted at Queens'; and the same year, or earlier, *Pedantius* (containing references to University life) was acted at Trinity.

In 1592 the University and County authorities forbade certain players to perform plays or Interludes within the district, when there was danger of infection. Nevertheless they performed at Chesterton, and braved the authorities by posting up their bills upon the College gates. The same year the town paid 10*s.* 'to the Queen's plaiers,' and twice that sum 'to Lord Strange's plaiers.' In the winter of that year, the Vice-chamberlain of Q. Elizabeth's household desired the authorities to prepare an English play against her coming. The Vice-Chancellor, John Still (author of *Gammer Gurton's Needle* acted at Christ's Coll. in 1566), begged for longer time, and that the play might be in Latin. In 1595, a comedy was acted at Queens' and two comedies and a tragedy at Trinity at Commencement, before a noble audience. For the tragedy, Thomas Nevile and the Seniors entreated Lord Burleigh to lend dresses for 'sondry personages of greatest estate' from 'the Office of the Roabes at the Tower.' In 1595 a comedy was acted at King's, when certain members of the University, being excluded, wreaked their vengeance upon the windows. In 1596—7, *Hispanus* and a Latin comedy *Sylvanus* were acted. In 1597 *Machiavellus* was acted [at St John's], and *Club Law* (in ridicule of the townsmen) was performed in Clare Hall.

In February 1600—1 some Trinity scholars pelted the Johnians who tried to come to their dramatic entertainment, and the matter was 'exhibited in the Vice-Chancellor's court.'

In 1602 (probably) was played at St John's the celebrated *Return from Parnassus, or the Scourge of Simony*, at Christmas. At the election of Bachelors 'in the College of the Holy Trinity was acted the comedy *Labyrinthus*.'

In February 1606—7 (as in 1595), there was window-breaking during a comedy in King's College: 'the like not known among scholars.'

Scyros a pastoral was attended by Prince Charles and the count Palatine at Trinity, in 1612.

On Mar. 2, 1614, *Aemilia* was acted before K. James in the hall of Trinity. Next day was acted in Trinity the comedy *Ignoramus*, by Geo. Ruggle of Clare. K. James was so much delighted with it that he returned to see it a second time. (Bp Corbet's verses on the subject are amusing.) On the 9th, *Albumazar* a comedy, and on the 10th *Melanthe* a pastoral; on the 13th the Piscatory *Sicelides* was performed at King's.

The following year was displayed an Interlude in a show; *Work for Cutlers, or a merry Dialogue between Sword, Rapier, and Dagger.* The second edition of *Exchange Ware at the Second Hand: viz. Band, Ruffe, and Cuffe, lately out, and now darned up,* &c. came out also that year.

At Christmas 1618, *Stoicus vapulans* made the spectators merry in St John's.

In 1622—3, *Loiola* a comedy was acted before K. James in the hall of Trinity, which was darkened; he ordered that the performance should be abbreviated from six or seven hours to four or five.

In March 1627, *Paria* was acted before K. Charles.

In 1632, *Senile Odium*, a comedy acted at Queens', was published.

Mr Riley, in the Appendix to the 1st Report of the Historical Manuscripts Commission, gives some extracts from the College Register or 'Sealing-book' of Queens' Coll., stating what dresses and properties were used or lent from the College treasury in the years 1636—8 (p. 72, *b*).

On Feb. 6, 1637—8, was acted in Queens' College, *Valetudinarian*, by W. Johnson, a Fellow of that Society.

In Feb. 1638, was acted, at Trinity, Cowley's *Naufragium Joculare*.

In March, 1641, was performed before Prince Charles, 'The *Guardian*,' by the same author.

About 1655, John Glendall, of Brasenose, who was *terrae filius*, a great mimic, at *Oxford* acted in several plays 'which the scholars before acted by stealth, either in the stone-house behind and southward from Pembroke Coll., or in Kettle-hall, or at Halywell-mill, or in the refectory at Gloucester-hall'.'

In 1701, the mayor and corporation of Cambridge, having given a company of actors leave to perform at *Sturbridge* fair; the University defended their own authority and swore-in 62 proctors. Bentley, then Vice-chancellor, committed the celebrated Dogget, the actor [and founder of the Thames watermen's badge], to gaol, and ordered the booth built for the theatre to be demolished. In the following spring, when Bentley had vacated his office, Sam. Cobb 'the Tripos' (of whom more anon) deplored the fate of the theatre in Trinity, for the Doctor,

' What *Collier* could never do, ruin'd the Stage.

· Sed aiunt ipsum non penitus evertisse sed tantum re-

---

[1] A. Wood, *Life*, 1660, Oct. 8.

formasse profanum illum locum in profaniorem vulgo dictum *a Tyring Room.'*

However, from a poem *The Long Vacation, a Satyr address'd to all disconsolate Traders* (London, 8vo., 1708), it appears that whatever might be the case in Trinity, Bentley's efforts had not been entirely successful at the Fair:

> ' The Actors too, must take the pleasant air,
> To *Oxford* some, to *Sturbridge* some repair,
> And quite debauch the hopeful Students there.'

Soon afterwards we catch sight of the dramatic interest at Oxford, where, in earlier years, the taste of the students had been so far respected that even the famous Mr Dryden was pleased to write several especial prologues and epilogues for their edification.

In 1712, Cibber visited their University with the company of his new theatre in Drury-lane. It had been a custom for the comedians while at Oxford to act twice a day; the first play ending every morning, before the College hours of dining, and the other never to break into the time of shutting their gates in the evening. This extraordinary labour gave all the hired actors a title to double pay, which, at the Act in King *William's* Time [says Cibber, *Life*, ed. 2, 1740, p. 383], I had myself accordingly received there.

But on this occasion, he says, the managers thought it better policy to have but one performance, though still to continue the double pay. Cibber proceeds to extol the good taste of the Oxonians who preferred

Shakespeare and Jonson, and were not carried away
with the 'false flashy Wit and forc'd Humour, which
had been the Delight of our Metropolitan Multitude.'
Addison's *Cato* had a run of three days' extreme
popularity, 'and Entrance demanded by twelve a
Clock at Noon, and before one it was not wide
enough for many who came too late for Places.'   On
leaving Oxford, the company had the thanks of the
Vice-Chancellor for their good behaviour, whereas, at
the Act in K. William's Time complaints had been
made of 'some Pranks of a different Nature:' and
having paid a remunerative visit, they contributed
£50 towards the Repair of St Mary's Church.

   In a number of the *Guardian* (95), in June, 1713,
are two or three humorous letters about the theatrical
companies arriving by wagon for the Act.

   Mr Geo. Powel (the well-known conductor of the
Puppetshow at the Opera in Covent Garden) is men-
tioned.   It is stated that 'we have sent to Town for a
Brick Wall which we forgot; the Sea is to come by
Water.'   Also in an accident on the road the High-
wayman 'broke the Mace for the Lord-Mayor of
London.   They also destroyed the World, the Sun,
and Moon, which lay loose in the waggon.   Mrs
Bartlett [the proprietor of the carrier's conveyance]
is frightened out of her Wits, for Purville (property-
man of the Theatre Royal) says, he had her Servant's
Receipt for the World, and expects she shall make it
good,' &c., &c.

   In 1737, the University of Cambridge complained
of the establishment of a Play-house by Joseph

Kettle, Esq., and an Act was passed for preventing such doings.

In April, 1747, was acted in Pembroke-hall a comedy called '*A Trip to* Cambridge, *or the Grateful Fair,*' by Kit Smart, Fellow of the Society. It is said to be the latest play acted in any College in Cambridge. The conclusion of the soliloquy of the Princess Periwinkle (who, entering '*sola* attended by *fourteen* maids of great honour,' complains that she is left alone—

> ' This bitter sweet, this honey-gall to prove,
> And all the oil and vinegar of love ;')

concludes thus :—

> ' *Pride, Love,* and *Reason* fight till they are cloy'd,
> And each by each in mutual Arms destroy'd.
> Thus when a Barber and a Collier fight,
> The Barber beats the luckless Collier...white ;
> The dusky Collier heaves his ponderous Sack,
> And big with Vengeance beats the Barber...black.
> In comes the Brick-dustman, with Grime o'erspread,
> And beats the Collier and the Barber...red ;
> Black, red, and white in various Clouds are toss'd,
> And in the Dust they raise the Combatants are lost.'

Notwithstanding the stringent enactment against theatrical entertainments here, a company of players from the theatres in London performed, in 1748, a pantomime called *Harlequin's Frolics, or Jack Spaniard caught in a Trap*, in Hussey's Great Theatrical Booth, the upper end of Garlic Row in Sturbridge Fair.

In 1772, in Stevens' theatrical booth in the Cheese fair at Sturbridge, were performed the *Clandestine Marriage*, the *West Indian*, the *Padlock, Douglas*, and the *Mayor of Garrat*.

In 1782, Mansel, writing to Mathias (author of the *Pursuits of Literature*), mentions[1] that he was at the theatre at Sturbridge. This was quite a fashionable resort about this time; and habitués of Barnwell theatre may think that Dr Farmer accompanied by other noted Shakespearian critics (Geo. Stevens and Malone) and Isaac Reed, whom Dr Barnes used to designate the *Shakespeare Gang*[2], used to sit in the critics'-row to see John Brunton (who succeeded Griffiths and Barritt), not many yards from where they now enjoy themselves. After sitting out the performance Farmer's party would adjourn to Emmanuel parlour.

In 1785 appeared in the *Gentleman's Magazine* a plea for the sanction of dramatic performances at *Oxford*.

A year or two later an opposition house was tried, by John Palmer, just at the end of Cheese fair: and another (which, being never used, was called from its projector '*Charles Day's* Folly') opposite to Parker's Piece.

Soon afterwards, Charles Humfrey built a theatre by the side of the *Sun* in Barnwell. His successor, Wilkins, erected the present theatre, which was opened in 1815 under the acting management of Mr Smith.

The *Cambridge University Calendar* for 1802 states that, on Sept. 18, '*Stirbitch* Fair' is 'proclaimed. The *Theatre* opens, and Plays are exhibited for about *eighteen* successive nights.'

[1] *N. and Q.* 2nd S. x. 41.
[2] Gunning's *Reminisc.* I. 173. 1854.

In 1806, the Old Theatre at Sturbridge Fair was pulled down, in consequence of the prevalence of an unfounded idea that it was unsafe.

In 1830, the 'Shakspeare Club' was founded; and three years later some seceding members formed the *Garrick Club*, who published an Album in 1836.

In Harrington's 'Supplie, or Addicion to Bishop Godwin's Catalogue of Bishops to the year 1608, entitled by Dr Chetwind, "a brief View of the State of the Church of England,"' he speaks of Dr Still, who examined him strictly, and after that answered him kindly, 'that the grace he graunted me was not of grace but of merit,' when he sued for his grace to be bachelor. (Harrington (*Nugae Antiquae Harringtonianae*, 1804, II. 158) says of Still: 'I must say this much of him; his breeding was from his childhood in good litterature, and partly in musique, which was counted in those dayes a preparation to divinitie, neither could any be admitted to *primam tonsuram*, except he could first *bene le, bene con, bene can,* (as they call it,) which is to reade well, to conster well, and to sing well; in which last he hath good judgement, and I have heard good music of voyces in his house.'

At Pembroke this degenerated into *bene nati, bene vestiti, moderate docti.*

Singing, at least to the degree which was indispensable for Clerks, was made a *sine qua non* in old times for the admission of scholars. This was the case at Winchester and New College (where William Wykeham gave lodgings for the Choristers or *Quiristers* on the same footing as the other students. In

later days one of their offices was to wait in hall, as
at King's College). This was the case also with some
of the 17th century foundations at Peterhouse, where
certain scholars were bound to attend choir-practice
once or twice a week. It is said of John Barwick,
about 1630, that to the study of Musick, 'which adds
so much Life and Ornament to Divine Worship, he
was always, by his Example as well as his Advice,
endeavouring to persuade such of his Fellow-Collegians, of the younger sort, as their Voices, their Age,
and their Genius rendered capable thereof.' In 1654
A. Wood, having 'obtain'd proficiency in musick, he
and his companions [Will. Bull, who, like himself,
played on the violins, Edm. Gregorie, B.A., and gent.
com. of Mert. coll., who play'd on the bass viol, Joh.
Nap, of Trinity, on the citerne, and George Mason of
the said coll. on another wyer instrument, but could
do nothing] were not without silly frolicks, not now
to be maintained.' By the next year he 'had genuine
skill in musick, and frequented the weekly meetings
of musitians in the house of Will. Ellis, late organist
of S. John's coll., situat and being in a house, opposite to that place whereon the theater was built.'
Wood mentions several of the parties who used to
play on the lute, theorbo lute, organ, virginal, coun-
ter-tenor viol, bass viol, lyra-viol, division-viol, treble-
viol, and treble-violin (which, till a little before the
Restoration, were less fashionable than viols), and
the harpsicon. Wood learnt the violin from Charles
Griffith, Jo. Parker, and Will. James (a dancing-master), but the instrument was then thought too vulgar

to be well taught in Oxford. In 1657, he thought Davy Mell the sweetest violinist (a London clock-maker), but 'Tho. Baltsar, an outlander,' the more nimble performer. In 1658, his opinion of this 'Baltzar, a Lubecker borne,' was enhanced, and he was himself obliged to play to draw out the lion. The musical meetings were held weekly at the house of Will. Ellis, when, by the demolition of cathedrals and organs in the Troubles, the publick instruments were destroyed.

In 1699, Humphrey Wanley, of University College, visiting Cambridge, writes to Dr Charlett: 'At night we were regaled with a very good concert of music; where I was much taken with some Italian songs, which Mr Pate brought from Rome; and a gentleman here sang excellently well.'

Uffenbach, visiting Cambridge in the summer vacation of 1710, tells how when they had spent an hour at the *Greek's* Coffee-house, 'Dr *Ferrari* came for us, and took us to the *Music club*, in *Christ's college*. This music meeting is held generally every week. There are no professional musicians there, but simply bachelors, masters and doctors of music, who perform. It is surprising, as they make such ado about music, and even create professors and doctors of music, still this nation achieves scarcely anything in it. I think however that their *ingenia* are not the least *musica*, as those of all frivolous men (*wie aller flüchtigen Menschen*); hence too all their compositions are very harsh, and cannot equal either the pretty manner of the *French*, or the tender manner of the

Italians. And so too this music, both vocal and instrumental, was very poor. It lasted till 11 *p.m.*, there was besides smoking and drinking of wine, though we did not do much of either. At 11 the reckoning was called for, and each person paid two shillings[1].'

We have already seen Uffenbach's praise of English organ-playing, and his distaste of their bell-ringing.

At Oxford, in August, 1721, Erasmus Philipps, 'Fellow-Commoner' of Pembroke[2], began to learn on the Violin of Mr Wheeler, to whom he paid 10*s.* entrance.

It appears from Nichols (*Lit. Anecd.* IV. 600 *n.*) that Battle had a spinet in his rooms at King's when an undergraduate, about 1723. Kirkman's harpsichords (says Mr G. V. Cox[3]) had not quite gone out at Oxford in 1805.

Poor Hearne, who preferred the Englishman's bell-ringing to the German's symphony, complains that in July, 1733, at the Oxford Act, 'one *Handel* a foreigner' was allowed the use of the Theater by the Vice-Chancellor, 'who is much blamed for it, however he is to be commended for reviving our Acts, which ought to be annual.' The performance begins a little after 5 o'clock in the evening, tickets 5*s.* 'This is an innovation. The players might as well be permitted to come and act.' Two days later (July 7):

---

[1] *Reise*, III. 12, translated by Mr Mayor.
[2] *N. and Q.* 2nd S. x. 443.
[3] *Recoll.* p. 53.

'half an hour after 5 o'clock...was another performance at 5*s.* a ticket, in the Theater, by Mr Handel
for his own benefit, continuing till about 8 o'clock.
N.B. His book (not worth 1*d.*) he sells for 1*s.*' He
performed again on Act Monday, Tuesday, and
Wednesday, July 11—13 ; Mr Walter Powel, the
Superior beadle of Divinity singing with them *all
alone.*

Dr Bliss asks (*Reliqu. Hearn.* III. 99), 'What would
have been the amount of Hearne's virtuous indignation, had he known that in May, 1856, Madame
Goldschmidt (Jenny Lind) sang at a concert in the
Sheldonian Theatre, the tickets being charged one
guinea, 15 shillings, and half-a-guinea each, according
to the situations filled by the audience, who flocked
to the music in immense multitudes ?'

The Music Room was erected in Oxford in 1742.
There is a Latin poem entitled *Odeum Oxoniense* in
the *Student, or Oxf. and Camb. Monthly Miscellany*
(II. 197, 1751), in which Powel and Handel are mentioned.   In the same volume (p. 372) it is described
as 'the *Temple* of *Harmony*, vulgarly called the *Music
Room.*'   There is, I believe, a collection of the pro-
grammes in the Bodleian Library.

About the middle of the century, music had taken
some root in the Universities.   The author of the
Academic (p. 22), in 1750, says, 'The money which by
Part of the University was formerly spent in midnight Drinkings to the ruin of their Health and Constitution is now employed in securing themselves
against those Complaints to which by a sedentary

and studious Course of Life they are particularly
exposed. And the Expences of the Students which
after the Example of their Leaders, were laid out to
much the same Purpose, are now devoted to a different Channel. A Taste for Musick, modern Languages, and other the polite Entertainments of the
Gentleman have succeeded to Clubs and *Bacchanalian Routs.'*

In 1750, 'Cantab.' wrote from Trin. Coll. to the
Student (I. 92[1]), to complain of the time wasted in
Fiddling, and of the foppery of those who were
infected by the '*scraping* Cacoethes.'

'Granticola,' dating his letter 'C. C. C. Cambridge,
April 5, 1750,' rejoins (I. 131), 'I see no reason
why our *schools* may not be frequented as well
as our *musick-meetings*, and NEWTON and LOCKE
still have their followers as well as HANDEL and
CORELLI.

'In an University, how much more agreeably is an
evening laid out by a select company of friends com-
posing a concert, than in carousing over a bottle, and
joining, to say no worse, in an unprofitable conversation? As to the concerts we frequently have in our
halls, do they not in some measure contribute, by
bringing us into company, to the wearing off that
rust and moroseness which are too often contracted
by a long continuance in college? And though these
meetings are frequented by some, so entirely on account of the company and conversation, that it has
been declared that the concert would have been

[1] See also II. 51, 105, 200, 224.

excellent, if there had been no MUSICK in it, yet in general we shall find it otherwise. If these were abolish'd, what a mortification would many of our smart *fellow-commoners* undergo, to be deprived of the pleasure of presenting tickets to the ladies, and ushering them into the hall! Add to this, that the banishment of MUSICK from our rooms, must necessarily be attended with the expulsion of the *harpsichord*, no inconsiderable part of our furniture. Not to mention the number of ingenious artists, that must by this means be reduc'd to a scanty subsistence, and that TIREMAN and RANDAL must then only rely on the organs of *Trinity* and *King's College* chapels.

'As to FIDDLING in particular, for my part, I see no absurdity in attracting the eyes of the fair by displaying a white hand, a ring, a ruffle, or a sleeve to advantage. Nor could any one, I imagine, blame the performer, nor could he himself be displeas'd with his art, if he was so successful as to *fiddle* himself into a good fortune.'

At Commemoration, in 1769, the Masque of *Acis and Galatea* was performed in the presence of an 'enormous brilliant audience[1];' as was the Oratorio of *Athaliah* on the evening of the 15th of June.

The comic concert is, to our shame be it spoken, an invention of our own time. Yet it is, perhaps, the necessary safety-valve provided for the relief of the exuberant spirits and lungs of undergraduates.)

[1] *Oxford in the Last Century*, p. 22, reprinted from the *Oxford Chronicle*, 1859.

It is at least rather more regular than the demonstrations of the Roarers in earlier days. The hubbub in Theatre, and even in Senate-house, is a symptom of the existence of a considerable class who are capable of little but inexplicable dumb-show and noise. In the earlier stage of the universities this was done systematically. In the exercise for every bachelor's degree at Cambridge, there was provision made in the person of the *Tripos* for jest, though this probably was not much abused in early times: while at the Act or summer Encaenia, there was a licenced jester, the *Varier* or *Praevaricator* at Cambridge, and at Oxford the *Terrae Filius*. But there were other customary buffooneries as well. By the Elizabethan Statutes of Cambridge, 1559 (*cap.* L. § 36), it was provided that 'no Master of the Games at Christmas shall be appointed under any name, *without the consent of the chancellor and the heads of the colleges.*'

One old custom at both universities was that of *salting*. This was a mock ceremony of initiating freshmen. It had been used, says Anthony Wood, time out of mind, but fell into disuse, and was forgotten at Oxford between 1647 and the Restoration. He describes his own initiation in the year mentioned, at Merton.

He had been entered upon the books on St Luke's day (Oct. 18): and from Allhallow e'en (Nov. 1) till Christmas there were charcoal fires in the hall a little after 5 p.m. The senior undergraduates would make the freshmen sit on a form, and one by one 'speake some pretty apothegme, or make a jest or bull, or speake some eloquent nonsense to make the company laugh.' If any were unsuccessful, 'some of the forward or pragmatical seniors would tuck him:' i.e., would wound his lower lip with his nail.

About Candlemas-day (Feb. 2, Feast of the Purification) all freshmen were instructed to prepare their speeches to be declaimed before the undergraduates and servants in hall on Shrove Tuesday. The Fellows got over their supper early and left the field clear, with an admonition 'that all things should be carried in good order.' The cook prepared the lesser brass pot full of 'cawdel' at the freshmen's expense, and each freshman in order had to 'pluck off his gowne and band, and, if possibly, to make himself look like a scoundrell.' Then a travestie of the academic exercises was performed. The victim had to stand on a form on the high-table, and to speak his speech. After which he was rewarded, according as he had acquitted himself well, indifferently, or ill, by having a draught administered to him of 'cawdel,' cawdel and salt, or salt and beer alone (whence, possibly, the expression of *paying for one's salt*), 'with *tucks* to boot.' Afterwards the senior cook administered an oath over an old shoe. The only fragment of the formula remaining is

Item tu jurabis, quod *penniless bench* non visitabis.

(This was a stone seat in the market, see the University regulation in 1584, *Oxoniana*, IV. 176, *N. & Q.* 1st S. I. 307, Warton's 'Panegyric on Oxford Ale,' *Companion to the Guide*.)

Wood gives his own speech on the occasion. It is not very interesting, and full of forced absurdity.

At the *salting* at Pembroke coll. in August, 1620, one of the *fathers* [senior sophs], and two or three of the *sons*, did 'excellently well.' 'A great deal of beer, as at all such meetings, was drunk.'

There is an old Statute prohibiting the *caeremonia saliendi recentes scholasticos.* At St John's they had *exceedings* in Hall on the occasion, and there was a charge for *salting* in the Tutor's bill, 3s. 4d. (*Diary of Symond's D'Ewes*, p. 15, *Parker*.) When the E. of Essex was at Trinity coll., Camb.[1], he was charged, in 1577, 'at the *saltinge* accordinge to the custome, vijs.' Something of the kind seems to have lingered as the *Fresh Treat*, for which freshmen paid *Fresh Fees* at St John's, Oxon., in 1714, see *Amherst, Terrae Filius*, Nos. 11, 41. Among Milton's juvenile later prose Works [*P. Works*, 852 foll.] is printed a Speech *in Feriis Aestivis Collegii* [Christi, apud Cantab.] *sed concurrente, ut solet, tota fere Academiae Juventute* [anno 1628, aetatis 19, *I. Miltoni* PATRIS (quem vocant) vice fungentis].

Professor Masson has quoted and translated the more interesting passages of this speech. The attempts at wit are perhaps superior to the *Sonnets on Master Hobson*, but now and then there is a jest which had better never have been uttered. And as a whole, we should now consider it tedious, especially as it is all in latin, with the exception of

[1] Cooper's *Annals*, II. 354.

the english verses, 'At a Vacation 'Exercise: the rest was prose' in english, which prose is lost.

But the most important personages who contributed towards the waggery of the Universities, were the *Tripos,* the *Prevaricator* (or *Varier*) and the *Terrae Filius.* Their office, as will appear, was at one period almost essential to the proceedings towards some of the academical Degrees. They may therefore have had some prototype in the ancient continental Universities. The positions of the *Tripos* and the *Praevaricator* or *Varier* at Cambridge, and of the *Terrae Filius* at Oxford, are not very clearly defined.

Perhaps the simplest way to impart what I know on the subject, is to begin by giving an account of the proceedings for degrees at Cambridge, from the Books of two Esquire Bedels. The former is Mr Stokys' book. 'He was (says Fuller) a zealous Papist, even unto persecution of others, which I note, not to disgrace his memory, but defend myself, for placing him before the Reformation, though he lived many years in the reign of Queen Elizabeth.' He was born at Eton, and formerly Fellow of King's College, University Registrary, 1558—1591, in which capacity he saved the University documents from the fate which too many suffered at the Reformation.

'*The order of the Questionists*[1]. In primis, the Questionists shall gyve the Bedels warnynge upon

[1] See Dean Peacock's *Observations on the Statutes*, Parker and Deightons, 1841. Appendix A. throughout.

the Le [i. q. *legibilis*] Daye, that they may proclayme before thordynarie Readers [the 4 Barnaby
Lecturers on Terence, Logic, Philosophy, and Mathematics, chosen on the 11th of June, the Feast of S.
Barnabas. *Ordinary* Lectures included comments
of the reader, *Cursory* Lectures consisted in simply
reading the text of the author with the common
glosses,] in the common Schooles thentrynge of their
Questions at the accustomed Hower, which is at
ix of the Clocke [this was the entering of *Priorums*,
or answering questions (*respondendum quaestioni*)
out of Aristotle's *prior* Analytics] at the which tyme
the Bedells, or one of them shall go to the Colledge, Howse, Hall or Hostell, where the sayed
Questionists be, and at their entryng into the sayed
Howse, &c. shall call and gyve Warninge in the
middest of the Courte, with thees words, *Alons*,
Alons, goe Mrs goe, goe. [It has been suggested
that the custom of the Bedel going with his wand
or staff to summon the candidates gave the name
Bachilour or *bacillarius*. The use of french formu-
las was perhaps derived from the University of Paris.
The french language, which was that of the Court,
was permitted equally with latin, to be used by
the scholars of the second set of foundations, at
Clare hall, King's hall, and at Oriel, Oxon.; but not
at Peterhouse, or at Merton, Oxon.], and then to
toll, or cause to be tolled the Bell of the Howse
to gather the Mrs. Bachilers, Schoolers and Questionists together, and all the companye in their
Habitts and Hoodds being assembled, the Bedells

shall goe before the Junior Questioniste, and so all
the Rest in their order shall folowe bareheadded,
and then the Father, [the Fellow of the foundation
who goes as patron of the candidates of his College who are called his *Sons*. In later times his
office has been swallowed in that of the *Praelector*],
and after all the Graduats and companye of the
sayed Howse unto the common Schooles in dew
Order; and when they do enter into the Schooles,
one of the Bedells shall saye, *noter mater, bona
nova, bona nova*, and then the Father being placed
in the Responsalls Seate, and his Chyldren standyng
over agaynst hym in order, and theldest standyng
in the hier Hand, and the rest in their Order ac-
cordyngly, the Bedyll shall proclayme if he have
any thynge to be proclaymed, and furder saye,
*Reverende Pater, licebit tibi incipere, sedere et coope-
riri si placet.* That done the Father shall enter
hys commendacions of hys chyldren, [they kneeling,
and the Bedells plucking their hoods over their faces],
and propounding of his Questions unto them, which
the eldest shall first aunswer, and the Rest orderlye;
and when the Father hathe added his conclusion
unto the Questions, the Bedyll shall brynge them
Home in the same order as they went : and if the
Father shall uppon his Chyldrens Aunswer replie and
make an Argument, then the Bedel shall knocke
hym out, [knock loudly at the door, so as to drown
his argument and bring it to a close], and at the
uttermost schoole Dore, the Questionists shall turne

them to the Father and the Company, and gyve thanks for their commyng with them.'

On Ash-Wednesday the bedell was to bring the Determiners, King's College being fetched last, to await the Vice-chancellor at 8 a.m. in St Mary's Church. If there were no sermon, there was to be Common Prayer. Then in the N. Chapel they swore '*Jurabitis quod Determinetis ad placitum Procuratorum*, and then the Proctours appoynt them their Senioritie:' [this constituted the *first Tripos List* as it was *afterwards* called, containing the names of the *Wranglers* and *Senior Optimes* or *Baccalaurei quibus sua reservatur Senioritas Comitiis Prioribus:* who, in early times were arranged according to the fancy of the proctors, though no doubt they paid some attention to merit. As lately as 1790, the Vice-chancellor and proctors had the right of placing one honorary *Senior Optime* apiece between the 1st and 2nd *wrangler*. This may puzzle us when we find Bentley, for instance, 6th on the first tripos, though he is rightly called 3rd wrangler. 'The second Tripos List, or of junior optimes (*quibus sua reservatur senioritas Comitiis Posterioribus*), which was formed on the second Tripos-day, had been, most probably, composed of those questionists, whose superiority was not already recognized, who had most distinguished themselves in the *quadragesimal* exercises[1].' The rest, οἱ πολλοί, had no seniority reserved till the general Bachelors' Commencement]. They then go to the

---

[1] Peacock, *On the Statutes*, Appendix A. p. ix. *n.* 2.

Philosophy Schools 'where Mr Vichauncellor, the Doctours, and other worshipfull Straungers shal be placed in the Stage provided for them. The Father shall be placed in the Responsall Seate, his eldest sone standyng at the Stalles ende upon hys right hande, Mr Proctour shall sytt under the hie Chaire of the Reader [the *lector ordinarius* in philosophy. The arrangement of the Schools must have been much as we find it now remaining from the days when Acts and Opponencies were commonly held there]. The Magistri non Regentes [every M.A. under one year's standing was expected to examine in the schools until the year 1785 : the M.A.'s first year from creation was his year *necessariae regentiae :* many of the friars and monks were chased out of the university in 1537, as well as other D.D. who swore to keep a longer term of regency, and it was found necessary to add to the *necessary* regency, first *one*, and then *two* years extra, which were not absolutely binding] in the upper stalles upon the Father's side ; and the Mr Regent Disputers shall sit in the first Stall. And when every man is placed, the Senior Proctor shall, with some oration, shortly move the Father to begyn, who, after his exhortation unto his Children, shall call fourthe his eldest sone, and animate hym to dispute with AN OULD BACHILOUR, which shall sit upon a A STOOLE before Mr Proctours, unto whome the sone shall propound 2 Questions, and in bothe them shall the sone dispute, askyng leave of Mr Proctour untyll the Proctour shall wyll hym to gyve Place unto hys Father. Then shall the Bedels, standyng before the Father, make

14—2

curtesye, and say in Frenche, *Noter Determiners, Je vous remercie de le Argent que vous avez donner a moy et a meis companiouns: pourquoy je prie a Dieu que il vous veuilles donner tres bonne vie, et en la Fin la Joye de Paradise.* And then make curteseye unto Mr Proctours and then to the Father agayne, sayinge, *Permissum est Dominationi tue incipere, sedere, co-operiri quando velis.* Then the Father askyng Licens of Mr Proctours shall dispute with the OLD BACHI-LOUR, and after hym two Regents; and when the sayed twoe Regents have ended at thappoyntmente of Mr Proctours, then shall the Father of thacte, puttynge of his bonet, propounde two other new Questions and discourse upon them in such manner as he wyll defende the same, agaynst whom two other Regents shall dispute so longe as shalbe thought good unto Mr Proctours, which with some convenient oration shall conclude this dayes dysputation, saying, *Nos continuamus hanc Disputacionem in Horam primam Diei Jovis post quartam Dominicam hujus Quadragesi-me.* And immediately a Sophister provided by the Proctour shall knele before the Responsall sett, and have for hys labour 4*d.* and 1 Lib. of Figgs. Then the Bedell havyng a Rolle of all the Questionists accordyng to their Senioritie, shall call them, and set them thorough the Responsall Seat, begynnyng with the Senior, at his entring the Proctour shall saye, *Incipiatis,* and pausyng a whyle, shall saye, *Ad opposi-tum,* then *Redeatis,* and last *Exeatis:* and with that the Questioniste senior shall goe fourthe of the Stall.' And so on with the rest. The next day four weeks virtually the same ceremony was performed. 'And when all have passed thorough the Stalle, then shall the senior Procurator saye, *In Dei nomine Amen. Authoritate qua fungimur, decernimus, creamus et pronunciamus omnes hujus anni Determinatores finaliter determinasse et actualiter esse in Artibus Bachalaureos.*' After this the 'Vichauncellour' and the rest had supper at the charge of the Determiners 'at what Howse the Proctours shall apoynte.' They were to provide the like on the Thursday before 'Shrove Sondaye:' also to give gloves to 'the Father, Mr Proctours, and the BACHILER AWNSWERYNGE,' and the proctors were to give to each bedel a pair for his pains. Another important point is, that 'All the Determiners dothe sytte in the New Chappel [attached to the divinity schools, afterwards part of the library; here each determiner was to say the *de profundis*, &c.] within the schools, from one of the Clocke untyll fyve upon the Mondaye, Tuesdaye, Wensdaye, and Thursdaye in the weeke before Shrove Sondaye abyding there examynation of so many masters [?Regents] as wyll repayre for that cause thether; and from three to four all they have a Potation of Figgs, Reasons, and Almons, Bonnes, and Beer, at the charge of the sayed Determiners, whereat all the Bedells may be present daylye: and upon the Thursdaye they be only examined in Songe and wrightynge. And twoe Magister Regents [afterward called *Moderators*] allowed and appoynted by the whole Universitie upon the Fryday folowyng, maketh by the senior of them an oration before the University, standyng by the chaire of the Vichauncelor, declaryng what Towardness they have found in the Tyme of their examination: and if they sayed Examiners do disalowe eny, he shall not procede.'

The bedels attend in their 'Hoods and Quoiffys... to brynge every Doctour or Mr of a Howse thorowghe the Prese with their Staffs turned.'

Beside this there was another ceremony called *Standing in Quadragesima*, which continued till rather more than a generation ago. All the Determiners had to stand in the schools every day from Ash-Wednesday till the last Act attended by one Sophister or undergraduate in the stage below himself; the two together being prepared (at the word of the Bedel *Incipiatis*) to defend 'three Questions of Dialecte and Philosophye wrytten fayer on a paper, and leyed before him in the Stall, unto the which he shalbe apoynted unto by Mr Proctours—' against all Scholars and Bachelors ; between the hours of 9 and 11 a.m. on *Lee* days (i.e. *dies legibiles*, days when lectures might be read), or between 1 and 5 p.m. on *Disses* (i.e. *dies disputabilés*, whereon the solemn disputations of the Masters of Arts, being preceded by *Dysses* or Dissertations, might be held. Beside these and their contraries,—*non le*, and *non dis*,—there were at the univ. of Paris *Le fe* or *dies legibiles festinanter*, when lectures were read *cursorie*, without elaborate comments). 'And one of the Bedels must daylye, at the ordenarye Lectures and at the Disputation, signifye thorder of their standynge, with thees words, or the licke, upon the Lee Dayes: *Noter Determiners,*

devaunt Diner sub spe, sub spe longa, vel sine spe.
And upon the Dis Dayes ; *Noter* &c. *Apres diner sub
spe* &c. [indicating, it may be, the various chances of
distinction in the morning disputation of the Le
days, and the afternoon arguments of the Disses.]
Upon the Daye of the last Acte the Bedell dothe
proclayme with thees wordes *Noter Determiners, apres
diner sine spe cum Patre.'* On the Saturdays each
Determiner was to sing Common Prayer and offer
1ᵈ. in St Mary's : 'and the Bedels for gyving their
attendance have every daye an Hundred Oysters and
Wyne to the same. *Item.* Every of the Proctours
appoyntethe one Questioniste to be Stewarde, and to
serve the Bevers, which for their labour are discharged
of their contribution unto the said Bevers and Suppers.' [The term *Bever* is I believe still applied in
some districts (Suffolk, for instance) to the labourer's
afternoon refreshment, 'his cold thin drink out of his
leathern bottle.' 'Ita postmeridianos vespertinosque
haustus in Collegiis academicorum et jurisperitorum
vocant Angli.' *Junii Etymologicon.*

'He is not one of those same ordinary eaters who
will devour three breakfasts and as many dinners
without any prejudice to their *bevers,* drinkings, or
suppers,' Beaum. and Fl. *Woman-Hater,* I. 2. *Bevere,
bibere, boire, beverage.* At Winchester school it was
thus described by Chr. Johnson about 1550 (afterwards 'Informator') in his school-boy poem, *De
Collegio:*

Tempore at aestivo data comessatio nobis,
Quando horae trinae pars dimidiata relapsa est.

The word was still in use when I was at school at Winton, for an intermission in schooltime on ' whole-school-days' from 3.30 to 4 p.m., when beer was served out at the (buttery) 'hatch.']

I have quoted thus at length from the account of the Bachelors' Commencement, because many of the points which do not immediately concern the office of the *Tripos* will be necessary for us to refer to, when we come to the next part of this compilation.

Before passing to the description of the proceedings given by another Bedell after the Restoration, I will just quote an account nearly contemporary with that given above.

At Q. Mary's visitation in 1556-7, 'On Asshewendesday, rayne and snow together. *It.* Mr Bronsted and I had in all the Bachelors before viii (at St Maryes), and shortly after the Vicechancellor began his sermon in S. Maryes, thuniversite Bell [the *School Bell*], and also St Maryes Bell rynginge to the same, the Mayre and Aldermen being presente. *It.* the acte began before x and continued tyll halfe howre after iii no senioryte given, no byll made nor none called, but only ii of the seniors the Vic. and D. Sedgewycke were present from the begininge to the latter ende, Mr Turner *Father*, Syr Whytgyfte *the bachelor*, [i.e. the famous master of Trinity and abp., then a B.A. (Syr), took the part of the BACHILOUR OF THE STOOLE], Syr Brydges the *eldest son*, Mrs Otway and Malyn replyed upon the bachelors and onlye Mr Hutton upon the Father[1].'

---

[1] *Peacock*, App. A. x. n. 2.

At Oxford, as at other European Universities at the time, the ceremonies of 'standing in quadragesima[1]' were much the same as here, 'with the exception of the powers given to the *collectors*, themselves likewise determiners appointed by the proctors, who distributed the other determiners into the different schools, and also assigned the order of their disputations[2].'

Dean Peacock published, in addition to the extracts from Bedel and Registrar *Stokys'* book, selections from Beadle *Buck's* book A.D. 1665. I propose now to cite some passages from this post-restorational document, contrasting them with the account already given from the pre-reformational record a century older.

'On Monday, Tuesday or Wednesday, [not Thursday, as before] either in the next or the next week save one after the said 12 day of Jan., the Questionists, at the appointment of the V. C. and Proctors, do sit in the Regent House, there to be examined by the Proctors, Posers and other Regents.' The senior makes a speech, as of old, setting forth their proficiency, and their graces are passed. The oaths are taken and the V. C. admits them 'in Dei nomine' &c. *ad respondendum Quaestioni.* Each having done 'his obeisance to M[r] V. C.' kneels at the upper table and 'giveth God thanks in his Private Prayers &c.' Before Ash-Wednesday, each has to *enter his Priorums:* i.e. he has to answer

[1] *Ibid.* App. A. XIV. *n.* 1.
[2] *Life of A. Wood.* 1655, April 25. 1679, Feb. 27.

a question out of *Aristotle's Priorums* (Prior Analytics) :—the Beadle having previously said 'with a loud voice *Bona Nova Mater Academia, bona nova*:' and having 'set up the *Father*,' and placed his *sons* before him, with the words *Honorande Pater, filiorum nomine, Gratias tibi agimus, liceat tibi sedere, cooperiri, et filios tuos affari, prout tibi visum fuerit.* 'It hath happened some time that 4 or 5 Colleges have kept their *Priorums* in the same morning: then all the 3 Bedles have employment enough to attend so many *Priorums*, and the Master of Arts *Disses*.' Between 7 and 8 A.M. on Ash Wednesday they are brought to St Mary's to a *Clerum*, by one intending to commence in divinity, or else to Litany.

Then to the School Yard; and, if there be no business, to the Consistory to fit themselves with gloves.

'Then one of the Bedles carrieth the Proctors, Father, Disputants TRIPOS and the 2 BROTHERS unto their several Seats...Last of all the Door is opened for the Bachelors, Sophisters and the rest of the Scholars to come in. After a little Pause the senior Proctor beginneth his Speech, and towards the end thereof, speaketh to the Father, to make an Exhortation to his Sons; which, after the Father hath done, the senior Proctor calleth up the TRIPOS and exhorteth him to be witty, but modest withall. Then the TRIPOS beginneth his speech or Position, made for the Illustration and Confirmation of his 1st Question. He may, if he will, speak something of his 2nd Question, but if he doth not, then the Senior Proctor commendeth the SENIOR BROTHER to reply upon the TRIPOS; and after him the JUNIOR BROTHER.' Meanwhile the Bedels 'are to deliver the TRIPOS'S VERSES to the V. C., Noblemen, D^n, &c. whilst the 2 BROTHERS are disputing upon him.' 'Then the senior Proctor desireth the Father to urge his Sons argument. The Father Propounding 2 or 3 Syllogisms in either Quaestion, Mr Proctor dismisseth him, and calleth up the first Opponent, being M^r of Arts. Now the Father may go out of the Schools, if he please, with a Bedle before him, and come in again when the 2nd opponent is disputing upon the 2nd Question. Then presently after the Father is in his seat, Mr Proctor doth end the TRIPOS his Act, with a word or two in his commendation, if he deserves it. Then Mr Proctor speaketh unto the Father to begin his Position towards an ensuing Act in Philosophy, and whilst he is reading it, the Bedles do deliver his VERSES to Mr V. C., the Noblemen, D^n, Proctors, Taxers, antient Bachelors in Divinity, and other grave men &c.'

The candidates had also to sit in the Schools from 1 to 5 P.M. (except on Saturdays and Sundays), every day for a month, to defend Theses against all comers: a practice which, with some modification, survived till within the last fifty years.

The speeches of the *Tripos* and his two *Brothers*—though originally intended to exhibit genius, rather than frivolity, and serving (it may be) in the first instance merely to raise the old standard ingenious fallacies and logical quibbles, which admitted of a certain degree of humour—tended, especially after the Restoration, to become boisterous and even scurrilous.

One *Tripos-speech* which was printed (and against which, as far as I know, no exception was taken by the authorities) has been preserved in the Bodleian Library. [*Pamph.* 318, also *Gough's Oxford Additions.*]

It is contained in a small publication called ' *News from both Universities*, containing

I. Mr *Cobb*s *Tripos* Speech at *Cambridge*, with a Complete Key inserted.

II. *The Brawny Priest: or the Captivity of the Nose.* A Poem. *London :* Printed for J. Roberts, near the *Oxford Arms* in *Warwick-Lane*, 1714.'

The Oxford contribution on this occasion is quite unworthy of type. It is not improbable that the *News* was an occasional publication uttered in defiance of authority, like the *Oxford Packet* of the same date, and issued by the same printer.

It appears that the senior members of the University were present in the Schools 'in robes demurely grave' (p. 20): and crowds of '*Sophs* in the Pit' (p. 19). The *Tripos* (Sam. Cobb of Trinity) entered, dressed probably in fantastic costume (p. 18), attended by his *two Brothers* carrying Catalogues for the Auction of Doctors.

Title : *Tripos Cantabrigiensis*, 19 *Feb.* 170$\frac{1}{2}$ [*S. Cobb*, B.A. 1698., M.A. 1702].

He begins : '*Ecce iterum* Crispinus—*Ego hîc regno*

Caesar; *sed periclitatur vita mea. Vos igitur* Sophistae! circumcingite Satellites...

> 'Twas well when our Forefathers did agree
> That the grave Doctors should sit there and see
> Their Follies banter'd by a Knave like me,
> And wisely manag'd to begin their *Lent*
> With one who swears he'll make you all repent.

[Then follows in English doggerel, alternating with
Latin prose and scraps of verse, a ludicrous satire on
several characters in the University. Foibles, rather
than grave faults, are censured.] Dr R[ichardso]n of
Peterhouse, the V.-C., is complimented, at the expense of his predecessor, *Bentley* (Master of Cobb's
college), as '*non similis antecessori suo neque ingenio
neque modestia neque aedibus.*'

Of the proctors *Jack Cooper* and *Sam. Awbery*,
they are *Caesar* and *Bibulus*, '*unum enim faciunt Pro-
curatorem.*'

Then follow the oracular dicta of the Tripos.

When are we to have decent *Taxors?* '*Cum non
sint* Regales.' [J. Haslop, King's, was Taxor.] It is
said, in 'Hints respecting some of the Univ. Officers,
by Robert Plumptre, D.D., Master of Queens', 1782,
p. 11, 'The Taxers office, it is to be feared, wants *attention* and *execution* rather than *reward.* It is an
office, however, in itself of much importance to the
Univ., and to the place in general.' The office was
originally appointed by the Univ. to prevent the original unattached students from being charged too
highly for their hostels or lodgings in the town. They
also assisted the proctors in making the assize of

bread and beer, and in other matters relating to the market. Their office was suspended between the year 1540 and 1546, while the Univ. was passing through its crisis of penury. The Commissioners, in 1852, recommended the abolition of the office; and this was carried out in accordance with the Composition of the Rt. Hon. Sir John Patteson, Knt., in 1856]. When may we expect to see Learning, Philosophy, Wit, and Theology combined? When 'the dumb doctor' is in the pulpit. ['He was a Fellow that had never preach'd'.] When may we expect the dissolution of the University? '*Cum tota Academia* gubernatur *sub* Lepore.' [Fras. *Hare* of King's, to whom, in 1713, Bentley dedicated his *Remarks on Freethinking*, till he offended him. Dean of S. Paul's 1725, bp. of S. Asaph, 1726]. Then visiting the buildings of his own Royal College, which were now, by *Bentley's* exertions, '*dignae futuro duce* Glocestrensi;' Cobb cannot help asking if the unity and beauty of the Court would not be enhanced, supposing his own windows ('which were the vilest in the whole College, scarce an whole Quarry in them') were sashed (*Shashandae*) as finely as the Master's Lodgings.

After deploring the fate of the Theatre in Trinity; for Bentley,—'what *Collier* could never do, ruin'd the Stage—*sed aiunt ipsum non penitus evertisse sed tantum reformasse profanum illum locum in profaniorem vulgo dictum,* a Tyring Room.'

After exorcising one of the proctors who was not favourable to the Tripos Speech, he laughs at an exproctor, Mr Noys, who used to drive over to Milton to preach, and was fond of looking at himself in the glass. He passes to another King's man, 'Judge' Bullock, 'a mathematician, and broad platter-fac'd Fellow,' who was supposed to be in love. He had also a passion for Architecture: whereupon Cobb takes occasion of alluding to the curious 'Custom at *King's* College, when a Lad comes in after Prayers to Dinner, to lay a Brick on his Trencher:'

> For they must needs be Architects
> Who are so us'd to eating Bricks. (p. 8.)

Reference is then made (p. 11) to the scandal that 'a Bishop's Son was made a Master of Arts, although a Boy, and of no standing in the University,' while a Bachelor of Arts had been appointed to the lucrative post of college Butler. [Charles Ashton, master of Jesus, mentions in his *Collectanea* on Univ. Stat. XX., that 'Bishops' sons have been of late years (at least 20 after Cobb's time) indulged this Privilege (of degrees as peers' sons, without statutable exercise), which is neither agreeable to the Statutes, nor the Interpretation, as I have shewn in *Collectan.*, p. 187.'] But the junior Proctor (who seems to have been an unskilful rider) must not be forgotten. There went of him 'a Story about *Ball's* throwing him:' 'Hip! Magister *Awbery! Quaeso des mihi veniam propter hanc offensionem, et posthac tui non obliviscar. Sed quoniam Reformator Academiae sum constitutus et mea plurimum refert universos pariter observare, tuam reformabo in equitando peritiam. Imprimis igitur, cum colles* Gogmagomianos *cum tuis* Jesuiticis *sodalibus, qui laborant morbo quem vulgo vocamus* the Hip, *acris im-*

bibendi gratia paullo ore hiscere velis, sic instructus sis.'

After some initiation in the rudiments of riding, the Buffoon makes a pretence of knighting the Proctor,

> 'Nor shall one *Iohnian* Doctor save his Bacon,'

as '*peregrinantem indefessum :* a Fellow, who is continually loytering about the Town:' but no great scholar.

> 'Nor Corner or College is free but he's in it;
> At the *Castle* and *Spittle-house-End* in a Minute;
> He seems like Juglers Tricks were-e'er he goes: ⎫
> Hey *Jingo*, Sirs, Where is he? at the *Rose;*   ⎬
> *Presto*, begone! he's at the *Market-Cross.'*   ⎭

Nor does the Master of Bene't College (a little fellow) escape, who 'when he was Vice-Chancellor forbad Plays, even so much as Puppet-Shows :' the Zeal o'the Land Busy of Sturbridge Fair.

> 'The Wise will say 'twas done with reason,
> For *Punch* was Jackish, and talk'd Treason.
> *   *   *   *
> But who can any Harm acquire
> From a small Gentleman in Wire?
> And what can e'er proceed that's odd
> From tiny things like Master *Modd?*

[A very little Man of *Trinity College.'* (Bentley's Vice-master; 'a feeble old man destitute of the requisite qualifications.' *Monk's* Life of *Bentley*, I. 409.)]

Next he quizzes *Waller*, the humanity lecturer at *Bene't* College, 'who order'd his Sophs to make Themes on unheard of things:' and set up for a pretty fellow. But his cure is beyond the skill of

Tripos: we must take him to '*Gonvil*, a small College where most of them study Physick:' and where the Doctor lives who keeps his cat as a weather-glass.

Then follows a mock *auction* of Doctors '*cum Privilegio Superiorum*. Catalogues may be had of me and my Brothers. [Two Lads spoke with him.]' These Commodities are knocked down for 3 groats to his assistants by Cobb, with the assurance that

> ''tis more than they're worth by a Shilling.'

However he cannot get 3*d.* for the scarce Remainders ; so he determines to

> 'send 'em beyond Sea; they'll pass with the *Dutch*.'

We may suppose perhaps that lists of the Doctors had been handed about among the Sophs, by the three Jesters, (*Tripos* and his *Brothers*), and when the boisterous merriment had reached its highest, and was beginning to subside; '*Mr Tripos* pulls a Halter out of his Pocket,' and after confessing and begging pardon for his freedom, proceeds to dispose of his effects :

> 'My Wit I leave, 'tis small, I grant it,
> To Doctors, and to those that want it ;
> And to the *Beaus* as 'tis my Duty
> I'll leave my Dressing and my Beauty.
> But now I hear my Fatal Knell,
> And so I take my last Farewell.'

Here perhaps he threw his mask and motley into the pit: meanwhile, possibly, the School's bell was tolled ; and as Tripos is being assisted by his

'Brothers' to his execution, 'the Sophs below in the Pit cry, *A Pardon, a Pardon, a Pardon.*'

Then on a monstrous sheet of paper is displayed the following Pardon, 'under which some Names were written, and seal'd with a Quart Pot:'

'To our Trusty and well-beloved the Worship-ful Mr *Vice-Chancellor*, and the Heads of the Colleges, in our Famous University of *Cambridge*, WE the Sophisters send Greeting.

'ACCORDING to Our Sovereign Authority committed to Us this Day, we pardon our Trusty and well-beloved *Sam. Cobb*, for all and every Offence he has committed against the Upper and Lower House.

Witness our Hand and Seal.'

The reprieved Tripos having thrown his rope to the Sophisters, makes his apology to the Senior members of the University and personally to the Vice-Chancellor.

> 'That I've been honest, you must needs confess.
> You've heard with how much innocence I spoke,
> No scurril Satire or ill-natur'd Joke;
> How from Obscenity I could decline,
> Which always grates a Doctor's ears and mine;
> How nothing tended to malicious Ends.
> Then let us all shake Hands and so part Friends.'

[The companion piece from the sister University, in this pamphlet the *Nasus Prehensus* written a dozen years later, of which a more perfect copy is to be found in *Bodl. pamphlets* 318, cannot, alas! make the same boast.]

A few quotations from regulations affecting this office will complete my notice of the *Tripos* or *Bachelor* of the *Stool:* and I shall then pass on to his kinsman the *Praevaricator.*

April 3, 1576, Decretum Praefectorum, 'It was declared to be the ancient and laudable custom of the University and therefore decreed and determined by Mr John Still, Doctor in Divinity and Vice-Chancellor, and the heads of colleges, viz. Mr Dr. Perne, Mey, Whitgift, Chadderton, Ithell, Bing, Legge, and Mr Norgate, that all those persons which should sustain the person of the FATHER, the ELDEST SON, the BACHELOR OF THE STOOL, and the disputers should keep their rooms and functions in the *latter act* and not to be changed but upon great and urgent causes, to be approved and allowed by the V. C., both the Proctors, and Masters of Colleges whereof any of the aforesaid persons so to be allowed or dispensed withall shall and do abide and remain, and of every of them.

'*Item* that every of the said two acts with the *father* and the *bachelor* should hold defend and maintain two questions which in no wise should be altered or changed.

'*Item* that the *Bachelor of the stool* answering both acts should and might account that, his two answerings, for one ordinary answering required by statute for and towards his degree, and for no more. But if he answered but one of the said acts, that then this be required for no answering towards his degree.'

I am enabled through the kindness of the Registrary, the Rev. H. R. Luard, to give the following account of the first volume of Triposes in his
custody.

It is a portly folio carefully indexed by the late
Mr Romilly. In the beginning are bound some slips
of paper containing the regulations which controlled
the Tripos and Praevaricator; and some proceedings
taken by authority against such as transgressed the
orders and statutes.

After a general order 'de morum urbanitate et
modestia.' (The copy being written probably about
the year 1630.) 'Prevaricatores etiam omnes et
Tripodes et alii disputantes a mimicis salutacoībus
et rerum politicarū magistratuū aliorumve nomina-
coībus, a iocis quoq: scurrilibus a gesticulacoībus,
obscaenitatibus anglicani sermonis, ineptiis dicteriisq:
omnibus penitus abstineant, sub paena suspencoīs vel
(si atrocitas facti postulaverit) expulsionis.'

Next comes a general Ordinatio of K. Charles, and
then a similar Interpretation '8°. May, 1626[1],' *de au-
ferendis morionum ineptiis et scurrilibus jocis in publicis
disputationibus.*

[1638.] 'Orders for Ashwednesday...Ra: Brown-
rigg procan:' No one to climb 'sedilia' or windows,
nor to make a noise by clapping, shuffling, beating,
laughing, hissing, or the like. All to appear 'in
habitu cum caputio.' The original order 'Praevari-
catores omnes et Tripodes' &c. is quoted: the punc-

---

[1] See Cooper's *Annals*, III. 185.

tuation of one passage being here 'obscaenitatibus, anglicani sermonis ineptiis.'

[In 1640, Seth Ward, M.A., Fellow of Sidney Coll., afterwards Bp. of Salisbury, being Praevaricator at the Commencement, Dr Cosins[1], the V.C., took offence at his speech, and suspended him from his degree, but restored him on the following day. The Praevaricator's speech for 1660 is described by the editor of D'Ewes' diary. See below.]

15 July, 1663. Mr Gower begged pardon for 'his speech made in the Commencement House.'

'*April* 19th, A.D. 1667. It is agreed at a meeting of the heades, that instedd of the vsuall performances of *prevaricators* in the *majora comitia,* and of the *Tripus* in the *first* or *latter Act* of the *minora Comitia,* That the *praevaricator* and *Tripus* respectively only mainteine what part soever of a question which hee pleaseth and make a serious position to mainteine it as well as he can, but shewing first his position to the vice chancellour, and the opponents without making any speech, to bring their serious Arguments: and if either the praevaricator or Tripus shall say any thing vpon the pretence of his position but what hee hath before shewen to the Vicechancellour and what hee hath allowed; or the opponents shall obtrude any sort of 'speech, or other arguments then serious and philosophicall, hee shall bee punished with the censure of expulsion,' &c.

'Fra: Wildford Vicechan:' &c.

---

[1] Cooper's *Annals,* III. 301.

'26 *Martii* 1669. Dᵃ Hollis' fellow of Clare Hall is to make a publick Recantation in the Bac. Schools, for his Tripos Speeche.' He was suspended. His submission is extant : '*In nomine*' &c.

'*Jul.* 28, 1673.' Mr Benj. Johnson, Proctor was admonished to appear, and in default was summoned for 28 Jul. 1673. He made his apology *Sep.* 22.

Sept. 26, 1673. John Turner's confession of his fault as 'Praevaricator at the commencement last past.'

'Dʳ Eachard of Catherine Hall suspended Dᵃ Smallwood from his B.A. degree for his scurrilous and very offensive speech made in yᵉ schooles upon yᵉ 26th of yᵉ aforesᵈ Month [March] when he undertook to performe yᵉ office of a Tripos.' He made his humble submission and was restored April 2, 1680[1]. [In the same year the *Praevaricator* was absurdly suspected of *depreciating* the Popish Plot.]

In 1683, three members of Sidney Coll., one of Jesus, and one of Caius, were rusticated for their outrageous combination to disturb the exercises of the latter Act.

[On the 7th of *July*, 1684, Peter Redmayne fellow of Trin. was expelled for some miscarriages in his Praevaricator's speech at the Commencement, but on the 18th of *October*, the King sent letters from Newmarket for restoring him in consequence of his former good behaviour[2].]

---

[1] Cooper's *Annals*, III. 586.
[2] *Ibid*. III. 601.

April 17, 1713. Mr Will. Law was suspended for 'his speech in the public schooles at the latter act.'

[In 1714, came Long's celebrated Music Speech which I shall soon have occasion to notice: Taylor's 1730.

In 1740-1, a strongly expressed grace was passed *Mar.* 19, against scurrility and the use of the English language in Tripos Speeches.]

Of the *Tripos Verses* there are 84 in MS., the earliest date borne by any is 7 *Mar.* 1574. They are in Latin verse of a serious nature on some special theme or question, ending with a couplet comprehending the conclusion, *ergo.* Next come thirty, most of which are in *Latin* verse, *printed* in pairs with an ornamental border, each concluding with an *ergo.* Each leaf contains a pair relating to some particular branch of science, *Theology, Medicine, Law*, &c. We may conclude that they were circulated at the acts of the several faculties, and bore reference to the thesis under discussion. Indeed I am inclined to suspect that several of the leaves bound in the collection are verses not of the *Tripos*, but of the *Philosopher*, the *Father*, or of some other disputant.

The last of the thirty above mentioned has no date affixed, but is supposed to belong to the year 1652, or thereabouts. On the back is a document relating to Richard Ireland and others, apprenticed to the trade and mystery of Stationers in Cambridge.

The next and all that follow bear a date.

In Comitiis prioribus, Feb 22, 169$\frac{3}{4}$.

1. Stoicorum ἀπάθεια non est admittenda.

2. Deus est Naturae Lumine cognoscendus.

The set for the latter Comitia of the same year follows. Then that for Mart. 7, 169$\frac{4}{5}$. That for Com. Posteriora, Mar. 19, 172$\frac{3}{4}$. About this period one of the sets generally takes the form of a Position 'Rectè statuit...'

The set for Com. Priora, Feb. 9, 1748—9, is important, as being the earliest which bears on its back *a list* of the *Wranglers* and *Senior Optimes*. This has been kept up in subsequent years: the paper for the *Com. Posteriora* bearing the names of the *junior* optimes. The verses for 1748—9 are of a lighter character.

1. Moriae Encomium (April Fools).
2. A defence of Berkeley on *Tar Water*.

In 1694—5 is the position '*Cartesiana* dubitatio non est optima philosophandi modus.' In 1723—4, and later years, *Newton* is defended.

From the year 1803 to 1858 one set of two appeared yearly on a double sheet. In 1859 (as since that date) there were four sets: by J. A. Willis, H. Sidgwick, G. O. Trevelyan, and J. H. Nelson. The volume ends with the verses for 1846, and some commemoration lines on the Tercentenary of Trin. Coll, 22° Dec. of that year. The second volume contains the verses from 1847 till the existing time. One or two sets of verses have been rejected from time to time; even within the last five and twenty years. The Provost of King's has a few sets which are not in the Registrary's Office. And in the Bodleian at Oxford is an imperfect collection of those between the

years 1782 and 1800. [*Gough, Adds. Camb.* 4°. 2.]
I propose to give a brief account of these, and of a
few others.

In the first place, when looking at a volume in
Bodley [*Gough, Oxf.* 58], I noticed a loose leaf folded
and lying in the book. On it were two sets of Latin
hexameters.

1. Ascensus et Descensus Mercurii in Barometro
pendent ex gravitate aëris et vi ejus elasticâ.

2. Idem Spiritûs non est aequè clara ac Idea Corporis. The concluding lines, at least, I recognized as
a translation of a passage in the *Rape of the Lock:*

'Tulit atque alienos Phyllis honores'

clearly represents

And Betty's prais'd for labours not her own.

But this paper is remarkable for having the words
Jul. 7, 1730, *Resp. in Die Comit.*, Gul. Trollope, *Aul.*
Pemb., *pro Gradu A.M.*

This, then, is something different from a Tripos
Paper. It belongs to the Comitia *Majora* or great
Commencement in the Summer, (and not to the
'first' or 'the latter Act' *Comit. priora* or *posteriora* of
the Comitia *Minora* or Bachelors' Commencement of
the Lent Term). By whatever name we are to call
them, they are clearly the verses to be distributed at
a Philosophy Act (when the *Praevaricator*, not the
Tripos, would be present) to be kept by W. Trollope,
B.A., Fellow of Pembroke, as an exercise for his M.A.
degree, which he appears to have taken in that year.

In 1676 were printed '*Musae* Subsecivae *seu Poetica
Stromata* auctore J. D.' This was the production of

James Duport (son of the Master of Jesus Coll.), who was Greek Professor, Vice-master of Trinity, Prebendary of *Langford Ecclesia* in Lincoln Cath., Archd. of Stow, and Dean of Peterborough. His earliest important publication was an *Epitaphium* on the death of *Bacon*, and his last act at Trinity was to take part in the election of *Newton* to a scholarship in 1664; and almost his last deed was, in 1679, to send *Barrow* a subscription of £200 for the building of Trinity Library. While he was an undergraduate in 1622—6 he wrote several *carmina comitialia*, which we call usually 'Tripos Verses.' A remarkable series of tripos verses are those by the unfortunate *Kit Smart*, who entered at Pembroke-hall in 1739, and took his B.A. degree in 1743.

It may be worth while to describe them.

I. in Com. Prior. 1740—1.

Datur Mundorum Pluralitas. A ride on Pegasus to visit the inhabitants of the planets Mercury, Venus, Mars, Jupiter, and Saturn, under the guidance of the witty old *Bernard le Bolivier Fontenelle,* (the first edition of whose *Entretien sur la Pluralité des Mondes* was published in 1686, and whose works had reached a 3rd English version in 1760, three years after his death).

II. In 1741—2.

Materies Gaudet Vi Inertiae. A description of the leaden Temple of Dulness in the heart of Ireland. Here the poet sees Zoilus, Bavius, Maevius, Spinoza, Pyrrho, Hobbes, and Epicurus. In front of the *Gothic* door stand four personages. *Sophis-*

tica, the eldest daughter of Matter, girt with 10 categories, bearing a club, and the net of a *retiarius;* clad in cobwebs she marches

> Quam lente Oxonii sollennis pondera cenae
> Gestant tergeminorum abdomina bedellorum.

Then with her diagrams comes *Mathesis.*

> incompta capillos
> Immemor externi punctoque innixa reclinat.
> doctasque sorores
> Fastidit, propriaeque nihil non arrogat arti.
> Illam olim duce Neutono, dum tendit ad astra
> Aetheriasque domos superûm, indignata volantem
> Turba mathematicûm retrahit, poenasque reposcens
> Detinet in terras, nugisque exercet ineptis.

Next *Microphile.*

> muscas et papiliones
> Lustrat inexpletum, collumque et tempora rident
> Floribus et fungis totaque propagine veris.

What joy is hers on the discovery of a Polypus !

> jam non crocodilon adorat ;
> Nec bombyx, conchaeve juvant : sed Polypon ardet,
> Solum Polypon ardet.

Last comes *Atheia*, sans everything but voice. The author tries to drink of the neighbouring stream, but is pulled up by the Muse.

III.   In 1742—3.

Mutua Oscitationum Propagatio solvi potest mechanice.

Momus, for ridiculing the birth of Pallas from the head of Jove, is condemned to bring forth *Polychasmia* the goddess of *Yawning.* Her compound creation, her patronage of Justices on the

Bench, Preachers who subdivide their text, Physicians with their gold-headed canes. But the *Soph* is particularly sedulous in his *cultus* of her, having often to argue on the question which heads the paper;—and to exemplify it. Which is now the case with the Author, who opens his mouth in vain for the draughts of Castaly which flow for Mr Pope alone, while himself waits as the hungry Sizar does for the Fellow to leave him some dainties.

In the *Student* or *Oxf. and Camb. Monthly Miscellany*, II. 238, 1751, is given an anonymous Tripos. 'Cantab. Comitiis prioribus, Feb. 21, 1750—51.' *Humani Corporis Topographia.*

In the Bodleian [*Topography Cambridge. Gough Camb.* 103], is one ' In *Comitiis Prioribus* Mar. 4, 1756.'

1. *Recte statuit Aristoteles de Terrae motibus.*

2. *Acta Philosophica celebris Academiae Lagadonensium.* The author gives an account of the ingenious idleness of that people, and the arguments of one of their professors.

In a volume of Miscellanies in the Camb. Univ. Library, [Nn. 4. 70], is bound *Carmen in comitiis prioribus* 1774. *Mola juventutis restauratrix*, (about 110 Latin hexameters). That in Com. Prior. Mar. 5, 1778, is on the subject of *Tobacco*.

For 1781, the verses on *Maps* [*d.* 1796] (Nicholson, the eccentric bookseller), printed in the *Camb. Univ. Calendar* for 1802.

The following are in the Bodleian (as has been stated).

In Comitiis Prioribus, Feb. 14, 1782.

1. *His nam plebecula gaudet.* (Street amusements.)

2. Οὐδεις ἀκαθαρτος εἰσιτω. [*sic,*] Temp. Hym. Pall-Mall. ' Casta fave *Lucina* ' &c.

[1783, Com. Prior. Mar. 6, on the study for degrees.]

Com. Prior. Feb. 10, 1785.

1. *Nulli fas castae sceleratum insistere limen.* The Spinning-house.

2. *Ille vel intactae segetis per summa volaret*
   Gramina ; nec teneras cursu laesisset aristas.

Bob. Foster, the *Flying Barber*, [*d.* 1799]. See pp. 135—7.

[1786, Com. Prior. Mar. 2.
Coll. Trin. Cespes. (Whishow, Trinity)].

Com. Prior. Feb. 22, 1787.

1. *Manicarum Laudes.* It will be remembered that according to *Gunning's Ceremonies* the Proctor or Moderator ought to present *gloves* to the writer of the verses. It appears that ladies who were careful of white hands wore their long gloves at night.

2. *Caeli mobilis humor.* Rain.

Com. Prior. Feb. 7, 1788.

1. *Pulmonem agitare solebant.* On Laughter.

2. *Spectatum veniunt.* Aspirations for a royal visit. Cp. Cooper's *Annals*, IV. 416. *Gent. Mag.,* LVI. 791. ' Cambridge Triumphant :' the king having visited Oxford in 1785, 1786.

Com. Posterior. Mar. 6, 1788.

1. *Dux Glocestrensis Cantabrigiam visens*, (Nov. 16, 1787, Cooper's *Annals*, IV. 423, 425).

2. *Concordia discors.* The Union Coffee-house, (see above, p. 142).

Com. Prior. 1789.

1. *Et canibus leporem, canibus venabere damas.* On hounds, (by *John Hookham Frere*).

2. *Immiscentque manus manibus, pugnantque lacertis.* A prize-fight between Humphrey and Mendoza, (by F. Wrangham).

[Woolaston was reprimanded for admitting Fr. Wrangham's verses in Com. Posterior, Mar. 26, 1789.]

Com. Prior., Feb. 18, 1790.

1. *Cartesii Principia* (by 'Bobus' Smith, see *Mus. Crit.* II. 226).

2. *Umbrosae penitus patuere cavernae.* An Address to Liberty on the fall of the *Bastille* (July 14, 1789).

Com. Posterior. Mar. 18, 1790.

1. *Cum vincamur in omni.*
Munere sola Deos aequat Clementia nobis.
The Slave trade. Cooper's *Annals*, IV. 426, 443. Pitt's motion (May 9, 1788), to consider the question next session.

2. *Cum prostrata sopore.*
Urget membra quies et mens sine pondere ludit.
Dreams.

Com. *Priora.* March 10, 1791.
1. *Romanis solenne viris opus utile famae.*
   Vitaeque et membris.
Fox-hunting.
2. *Bellum, Pax rursum.*
Gibraltar.

[Com. Posteriora, 1791. *Platonis Principia,* by 'Bobus' Smith, see *Mus. Crit.* II. 227.]

Com. Prior. Feb. 23, 1792.
1. *Newtoni Systema Mundanum,* by 'Bobus' Smith (*Mus. Crit.* II. 230).
2. ’Εν δ’ ’Ερις ἐν δὲ Κυδοιμὸς ὁμίλεον. A debate in Paris. Reference to the late National Assembly sitting in the Riding School. A satirical account of French *assignats* (which were issued Dec. 1789. This was printed a few days after Pitt's budget speech on the flourishing condition of our own country).

Com. Prior, Feb. 14, 1793.
1. *Non sibi sed toti genitum se credere mundo.*
Love of our country.
2. Πολύδακρυς ‘Ηδονή.

Com. Posterior, March 14, 1793.
1. Μέγας οὐρανὸς, Οὔλυμπόστε. [*sic.*]
A semi-heathen, semi-scriptural cosmogony with praise of Newton.
2. ‘Ο πρὶν παλαιος ὄλβος ἦν πάροιθε μὲν
   ὄλβος δικαίως, &c.

Troubles in France, England exhorted to suppress the Revolution. (War was declared by Great Britain, Feb. 11, 1793. Jan. 5, 1793, a dumb peal had been rung in Great St Mary's for Louis XVI. Cooper's *Annals*, IV. 447, and in March a subscription was raised in Cambridge for the French refugee clergy.)

Com. Prior. Mar. 6, 1794.

1. Οὗτός γε

'Αμφότερον, βασιλεύς τ' ἀγαθός, κρατερός τ' αἰχμητής.

Augustus prays to Liberty to give peace to the Moselle. The treaty of Commerce had been made with Russia, March, 1793.

2. 'Εν δ' ὁ πυρφόρος θεὸς

σκήψας ἐλαύνει λοιμὸς ἔχθιστος.

Pestilence on the Delaware.

Com. Prior. Feb. 19, 1795.

1.   *Virgo,*
              Floridis velut enitens,
              Myrtus Asia ramulis,
              Quos Hamadryades Deae
              Ludicrum sibi roscido
              Nutriunt humore. [Catullus.]

Wishes a fair voyage to Caroline, Princess now of Brunswick, who was married to the P. of Wales, April 8, 1795. (A congratulatory Address on the occasion was presented at St James' by the d. of Grafton, and the V. C., W. Pitt, e. of Euston, d. of Rutland, 6 bishops, &c. April 29, 1795.)

2. ῞Ος θεσπιῳδεῖ τρίποδος ἐκ χρυσηλάτου,
μέμψιν δικαίαν μέμφομαι ταύτην.

Auctor cum Tripode colloquitur. A somewhat fescennine dialogue with the Tripos, whom, with a *pace Prisciani*, he calls *felina* (apparently because a cat, like the Manx *Tre Cassyn*, or trinacria, always falls on its legs). Various town or university topics are introduced.

Litem
Composuere gravem Ποδαλείριος ἠδὲ Μαχάων.

There is a description of drivers, walkers, who come home splashed. Early-rising sportsmen. The *bucks* sunning their sleek locks as spruce as any Narcissus of the Isis. How deliberately they lounge: how rudely they stare, not deigning to wear their gowns and battered caps: these pupils of bully Dawson!

What is the allusion in the following?

> Saepe Gradus errant, etenim lex unica jussit
> Parcere Germanis, sed quid tibi *Curia* fecit
> Ut brevior fiat quam cum Romana fuisset?

Does the last line refer to some false quantity such as Kipling or Watson were capable of making, or to some small meeting of the Senate?

The affectation of archaisms in Latin verse is satirized, and the free use of conjunctions. He concludes with an address to the vagrant poem:

> Uraris *Tineo* non impunitior ipso
> Cum tua membratim jactu dispersa faceto
> Frustula calcabit belle soleata juventus.

Comit. Poster. Mar. 19, 1795.

1. A passage from *Plato*. The Immortality of

the Soul, by 'Bobus' Smith (*Mus. Crit.* II. 57). [Good authority however ascribes this to *Jo. Keate.*]

2. Θαλασσίπλαγκτα
λίνοπτερ' εὗρε ναυτίλων ὀχήματα.
Progress of Navigation.

Comit. Prior. Feb. 11, 1796.
1. Εὐγραφέων καλάμωι. The Old Masters, (by Tower of St John's).
2. Οἰκτρὸν γὰρ πόλιν τήνδ' ὠγυγίαν, &c.
(Aesch. *S. C. Thebas*, 321—3).

Roma Alarico Getarum Rege, capta, spoliata; A. U. C. 1163 (by Harris).

Com. Prior. Mar. 2, 1797.
1. Αὖραι ἡδύπνοοι καμάτου ἀνάπαυσιν ἔχουσαι.
Epidemics, consumption, &c., by W. Frere (*Mus. Crit.* I. 323).
2. *In varias doceo migrare figuras.* 'Dialogue of the Dead between Pythagoras, Ennius, and Charon,' (by S. W. Gaudy).

Com. Posterior. Mar. 30, 1797.
1. Σᾷ δ' ὑπὸ σδεύγλᾳ κρατερῶν λεπάδνων
Στέρνα γαίας καὶ πολιᾶς θαλάσσας
Σφίγγεται· σὺ δ' ἀσφαλέως κυβερνᾷς.
Ἄστεα λαῶν. *Erinna.*

The death of the empress Katherine of Russia, (*Nov.* 17, 1796).
2. *Securum iter et fallentis semita vitae.* 'Latin *elegiacs*, on the Pleasures of a retired Life,' (by Clem. Leigh).

Com. Prior. Feb. 22, 1798.

1.   *Quicquid agunt homines, Votum, timor, ira, Voluptas,*

   Gaudia, discursus nostri est farrago iibelli.

An account of a theatrical entertainment.

2.   *An imprimis quasi ceram animum putamus et memoriam esse signatarum rerum in mente vestigia.* A statement of a theory of Impressions, by W. Frere, (*Mus. Crit.* I.).

[Com. Posterior. 1798.
In Phantasiam, by H. V. Bayley, *Mus. Crit.* I. 323.]

Com. Prior. Feb. 7, 1799.

1.   Ὁ δὲ θεὸς εἶπεν, &c., 1 Chron. xxviii. 3.

The son of k. Henry, a man of Peace builds King's Coll. Chapel.

2.   *Atque hic undantem bello magnumque fluentem Nilum et navali surgentes aere columnas.*

The Battle of the Nile, *Aug.* 1, 1798.   There was an illumination in honour of the victory in *Oct.* 3, 1799, and a General Thanksgiving, *Nov.* 29.

Com. Prior. Feb. 1800.

1.   ἀλλ' ὅμως ἐν οὐρανῷ
       ναίουσι, &c.   *Edwy and Elgiva.*

2.   Latin Elegiacs on *Paris et Oenone,* (by G. L. Newnham).

Com. Posterior. Mar. 27, 1800.

1.   *Immensos Lapponiae montes, miracula naturae. Joan. Luxi. prolegg.* iii. 18.

Lapland and gnomes.

2. *Quae supra nos nihil ad nos.*
The futility of speculations on the unknown.

[Com. Posteriora, 1802.
Ars Piscatoria, by James Parke (*Mus. Crit.* I.)]

In the lists of names on the backs of the verses, there are often subdivisions in the classes, indicated by spaces left between the names: and those who took *aegrotat* degrees were assigned to the several classes by the moderators.

We will now pass to the *Act* or *Great Commencement* in the summer; till which time the *seniority* of the honour men was reserved from the *first Act* generally in February (*Comitia Priora* of the Wranglers and Senior Optimes) and from the *latter Act* of the 'Bachelors' Commencement' (*Comitia Posteriora* of the Junior Optimes): so that they kept their place above any of the πολλοὶ, or ordinary-degree men.

At this Great Commencement (*Comitia Majora*) the higher degrees were given, and the PRAEVARI-CATOR held a similar position to that which the *Tripos* had taken on the earlier occasion.

The following account is taken from esquire bedel *Matt. Stokys'* Book[1], just before the Reformation.

'*The Vepers in Arte.* [Vesperiae ante Comitia maxima]...In the mornyng att vii off the Clocke all the Inceptours in Arte shall assemble att the College or Place where the FATHER [In later days the Proctor

---

[1] Dean Peacock, *On the Statutes*, 1841. Appendix A. pp. xx—xxi.

took this office at the great Commencement] is aby-
dyng. Than the Father shall call hys chyldren lyke
as he wyll have them in Senyoryte, begynnyng at the
eldyst,...so they shall take upp the Scolys; fyrst the
Comyn Scolys, the Master in Ordynarye redyng in
everye Scolys, as the Facultye requyryth : And so in
everye Howse of Fryers, where any Regent is...[Then
after some Questions and notice of Disputations : the
'eldyst sonne' beginning to rehearse his arguments
'shall be clappyde out,' see p. 209] Than the Proctour shall make as many ley ther handys on the
Boke as may, and he shall say, *Jurabitis quod nunquam resumetis Gradum Bachalariatus in eadem facultate de cetero.* [i.e. 'hereafter.' The Oxonian formula
was quaintly personal : *Magister tu jurabis quod nunquam consenties in reconciliationem Henrici Simeonis,
nec statum Baccalaureatus iterum tibi assumes.* It is
thought that the culprit had, to gain some end, dis-
sembled his degree in king *John's* reign.] After
that the Father shall rede hys Comendatyon, hys
Chyldren folowing and there whodys pluckydde on
there Hedys, [to hide their blushes ;] and that don,
the Bedyll shall say, *Honorande Magister, solent queri
Questiones.* [The Father repeats ; adding, *sub quo?
quando? et ubi?*] *Sub quo? Sub meipso, Deo dante.
Quando? Die Lune. Ubi? In ecclesia Beate Marie
Virginis.* And thus endyth the Vepers in Arte.

Nota. That the Fathers and the Bedellys shall
dyne wyth the eldest Inceptour that Daye.

The Commcnsment in Arte. In the Mornyng on
the Commensment Day all the Inceptours shall as-

semble att the Father's Place, as they dyd the day off the Vepers: than the yongest shall go fyrst, and the Father shall cumme behynde wyth hys eldyst Sonne next hym all to Saynt Marye Chyrche. The Father shall sytt before the Auter, & as many off his Chyldren as may. Iff there be Commensment in Divinite & Lawe that Day, the Father of Dyvinite shall sytt in the middys of the Gresynge [*step*] before the Hyghe Auter, covered iff he wyll, & hys eldyst Sone....Than next hym the Father in Lawe. [The Father in Art and each Inceptor offers 1*d*. Mass is said. Then] the Proctour shall say *Incipiatis.* Than the Father shall rede a Texte in Phylosophye, & say, *Ex isto Textu eliciuntur duo Articuli ad præsens disputandi:* & he shall reherse the Questyons that shall be dysputyde. Then shall stonde upp THE YONGEST REGENT THAT COMMENSYDE THE YERE BEFORE [i. e. the PRAEVARICATOR or VARIER; who had at the preceding Commencement sworn, in addition to the ordinary oath, *Jurabis etiam quod sequenti anno in proximis comitiis per te, vel per alium,* VARIABIS, *determinabis questionem, &c.* Compare Peter Gunning's account of himself: ' In the year of our Lord 1632 I commenced bachelor of arts, and was made senior brother. In the year of our Lord 1632, ending on new year's day, January 1, I was chosen fellow of the college, (Clare hall,) when I was nineteen years old. At the same year, ending at the latter act, I was made *tripus.* In the year 1635, in July, I commenced master of arts, and was sworn *praevaricator.*' *Baker-Mayor,* 234—5; see also the quotation given by Mr *Mayor* in the notes, p. 648, where Edw. Stillingfleet is described as giving a 'witty and inoffensive speech' as Tripos: and in 1660 the Praevaricator, Mr Darby, is said to have been 'witty and innocent.'] 'He was required to preface his argument with an Oration, in which he was authorized by custom, like the TRIPOS at the *lesser comitia*, (in the spring,) to use considerable freedom of language; a privilege which was not unfrequently abused. The praevaricator was so named (says dean Peacock) from *varying* the question which he proposed, either by a play upon the words, or by the transposition of the terms in which it was expressed. A beautiful specimen of such a speech has been preserved, which was made by Dr James Duport in 1631,' see p. 234. [It will be found quoted in the *notes.*] 'And he shall ansure to one argument in both maters; fyrst to the Sone & after to the Father, iff he may have reason therto, he shall certyfye the Argument off hys Sone. After the Proctour hath sayde, *Sufficit*, shall stonde up the non Regent & reherse the maters, & the way off *the yong Regent:* after he shall rede hys Lesson, & ansure to the Sone, to the Father, & the non Regentys, in lyke Forme as is sayde in the Vepers. Whan all have arguyde, the Proctour shall say, *Ad Oppositum.* The Sonne shall ansure, *Est Philosophus.* Than the Yongest Doctor off Divynite shall take the Conclusyon, and say thus, *Has Conclusiones, assero et determino esse veras.* [Then an Oath is given to continue regency for five years, and not to incept or read in the faculty elsewhere, except at Oxford. The

Inceptor then sits and gives his final *determination* of
the questions in the ear of the Father (*Magister*),
and as he is going, on off [i. e. *one of*] the Bedellys
shall stonde there & say, *Nouter Mater*, [maître,]
Mater N. pronounsyng by name...[After the *Vepers
in Gramer* follows the Act or *enteryng of a Master in
Gramer :* which, though beside our question, is too
quaint to be passed over.   After beginning with
Mass, &c., as in Arts,] Whan the Father, [sitting aloft
under the 'Stage for Physyke' in St Mary's church,]
hath arguyde as shall plese the Proctour, the Bedyll
in Arte shall bring the Master of Gramer to the Vice-
chauncelor, delyveryng hym a Palmer, [some sort of
ferule or cane,] wyth a Rodde, whych the Vycechaun-
celor shall gyve to the seyde Master in Gramer, & so
create hym Master.   Than shall the Bedell purvay
for every master in Gramer a shrewde Boy, whom the
master in Gramer shall bete openlye in the Scolys, &
the master in Gramer shall give the Boye a Grote for
hys Labour, & another Grote to hym that provydeth
the Rode & the Palmer, &c. *de singulis.*   And thus
endythe the Acte in that Facultye....

Nota.   That the Inceptour in Gramer shall gyve to
the Vicechauncelar a Bonett, and to the Father, and
to eche off the Proctours a Bonett...

ᐯ   [Then comes an account of the Vespers in Divinity, and of the Divinity Act which was to take
place after 'the Actys in Gramer, Art, Musyke,
Physyke, Cyvyll, Canon. ']...M^d. Iff ther commense
ij Fryers Doctours in on Howse, the on is Regent
Claustrall, and shall rede his Lesson in hys owne

Scholys, and the other shall rede in the commyn Scolys; and lyke wyse wyth the Dysputatyons... Whan the Dysputatyon is don the Doctour shall not say the Prayers, but be brought home wythe the Bedellys, and the Opposers, and there he shall gyve them Drynke: and the Responsall shall gyve hym xx*d.* towarde the Costys of thys Drynkyng. ...*The Vepers in Canon and Civell...The commens-ment in Canon and Civyll...*

M^d. ...The Bedell shall gather of every Doctour Comensar for every Doctour ther being present, a Grote for hys Pylyon, and iff ther be moo Commensars Doctours than on, he shall gather of the yongar Commensar a grote for the elder Commensar.'

The following extracts[1] are taken from Bedel *Buck's* Book, 1665. '*In Vesperiis Comitiorum.* The Bedels are to go to the several Colleges, and bring the Inceptors in Arts to the Father in *Philosophy* by 7 of the Clock that morning, in Hoods black. After a little stay at the Father's chamber, we go to the Father of *Physick*...to the Father in *Civil Law*...to the Father in *Divinity*...to the V. C.

The Inceptors in all Faculties go this day with Black Hoods turned, and their Caps off. When we come at the V. C^n. Lodgings, after a little stay there, we are to go to the Schools...The V. C., ...not being a Father, is in his Scarlet Gown, his Cap being garnished with gold Lace; but if he be a Father, then he goeth in his Cope; and so do the other Fathers with their Caps garnished.

---

[1] Peacock, *On the Statutes*, 1841. Appendix B. LXXIX—LXXXVII.

The Proctors go in white Hoods, and their Caps garnished with gold Lace, carrying their Books in their hands. The Father in Philosophy goeth in like manner, save only he carrieth no Book. When we are come into the Philosophy Schools, one of the Bedels saith unto the Lecturer there reading, *Venerabilis magister, haec tibi sufficiant.* Then he leaves off his Reading. The Bedel then readeth all the Quaestions *in hunc Modum. Quaestiones his nostris Comitiis disputandae sunt hujusmodi; In Schola Theologica.*—Then he reads them. *In Schola Juris Civilis—In Schola Medica—In Schola Philos.*—He readeth likewise all the Questions for these 3, *in Vesperiis Comitiorum, in Die Comitiorum.*

Then another Bedel saith to the Lecturer, in French, *Monsieur, une Parole s'il vous plaist. Les Seigneurs de notre Commencement vous prient, qu'il vous plaist d'etre present Demain à leurs commencements dans l'Eglise de notre Dame.*

Then the Reader comes down out of his seat; and from thence we go to the Logick Schools, and there do the like ; and from thence to the Rhetorick, and so do there likewise...[The Fathers take a high seat in their several schools, and a Bedel goes to each, and summons him to the Benedictions 'which are usually very short.' Then they go to S. Mary's Church ; where all take their places on the Stages, &c.] Mr V. Ch. (if he be a Divine) doth moderate this Divinity Act, and beginneth with a Prayer ; then he maketh a short Speech, at the end of which, he desireth the Father to begin : who, at the end of his speech, calleth up the *Answerer*, who, after his Prayer, readeth his Position. In the mean Time the Bedels deliver his *Verses* to the Vice-Chancellor, Noblemen, &c.

The Position being ended, the Father doth usually confute it, but very briefly, and then he disputeth upon his Son ; who, after he hath repeated the first syllogism, doth endeavour to answer the Objections the Father used against it. Now he falleth to his arguments again, and having disputed a little while upon both Questions, the V. C. taketh him off, and calleth up the Senior Opponent ; and so all the rest in their Seniority. They having all disputed, the V. C. dismisseth the *Answerer*, with a word or 2 in his commendation, if there be cause for it. Then he beginneth his Determination : which being ended, and also his Prayer, the *Respondent*, and all his Brethren standing with him by the Seat, do take this Oath, which the Proctor giveth, [against taking the degree again.].. Then they are to sit upon the Form before the respondents Seat ; and the Bedel having covered their faces with their Hoods, he holdeth up his Staff and saith, *Honorande Pater, ad Commendationem :* which being ended the Bedel doth uncover the Inceptors' Faces and saith again, *Honorande Pater, solent quaeri Quaestiones,* &c. [see p. 245. They then adjourn to dinner at the Answer's college hall.] The University Musicians usually standing by the College Hall, welcome them thither with their loud Music.

At 3 of the Clock the School Bell rings to the

Act, and the V. C. and all the Company with him go to the Commencement House, and so soon as they are placed, the Proctor sitting on the South side, beginneth with a short oration.

Then the *Father in Philosophy* sitting on the North side, with his eldest son on his right Hand, doth begin his exhortation : and after he hath ended his Speech, the Proctor calleth up the VARIER or PRÆ-VARICATOR, who having ended his *Speech*, is dismist by the Proctor : and then the PHILOSOPHER is called for by him : and whilst he is reading his *Position* the Bedels deliver out his *verses* in the like manner as they did in the morning at the Divinity Act. [A short account of the *Law Act*, and of *the Physick Act*, follows : at the former, if not at both, *verses* were distributed.]

In Die Comitiorum... we all go directly to St Mary's, where the V. C. is placed with the Dⁿ· of his own Faculty in the upper stage at the West end of the Church. The Father in divinity sitteth in the lower stage, with his Sons on his right hand.

The Lady Margaret's Professor (who is usually the Moderator this Day) sits on the South Side in the same seat the V. C. did the day before...All being placed, the *Moderator* beginneth with a Prayer, and a short Speech : which being ended, The *Father in* Divinity maketh a Speech ; and when that is done, the Proctor saith, *Honorande Pater, ad Creationem:* Wherein a *Cap*, a *Book*, a *Ring*, a *Chair* and a *Kiss* are used.

Then the Father calleth up the *Answerer*, and showeth him his sons, whom he encourageth, &c.

Then the Answerer beginneth his *Prayer* and *Positions*, and when the Position is reading, the Bedels deliver *verses* and Groats to all Dⁿˢ present, as well Strangers as Gremials [Others reply in turn :] Every Inceptor...is to make a short speech...in which he thanketh the University, and likewise his Father. [Then come *Commendations* and *Prayer:* the Bedel says *Incipe: Ad Oppositum: Pone dextram in Manum Dⁿⁱˢ.* and gives him the oath as in p. 247, and a *Profession* concerning Holy Scripture. With that exception the same order is observed in the other faculties : the Proctor dismissing each with *Exito.* In the *Philosophy* Act the Father having created his Son ;—] the VARIER or PRÆVARICATOR maketh his *Oration.* Then the *Son* maketh a short speech, and disputeth upon him. Then the *Answerer in Philosophy* is called forth, and whilst he is reading his Position the Bedels distribute his *verses* &c. When the Position is ended, the eldest son, and 2 masters of Arts reply upon him. The Senior Mʳ. of Arts usually makes a Speech, before he replieth ; but the 2ᵈ. *opponent* doth not...

After some 10 or 12 are thus created [as described on p. 248] in the Church, the Proctor standeth up, and saith, *Reliqui expectabunt Creationem in Scholis Publicis.*

[They adjourn for that purpose. Next morning *the Law Act* is performed : *Groats* and *Verses* are distributed to the Dⁿˢ· present ; verses alone to noblemen and strangers.   Then *the Physick Act* begins.]

Now if there be no *Music Act*, Mr Proctor maketh a short Speech, thanking the Auditory for their patience and desireth their pardon in case there have been any Slips or mistakes in such variety of exerciseș

Mem. That the VARIER to be in the future Commencement hath this Oath added, *Jurabis* etiam, &c. [as described p. 246]. *He is sworn last, tho' he be one of the first that is called.'*

Gunning's edition of Wall's *Ceremonies* (1828), shews that the forms *Incipe*, *Ad Oppositum*, &c., remain unaltered in the Divinity *Commencement.* The office of *Tripos* and Prevaricator have gone; the name of the former has come to signify the *list* on the back of which the verses are printed (and in later times even the *examination* which results in that list).

Under the section concerning the *First Tripos.* Gunning says, 'Each of the Proctors provides a copy of verses in Latin, which he sends to be printed at the University Press.

The Junior Proctor gives directions about the printing, and orders a number of copies to be sent to the vestry, to be distributed by the company to persons in *Statu Pupillari*, who assemble in the Law Schools in order to obtain them....The Vice-Chancellor, Noblemen, Doctors, and University Officers, fit themselves with gloves, which are provided by the Junior Proctor.   Gloves also are given to the Writers of the Tripos Verses, the Marshall, the School-keeper, the

Yeoman Bedell, the Vice-Chancellor's servant, the Proctor's men, and the Clerk of St Mary's...

Each of the Proctors makes a Speech[1] ['now discontinued'], and the Tripos papers are thrown amongst the Undergraduates.

A Bedell reads from a Tripos paper:

'Baccalaurei quibus sua reservatur Senioritas Comitiis prioribus."'

The like was done at the *Second Tripos* (of the 'Junior Optimes,' *Comitiis Posterioribus*).

In a letter[2] to *Alexander Gill*, dated *Cambridge, July*, 2, 1628, Milton writes; 'One of the fellows of our college, who was to be the respondent in a philosophical disputation for his degree, engaged me to furnish him with some verses which are annually required on this occasion; since he himself had long neglected such frivolous pursuits, and was then intent on more serious studies. Of these I send you a printed copy.'

Of the symbolism of the *insignia doctoralia*[3] Bentley gives an account, well worth perusing, in the Introduction to his edition of Terence. In the Elizabethan statutes the Doctors are called emphatically *pileati*, cap-wearers. Bentley explains the solemn delivery of the *Cap* to the Inceptor to mean that he was free, and also that he was to set out on a toilsome journey, eloquent like Ulysses, cunning like Mercury,

---

[1] Cp. Gunning's *Reminisc.* (1854), II. 80.

[2] Translated from the Latin by *Ro. Fellowes*, A.M. *Oxon.* Milton's Prose Works, 1834, p. 951. The original Latin is given *ibid.* 831.

[3] Cp. *Fr. Burman's* Visit to *Cambridge* in 1702. Mr. Mayor's *Cambridge in Q. Anne's Reign*, p. 116.

workman-like as Vulcan: the three who are especially represented in antiques with *petasi*. The *Bible* was handed to them; firstly *shut*, as mysterious; secondly *open*, as to learned expositors. The *Ring* too symbolizes *liberty*; it is also a sign of *birth* to the doctor's degree; of *betrothal* to the chaste spouse Theology. [The gold ring, with the motto COMMENDAT RARIOR VSVS, was the symbol of authority handed by the Head-master (*Informator*) at Winchester to the *Praefect of Hall*, as a sign that a 'Remedye' or whole-holiday was granted. It was returned on the morning of the next 'whole-school-day.' This custom is known to have been as old as 1550, and expired only a few years ago]. The *Chair* represents stability: it invites the Inceptor to aim at succeeding the Professor: it calls him to the episcopal Throne, or the decanal Stall. It seems luxurious at first, but it will prove hard to fill. Then the *Kiss:* that is a token of *pardon*, of *goodwill*, of *kinship* with Alma Mater. It is no kiss of dalliance (*suavium*), but a kiss of holy love (*osculum*).

John Dunton in his *Life and Errors* (1818, p. 683), gives some quaint reflections in a letter to a friend on the ceremonies which were performed at the Scotch Commencement in 1709, when Edmund Calamy *tertius* had a degree conferred upon him.

He says, that 'Doctor...is a title that was in the Apostles' days;...and Gamaliel is called a Doctor of Law...When University Students have got a Degree in the Arts, then they have a gown and a cap for the sign of it. [He gives also an explanation of the symbolism of the *doctoralia*.] The first Degree is Bachelor of Arts, in Latin *Baccalaureus;* which implies as much as Laurel-berries; which puts me in mind of those Romans who accounted Apollo their God of Wisdom.'

Dr Donaldson, in his Latin Grammar[1], ingeniously derives the word from *bas chevalier,* who, according to the old French feudal system, might not like a *knight banneret* unfold a banner, but was himself a follower. Professor Malden in his essay on the *Origin of Universities*[2], gives a similar explanation. May it not with greater probability be connected with *baculus* or *bacillus,* the Bedel's staff which always was prominent in the ancient ceremonies of admission to degrees[3]? (See Helfenstein, *Contemp. Rev.* IV. 247.)

As to the name *Praevaricator;* several instances of the word are cited in Todd's Johnson's *Dictionary*[4]. Archbishop Trench says, ' " *to prevaricate*" was never employed by good writers of the seventeenth century, without nearer or more remote allusion to the uses of the word in the Roman law courts, where a " praevaricator" (properly a straddler with distorted legs) did not mean generally and loosely, as now with us, one who shuffles, quibbles, and evades; but one who plays false in a particular manner; who undertaking, or, being by his office bound, to prosecute a charge, is in

---

[1] P. 471, ed. 1860.   [2] P. 23 (1835).

[3] See J. Helfenstein in *Contemporary Review,* IV., p. 247, on *Mediaeval Universities.* Also *Diez, Vergleichendes Wörterb. der roman. Sprachen,* ed. 3, p. 43, who rejects both these derivations and also that of *Littré* and *Gachet* from *vassal.*

[4] E. g. *Apology for Smectymnuus* (1642). *Milton's Prose Works,* p. 78. *Hacket's Life of Abp. Williams,* and *Bp. Wren's Monarchy Asserted* (Preface).

L. B. E.   17

secret collusion with the opposite party; and betray-
ing the cause which he affects to support, so manages
the accusation as to obtain not the condemnation,
but the acquittal of the accused; a "feint pleader," as,
I think, in our old law language, he would have been
termed.   How much force would the keeping of this
in mind add to many passages in our elder divines.'
English Past and Present, Lect. IV.

Cicero, in his Second Philippic, says, 'I shall seem,
quod turpissimum est, praevaricatorem *mihi apposu-
isse:*' (i. e. to have set up Antony as *a man of straw*
to argue with me, merely to bring out my own powers).
It is very easy to see how such an office in academical
disputations would degenerate into *badinage.*

Beside the annual Acts at the Commencement in
the summer, there was, on grand occasions at that
time of year, a *public Commencement,* answering to an
especially grand Commemoration at Oxford, on the
Accession of a Sovereign, the Installation of the
Chancellor: (as of the D. of Newcastle, July, 1749.
Cooper's *Annals,* IV. 269—272) or the visit of some
other personage of note.   There were elaborate disputations prepared by the doctors, &c.: some of which
are described in Nichols' *Royal Progresses of James I.*
in 1614, when there was a *Varier* taking part in the
proceedings.   On that occasion 'the Philosophy Act
[on the question *an canes possint facere syllogismos!*]
made amends, and indeed was very excellent, insomuch that the same day the Bishop of Ely [Dr An-
drewes] sent the Moderator, the Answerer, the Varier
or Prevaricator, and one of the Repliers, that were all

of his House [Pembroke] twenty angels apiece.'
Nichols' *Progresses of James I.*, Vol. III. 56. Also,
Hacket's *Life of Abp. Williams* (ed. 1693, I. p. 23),
who was Proctor at the time of the visit of the Elector
Palatine of the Rhine and Prince Charles to Cam-
bridge in 1612—3.

(In addition to the *praevaricator,* there was some- ✓
times at the *Public* Commencements (and on those
occasions only), a MUSICK SPEECH. This was very
much of the same nature as the *Tripos' Speech* at the
Lesser Act in the spring.

In June, 1714, was delivered the famous *Music
Speech* of *Roger Long*[1], M.A., Fellow of Pembroke
Hall, afterwards Master, Lowndes' Professor, and author of a work on Astronomy. The Speech consists
of a medley of Latin prose and English verse, which
was spoken *in St Mary's church.*)

I will first give *Ralph Thoresby*, F.R.S., the Leeds
antiquary's account of his visit to the Commencement
at Cambridge in 1714, and then proceed with some
extracts from *Roger Long's* speech. Thoresby writes
in his *Diary* (ed. *Hunter*, 1830):

'*June* 24. [Friday.] Walked to Bishopsgate-street
about the coach for Cambridge.

July 5. [Monday.] After a weary night, rose by
three; walked to Bishopsgate to take coach for Cambridge, was in time...We passed through...Epping
Forest...thence through Woodford to Bishop Stort-
ford where we dined; thence by Quenden-street and

---

[1] Cooper's *Annals*, IV. 115. Dyer's *Privileges*, Vol. II. (Supplement
to Hist. of Camb. part 2), pp. 81, 126. Nichols, *Lit. Anec.* IV. 492, 663.

Newport to Littlebury...Had a view of Audley-end...
and of Saffron Walden; the country people were
planting that valuable crocus; thence over Gog-ma-
gog's-hill...to Cambridge after a prosperous journey.
Escaped a great danger in the town itself, one of the
wheels of the coach being just off, and the man driving a full career, as is too usual with them. I made
my first visit to Mr Milner, [formerly Vicar of Leeds,]
at Jesus College, and after my return was at a loss
for a lodging, my worthy hostess having let the room
I had agreed for to another for a greater rate, this
busy time of the Commencement. Mr Dover [one of
his coach-mates] and I went to the Red Lion (Mr
Reyner's, a Yorkshireman), where we fixed.

[*Tuesday, July*] 6. Had Mr (now Sir William)
Milner's company to see the public schools and library, but the then keeper could give me little satisfaction. Then to the Commencement, at St Mary's:
our countryman, Dr Edmundson, had kept the Act
yesterday, Mr Waterland, Master of Maudlin, did the
like to-day. Dr James, Dr Edmundson, Dr Gibbons,
and Dr Sherlock (which three commenced yesterday)
were opponents, and Dr Jenkins (Master of St John's)
was moderator; all performed excellently, and the
Praevaricator's speech was smart and ingenious, attended with volleys of hurras : the vocal music, &c.
was curious; and after seven or eight hours' stay
there, being sufficiently wearied, I went thence to
visit Mr Baker (a learned antiquary) at St John's,
whom I never saw before, though I corresponded with
him many years ago,' &c.

[*Wednesday, July*] 7. Early to bespeak a place in the coach, but there was none empty till Friday...I dined at Jesus College...Was after at Trinity College to visit Dr Colbatch, Casuistical Professor of Divinity; after prayers in the delicate Chapel there. [The work of decorating the Chapel had been begun in 1707, under Cotes' directions; but Bentley did not complete it till 1727, when he civilly gave Colbatch the old clock for his church at Orwell.] He very courteously showed me the stately library, of which the obliging Mr Claget is keeper, whose company I also enjoyed. The courteous Professor, Dr Colbatch, would constrain me to sup with him in the College Hall.

[*Friday, July*] 9. Morning, rose before four; then by the care of Dr Colbatch, my very kind friend, was placed in one of the three coaches, where I had better company and accommodations.'

Long was assisted by *Laurence Eusden.*

The
Music Speech
spoken at the
Public Commencement
in
Cambridge
July the 6th 1714
By *Roger Long* M.A.
Fellow of *Pembroke-Hall.*

The *humble Petition* of the Ladies who are all ready to be eaten up with the Spleen,
To think they are to be lock'd up in the Chancel, where they can
· neither see nor be seen;

But must sit i' the Dumps by themselves all stew'd and pent up,
And can only peep through the Lattice, like so many Chickens in a
    Coop;
Whereas last Commencement the Ladies had a Gallery provided near
    enough,
To see the Heads sleep, and the Fellow-Commoners take Snuff.
'Tis true for every Particular how 'twas order'd then we can't so cer-
    tainly know,
Because none of us can remember so long as Sixteen Years ago;
Yet we believe they were more civil to the Ladies then, and good
    Reason why, -
For if we all stay'd at home your Commencement wou'dn't be worth
    a Fly:
For at *Oxford* last Year this is certainly Matter of Fact,
That the Sight of the Ladies and the Music made the best Part of
    their Act.
Now you should consider some of us have been at a very great
    Expence
To rig ourselves out, in order to see the Doctors commence:
We've been forc'd with our Mantua-makers to hold many a Consul-
    tation,
To know whether Mourning or Colours wou'd be most like to be in
    Fashion;
We've sent to Town to know what kind of Heads and Ruffles the
    Ladies wore,
And have rais'd the Price of Whalebone higher than 'twas before;
We've got Intelligence from Church, the Park, the Front-box and
    the Ring,
And to grace St. *Mary's* now wou'dn't make our Cloaths up in the
    Spring.
In Flounces and Furbelows many Experiments have been try'd,
And many an old Gown and Petticoat new scour'd and dy'd.
Some of us for these three Months have scarce been able to rest,
For studying what sort of Complexion wou'd become us best;
And several of us have almost pinch'd ourselves to Death with going
    strait lac'd,
That we might look fuller in the Chest, and more slender in the
    Waste.
And isn't it now intolerable after all this Pains and Cost,
To be coop'd up out of Sight, and have all our Finery lost?
Such cross ill-natur'd Doings as these are even a Saint wou'd vex
To see a Vice-Chancellor so barbarous to those of his own Sex.

We've endeavoured to know the Reason of all this to the utmost of
  our Power,
What has made the Doctors contrive to take us all down a Peg lower,

. . . .

As for that Misfortune the Ladies might e'en thank the Prevaricator,
Who was so extremely arch they were ready to burst their Sides with
  Laughter,

. . . .

LADIES, you see by this Petition.
How much I pitied your Condition ;
And had the Doctors thought it safe,
You'd had a better Place by half :
But 'tis too late now to complain,
I was your Advocate in vain ;
Howe'er you may by my Assistance,
Know what's been doing at a Distance.

The Doctor there, now so smugg'd up to win ye,
Yesterday play'd the Part of *Nicolini ;*
An excellent Performer, though I fear
You thought his Cat-call wasn't quite so clear,
Nic oft the Lyon, who has at him flown,
Like any *London-Prentice* has o'erthrown ;
But all that Battle's nothing at the Opera,
To th' Doctors here with *Heresy, Schism,* and *Popery ;*
Nic charm'd you in a Tongue not understood ;
Here you had *Latin,* is n't that as good ?

With Ring and Kiss the second Act you saw
Our new Professor married to the Law :
'Tis such a Shrew that few wou'd care to venture,
But for that all-prevailing Charm, the Jointure.
He can assist, if you desire, to wed
When by the Almanack it is forbid ;
Or Licence grant without the Banns to marry,
If for three Holidays you're loth to tarry.
For those Transgressions which the Law thinks meet
With Wand be expiated and white Sheet,
He can procure for Criminals of Fashion,
The easier Punishment of Commutation.

Our Physick Doctor next took his Degree,
In hopes the *Title* may enlarge the Fee,
The *Ladies Doctor*—let him feel your Pulse,
I'm sure he need desire no Business else.
He hopes to hear Complaints from some of you,
Doctor I find my self I can't tell how!
At first your Case will put him to a stand,
Till the Broad-piece is slid into his Hand, .
Then he considers—and there's all the Reason
To think the *Bath* may do you good this Season.
You soon resolve to try a Course once more
From which you found such Benefit before:
This shows your Ailment rightly understood,
Nothing but Company had done you good.
And don't you now like that Physitian best,
That in prescribing hits the Patient's Taste?
But since the Vulgar can't hope to command
Fees worthy of a Graduate Doctor's Hand,
He has for publick Good made such Provision,
Every one here may be her own Physitian;
And I, though not equipt in gaudy Jacket,
Have undertaken to retail his Packet.

Are any of you troubled with
The Scurvey that destroys the Teeth
And often causes stinking Breath;
In short, from whose prolific Womb
Almost all our Diseases come.
Do any of ye suffer ever
Obstructions in the Spleen or Liver,
Weakness of Stomach, Back or Reins,
Rheumatick or Nephritick Pains,
Colicks, Consumptions, Dropsies, Itches,
Jaundies, Stone, Gravel, Cramps or Stitches;
Are any here afflicted by
Melancholy they can't tell why;
Does any one the Megrim dread,
Or the Vertigo in the Head,
The Doctor here by me assures ye
He'll take no Mony till he cures ye.
He quickly can remove the Smart,
Of th' Palpitation of the Heart;

And what the hardest Part of th' Trade is,
Of Fits o' th' Mother cure the Ladies.
Is any Husband here chagrin
Because his Wife has got the Spleen,
The Doctor tells you in a trice
Whence the Distemper took its Rise,
Whether the Coach too long has wore,
Or wants a Pair of Horses more;
Whether she has at Ombre lost,
Or is outshin'd by some new Toast;
Has by Gallant been left i' th' Lurch,
Or some Body took her Place at Church;
Her fav'rite Bason has let fall,
Or wa'n't invited to a Ball,
Or silver Tea-kettle was shown
Of newer Fashion than her own.
Is any one in mortal Fear
She shou'dn't have a Son and Heir
The Doctor a Prescription hath
Wou'd save a Journey to the *Bath.*
Whereas Carbuncles sometimes vex
The Faces of the tender Sex,
You've his Cosmetic Secret here,
Wou'd ev'n a Face of Wainscot clear;
Take away Sun-burn, Tan, or Morphew,
And Freckles be they many or few:
And make a *Cambridge* Beauty bright,
At Distance or by Candle-light.
The Doctor can a Dye prepare,
To change the Colour of the Hair,
Teeth when decay'd draw out or clean,
And artificial ones set in.
Are any here disorder'd by
The Tweer or Rolling of the Eye,
Not *Bickerstaff* cou'd cure you better,
By's famous Circumspection-Water.
He has an excellent Receipt
To make young Damsels eat their Meat,
Leave Chalk and Oatmeal, and such Trash,
To diet upon wholesome Flesh.
Besides his Skill in Physiology,
He has been Student in Astrology;

Can tell, if any wants to know
How her Affairs are like to go,
Whether the Cards will her befriend,
Or how a Suit of Law will end.
He can, by Help of Magick Glass,
Shew a young Wench her Sweet-heart's Face:
I' th' Stars or on her Hand can read
How long she's like to live a Maid.
He can with Ease recover soon
The Thimble lost, or silver Spoon;
And help you to find out the Thief,
As well as by the Sheers and Sieve.
Should an old Spark inconstant prove,
By Spells he can renew his Love;
His Blood with Flames rekindled sieze,
As if he'd drunk *Cantharides.*
He has an Amulet or Charm,
Put it but on, you'll take no Harm,
Though you should hear the Schriech-Owl shriek,
Or Cricket chirp, or Death-watch strike;
From the ill Omen it would screen,
Should you at Table make Thirteen;
No Danger need you fear at all,
Should you the Salt-seller let fall,
Or hear the Raven thrice cry *Pork,*
Or lay across your Knife and Fork.
Alas! that he no Herbs can find
To ease the Pain of a love-sick Mind!
But there's no Help in that Disease,
From *Galen* or *Hippocrates:*
All can be done on that Occasion,
Is gaining th' Object of your Passion;
Should that impossible appear,
Then change your Mind, and fix elsewhere;
For this *Probatum* none can doubt,
One Nail will drive another out.

Well then, since here (a Sight that's very rare)
Men much more plentiful than Women are,
Out of this Company, 'tis my Advice,
You unprovided Ladies take your Choice.

Here is Variety enough, you have
The gay, the wise, the witty and the grave.
How do our Proctors there your Fancies hit?
The one for Beauty fam'd, the other Wit.
I shou'd the *Oxford* Doctor first have shown,
But that we've Doctors plenty of our own;
Besides, he'as little need of our good Wishes,
Of whom so many of you long for Kisses.
Some here, since Scarlet has such Charms to win ye,
For Scarlet Gown have laid out many a Guinea.
Though, I shou'd think, you had far better wed
The young in Sable, than the old in Red.
There 's one amongst our Doctors may be found,
Values his Face above a Thousand Pound;
But if you stand, he'll something 'bate perhaps,
Provided that you don't insist on Shapes:
Some of our Dons, in Hopes to make you truckle,
Have for this two Months laid their Wigs in buckle;
If clear-starch'd Band and clean Gloves won't prevail,
Can the laç'd Gown or Cap of Velvet fail?
What though th' Squire be awkward yet and simple,
You'd better take him here than from the *Temple.*

Amongst that fine *Parterre* of handsome Faces,
Do any like a Joynture in *Parnassus?*
Upon us *Fellows* your Affections fix,
But then you can't expect your Coach and Six;
What if we're not o'erstock'd with Land or Money,
We'd gladly settle—our Affections on ye,
And then such Constancy 'mongst us appears,
That some of us can court for twenty Years:
But most of you, I fear, wou'd be but loth
So long before you dine to lay the Cloth.

Will Beaus and Butterflies then please your Fancies ⎫
Well vers'd in Birthrights, Novels and Romances ⎬
Scandal, Plays, Opera's, Fashions, Songs and Dances, ⎭
We'll show you those that most politely can,
Or tap the Snuff-box, or gallant the Fan.
Or do your Inclinations bid you fix
Upon some learn'd Adept in Politicks,
We've those wou'd almost stun ye with the Din
Of who's to be turn'd out and who put in;

Those that can tell you how you ought to like
The new Canal that's cutting at *Mardyke* ;
How far the *Bill* does th' Toleration touch,
Or if we by our Trade shou'd get too much,
What Umbrage it may give our Friends the Dutch ;
How many Grains must to each Power be giv'n
To make the Balance of all *Europe* even :
In short, no Difficulties of State but vanish
When once their Noses are well cram'd with *Spanish*[1].

I've but an Offer more for you to choose,
And that is such I'm sure you can't refuse ;
Our Youth of Quality—ay, there's a Charm
The coldest Virgins Heart will quickly warm ;
Which of you wou'dn't be well pleas'd to sit
In the gilt Chariot grac'd with Coronet,
Diamonds all o'er in the Front-box appear,
And have the grateful Sound salute your Ear
Where-e'er you go—*My Lady* Flounce's *Servant there.*

But whilst we thus lash the Coquet and Prude[2],
Let us not seem to modest Merit rude ;
In blaming Vice we do the Virtuous praise,
Thus Foils the Diamonds Lustre higher raise ;
Thus Shadows stronger make the Light appear,
And *Venus* near an *Ethiop* seems more fair.
To you, ye Fair and Chaste, whose Eyes inspire
Though a resistless yet an awful Fire,
The Muse wou'd fain her humble Tribute bring,
Such Virtues honour, and such Beauties sing,
But for the daring Flight too feeble finds her Wing :
In every thing but her good Wishes poor,
Of them she gladly heaps a boundless Store.
May every rising Sun each circling Year
To Joys untasted be a Harbinger ;
Pleasures unmix'd the happy Hours beguile,
And Love and Fortune on you ever smile ;
May Truth and Honour only know you kind,
And every *Marcia* here a *Juba* find.

[1] A kind of Snuff.
[2] [N.B. *I han't meddled much with the Coquet or Prude under these Characters, but I wanted a Rime to rude.*]

May every Fair—
But see the Sons of Harmony prepare
A Feast might entertain a Cherub's Ear :
Into such Notes *Israel's* prophetick King
Of old awaken'd every sounding String,
When in like Numbers Priests and *Levites* spoke,
Of *Salem's* Temple the Foundation shook.
Attend ye Winds—the hallow'd Sound convey
O'er Heav'n's high Arch to Realms of lasting Day ;
There the Almighty's vengeful Pow'r withstand,
And wrest the Thunder from his threat'ning Hand ;
Call inexhausted Show'rs of Blessings down,
And rain 'em all on pious ANNA's Throne.

(At Cambridge there was no *public* commencement
between 1714, when *Roger Long* gave his MUSIC
SPEECH in *St Mary's* church, and 1730, when John
Taylor[1], M.A., St John's (editor of *Lysias* and of *Demosthenes*), made one in the Senate-house on the occasion of the opening of that building.) It had been
commenced in 1722, but the west end was not completed till about 1768.   It was also called the '*New
Regent House*,' and even '*the Theatre*' (in Ansell's
Authentic Narrative, 1751).
(Taylor also wrote an Ode for music which seems
not to have been performed (Cooper's *Annals*, IV. 208),
but Greene set to music an edition of the Ode to S.
Caecilia's Day which Pope altered for the occasion.
Taylor's *musick speech*[2] however was spoken: and it
has been preserved.) I transcribe it from the reprint
by John Nichols and Son in 1819.   Besides this that

---

[1] Nichols' *Lit. Anecd.* IV. 662 n.
[2] Monk's *Bentley*, II. 294.   Cooper, IV. 208.   Nichols' *Lit. Anecd.*
I. 436, IV. 492, 533–5, 662.

Pamphlet contains other poems by Taylor, a biography of him and of Roger Long, with the *Latin* portion of Long's *Musick Speech* as well as the English verses which I have quoted already.

The Music Speech
at the
Public Commencement in Cambridge,
July 6, 1730.
To which is added
An Ode designed to have been set to Music
on that Occasion.
by
John Taylor, M.A.
Fellow of St. John's College.

DIGNISSIME DOMINE, DOMINE PROCANCELLARIE,
NOBILISSIMA FREQUENTIA,
VENERANDA CAPITA,
DIGNISSIMI DOCTORES,
CORONA HOSPITUM JUCUNDISSIMA,
VIRI SPECTATISSIMI,
JUVENTUS ACADEMICA,

Si, quod mihi in animo vehementer exoptandum semper judicavi, ullum unquam extaret tempus, ubi mea vox et oratio, non dicam apud aures vestras cum laude versari, sed cum aliquâ saltem patientiâ exaudiri posse videretur, illud profectò hodierno die mihi penè consecutus videor. Eorum enim hominum vultus intueor et sensus appello, quibus, tametsi munus et contentio dicendi tota est nostra, gratulatio tamen mecum pariter est communis. Neque profectò cuiquam vestrûm levius hoc aut incredibile videatur, si palàm profitebor, nobis quodammodo ex ipsâ ratione dicendi accedere quandam vim et ubertatem orationis. Nam cum omnem ferè doctrinae humanioris rationem et literarum aciem hebescere intelleximus, nisi adjungatur ornatus et cultura quaedam liberalior, perfectum est summâ Academiae fortunâ, bonorum omnium desiderio, Procancellarii optimi consiliis, laboribus et constantiâ singulari, ut Musas diuturno situ squalentes in nitorem, et munditiem dicam, an elegantiam? hodie vindicatas gratulemur. Non ampliùs intra barbaros penè parietes et iniquis occlusa spatiis versabitur acies ingenii. Vicit,

vicit hodierno die Academiae faustitas, nos aliquando studia, quae privatim cum jucunditate recolimus, posse publicè cum dignitate profiteri.

Jam diu est quod Philosophia caeteráque adeo optimarum artium studia, excussâ illâ quae per tot retro saecula inveteravit barbarie, cultiorem nacta sint disciplinam, et nostrorum hominum ingeniis vindicata in sempiternam famam et uberiorem usuram latiùs emanaverint. Dolebat interea bonis omnibus Academiam ipsam, quae tantae causae vindex esse potuit, deteriori uti fortunâ; et huic eam deesse culturam per quam est effectum ne caeteris omninò artibus deesset. Indigna nimirum et miseranda sanè conditio, Academiam, quae foris et in acie cunctis facilè placebat, domi et in otio sibi soli placere non potuisse; et uti eam praesertim taederet privatae fortunae, cujus publicae disciplinae pigebat neminem.

Haec fuit nobis domesticarum rationum luctuosa facies, cùm eum, quem EUROPA toties experta sit vindicem, toties BRITANNIA delicias compellavit, patronum nacta sit ACADEMIA. Injurius essem et vestrae virtuti gravissimus, si eum ulteriùs nominarem, quem penè gratissima vestra recordatio, praesentes Academiae fortunae, et hi ipsi parietes, pleniùs et expressiùs quam Oratio nostra designabit. Jam ille qui toties saluti aliorum invigilaverit, suae tandem gloriae deesse noluit. Cui quoniam feliciori viâ consulere non potuit, Academiae prospexit fortunis, et futuris literarum moenibus literarium jecit fundamentum. Testor clarissimum illud doctrinae lumen pariter et hortamentum, instructissimam illam librorum copiam, quâ nostrorum hominum ingenia eâdem operâ acuit et devinxit, et tot suae memoriae impressit vestigia, tot vel privatae gloriae monumenta struxit, quot ex uberrimo isto disciplinarum fonte vel universa literarum Respublica sperare possit ornamenta. Quid? annon incredibile prorsus et penè divinum istud beneficium praedicemus, quod non solùm vota exsuperavit, sed penè facultatem capiendi? Noluit non solùm vulgari donandi ratione, verùm etiam nostris parietibus suam contineri et terminari benevolentiam; et quanto illustriorem sibi comparavit laudem superiorum beneficia exsuperando, tanto difficilius reliquit posterioribus negotium aequiparandi sua.

And now a while let sterner Science rest,
While Verse and Music hail the softer guest;
To Beauty sacred are the chord and song,
And homage-numbers speak from whence they sprung;
Theirs is the well-turn'd verse and glowing note,
Whatever Orpheus swell'd, or Prior thought:

By them inspir'd, I draw th' adventurous line;
Theirs all its graces, all the failings mine.

Ladies! our homely simile would say, ⎫
That by the model of this single day ⎬
The gremial doctor shapes his awkward way; ⎭
Rubs, frets, disputes, and thinks his compass through,
Till fifty winters mellow on his brow:
His Noon of Life in reverend slumber past,
His Evening soul to Love awakes at last.
The late, the closing science is a Wife;
And Beauty only cheers the verge of life.

Now will those *Oxford* Wags be apt to fleer
At these old-fashion'd tricks we practise here.
Those enterprising Clerks, I've heard them say,
Have found a better and a nearer way:
Philo with *Hymen* they have learn'd to blend,
And jointure early—on their Dividend.
There Marriage-deeds with Buttery-books can vie;
They storm and conquer—whilst we toast and sigh.

Ladies! we own our Elder Sister's merit;
The forward Girl had e'er a bustling spirit.
'Tis there politeness every genius fits;
Their Heads are Courtiers, and their Squires are Wits:
There *Gentleman* 's a common name to all,
From *Jesus College* down to *New Inn Hall:*
'Tis theirs to soar above our humble tribe,
That think or love as Statutes shall prescribe:
They never felt a fire they durst not own,
Nor rhym'd[1] nor languish'd for a *Fair Unknown:*
Nay Verse, that earnest Pleader with the Fair,
Has found a Portion and Professor[2] there.
Whilst We our barren, widow'd boys regret,
And *Cambridge* Muses are but Spinsters yet.

---

[1] *Taylor* himself wrote some Stanzas '*to the* Fair Unknown [Mrs. Abthorp] *on seeing her at the* Musick-booth at *Sturbridge Fair.*' The verses are printed in the pamphlet from which I am quoting as well as in Nichols' *Anecdotes.*

[2] 'The Poetry Professorship at Oxford had then been recently established by the bounty of Dr. Henry Birkhead.'

By this plain-dealing will the Fair-ones guess
Our clumsy-breeding, and our lame address.
'Tis true our Courtship's homely, but sincere,
And that 's a doctrine which you seldom hear.
Nay, I expect the flatter'd Fair will frown :
I see the pinner o'er the shoulder thrown ;
See every feature glowing with disdain,
The awful rap of the indignant fan ;
The head, unmindful of its glories, tost,
And all the business of the morning lost.

- I hope the charge is not so general yet,
As no good-natur'd comment to admit.
Pray cast your eyes upon our Youth below,
And say what think you of our *purpled* Beau?
For, if the picture 's not exactly true,
The thanks to white-glov'd *Trinity* are due.

What though our *Johnian* plead but scanty worth,
Cold and ungenial as his native North,
Who never taught the Virgin's breast to glow,
Nor rais'd a wish beyond what Vestals know ;
Nor *Jesuit*[1], cloister'd in his pensive cell,
Where vapours dank with contemplation dwell,
Dream out a being to the world unknown,
And sympathize with every changing Moon ;
Though Politicks engross the Sons of *Clare*,
Nor yields the State one moment to the Fair ;
Though *Bene't* mould in indolence and ease,
And whist prolong the balmy rest of *Kay's* :
And one continued solemn slumber reigns,
From untun'd *Sidney* to protesting *Queens'* :
Yet, o ye Fair !—
Let this one dressing, dancing race atone
For all the follies of the pedant gown.
The Templar need not blush for such allies ;
Nor jealous *Christ Church* this applause denies.

How sleek their looks ! how undisturb'd their air,
By midnight vigils, or by morning prayer !

[1] 'Jesus College is in a sequestered situation.'

L. B. E.   18

No pale reflection does those cheeks invade,
No hectic Student scares the yielding Maid.
Long from those shades has learned dust retir'd,
And Toilets shine where Folios once aspir'd.

. Pass but an age—perhaps thy labour[1], *Wren*,
Rear'd to the Muse, displays a softer scene.
Polite reformers ! luxury to see
The pile stand sacred, Heidegger, to Thee.
Where Plato undisturb'd his mansion keeps,
And Homer now past contradiction sleeps,
The Vizard Squire shall hear the Concert's sound,
And Midnight Vestals trip the measur'd round.
I see the Classes into Side-boards flung,
And musty Codes transform'd to modern Song ;
The solemn Wax in gilded Sconces glare,
Where poring Wormius dangled once in air.

Yet still in justice must it be confess'd,
You'll find some *modern* Scholars here at least.
Profound Adepts, which Gallia never knew !
For who would seek Ambassadors in you ?
An handsome Envoy is no blunder yet,
A well-dress'd Member, or a Treasury Wit :
Toupees in Britain's Senate may have rose,
But who e'er read of balance-holding Beaux ?
For, oh ! unhappy to your powder'd heads,
'Tis sure that Brancas thinks, and Fleury reads.

'Tis yours in softer numbers to excel,
To watch how Modes, not Empires, rose and fell ;
Prescribe the haughty Prude a narrower sphere,
And sigh whole Years in treaty with the Fair ;
To parley ages on a Snuff-box hinge,
And mark the periods of the Bugle-fringe.

Memoirs like these, well gilded, may adorn
The ebon cabinet of Squires unborn ;
With what serene composure of the brain
Shall future Beaux turn o'er the rich remain !
The well-spelt page perhaps with rapture dwells
On Pepys' gilded show or Woodward's shells :

[1] Trinity College Library.

Important truths are couch'd in every line;
What *Cambridge* Toast excell'd in Twenty-nine,
What new Embroidery this Commencement grac'd,
And how complexions alter'd since the last.
Ev'n China Nymphs shall live in Sonnet there,
Or Polly Peachum stroll'd to Sturbridge Fair.

Perhaps, though schemes ill suit so soft a pen,
The gilded leaf some secrets may contain.
What shower-drench'd Sinner reeling from the Rose,
Did first the hint of Hackney-chairs propose :
Who bade Sultanas clasp the well-shap'd Maid :
Who first projected Caesar's Cavalcade :
Who fond of planting Opera Statutes here,
Struck out the modish thought of ticketing the Fair.

The moral of my tale might fairly show
The Northern Vicar that *commences* now,
How Alma Mater better days expects,
And Reformation thrives against the next.
But oh, ill-fated Youth ! he sees the last,
And Trent, like Styx, for ever holds him fast :
Before him flits some visionary scene,
He sees *Commencement* rise on every green ;
The red-rob'd Doctor struts before his eyes,
The Galleries of Southern Beauties rise ;
Then moulds his scanty Latin, and less Greek,
And *Hereboords*[1] his parish once a week.

Perhaps, if flames can glow beneath the Pole,
Some distant Caelia fires his youthful soul,
Proud to retail the little All he knew,
He vends his College-stock in Billet-doux ;
Whate'er his Tutor taught his greener age
Of Muses breathing o'er the letter'd page ;
Whate'er our Legendary Schools instill'd,
Or raptur'd Bards with holy transports fill'd,
The Tale, ye Fair-ones, with distrust survey,
There's not one word of truth in all they say.

[1] In quibusdam Codd. '*Harry Hills*' [a retailer of cheap-printed Sermons].

*poterant contradicendi subtilitate veritatem philosophi-
cam eluserunt, et Tripodes sua quaesita ingeniose et
apposite defenderunt,* they ordered that every future
Praevaricator or Tripos who should transgress [p. 84]
the rules of decorum by ridiculing any person or office
or ordinance whatever, should be degraded or imprisoned; and if the case should seem to deserve a
severer punishment, that he should be expelled.

' These stringent regulations may have checked the
licence for a season; but in the year of the Restoration [1660], when the whole University was too outrageous in its mirth to think of any rigid enforcement
of the Statute, it appears from a copy of his speech
still in existence, that the Praevaricator's jibes were
launched forth at all present without mercy and without distinction.'   [The editor of Sir Symonds D'Ewes,
Diary, p. 84, proceeds to give a summary of the speech
to which the reader is referred.   After ridiculing the
Undergraduates, Doctors and Proctors, he compliments a Johnian who had just demolished the arguments of Popery in his public exercise—'*Suis* et ipsa
Roma viribus ruit.'   The Physicians are asked whether
Homer died of the *Iliaca passio*.   He banters those
who have waited through the Troubles for their M.A.
degree,—the Doctors, and the visitors from Oxford.
He proceeds to his Questions 'omnis motus est circu-
laris' and another.   Then after personalities he begs
for quarter from his hearers.]

Such was the audacity of the praevaricator in 1660.
In 1667 he was threatened with expulsion if he should
admit anything into his speech which had not been

previously submitted to the Vice-chancellor for approval. In 1680, in consequence of a report[1] that he had thrown ridicule upon Oates' plot, the University was visited with a sharp reprimand, and threatened with the interference of Parliament. This blow he never recovered; and although in Dr Long's speech in 1714, he is represented as having exerted his jocularity with most marvellous effect,

> ['the Ladies might e'en thank the Prevaricator
> Who was so extremely arch they were ready to burst their Sides
> with Laughter,']

he soon after became defunct. A few chastened and refined traces of spirit may sometimes be found in those annual verses which still bear the name of Tripos, and in one or two unaccredited effusions which had been circulated under the name we are reminded of his pristine audacity. His *joci scurriles* have occasionally been heard from the upper regions of the Senate-House (D'Ewes, *Diary*, p. 89). 'After an interval of a month from the first Act belonging to the Bachelors' Commencement came "THE LATTER ACT" [*Comitia Posteriora*, in Comitiis Minoribus, Thursday, *March* 30]. The *Tripos* on this occasion was a friend of Symonds [D'Ewes, *Diary*, 1620, p. 99], "one Sir Barret" of St John's, the author of the Latin Comedy, which had been acted in the Hall at the preceding Christmas: and we are informed that "both in his position, and in his extempore answering, he made a great deal of sport, and got much credit."

---

[1] Cooper's *Annals*, III. 586.

The *senior Brother* also was one of Symonds' friends, a fellow-commoner of Jesus, by name Saltonstall; and the *junior Brother* was "Sir Tutsham of Trinity a very good scholar" [author of an ode upon the birth of the princess Mary]. The whole was concluded by a disputation between one of the Proctors [p. 100], termed "the *Father*," and two Masters of Arts of St John's.

'Now approached the *Majora Comitia* or GREAT COMMENCEMENT; and the Divinity exercises in the schools came so thick and frequent, that twice in the same day had Symonds the gratification of attending a *Clerum*.... (Symonds [Sir Simonds D'Ewes, *Diary*, 1620, p. 104] proceeds to give an account of an ACT IN MUSIC. A Sophister "came up" in the schools bringing with him a viol: and he commenced his proceedings by playing upon this viol an original *lesson* or exercise. After this he entered upon his *position* "of sol, fa, mi, la," which he defended against *three opponents*. When the opponents had left him master of the field he played another piece, probably in a triumphant strain; which gave the *Moderator* occasion to observe that *ubi* [p. 105] *desinit philosophus, ibi incipit musicus*. This Symonds had recorded as "a very pretty jest."'

Hobson having failed to bring the parcel with his new clothes, D'Ewes presented himself in his old suit on *Sunday* morning, *July* 2, 1620, 'amid the throng in *St Mary's* church. The only seat he could find was upon the highest part of the scaffolding behind the pulpit; "very commodious," but an indifferent place for hearing.' He complains that the *sermon* was 'palpably read:' but that in the afternoon was preached *memoriter.* 'On the morning of *Monday* [July 3], the competition for seats was so eager that Symonds found it expedient to "rise betimes and take an early breakfast, and pass onwards to *St Mary's*" with as little delay as possible; and he whiled away the time until the business of the day commenced, partly in conversation, partly with a book. At length the Vice-Chancellor, Dr Scott of Clare-Hall, opened the proceedings of the day by a speech. After this, the King's Professor of Divinity, Dr Collins, who filled the office of *Father*, "oratorized as his manner was most excellently"...: the *Respondent* in the DIVINITY ACT, Dr Beale, afterwards the Master of St John's and a distinguished royalist, came forward to read the questions of his position. Upon these questions the Professor was about to dispute when he was "cut off" by the Vice-Chancellor who acted as *Moderator;* and the several *opponents*, all Doctors in Divinity, were directed to proceed with their work. After the disputation was finished the Moderator pronounced a learned and copious determination, and the Father dismissed his *son* the Respondent with some merited encomia. This was "the full catastrophe." It being "about *one* of the *clock*" the assemblage broke up, excepting such as like Symonds [D'Ewes, *Diary*, 1620, p. 107] desired to keep their places; and they adjourned for dinner.

[p. 108.] 'At *three o'clock* the combatants were ready for their afternoon's exhibition, which was an ACT IN LAW. After an oration by each of the *Proc-*

tors, the *Praevaricator* "came up;" and when he "was hushed," the disputing commenced. Symonds tells us little of the proceedings, excepting that the wit of the Praevaricator was "indeed pitiful." After all was ended, being invited to supper by the *Junior brother*, who was "of our house," Symonds had his share of the "great feasting" which prevailed.

'On the *Tuesday* morning, Symonds [D'Ewes, *Diary*, p. 108, *July* 4, 1620] came late, and was "fain to rest contented with a very incommodious seat." In the DIVINITY ACT this day, the *Moderator* was the Lady Margaret's Professor, Dr Davenant, a learned theologian of the Calvinistic school; and the *Respondent* was Symonds's friend Micklethwaite, afterwards Preacher at the Temple. The *opponents* were seven commencing Doctors. When the Act was ended, the *Regius Professor* addressed them in a speech, and then "gave them the final complemental *investiture*." There was no interval allowed for dinner: our friend Symonds, however, went to dine with a friend at Trinity, one of the party being George Herbert, then Public Orator. When he returned to St Mary's he found that the PHILOSOPHY ACT had commenced, and that the *Praevaricator* was in the midst of his speech. The *senior Brother*, that is, the senior commencing Master of Arts, "disputed upon the Praevaricator," and the several *opponents* took their turn with the *Respondent*. Then followed the *oaths*, and the *investiture*. After this was a LAW ACT; and with it "our Commencement had a full end." The festivities in the evening were kept up till a late hour: supper was not over "until ten of the clock," and Symonds laid not his head upon his pillow until after twelve. The next morning he "slept chapel."'

At *Oxford* the Act is the first Tuesday in July, and corresponds with our Commencement ; being the occasion when the *acts* or exercises were finished, qualifying students to *commence* as Bachelors of Arts.

The Public Commencements at Oxford were scarcely less frequent than with us; but they created considerable interest in the country at large.

Colley Cibber says, in his *Autobiography* (ed. 2, 1740, p. 382), 'After the Restoration of King *Charles*, before the *Cavalier* and *Roundhead* Parties, under their new Denomination of *Whig* and *Tory*, began again to be politically troublesome, publick Acts at *Oxford* (as I find by the Dates of several Prologues written by *Dryden*, for *Hart*, on those Occasions) have been more frequently held than in later Reigns. Whether the same Party-Dissensions may have occasioned the Discontinuance of them is a Speculation not necessary to be entered into. But these Academical Jubilees have usually been looked upon as a kind of congratulatory Compliment to the Accession of every new Prince to the Throne, and generally as such they have attended them. King *James*, notwithstanding his Religion, had the honour of it ; at which the Players, as usual, assisted.' Cibber then tells an anecdote how *Tony Leigh*, by a piece of impromptu *gag*, in the character of *Teague* in 'the *Committee*,' raised a laugh against *Obadiah Walker*, master of University College, who had become a pervert to Rome.

The following Letter from *James Howell* to his 'Brother, Dr *Howell* at Jesus Colledg in *Oxon.*,' will give some idea of the splendour of the entertainments. (*Epistolae Ho-Elianae*, I. § 5 [misprinted '4'], p. 197): '*Brother*, I have sent you here inclosed Warrants for four brace of Bucks, and a Stag; the last Sir *Arthur Manwaring* procured of the King for you, towards keeping of your Act, I have sent you a Warrant also for a brace of Bucks out of *Waddon* Chace; besides, you shall receive by this Carrier a great Wicker Hamper, with two jouls of Sturgeon, six barrels of pickled Oysters, three barrels of *Bologna* Olives, with some other *Spanish* commodities. [He then offers to present him, on the next vacancy, to the rectory of *Hambledon*, worth £500 a year *communibus annis*, 'as good as some Bishopricks.'] I thank you for inviting me to your Act, I will be with you the next week, God willing; and hope to find my Father there; So with my kind love to Dr *Mansel*, Mr *Watkins*, Mr *Madocks*, and Mr *Napier* at *All-souls*, I rest your loving brother, J. H.

'Lond. 20 *June*, 1628.'

It does not appear whether this were a public Act, or no. A list of the occasions in later years is given in Dr *Rawlinson's MSS*. s. a. 1733 (*Oxoniana*, IV. 282.)

1661. A public act on the first opening of the Theatre. [Is not this a mistake?]

1664. Another. [The building of Theatre it is said was commenced this year. Evelyn and Boyle speak of their visit to the Act, at the opening of the Sheldonian Theatre in 1669. Evelyn had also been at the Act in 1654, and went again in 1675 : see below.]

1678. No Act because there was no D.D. forthcoming, Wood says it was rather because the Univ. didn't choose to bring trade to the town : another report was that they were afraid of the rudeness of the dragoons.

1680. Another.

1693. Another.

1702. On Q. Anne's visit.

1703. Another.

1704. On the victory at Blenheim.

1706. On the celebration of Frankfort University. [See the 2nd Part of this Essay.]

1707. On the visit of the Armenian archbishop.

[1708. The dean of Ch. Ch., *Aldrich,* proposed an *encaenia* for young gentlemen to speak verses and speeches once every term ; but that was not complied with. *Hearne-Bliss,* I. 141.]

1713. On peace with France.

[*Amherst* says (*Terrae Filius* XLVII.) 'I pass therefore to the statute (VII. 1) which ordains *a publick act* to be kept every year. This is now in a manner quite worn out (1721) ; for, of late, there has not been a *publick act* above once in *ten* or *twelve* years ; and then only upon extraordinary occasions, such as a *restoration,* or some *triumph of the church ;* the last that we had, was upon the *glorious peace* in 1712, an *Aera* which the *university dons* were resolved to commemorate, even at the expence of *observing their statutes.* But they would not, however, be too punctual in performing their duty ; and therefore stopt the mouth of the *Terrae-Filius* (who is the *statutable* orator at this solemnity) having intelligence that he design'd to utter something in derogation of the reverend Mr *Vice-Chancellor.*' The intended Speech was printed, and a copy is preserved in the Bodleian, *Pamphlds* 308. It is a ribald attack upon members of the University. See the *Guardian,* nos. 72, 95. Then there seems to have been a long interval as at *Cambridge :* and the next was in—]

1733. Another. [On this occasion also the *Terrae Filius'* Speech was suppressed and printed. A copy is in the Bodleian, *Pamph.* 384.]

At Oxford, as at Cambridge, the Act had from early times been held in the University Church ; but in Oxford the *Theatre* was built eighty years before the *Senate-house* at Cambridge. The following are descriptions by two eminent men who were present at the Inauguration of the Sheldonian Theatre.

John Evelyn was present at the Act in Oxford in the years 1654, 1669, 1675.

On the first occasion he was accompanied by his wife.

July 8, 1654. 'Was spent in hearing several exercises in the schools and after dinner yᵉ Proctors opened yᵉ Act at St Marie's (according to custome) and yᵉ Prevaricators their drolery. Then the Doctors disputed. We supped at Wadham College.'

In 1669 the Act was transferred from St Mary's Church to the new Sheldonian Theatre. On July the 9th, the proceedings lasted from 11 A.M. to 7 P.M.

A letter from Mr *John Wallis* to the Hon. *Ro. Boyle*, dated from *Oxford*, July 17, 1669 (and quoted in a note to Neal's *Hist. of the Puritans*, ed. 3, vol. III. p. 163), gives the following account of the opening of the *Sheldonian Theatre.*

'SIR. After my humble thanks for the honour of yours of July 3, I thought it not unfit to give you some account of our late proceedings here. Friday, July 9, was the dedication of our new theatre. In the morning was held a convocation in it, for entering upon the possession of it ; wherein was read, first the archbishop's instrument of donation (sealed with his archiepiscopal seal) of the theatre, with all its furniture, to the end that St Mary's-church may not be farther profaned by holding the act in it. Next a letter of his, declaring his intention to lay out 2,000*l*.

for a purchase to endow it. Then a letter of thanks to be sent from the university to him, wherein he is acknowledged to be both our creator and redeemer for having not only built a theatre for the act, but, which is more, delivered the Blessed Virgin from being so profaned for the future : he doth, as the words of the letter are, " non tantum condere, hoc est creare, sed etiam redimere." These words, I confess, stopped my mouth from giving a placet to that letter when it was put to the vote. I have since desired Mr Vice-chancellor to consider, whether they are not liable to just exception. He did at first excuse it ; but upon farther thoughts, I suppose he will think fit to alter them, before the letter be sent and registered. After the voting of this letter, Dr South, as university-orator, made a long oration ; the first part of which consisted of satirical invectives against Cromwell, fanatics, the Royal Society, and new philosophy. The next, of encomiastics ; in praise of the archbishop, the theatre, the vice-chancellor, the architect, and the painter. The last of execrations ; against fanatics, conventicles, comprehension and new philosophy ; damning then, *ad inferos ad gehennam.* The oration being ended, some honorary degrees were conferred, and the convocation dissolved.

'The afternoon was spent in panegyric orations, and reciting of poems in several sorts of verse ["interchangeably pronounc'd by the young students plac'd in the rostrums, in Pindarics, Eclogues, Heroics, &c.," *Evelyn's Diary*], composed in praise of the archbishop, the theatre, &c., and crying down fanatics. The

whole action began and ended with a noise of trumpets; and twice was interposed variety of music,
vocal and instrumental; purposely composed for this
occasion.

'On Saturday and Monday, those exercises ap-
pertaining to the act and vespers, which were wont
to be performed in St Mary's church, were had in
the theatre. In which, beside the number of proceeding doctors (nine in divinity, four in law, five in
physic, and one in music), there was little extraordinary; but only that the *terrae filii* for both days
were abominably scurrilous; and so suffered to proceed without the least check or interruption from vice-
chancellor, pro-vice-chancellors, proctors, curators, or
any of those who were to govern the exercises;
which gave so general offence to all honest spectators, that I believe the university hath thereby lost
more reputation than they have gained by all the
rest; all or most of the heads of houses and eminent
persons in the university with their relations being
represented as a company of...and dunces. And
among the rest the excellent lady which your letter
mentions...During this solemnity (and for some days
before and since) have been constantly acted (by the
vice-chancellor's allowance) two stage-plays in a day
(by those of the duke of York's house) at a theatre
erected for that purpose at the town-hall; which
(for aught I hear) was much the more innocent
theatre of the two. It hath been here a common
fame for divers weeks (before, at, and since the act)
that the vice-chancellor had given 300*l.* bond (some

say 500*l.* bond) to the *terrae filii,* to save them harmless whatever they should say, provided it were neither blasphemy nor treason. But this I take to be a slander. A less encouragement would serve the turn with such persons. Since the act (to satisfy the common clamour) the vice-chancellor hath imprisoned both of them: and it is said he means to expel them.'

John Evelyn, who (as we have seen) was also present at the opening Encaenia, complains that 'the *Terrae filius* (the *Universitie Buffoone*) entertain'd the auditorie with a tedious, abusive, sarcastical rhapsodie, most unbecoming the gravity of the Universitie, and that so grossly, that unlesse it be suppress'd it will be of ill consequence, as I afterwards plainly express'd my sense of it both to ye Vice-Chancellor and severall heads of houses, who were perfectly asham'd of it, and resolv'd to take care of it in future. The old facetious way of raillying upon the questions was left off, falling wholy upon persons, so that 'twas rather licentious lyeing and railing than genuine and noble witt.' (Diary of *J. Evelyn,* July 10, 1669.)

It may be worth while in this place to give a full summary of '*An Act at* Oxford. *A Comedy: By the Author of the* Yeoman o' Kent. [*T. Baker.*] *Vicit vim virtus.* London: *Printed for* Bernard Lintott *at the* Middle-Temple-Gate *in* Fleetstreet, 1704.' (pp. 60, 4to., dedicated to the Rt. Hon. *Edward* lord *Dudley* and *Ward.* Bodl. 'Malone, 92.') It 'was not thought fit for Representation:' but the cast of

Characters is given in the Dramatis Personae; as follows:

MEN.

Bloom, A Gentleman Commoner of a good Estate.	Mr *Wilks*.
Captain *Smart*, A Man of Honour, formerly a Pretender to *Berynthia*, but having had his Misfortunes is slighted by her.	Mr *Mills*.
Lampoon, a Ridiculous Mimicking Fellow.	Mr *Cibber*.
Squire *Calf* of *Essex*.	Mr *Bullock*.
Deputy *Driver*, a Stock-jobber and Reformer of Manners.	Mr *Johnson*.
Chum, a Serviter.	Mr *Pinkethman*.

WOMEN.

Berynthia, a fine Lady of large Estate, at *Oxford*.	Mrs *Rogers*.
Arabella, Wife to the Deputy, a Modern City Lady.	Mrs *Moor*.
Mrs *ap Shinken*, a Welch Runt.	Mrs *Lucas*.

Scene, the University.

Act I. *Sc.* I. *The Physick Garden*. Bloom, the gentleman-commoner, is glad to lay aside his Homer, and welcomes Capt. Smart, who has come from London, as we should say now *to Commemoration*, when, as even the Town Spark confesses, 'the lively Season o' the Year, the shining crow'd assembl'd at this time, and the noble situation o' the Place, gives us the nearest shew of Paradise.'

'*Bloom*. Why, faith, this publick Act has drawn hither half the Nation, men o' Fashion come to shew

·some new French Cutt, laugh at Learning, and prove their want of it. The Company, the Diversion, have rais'd us a pitch above ourselves; the Doctors have smugg'd up their old Faces, powder'd their diminutive Bobs, put on their starch'd Bands and their best Prunello Cassocks, with shining Shoes that you might see your Face in. The young Commoners have sold their Books to run to Plays. The Serviters have pawn'd their Beds to treat their shabby Acquaintance, and every College has brew'd.

Smart. But what's the Nature of this publick Act?

Bloom. The Pretence of it is florid Orations and Philosophical Disputes, which few understand, and fewer mind; but in fact 'tis to bring honest Fellows together; for ev'ry College you pass thro', you're accosted thus,—*Sir, will you walk into the Buttery and take a Crust, and a Plate o' Beer* [A *Plate of Ale* is the expression still used at Trin. Coll., Camb., for one of the silver tankards purchased by fellow-commoners for their own use, and left by them as a parting present to the college] *or a Commons* with *us at the Burser's Table;* [*Cōmuna,* or *Cōmina,* the rations provided in hall at *Oxford:* which at *Cambridge* may be supplemented by *Sizings:* at *Cambridge,* the term is now used chiefly for the supplies of bread, butter, &c., taken from the butteries; which answer to the *Battels* at *Oxford*] and then you're carry'd to the Nick-nackatory, where the greatest Curiosity is threescore emperors carv'd upon a Cherrystone, which proves mathematically that threescore grave Faces at *Oxford* may

19—2

make one good Head-piece. [Cp. *Terrae-filius*, No.
XXXIV. 'I went with two or three friends who were
members of the university to the *musaeum*, (vulgarly
called the *Nick-nackatory*,) and the *theatre;* at the
last of which places the *fair young lady* who keeps
the door...shewed me that antiquated *machine* where
my predecessors of witty memory gained such immortal reputation.']

Smart. And what fine Ladies does the Place
afford?

Bloom. Why, this Occasion too has brought in the
Country Dames with their awkward Airs; from Mrs
Abigail Homely, the Beauty o' *Bristol*, to *Nell Simper*
o' *Shrewsbury* that has lost all her Teeth with eating
sweet Cake; but the Tost o' the University is the
fair *Berynthia*...'

Then comes in Mr Deputy *Driver*, a member of
the *Calves-head Club*, a hypocritical rogue, who makes
a trade of the profession of being 'a Bustler for Reformation.'

The Reforming Society which exerted itself in 'demolishing a poor Sunday apple-stall, setting the Beggars at work, that you mayn't be teaz'd to give 'em
anything;' and in attending 'Committees for suppressing *Bartl'mew* Fair,' was not likely to find quarter at
the hands of a dramatic author. *Driver* is made to
say, 'The University has suffer'd the Players to come
down among 'em to affront the *London* Grand Jury,
who have voted 'em Corruptors of Virtuous Prentices,
and modest Chambermaids, and order'd their wicked
Bills to be torn down by the Religious Counter Offi-

cers.' [See *Colley Cibber's* Autobiography: he learnt the character of *Lampoon* in this Play; in which capacity he was to say, in this scene,

'Gentlemen, you'l be at the Play,' we all go this Ev'ning out o' pure Religion.

Smart. Religion?

Lampoon. Ay, Sir, for the Town of *Oxford* has oblig'd the Players to give a Night towards rebuilding the Church that fell down.']

The Deputy continues;—'Sir, I have no Opinion of *Oxford* Education, it breeds nothing but Rakes, and rank Tories; I have a Son at University-learning, with pious *Noncon* in —— ; neither do I approve of your School Authors; *Horace* was a drunken Rogue..., therefore I had the *Pilgrim's Progress* turn'd into Latin by a Scotch Anabaptist for the use of my Son *Bob.*'

As for *Lampoon,*—'an affected carping Fellow,' who has not had the advantage of an university education, and professes to hate 'your odious Gowns, like so many Draggletail Questmen, and your filthy square Caps that seem only to teach one to squint;'—who is one of the 'Criticks that affect to be short-sighted, and peep up at ev'ry Woman they meet, to see if she wears her own Face:'—who says of himself, 'I had a Place at Court...the Quality round me wou'd drop down with laughing 'till I was turn'd out for ridiculing People of Rank, which I thought as Honourable as a witty *Turrae filius* here that's expell'd the University for fear of infecting the Men of burthen'd Learning and prodigious Memory:'—*he* too declares himself no better pleas'd with his visit.—'Well, this Act Medley

wou'd make one die with their Latin Speeches and
Poppet Shews, the *Turrae filius*, [so the visitors seem
to have pronounced it]: and the dancing of the
Ropes, they shou'd e'en put a false Hide upon one o'
the senior Aldermen, and shew him for the *Lincolnshire* Ox.'

Squire *Calf* of *Essex* has come up too: 'the Town's
so full I was forc'd to put my Horses into the *College
Library:*' his object is to make merry with his old
toping friends, and 'to hear the *Turrae Filius*, they
say he designs to be violently witty, and I love an
Oxford Turrae filius better than *Merry Andrew* in
Leicester Fields...I, Sir, was seven years a Gentleman-
Commoner here, and you may see my name every
Day i' th' Buttery Book—*Cormorant Calf* of *Ba-lial
College*, Esq.; sixteen-pence boil'd Beef, eight-pence
Bacon, a penny-half-penny Bread, and a farthing
Carrot.'

Then we have a specimen of an argument on the
merits of the university education between two excellent judges: the worthless Londoner, and the debauch-
ed country squire who had dishonoured Oxford with
his evil habits and by a pretence of learning Latin,
Greek, and Hebrew, geometry, trigonometry, and...
vice. We can hardly credit him with carrying away
even a smattering of any but the last. His principles
would not suit political economists: 'I eat great store
of Beef, that an Ox may bear a good Price, wear Flan-
nel Shirts to encourage the Woollen Manufacture,
and make ev'ry Body drunk to promote the Duties
upon Malt, Salt, Mum, Syder, Pipes, and Perry.'

'*Chum*, whose Father's a Chimney-sweeper, and his Mother a poor Gingerbread Woman at *Cow-Cross*, a Gentleman-Serviter of *Brazen-Nose* College,' whose business is 'to wait upon Gentlemen Commoners, to dress 'em—clean their shoes, and make their exercises;' takes the place of the faithful slave in the old comedy, and by personating a wealthy suitor wins *Berynthia* for his master *Smart*. The poor fellow, whose fortune is soon told,—'the reversion of old shoes which Gentlemen-commoners leave off, two raggs call'd shirts, a dogs-ear'd *Grammar*, and a piece of an *Ovid de Tristibus*',—is rewarded by a present of 500 guineas.

As an interlude in *Act* IV. Sc. 2, the *Theatre at Oxford is discovered* 'A Semi-Circle of the Doctors, to the extent of the Stage. The pupils over them, ladies rang'd on each side, and *Bloom* as *Terrae Filius* seated high, nearer the audience.

A performance of trumpet-musick, and the following ode sett and sung by Mr *Leveridge*.

> Dum cantat Orpheus carmina montibus &c.
>
> .   .   .   .   .   .
>
> Sic en perito cum fidibus tubae
> Clangore misto nascitur altius
> Sublime Sheldoni Theatrum
> Oxonio Decus et Camoenis.'

After the stanzas which are not worth quoting in full; *Bloom*, who is chosen terrae filius, starts up, and delivers an apology for a speech: or rather, an apology, because 'you shall no more have a *Terrae filius* than a *Musick Speech*:' [which was not peculiar to Cambridge, see Wood's *Life*, s. a. 1681].

It is not worth while to transcribe his excuse, inasmuch as it can hardly be a fair specimen, as it was
intended for a town audience. We gather merely
that it depended for effect on its bold and impudent
satire without distinction of person: that it was delivered (to judge from the printing) *in jerks*, either to
give room for applause, or 'to beget an awful expectation in the audience.' It contained scraps of verse
in English or 'the learned languages.' It was 'generally made by a Club:' (so Act IV. Sc. 2, p. 40, Bloom
says; 'the Speech is made by the *Scandal Club*; for
at *Oxford* there must be more heads than one to write
a sensible witty thing).'

Shall we subscribe to the conclusion—'consequently good for nothing'?

The following list of *terrae-filii* is taken from *Oxoniana*, I. 104—110, and Bliss *Life* of A. Wood (1848),
108, 185, 232, 237, 238, 245, 246.

1591. *J. Hoskyns*, M.A. of New College, who afterwards revised
Raleigh's *History of the World*, was expelled for being so 'bitterly
satyrical.'

1632. Mr *Masters*, expelled for his speech. He was restored in
1638.

[1648. A printed speech denouncing the slowness of the Parliament in executing the King.]

1651. The first Act that was kept after the Presbyterians had
taken possession of Oxford. *Tho. Cardes* of Balliol, and *Will. Levint*,
terrae filii.

[1654. Evelyn was present at an Act.]

1655. *Ro. Whitchall*, Ch. Ch. (author of *The Marriage of Arms
and Arts*). The Act was then in St Mary's church: as there had
been none kept for several years, 'it was such a novelty to the
Students...that there was great rudeness committed, both by them
and by the concourse of people who attended, in getting into places
and thrusting out strangers, during the time of the solemnity. Where-

upon the V. C., Dr Greenwood of B. N. C., a severe and choleric governor, was forced to get several guards of Musquetiers, out of the Parliament garrison then in Oxford, to keep all the doors and avenues, and to let no body in, except those the V. C. or his Deputies appointed. There was then great quarrelling between the Scholars and the Soldiers, and thereupon blows and bloody noses followed.'

The other *terrae filius* was *John Glendall* M.A., fellow of B. N. C., 'a great mimic, and acted well in several plays, which the Scholars acted by stealth, either in the stone house behind and south-ward from Pembroke College, or in Kettle Hall, or at Holywell Mill, or in the Refectory at Gloucester Hall. A. W. was well acquainted with him and delighted in his company.'

1657. *Danvers* of Trinity.

1658. *Tho. Pittis* of Trinity, then of Lincoln. His speech being 'much disliked by the *godly party* of those times,' he was expelled. His colleague was (dean) *Lanc. Addison*, (father of Joseph,) who had to recant.

1660. No Act.

1661. *Field* of Trin.

1662. No Act.

1663. *John Edwards*, Trin. (*Saturni.*) *Jos. Brooks*, Ch. Ch. (*die Lunae*).

1664. *Ric. Wood*, Joan. *Sat.*

Wm. Cave, Magd. *Monday.*

1665—8. No Acts, the Theatre in building.

1669. *Hen. Gerard*, Wadh.

Tho. Hayes, B. N. C., who then took his M.D. degree. This was the occasion of the Inauguration of the Sheldonian Theatre. Evelyn was present, and was shocked. *South* made an Oration.

1670. No Act.

1671. *Sat.*

Nich. Hall. Wadh. *Monday.*

1673. *John Shirley*, Trin, reflected upon Wood's antiquarian tastes in 'a speech full of obsenity and prophaness...' saying that ' the society of Merton would not let me live in the College, for fear I should pluck it down to search after antiquities, that I was so great a lover of antiquities that I loved to live in a cockleloft rather [than] in a spacious chamber, that I was Vir caducus, that I intended to put the pictures of mother Louse, and mother George two old wives into my book, I would not let it be printed, because I would not have it new and common.'

1675. *Venables Keeling*, Ch. Ch. [Evelyn present.]

[1680. A Public Act.]

1681. *Moore* [qu. *John Mower*] Merton, 'came up on the Saturday, very dull, and because he reflected on Sr. Tho. Spencer's doings..., his son, who was there, cudgelled him afterwards in the Row-Buck yard, dogged him to the place with another...

Monday, [*Mathias*] *Henvill* of New-Inn hall, (a married man) and the other *Terrae filius* made up what was wanting on Saturday, full of waggery and roguery, but little wit.'

1682. [*Henry*] *Bowles* of New Coll. on Saturday, much against Ch. Ch. *James Allestree* of Ch. Ch., Monday, much against New College and the *Terrae filius* of Saturday, but replyed by the said *Terrae filius* being proproctor, for Dingley junr. proctor, both very well, and gave great content.

[In 1693 [1], 1702, 1703, 1704, 1706, 1707, there were public acts.

In the *Oxford Packet*, (printed in 1714, by the publisher of *News from Both Universities*), is advertised '2nd edition of the *University Miscellany* or *More Burning Work for the Oxford Convocation*: viz.,

Two Speeches spoken by the Terrae Filius, *Mr* R—s of Magdalen Hall, *in the Theater at the Publick Act* 1703.']

Oct. 3, 1713. Dr Gardiner, chosen V. C. again the third time for the year ensuing. At the same time a Libel called a speech that was intended to have been spoken by the Terrae Filius, was by order of the convocation burnt by the hands of the common Bedel in the Theatre yard. [Bodl. *Pamphlets*, 308.]

This Act seems to have created considerable excitement in the country. In the *Guardian*, June 1713, (Nos. 72, 96), are several whimsical notices of the migration of the Players to Oxford, and some anxious reflexions as to the probable conduct of the *Terrae-*

---

[1] Compare 'the *Oxford-Act*: A Poem, *London*; Printed for *Randal Taylor*, near *Stationers-Hall*, 1613.' This is a misprint for 1693. 4to. pp. 22. [Bodl. C. 6. 14. *Linc.*]

filius. Mr Ironside says, 'In my time I remember the *Terrae-filius* contented himself with being bitter upon the Pope, or chastising the *Turk;* and raised a serious and manly Mirth, and adapted to the Dignity of his Auditory, by exposing the false Reasonings of the Heretick, or ridiculing the clumsy Pretenders to Genius and Politeness. In the jovial Reign of King *Charles* the Second, wherein never did more Wit or more Ribaldry abound, the Fashion of being arch upon all that was Grave, and waggish upon the Ladies, crept into our Seats of Learning upon these Occasions. This was managed grosly and awkwardly enough, in a Place where the general Plainness and Simplicity of Manners could ill bear the Mention of such Crimes, as in Courts and great Cities are called by the specious Names of Air and Galantry[1].'

It was, I suppose, of a terrae filius about this period that Amherst speaks (*Terrae-F.* No. I.). 'One of these academical *pickle-herrings* scurrilously affronted the learned president of St *John's* College (in defiance of the statute *de contumeliis compescendis*), by shaking a box and dice in the theatre, and calling out to him by name as he came in, in this manner, *Jacta est alea, doctor, Seven's the main,* in allusion to a scandalous report handed about by the doctor's enemies, that he was guilty of that infamous practice, and had lost great sums of *other people's* money at dice.'

The following is the account of the Oxford Commencement given by John Ayliffe, LL.D. (who vacated his fellowship at New College), in his *Antient*

---

[1] *Guardian,* 72.

and Present State of the Univ. of *Oxford*, 1714
(ii. 131—135).

    'There is a general Commencement once every Year in all the
Faculties of Learning, which is called the *Act* at *Oxford*, and the
Commencement at *Cambridge*, which *Act* is opened on the *Friday*
following the 7th of *July*, and Exercises perform'd in the Schools
on *Saturday* and *Monday* ensuing the opening thereof, and also in
the publick Theatre with great Solemnity. On *Saturday*, in the
Forenoon, all the Professors and Lecturers read in the several Arts
and Sciences, all cloathed in their proper Habits, as was heretofore
usual at the *Vespers* or Evening Exercises, which are only now Disputations in the several Parts of Learning, from One o'Clock till
Five in the Afternoon, the *Artists* Disputations being had in the
Theatre, and those of *Divinity, Law* and *Physick*, in their proper
Schools. The Inceptors in Arts dispute on three *Philosophical* Questions, and one of these Inceptors (for so are the Masters called, who
stand for their Regency in this solemn *Act*) to be appointed by the
Senior Proctor, has the Place of the Respondent. And first, the
Senior Proctor opposes on all the Questions, and confirms an argument on the First; then the Pro-Proctor and *Terrae-Filius* dispute
on the Second; and lastly the *Junior* Proctor on the Third Question; and all the Inceptors are oblig'd to attend these Disputations
from the Beginning to the End, under the Pain of 3*s*. 4*d*. At the
equal expence of all the Inceptors, there is a sumptuous and elegant
Supper at the College or Hall of the *Senior* of each Faculty, for the
Entertainment of the Doctors, called the *Act-Supper*. On *Sunday*
between the *Vespers* and the *Comitia* (for so are the Exercises of
Saturday and *Monday* stiled) there are two Sermons in the *English*
tongue, at St *Mary's* Church, preach'd by any one of the Inceptors,
as the Vice-Chancellor shall appoint, being Doctors of *Divinity*, in
this *Act*. On *Monday* at Nine a Clock, all the Inceptors go with
the Beadles of their several Faculties to St *Mary's*, and there, after
Prayers at the Communion-Table, make Oblations; and if any Person shall absent himself, or be irreverently present, he shall be
mulcted five Shillings, and moreover punish'd at the Vice-Chancellor's Pleasure. Then the Comitial Exercises beginning, the *Senior*
Proctor mounts the Pew on the *West* side of the Theatre, and the
Junior Proctor the Pew opposite to him on the *East* side. The
Professor of Physic, with his Inceptors, on the *West*; and the Law
Professor, with his Inceptors, on the *East* Side thereof; and the

Divinity Professor, with his Inceptors, on the *North* side, under the Vice-Chancellor; and the Inceptors in Musick, with their Professor in the Musick Gallery, on the *South*; and at these *Comitial* Disputations, the same method is used in respect of the Agents, as at *Vespers, viz.* first, the *Senior* Proctors; then the *Terrae-Filius*, and Pro-Proctor; and lastly, the *Junior* Proctor; and he who was Respondent the year before, is the *Magister Replicans* this year. The first *Opponent* among the Inceptors has a Book given him, at the End of Disputations, by the *Senior* Proctor (who in respect of the *Artists* Inceptors, is called *Father* of the *Comitia*) and is also created Master by a kiss, and putting on his Cap. After the *Comitial* Exercises in Arts are ended, if there be any Person taking a Musick Degree, he is to perform a Song of Six or Eight Parts on *Vocal* and *Instrumental* Musick, and then he shall have his Creation from the *Savilian* Professors, &c. After the performing of the Exercises, and the Creation of Doctors, according to a prescript Form in each Faculty, the Vice-Chancellor closes the Act in a solemn Speech; wherein it is usual for him to commemorate the Transactions of the year past, and especially such Benefactions as have been given to the University. And after the end of the *Act*, the Vice-Chancellor, with the Regents of the foregoing year, immediately assemble in the Congregation-House; where, at the supplication of the Doctors and Masters newly created, they are wont to dispense with the wearing of *Boots* and *Slop Shoes*, to which the Doctors and Masters of the Act are oblig'd, during the *Comitia*. On *Tuesday* after the *Comitia* a *Latin* Sermon is preach'd to the Clergy, at Eight in the Morning in St *Mary's* Church; the Preacher to be either some Doctor, or Batchelor in *Divinity*, and of the Vice-Chancellor's Appointment, with a *Pre-monition* for this End from the Vice-Chancellor for three months before hand. The Questions to be disputed on in each Faculty, are to be approved by the congregation of Masters some time before the Act; and because that *Civilians* ought to know the differences between the Civil and our own *Municipal* Laws, one of the Law Questions ought to have some Affinity with the *Common Law* of *England*; wherein the Professor, by a short Speech, ought to shew, what the one and what the other Law maintains. If any Contumelious, Reproachful, or Defamatory Language be given in any Speech or Argument at Disputations, the Vice-Chancellor may convene the Person before him, and command a Copy of his Speech; and if he pretends that he has no Copy, he may convict him by Oath, and punish him according to the Heinousness of the Offence, in respect of Persons and other circumstances, either by publick

Recantation, Imprisonment, or Banishment from the University, as a Disturber of the publick Peace; besides the satisfaction he is oblig'd to make to the Party injur'd; so that there is not that Licence given for an impudent Buffoon, of no Reputation in himself, called a *Terrae-Filius*, to sport and play with the good Name and Reputation of others; but the business of this *Terrae-Filius*, is a solemn and grave Disputation. And although this manner of sportive Wit had its first original at the Time of the Reformation, when the gross Absurdities and Superstitions of the *Roman* Church were to be exposed, and should have been restrain'd to Things, and not have reached Mens Persons and Characters; yet it has since become very scandalous and abusive, and in no wise to be tolerated in an University, where nothing ought to appear but Religion, Learning, and good Manners.'

In the year 1721 (*Jan.* 11, to *July* 6), Nicholas Amherst published his 50 numbers of the '*Terrae Filius*: Or, the Secret History of the University of of *Oxford;* in Several Essays.' In the first number he writes,

'It has till of late been a custom, from time immemorial, for one of our family to mount the *Rostrum* at *Oxford* at certain seasons, and divert an innumerable crowd of spectators, who flocked thither to hear him from all parts, with a merry oration in the *Fescennine* manner interspers'd with secret history, raillery, and sarcasm, as the occasion of the times supply'd him with matter.'

The frontispiece of the edition of 1726 is an engraving by *Hogarth*. In it is depicted the interior of the Theatre. In the gallery is a crowd of academical personages, one of whom is waving his arm and yelling: another climbs down over the railings. The Vice-chancellor is seated on a throne, and in a chair on his right hand below the steps is a proctor (perhaps); while others are sitting in the seats below the gallery. In the foreground is a structure which may be intended for 'that antiquated *machine*' mentioned in No. XXXIV., the *rostrum* of the *terrae filius*. On one side stands a portly *don* who has torn the *Terrae filius* speech, while the miserable culprit is being attacked by a crowd of doctors and infuriated *toasts*, one of whom has laid hold of his cap, another of his wig, while two *dons* ungown him, and a dog is barking at the noise. In spite of the efforts of Amherst there was no public act at Oxford between the years 1713 and 1733. In Nichols' Annals of Bowyer's Press (*Anecd.* Vol. II.), it is stated that the year 1733 was 'rendered remarkable in the literary world by the brilliancy of the Public Act at Oxford.' Then was published '*Bellus Homo et Academicus* Recitârunt in Theatro *Sheldoniano* ad Comitia *Oxoniensia* 1733, *Lodovicus Langton* et *Thomas Barber*, Collegii Div. *Magd.* Commensales. By *W. Hasledine* of *Magdalene* College. Accedit Oratio *Petri Francisci Courayer*, S. T. P. habita in iisdem Comitiis 5 Id. *Julii.' Will. Bowyer*, Esq., F. R. S., printer, himself wrote 'an English Poem called *the Beau and the Academick*, a Dialogue in Imitation of the *Bellus Homo et Academicus* spoken at the late Publick Act at Oxford; addressed to the Ladies.' The Latin poem is printed in *Selecta Poemata Anglorum...Accurante* Edwardo Popham, *Coll.* Oriel. Oxon., *nuper Socio.*

Splendid though the Act may have been, the *Terrae filius* was no better behaved than on the preceding occasion. His speech also was suppressed:

but there is a copy of it in the Bodleian (*Pamph.* 384). The late Mr R. Robinson of Queen's gave the more interesting points in it in the *Oxf. Undergrad. Journal*, May 29, 1867.

The *Terrae filius* 'begins by apostrophizing the Bishop (of Oxford I presume) as a "mitred Hog," and by asking what he has to do with a wife of eighteen. *Ch. Ch.* was unpopular: the place was indeed at its zenith, it had its fill of rich aristocrats, its Tutors were intelligent, and appreciated the value of their connexion with Westminster, it could boast of West (the "Favonius," who always was "to have a front box in the theatre of" Gray's "little heart,") and of Budgell; but the men gave themselves airs, with wonderful ignorance and conceit they claimed to belong to an House, not to a College; those of other Colleges were 'squils' and 'hodmen,' they were accustomed with suppressed blushes to style their foundation "royal and ample;" Gibbon was wrong in saying that Locke was expelled on speculative grounds, but they understood him as little as they saw why such a fuss should be made about Handel: accordingly this Terrae Filius sneers at the establishment, and brands the Dean [*John Conybeare*, elected the preceding year] as a courtier. "Long, little President of *Trinity*," [Geo. Huddesford,] he proceeds, "hast thou expected the Lash and screened thyself for Fear behind thy Barrel-gutted Fellows." The "worthy Head [Theo. Leigh] and men of *Balliol*— I mean Belial" had yet to make their character and that of their house; the shape of the seats of their chairs at the high table was indeed unexceptionable, and must have been excogitated with deep thought, —but many of the men ate raw turnips, the Dons used to punish some delinquents by sending them to the Sacrament, and others by heavily fining them. '*Lincoln* always was and always will be under the devil's inspection,' but whether the devil was the statue over the College or John Wesley I can't say. *S. John's* boasts its "Jacobite topers." In *Worcester* "there cannot be found [a Parson] who can easily read [Prayers] in English, much less in Latin;" perhaps Shadwell's Lady Cheatly got her chaplain there. *New College* is a place where boys elect a boy as their Warden [John Coxed]. The Fellows of *Queen's* are "haughty and imperious" Aristotelians. In *All Souls'* "live your Smarts, your gallant gentlemen;" by their sensual habits (which bear out another satirist in coupling them with Johnians) you would think them all bodies and no souls at all; they got so drunk as to prove that *Homo* is not necessarily a *noun substantive*, by way of maintaining their Tudor reputation of being swashbucklers. *Brasenose* engrosses good livings, and brews ale which flies to the seasoned head of an Essex Squire; in a play, a man who wishes to be taken for a Fellow of that College has to use a large pillow for a stomach. [Miller's *Humours of Oxford*, Act. IV.] *Exeter* is "governed by old women" (who, when Shaftesbury was there, enfuriated the men by empoverishing the beer). [Jos. Atwell, Rector, 1733.] *Jesus* College is verminous and smells of toasted cheese. The

L. B. E. 20

Oriel men are all in debt. The *Magdalen* Dons are loose livers. The *Merton* men are "Lollards" (perhaps Low Church) and, as Meadowcourt, Hanoverian.'

In 1763 the Encaenia 'was selected by the Academical body as the occasion for giving effect to its approval of the management of public affairs; and this they did by some accessories to the ordinary display at Commemoration designed to mark it as an event "in honour of the peace." But there was nothing after all in the three days' demonstration, which gives it a title to the character of a remarkable occurrence, or calls for more than this general notice; unless we may advert to the appearance on the stage of a Terrae Filius, who, despite the danger of an academical mittimus to the Castle or Bocardo, rose up to assert "the privilege of his family." He was not, however, a veritable descendant of those quasi statutable personages who claimed a right, as established by the ancient forms of the University, to exercise their talents for satire and raillery at every celebration of the Act, and who, as the occasion of the times supplied matter, were accustomed to make very free on the Rostrum of the Theatre with the public and private character of those drest in authority, until at length their freedom of speech, exceeding all bounds of moderation or decency, brought about a discontinuation of their office. He, notwithstanding, though announced as a mere out-door actor, produced by the programme of his intended performances, no little consternation among unmatriculated, as well as matriculated, equally in dismay at anticipated revelations, as if the sallies of his wit could not touch a gown and cassock without glancing off upon the fame of town celebrities. It was rumoured that the Mayor and Corporation were first seized with the panic, and were for taking steps ; but, upon its being held to be an University business and to fall more properly under the cognizance of the House of Convocation, ",from the body corporate," so says our authority, "the cause was removed, by a new kind of *certiorari,* to the body academical." Yet after all, Terrae Filius—and we believe he is the last that appeared in any shape—proved in the end a harmless satirist, and did nothing seriously to disturb the usual course of the solemnities and festivities.' (*Oxford during the Last Century,* pp. 12, 13, reprinted from the *Oxford Chronicle,* 1859.)

The name however was still remembered in 1779, when Mrs Cowley puts into the mouth of *Gradus,* an awkard wooer from B.N.C., the following sentiment : 'There is something in her eye so sarcastic, I'd rather pronounce the *terrae filius* than address her.' (*Who's the Dupe?* I. 3.) Evelyn speaks of the *Praevaricator* at Oxford : but it is most probable that this was a loose way of applying the term peculiar to one university to a class existing at the other. In the same way, the term *Fellow-commoner* used at Oxford to be convertible with *Gentleman-commoner.* Eachard in his *Grounds and Occasion of the Contempt of the Clergy,* 1670, p. 37, mentions in one clause the *Tripus Terrae filius,* and *Praevaricator.*

20—2

ᴸ⸝ ⟮At Oxford, as well as at Cambridge, there were
Musick Speeches (so called in *Life of* A. Wood, s.a.
1681), more commonly known there as *Musick*
Lectures. The following list is taken from Wood's
Life, *sub annis* 1660, 1679, 1681, 1682, 1683.

1660. 'There was a most excellent musick-lecture of the practick
part in the public school of that facultie (*May* 24), when A. W. performed a part on the violin. There were also voices, and by the direction of Edw. Low, organist of Ch. Church, who was then the deputy
professor for Dr Wilson, all things were carried very well, and gave
great content to the most numerous auditory. This meeting was to congratulate his majestie's safe arrival to his kingdomes.'

1661. [Richard] Torless of St John's.
    [John] Fitz-Williams of Magd. coll. [probationer.]
1664. Mr [Thomas] Jeamson of Wadh.
1672. ——
1673. [Anthony] Wolveridge, All Souls.
1674. Charles Holt of Magd. coll.
1675. [Francis] Slatter of C. C. C.
1676. —— —— Jesus coll.
1677. [Richard] Strickland of Magd. coll. [fellow.]
1678. John Grubb of Ch. Ch.
1679. James Allestree of Ch. Ch. in the *Theatre:* a dispensation
was passed in *June* to remove it thither from the *Music school:* 'and
the 12 *July* following it was solemnly and well done at 7 and 8 in the
morning.'

1680. —— 's Northon of Ch. Ch. in the Theatre.
1681. [Thomas] Sawyer [demy] of Magd. coll. in the Musick
school. 'The reason, as was pretended, why he did not speak it
in the Theatre was, because the Bp. said, people broke down many
things there to the charge of the university; but we all imagined the
true reason to be because he was not a Ch. Ch. man, [like his predecessors Allestree and Northon,] and therefore would not allow the Theatre
to grace him. Grand partiality !'

1682. Wm. Lloyd of Jesus coll. in the musick school.

At Oxford the nearest approach to the Cambridge
Tripos verses is to be found in the *Carmina Quadra-*

gesimalia or Lent Verses, which bore a close resemblance to the early *carmina comitialia* of Duport and others at our University. They are something of the nature of the Winchester '*vulgus:*' still more of that of the Westminster epigrams. They are described in the second *fasciculus* (edited by Ant. Parsons) in 1748, as Verses recited publicly in the schools on the First Day of Lent by the determining Bachelors of each college. They are composed on the theme of the disputation, which is to follow their recitation, as one of the exercises *in Quadragesima* qualifying for the degree. They are epigrammatical illustrations of the subject: not always very philosophical, but elegant. Este collected one volume of those composed by Christ Church men, and Parsons another: the two appeared respectively in the years 1723 and 1748.

Amherst (*Terrae Filius*, No. L.) says that the courts of justice were not 'the only places in which the *constitutioners* [Members of the Oxford *Constitution* Club about 1715] met with unjust and scandalous usage: *St Mary's Golgotha*, [in the old Clarendon buildings,] the *Theatre, Convocation-house,* and *Schools,* eccho'd with invectives and anathemas against them. The most scurrilous reflections on them were constantly thrown out in the *Lent verses*, sermons, declamations, and other publick exercises.'

Specimens of the Lent Verses will be found in *Selecta Poemata Anglorum Latina*, accurante *Ed. Popham*, coll. *Oriel. Oxon.*, nuper Soc. (Dodsley, 1774, 1779, &c.). The following references to several of those in Este's, and in Parsons' volumes, will give a notion of their scope :—

CARMINA QVADRAGESIMALIA.   Vol. I. 1723 (edited by *C. Este*).

Page 1.   An Idem semper agat Idem?   *Affr.*   The monotonous life of a Fellow.

> 'Conviva assiduus, lumbo venerandus ovino
> Pascitur, et totos credo vorasse greges.'

By the Common-room fire

> 'tria sumuntur pocula, tresque tubi.'

[In my copy this is assigned to 'Ja. Bramston 1717.' See however *Wrangham's Zouch* lxvi, where abp. *Markham's* name is mentioned.

Page 14.　The *Masquerade* (so also p. 71).

　,,　15.　*Cobb*, the fat Innkeeper.

　,,　23.　' Tyro magis sapiens quo toga scissa magis.'

　,,　25, 137.　Sign-boards.

　,,　32.　Bellringing.

　,,　36.　A Cantab borrows fine clothes (*gômers*, we called them at Winchester) and money to go home.

Page 37.　The Physick Garden.

　,,　38.　The Lownger.

　,,　39.　Perhaps the *Beefsteak* Club ' *Eastcourto* Praeside.'

　,,　41.　Statue of the Muses on the *Clarendon*.

　,,　43.　*Ogilvy's* Aeneid.

　,,　44.　*Pinkethman*, the comic actor.

　,,　51.　Drawing lots on S. *Valentine's* Day.

　,,　53.　*Falstaff* at *Oxford*.

　,,　60.　Perhaps a *Winchester* Carrier, who carries no watch in his pocket.

Page 66.　*Busby's* monument.   (See the *Spectator*, No. 329.)

　,,　78.　Panegyric on Ale.

　,,　89, 90.　*Vesey*, the beadle.

　,,　91, 92, 142.　*Clusius*.　Probably ' Great Tom,' the Ch. Ch. bell.

Page 93.　A lady's Fan.

　,,　98.　Tennis.

　,,　102.　Grinning through horse-collars.　(cp. *Uffenbach Reisen*, iii. 159. Hughes, *Scouring of the White Horse*.)

Page 104.　The bewilderment of an old Bedmaker.

Page 110. The Oxford Almanac 1702.

,, 115. The Wooden Horse, a punishment for thieves and those who cried *An Ormond.*

Page 115. *Procter*, a sorry horsedealer.

,, 117. *Thames* and *Isis.*

,, 118. *Cloe's* Watch.

,, 118. The punishment of *Curll* by the *Westminster* Scholars for publishing a surreptitious and incorrect edition of a Speech.

Page 120. Blindman's Buff.

,, 124. Different opinions on the discovery of a Roman pavement near Woodstock in 1712.

Page 125, 126. The doctors *Abel, Read,* and Mrs *Kirby.*

,, 130. *Chloe's* hoop-petticoat.

,, 131. *Sanga's* Christmas pies.

,, 136. Automata pictures.

,, 139. *Addison's* Ovid. (Smalridge, 1718.)

,, 150. *Shotover.*

,, 152, 155. The mysteries of Housewifery.

,, 157. Cocoa.

,, 160. Tythe-pig.

,, 162. The horse who 'knelt for queen *Anne* and stampt for the Turk.'

Page 165. An 'Oxford Nightcap.'

References are made to the *Tatler, Spectator, Guardian*; to *Prior, Garth's* Dispensary, *King's* Miscellanies, 'Three Hours after Marriage,' 'Tale of a Tub,' &c. &c.

The list of Authors as noted in MS. in my copy is as follows (the numbers relating to the *page* on which a set of verses *begins*) :

Adams 33.
Alsop 33, 96, 110, 158.
Battely 41.
Bold 53, 142.
R. Booth 22, 86, 121, 121, 125, 145.
Ja. Bramston 1, 10, 14, 32, 36, 44, 130.
Burton 14.
Cade 7, 41, 127.
Davis 23, 66, 87.
B. Dowdeswell 129, 144.
Dwight 109.

In Vol. II. 1747—8, edited by *A. Parsons*, the following may be noticed :

Page 3. Fair *Rosamond.*
 „   7. *Oxford* Meadows.
 ,, 21. The herb *Margelina* or Poor Man's Weather Glass.
 ,, 23. *Chloe* cutting figures in paper.
 „   24. The Death of Dr *Freind.*
 ,, 35. *Fontaine.*
 „   53. *Gay's* Black Ey'd *Susan.*
 „   56. Dr *Hales.*
 ,, 58. Carrier pigeon.
 „   66. An imitation of the last canto of the *Rape of the Lock.*

    ' The bells she jingled and the whistle blew,' &c.

 „   68. *Heloise* to *Abaelard.*
 „   69. The Seven Ages of Man.
 „   73. Milton's *Sabrina.*
 „   109. Nautilus.
 „   116. *Rape of the Lock*, v., where 'all things lost are treasured.'
 ,, 129. The Witches' broth, *Macbeth.*
 ,, 137. *Wolsey's* Speech.

Reference is made to *Addison's* Travels, the *Spectator, Dryden's* Knight's Tale and ' All for Love,' The *Pleasures of Imagination. Milton* and *Othello.*

The authors noted in my copy are

Bale 71.
Ro. Bedingfield 14, 72, 86, 104.
Bruce 13, 77, 81, 89, 90.
Crackenode 144, 147, 148.
Cretcheley S. 54.
Dowdeswell 52.
Freind 53.
Gilpin 40.
Ld. Harley 13, 98, 101.
Hay 25, 27, 33.
Impey 7, 11, 16, 85, 96, 97, 118, 121, 133, 134, 145.
Jubb 35, 76.
Kendal 123, 139.

Lent verses were written also by *Lowth, South, Johnson, Vincent Bourne, &c.*

At Cambridge '*Lent term* (which for many years had been a time of great disorder by reason of divers undue Liberties taken by the younger Scholars, an Evil that had been much complained of; and all Exercise had either been neglected or performed in a trifling ludicrous manner) was made a regular term, and the Disputations were conducted with the same good Order as in the others, which effectually put a stop to all such Complaints for the future.' This was done by the influence of Dr *Matthias Mawson*[1], master of Bene't, when Vice-chancellor in 1730, 1731.

The Lent Disputations, and 'standing *in Quadragesimâ*,' or *Determining* [one or more questions in a strictly logical or syllogistic form] were common to

---

[1] *Masters'* Hist. of *C.C.C.C.* p. 196, ed. 1753.

almost all ancient universities[1]. As a pendant to the accounts given above from the Cambridge Bedell's Books, it will be well to add one or two notices relating to Oxford.

It is stated in (Walker's) *Oxoniana*, I. 61, that 'Dr Fell, when Vice-chancellor, (1646, 1647,) reformed several abuses in the schools, and "because *coursing* in the time of *Lent*, that is, the endeavours of one party to run down and confute another in disputation, did commonly end in blows, and domestic quarrels (the refuge of the vanquished side), he did, by his authority, annul that custom. Dr Fell, that he might, as much as possible, support the exercises of the University, did frequent examinations for degrees, hold the examiners up to it, and if they would, or could not do their duty, he would do it himself to the pulling down of many. He did also, sometimes, repair to the Ordinaries [see above, p. 208], commonly called *Wall Lectures* (from the paucity of auditors), and was frequently present at those exercises called *disputations in Austin's*, when he would make the disputants begin precisely at one, and continue disputing till three of the clock in the afternoon; so that upon his appearance more auditors were then present than since have usually appeared at those exercises[2]."' In his Diary, however, *A. Wood* thus comments on the conduct of dean Fell:

'1683, *Feb.* 17. Egg Saturday, but one bachelor of Mag. hall presented *ad determinandum*, whereas since the king's return they were never without 6 or 8 or

---

[1] Peacock, *On the Statutes*, App. A. xiv. *n.* 1841.
[2] *Athenæ Oxon.* II. 796, ap. *Oxoniana*, I. 61.

12, and Exeter coll. not one, who used to have commonly 12. About 20 matriculated before Egg Saturday for Lent term.

'120 Bachelors determine, whereas there never used to be under 200. *Lent disputations* decay, the bachelors don't dispute, or will not, unless the superiors (boyish regents) are present; some senior masters go to hear disputations, particularly Mr Huntingdon, after his long absence, but they will not dispute, and stand silent, while their abetters sneer and grin; *this we got by having* coursing *put down by Dr* Fell.' His autobiography in earlier years shews that his reckoning was exaggerated. Thus:

' 1678, *Mar.* 23. *Saturday* the junior proctor made his speech; 180 bachelors this last Lent, and all things carried on well, but no *coursing*, which is very bad. Quaere the reason?'

' 1681, *Feb.* 10. One hundred and ninety-two bachelors to determine this Lent, but 23, or thereabouts, were not presented on Egg Saturday, their time for determining short, that is to say, every bachelor was to determine twice between the 17 *Feb.* to 7 *March*, because the king was to come soon after, and the Parliament to sit on 21st *March.*

' Note, that the Divinity school hath been seldom used, since altered and changed (but before 'twas a pig market), but now this Lent, because the Geometry, Astronomy, and Greek schools were fitting for the house of lords, and twice every day, or three at least, were appointed to determine there.'

The obsolete exercise of '*doing Austin's*' is said to

have derived its name from the custom of scholars disputing with the *Augustine monks*[1], who had acquired a great reputation for exercises of this kind. They are termed in the old Oxford Statutes, *Disputationes in Augustinensibus*. The Proctor chose his *collector in Austin's*, who had the power of matching disputants together at his own discretion[2].

In 1655, Edward Wood, fellow of Merton, when junior proctor, chose his brother Anthony as his collector in Austin's, 'which office he kept till he was admitted Master of Arts' nine months later, his brother having died in the first month of his proctorate.

In 1679 Wood exclaimed, 'Is it not a shame that it should be accounted unusual for scholars to go to Augustin's disputations, and that the masters of the schools speak English to them?'...'This Lent the collectors ceased from entertaining the bachelors by advice and command of the proctors. Van der Hwyden of Oriel was then a collector; so that now they got by their collectorships, whereas before they spent about 100*l.* besides their gains, on cloaths or needless entertainments.'

In 1658 he had noticed the death of Will. George, B.A., student of Ch. Ch., who had been accounted 'a noted sophister and remarkable *courser* in the time of Lent in the publick schooles. He was poore, and therefore ready to make the exercise of dul or lazy

---

[1] *Oxoniana*, I. 45.

[2] See Amherst, *Terræ Filius*, No. XLII. quoted in the next *Part* of this Essay.

scholars. He look'd elderly, and was cynical and hersute in his behaviour.'

The *Wall Lectures* were so called, as being delivered to the bare walls. Uffenbach[1], from hearsay, describes the same thing at Cambridge in 1710. '*Nur den Winter drey oder vier Lectiones von den Professoribus gehalten werden, die sie vor die Wände thun, dann es kommt niemand hinein.*'

The ceremony of *circuiting* was prescribed by the Oxford Statutes (IX. v. 1). It consisted in the intended graduate following bareheaded his Presenter and the Bedells to the lodgings of the Vice-chancellor, and of each of the Proctors, to sue for their attendance at a Congregation for his Degree next day.

On April 4, 1722, Erasmus Philipps, 'Fellow-Commoner' of Pembroke, *Oxon.*, 'went *a circuiting* wth Mr Collins of our College. This is an Exercise previous to a Master's Degree.' (*N. and Q.* 2nd S. x. 444) This custom however is not mentioned in 'Consideration on the Public Exercises, &c., Oxford, 1773.'

It has been already explained (p. 283) that the *Act* at Oxford (on the first Tuesday in July) was properly only a solemn season for the conclusion of academical exercises and for full admission to degrees.

COMMEMORATION (which fell nearly at the same time of the year and which now lends its name to the ceremory for conferring honorary degrees, the recitation of prize compositions in the Sheldonian

---

[1] *Reisen*, III. 2. 1754.

Theatre, and the display of gaiety and hospitality which of old accompanied the public Act) is, strictly speaking, the *Encaenia*, or Celebration of Founders and Benefactors, now held in June, in the Theatre (which was opened formally July 9, 1669). In the *Gentleman's Magazine*, for 1750, is a description of Oxford Commemoration in that year. 'Monday, *July* 2. The Doctors &c. were entertained at lord Crewe's expence in New College hall. At 4 o'clock there was a *procession* to the theatre. (*Music* was performed. The orator stood in the *rostrum* which had been moved into the centre of the *area*. Letters from the Chancellor were read, and an *honorary degree* conferred on the rt. hon. earl of Plymouth. The *orator's speech* lasted above an hour. An *ode* set by professor Hays (*William* Hayes who was succeeded by *Philip* Hayes in 1777). The theatre was quite full, a very handsome appearance of ladies ; and the whole was conducted with great decorum.' In *Gent. Mag.* XXXIII. is an account of the Oxford *Encaenia* in 1763 ; and in vol. XLIII. that of 1773 is described as 'the grandest that ever was.'

It is interesting to us, who witnessed the visit of Alexander, Archbishop of Syros, Tenos, and Melos, in the spring of 1870, to know that in 1701 while Bentley was Vice-chancellor, 'a Greek Prelate, Neophytos, Archbishop of Philippopolis [Exarch of all Thrace and Drovogia], visiting England at the time, came to Cambridge and was presented to a degree of Doctor in Divinity by the University. On this occasion the Vice-chancellor, with great good-nature and propriety, directed that he should be presented by the Greek Professor, Joshua Barnes; who was thus gratified with the opportunity of delivering a Greek oration, a copy of which is still preserved[1].' It seems that the archbishop replied, as Mr Cooper (*Annals*, IV. 46, *n.* 3) refers to a speech made by him on that occasion. As the title of the oration is not printed quite correctly in the notes to that valuable collection, I quote it from a copy which is bound up in a volume of tracts in St John's College library, Cambridge [Ee. 12. 10.], "λόγος τοῦ ἱερωτάτου καὶ σεβασμιωτάτου Νεοφύτου μητροπολίτου τῆς Φιλιππου-πόλεως πρὸς ἀκαδημίαν τῆς Κανταβριγίας, ιγ σεπτεμ-βρίου. Ὅτ᾽ εἰς τὴν τάξιν τῶν ἐκεῖ ἱεροδιδασκάλων τῆς θεολογίας ἐνεγράφθη. *Oratio* Sanctissimi et Reverend-issimi Viri *Neophyti* Metropolitae *Philippopolis*, Ad Academiam *Cantabrigiensem*, XIII Septembris, cum ad gradum Doctoratus in S. Theologia admitteretur. *Cum Versione Latina.* Imprimatur, *Ri. Bentley*, Acad. Cantab. Procancellarius. *Cantabrigiae*, Typis Aca-demicis. MDCCI." pp. 7.

The speech begins with an elegant and complimentary comparison of the University to bees, which not only gather honey but impart their sweets to others. We are fishers of men using the tackle of Wisdom and Learning, and in our turn we are enclosed in the net of God. Again, Man is light, as by wisdom he traverses all things, but he is in turn brought to the one Source of Motion, the very Wisdom, and the Light which lighteneth every man that cometh into the world.

A threefold Wisdom is known to our Greek theologians; first Natural Wisdom, and next Supernatural Wisdom of two kinds, viz. *Create* (which is Faith) and *increate* which is the Subsisting Wisdom

---

[1] Monk's *Life of Bentley*, I. 152, 153.

(ἐνυπόστατος σοφία) of God, the Son and Word of God the Father, our Lord Jesus Christ.

The first Wisdom leads to the second and the second to the divine Person of Wisdom: and without the first (natural wisdom) we cannot find the way which leads to Jerusalem which is above through the searching of the Scriptures.

Then follows a comparison of the Chancellor (the duke of Somerset) and the Vice-Chancellor (Bentley) to the Silver Trumpets mentioned in the Book of Numbers (x. 2, 8.). Δύο τοιαύτας σάλπιγγας φημὶ ἐγώ, τόν τε ὑψηλότατον καὶ μεγαλοπρεπέστατον Καντζηλάριον, Δούκαν Σωμερσετίων, καὶ τὸν Βιτζηκαντζηλάριον τῆς περιφήμου ταύτης Ἀκαδημίας τῆς Κανταβριγίας. Ὡς γὰρ αἱ Σάλπιγγες χρῶνται πνεύματι ἐκ τῶν ἐντοσθίων ἐξερχομένῳ· οὕτω καὶ ἡ ὑμετέρα ὑψηλότης, ὦ ἱεροὶ διδάσκαλοι, προσχρῆται τῇ ἔσωθε διδασκαλίᾳ τοῦ πνεύματος ἧς ἐξερχομένης πραγματεύεται ἡ σωτηρία τῶν ἀνθρώπων.

But I have not words to enumerate the excellences of the Chancellor the V.C., D.D's, and all the rest. And who can sufficiently praise the harmony, proportions, and elegance of the Colleges, especially the most noble and beautiful college of Trinity? (τὸ τῆς ὑπερουσίου Τριάδος περικαλλέστατον καὶ ὡραιότατον;).

He concludes with a solemn prayer, (Δέομαι μόνον τῆς μακαρίας καὶ ζωοποιοῦ καὶ ἀδιαιρέτου καὶ ἀσυγχύτου Τριάδος, ἑνὸς τῇ φύσει καὶ μόνου Θεοῦ,) for king William, the archbishop of Canterbury, and all the other archbishops and bishops of the English Church, as well as all the members of the University.

The speech is signed Ὁ ταπεινὸς Μητροπολίτης Φιλιππουπόλεως Νεόφυτος.

Mr George Williams remarks (*The Orthodox and the Nonjurors*, XXIII.) that the original Oration delivered by the Archbishop of Philippopolis before the Chancellor and Senate of our university, Sept. 13, 1701, is preserved in the British Museum (*Brit. Mus.* Addit. MSS. 22, 911, ff. 4—7) among the papers of Dr John Covel, master of Christ's, who had been chaplain to the embassy in Constantinople from 1670 —77, and to whom Archbishop Tenison gave Neophytus an introduction (*The Orthodox and Nonjurors*, LIX.).

L. B. E.   21

Mr Williams adds that he has not been able to find the name of the Greek archbishop among the Graduati Cantabrigienses; yet that it is certain he was decorated with the same distinction at Cambridge as at Oxford. I am enabled by the kindness of the Reverend H. R. Luard, the Registrary of the University, to confirm this statement. There is indeed no entry in the Orator's Book between the years 1700 and 1706; the grace for the degree was never entered in the book, nor is the original grace itself to be found; none of the Greeks signed their names in the book of the subscriptions to the Three Articles; but there is a transcript in the grace book of the following grace which clearly proves that the degrees were conferred, though the unusual circumstances of the inauguration, happening as it did in vacation-time, may have led to the omission of some of the ordinary formalities.

'*Lect: et Concess: Sep^{tbris}* 13mo] Placeat vobis, ut Archiepiscopus Philippopolitanus una cum quatuor ex ejus comitatu habeant literas testimoniales graduum suorum apud nos susceptorum Academiae sigillo signatas.'

The archbishop's previous visit to Oxford is thus described by E. Thwaites, fellow of Queen's and Greek Professor at Oxford, in a letter to Dr Charlett, master of University. [Walker's] *Oxoniana*, iii. 146 —148[1].

'*Sept.* 2, 1701. Rev. Sir, Yesterday at three

[1] The Rev. G. Williams B.D. gives a reference to the original 'Ballard MSS. in the Bodleian, Vol. XIII. art 22.' and adds that the

o'clock the Archbishop of Philippoli (*sic*) was created Doctor of Divinity, in the Convocation House, his physician made D. Med., and his presbyters and deacon[1] Masters of Arts; 'twas a mighty show, and the solemnity was very decent. After their admission, his grace made us a very excellent speech, all in plain, proper Hellenistic Greek, and continued speaking nearly half an hour; all with great respect to the house, great gravity, great boldness, and a very manly voice. If you have not seen him, I hope you will in London: he is a man of admirable air, and makes a graceful appearance.

'He commended the English nation for hospitality, the Church of England, the University, the Chancellor's [duke of Ormond's] civility to him, the Vice-chancellor's [Dr Roger Mander of Balliol's] kindness, &c., in very round periods.

'After that we went to the theatre, had a Latin song or two, which made about half-an-hour's music, and the company dispersed. The concourse was so great, I have not seen it greater, except at the Act.

'The forms of presentation had nothing singular in them, except the last by the Orator [*Will. Wyatt*, student of Christchurch, principal of S. Mary Hall], we had one of his rants. *Praesento Vobis hunc egregium Virum, Athanasium, diaconum, nomine suo apud omnes orthodoxos venerandum, ut gradu Magistri in*

---

letter is given in extenso in the *Union Review*, Vol. II. p. 650. London, 1863.

   [1] 'Athanasius, Archdeacon; Neophitus, Archimandrite; and Gregorius, Protosyncellus.'

Artibus insignitus tandem fidem acrius, quam ipsi Episcopi, tueatur: they are the words as I remember.

'I am very sorry you were not here at the reception and entertainment of this great man for reasons I cannot tell you in writing.

'Indeed Dr Woodroof has exerted himself and shewn us that he does understand Greek.'

'Benjamin Woodroffe, canon of Ch. Ch., who was Principal (1692—1712) of Gloucester Hall (which in 1714 became Worcester College), had the charge of the five youths from Smyrna placed in that hall about 1694. Mr George Williams (formerly senior fellow of King's Coll. Camb.) has shewn in his *Orthodox Church of the East in the eighteenth century,* pp. xix. xx. (Rivington's, 1868), that this colony of Greek students in Oxford was formed at the suggestion of Joseph Georgirenes, metropolitan of Samos (then a refugee in London), who, about 1682, or 1683, petitioned archbishop Sancroft to further his scheme for the education in England of twelve Greeks, with a view to their returning to preach in their own country 'the true doctrine of the Church of England.'.

It will perhaps be remembered that in 1616 Metrophanes Critopulus (afterwards patriarch of Alexandria) was sent by Cyril Lucas, patriarch of Constantinople, to be educated at Balliol. Accordingly about the year 1689 a 'Greek College' was founded in Gloucester Hall for the education of twenty youths of the Greek communion in five years' residence. They were to be all alike habited in the gravest sort of habit worn in their own country, and to wear no other either in the University or anywhere else[1]. They were not to go out of the college without special leave, or without a companion, and were to have no vacations. Three of them were unfortunately enticed away to the continent by agents of the Roman Church; among other adventures they were kept at Louvain for five months by order of the pope. Two of them escaped back to England, and were sent home to Smyrna by Mr. E. Stephens, a loyal phil-hellen. But that gentleman received in 1705 a letter from the Registrar of the Greek Church at Constantinople, stating that 'the irregular life of certain priests and lay-men of the Eastern Church, living in London, is a matter of great concern to the Church. Wherefore the Church forbids any to go and study at Oxford, be they never so willing[2]."

In 1768 the king of Denmark, having received an honorary degree at Oxford, paid Cambridge a visit in the month of August, and was made to tremble by the portrait of Oliver Cromwell at Sidney[3].

On the 16th of October, 1775, 'the Prince of Hesse and the Danish ambassador arrived in Cambridge and, after viewing the public buildings, proceeded to Newmarket races[4].'

In April 1797 'the Prince and Princess of Orange

---

[1] Mr Moore's *Historical Hand-book and Guide to Oxford*, p. 21. Shrimptons, 1871.

[2] Mr G. Williams, *The Orthodox and the Nonjurors*, XXIII—XXV.

[3] Cooper's *Annals*, IV. 351.

[4] *Ibid.* 378.

visited Cambridge, and attended the University Sermon on Sunday[1]'

It has been already mentioned incidentally (*supra*, p. 237), that king George III. visited Oxford in 1786). Of this occasion we have a most lively record in the *Diary and Letters of Madame D'Arblay* (III. 76 —107), who, then known as Miss Burney, the authoress (in 1778, 1782) of *Evelina and Cecilia*, was spending her life as a keeper of the robes to queen Charlotte. It was unfortunately in the vacation time, in August, not many days after the attempt made by the maniac Margaret Nicholson upon the life of the king; and the severe etiquette of the court would not permit Miss Burney to enjoy at her ease haunts so congenial to her nature. She describes the reception in the Sheldonian theatre, the queen and princesses shedding tears at the mention in the address of the good king's escape. 'Next followed music: a good organ, very well played, anthem-ed and voluntary-ed us for some time' (III. p. 97). The scenes in Oxford on this occasion must have been very strange: the younger men were not in residence, and the University was represented by old and grave men, most of whom were very shy and unaccustomed to the ceremonies of the court. She describes humorously the awkward attempts made by the 'worthy collegiates' to kiss the king's hand: 'many in their confusion fairly arose by pulling his majesty's hand to raise them' (*ibid.* 98). A strange contrast with the

---

[1] Cooper's *Annals*, IV. 458,

graceful retrograde march which, in spite of a sprained ancle and a cumbrous train, lady Charlotte Bertie made before the king, no doubt to the admiration of doctors and masters no less than of Miss Burney herself. However it is not surprising that she, who from her childhood had watched Dr Johnson, 'the greater Bear,' swallowing cup after cup of bohea, should have taken goodnaturedly such compliments as were awkwardly proffered her. And though she had to endure tedious hours of standing and, fasting, and then was forced to hide suddenly the smuggled apricots and bread when the queen came unexpectedly upon her retreat in the master's parlour at Wolsey's college (Magdalen, where Dr Horne was president): yet she felt well repaid with a sight of her father's and her own friend Sir Joshua Reynolds' window in New College ante-chapel. And even when she might not sit down in the royal presence, nothing prevented her from pulling down book after book while she was waiting in Trinity College library. Doubtless too she entered into the humour of the situation when in attendance on the royal party feasting in Christchurch hall, the dons, slily provided the back row of maids of honour and equerries 'with tea, coffee, chocolate, cakes, and bread and butter,' while some took it in turns to stand demurely as a screen between the royal banquetters and those in waiting who were engaged in a humbler way at the same employment.

The question of the admission of ladies to the studies of the English universities was not (as far as I am aware) moved in the eighteenth century. There are however instances recorded of their admission in the infancy, and also in the riper years, of the great rival of the University of Paris.

'One of the most singular points in the history of the University of Bologna' (writes Professor *Henry Malden*, in his *Essay on the Origin of Universities*, 1835, pp. 63, 64) 'is the admission of the female sex to its honours and offices. There is mention in early times of learned women on whom degrees were conferred. It is said that Novella d'Andrea [died in 1366] read lectures on jurisprudence, but took the precaution of drawing a curtain between herself and her auditors. Mrs Piozzi mentions la Dotteressa Laura Bassi [1711, †1778], who taught mathematics and natural philosophy; and Lady Morgan has introduced us to Signora Clotilda Tambroni [1758, †1817], a learned professor of Greek. But the boldest inroad into the scientific province of the ruder sex was made by Madonna Manzolina, who lectured on anatomy.'

The following story is told by Ovid's friend and Augustus' freedman *Hyginus* (no very good authority indeed, *fab.* 274, '*Of Inventions*'). There was a law at Athens that no woman should practise midwifery. But a certain lady named Agnodice, perceiving the inconvenience of the present custom, cut off her hair, and, disguising herself as a man, went to the lectures of Hierophilus, and subsequently attended ladies. The faculty, getting wind of this, trumped up an accusation against her in Areopagus, and when Agnodice had cleared herself of the scandal, they alleged the then existing law against obstetrices. But the court was so much moved by a deputation of Athenian matrons, that they not only acquitted Agnodice, but made it lawful for ladies (*ingenuae*) to study medicine.

There had been a great falling-off in the literary culture of English gentlewomen[1] from the days of Roger Ascham and queen Elizabeth and the time of the Revolution; just as Cornelia mother of the Gracchi had been succeeded by the matrons of Cicero's time, most of whom were ignorant, or else, like Sempronia wife of Decimus Junius Brutus, had but this one excellence of those which ennobled Cornelia, and so, though a few Roman wives might still have a taste for literature, the children of Rome were allowed to grow up without knowing even the laws of the Twelve Tables, which had in Cicero's own childhood[2] been as regular a lesson as the Church catechism with ourselves. Then, just as under the empire the past literature of Rome was a sealed book to Horace and to those who heard or read his poems, so too Addison found Chaucer forgotten and already almost unintelligible[3].

The study of the works of former years and generations received an impetus in the Roman empire

---

[1] Strype's *Life of Parker*, b. II. ch. xxv.

[2] 'Discebamus enim pueri XII, ut carmen necessarium: quas iam nemo discit.' Cicero, *de Legibus*, II. XXIII. 59.

[3]   'Till Chaucer first a merry bard arose,
    And many a story told in rhyme and prose:
    But age has rusted what the poet writ,
    Worn out his language and obscur'd his wit.

from the imitative character of the composition of
the Flavian period: and such studies were fostered
no doubt by the first imperial rhetoric professorships
which were founded by Vespasian[1].

A generation later we find Juvenal[2] complaining
of learned ladies.

But in England the revival of literary taste was
not immediately due to any educational establishment: we are indebted for our acquaintance with the
works of Shakespeare (which had been ill edited and
then well-nigh forgotten) to the admiration expressed by Steele in the *Tatler*[3]; while Milton's poems
would hardly have been so well known as they have
been, were it not for the criticisms published by
Addison in the *Spectator*[4].

One of the chief evils of society which the es-
sayists strove to remedy was the low intellectual and
moral tone of persons of fashion and especially of
ladies. 'If fathers and brothers' (says Steele) 'will
defend a lady's honour she is quite as safe as in her
own innocence. Many of the distressed who suffer
under the malice of evil tongues are so harmless that

In vain he jests in his unpolished strain
And tries to make his readers laugh in vain.'

Addison's *Account of the greatest English Poets* to Mr H. Sacheverell, April 3, 1694. (Written when 22 years of age.) Compare the
commentators on Horace, *Epist.* II. i. 86.

[1] Suetonius, *Vesp.* 18. Merivale's *History of the Romans under the
Empire*, ch. LXIV.

[2] Juvenal, VI. 434—456.

[3] *Tatler*, Nos. 8, 41, 68, 90, 111.

[4] *Spectator*, 267 to 463 *passim*.

they are every day they live asleep till twelve at noon; concern themselves with nothing but their own persons till two; take their necessary food between that time and four, visit, go to the play, and sit up at cards till towards the ensuing morn.' What wonder they grew up to be thoughtless mothers[1]; or that such mothers found their children wilful. What more graphic pictures can there be of the viciousness of abused society than in Sheridan's *School for Scandal*, and in the select lounge in the dressing-room of the countess in Hogarth's *Marriage à la mode*[2].

The account of a gentlewoman's daily occupations quoted above from Steele is hardly in excess of that given in Swift's specimens of modern polite conversation, or even of the evidence of Vanbrugh's Sir John Brute, when in his wife's clothes he 'scandalizes the women of quality.' At the commencement of the century few Englishwomen were known for their mental accomplishments except Pope's rival lady Mary Wortley Montagu. But the good heart of Steele led him (with the help of Addison and John Hughes) to make great efforts for the increase of the number. The papers in the *Spectator*[3] relating to books for ladies' reading, are familiar to us. Steele, who in the 248th number of the *Tatler*, in 1710, had promised some such undertaking, edited

---

[1] *Spectator*, 246.

[2] Pope's *Rape of the Lock*, 1.
    At every word a reputation dies:
    Snuff and the fan supply the pause of chat,
    With singing laughing ogling and all that.

[3] Nos. 37, 92, 140, 163, cf. *Tatler*, No. 248.

in 1714 *The Lady's Library* in three volumes oc-
tavo[1]; a book which breathes, no less than his *Christian Hero*, that spirit of purity and religion with
which he often sighed.   Their efforts were not altogether vain.   'My fair readers' (writes Addison in
the *Spectator*, No. 92) 'are already better scholars
than the beaux.   I could name some of them who
talk much better than several gentlemen that make
a figure at *Will's*; and, as I frequently receive letters
from the fine ladies and pretty fellows, I cannot but
observe that the former are superior to the others,
not only in the sense, but in the spelling.' The
picture drawn, in No. 37, of a literary lady's library
is very suggestive.   And as the century advanced,
we find a small coterie of gentlewomen gathering
round Dr Johnson, while another party rallied round
the knight of the Blue Stocking, Mr Benjamin Stillingfleet[2] (1702—1771), the grandson of the bishop
of Worcester.   The following list of literary ladies
might be greatly increased.   Eliz. Carter (1717—
1806), Eliz. Montagu (1720—1800), Hester Lynch
Piozzi (1739—1821), Sarah Trimmer (1741—1810),
Lady Eleanor Fenn (1743—1813), Anna Laetitia
Barbauld (1743—1825), Hannah More (1745—1833),
Frances Burney (1752—1840), Joanna Baillie (1762
—1851), Maria Edgworth (1764—1849), Amelia Opie
(1769—1853), Jane Austen (1775—1817).

---

[1] '*The Lady's Library*, written by a Lady.   Published by Mr *Steele*.'
Tonson, 1714, 3 vols. 8vo. in Cambridge University Library '30. 6.
88—90.'

[2] Boswell's *Life of Johnson*, s. a. 1781.

It was hardly to be expected that institutions which were governed by a law of celibacy like the universities, should fall much under the consideration of intellectual ladies. There was however at least one who must not be forgotten, *Ann Jebb*, the wife of an important mover in the Cambridge world, John Jebb,

(who was son of Dr John Jebb, dean of Cashel, born in 1736, and after spending some time at eight places of education, including Shrewsbury and Dublin University, was admitted pensioner of Peterhouse, Nov. 9, 1754 [where his uncle Samuel Jebb, M.D. the non-juror, had been sizar, B.A. 1712, died 1772], second wrangler in 1757, Professor Waring being senior, second members' prizeman in 1758, being beaten by W. Roberts [afterwards Provost of Eton]. He was confirmed fellow of Peterhouse in 1761, after the regular year of probation. In 1762 he was ordained deacon by the bishop of Lincoln, and priest fifteen months later, on which occasion he preached the ordination sermon. As moderator in 1762—3, when Paley was senior wrangler, and as taxor in the two following years, he was colleague of Ri. Watson who speaks of him as in 1774 'a very honest and intelligent but unpopular man[1],' but a friend of whom he was himself proud[2]. Jebb was again moderator in 1763—4 with Fairclough, and in 1767—8, when Watson was once more associated with him, as well as in the two following years. After commencing the study of Hebrew in 1764, he was collated to the vicarage of Gamlingay, *co.* Beds., on the recommendation of Dr Edm. Law, master of his college; in less than four months he was instituted to the University living of Ovington, *co.* Norfolk.)

On the 29th of December, 1764, just a fortnight after he had been instituted to the rectory of Ovington, he married *Ann Torkington*, eldest daughter of the rector of Little Stukely, *co.* Huntingdon, and of lady Dorothy Sherard. One of her brothers succeeded their father as rector of Stukely. The other was master of Clare Hall.

[1] *Anecdotes of the life of Ri. Watson, bp. of Llandaff*, 1818, I. 48.
[2] *Ibid.* I. 101.

After an attempt to reside near Gamlingay, he gave up that vicarage and returned to Cambridge; where he entered on the curacy of S. Andrew's parish, and the lectureship which Henry Hubbard [B.D. Emmanuel, univ. Registrary 1758—1778: see notes on '*a Fragment*' relating to the disorders in 1750 mentioned above, p. 66, where he figures as *Harry*] had held 'near twenty years.'

In 1768 and 1770 he was an unsuccessful candidate for the Arabic Professorship, having studied that language for four or five years. In the spring of 1769 he declared himself an opposer of the tory party in the university by voting in a minority of two, with Michael Tyson of Bene't (Corpus Christi, B.A. 1764) College, against the loyal address to King George III. on March 17. Within a few months John Jebb was presented to the vicarage of Flixton and the united rectories of Homersfield and St Cross, *co.* Suffolk, and was nominated chaplain to Ro., earl of Harborough. A year later he resigned the university living of Ovington. It appears that in 1771 Jebb took considerable interest in the case of Robert Tyrwhitt of Jesus (grandson of bishop Gibson[1]), who had proposed to argue questions on the Socinian side in the theological schools, but had changed his theses at the instance of Professor Rutherforth. Later in the same year Jebb joined with Tyrwhitt and others in attempting to remove the rule requiring persons to subscribe the XXXIX. Articles on their admission to the degree of B.A.

This grace was rejected by the caput; as had been another, for removing subscription to the Three Articles of King James, which Tyrwhitt had proposed in the summer.

The following anecdote gives us a glimpse of the discussions on this subject at the time.

'There was a society established at Cambridge, in the year 1757, by the Wranglers when Dr Waring was senior and Mr Jebb second, called *The Hyson Club* [see above, p. 158, where 1758 is the date given]. The members were accustomed to meet for the purpose of drinking tea and holding rational conversation. Several of the highest characters in the university were already enrolled amongst its members, when Doctor, then Mr Paley [B.A. 1763] became an associate, soon after his establishment [1771] in the tuition of Christ's College. No particular subjects of discussion were proposed at their meetings; but accident, or the taste of the individuals, naturally led to topics in which literary men might fairly unbend themselves from severer pursuits. In a debate, one evening, on the justice and expediency of making some alteration in the ecclesiastical constitution of the country, for the relief of tender con-

---

[1] Dyer's *Life of R. Robinson*, p. 317.

sciences, Doctor Gordon[1], fellow of Emmanuel College, and afterwards precentor of Lincoln [B.A. 1748], an avowed tory in religious politics, when vehemently opposing the arguments of Mr Jebb, a strenuous supporter of all such improvements, exclaimed, with his usual heat, "You mean, Sir, to impose upon us a new church government." "You are mistaken, Sir," said Mr Paley; "Jebb only wants to ride his own horse, not to force you to get up behind him.[2]"

But Jebb was not content with private discussion. He attended the general meetings of 'numbers of the clergy who called themselves of the established church, Archdeacon Blackburn at the head of them[2],' in the *Feathers' Tavern* in London (July 17, 1771, &c.) and was a member of the committee which prepared a petition (Dec. 11) to the House of Commons. Meanwhile he was writing letters in the *Whitehall Evening Post* under the signature of *Paulinus*, while Dr Sam. Hallifax, of Jesus [B.A. 1754, afterwards Bp. of Gloster], was preaching and publishing three sermons on the other side, and being answered by Sam. Blackall, fellow of Emmanuel [B.A. 1760].

The petition was presented Feb. 6, 1772, by Sir W. Meredith, seconded by Tho. Pitt (lord Camelford). The motion that the Speaker leave the chair to resolve the Commons into a Committee of the whole House was lost by 159 against 67.

Dr Will. Sam. Powell, Master of St John's, had just before this printed the fourth edition of his Commencement Sermon which he had preached in 1757 in defence of subscription. 'A most impudent letter addressed to him[4]' appeared under the signature of '*Camillus*' in the *London Chronicle*, of Jan. 22, 1772. 'It was probably forged at Mr Jebb's anvil: though he even condescends to be an advocate for the Methodists, rather than not find matter of abuse: for I suppose Mr H. means Mr *Hill*, then a young Scholar of St John's College; who while he was Undergraduate and not in orders, went preaching about in Cambridge, and the neighbouring villages, and particularly in a barn at Waterbeche where was a numerous seminary of the disciples of Mr Berridge of Clare Hall, called from him *Berridges*, and who to this day send out preachers, gardeners, collar-makers, shop-keepers, &c. into

[1] Author of a *New Estimate of Manners and Principles*. See Mayor's *History of St John's*, 711, l. 18, 1022, l. 23. In the index to Mr Mayor's book Gordon's Christian name is misprinted *Jas.*, for *John*.

[2] *Facetiæ Cantabrigienses*, ed. 3, 1836, p. 91. Meadley's *Memoirs of Paley*, 1809, pp. 37, 46, 47.

[3] Cole *ap.* Nichols' *Lit. Anecd.* i. 570.

[4] *Ibid.* i. 572.

many of the adjacent villages. It was for this irregularity, perhaps, that the master thought proper to refuse a testimonial. He is son, I think, of Sir Rowland Hill, and is now in orders, and in repute with his people; and has this year, 1777, printed a warm pamphlet against Mr John Wesley, one of the patriarchs of his order[1].'

On Sunday, Dec. 27 (St John's Day), 1772, Jebb preached on the question of 'subscription' (Acts xv. 10) before the University: and again, on the Holy Innocents', on the Spirit of Benevolence (reprinted 1780—82). In the spring he was again busied with 'subscription' and 'annual examination;' and at the close of the year he was enduring the disappointment of the hopes which he had fostered, that the new Vice-Chancellor, Dr W. Cooke of King's, would support his 'long projected institution' of a yearly examination[2] in the greek and latin classics, and the elements of geometry and algebra, without respect of noblemen and fellow-commoners, who were to be subjected to a second examination in Locke's *Essay on the human understanding*, natural philosophy and modern history. Early in 1773 he published two editions of ' *Remarks*,' and a postscript on that subject. But it was on May 8 of that year that this most important scheme was brought officially before the University, by the presentation of his first grace for an annual examination. This having been rejected by the caput he offered three other graces in succession four days later, but they met with the same fate, Dr Powell of St John's having even contemplated to prevent Jebb by a grace from offering any more. Dr Law (the Master of his old College, Peterhouse) stood resolutely Jebb's friend. 'Several Johnians' he adds 'were for me, though their master was against me so bitterly. Dr Watson, and many men of Trinity, were strenuously my friends.' He was determined to bring his proposal through the caput to the senate at all hazards.

He had left Cambridge for Bungay only ten days in the summer of 1773, when a grace was offered to the senate (July 5) by the Vice-Chancellor himself that a syndicate should be appointed to consider the question, and was carried without opposition! However the syndicate was called early in the October term, and the scheme was rejected. In December when Dr Lynford Caryl of Jesus was Vice-Chancellor, Jebb made a fruitless attempt to rescind the report of the syndicate as having been made too early in the term: but another more promising syndicate was appointed, though the scheme was lost owing to the opposition of Dr Thomas (dean of Ely), Dr Powell (master of St John's), Dr Sam. Hallifax (Jesus and Trin. Hall), Stephen Whisson of Trin. the univ.

[1] Cole *ap*. Nichols' *Lit. Anecd.* 1. 574.
[2] Jebb's *Works*, ii. 314.

librarian (who had been proposed for nomination at the previous election of Vice-Chancellor, though not 'head of a college') and 'the Emmanuel' men[1]' including Dr Ri. Farmer. It is said by Disney 'from good authority[2]' that it was even proposed by this party to strike a medal with the inscription ' Academia liberata, Apr. 19, 1774.'

In August, 1773, Jebb had confided to his friends that he was about to resign his preferment in the Church of England. For a time he ceased to read the prayers, though he preached occasionally. At the visitation in his church at Flixton, Jebb preached against ' subscription ' (his university sermon of the preceding March), for which archdeacon Goodall of Suffolk ' although a Wollastonian' rebuked him before the clergy at the public house where they met. In the following spring Theophilus Lindsey confided to him his own intention of secession and of ' his earnest wishes of meeting with a society of unitarian christians.' Jebb shewed great interest in this proposal, and, when afterwards he resided in London, was a constant attendant at the chapel in Essex-street. In June, 1774, he finally left Bungay, and, after spending two months with his father at Egham, saw his propositions for the annual examination passed the caput but thrown out in the senate by one vote in the black-hood, or non-regent, house. A few days earlier ' *A letter to the author of the plan for the establishment of public examinations*' had appeared; and in the following month (November) ' *An observation on the design of establishing annual examinations*' [by Dr Powell, 1774]. To these ' Priscilla' [Mrs Ann Jebb] rejoined in ' *A letter to the author of an observation.*'

In March, 1775, Jebb in deference to advice abandoned his intention of immediately prosecuting his examination scheme by moving an application to the Chancellor, and turned his attention to the American slave question.

In September the vacancy of Homersfield rectory and Flixton vicarage by his resignation was declared.

In November he published ' *A Short Statement of the Reasons for his late Resignation, To which are added Occasional Observations, and a Letter to the Right Rev. the Bishop of Norwich.*' 1775.

He still remained at Cambridge and declared his intention of presenting on Feb. 21, 1776, a grace for annual examination. The Vice-Chancellor informed him that he had forfeited his vote according to the statute of 1603, ' *De oppugnatoribus ecclesiae anglicanae.*' He was however suffered to present the grace: to which inconsistency he called public attention. The votes on which he had counted dwindled away,

---

[1] Disney's *Jebb*, 62.   [2] *Ibid.* p. 71.

and the measure was again lost. He was attacked in a pamphlet
'*Resignation no Proof, a Letter to Mr* Jebb, *with occasional Remarks on
his Spirit of Protestantism.*' The second issue bore the name of the rev.
E. Tew, M.A. late fellow of King's. On the other hand his sincerity
was applauded in '*A letter to the rev. John Jebb, M.A. occasioned by his
Short View.*'

Being unable to get a livelihood in Cambridge by his lectures in
mathematics and natural philosophy, he took sir Ri. Jebb's advice and
attended Dr Colignon's anatomical lectures with a view to following the
example of his uncle Samuel Jebb (sometime secretary of Jer. Collier)
who, having been educated at Peterhouse, had as a non-juror resigned
his clerical functions to practise medicine. In Sept. 1776, John Jebb
settled in Craven street, London, giving greek testament lectures while
he went through two years probation (which was technically unnecessary
after his university degree) before he began to practise medicine,
attending the lectures of Hunter and others. March 18, 1777, he
received his diploma as doctor of physic from S. Andrew's university,
and was admitted licent'ate of the coll. of physicians, June 25. In the
same year Dr Priestley dedicated to him his '*Doctrine of Philosophical
Necessity.*'

Feb. 5, 1778, Dr Jebb began to practise, and was admitted F.R.S.
a year later. In his attention to professional duties he several times
caught serious illnesses which did not dissuade him from his practice,
though in Nov. 1780 he admitted himself of Lincoln's inn with the
thought, which he soon abandoned, of taking up the legal profession.
In Feb. 1780 he proposed Fox as candidate for Westminster, and was a
staunch supporter of that politician till his coalition with lord North in
1783. In 1780 he contributed notes to Priestley's '*Harmony of the
evangelists in English.*'

He died March 2, 1786, and was buried in Bunhill-fields. In that
place, which was opened under act of parliament to the public for
purposes of peaceful recreation on Thursday, Oct. 14, 1869, lie also
John Bunyan, I. Watts, Sam. Neal, Susannah mother of the Wesleys,
Dan. Defoe, Will. Blake, J. Dunton, Jos. Ritson and others.

While John Jebb had been engaged in the contro-
versial strife at Cambridge, his wife had accompanied
him to the battle on more than one occasion. While
he was attacking 'subscription,' 'this lady, under the
assumed title of *Priscilla,* assailed the most formi-

dable of her husband's opponents, answering their arguments, detecting their weak points, and rebuking their invectives, with great acuteness, poignancy, and effect[1].'

Again in 1772, 'in the stormy controversy which ensued' on his proposal for an annual public examination which should include every order of student, 'Mrs Jebb again took an active part, following her spouse to the contest like another Gildippe—*sempre affissa al caro fianco.* After scattering a few missiles in the Whitehall Post, she published a letter to the author of "An Observation on the Design of establishing annual Examinations at Cambridge," generally ascribed to Dr Powell; and it must be confessed, that the objections of the observer and his adherents were repelled with sufficient spirit and acuteness[2].'

Dr Disney in his life of Jebb, though he does not choose to enlighten the reader on the identity of Priscilla and Mrs Jebb, seems to hint that it was generally known: 'it will be sufficient for me to say, that it (A letter to the author of an Observation, whom he identifies with Dr Powell) was written by a lady....The notification of her victory may probably be more readily admitted upon the judgment of others than upon my own, and the citation of their testimony will acquit me of the imputation of a compliment[3].'

[1] *Discourse of* Wm. Sam. Powell, *D.D.* prefixed to the rev. Tho. Smart Hughes' *Divines of the Church of England,* no. 21, p. xii., *ap.* Mayor's Baker's *Hist. of St John's,* p. 1057, l. 27.

[2] *Ibid.* p. xvii. *ap.* Baker-Mayor, 1058, l. 36.

[3] Disney's *Jebb,* 1. 81, 82.

The following is an extract from the account of Mrs Jebb printed by Dyer, who mentions also that Meadley, the biographer of Paley, published a short sketch of her life.

'Mrs Jebb was not content with being a silent observer; she became the active opponent of Dr Powel, the master of St John's College, who conducted the other side of the controversy on annual examinations, and who felt as sensibly the point of Mrs Jebb's pen, in the public prints, as he did those of the learned Doctor's. It was in reference to the force of argument contained in a smart Letter, written by Mrs Jebb, against Dr Randolph of Oxford, ["The Reasonableness of Subscription to the Articles of Religion, from Persons to be admitted to Holy Orders, or a Cure of Souls, vindicated in a Charge delivered to the Clergy in the Diocese of Oxford in Dec. 1771."] under the signature of "Priscilla," that the late Dr Paley said at the time, [in his *Defence of Bishop* Law's *Considerations*,] "The Lord had sold Sisera into the hands of a woman[1]."

'When Dr Jebb (having embraced some speculative opinions, which he thought made it necessary for him to resign his preferment and to leave the church) settled in London, he became a physician, and a strenuous political reformer. No name is better known among the advocates of parliamentary reform than that of Dr Jebb; and the active energy of Mrs Jebb is also well known: being an invalid, she

[1] Meadley's *Life of Paley*, ed. 1810, 97, 98. Disney's *Jebb*, I. 81 n.

lived a retired life ; but her zeal rose to the full level of her husband's—she saw with the same quickness, glowed with the same ardour, and wrote, occasionally, with the same spirit.

'But Mrs Jebb was not more distinguished for the vigour of her mind, than the qualities of her heart. She was a Christian, without bigotry ; a moralist without severity ; a politician without self-interest or ambition ; a sincere friend, without disguise and without reserve. With considerable powers of mind, she possessed all the amiable softness of the female character. With as few failings as could well fall to the lot of humanity, she exercised an unlimited candour in judging those of others. Candour and benignity were the prominent features of her character. Her friends therefore were numerous, and she could not have a single enemy.

'These superior qualities of mind and heart were lodged in a body of the most delicate texture. In figure she was small : her frame was extremely feeble, her countenance always languid and wan. She used to recline on a sofa, and had not been out of her room above once or twice these twenty years—she seemed the shadow of a shade, or rather all soul and intellect, like one dropped from another sphere. For her ardour and patriotic firmness, mixed with urbanity and gentleness, and occasionally brightening with innocent playfulness, gave that to her countenance which the mere bloom of health cannot bestow, nor the pen describe ; it gave a singular interest to her character : it can only be felt, and will be lastingly remembered, by her surviving friends. Mrs Jebb died at her house in Half-moon Street, Piccadilly, Jan. 20, 1812.' Dyer's *Supplement to the Hist. of Camb.* II. (= *Cambridge Fragments*) pp. 168, 169. *Privileges of the Univ. of Camb.* II. London, 1824, quoting the *Morning Chronicle*, &c., Jan. 27, 1812.) ' The *fugitive pieces* of Mrs Jebb (for they have never been collected into a regular volume) appeared in different news-papers, the London Chronicle and Whitehall Evening Post, between the years 1771 and 1774, in numerous Letters and under different signatures, though most often under that of *Priscilla;* being Answers—to Dr Randolph's *Reasonableness of Subscription...*Dec. 1771;—to Dr Hallifax's (afterwards Bishop) [Sam. Hallifax of Jesus, B.A. 1754, M.A. 1757, Trin. Hall, LL.D. 1764, D.D. per lit. regias 1775, bishop of St Asaph, regius professor of Laws 1770—82. His syl-labus of lectures, *An Analysis of the Roman Civil Law*, 1795, ed. 4. In 1768 he had defeated Jebb when he was for the first time candidate for the Arabic professorship. He called on Wilkie the pub-lisher, to advise him not to print any more of Mrs Jebb's letters[1].] *Three Sermons preached before the University of* Cambridge, *occasioned by an attempt to abolish Subscription to the* 39 *Articles*, published in 1772;—to Dr Powel's *Defence of the Subscription re-quired by the Church of England, a Sermon preached before the University of* Cambridge *on the Commence-ment Sunday*, first published in 1757, republished in

---

[1] *Hist. of St John's coll.* Baker-Mayor, 1067, l. 37.

1772;—to Dr Balguy's *Charge to the Clergy and Arch-deaconry of* Winchester, 1772.

' In 1774 Mrs Jebb published a *Letter to the Author of* the Design of Establishing Annual Examination at *Cambridge*, which was generally ascribed to Dr Powell, master of St John's; in 1792 a little piece, entitled *Two Penny-worth of Truth for a Penny; or a true State of Facts, with an Apology for* Tom Bull, *in a Letter from Brother* John; in 1793 *Two Penny-worth more of Truth*, &c. These were a sort of playful replies to a pamphlet under the title of *One Penny-worth of Truth, from* Thomas Bull *to Brother* John, and relate to the French Revolution[1].'

When John Jebb wrote to congratulate bishop Ri. Watson on the publication of his *Apology for Christianity* in 1776, he thus assures him[2];—' My wife who has a veneration for you is also prodigiously satisfied; she is only a little alarmed lest you have found out a greater mathematician than her friend Waring.' [coll. S. M. Magd., Lucasian prof. mathemat. 1760—1798.]

In pre-reformational times the members of the colleges had no more thought of marriage in that condition than had the inmates of any religious house.

Soon after the Norman conquest celibacy had been enjoined on the English clergy down to the order of subdeacon. In the time of pope Gregory VII. (Hildebrand) the first canon of the synod of bishops held

---

[1] Dyer, *Priv. Camb.* II. part 2, pp. 168, 169.
[2] *Anecdotes of the Life of* Ri. Watson, *by himself*, I. 101, ed. 1818.

at Winchester in 1076, when Lanfranc was archbishop of Canterbury[1], had prepared the way for the more decided decree of 1102 under his successor Anselm.

In Lanfranc's days (says dean Hook), 'in those cathedrals which were served by the secular clergy, the canons were generally married men.' About 1130, when archbishop William of Corbeuil as legate demanded the enforcement of the canon, the king made it a subject for dispensation[2]. In the 30th canon of the council of Osney, near Oxford, at which archbishop Stephen Langton presided in 1222, mention is made of sons of the clergy, but there, as in the 28th canon, their wives are stigmatised as *concubinae*[3].

In the following centuries the appearance at least of celibacy was kept up if it was not enforced farther down the scale of orders. For instance it was ordered in 1440, that when the bishop of Lincoln visited his cathedral (which was in the hands of *seculars;* and so, strictly speaking, not a 'minster,') he should take with him into the chapter-house *notarium proprium, et unum clericum quem uoluerit, honestos uiros non coniugatos.*

Some interesting documents, which will probably throw a new light upon the condition of some of the English clergy previous to the reformation, have lately been discovered by an eminent Lincolnshire antiquary, and will soon it is hoped become *publici juris.*

[1] Hook's *Lives of the Archbishops*, II. 147.
[2] *Ibid.* p. 317.   [3] *Ibid.* p. 752.

In 1535 began the business of dissolving the monasteries; but four years later, when the king was already in treaty for a fourth consort, a cruel sting was put in the third and fourth tail of the *six articles*, in shape of an injunction of celibacy on all the clergy; while at the same time the regulars were reminded that they were still bound by their vow even though they had been unhoused from their retreats, not excepting any who took no benefice. (31 Hen. VIII. *cap.* 14, §§ 5, 7—10.)

In the following year (32 Hen. VIII. *c.* 10, § 1) it had been found impossible to exact the penalty of death in the numerous cases which had arisen, and it was commuted for forfeitures.

In 1547—9 king Edward repealed the above-mentioned statutes of his father (1 Ed. VI. *c.* 12, § 3) and 'all and every law and laws positive, canons, constitutions and ordinances heretofore made by authority of man only' which forbade marriage to any ecclesiastical or spiritual person (2 & 3 Ed. VI. *c.* 21, § 2), at the same time recommending celibacy and excluding anticipators from the benefit of the act. In 1551 —2 it was found necessary to support by the authority of a fresh statute those who took advantage of that which has just been cited: and in the latter year the XXXI st Article (answering to the first clause of the existing Articles of Religion of 1571) confirmed the law for ecclesiastical persons. Even in one particular case the king gave special licence to a vice-master of Trinity college, Cambridge (Thomas Dovel, B. D.), to enjoy his fellowship and vice-mastership, although he was married: *anno* 1551[1].

In 1553—4 (1 Mary *sess.* 2, *cap.* 2) the queen revived the old ecclesiastical laws by repealing 2 & 3 Ed. VI. *c.* 21 and 5 & 6 Ed. VI. *c.* 12. It does not appear from Law's *Ecclesiastical Statutes at large* (1847) that 1 Ed. VI. *c.* 12, § 3 was formally repealed. It is declared moreover in Burn's *Ecclesiastical Law,* (art. *marriage,*) that it 'finally repealed' 31 Hen. VIII. *c.* 14. On the other hand, it is stated generally in the following page (II. 453), that 'in Queen Mary's time, King Edward's laws being repealed, the clergy were again brought under the severe laws of King Henry VIII., and so continued during all that reign, and (which is remarkable) during also the whole reign of Elizabeth.' At all events, it appears from the case of John Rogers in 1555, and others, that queen Mary's chancellor (bishop Gardiner) and council proceeded under the statute of her father. Thus *all* who would continue in their benefices were forced to renounce their wives, and those who had formerly been *regulars* were not only deprived but forced to be separated from their wives as well[2]. Though this was a literal revival of her father's law, it was practically a dealing of much harder measure upon seculars[3] who like Rogers had returned to England at a time when married clergy were recog-

---

[1] Cooper's *Annals,* II. 58, referring to Strype, *Eccl. Mem.* II. ii. 12.

[2] See *Henry Wharton* ap. Wordsworth, *Eccl. Biog.* II. 336 n.

[3] *Ibid.* II. 304, n. (*pace* Fox). See also II. 315, 316, 330—4, 343, 376, 422, ed. 1839.

nized by law. Such rigour was contrary to the first canon of the council of Winton (1076), to the fifth of the apostolic canons, and to the example of St Peter, of whom S. Clemens Alexandrinus[1] relates that his wife was comforted by him and went before him to martyrdom. The rule of enforced clerical celibacy, which was at least improbable from the Bible, contrary to some of the earliest canons (e.g. *Gangran* IV., A.D. 324, which was received by the undivided Church; *Trullan* XIII., A.D. 692, the existing rule of the Eastern Church, according to which the bishops only are bound to be unmarried[2]), and proved by experience to be impracticable, has been abrogated for the Church of England by the XXXII nd Article, which was revised and passed by convocation, set forth by royal authority, and enjoined for subscription by act of parliament in 1571, 13 Eliz.

It was not however till 2 James I. *c.* 25, §§ 49, 59, that 1 Mary, *sess.* 2, *c.* 2, was formally repealed, and 2 & 3 Ed. VI. *c.* 21, and 5 & 6 Ed. VI. *c.* 12, made perpetual. It may have been that queen Elizabeth did not choose that parliament should appear to have any special prerogative in ecclesiastical matters. 'Or perhaps, in order to have the clergy more dependent, she might be willing that this matter should continue doubtful.' (Burn's *Eccl. Law*, II. 453 = [454].) Her policy in the case of the universities was unmistakeable.

---

[1] *Strom.* 7, ap. Euseb. *H. E.* III. 30.

[2] Other authorities will be found in the Bishop of Ely's Exposition of Article XXXII.

With remarkable foresight bishops Hugh de Balsham and Walter de Merton had set the example of
founding colleges in connexion with the secular and
not with the regular clergy towards the close of the
thirteenth century. Accordingly, at the dissolution
of monasteries in the reign of Henry VIII., their
foundations remained and formed the model for new
corporations, such as Trinity and Christ-Church, to
rise out of the dissolved religious houses. The clerical members of the universities would have lived
therefore, as a general rule, under the same condition
in queen Elizabeth's reign as other clerks who had
taken no vows. But there were other regulations
which affected them. · Many were already bound to
celibacy (so long as they remained upon the foundation) by the old statutes of their colleges, and it
can hardly be thought that these were over-ridden
by the XXXI st Article of 1562 which was promulgated by royal authority; for the queen had, only
a few months previously, in 1561, sent an ' Injunction
that no Head or member of any College or Cathedral Church being married, shall keep his Wife or
family within the Precincts of the same on Pain of
forfeiting all his Ecclesiastical Promotions there.'
(Dated *Ipswich, Aug.* 9, 1561[1].) It is mentioned
that of late ' within certain of the same Houses as
well the chief Governors, as the Prebendaries, Students, and Members thereof being married, do keep
particular Households with their Wives, Children, and
Nurses, whereof no small Offence groweth to the

---

[1] Dyer's *Privileges of Cambridge*, I. 49, 131.

Intent of the Founders, and to the quiet and orderly Profession of Study and Learning within the same.' The reason assigned for royal interference was 'least by Sufferance thereof, the rest of the Colleges, specially such as be so replenished with young Students as the very Rooms and Buildings be not answerable for such Families and young Children, should follow the like examples;' and it will be observed that the objection is laid, not to the infringement of celibacy, but to the inconveniencing of scholastic habits.

At the same time the will of queen Elizabeth cannot be disguised. 'When secretary Cecil sent this injunction to the Archbishop [M. Parker], he knew that it could not be well taken by him who was himself a married man, and much for the Clergy's liberty of marriage ; and so was Cecil himself : but he plainly told the Archbishop how the Queen still continued an enemy to the state of matrimony in Priests ; and was near at a point to have forbidden it then absolutely, had he not been very stiff at this juncture[1].'

Among other of the archbishop's suffragans, bishop Cox of Ely was not well pleased with the injunctions dutifully forwarded to him. He was afraid that the enforcement of them in the cathedral, where separate houses were provided for deans and prebendaries, would give rise to the evil of non-residence. In his own cathedral however there was only 'one Prebendary continually dwelling with his family in Ely

---

[1] Strype's *Life of Matthew* (Parker) *Archbishop of Canterbury*, II. ch. 8, anno 1561.

church.' 'Turn him out' (the bishop writes), 'daws and owls may dwell there for any continual house-keeping[1].' At the same time he thought it 'very reasonable that places for students should be in all quietness among themselves, and not troubled with any families of women or babes.' He was a good authority on this point, for (according to Cole in his *Athenae Cantabrigienses*) his own wife was introduced into Christ-Church while he was dean there about 1550, and she with the wife of Peter Martyr, one of the canons of that cathedral, were 'the first women ever introduced into a cloister or college, and upon that account gave no small scandal at the time.'

How far the injunctions were obeyed we may gather from a fact related by Strype in the next chapter of his Life of Parker (II. ix.); that the Arch-bishop himself and the bishop of London, only a few weeks later in the same year 1561, procured the admission of Laurence Humfrey as President of Magdalen College, Oxford, though one of the objec-tions urged against him by the fellows of that society was that he was a married man.

In June 1604 a bill entitled 'An Act prohibiting the Residence of Married Men, with their Wives and Families, in Colleges, Cathedral Churches, Collegiate Houses and Halls of the Universities of Oxford and Cambridge,' was sent up to the house of lords but stopped in committee after the second reading[2]. In

---

[1] Strype's *Life of Matthew* (Parker) *Archbishop of Canterbury*, II. ch. 8, anno 1561.

[2] Cooper's *Annals*, III. 5.

1605—6 it was again introduced and, after some technical difficulties had obstructed its progress, was finally lost on the second reading in the house of lords[1].

In the Elizabethan statutes of 1570 (which as has been remarked were given 'under the broad seal; but not confirmed by act of Parliament, as most of our Charters are,' Dyer, *Priv. Camb.* I. 158) is the following (*cap.* 50, De ordinationibus collegiis praescriptis, § 33) : *Socios collegiorum maritos esse non permittimus, sed statim postquam quis uxorem duxerit socius collegii desinat esse: ordinem tamen gradus sui in academia tenere potest.*

Dyer had remarked in another place (*Hist. Camb.* I. 94), 'Let it be noticed, that the old statutes by using the word *ecclesiasticos*, ecclesiastics, as effectually barred the heads of houses from marrying as fellows. Cranmer, in the old statutes, pared down the word *ecclesiasticos* to *socios*, leaving the door wide enough for masters to enter, though too narrow for fellows : still the authority, even for the marriage of the masters, was not positive, but left room for dispute. The cause was agitated ; and, in 1575, the masters triumphed in the person of Dr Goad, and on the ground that queen Elizabeth's statutes said nothing on the subject.'

The accusations laid against provost Goad by his fellows were various, and he came off with flying colours. It is hinted by Strype[2] that there was mali-

---

[1] Cooper's *Annals*, p. 20.

[2] Strype, *Annals*, II. ii. (p. 39, ed. Oxon.) = 421.

cious personal feeling in the case. 'One of these fellows was Lakes, of a haughty disposition, who had been provoked by the provost, having reproved him for his habit unbecoming a scholar. For he wore under his gown, a cut taffeta doublet of the fashion [1575] with his sleeves out, and a great pair of galligastion hose. For this disguised apparel, so unmeet for a scholar, the provost punished him a week's commons. This had ever after stuck in his stomach, and he had sundry expostulations afterwards with the provost about it: such was his stout nature and impenitency to be reproved.' Provost Goad was a strict disciplinarian. When acting as deputy vice-chancellor he reprimanded Mr Newman, Mr Pricke and Mr Nanton, who were found walking in King's college chapel, and bound them over in virtue of the oath which they had previously taken to obey the vice-chancellor and his deputy.

But for provost Roger Goad himself, one of the complaints laid against him was 'of his wife; that she came within the quadrant of the college; (though she came never twice within the quadrant, but kept within the lodgings). That their statutes did forbid the provost to marry; though the statutes, as the provost in his answer shewed, did not forbid the provost's marriage: and that the visitor's statutes in the beginning of the queen's reign, and the university statutes lately made, allowed heads of colleges to marry.'

In Loggan's *Cantabrigia Depicta*, published about 1680—90, the master's wife is represented taking the air in his trim Dutch garden in Jesus college, fan in

hand, accompanied by her spaniel. The like is depicted in his engraving of Trinity Oxon. in 1672—3.

Early in the reign of king George III. some of the
fellows of colleges began to demand that the same
privilege should be granted themselves as had been
conceded to the heads of several of the colleges. The
earliest mention of the subject at that period which
I have seen is in the Bodleian [*Gough*, Camb. 36],
'The Council in the Moon. *Alitur Vitium vivitque
tegendo.* VIRG. *Cambridge. Sold* by *Fletcher* and
Hodson on the Market Hill. Sold also by Messrs.
Wilson and *Fell*, in Paternoster-Row, *London*, and all
other Booksellers in England. 1765.' pp. 23. It is a
miserable production.

In Cooper's *Annals* (IV. 340) is printed a letter from
Edward Betham, fellow of King's, to Cole in the following year (31 Jan. 1766). "In the University we have
all of late been in a most violent flame, labouring
under the same disorder that carried off poor Dr M.
some years agone. Young and old have formed a
resolution of marrying....But it must be confessed indeed they go on with more prudence than your honest
and simple friend...The scheme therefore is—a wife
and a Fellowship with her. For this purpose the
University is to Petition the Parliament, to release
the Fellows of the several Colleges from the observance of all such Statutes of our Founders, as oblige
them to Celibacy....This affair has been canvassed
and warmly agitated among us between two and
three months. There were those, who would not
believe it was or could be intended in earnest: who

imagined it to be a jest only. However, the projectors and abettors of the, scheme were in earnest. Accordingly a Grace was drawn up, and on Friday last brought into the House. Mr Ashby [Geo. Ashby, St John's, B.A. 1744], who, in a manner with the whole of St John's, was exceeding warm and zealous in the cause, was fixed upon to present the Grace: but for some reason or other then declined it.   There was the greatest confusion imaginable in the House: this added to the tumult; did not in the least allay or abate: but excited and heightened the warmth and ardour of the Partizans.   The Grace was shewn, but not in form proposed to the Vote of the whole House. Nothing therefore was determined at the Congregation.   The party however continues hot, and is in hope of downing to the ground with Celibacy.

"The Preamble of the Grace is, Cum Celeberrimae quaeque et florentissimae Universitates apud exteras gentes quae ad reformatam Fidem accesserunt, liberam Matrimonii celebrandi Potestatem Academicis suis permiserint, ut se in libertatem cum Politicam tum Christianam vindicent in Nostra Academia socii: Placeat vobis, &c. ['The grace is in full in MS. Cole, xxiii. 73 *b*.']...You observe the foundation they go upon.   The restraint from marrying they look upon as a Remnant of Popery...   This is an affair of so extraordinary a nature that I thought you would like to have some account of it."

In 1783 a bill passed the House of Commons (3rd. reading Jan. 24) to remove the restriction of celibacy. from the *Heads* of such colleges as were still bound ιy their statutes in that respect. It appears however hat in committee the name of Cambridge was re-noved from the bill[1].

It appears that while the case of these *masters* ιf colleges was before the public, the grievances of he *fellows* were again brought up. In the *Gentle-nan's Magazine* (LIII. 129) married fellowships are ιdvocated : and it was (I should conjecture) on this ιccasion that there appeared on the same side ' *A Fair Statement: περὶ πάντων ἐρῶ καθέκαστον ἐφεξῆς ιαὶ οὐδὲν ἑκὼν παραλείψω.* Dem. pro Cor.' pp. 11: *M. Watson*, Printer, *Cambridge.* [Bodl. *Godwin* Pamph. 908. No title or date.] In the opening of this pamphlet the abolition of the restriction of celi-bacy in the case of Cambridge fellows is said to be 'a measure loudly called for by the great body of the University' on the ground that fellows are exempted as 'ecclesiastical Persons' by 1 Jac. I. XXV. 48—50, and inasmuch as compulsory celibacy is con-trary to Scripture.

There is evidence of a fresh stir in the matter about the years 1793—8.

In 1794 'A Letter on the Celibacy of Fellows of Colleges' was published by *Johnson*, St Paul's Church Yard, and in 1798 appeared 'Reflections on the Caelibacy of Fellows of Colleges. *Semper nocuit differre paratis.* Lucan. — *Cambridge*, Sold by *J. Deighton*, 1798. Price sixpence.' pp. 25. [Bodl. *Gough*, Camb. 66.] This had been *written* in October, 1793, which is made an excuse ' to account for allusions...

[1] Cooper's *Annals*, IV. 407.

to books which are now, or ought to be forgotten.'
The books referred to are, I believe, Frend's *Peace
and Union* (1793), Godwin's *Political Justice* (1793),
and, possibly, Paley's *Elements of Moral and Political
Philosophy* (1785). It is stated in the pamphlet before us (p. 8), that compulsory celibacy has an evil
effect on the character and the reputation of fellows. It is proposed (p. 21) that the tutor should
be the only married man who should occupy rooms
in college, and even he should not have his family
within the walls. On page 19 it is recorded that
'since writing this a member of the university of
Cambridge has had it in contemplation to present a
grace to the senate, to prevent colleges from admitting more young men than can be accommodated
with appartments within the walls of the colleges.'

Both the 'Letter' and the 'Reflections' are quoted
in ' *Toleration of Marriage in the Universities*, recommended to the attention of the Heads of Houses;
with remarks on the provisions with which it should
be guarded. By *Charles Farish*, B. D., Fellow of
Queen's [*sic*] College, Cambridge, *Crudelis quoque tu
neque alma mater*.—Cambridge ; *printed by* Francis
Hodson, *and sold by* J. Deighton. *Price Two Shillings*.' Farish's is by far the most interesting pamphlet which appeared on the subject. 'On the 23rd
of March (1798) an unsuccessful attempt was made
to pass a grace for appointing a syndicate to decide
on the best means of abolishing the law by which
fellows of colleges are bound to a life of celibacy[1].'

[1] Cooper's *Annals*, IV. 462.

· The dissatisfaction on this point seems to have kept up a smouldering existence, for there is in my father's possession a copy of a pamphlet which belonged formerly to Mr Geo. Dyer (who however does not mention it in his *History of Cambridge*, I. 94 *n.* 1814). It is

'*Forbidding to Marry*, a Departure from the Faith: A Sermon, preached before the *University of Cambridge* at Great St. Mary's Church, on Sunday, Nov. 8, 1812. By *James Plumptre*, B.D., Fellow of *Clare Hall*, and Vicar of *Great Gransden* in *Huntingdonshire.* Cambridge: *printed by* J. Hodson: *and sold by* J. Deighton *and.* J. Nicholson, Cambridge: *and by* F. C. & J. Rivington, St. Paul's Church Yard; *and* J. Hatchard, no. 190, Piccadilly, London. *Price one shilling.* 1812.' [pp. 15, with a curious list of Books by the same author, including a Sermon on the Small-Pox and Cow-Pock, another on sea-bathing at Margate, the Camb. Bible Society, and works relating to the expurgation of the drama, and Aikin's Songs.] Dedication to the Chancellor, V.C., representatives in parliament, heads, and senate. Reference is made to Farish's pamphlet, to Reflections on the Celibacy, &c., and also to *Ro. A. Ingram's* '*Disquisition on Population, in which the Principles of the Essay on Population by the Rev.* T. R. Malthus *are examined and refuted*'; and to the *British Critic* for Sept. 1811, Vol. XXXVIII. p. 290, besides Henry Wharton's erudite Treatise on the Celibacy of the Clergy printed more than a century earlier.

Oxford men will not need to be reminded of the doings at Merton which Anthony Wood deplored in his *Life* when about a twelvemonth after the restoration Sir Thomas Clayton was made warden and found his way into the college in spite of the attempts of the fellows for a fortnight or 3 weeks to bar him out; and how he learnt that the key of the stables would unlock the chapel door. But though A. W. complains bitterly of the cost to which the College was[1] put by the 'great dislike...taken by the

[1] Cooper's *Annals*, II. 348.

lady Clayton to the warden's standing goods, namely chaires, stooles, tables, chimney-furniture, the furniture belonging to the kitchin, scullery, &c. all which was well liked by Dr Goddard, Brent, Savile, &c.... Secondly, the warden's garden must be alter'd, new trees planted, arbours made, rootes of choice flowers bought, [Rootes of flowers, which cost 5 shil. a root] &c. All which tho unnecessary, yet the poore coll. must pay for them, and all this to please a woman. Not content with these matters, there must be a new summer-house built at the south-end of the warden's garden, wherein her ladyship and her gossips may take their pleasure, and any eaves-dropper of the family may hearken what any of the fellows should accidentally talk of in the passage to their own garden.' And well they might complain, for there sure enough in Loggan's view of Merton (which must have been drawn in warden Clayton's time) is shewn, beside the arbour on the north, a lordly watch-tower built on the wall of the south terrace walk, a considerable stone building mounted by 16 steps and commanding a fine view of the meadows, which however might have been had before from 'the larg bay-window...at it's south-end¹.' Though he further complained of his 'burdning his accompts with frivolous expences to pleasure his proud lady, as (1) For a key to the lock of the ladies seat in St Marie's church, to which she would commonly resort. (2) For shoes and other things for the foot-boy'—[and the grievance

---

¹ *Ibid.* p. 122. Ed. *Oxon.* 1848.

did not cease, for as late as 'Hilary terme 1674,' the bursar had to pay about 10 *li.* 'for a very larg looking-glass for her to see her ugly face and body to the middle:' which looking-glass they did carry 'to their country seat, called *the Vach*' in Buckinghamshire] still it would not be true to say that the fellows' dislike of warden Clayton was due to his bringing a wife into college, any more than it would be correct to refer the opposition shewn to D[r] Bentley, at Trin. Coll. Cambridge, half a century later, to his wasting the goods of the College. Bentley built a new summer-house contiguous to his own study[1], he laid out the garden of the Lodge and made a terrace at the expense of the College, but without any order from the seniority. Clayton did the like. The-master of Trinity extorted leave to erect a handsome new staircase[2] &c. at a cost far above his estimate: warden Clayton's summer-house cost about five times the 20 pounds which he had asked at first[3]. Each of these heads with profuse meanness consumed in their own houses the fuel which belonged to the College. But these offences were not the first grounds of the unpopularity of either: each of them was disliked before he set foot within the College which he was to govern. Otherwise it is not impossible that Bentley might have built his noble staircase without hearing a murmur from the fellows, and Clayton might have brought his wife into College in 1661 without provoking much discontent. But the warden

---

[1] Monk's *Bentley*, II. 23, 24.   [2] *Ibid.* I. 175.
[3] *Ibid.* II. 201. Cp. A. Wood's *Life*, p. 122.

of Merton was known to be 'the very lol-poop of
the university,' a person of scandalous life, a turn-
coat, who 'had sided with the times after the grand
rebellion broke out in 1642,' and a stranger[1]; while
the master of Trinity, as all were aware, had been
a Tartar to those who had thought to catch him, and
a Johnian.

The late professor Conington, in his answers in
evidence (p. 116) to the Oxford University Commission, 1852, speaks thus of the restriction of celibacy of fellows: 'Like that of Orders it is not purely
arbitrary but serves a distinct purpose, though scarcely
that which originally suggested its introduction. Yet
it would be difficult to make out that the end here,
any more than in the case of Orders, either justified
or necessitated the means employed. The end. I
take to be two-fold:—to carry out the Collegiate
system by securing the residence of tutors within
the walls, and to expedite the succession to Fellowships by increasing the chance of vacancies. The
first thing to be observed is that these considerations,
taken at their best, obviously apply to a part of the
body of Fellows, not to the whole...Those for whom
residence within College walls is desirable are clearly
the tutors: those whose Fellowships it is important
to make terminable must be the sinecurists and the
non-residents...So long as married heads of Colleges
occupy a part of the College buildings a proposal
to allow a similar privilege to married tutors is not

---

[1] Ant. Wood's *Autobiog.* pp. 118, 119. Bliss, 1848.

to be treated as an absurdity ; much less to be put down by paltry sneers about domestic details.'

On the other hand the Cambridge Univ. Commission, 1852, reports (p. 172) that 'We notice the condition of celibacy which by law or practice is now invariably attached to the tenure of all Fellowships in Cambridge, only to say that it cannot in our opinion be conveniently separated from the Collegiate system. We do not doubt, however, that the condition has tended to prevent many men of ability and eminence from continuing their residence in the University so long as might have been desirable. We have accordingly proposed a scheme for the extension of the Professorial body and the creation of an entirely new one under the name of Public Lecturers, which, among other recommendations, appears likely to compensate for the difficulties experienced in retaining the most eminent Graduates in the immediate service of the University owing to the condition of celibacy attached to all the Fellowships. Upon this point we may remark that the Statutes of some Colleges are silent, probably because in Roman Catholic times the celibacy of the Fellows of a College was assumed to be indispensable and no express law was required to enforce it. It is, however, understood that, in the case of the Colleges referred to, one of the "Ordinances prescribed for Colleges" contained in Cap. L. of the Statutes of the University (xii. Eliz.) has supplied the omission of the condition in their particular Codes.

'The following is the Ordinance in question :

" Socios Collegiorum maritos esse non permittimus, sed statim postquam quis uxorem duxerit, socius Collegii desinat esse : ordinem tamen gradus sui in academia tenere potest."

'In revising the Statutes of the University and of the Colleges, it will be necessary to make provision for the continuance of this rule.'

At the present time, in some Colleges and under certain conditions fellows do not at once vacate their fellowships by marriage, but in no case can their families reside within the walls.

While Dr Goad was Vice-chancellor in 1576—7, it had been his duty to commit the Minister of Trinity parish to prison for having solemnized an irregular marriage between John Byron (of Newstead, *co.* Nottingham), scholar of Queens', aged 19, and a daughter of Nic. Beaumont of Cole Orton. Two masters of arts who had been present at the ceremony were also imprisoned.

The Injunctions of king Charles I. (dated *Newmarket,* Mar. 4to 1629) speak of another difficulty:

'We have been informed that of late years many Students of...our university, not regarding their own birth, degree and quality, have made divers contracts of marriage with women of mean estate and of no good fame in that town [of Cambridge], to their great disparagement, the ·discontent of their parents and friends, and to the dishonour of the government of our university: We will and command you, that at all times hereafter if any taverner, victualler or In-holder, or any other inhabitant of that town or within the jurisdiction of that University, shall keep any daughter or other woman in his house to whom there shall resort any scholars of that University of what condition soever, to mispend their time, or otherwise to misbehave themselves, or to engage themselves in marriage without the consent of those that have the guardiance and tuition of them ; that...you command the said woman or women, thus suspected (according to the form of your charter against women *de malo suspectas*) to remove out of the said University and four miles of the same.'

In 1712 a case of this kind came to light[1], for in that year Sarah Howel and Car. Morgan were prosecuted for entertaining scholars and carrying on courtships between them and certain women. It was owing perhaps partly to laxity of discipline, and partly to the fact that the inmates of the Universities were drawn in less proportion from gentlemen's families than at present, that there was more common intercourse between them and the families of tradesmen in the University towns. The custom of drinking toasts must also have contributed in some measure to the same result. The consequence was that academics used to keep company with such well-dressed young women as found nothing better to do, something in the way in which young 'prentices may now be seen making holiday on Sunday afternoons: but in the days of ceremony, snuff-boxes and fans.

It appears from Dr Rawlinson's MSS. that early

---

[1] See Index I. in the Registrary's Office, *Acta Curiae.*

in the last century a good deal of attention was paid
to the promenades and gardens of Oxford.　In 1706
'Trinity Coll. Grove altered, and Merton Coll. Summer House built.'　The latter was, I suppose,
a rival edifice to Mrs Clayton's watch-tower [*supra*
p. 358].　In the following year he records 'A new
terrace walk in Merton Coll. Garden, made upon
the Town Wall, 74 yards long.'　Zachary Conrad
v. Uffenbach, who was there a few years later (Sept. 3,
1710), after mentioning the sun-dial in the court
whereof the gnomon is a pillar, adds that the representation of the history of John Baptist shewn him
over the door by the worthy 'Socius Collegii' who
lionized him was nothing remarkable.　'Nor is the
Garden, which is considered however the finest in
Oxford.　It consists of a grove or some dark low
walks, which, as they have no proper air, are not
pleasant.　At the side is a raised path and a poor
pleasure-house[1].'　Three days later he walked in the
allée behind Magdalene.

Merton Garden had been celebrated by bishop
John Earle [of Worcester and Sarum, dean of West-
minster, translator of *Icôn basilikê*, and of Hooker's
Ecclesiastical Polity, and author of '*Microcosmographie,
or a Peece of the World discovered*; in Essayes and
Characters,' 3 editions in 1628.　Reprinted lately by
Mr *Arber*] in his poem, *Hortus Mertonensis*[2], written

[1] Uffenbach, *Reisen*, III. 152.
[2] Ap. Jo. Aubrey's *Natural Hist. and Antiq. of Surrey*, IV. 167, &c.
quoted à *propos* of Howard's 'long *Hope*,' i.e. according to Virgil,
deductus vallis,

while a fellow of that society [M.A. 1624]. He contrasts the natural growth of the trees under the care of Thomas Hawkins, the old gardener, with the fashionable stiff Dutch clipping of shrubs into grotesques. He mentions the game of bowls and the rustic seats there.

Z. C. von Uffenbach, at the close of his account of a visit to S. John's Coll., Oxford in 1710, Sept. 25, says, 'the hall is small but tolerably clean, and smells not so ill as the rest generally. There hang certain portraits of sundry benefactors of the college therein. Next we went on to a garden, which they call Paradise Garden. This is hard by an end of the town near a tavern, which is in connexion with it, and at the back of which on the water are countless little boxes partitioned by hedges, where the fellows drink in summer. [*In dem hinten an dem Wasser unzchliche kleine Cabinete von Hecken gezogen neben einander sind, da die Heeren* Fellows (Socii) *im Sommer darinnen trinken*[1].]

'The garden in itself is not otherwise remarkable, and is for the most part devoted to the kitchen; however, there are beautiful fruit-trees, and in particular many yew-trees there. I have never before seen such plenty of these together, as there is a whole nursery of young ones in this place. Those in the walk had, all of them at least that were young, a kind of fruit which I had not seen before. They are little red berries hollow inside, just like raspberries, except that these are rather smaller, rounder, and quite

---

[1] Uffenbach's *Reisen*, III. 171.

smooth. Their colour and transparency, as well as the opening in the centre, is in other respects similar. Mention of this fruit has already been made in *Borrichius*. [Olaus Borch, a Danish medical writer 1626,+1690.] Also the door or wicket of this garden is worthy of notice.'

This pleasaunce appears in the map of T. Neale and Radulph Agas (1566—78), engraved by Loggan a century later, as 'Paradise;' and in Loggan's own (1675) as 'Paradise garden,'—at the bend of the river to the south of the Castle. 'Paradise Walks' is the scene of the three first acts of *The Humours of Oxford*, a play by James Miller of Wadham (1703,+1744). In the third report (1872) of the Historical MSS. Commission is mentioned 'a curious drawing of Wadham College Gardens, A.D. 1711, and pen-and-pencil sketches of the heads of Oxford authorities of the period,' in Vol. XLIII. of the MSS. of the Reverend Sir William Cope, Bart., at Bramshill House, *co.* Hants.

'The Oxford Packet, *London*, Printed for *J. Roberts*, 1714.' [in St John's Coll. library Cambridge, Hh. II. 27] contains 'I. News from Magdalen College [Sacheverell's Inscription on a piece of Plate].—II. Antigamus: or a Satire against Marriage, Written by Mr Thomas Sawyer.—III. A Vindication of the *Oxford* Ladies, wherein are displayed the Amours of some Gentlemen of *All Souls* and St *John's* Colleges.'

In 1716 'the wall under the town wall (commonly called the Dead-man's wall, from being so warm as to revive a man almost dead with cold, and by others Montpelier) at the back of Merton College was raised.

At the same time Christ Church White Walk was made wider, and part of the said wall rebuilt.

'1717, Aug. 14. The back-door to Merton College Garden was shut up, on account of its being too much frequented by young scholars and ladies on Sunday nights. And June 17, 1718, for the same reason, by order of the warden and fellows, the garden was to be kept locked every Sunday[1].' Hearne has recorded[2] the incident which immediately occasioned the former step.

'Aug. 23, 1717...Last week was published a six-penny pamphlett, written in verse by one (as 'tis said) of St. John's Coll., called *Merton Walks, or the Oxford Beauties.* Though 'tis but poor stuff yet it was mightily bought up [a copy now in the library of St John's Coll. Camb., classed Gg. 7. 16]. The characters are so far from being different that there is, as it were, the same character running throughout, and that is the praise or commendation of the ladies. The society of Merton college have since ordered the garden to be kept close and the steps to be pulled down. One of the beauties in this pamphlett is one Mrs Fiddes that lodges against the Angel Inn at Shipway's the barber's. She is daughter of Mr Fiddes, S.T.B....very conceited but void, as it were, of understanding.' This young lady was nicknamed, after her father's work, the 'Body of Divinity[3].' 'Thereupon the young gentlemen and others betook

---

[1] Dr Rawlinson's MSS. ap. [Walker's] *Oxoniana*, IV. 229.

[2] *Reliqu. Hearn.* Bliss, II. 51, 52 (ed. 1869).

[3] *Ibid.* II. 223.

themselves to Magdalen college walk, which is now [1723] every Sunday night in summer time strangely filled, just like a fair, which hath occasioned a printed letter giving an account of an accident which happened between a young gentleman and a young woman[1].'

Hearne mentions Alderman White's daughters as being Oxford Toasts[2].

We find again that in 1727, 'Aug. 12, Merton Coll. back-gate that led into the fields was shut up, and another opened through the grove[3].'

Erasmus Philipps, when a 'Fellow Commoner' (gentleman commoner) of Pembroke Coll., Oxon., paid 10*s*. for a key of the college garden, Aug. 4, 1720 (as Gibbon, when gentleman commoner at Magdalene, was presented with a key of the library), which, in Sept. 1722, he made over to Mr Andrew Hughe, scholar of the college[4].

On April 21, 1721, appeared the 28th number of *Terrae Filius*, wherein Amherst gives his sketch of the Oxford Ladies or Toasts of the time. He hints that from prudential motives their lives were respectable (p. 157), that they were frequently daughters 'of the *townsmen* of *Oxford* (who are, many of them, *matriculated* men), who would marry them 'to advantage, if they could, in which I can see no great harm on their parts' (p. 153).

After speaking of the Royal letter sent to our

---

[1] Rawlinson, MSS. ap. *Oxoniana*, II. 170.
[2] *Ibid.* II. 89.　　[3] *Ibid.* IV. 241.
[4] *Notes and Queries*, 2nd S. pp. 365, 444.

university in 1629, he proceeds to say : ' Happy is it for the present generation of *Oxford* TOASTS, that *King* CHARLES I. (so much unlike that accomplish'd *gentleman*, his son) was long ago laid in the dust ! Were that *rigid* king now alive, my mind misgives me strangely, that I should soon see an end of all the *balls* and *cabals*, and *junketings* at *Oxford;* that several of our most celebrated and right beautiful madams would pluck off their fine feathers, and betake themselves to an *honest livelihood;* or make their personal appearance before the *lords of his* majesty's privy-council, *to answer their contempt, and such matters as should be objected against them.*

But HE is dead ! and the *sculls*, as much as they talk for him at *some certain seasons*, have not respect enough for him, or have too much respect for the *ladies*, to take his advice in this particular. I do not charge all the *Oxford* TOASTS with the same *ill fame*, or the same *ill designs;* nor would I, knowingly, charge any one of them with any one thing of which she is guiltless : but an OXFORD TOAST, in the common acceptation of that phrase, is such a creature as I am now going to describe.

She is born, as the *King* says, of *mean estate*, being the daughter of some insolent *mechanick*, who fancies himself a *gentleman;* and resolves to keep up his *family* by marrying his girl to a *parson* or a *school-master :* to which end, *he* and his *wife* call her *pretty Miss*, as soon as she knows what it means, and send her to the *dancing-school* to learn to hold up her head, and turn out her toes : she is taught, from a child, not to play with any of the dirty boys and girls in the neighbourhood; but to mind her *dancing*, and have a great respect for the *gown*.   This foundation being laid, she goes on fast enough of herself, without any farther assistance, except an *hoop*, a *gay suit of cloaths*, and *two* or *three* new *holland smocks*.   Thus equipt, she frequents all the *balls* and *publick walks* in *Oxford*; where it is a great chance if she does not, in *time*, meet with some raw coxcomb or other, who is her *humble servant*; waits upon her home; calls upon her again the next day; dangles after her from place to place; and is at last, with some art and manage-ment, drawn in to *marry* her.

She has *impudence—therefore* she has *wit*;

She is *proud—therefore* she is *well-bred*;

She has *fine Cloaths—therefore* she is *genteel*.'

In one of his papers of Advice 'to all gentlemen *School-Boys* in his majesty's dominions, who are de-sign'd for the university of *Oxford*' (*Terrae Filius*, XXXIII.) he refers to the same subject in terms which, if not to be taken *cum grano*, need at least, like all dishes served up by a malcontent cook, to be swal-lowed warily in suspicion of heat and seasoning.

'Have a particular regard how you speak of those *gaudy things* which flutter about *Oxford* in prodigious numbers in summer time, called TOASTS; take care how you reflect on their parentage, their condition, their Virtue, or their beauty; ever remembering that of the Poet,

'Hell *has no* Fury *like a* Woman scorn'd,'

especially when they have *spiritual bravoes* on their

side.' (Hogarth's frontispiece to the Terrae Filius Essays when collected in 1726, represents that personage as torn to pieces by enraged Toasts and Dons.)

'Not long ago, a bitter lampoon was published upon the most celebrated of these *petticoat-professors ;* as soon as it came out, the town was in an uproar, and a very severe sentence was passed upon the author of this anonymous libel: to discover whom, no pains were spared; all the disgusted ill-natured fellows in the university were, one after another, suspected upon this occasion. At last, I know not how, it was peremptorily fixed upon *one ;* whether justly or not, I can't say; but the parties offended resolved to make an example of *some body* for such an enormous crime, and *one* of them (more enraged than the rest) was heard to declare [with an oath] that, right or wrong, that *impudent scoundrel* (mentioning his Name) *should be expelled ;* and that SHE *had* interest enough with the PRESIDENT *and* SENIOR FELLOWS *of his College to get his business done.* Accordingly, within a year after this, he was (almost unanimously) *expelled from his Fellowship*, in the presence of some of the persons injured, who came thither to see the execution.

'*Felix, quem faciunt* aliena pericula *cautum*, was the *Thesis* pitch'd upon by the *excluding doctors* for the *undergraduates* to moralize upon in a public exercise upon this occasion.'

In the library of St John's Coll. Camb. is bound up with 'Merton Walks, or The Oxford Beauties: &c. 1717, pp. 31. [Gg. 7. 16.] a copy of *Strephon's*

Revenge: A Satire on the *Oxford Toasts.* Inscribed to the Author of *Merton Walks,*' 2nd ed. corrected, 1718. It begins with a complaint of 'the almost universal corruption of our youth, which is to be imputed to nothing so much as to that multitude of Female *Residentiaries'* who encourage idleness and foppery. These ladies, it appears, went about without chaperons; and many of them were children of poor tradesmen[1]. Page iv. describes one of their hangers-on: 'A College-*Smart* is a Character, which few perhaps are acquainted with; He is one that spends his Time in a constant Circle of Engagements and Assignations; He rises at Ten, tattles over his Tea-Table till Twelve, Dines, Dresses, waits upon his Mistress, drinks Tea again, flutters about in Publick 'till it is dark, then to the Tavern, knocks into College at Two in the morning, sleeps till Ten again,' and so on.

This account does not differ much from the description of 'the Lownger' in the *Oxford Sausage,* which was first published in 1764.

'I rise about nine, get to Breakfast by ten,
   Blow a Tune on my Flute, or perhaps make a Pen;
   Read a Play 'till eleven, or cock my lac'd Hat;
   Then step to my Neighbours, 'till Dinner, to chat.
   Dinner over, to *Toms,* or to *James's* I go,
   The News of the Town so impatient to know;
   While *Law, Locke,* and *Newton,* and all the rum Race,
   That talk of their Modes, their Ellipses, and Space,
   The Seat of the Soul, and new Systems on high,
   In Holes, as abtruse as their Mysteries, lie.

[1] Or college servants. *Terra Filius,* No. xxxv.

From the Coffee-house then I to Tennis away,
And at five I post back to my College to pray:
I sup before eight, and secure from all Duns,
Undauntedly march to the *Mitre* or *Tuns;*
Where in Punch or good Claret my Sorrows I drown,
And toss off a Bowl " To the best in the Town:"
At One in the Morning, I call what's to pay,
Then Home to my College I stagger away,
Thus I tope all the Night, as I trifle all Day.'

These lines had appeared previously in the *Student*
II. 279, in 1751, with the slight variations of six,
for five, as the hour of Chapel service, and *Clapham's*
(for *James's* which is mentioned in *Tom Warton's*
'Panegyric on *Oxford* Ale:' see p. 146 supra), which
and *Tom's* are described at the foot as 'Noted coffee-
houses in *Cambridge.*' In an earlier number of 'the
Student or Oxf. and Camb. Monthly Miscellany[1]'
we are told that 'In every college there is a set of
idle people called *Lowngers* whose whole business is
to fly from the painful task of thinking...Whomsoever
these *Remoras* of a college adhere to, they instantly
benumb to all sense of reputation, or desire of learning.' In the summer of 1711, Steele had described
a new sect of philosophers at Cambridge, called
Lowngers in the language of that university. 'Our
young students are content to carry their speculations
as yet no farther than bowling-greens, billiard-tables,
and such like places.' Steele, who had been at
Oxford (of Merton College) about fifteen years earlier, goes on to say 'I must be so just as to observe,
I have formerly seen of this sect at our other uni-

[1] 1750, I. p. 21.

versity; though not distinguished by the appellation which the learned historian, my correspondent, reports they bear at Cambridge. They were ever looked upon as a people that impaired themselves more by their strict application to the rules of their order, than any other students whatever. Others seldom hurt themselves any further than to gain weak eyes, and sometimes headaches; but these philosophers are seized all over with general inability, indolence, and weariness, and a certain impatience of the place they are in, with an heaviness in removing to another[1].'

A letter from *Leo* the Second, dated at his Den in — college in *Cambridge,* in the summer of 1713[2], records that there is 'at present a very flourishing Society of People called *Lowngers,* Gentlemen whose Observations are mostly itinerant, and who think they have already too much Good-sense of their own to be in need of staying at home to read other Peoples.'

The following sketch was published in the *Con-noisseur,* Aug. 21, 1755[3].'

'A Lownger is a creature that you will often see lolling in a coffee-house, or sauntering about the streets, with great calmness, and a most inflexible stupidity in his countenance. He takes as much pains as the Sot to fly from his own thoughts; and is at length happily arrived at the highest pitch of indolence, both in mind and body. He would be

[1] *Spectator,* 54.

[2] *Guardian,* 124.   [3] *Connoisseur,* 82.

as inoffensive as he is dull, if it were not that his idleness is contagious ; for like the *torpedo*, he is sure to benumb and take away all sense of feeling from every one with whom he happens to come in contact.'

The Oxford *Smart* in 1721, is described in the 46th No. of Amherst's *Terrae Filius* :—

' " *Oxford* a boorish place !—poor wretch ! I am sorry for thy ignorance. Who wears finer *lace* or better *linnen* than *Jack Flutter?* who has handsomer *tie-wigs*, or more fashionable *cloaths*, or *cuts a bolder bosh* than *Tom Paroquet?* Where can you find a more handy man at a *Tea-Table* than *Robin Tattle?* Or, without vanity I may say it, one that plays better at *Ombre* than him who subscribes himself as an enemy... *Valentine Frippery.*" [Dated 'Christ-Church College, July 1.']

'He is a SMART of the first rank, and is one of those who come, in their *academical undress*, every morning between *ten* and *eleven* to *Lyne's* coffee-house; after which he takes a turn or two upon the *Park*, or under *Merton-Wall*, whilst the dull *regulars* are at dinner in their hall, *according to statute*; about *one* he dines alone in his chamber upon a *boil'd chicken*, or some *pettitoes*; after which he allows himself an hour at least to dress in, to make his afternoon appearance at *Lyne's*; from whence he adjourns to *Hamilton's* about *five*; from whence (after strutting about the room for a while, and drinking a dram of citron) he goes to chapel, to shew how genteely he *dresses*, and how well he can *chaunt*. After prayers he drinks Tea with some celebrated *toast*, and then waits upon her to *Maudlin* Grove, or *Paradise-Garden*, and back again. He seldom eats any supper, and never reads any thing but *novels* and *romances*.

'When he walks the street, he is easily distinguished by a stiff *silk gown*, which rustles in the wind, as he struts along; a *flaxen tie-wig*, or sometimes a long *natural* one, which reaches down below his rump; a broad *bully-cock'd hat*, or a *square cap* of above twice the usual size; *white stockings*, thin *Spanish leather shoes;* his cloaths lined with tawdry silk, and his shirt *ruffled* down the *bosom* as well as at the *wrists*. Besides all which marks, he has a delicate jaunt in his *gait*, and smells very *philosophically* of essence.

'This is a true description of my correspondent; and I leave the reader to judge, whether this is properly good *breeding*, or ridiculous grimace, and inconsistent *college foppery*. There is not, I agree with Mr. *Frippery*, a deficiency of this sort of politeness in OXFORD; but

a man, in my opinion, may be very *ill-manner'd* under a *silk gown*, and
do very uncivil things, for all he wears *lawn ruffles*. For instance, why
may not one of these *well-dress'd* sparks *damn all* strangers, *or knock
them down*, (provided he has a mob to defend him,) as well as a *ragged
servitor* of *Jesus*, or an *half-starv'd scholar* of *St. John's?* Is he ever
the *better bred* for being *better clad?* Or do *good manners* consist in
tufts or *silk stockings?*—That a gay suit of *cloaths* often hides a *bad skin*,
and that a *light wig* sets off a dirty countenance, I am well enough
convinc'd; but that they can hide too a multitude of *rudenesses* and *ill
manners*, or atone for them, is what I never yet read either in *holy
scripture*, or *profane philosophy*. I should not, for my part, like a *kick
of the breech* ever the better from having it from a *red topt* shoe; nor do
I think that a *broken head* would smart the less, tho' it were to be done
with a *clouded cane*.

'I know it is an hard thing to make any of my wary readers believe
that *beaux* can be quarrelsome; but I can assure them, upon the word
and honour of an *English* author, that *five* or *six* years ago, some
twenty or *thirty* of these *Oxford smarts* did actually frighten *three* or
four poor-spirited *foreigners*, and kick a *presbyterian parson* out of a
coffee-house.

'My dear friends the *smarts* have another very scurvy trick. Would
they be content to be *foppish* and *ignorant* themselves, (which seems to
be their sole study and ambition,) I could freely forgive them; but they
cannot forbear laughing at every body, that *obeys* the *statutes*, and differs
from them; or (as my correspondent expresses it, in the proper dialect
of the place) that does not *cut as bold a bosh* as they do. They have
singly, for the most part, very good *assurance;* but when they walk together in *bodies*, (as they often do,) how impregnable are their *foreheads!*
They point at every soul they meet, laugh very loud, and whisper as
loud as they laugh. *Demme*, Jack, *there goes a prig! Let us blow the
puppy up*—Upon which, they all stare him full in the face, turn him
from the wall as he passes by, and set up an *horse-laugh*, which puts the
plain, raw novice out of countenance, and occasions great triumph
amongst these *tawdery desperadoes*.

'There is, I confess, one thing in which the aforesaid *gownmen* are
very *courtly* and *well-bred;* I mean in paying their debts: for you are
not to suppose that they wear all this rich drapery at their own proper
costs and charges; all the SMARTS in OXFORD are not *noblemen* and
gentlemen-commoners, but chiefly of a meaner rank, who cannot afford
to be thus *fine* any longer than their *mercers, taylors, shoe-makers*, and
perriwig-makers will *tick* with them; which now and then lasts *three* or

four years; after which they brush off, and return, like meteors, into the same obscurity from whence they arose.

I have observed a great many of these *transitory foplings*, who came to the university with their fathers (rusty, old country farmers) in linsey-wolsey coats, greasy sun-burnt heads of hair, clouted shoes, yarn stockings, flapping hats, with silver hat-bands, and long muslin neckcloths run with *red* at the bottom. A month or two afterwards I have met them with *bob-wigs* and *new shoes, Oxford-cut;* a month or two more after this, they appear'd in *drugget cloaths* and *worsted stockings;* then in *tye-wigs* and *ruffles;* and then in *silk gowns;* till by degrees they were metamorphosed into compleat SMARTS, and damn'd the old country *putts,* their fathers, with twenty foppish airs and gesticulations.

'*Two* or *three* years afterwards, I have met the same persons in *gowns* and *cassocks,* walking with demure looks and an *holy leer;* so easy (as a learned divine said upon a *quite different occasion*) is the transition from *dancing* to *preaching,* and from the *bowling-green* to the *pulpit!*'

It is interesting to compare with this the account given by bishop Earle[1] an old Merton man, of '*A meere young Gentleman of the Vniuersitie*' in 1628:

'one that comes there to weare a gowne, and to say hereafter, hee has beene at the Vniuersitie. His Father sent him thither, because hee heard there were the best Fencing and Dancing Schooles, from these he has his education, from his Tutor the ouersight. The first Element of his knowledge is to be shewne the Colledges, and initiated in a Tauerne by the way, which hereafter hee will learne of himselfe. The two markes of his Senioritie, is the bare Veluet of his gowne, and his proficiencie at Tennis, where when hee can once play a Set, he is a Fresh-man no more. His Studie has commonly handsome Shelues, his Bookes neate Silke strings, which hee shewes to his Fathers man, and is loth to vntye or take downe for fear of misplacing. Vpon foule dayes for recreation hee retyres thither, and looks ouer the prety booke his Tutor Reades to him, which is commonly some short Historie, or a piece of *Euphormio;* for which his Tutor giues him Money to spend next day. His maine loytering is at the Library, where hee studies Armes and bookes of Honour, and turnes a Gentleman-Critick in Pedigrees. Of all things hee endures not to be mistaken for a Scholler,

---

[1] *Microcosmographie,* § 23 (Mr Arber's reprint).

and hates a black suit though it bee of Sattin. His companion is ordinarily some stale fellow, that ha's beene notorious for an Ingle to guld
hatbands, whom hee admires at first, afterward scornes. If hee haue
spirit or wit, hee may light of better company, and may learne some
flashes of wit, which may doe him Knights seruice in the Country
hereafter. But hee is gone to the Inns of Court, where hee studies to
forget what hee learn'd before, his acquaintance and the fashion.'

The *Gradus ad Cantabrigiam*, 1803 *and* 1824, re-
cognizes the term 'Lounger,' 'to Lounge,' 'to take a
Lounge,' and 'Lounging Book.' This last is explained to mean 'a novel, or any book, but a mathematical one. The late Mr Maps, of Trumpington-
street, possessed the most choice collection of *Lounging Books* that the genius of Indolence could desire.
The writer of these pages recollects seeing *Rabelais*
in English; several copies of the *Reverend* Mr Sterne's
Tristram Shandy; Wycherly and Congreve's Plays;
Joe Miller's Jests; Mrs Behn's Novels; and Lord
Rochester's Poems, which are very *moving!* And to
these we beg to add [ed. 1824]—The *Cambridge
Tart*, and *Facetiæ Cantabrigienses.*' The first edition
of the work just quoted, in 16mo. 1803, containing
about 150 pages, is said, in the Dedication, to have
been adapted to the pocket with a view to being a
complete *Lounging Book*. So also 'Tavern Anecdotes...By One of the Old School,' 1825, professes on
its title-page to be 'Intended as a *Lounge-Book* for
Londoners and their Country Cousins.'

This is the proper place to mention the '*Mappesian
Library;* founded by the late Mr John Nicholson,
alias *Maps* [His portrait which now, in 1824, adorns
the stair-case of the Public Library, was presented by

the Undergraduates], of Trumpington-street. Mr
Maps, if Fame lie not, was originally by profession a
staymaker, which, strange to relate, had not *attraction*
sufficient to bind him'to it long. He afterwards took
to crying and hawking of *maps* about the several Colleges in the University, whence he acquired *all* his
claim to eccentricity!!' (*Gradus ad Cantab.*) Gunning, in his *Reminiscences*[1], says, that this character
was universally known by the name of *Maps*, though
his only son, to whom he left a handsome property,
discovered he was entitled to the name of Nicholson.
When he first began business, he was a seller of maps
and pictures, which he exhibited in the streets on a
small movable stall; but when I came to College [in
1784] he was living in an old-fashioned, but large and
commodious house belonging to King's College, and
adjoining to what was then the Provost's Lodge. He
had a very large stock of books required at college
lectures, both classical and mathematical; and I do
not believe I expended during my undergraduateship
twenty shillings in the purchase of books for the lec-
ture-room. His terms of subscription were five shillings and threepence per quarter, but were afterwards
increased to seven shillings and sixpence. When his
house was pulled down to make way for the Screen
which connects the Chapel of King's with the New
Building, he built and removed to the house now occupied by Macmillan. He was indefatigable in pursuit of business, and was to be seen most part of the
day loaded with books going from room to room in

---

[1] Ed. 1854, I. 198—200.

the different colleges, and announcing himself by shouting MAPS as he proceeded. Persons requiring themes or declamations, or compositions on occasional subjects, were in the habit of applying to him, and if they had no objection to pay a high price, were furnished with articles of considerable literary merit. It was said that manuscript sermons might be obtained through him; but in every transaction of the kind he strictly concealed the names of the parties concerned. By the desire of Dr Farmer [of Emmanuel], his truly characteristic portrait was placed on the staircase of the Public Library, a distinction he was better entitled to, than a *smirking Professor* in scarlet robes who hangs very near him.'

Mr Geo. Dyer mentions[1] the full-length portrait by Reinagle, and states that Nicholson began by selling maps about the country, and also that 'the gownsmen and he lived in the exercise of constant depredations on each other. The fact seems to be, that the former began first to crib the books of the latter, and the latter was, therefore, compelled to make reprisals, or, otherwise, he must at length have had an empty shop. Maps's tricks came under the act of *se defendendo;* so that, though the gownsmen were often obliged to watch him like a sharper, still he was allowed, by general consent, to have deserved the character of an honest man.' He has won for his portrait a place among the town worthies in the Free Library, as well as in that of the university.

---

[1] *Cambridge Fragments,* pp. 88—90 in Vol. II. of *Privilges of Cambridge.*

In the *Cambridge Tart* 1823, p. 135, are some

> 'Lines on seeing the portrait of "Old *Maps*," a well-known biblio-thist of Cambridge, placed over the door of a country library.'

I reprint them without attempt at emendation.

> ' Can I forget thee, *Maps?* no! scanty praise
> Our learned Granta fail'd not to resound,
> As erst thy hasty steps pac'd classic ground.
> Thou bustling caterer for letter'd bays !
> When judgment sound might wrangler's honours rise
> How hast thou bid my spirits to rejoice
> When not a surly *dun*, but thine own voice,
> Welcom'd no trifling novel of the day ;
> 'Twas armful large !—a soil'd and tatter'd stock :
> *Euclid*, and *Conics*, *Algebra*, and *Locke*,
> And *Newton*, philosophic head supreme !
> And all the minor morals in array.
> Now, 'tis but Sonnetteer can sound thy fame,
> Thy son's superior merit dignifies the name.'

This looks not unlike a puff of John Nicholson, junior: the following *is* a *bona fide* advertisement, the only one on the original indigo-coloured boards of the Camb. Univ. Calendar for 1802 which he published:

'*Nicholson's Circulating Library*, near the *Senate-House, Cambridge*, Established *Fifty* Years. *Subscription*, 7s. 6d. per Quarter ; For which each *Subscriber* is allowed to have *Fifteen Books* at once. A Quarter's advance to be paid at the time of Subscribing. *Stationary*, Of all Kinds, and of the best Quality, and on the lowest Terms. *New Publications* and Books of every Description, procured on the shortest Notice. *Bookbinding* executed in a variety of plain or elegant Fashions. *Cambridge: printed* by *F. Hodson*.' [Corner of Green-street.]

In the same calendar, pp. 19, 20, is a note to the
effect that '*A Syllabus* of *each* Public Lecture (Modern History excepted) may be had at *Nicholson's*
and *Deighton's*, to the latter of whom the names of
the Attendants at the different Lectures are requested
to be delivered.' In the Introduction to the same
volume, *l—lii*, is a 'copy of Verses, which appeared
on a *Tripos* paper:' in fact the Tripos verses for 1781
when the subject of them was yet alive.

' Πολλά τε ἤδη

ΜΑΨ

HOM. *Il.* II. 213.

'O Tu Tyronis pariter, pariterque Sophistae
Deliciae! si vel mavis *Grantanus Apollo*,
Seu magis illustri titulo MAPS nomine gaudes,
Nunc ades, et felix audacibus annue coeptis.

Nil mihi Pierides: Parnassi somnia nulla:
Nec sitiens unquam properavi Heliconis ad undas;
Attamen aggrediens vestrae praeconia famae
Mirifico videor perculsus Numinis oestro,
Intùs et insolitos patiens inflarier ignes,
Heu rapior! flagranti animo, prodire Poëta.

Haud procul à celebri statuit quam Granta Palaestrâ
Aemula quà Pubes contorta Sophismata vibrant,
Stat domus; haud equidem Pariis innixa columnis,
Neve minans albo irrumpere in aethera tecto;
Cujus Apollinea clarus tamen Incola in arte,
Grammaticus, Rhetor, Geometres, omnis in usum
Ornatumque sciens artis, summusque Magister.

Oh ego si potui (catus utpote *Bunbury*) vivam
Effigiem vultumque viri depingere; chartis
Perpetuò nostris tua, MAPS, spiraret Imago.
Qui decor obsequii! blandi quae gratia Vultus!
Tu quoties properans Juvenum succurrere votis
Suaviter arrides; tu scilicet omnibus Idem,
Dona tuas quicunque rependunt annua ad aras.

Fallor! an ante oculos subitò sese atria pandunt
Templi—(Fama noces mendax—infama *Tabernae*
Nomen quae dederis,) premit undique turba togata,
Quisque sibi *Lucem spondens et Pocula sacra;*
Hic petit Euclidem; Newtonum deperit ille,
Tertius exorat Mopsae et Corydonis amores,
Quos legat ignavo solvens sua membra cubili.
Nonne vides? quam mente vacans! Incuria frontis
Regna tenens, sensus Lethaeo rore soporat.
Auctores titulosque librorum agnoverit ille
Tanquam ungues digitosque suos; quicquid tamen intùs
Lockius erudiit, Mentisque Animique recessus
Arcanos pandens, vix altera saecla docebunt.
Rarior has sedes visit tamen ille, capillis
Incomptis scissâve togâ qui mente capaci
Newtono invigilans nocturnam absumit olivam.
Summa Mathematicae referet mox praemia palmae
Victor, et agminâ gradietur Epomide Primus.

Haud tamen exercet MAPS sola domestica cura,
Nec satis esse putat proprios coluisse Penates,
Impiger excurrit per vicos; quaeque tulere
Seu *Veterum* gravior Sapientia, sive *Recentum*
Acrius ingenium; nulli non commodus offert.
Et quamvis humeris graviter tibi Musa, Mathesis,
Incumbant, Sophiaeque omni farragine pressus
Incedas, et fessa labet sub pondere cervix,
Frons tua laeta tamen, mira est tibi gratia Risûs.
Et veluti quondam sylvas Rhodopeïus Orpheus
Immitesque tigres et saxa sequentia duxit,
Vox tua si nostras veniat fortasse per aures,
Te subitò petimus properi, oblitusque laborum
Quisque, tibi sua Sacra refert et Numen adorat.

Si quem dura premant *Tutoris* jussa, Minervâ
Invitâ ut multum sudet miserabile carmen,
Scilicet elatus quia Majestate Sophistae,
Noctu finitimis voluit fera bella fenestris;
Thure pio supplex tibi si cumulaverit aras,
Huc Flacci rediisse Sales, tonitruque Maronis
In superas iterum jures revocarier auras.
Rhetoris an labor impositus? male sordidus esset
Qui per avaritiam patitur dispendia famae:

Ah potius tribuens sua MAPS munuscula, summus
Prodeat Orator Cicerone disertior ipso.
Jamque oro veniam, si nomen, Delie, vestrum
Ille ferat posthac; nec det ceu Marsya poenas,
Judice quo—famâ pariles sunt MAPS et Apollo.

Si te fatidicae praesse putaveris arti,
Ex *Tripode* ea nostrum fundentem Oracula Vatem,
Neve magis quam MAPS praenuncia Pythia Veri.
Seu jactes medicinam! at noster Bibliopola
Aegrotis Opifer longe praeclarior audit:
Scilicet hic nunquam vacuus queribundus in aures,
"*Heu Domino haud prosunt quae prosunt omnibus Artes.*"
Roma Palatinos tibi si decreverit arces,
Annon ipse vides assurgunt huic quoque templa,
Queis pretiosa magis, minus etsi lauta supellex?

Ter venerande Pater! si quid mea carmina possunt,
Nulla dies unquam memori tete eximet aevo.
Virgilius citiùs morietur; Horatius ipse
Ovidiusque simul; "quos non Jovis ira, nec ignis
Nec poterit ferrum, nec edax abolere Vetustas;"
Quam, MAPS, ulla tuae venient oblivia famae.'

'Previous to the Senate-House Examinations, *Maps* annually made an arrangement of the *Honors* with a foresight almost oracular[1].'

I noticed lately in Mr E. Johnson's shop a well-worn copy of Ludlam's Algebra. Within the first board was a label of Nicholson's Circulating Library almost effaced. Some borrower had written the name 'Mapps' in it, for which young Nicholson had substituted his own name. A later hand had then written 'Do not be ashamed of y^r name, your Father never was. Μαψς αυτον καλεουσι θεοι ανδρες δε Νιχολσον.'

In a volume of tracts in the Cambridge Free Li-

---

[1] *Camb. Univ. Calendar*, 1801, p. lii.

brary [B. 13. 50] is an advertisement of *Stevenson's* (late *Nicholson* and Son's) Circulating Library.

From the *Year Book* of 'ingenuous Hone' (*col.* 682), we learn that old Nicholson died Aug. 8, 1796, aged 66, lamented by an unparalleled circle of friends; it is said that he was known 'by the name of "Maps and Pictures." He presented to the University a whole length portrait of himself, loaded with books, which hangs in the staircase of the public library, and under it a print engraven from it.'

It was to oblige 'Maps' that, in 1786, Porson added some notes to an edition of Hutchinson's Xenophon's Anabasis, which was then about to be published[1].

Lending libraries were first tried in England a few years before the middle of the eighteenth century; but William Jones of Nayland (1726—1800) complains, in *Letters from a Tutor to his Pupils*, No. v, of the prevalence of novel-reading: 'this fashion, which has increased so much of late years, as nearly to swallow up all other reading; like the lean kine of Pharaoh, which swallowed up all the fat ones, and did not look the better for it.'

In the Bodleian [*Gough*, Oxford 90] is a paper relating to James Fletcher's Reading-Room for fifty subscribers, about 1780. In [Dr Caswall's] '*A New Art teaching how to be Plucked*,' &c. by Scriblerus Redivivus, Oxford, *J. Vincent*, ed. 3, 1835, pp. 17, 18, it is stated that 'there be four places in Oxford where

---

[1] *Life*, by Watson, p. 49.

novels are to be got; Mr Weatherstone's, Mr Dewe's,
Mr Hawkins', and Mr Richards'; whereof the first,
which is the oldest, is in St Aldates'; the second,
which hath many new books and various, is in Broad-
street; the third, in High-street; and the fourth, in
Magdalen-street.'

A passage in Nevile's *Poor Scholer*, 1662, *Act* ii.
sc. 4, shews that hiring books was an old shift, though
(we may hope) not often practised with so sinister a
design.—'*Pege.* Thus you must steer your course,
step to a Book-sellers, and give him this angel [*puts
money out of 's pocket*] which I'le lend you, for the use
of (the many-languag'd Bibles lately publisht) for a
week, their price is 12 pound, when you have once
got 'um into your study, invite your father to your
chamber, show him your Library, and tell him you
are 12 *l* out of purse for those large volumes.'

I have already mentioned (p. 144) the library in
Emmanuel coffee-house in 1763, and on pp. 151, 152,
I have quoted from *An Account of several* Public
Buildings *in* Oxford, *never before described*, in the
Student, Vol. II. No. 10 (July 3, 1751). In that paper
is included the following humorous sketch :—'In the
university there are several *libraries* (besides those of
RADCLIFFE, BODLEY, and of private *colleges*), which
were instituted to remedy the great neglect of reading so prevalent amongst us, as well as for the benefit
of those gownsmen who are incapable of reading
Greek or *Latin* [p. 374], and also to promote that
most edifying practice of *lownging.* For as, according
to the old maxim of PLINY, *mallem nihil agere quàm*

agere nihil, i.e. I had rather do nothing than have nothing to do; so is it better surely to read books of no use at all, than to read no books at all. Therefore, these *libraries,* to render them the more universal, are conjoin'd with the several *coffee-houses:* but the most remarkable is that lately erected near *New-College,* which, from the matter it contains, has obtained the appellation of ΠΑΜΦΛΕΤΙΚΟΝ. The number of *books,* which, for a very plain reason, are entirely in *English,* still daily encrease. But, for further particulars, we must refer the curious to its original founder and present librarian, the *great* Professor JOHNSON. It seems to be an universal maxim for the *students* in these *libraries* to keep a profound silence. At one of them in particular, near *St. Mary's,* is a place purposely set apart for those of a superior degree, who have sense enough to hold their tongues. This is call'd the *Temple of Silence.* The disciples are directly opposite to those of PYTHAGORAS: for, instead of being silent from the first seven years from their coming to the University, they are allow'd to talk a great deal of nothing for that time, but ever after never to open their lips.'

The paper concludes with a promise to the reader of a more complete book, 'already in the press,' on the subject. It was not, I believe, until 1762, that a fuller *jeu d'esprit* of that nature was published, no doubt by the same author, Tom Warton junior, fellow of Trin. Coll., Oxon. (though it has been asserted by A. Chalmers, in his *English Poets,* I. xiv., that 'The "Guide to the Companion" was the production

of Mr Huddesford'). Though it was re-edited in
1806 by Mr Cooke of Oxford, with the original cuts,
it is now a scarce book. I will, therefore, quote the
title at length, and a passage which bears upon p. 151
of this present compilation, as well as on the topic of
coffee-house-libraries.

'*A Companion* to the *Guide* and a *Guide* to the
Companion[1]: being a Complete supplement to all the
Accounts of *Oxford* hitherto published. Containing
An accurate Description of several *Halls, Libraries...*
&c. The whole interspersed with Original *Anecdotes*,
and interesting *Discoveries*, occasionally resulting from
the Subject. And embellished with perspective *Views*
and *Elevations* neatly engraved.

> *Avia Pieridum peragro loca: Nullius ante*
> *Trita solo......* LUCRET. IV. I.

London: Printed for *H. Payne*, at Dryden's Head
in Paternoster Row: and sold by the Booksellers of
Oxford. [Price Sixpence].' (No date, pp. i—iv, 5—40.
Bodl. Douce O. 56).

Page 8. ' I have discovered no less than

TWELVE HALLS,

never yet enumerated nor described, namely,

TIT-UP HALL,		FOX HALL,
CLAY HALL,		FEATHER HALL,
CABBAGE HALL,		KETTLE HALL,
CATERPILLAR HALL,		TRIPE HALL,
STUMP HALL,		WESTMINSTER HALL.
LEMON HALL,		

---

[1] 'Tu tibi Dux Comiti; tu Comes ipsa Duci.'
Ovid, *Heroid.* XIV. 106.

Lastly, to these we must add,

KIDNEY HALL,

which has been long in esteem as a noted *Seminary;* and has lately been re-founded by the Name of DIAMOND HALL.

·'With these HALLS we must mention a Thirteenth, formerly distinguished by the name of REDCOCK HALL: This House has been for some years [p. 9] unhappily alienated from the purposes of Literature, and is at present inhabited by two widow gentlewomen.

'The notion is equally erroneous with regard to the number of our LIBRARIES. Besides those of *Radcliffe, Bodley,* and the private colleges, there have of late years been many Libraries founded in our *Coffee-Houses,* for the benefit of such of the Academics as have neglected, or lost, their Latin and Greek. In these useful Repositories *Grown-Gentlemen* are accommodated with the *Cyclopaedia* in the most expeditious and easy manner.—The MAGAZINES afford History, Divinity, Philosophy, Mathematics, Geography, Astronomy, Biography, Arts, Sciences, and Poetry.—The REVIEWS form the complete Critic, without consulting the dry rules of Aristotle, Quintilian, and Bossu; and enable the student to pass his judgment on volumes which he never read, after the most compendious method.—NOVELS supply the place of experience, and give lectures of Intrigue and Gallantry.—OCCASIONAL POEMS diffuse the itch of rhyming, and happily tempt many a young fellow to forsake Logic, turn *smart,* and commence Author, either in the Pastoral, Lyric, or Elegiac way.—POLITICAL PAMPHLETS teach the inexpediency of Continental Connections; that for the punishment of French Perfidy, we should wage perpetual war with that nation; and that our Conquests in America will raise the jealousy of all *Europe.* As there are here Books suited to every Taste, so there are Liquors adapted to every species of reading. Amorous Tales may be perused over *Arrack Punch* and *Jellies;* Insipid Odes over *Orgeat* or *Capilaire;* Politics over *Coffee;* Divinity over *Port;* and Defences of bad Generals and bad Ministers over *Whipt Syllabubs.* In a word, in these Libraries Instruction and Pleasure go hand in hand; and we may pronounce, in a literal sense, that Learning remains no longer a *dry* pursuit.

'The most ancient and considerable of these, is that in New College-Lane, founded by the memorable Mr *Johnson.* He was accordingly constituted the first Librarian, and upon his retiring to the *Isle of Wight,* for the private pursuit of his Studies, was succeeded by Librarian *Hadley,* who, though now removed, still accommodates *Students* on their way to *London:* and a *female* Librarian at present fills this important department with applause.

'With regard to the *Manuscripts* of these Libraries, they are oblong
folios [p. 11], bound in parchment, lettered on the plan of Mr *Lock's*
Common Place Book; are written by, and kept under the sole care of
the Librarian. These Manuscripts, which in process of time amount
to many volumes, are carefully preserved in the *Archives* of each respective Library.

'That the reader may not be surprised at our mentioning a female
Librarian at *Oxford* (which indeed would be less extraordinary if our
Fellows of Colleges were allowed to marry), it must be remarked that
the other Libraries, established on this plan, viz. *James's*, *Tom's*, *John's*,
&c., are also conducted by Females; who, though properly the *sub-
Librarians*, have usurped the right of their Husbands in the execution
of this office.'

Gray, writing from Peterhouse to his friend Wharton, April 26, 1744, mentions that the bars at Dick's
and the Rainbow coffee-houses were kept by women.
It appears also from Cradock's *Memoirs*, IV. 226,
quoted in Gray's works, I. lxvi, that 'it was the custom at Cambridge, when a book was ordered at a
coffee-house, that four subscribers' names should be
previously signed.'

The Book Club, or Society for Promoting Useful
Knowledge, was established at Cambridge in 1784,
and met in the Bull Inn till about 1841[1].

Having given references already (pp. 153—155) to
the tory *high borlace* (1732—65) and the lady patron-
esses of that club, it must be said that this was not
the only society of the kind at Oxford. It is recorded
by Chalmers, in his *English Poets*, XVIII. 76, of Tom
Warton, that 'in 1747 and 1748 he held the office of
poet laureate, conferred upon him, according to an
ancient practice, in the common room of Trinity Col-

[1] Cooper's *Annals*, IV. 409.

lege. The duty of this office was to celebrate the lady chosen by the same authority, as the lady patroness, and Warton performed the task, on an appointed day, crowned with a wreath of laurel. The verses, which Mr Mant says are still to be seen in the common-room, are written in an elegant and flowing style, but have not been thought worthy of transcription.'

A notice of university wits and poets must be reserved for the second division of this compilation.

The custom of naming a lady as 'an excuse for the glass' seems strange and unnatural to us who are not 'to the manner born:' but it was customary at the universities as early as 1730[1]; and we read of Dr Ri. Farmer, that, 'from his first coming to College, he always gave Miss Benskin as a toast, and never could mention her name without evident feelings of the most ardent affection[2].' Compare also *supra*, p. 160.

In 1710 Uffenbach was particularly pleased with Clare walks. He also admired the fine new buildings behind that college, or hall, as it was then more euphoniously called. His taste was that of the times; and so he despises the old buildings of Queens' as not much better than 'Magdalene College[3].' In the last century there was a general detestation of anything gothic : pointed arches were studiously reduced to a horizontal, and the world went mad over Italian and classical decoration.

---

[1] James Miller's *Humours of Oxford*, Act IV. Sc. 1,
[2] Gorham's *Martyns*, p. 99.
[3] Reisen, III. 7, 24.

Bentley had mutilated the south-west of the great court of Trinity, Sir Nathaniel Lloyd had left a legacy (1735) for the facing or defacing of Trinity Hall. But in the middle of the century the most ancient foundation set the example of 'improvements.'

In 1762 the fellows of Peterhouse, in the absence of the Master (bishop Law), voted to face the court with stone, the windows were made square, and everything smoothed clean away. In the guide-book, printed after 1763, it is described as 'entirely new cased with stone in an elegant manner. The lesser court, next the street, is divided by the chapel; and on the north side is a lofty elegant building, faced with stone, lately erected.' In the edition of 1796 this is described as 'a lofty modern building faced with stone:' novelty and elegance being of course synonymous. In 1773 St John's followed this example, and faced the first court, on the south side, 'at such an expence as it would be preposterous to go on in the same manner[1].' This, says the guide-book, 'makes a handsome appearance.'

The highest praise was lavished on '*Emanuel College*. On the west, next the street, is erected a very handsome building (of which the plate annexed is an exact representation), which makes the principal court a very beautiful one, having on the south an elegant uniform stone building, adorned with a balustrade and parapet; and opposite to it, on the north, the hall, combination-room, and master's lodge; on the east is a fine cloister with 13 arches, and an hand-

[1] Cole ap. Mayor, 611. 19.

some gallery over it, well furnished and adorned with portraits of the founder, several of the benefactors, and former members of the college. In the middle of the cloister is the entrance into the chapel.

'The chapel, including the ante-chapel, is 84 feet long, 30 broad, and 27 high; and is extremely well adorned and furnished. The altar-piece is a very grand painting of the prodigal son, by Ammiconi: the floor is marble, and the ceiling stucco. There is a neat organ, and a gallery for the master's family. In the middle of the chapel hangs a curious glass chandelier, which has a beautiful appearance when lighted.

'The hall is one of the most elegant in the university, having been fitted up in a grand taste; the carved work, wainscotting, and fret-work of the ceiling being highly finished. There are two fine bow-windows, opposite to each other, at the upper end of the hall, and a gallery for music over the screens. The gardens are extensive and pleasant, with a bowling-green, and cold-bath, over which is a neat brick building, sashed in front, containing a commodious little room to dress in. The curious take notice of a fine young cedar-tree in this garden.'

At the same time the buildings of Queens' are dismissed as 'two courts besides a pile of buildings near the gardens:' but the readers are comforted by the information that 'The front of the college next the water, including the president's lodge, is intended to be rebuilt in an elegant manner, part of which is already finished, and when the whole is completed, it will make an exceeding grand front (see the annexed plan).'

Of course they would have done well to have put themselves under the guidance of Sir James Burrough, master of Caius (1754—64), the leader of the vandal revival. Still we shall not quarrel with the Guide for commending Queens' 'grove and gardens; which, lying on both sides of the river, are connected with each other and the college by two bridges of wood; one of which is of a curious structure, built of one arch upon piers of stone: the gardens being very extensive, well planted with fruit and adorned with rows of elms, and fine walks, make it a very agreeable retirement for students.'

The following extracts from *A Pocket Companion for* Oxford, 1761, should have come a few pages earlier.

Magdalen. 'One unparalleled Beauty belonging to this College is the extensive Out let. The Grove seems perfectly adapted to indulge Contemplation; being a pleasant kind of Solitude, laid out in Walks, and well planted with Elms and other large Trees. It has likewise a Bowling-Green in it, and having some beautiful Lawns, feeds about forty Head of Deer.

'Besides the Walks which are in the Grove there is a very delightful and much frequented One, round a Meadow containing about 13 Acres, and that surrounded by the several Branches of the *Cherwell;* from whence it is called the *Water-Walk;* which yields all the Variety could be wished: Some Parts of it running in straight Lines, with the Trees regularly cut; others winding, and the Trees growing little otherwise than as Nature directs: There is plenty of Water as well as Verdure, and an agreeable View of the Country adjacent.'

St John's College. 'The Gardens belonging to this College are extremely agreeable, very extensive, and well laid out. They still retain the Names they formerly had, when they had nothing to boast of but a Plantation of tall Elms, *viz.* the *outer* and *inner Grove.* But now the outer one is disposed in regular Walks and Grass-Plots, the Walls thereof covered with Evergreens and neatly cut, and finely shaded by Trees of various Kinds, *viz.* the middle Walk by a Row of Lime Trees on each Side cut arch-wise, a Row of cut Elms by the Side-Walks, and at each End and across the middle two Groups of beautiful Chestnut Trees. The inner Grove is of quite a different Cast to this, being so contrived as to satiate the Eye at once, but its various Parts present themselves gradually to view. No Spot whatever is calculated to yield a more pleasing Variety; for, except Water, it has all that could be wished.'

Merton College. 'The Gardens are very pleasant, having the Advantage of a Prospect of the adjacent Walks and Country from the South Terrass.'

Christ Church. 'Next to the Buildings of *Christ-Church*, their long Gravel walk, planted on each side with Elms, deserves our Notice, being a Quarter of a Mile in Length, and of a proportionate Breadth. This is much the finest Walk about *Oxford*.

'Parallel to this is another Walk under the Walls of *Corpus-Christi* and *Merton* Colleges, which is much resorted to by *Invalids*, on account of its being sheltered from the North Winds by the Colleges abovementioned.'

New College Library. 'From hence we pass through the middle Gate into the GARDEN-COURT, which widens by Breaks as we approach the Garden. This Court is separated from the Garden, by an Iron Gate and Palisade which extend 130 Feet in Length, and admit of a most agreeable Prospect of the Garden through them. In the middle of the Garden is a beautiful Mount with an easy Ascent to the Top of it, and the Walks round about it, as well as the Summit of it, guarded with Yew Hedges. The Area before the Mount being divided into four Quarters, in one is the King's Arms, with the Garter and Motto; in that opposite to it the Founder's; in the Third a Sun-Dial, and the Fourth a Garden-Knot; all planted in Box, and neatly cut.

'The whole is surrounded by a Terras. On each Side are Lime-Trees planted; and on the North Side in particular there is a *serpentine Walk* planted with *flowering Shrubs*. Behind the Mount likewise is a fine Collection of Shrubs so contrived as to rise gradually one above the other, and over them, a Row of Horse Chestnut Trees, which spread in such a Manner as to cover the Garden Wall, and carry the Eye on to a most beautiful Mantle of tall Elms, which terminates the View, and seems to be the only Boundary to that End of the Garden; but we are obliged to *Magdalen* College Grove for this additional Beauty.

'At the South East Corner of the Garden we enter the BOWLING-GREEN; which is in all Respects neat and commodious. Opposite to the Entrance is a *Pavilion* or *Temple;* on the Right a Terras with flow-ring Shrubs, and a Row of Elms to shade the Green in the Evening, that Side being almost due West; and on the Left a Row of Sycamores which are mentioned by Dr *Plot,* in his *Natural History* of *Oxfordshire,* as a great Curiosity; being incorporated from one End of the Row to the other.

'Having conducted our Reader to the furthest Part of the College, we would recommend to him a View of the Building from the Mount; whence the Garden-Court, in particular, has a very grand Effect: For from thence the Wings appear properly display'd, and the whole is seen at a convenient Distance. The Perspective View annexed was taken from the first Landing-place, and may be compared with the Original. From the top of the Mount likewise there is an extensive and agreeable Prospect of the Country, and of some other Buildings in the University.'

As an example of the critical taste of the time we may select the following from the Account of *Trinity College:* 'The Chapel here is exqui-sitely finished; its Screen and Altar-Piece are of Cedar curiously work'd, and the latter is embellished with Carvings of that eminent Artist Mr *Guibbons;* the Floor is laid with black and white Marble; the Cieling adorned with admirable Stucco of a very high Relief, in the Middle of which is an *Ascension* finely painted; and that which appears to be the Frame round this Picture is a curious *Deceptio Visus,* or Deception of the Sight; for it does not really project, but is on a Level with the rest of the Cieling. In a Word, this Chapel is a Pattern of Elegance joined with Simplicity.

'The Hall is a handsome *Gothick* Room, adorned with the Pictures of their Founders and Benefactors.'

The contemporary descriptions of other college chapels must be reserved for the third, and those of the Physick or Botanick Gardens, for the second part of this Compilation.

Feb. 10, 1779, the Corporation ordered the trees on Erasmus's walk at the north end of Queens' Green to be sold[1], but the University paid 50*l.* to preserve

---

[1] Cooper's *Annals,* IV. 389.

them, Sept. 26, 1780. So in an engraving of King's College Chapel, published in 1793 (by W. & J. Walker, from an Original Drawing by J. Walker, figures by Burney), a party of ladies and university men are depicted as enjoying a summer's afternoon on that walk, while others are punting themselves and their friends on the river, the larger barges being towed by horses who wade in the water.

In one of Loggan's views of Clare Hall (about 1690), two men, in business-like costume, are rowing two ladies and a beau, who sit under an awning in the stern, while another pleasure party watch them over the wall of the fellows' garden.

William Pattison, the poet of Sidney Sussex College, who used to amuse himself with fishing, also, about 1725, wrote a poem to the *Cambridge Beauties* Aureuchia, Sylvia and Delia, Belinda and Flora. A few years later appeared 'A Poem, in answer to a Lampoon, which was wrote on the *Cambridge* Ladies, London, 1731.' [Bodl. *Gough*, Camb. 103]. It relates to the virtues of the Beauties who attended the Cambridge churches: as, Alinda, Flavia, and Flora at the University Church; Clarissa a 'Less St Marian;' 'thy fair oh *Benne't*;' 'the *Andrian* fair;' and 'the fair *Botolphian* maid.'

> 'Surprized I gaze on each unerring Fair,
> Whom health requires to take refreshing Air,
> To *King's* cool shades where restless Lovers walk,
> In different Ways on diff'rent Subjects talk.
> But ah how fatal oft these Walks do prove
> To injur'd Innocence, and constant Love,
> Let LUCIA witness.'

The following passage from 'The Friendly and Honest Advice of an Old Tory to the Vice-Chancellor of Cambridge,' 1751 [Bodl. *Gough*, Camb. 36, 47], p. 26, describes a condition of things very strange to us.

'The Wranglers I am told on the first Day of their Exercise have usually expected that all the *young Ladies* of their Acquaintance (whether such as have sometimes made their Bands, or who are more genteely employed in keeping the Bar at a Tavern or a Coffee-house) should wish them Joy of their Honours. To give them an opportunity of doing so, their Manner has been to spend the Morning in going to several of their Houses.'

The second volume of the Student or Oxford and Cambridge Monthly Miscellany contains several papers written by 'the Female Student,' and dated from Cambridge in 1751, though I have my suspicions that they were written by an Oxonian. The career of a Toast or Beauty is sketched in a lively manner. She is the daughter of a fellow of a college who was secretly married to the daughter of a 'matriculated tradesman' (a barber, a bookseller, a butler or cook of college, II. 256; a tailor's daughter is mentioned, *ibid.* 303). She had picked up as much information as she could from the inside of wig-boxes and from the curling papers twisted round pipes (p. 49), and her unknown father had carefully taught her Latin and one science after another. After she had ceased to be the care of freshmen of fortune over the tea-table and of gold tufts and 'the genteelest, or (in the modern dialect) the *jemmiest*' of all our violin-playing fellow-commoners at concerts (I. 131, II. 51, 105), she, by her wit, becomes a favourite with older members of the university. What she might come to in time is shewn in the description of her predecessor, Miss Betsy Peevish (II. 349), an old maid who 'goes to church constantly (with a large quarto bible under her arm) twice a day; and after prayers are over, she confabulates with some *pious* old woman about the faults of her neighbours.'

It must have been shortly after this that Goldsmith wrote his *Double Transformation. A Tale.*

> 'Secluded from domestic strife
> *Jack Book-worm* led a college life;
> A Fellowship at twenty-five
> Made him the happiest man alive,
> He drank his Glass, and crack'd his Joke,
> And Freshmen wonder'd as he spoke.
> Such Pleasures unalloy'd with Care,
> Could any accident impair?
> Could Cupid's shaft at length transfix
> Our Swain, arrived at thirty-six?
> O had the Archer ne'er come down
> To ravage in a Country Town!
> Or *Flavia* been content to stop
> At triumphs in a *Fleet-Street* Shop!
> *   *   *   *   *   *   *
> Skill'd in no other arts was she
> But Dressing, Patching, *Repartee.*
> And, just as Humour rose or fell,
> By turns a Slattern or a *Belle.*'

I have already given an extract (on p. 158) from T. Warton's *Progress of Discontent*, which was composed not much before this time. The hero of that piece, having given up his fellowship to take a living and to marry 'a cousin of the 'squire,' repents at his leisure, and sighs for his old college days :—

> 'No cares were there for forward Peas
> A yearly longing wife to please;
> My thoughts no Christ'ning Dinners crost,
> No children cry'd for butter'd Toast;
> And every Night I went to bed
> Without a *modus* in my head.'

After all, the universities had no great reputation for politeness. [Bishop] John Earl (1628, when fellow of Merton) in his *Microcosmographie*, § 20, says, of *A downe-right Scholler* that

'His scrape is homely and his nod worse. He cannot kisse his hand and cry Madame, nor talke idly enough to beare her company. His smacking of a Gentle-woman is somewhat too sauory, and he mistakes her nose for her lippe. A very Wood-cocke would puzzle him in caruing, and hee wants the logicke of a Capon. He has not the glib faculty of sliding over a tale, but his words come squemishly out of his mouth, and the laughter commonly before the iest. He names this word Colledge too often, and his discourse beats too much on the Vniversity. The perplexity of mannerlinesse will not let him feed, and he is sharp set at an argument when hee should cut his meate. He is discarded for a gamester at all games but one and thirty, and at tables he reaches not beyond doublets. His fingers are not long and drawn out to handle a Fiddle, but his fist is cluncht with the habit of disputing. Hee ascends a horse somewhat sinisterly, though not on the left side, and they both goe iogging in griefe together. He is exceedingly censur'd by the innes a Court men, for that hainous Vice being out of fashion. He cannot speake to a Dogge in his owne Dialect, and vnderstands Greeke better then the language of a Falconer. Hee has beene vsed to a darke roome, and darke clothes, and his eyes dazzle at a Sattin Doublet. The Hermitage of his Study, has made him somwhat vncouth in the world, and men make him worse by staring on him. Thus is hee silly and ridiculous, and it continues with him for some quarter of a yeare, out of the Vniuersitie. But practise him a little in men, and brush him ore with good companie, and hee shall out balance those glisterers as much as solid substance do's a feather, or Gold Gold-lace.'

A dramatist's opinion is thus expressed by Farquhar (*Love and a Bottle*, II. 2) in 1698:

' *Widow Bullfinch.* Champagne is a fine liquor, which all your great beaux drink to make 'em witty.

' *Mockmode.* We dare not have wit there [at the university] for fear of being counted rakes. Your solid philosophy is all read there, which is clear another thing.'

Jack Lizard is represented in the *Guardian* of April 8, 1713 (No. 24), as coming home for his first vacation (he was only about fifteen years old), and making his friends uncomfortable by applied science of a disagreeable description, and by telling, in company, long stories about the college cook. The 77th number of Hugh Kelly's *Babler* illustrates, in the person of Tom Welbank, the ignorance of the world displayed by a university man when in company with Mr Pope and Lady Mary Wortley Montague. The testimony of Nic. Amherst, in *Terrae Filius*, ed. 2, p. 193, is in the same direction.

In 'the Author's Farce, and the Pleasures of the Town,' I. 5, *Witmore* is made to say, ' But for a man to preach up Love and the Muses in a Garret, it wou'd not make me more sick to hear Honesty talked of at Court, Conscience at *Westminster*, Politeness at the University.'

And Swift says,

'A scholard when just from his college broke loose,
Can hardly tell how to cry *Bo* to a goose.'

The Female Student, however, makes a distinction.

Speaking of masters of arts she writes (*Student, or Oxf. and Camb. Monthly Miscellany*, 1751, II. 301, 302):

'A magisterial strut, a wise gravity of countenance, and a general stiffness in all his actions denote him for a man of consequence. He is taught to entertain a sovereign contempt for undergraduates, and, forsooth scorns to demean himself by conversing with his inferiors. Hence the whole scene of his life is confin'd to those of his own standing: and the college-hall, the common-room, the coffee-house, and now and then a ride on Gog-magog-hills, is all the variety he has a taste for enjoying. One half of the human creation, (which men have complaisantly term'd the *Fair*) he is an utter stranger to; and that softness, that delicacy, that *je ne scai quoy* elegance of address, which our company imperceptibly inspires, is in his eyes a foolish impertinent affectation. Thus does he gradually degenerate into a mere —— what I don't care to name; 'till at last he has liv'd so long at college, that he is not fit to live any where else.

'That I have traced the true source of ACADEMICAL ILL-BREEDING, is plain from the awkward carriage of our rusty *dons*, whenever they are *saddled* with the company of strangers. But at the same time let me do justice to those of our *younkers* (especially among the fellow-commoners) who by studied grimace, formal elocution, and forc'd action, are equally excessive in the practice, as others are in the neglect of POLITENESS. This affectation I attribute to the vain ambition of monopolizing the regards of what they call BEAUTIES amongst us, who (poor souls!) deal out their good graces indiscriminately to all that dance after them. However, as the honour of sauntering with them in publick, is seldom indulg'd but to the *jaunty*, he is sure to have the *reputation* at least of being a favourite, who by this mark of their esteem is preferr'd for POLITENESS.'

Richardson; in *Sir Charles Grandison* (1753), gives an amusing sketch of Mr Walden, a pedantic and conceited 'Oxford Scholar of family and fortune; but quaint and opinionated, despising every one who had not had the benefit of an university education.' Harriet Byron writes thus to her confidential friend, Miss Selby (*Letter* X.): 'By the way let me ask my uncle if the word "*scholar*" means not the *learner* rather than the *learned?* If it originally means no more, I would suppose that formerly the most learned men were the most modest, contenting themselves with being thought learners.'

Judging from the specimens which she gives of their conversation at table, we should now say that all the gentlemen were impolite (perhaps they were drawn so intentionally to lead up to the immaculate Sir Charles); but Mr Walden is offensively and excessively rude. This is the style of his conversation (*Letter* XII.):

'It has been whispered to me that you have had great advantages from a grandfather, of whose learning and politeness we have heard much. He was a scholar. He was of Christ Church in our university, if I am not mistaken. You have thrown out some extraordinary things for a *lady*, and especially for so young a lady. From *you* we expect the opinions of your worthy grandfather, as well as your own notions.

'Have you, madam, read Swift's *Tale of a Tub?* There *is* such a book, Sir Hargrave...'

'I have, sir.'

'Why, then, madam, you no doubt read, bound up with it, *The Battle of the Books:* a very fine piece written in favour of the ancients, and against the moderns.' One of the other gentlemen puts in maliciously, 'The young gentlemen at both universities are already in more danger of becoming *fine gentlemen* than *fine scholars.*' (*Letter* XIII.) However, Mr

26—2

Walden is said to have had 'very few admirers in the university to which, out of it, he is so fond of boasting a relation:' and we can sympathize with Miss Clement's whispered thanksgiving that 'all scholars are not like this.'

If we may trust a lady's account, scholars were ignorant of the fashionable slang. (Mrs Cowley's *Who's the Dupe?* 1779, I. 3.)

'*Charlotte.* Knowledge, as you manage it, is a downright bore.

'*Gradus.* "Boar!" what relation can there be between knowledge and a "hog!"

'*Char.* Lord bless me! how ridiculous. You have spent your life in learning the dead languages, and are ignorant of the living. Why sir, "bore" is all the "ton."

'*Grad.* "Ton!" "ton!" What may that be? It cannot be orthology: I do not recollect its root in the present languages.

'*Char.* Ha, ha, ha! better and better. Why, sir, "ton" means—"ton" is—Pho! what signifies where the root is? These kinds of words are the short hand of conversation, and convey whole sentences at once. All one likes is "ton," and all one hates is "bore."'

How far ignorance of the world may have been produced by the difficulties of locomotion, it is not easy to say. Only a small proportion of the Oxonians can have enjoyed the fashionable society of Astrop wells (*Spectator*, No. 154, and compare p. 105 *supra*), and still fewer the more fashionable 'watering-place' the Bath, like John Thorpe in Miss Austen's *Northanger Abbey.*

Since the time when master Hobson jogged between Cambridge and the *Bull* in Bishopsgate-street, there had been considerable advance in the facilities of conveyance; but still communication between distant counties was no trifling matter.

About 1670 the *Flying Coach*[1] performed the journey from London to Oxford in 13 hours in summer: in cold weather it took two days.

Dr Bliss says[2] that in 1724 Haynes's *flying coach* from Oxford to London took two days in winter, and one in summer, when they ran three days a week. In 1707 there was only one carrier once a fortnight between Oxford and Bath, Oxford and Birmingham, Oxford and Reading. To Shrewsbury once a month; to Exeter once in five weeks; to Westmoreland thrice a year. In Nov. 1731 the licensed waggoners, Mr Thos. Godfrey and the widow Stafford, put one Barnes into the Vice-Chancellor's Court for having set up a waggon to carry goods to and fro from London without his licence[3].

July 17, 1702, Fr. Burman left London in a coach and four at 5 in in the morning and reached Cambridge at 8 p.m.

Aug. 16, 1710, when Z. C. von Uffenbach[4] was driving from Bicester to Oxford, one of the wheels of his coach broke, and the passengers had to walk the remaining ten miles.

Ralph Thoresby's journey and narrow escape from a similar accident in the summer of 1714, has already been quoted (pp. 259, 260).

June 24, 1741[5], a daily post was established between Cambridge and London by the Postmaster-General. Mr Cooper (*Annals*, III. 463) quotes an advertisement of the autumn of 1654: 'A Stage Coach goes from the Swan at Grayes Inn Lane end in Holborn to the Rose in Cambridge every Monday, Wednesday, and Friday for 10s., and from the Rose in Cambridge every Tuesday, Thursday, and Saturday for 10s. Letters and small packets are sent by them.' 'This seems to have been the coach afterwards called the Fly, which went by the Epping road, and which many years since put up at the Queen's Head, in Gray's Inn

---

[1] Hone's *Year Book*, col. 269.
[2] *Reliqu. Hearn.* Bliss, II. 215 n.   [3] *Ibid.* III. 77.
[4] *Reisen*, III. 85.   [5] Cooper's *Annals*, IV. 243.

Lane, till removed to the George and Blue Boar in Holborn. It continued to run from the Rose till the 11th of April, 1808, when it started from the Red Lion. From Chamberlayne's *Angliae Notitia*, 1671, it appears the coaches from London to Cambridge performed the journey in 12 hours ['at a low price as about 1*s*. for every 5 miles.' Hone's *Year Book*, col. 1451, where reference is made to the flying-coaches of 1720], "not counting the time for dining, setting forth not too early and coming in not too late." In the early part of George the Second's reign, especially in the winter season, although the coaches had six horses, they were frequently two days in performing the journey hence to London.'

The fares for hackney coachmen[1] between Cambridge and Sturbridge fair in 1688 were fixed at 1*s*. for one, two, three, or four persons from sunrising to sunset; and after sunset 18*d*. In 1729[2] the fare was only 3*d*., and was raised to 6*d*. by day, and 1*s*. in the evening.

About 1749 the University licensed eleven letter-carriers: and there were two coaches to London.

According to the *Cambridge Guide*[3], about the year 1770, there were

'*Post days* at *Cambridge*.

'*London*. In every day (except Monday) at 9 in the morning [8, ed. 1796]. Out every night (except Saturday) at 9 o'clock [alternate days at 5 or 6 p.m. in 1763].

'*Caxton* [*Huntingdon*, 1766] *and the North*. In every day (except Sunday) at 9 in the morning [10, 1763; 8, 1796]. Out every day (except Monday) at 9 in the evening.

'*Norfolk, Bury, &c.* In every day at 9 [8, 1796] in the morning. Out every night at 9 o'clock.

'*Ely*. In every Wednesday, Friday, and Sunday, at 9 in the morning [every evening (except Saturday), 1796]. Out the same mornings at 10 o'clock [every night at 7 o'clock (except Monday), 1796].'

In the same *Guide* eight *Coaches* are mentioned (in 1763 only three). Among these are: '*The Fly* for 4 passengers at 14*s*. each [12*s*. in 1763; 18*s*. in 1796], which goes to London every day by Chesterford, Hockerill, and Epping; set out at 7 o'clock from the Rose, in the marketplace, and arrives at the Queen's Head, Gray's Inn Lane [George and Blue Boar, Holborn, 1796], at 5 o'clock the same evening; from whence another Fly sets out every morning at 8 o'clock for Cambridge.' ['Whereas many Gentlemen of the University and others have much

---

[1] Cooper's *Annals*, III. 540.
[2] *Ibid.* IV. 205, 206.   [3] *Ibid.* IV. 273.

desired they might be at Liberty, when travelling in the FLY, either to Dine, or not, upon the Road: We the Proprietors of the said Fly, for the more speedy Conveyance of Passengers, do not stop on the Road to dine (except desired), by which means near an Hour will be saved in the Journey; and nothing shall be wanting to render the said Machines in all other respects, as compleat, safe, and expeditious as any in the Kingdom, By A. S. Forlow & Co.' of the Rose. He took the credit of being 'the first Undertaker of conveying Gentlemen, in this expeditious manner, to and from London.' Cooper's *Annals*, IV. 336.] 'The London and Cambridge Diligence for 3 passengers at 15*s.* each' [1*l.* in 1796], 8 a.m. to 4 p.m. from the Hoop to the White-Horse, Fetter Lane. 'Woodward and Co.'s Ipswich Stage,' 'Smith and Co.'s Post Coach from Cambridge to Birmingham in 2 days, at 1*l.* 10*s.* each,' &c. &c. E. Gillam's, J. Burleigh's, J. Cock's, and Oliver's *Waggons,* and several carriers are enumerated. In 1764 there was also a *Fly* to Ely, six horses, on week-days, 8 a.m. to 11 p.m. Return 3 p.m. to 6 p.m. Insides 4*s.* outsides 2*s.*

The first mail coach direct from London to Cambridge (in 7¼ hours) was that from London to Wisbech, which began to run Feb. 6, 1792.

The *Cambridge Chronicle*[1], price 2½*d.* was first published Sat., Oct. 30, 1762. With it was afterwards incorporated the *Cambridge Journal and Weekly Flying Post*, which first appeared in Sept. 1744.

In March, 1785, Cambridge bags were sent to and brought from Bournbridge[2], when the plan of Mr Palmer of Bath for mails was set on foot between London and Norwich. 'Before that time letters were conveyed on horseback, and I have seen' (says Professor Pryme) 'the post-lad with a portmanteau strapped behind him on his horse, of which he could so easily have been robbed, riding between Newark and Nottingham.

'Pack-horses were used for conveying goods, and I have seen long strings of them with their panniers in the North of Yorkshire and in Devonshire.

'A gentlemen of olden time travelled, when alone, by "riding post," that is, hiring for eightpence a mile at each stage two horses, with a post-boy, who carried the portmanteau behind him, and took the tired horses back when fresh ones were had. Every gentleman visited London at least once in his lifetime. Pillion was the usual mode of conveyance for women among farmers, and even the gentry. I have seen hundreds riding so[3].'

---

[1] Cooper's *Annals*, IV. 323, 249.   [2] *Ibid.* IV. 415.
[3] *Autobiog. Recoll. of Geo. Pryme*, 1870, pp. 62, 63.

At the end of the *Camb. Univ. Calendar* for 1802 are advertised nine coaches: The *Telegraph* light Coach, *Mail, Fly, Heavy, Lord Nelson, Bury, Birmingham, Old Birmingham,* and *Ipswich.* When the *Telegraph* was first announced to do the distance between this and London in the time there stated (7 hours)[1], 'people anticipated that it would never last, and that the horses would shortly break down from fatigue. The coaches went very slowly: a man walking between Bury St Edmund's and Newmarket was offered a lift on one as it passed him. He had been in the habit of accepting it, but on this occasion said, "No, thank you, I'm in a hurry to-day." I myself have travelled with my uncle from Nottingham to Hull by coach, when it took two days to perform the journey (72 miles), and have witnessed two men, who spoke to the coachman as he left Newark, arrive on foot at the half-way house between that and Lincoln, a distance of 16 miles, just as we drove out of it after baiting the horses.'

Among Dighton's caricatures is *A View of the* 'Telegraph, *Cambridge,* May, 1809, a portrait of 'Dick Vaughan,' in black hat, brown top-coat, white neckcloth, yellow waistcoat and top boots, employed in knotting his long coaching whip.

In the *Cambridge University Calendars* a list of Coaches precedes the Index from the year 1805 onwards. But in 1842 'the list of Coaches is altogether omitted as, owing to the frequent changes in the time of their starting, consequent upon the progress of the different railroads, &c., its insertion would not have given information that could have been depended upon.' There is an advertisement of the Post Office in Sidney Street.

I have heard it said that our *Floralia* in the 'May term' have become quite a different thing within the memory of our elder residents, since railways have brought up our aunts and cousins from a distance.

It would be a hopeless task to attempt to enumerate all the trivial particulars in which modern invention have altered or modified the habits of the university. Gas, for instance, has in most places supplanted oil-lamps in the courts and on the staircases, though we may still be proud to retain tapers in the Chapels

---

[1] *Autobiog. Recoll. of Geo. Pryme,* pp. 61, 62, *s. a.* 1804.

of some of our colleges. Mr E. Johnson, of Trinity-street, has a caricature ('Topham fecit') of the under-porter of Trin. coll.; he carries a lamp-lighter's ladder and a capacious oil can, like a garden watering pot : just such an one as that from which the unconscious lamplighter is pouring oil into the open chair in Hogarth's 4th cartoon of the *Rake's Progress*, on S. David's day.

Gunning records[1] a curious story relating to this custom. 'Castley [of Jesus] was a man of penurious habits, of which the following may be taken as an illustration :—John Brooke, whose rooms were on the same staircase, proposed that they should furnish a lamp at their mutual charges, to prevent the recurrence of much inconvenience to which they had been subjected of an evening from the darkness of the staircase. Castley said he considered it a piece of needless extravagance ; but after a time he agreed to the proposition, with the condition that he should be allowed to furnish the oil on alternate nights, for he thought the porter, whom Brooke had proposed to employ, would charge too much. This was agreed to.

'To Brooke's great surprise, he frequently found the lamp on Castley's nights burning brightly at a late hour, whereas, when the porter lighted it on his night, it had burnt out much earlier. One evening when Brooke was reading in his room with his door *sported* (fastened), he heard *a very quiet step* on the landing-

---

[1] *Reminiscences*, II. 139, 140.

place; and opening his door *gently* he surprised Castley in the very act of puffing out the lamp, by which
dexterous manœuvre, on alternate nights, he was enabled to shirk the expense of providing oil!'

Mr Mayor says (*Hist. of St John's*, 1095, l. 10), 'As
an undergraduate Dr Wood "kept" in a garret in the
2nd court letter O. The college tradition that he
studied by the light of the rush candle on the staircase, with his feet in straw, not being able to afford
fire and candle, is confirmed by H. T. Riley, esq.,
who heard it from Dr Wood's bedmaker.'

Dr Ro. Plumptre, in his *Hints respecting some of
the university Officers* in 1782 (p. 23), asks 'If...we
cannot well afford to *pave* the streets, would it not be
as well to *light* them?' Both were done by the act
of 1788.

It has been seen already (pp. 101 foll.) that in old
days the sizars, servitors, battelers, and poor scholars,
undertook, to a great extent, the menial offices, which
in time devolved upon college servants: the cook,
steward, and barber, being as much parcel of the
foundation as the college porters and chapel clerks.

In 1625 (J. Gostlin, V. C.), a decree of the heads was
made to prohibit the admission of bedmakers, illiterate
boys and men, and even women, into colleges to perform those menial offices which had aforetime been a
source of income to poor scholars—'*a studiosis egenis
ad eorum impensas sustentandas.*' John Strype, writing
to his mother, 16 Aug., 1664, from St Katharine-Hall,
Cambridge, says of his tutor's account, 'Bedmaker
and Laundresse are set down for a whole last Quarter.'

Among Vincent Bourne's Latin poems is a notice of Isaac Newton's (male) bedmaker at Trinity.

'AD JOHANNEM PERKINS,

astrologum cantabrigiensem.

'Lusit, amabiliter lusit Fortuna jocosa,
    Et tunc, siquando, tunc oculata fuit;
Cum tibi, Johannes, Newtoni sternere lectum;
    Cum tibi museum verrere diva dedit.
Nam dum ille intentus studiis caelestibus haesit,
    Concipiens ambos mente capace polos:
    *   *   *   *   *   *   *   *

Tu quoque cognatus stellis, Martique Jovique,
    Mercurio et Veneri non rudis hospes eras:
    *   *   *   *   *   *   *   *

Cum musis musae famulantur, et artibus artes,
    Majori (ut fas est) obsequiosa minor;
Nec melior lex est nec convenientior aequo,
    Quam siet astronomo seruus ut astrologus.'

The same author wrote some elegant Latin elegiacs to Charon 'in obitum Roussaei, collegio Trinitatis servi a cubiculis, anno 1721,' who was drowned in the Cam on which he had so often rowed.

The following extract is from the *Student or Oxford and Cambridge Monthly Miscellany*, I. 55: 'T'other day I caught my bedmaker, a grave old matron, poring very seriously over a folio that lay upon my table...*Lord bless you master*, says she, *who I reading.*'

Reference to college barbers has been made above, pp. 130—8.

Though I gather from the reminiscences of a friend who was at Cambridge in 1812, that there has not been any great addition to the articles of furniture usually found in college rooms since his time, there has clearly been a considerable advance in luxury even in the last dozen years, in expence, ease, and ornament. However, I gather from a note on p. 13, of *Hints to Freshmen at the Univ. of Cambridge* (ed. 4, 1822), that *sofas* had not universally a place in undergraduates' rooms. The change since the last century is still more clearly marked. In the illustration to the poem of 'the Lounger' (see p. 372), in the *Oxford Sausage* of 1764, the hero sits in a bare room, with one little round table, one chair, an empty grate, and (above the chimney-piece, which is quite unadorned), something which may stand either for a map of England or for a much fractured oblong mirror. Gray, in a letter written 9 Oct., 1740, says that he 'saw in one of the vastest palaces in Rome...a bed that most servants in England would disdain to lie in, and furniture much like that of a soph at Cambridge for convenience and neatness.'

The *Oxford Guide* for 1761, however, records that at *All Souls* 'The private Apartments of the College are generally very neat and convenient. The room in the old quadrangle, which was formerly the library (before the new one above described was finished), is lately fitted up, by one of the Fellows, in a very elegant manner, in the Gothic taste; and is deservedly esteemed one of the curiosities of the house.'

William Whiston tells in his *Memoirs* (ed. 1. Vol. I. p. 23), that, when an undergraduate at Clare-Hall in 1687, he was much concerned at finding his sight impaired, till a narrative of Mr Boyle suggested the cause and the remedy. 'For I and my Chamber-

Fellow had newly-whitened our Room, into which almost all the Afternoon the Sun shone, and where I used to read. I therefore retired to my Study [probably the *museum* or recess in their common "keeping-room," see above p. 89], and hung it with Green, by which means I recovered my usual Sight, which God be praised, is hardly worse now, that I perceive, at fourscore years of Age, than it was in my youthful Days.' Whiston writes in 1746 of his residence at Clare about 1686: 'had the Expences of a Collegiate Life been as extravagant then as they are now come to be, or had I not lived as frugally as possible, she [his Widow Mother] would not have been able to have given me my Degrees; especially that of Master of Arts. In which the Present of £5 from Bishop *Moor*, was then a kind and seasonable Addition; and partly an Occasion of my Acceptance of the Place of his Chaplain afterwards. However I find from my Accounts still preserved, that tho' I was a Pensioner for the last half Year, yet did my whole Expences for the last three Years and half, till my first Degree inclusive, not amount to so much as 100*l.* See Dr *Newton's* very prudent Pamphlet, called *The Expence of University Education Reduc'd.*' (*Ibid.* I. pp. 25, 26.)

George Whitfield, when a servitor of Pembroke coll., Oxon. (1728), did not cost his relations more than 24*l.* in three years, having a kind tutor and being a handy and popular servitor. But about 40 years earlier Sam. Wesley the elder had managed to keep himself as a 'poor scholar' at Exeter coll. with less than three guineas, and by frugal living, by taking pupils, and

writing exercises for money, to bring away with him
10*l.* 15*s.*[1]   27 Jan. 1776, the master and seniors of St
John's, Cambridge, made a strict rule for the quarterly
payment of the cook's bills[2].

Beloe, in the *Sexagenarian*, I. 29, 30, mentions a
letter from a good authority at Balliol in 1760, who
says that 80*l. per annum* was enough, but a gentlemen-
commoner spent 200*l.* About 1620 a fellow-commoner's expenses at St John's, Camb., did not exceed
60*l.*[3] Edmund Burke spent about 150*l. per annum* at
Trinity, *Dublin*, in 1745. Sir Erasmus Philipps, when
'fellow-commoner' of Pembroke, *Oxon*, about 1720, paid
2*l.* to the esquire bedell of divinity at matriculation;
10*l.* 'caution money' to the college, which sum on
leaving he handed over for the use of the society; 10*s.*
on admission to Bodley's library. Charles Simeon's[4]
whole income, when at King's about 1780, was 125*l.*
per annum: he used to dispose of one-third of that
sum in 'charity.'

Daniel Wilson[5] (bp. of Calcutta), at S. Edmund
Hall, 1798—1801, had an allowance of 100 guineas a
year; and he continued to make it suffice. The college records shew that his *battels* averaged about 8*s.*
a week.

In 1790 'The price of Hair-dressing, Room-rent,
Washing, Attendants, &c. &c. is even lower than at
most places. The Collegiate and University dues are

---

[1] Philip's *Whitfield*, p. 27; Southey's *Wesley*, I. 47.
[2] Mayor, 1085, l. 30.
[3] *Life of Sir Symonds D'Ewes*, I. 119.
[4] *Life*, by Carus, p. 22.   [5] *Life*, by Bateman, p. 56.

peculiarly trifling. The charges of Tuition are, according to your own confession Sir, even culpably inconsiderable. And the sum paid by Pupils for attendance at the different Public Lectures is by no means equal to the sum required in London by the Professors of the Experimental branches of Science[1].' Many of the Public Schools are nearly as expensive as Oxford: Private Tuition, the Army, Law and Medicine, more so[2].'

In very early times it had been found necessary to devise expedients for the defence of scholars against the exorbitance and oppression of the town's people. 'Frederic II. when he founded his university at Naples, fixed a *maximum* price for lodgings, and enacted besides that all lodgings should be let according to the joint valuation of two citizens and two scholars. [*Conring.* Diss. v. s. 9.] The latter regulation was in force in the English universities. At Bologna, in like manner, four taxors were appointed to regulate the price of lodgings. Elsewhere it was provided, that when a scholar had once hired lodgings, he should not be disturbed in possession of them so long as he paid his rent[3].' See the letters patent of K. Henry III. 1231[4].

When colleges had been built at Cambridge, the office of *Taxors* or *Aediles* (*Taxatores*) was to superintend the assize of bread[5].

---

[1] Philalethes, *Answer to V. Knox*, p. 10.   [2] *Ibid.*
[3] Prof. H. Malden *On the Origin of Universities*, p. 32.
[4] Peacock *On the Statutes*, pp. 25, 26 n.
[5] Ashton's *Collectanea* in Stat. xxxvii. fol. 29.

Fuller says, *Hist. of Univ. Camb., Introd.* § 38,
'Their name remains, but office is altered at this day
[1655]. For after the bounty of Founders had raised
Halls and *Colledges* for Scholars free abode, their liberality gave the Taxers a *Writ of ease*, no more to
meddle with the needless prizing of Townsmens
houses. However, two Taxers are still annually chosen, whose place is of profit and credit, as employed
in *matters of weight*, and to see the true gage of all
measures, especially such as concern the victuals of
Scholars. For, where the belly is abused in its food,
the brains will soon be distempered in their study.'

In this respect they were like the Roman *aediles*,
who were also *curatores annonae:* compare

> ' sese aliquid credens italo quod honore supinus
> fregerit heminas Arreti aedilis iniquas.'
>
> PERSIUS, I. 129.

and

> ' praetextam sumere mauis,
> an Fidenarum Gabiorumque esse potestas
> et de mensura ius dicere, uasa minora
> frangere pannosus uacuis aedilis Ulubris?'
>
> JUVENAL, X. 100.

By the Award between the University and Town
of Camb., *anno* 1502, at the instance of Margaret
Countess of Richmond and Derby and mother of
K. Hen. VII., it was agreed *inter alia*, 'That every
Burgess and Dweller in the Town shall have all his
Corn, Grain, Coal, and other Things measured at the
Water Side by the Taxor's Bushel; or with their own,
sealed by the Taxors, for 4*d.* only, for a whole year.

'That neither Proctors nor Taxors shall take of

any one, for setting up Baking or Brewing in the Town, more than 3*s.* 4*d.*'

The office of taxor, however, required to be revived in 1546[1], having been merged in the proctor's in 1540 on account of the miserable poverty of the university[2].

By the Elizabethan Statutes (*cap.* xxxvi.) in 1570, two regents or non-regents were to be nominated every year by a pair of Colleges (after the same combination as the proctors had been since the year 1557) as *Ediles* or *Taxors:* the Heads of their Colleges were to present them before Sept. 1, and the Regents were to elect them. The custom of presentation had died out, and was revived by a grace of Oct. 13, 1722.

In the curious painting kept in the Registrary's office, executed in bedel Stokys' time in 1590, in the right-hand corner are represented two taxors in academicals, and two tradesmen with aprons, weighing loaves out of a basket. In three compartments of the picture are painted various weights and measures. There are also scrolls containing tables of the same, and '*the Gagers marke with five differences.*' In the same room is preserved a measure bearing the date 1641, C. R. and royal arms.

Dr Ro. Plumptre of Queens', in his *Hints respecting some of the University Officers*, 1782, p. 11, says, that the taxors in his time were paid quite as well as they deserved.

Among the Bowtell collection at Downing College

[1] Cooper's *Annals*, I. 441.
[2] Peacock *On the Statutes*, p. 26 n.

is a memorandum (which Mr H. T. Riley assigns to Q. Elizabeth's time, *Hist. MSS. 3rd Report*, p. 325) of '*Quae reddenda Taxatoribus*. Imprimis, a brasen busshell, with a strike of woode. Item, a gallon, a pinte of brasse. Item, a tubb with one busshell of musterd seede, and a keler. Item, 2 payre of scales for breade, with 2 piles of brasse. Item, 2 scales for barrells, and another for the busshell of the towne. Item, a key for the markett-bell.'

'In Sept. 1733 there was a dispute between the University and the Corporation as to the right to weigh hops at Sturbridge fair, as there had been in several previous years. The matter was referred to the Commissary of the University and the Recorder of the Town, who decided in favour of the University. A paper on the subject was drawn up and published by Thomas Johnson, of Magd. Coll., one of the taxors[1].'

March 26, 1784, the work of the taxors was increased, and more definitely stated by a grace of the senate[2].

The Camb. Univ. Commissioners, in their Report of 1852 (p. 11), recommended the discontinuance of the office. It was abolished by the award of sir John Patteson (Aug. 31, 1855) between the town and university. The taxors are not mentioned in the Bill ('the *Cambridge Award Act*') which confirmed the award in the following year.

The reverend Richard Shilleto wrote to me on

---

[1] Cooper's *Annals*, IV. 213.   [2] *Ibid.* IV. 411.

St Swithin's, 1872: 'The very names of men once specially recommended in the Bidding Prayer are utterly
unknown! Dr Gifford did some years ago, having
an antiquated copy, recite the once well-known words,
"the Proctors, T a x o r s, and all that bear office in
this our body." I told him immediately after his sermon that I for one should not come to hear him next
Sunday. "You are a rank Papist." Of course he
asked the grounds of this grave accusation. "Why,
you have been praying for men who have been dead
to my certain knowledge some ten years ago." I do
not think they have been prayed for—or rather bid-
den to be prayed for—since.' The Vice-Chancellor
has still magisterial jurisdiction with the mayor: and
the proctors, and their deputies, have constabular position within the circuit of the university[1].

Dr Waterland[2], when at Magdalene, maintained the
rights of the university against some magistrates of
the town, who had bailed a person committed by the
vice-chancellor.

In 1705 the mayor was discommuned[3], and read a
confession of his offence in the University Church, for
having refused precedency to the Vice-Chancellor in
the joint seat in the Guildhall.

Izaak Walton mentions that Ro. Sanderson (of
Lincoln college, Oxon.), when senior proctor in 1616,
'did not use his power of punishing to an extremity;

---

[1] 1732—3, Cooper's *Annals*, IV. 212; 1749, *ibid.* IV. 274; 1765,
ibid. IV. 336; 1771, *ibid.* IV. 362; 1785, tripos verses.

[2] Van Mildert, I. i. 34.

[3] Cooper's *Annals*, IV. 73, 74.

but did usually take their names, and a promise to appear before him unsent for next morning: and when they did, convinced them with such obligingness, and reason added to it, that they parted from him with such resolutions as the man after God's own heart was possessed with, when he said to God, *There is mercy with thee, and therefore thou shalt be feared.* (Psal. cxxx.) And by this, and a like behaviour to all men, he was so happy as to lay down this dangerous employment, as but few, if any have done, even without an enemy.'

Fra. Dickens, a friend of Tho. Baker, fellow of Trinity Hall, was twice proctor, and executed the office 'with great lenity and tenderness[1].'

Dr Tho. Townson, fellow of Magd. coll., Oxon. was senior proctor in 1749, 'and it is remembered[2] of him that, in performing the duties of that difficult office, he so tempered salutary discipline with just lenity, and so recommended whatever he did by the manner of doing it, that he was universally esteemed and beloved. The Radcliffe Library was opened this year with a speech by the famed orator, Dr King; and the celebrity, graced with a large and splendid company of the friends of the university, was distinguished also by conferring degrees on the trustees of Dr Radcliffe's benefaction.'

Townson, in his speech at the end of his year of office as senior proctor, applauds the elegance of Dr King, and makes honourable mention of Drake

---

[1] Masters' *Baker*, 110.
[2] *Life*, by Archdeacon Churton, p. xv.

(his companion in travel), and Bagot (his pupil, lord Bagot), who had received degrees. He also bestows a generous compliment on Lowth, professor of Poetry, and author of *Praelections on Hebrew Poetry.*

From the earliest times there has frequently arisen discord between the townsmen and the members of the university, their neighbours.

As Dr Whewell says (*Principles of English University Education,* 1837, p. 129) : 'If by ancient usage the students wear a peculiar dress, their position will generate the turbulence and the pride of *the gown.* If they are not so distinguished from their fellow-townsmen, they will soon find means themselves of marking the difference between the *Bursch* and the *Philister.*' This distinction has sometimes led to internecine strife, scarcely less deadly than the affrays of the *caterua* at Caesarea of Mauritania, which the preaching of S. Augustine quelled: 'pugnam ciuilem, uel potius plus quam ciuilem, quam cateruam uocabant: neque enim ciues tantummodo, uerum etiam propinqui et fratres, postremo parentes ac filii lapidibus inter se in duas partes diuisi, per aliquot dies continuos, certo tempore anni, sollemniter dimicabant, et quisque ut quemque poterat occidebat[1].'

At Oxford, in 1354, 'on the Feast of St. Scholastica, the Virgin [Feb. 10, 548 A.D. sister of S. Benedict, founded a convent in the valley of Monte Cassino], several Scholars going to a Tavern then called *Swyndlestock,* and in some modern Deeds *Swynstock*

---

[1] *De doctrina Christiana,* IV.

(but lately known by the Name of the *Mermaid*), at *Cairfax* ["Quatervois" or *Carfax*], and being served with bad Wine, order'd the Vintner [John de Croydon] to change the same for better, and for his sawcy Language they broke his Head with the Flagon; who thereon went and laid the matter of his Grief before his Servants and some of his Neighbours[1].' They rejoiced to have a good occasion for a fray, and rang the bell of S. Martin's to summon the Townsmen, who fell upon the Scholars and even the Chancellor, Humphrey de Charleton. By his orders S. Mary's bell was tolled, and the Scholars then 'defended themselves till Night parted them, without any Mischief done on either side.' Next morning the Chancellor issued proclamation that both sides should lay down their arms, but the Townsmen going to the *Austin* Schools 'assaulted a D.D. in his Determinations together with his Auditory, and then by the means of an Ambuscade of 80 Persons plac'd in St *Giles's* Church, they surrounded the Students in the Fields called the *Beaumonts*, and soon put them to flight, being without Arms, some getting into the *Austin* Convent, and others into the City, with the loss of one slain, and others miserably wounded.'

The Scholars were much harassed, and many of their Halls burnt, priests insulted, and all the friars' crosses overthrown, the peasants having been induced to break open the city gates, which had been shut against them. A royal proclamation restored peace;

---

[1] Ayliffe's *Antient and Present State of Oxford*, I. 126. 1714.

and the authorities were summoned to appear before K. Edward III. at Woodstock. The bishop of Lincoln (John Gynewell), in whose diocese it then was, put Oxford under an interdict to be published every Sunday and holyday. All the scholars went into rustication, with the exception of those of Merton. But having surrendered their privileges to the king, they returned by degrees, and were exhorted by him to resume their studies regularly: for, 'as it is said to have formerly happen'd at *Athens*, on a Quarrel of the like Nature, between the Scholars and Citizens; where the Sophists, on refusal to do any publick Exercises, taught the Youth in their private Houses; even so here were the Scholars altogether instructed in private for some time, until the King publickly open'd the Mouths of the Lecturers; and, for an Encouragement, now granted to them the most ample Charter yet obtain'd, containing many antient and modern privileges, some of which were taken away from the City and conferr'd on the University[1].'

In 1357 the bishop took off the Interdict on condition 'That the City on St *Scholastica's* Day, should celebrate so many Masses at the City's Expence, for the Souls of the Scholars and others kill'd in this Tumult: Others say that the Mayor and Bailiffs, with 60 of the chief Burgesses, were obliged on that Day at St *Mary's*, to swear Observance of the customary Rights of the University, unless they have a Cause of Absence to be approv'd by the Vice-Chancellor; and

---

[1] Ayliffe, I. 131. See further [Walker's] *Oxoniana*, I. 119—128.

also, at their own Costs, there to say Mass by a Deacon or Subdeacon, for the Souls of the slain: and it was further ordered that the said Number of Citizens should after Mass ended, singly offer up a Penny at the high Altar, of which forty Pence was to be distributed to Poor Scholars, and the Residue to the Curate of St *Mary's.*'   As long as this was performed the City was exempt from their engagement to pay 100 marks, 'till Q. *Elizabeth's* Reign, when the Scholars impleaded them in the Summ of 1500 Marks, for omitting the same for 15 Years, by reason of a Prohibition to celebrate Mass according to the Tenor of the said Agreement: wherefore it was order'd by the Privy Council, that instead of the Mass on this Day, there should be a Sermon and Communion at this Church, with the aforesaid Offering, and at length this came only to publick Prayers, with the Oblation of sixty Pence as now in Use. *Londinensis* says, that the Mayor was obliged to wear a Halter or Rope about his Neck in this Procession, which through the Dignity of his Office was afterwards chang'd into a Silken Ribband [compare the tradition of the Burgomasters of Ghent], with whom I cannot agree, tho' 'tis certain the young Scholars were wont to rally him with much Contempt on this Occasion, till this Insolence was restrain'd by a Statute, under the Pain of Imprisonment[1].'   In process of time the City authorities began to rebel against this indignity.

1681, *Jan.* 13. 'News that alderman W. Wright, a

---

[1] Ayliffe, I. 132—134.

burgess of the city, had lately made a motion to a committee to have the formality of St Scholastica's day laid aside. Townsmen go about into London, grow insolent as in 1641. *Feb.* 10, St Scholastica; the mayor (J. Barell), and about 20 citizens or more, came to St Mary's according to custom; heard prayers, and would have offered 65 pence, but the vice-chancellor refused unless all were there. The rest, out of contempt, would not come as 'in 1641, merely encouraged for what they do by the late demeanour of the parliament.

'1682, *Feb.* 10. Friday, the burgers or citizens of Oxford appeared in their full number on St Scholas-tica's day at St Mary's. Alderman Wright, their oracle, told them that if they would not appear, there might be some hole picked in their charter, as there was now endeavouring to be done in that of the city of London; he told them, moreover, that though it was a popish matter, yet policy ought to take place in this juncture of time[1].'

'In the year 1800, another attempt to evade this customary ceremony was made by the then mayor, Richard Cox, esq., who neglected to attend at St Mary's church. For this contempt the university de-manded and recovered the fine of 100 marks of Mr Cox. But at the close of 1824, the mayor and coun-cil applied to the university for a total abolition of the custom[2].' This was granted under the university

---

[1] *Autobiography of A. Wood.*

[2] Dr Bliss' note to Wood's *Autobiography*, p. 224. Cp. *Recollections of Oxford*, by G. V. Cox.

seal in convocation, Feb. 1, 1825, for which favour the city returned their thanks. I find in the
Oxford Univ. Calendar for 1822 among the ceremonies: 'Feb. 10, Sexagesima Sunday, *Scholastica*.
Litany read at the altar of St Mary's church, after
which the Mayor, the two Bailiffs, and sixty of the
burghers of the city of Oxford, make an offering of
a silver penny each, as an atonement for the murder
of some scholars, which took place in affray in the
year 1353, 27 Edward III.' An oath, however, was
exacted annually until about 1854, binding the city
to hold intact the ancient privileges of the university[1].

Will. Soone, who was in 1561 regius professor of
Civil Law till he turned papist, writes to Geo. Bruin
from Cologne, eve of Pentecost, 1575, a curious account of the manner of our university.

'The common dress of all is a sacred cap (I call it
sacred, because worn by priests); a gown reaching
down to their heels of the same form as that of
priests. None of them live out of the colleges in the
townsmen's houses; they are perpetually quarrelling
and fighting with them; and this is more remarkable
in the mock fights which they practise in the streets
in summer with shields and clubs. They go out in
the night to shew their valour, armed with monstrous
great clubs furnished with a cross piece of iron to
keep off the blows, and frequently beat the watch.
When they walk the streets they take the wall, not

[1] Moore's *Historical Handbook to Oxford*, p. 40. Shrimpton's, 1871.

only of the inhabitants, but even of strangers, unless persons of rank. Hence the proverb, that a Royston horse, and a Cambridge Master of Arts, are a couple of creatures that will give way to no body... In standing for degrees, the North country and South country men have warm contests with one another; as at Oxford the Welsh and English, whom the former call Saxons[1].' He concludes, however, by asserting that he would prefer Cambridge life to a kingdom.

Ant. Wood speaks of a *Town* and *Gown* riot, which lasted a week at Oxford, on the election of Ant. Hall, vintner, as mayor in Sept. 1673. 'A scholar of Brase Nose his arm broke, another his head; began by servitors, and carried on by them, and commoners, and townsmen of the meaner sort.'

In March 1788 a drayman was killed in a street fight at Cambridge, by Tho. ('Turk') Taylor of Trinity[2].

In Dec. 1792 the riot act was read, and the townsmen convicted for attacking meeting-houses[3].

Mention has already been made (pp. 41—43, 48) of misdemeanours of that character, and similar instances of misconduct will be noticed in the third part of this Essay.

The question of the rating of our University is discussed in *The Rights and Privileges of both the Universities, and of the University of* Cambridge *in*

---

[1] Bruin, *de præcipibus totius universi urbibus*, II. I. in *Gent. Mag.* XLVI. 201. Cooper's *Annals*, II. 329.

[2] Gunning, *Reminisc.* I. 116. Cooper's *Annals*, IV. 430.

[3] *Ibid.* IV. 445.

particular, Defended in a Charge to the Grand Jury, At the Quarter Sessions for the Peace, held in and for the Town of Cambridge, *The Tenth Day of October,* 1768. *Also, An Argument in the Case of the Colleges of* Christ *and* Emmanuel. *By* James Marriott, *LL.D.,* Cambridge, *Printed by* J. Archdeacon, &c., &c., *London,* 1769. For the Benefit of the *Hospital* at *Cambridge.* Price 1s. pp. 36 [Bodl. *Gough Camb.* 66.] Reference is made to transactions in the years 1650, 1748—51, 1768.

The Arguments of Mr Mansfield, *Mr* Dunning, *and Mr* Pemberton, *on the Special Case between the Society of* Catherine-Hall *and the Parish of St* Botolph, Cambridge...*by a Gentleman of the* Middle Temple, 1774, and p. 22 of *Hints respecting some of the University Officers, its Jurisdiction, its Revenues, &c., Submitted to the Consideration of the Members of the Senate of the University of* Cambridge. *By* Robert Plumptre, *D.D., Master of* Queens' *College.* Cambridge, *Printed by* J. Archdeacon, *&c.,* 1782.

The state of morals and discipline in the university seems to have reflected pretty much the condition of the country at large: and if we condemn the members of the Westminster and Constitution Clubs (pp. 50, 70), we must not forget that we are thinking of the days of the *Mohocks,* celebrated by Steele and Swift, and in the artificial comedy of that era, and of the *Scowrers* (Gay's *Trivia*): just as we ought to measure the religious and political intolerance of the universities, not by our own sentiments, but by the current notions of those times.

The author of the *Academic* [Dr John Green] in 1750 says (p. 21), that it was asserted that 'modesty, sobriety, in a few years, have made a swift Progress among all Orders:' and if the Benefactions 'appropriated by their Donors to luxurious Uses' according to the spirit of past times, had, in the university, somewhat retarded the improved state of feeling which was become prevalent in the country, private expences there ran rather in healthy exercise than in bacchanalian entertainments. It was only a few years earlier, in 1741, that Kit Smart had attached to the members of Gonville and Caius College the epithet which has become familiar to us through Trevelyan's *Horace at Athens:*

> The sons of culinary Kays,
>   Smoking from the eternal treat,
> Lost in ecstatic transport gaze
>   As tho' the Fair were good to eat;
> E'en gloomiest Kingsmen pleas'd awhile
> " Grin horribly a ghastly smile."

As to drinking, even Dr Johnson (perhaps with some feeling of pleasure in emulating the Socrates of the Platonic *Symposium*) remembered that he had 'drunk three bottles of port without being the worse. University College has witnessed this.'

In 1644 A. Wood and his mother sent *sack, claret,* cake, and sugar, to welcome Dr Bathurst and his bride. Before this, Ro. Herrick, of St John's and Trinity Hall, had sung of the maiden-blush:

> ' So purest diaper doth shine
> Stained by the beams of *claret* wine.'

Hearne, in 1706, speaks of *claret* which cost 1s. 6d. *per* bottle[1].

In Fielding's *Tom Jones*, Squire Western asks (xviii. 12), 'Wut ha' Burgundy, Champagne, or what?' and the landlady at Upton (x. 3) serves Worcestershire perry for mulled wine, champagne, sack, white wine, and what not. The 'Man of the Hill' offers Jones *brandy*, which he has kept 30 years.

In Smollett's *Roderick Random*, 1748, they call for 'French wine' (ch. 46). Narcissa's brother at Bath drinks 'no other sort of wine than *port*' (ch. 56). Roderick and his friend drink 'small French *claret*' against 'Bruin's' *port* (ch. 57).

In Fielding's *Amelia* (1751) *champagne* is drunk at dinner (ix. 3).

In Smollett's *Peregrine Pickle* (1751) *champagne* is on the sideboard at the masquerade ball in the Haymarket, *burgundy* in the eating-room (ch. 76).

In his *Humphry Clinker* (1771), 'Jack Holder is now at the Bath driving about in a phaeton and four, with French horns. He has treated with turtle and *claret* at all the taverns in Bath and Bristol.'

'At half an hour past eight in the evening he [Quin] was carried home [from his Club at the Three Tuns] with six good bottles of *claret* under his belt.'

Matthew Bramble, in the same novel, writes to Dr Lewis contrasting country and town life: 'At Brambleton I drink the virgin lymph pure and crystalline

---

[1] *Reliqu. Hearn.* I. 122.

as it gushes from the rock, or the sparkling beverage *home-brewed malt* of my own making; or I indulge with *cyder* which my own orchard affords, or with *claret* of the best growth imported for my own use by a correspondent on whose integrity I can depend... Now mark the contrast at London... If I would drink water I must quaff the mawkish contents of an open aqueduct exposed to all manner of defilements, or swallow that which comes from the river Thames impregnated with all the filth of London and Westminster. This is the agreeable potation extolled by the Londoners as the finest water in the universe. As to the intoxicating potion sold for wine, it is a vile unpalatable and pernicious sophistication balderdashed with cyder, corn-spirit, and the juice of sloes. In an action at law laid against a carman for having staved a cask of *port*, it appeared from the evidence of the cooper that there were not above five gallons of real wine in the whole pipe which held above a hundred, and even that had been brewed and adulterated by the merchant at Oporto... I shall conclude this catalogue of London dainties with table-beer guiltless of hops and malt, vapid and nauseous.' In the next letter from J. Melford to sir Watkin Phillips, Bart. of Jesus Coll. Oxon., we read that ' S—— lives in the skirts of the town, and every Sunday his house is open to all unfortunate brothers of the quill, whom he treats with beef pudding and potatoes, *port*, punch, and Calvert's entire butt-beer.'

In another letter it is complained that a hospitable foreigner, ' when he afterwards meets with his guest in London, is asked to dinner at the Saracen's Head, the Turk's Head, the Boar's Head, or the Bear, eats raw beef and butter, drinks execrable *port*, and is allowed to pay his share of the reckoning.' Just afterwards J. Melford describes a trick he played at Harrowgate: 'I dexterously exchanged the labels and situation of his bottle and mine: and having tasted his tincture, found it was excellent *claret.*' The pretended patient protested that "it was a varra poorful infusion of jallap in *Bourdeaux* wine." What he had drunk was genuine wine from Bordeaux, which the lawyer had brought from Scotland for his own private use.' In Argyleshire 'they find means to procure very good *claret* at a very small expence.'

Mackenzie, who had lived almost all his life in Scotland, calls *claret* the fashionable drink in 1771 (*Man of Feeling*, ch. 33).

About the same year the bursar of Peterhouse paid Juba Fortune 5*l.* 8*s.* for four dozen of *Sherry*.

1773. For eight dozen, 9*l.* 12*s.*
       Calcavella, per gallon, 6*s.* 8*d.*

1772. Fine old *Madeira*, per dozen, 1*l.* 16*s.*
       A 'share' of a dozen of *Madeira*, 1*l.* 4*s.* 9*d.*
       Brandy, per gallon, 12*s.*
       Geneva, per gallon, 5*s.* 6*d.*

1769. *Port*, per pipe, 34*l.* 1*s.*

1771. Red *port*, at 18*s.*

1773. *Port*, per dozen, 17*s.* 6*d.* and 17*s.* 4*d.*

1774. *Port*, per dozen, 17*s.*
       Lisbon, per dozen, 16*s.* 6*d.*
       Ditto, per hogshead, 21*l.* 4*s.*

1775.   *Rum,* per dozen, 1*l.* 15*s.*
      Fine *Porter,* per barrel, 1*l.* 16*s.*

1780.   *Tent* and *Sack,* per pint, 2*s.*
      Lisbon, per hogshead, 24*l.*
      Bottles were charged 3*s.* 6*d.* per dozen.

In the most amusing *New Art of Pluck,* by *Scriblerus Redivivus* [Dr Caswall], Oxford, ed. 2, 1835, book ii. ch. 9, it is said that 'Wine drinking produceth Pluck each year in the proportion following: Sherry 72, Claret 23, Madeira, 27, Champagne 13, Port 90. The reason whereof is, that Port is most drunk, Champagne least, and the rest in proportion. Of late also hath Beer contributed not a little to produce Plucks, for indeed beer is a good thing for making the mind heavy and loaded. Nevertheless, as yet beer hath not such consequence in Oxford as in Cambridge, being a new fashion in this place.'

So utterly have tea and coffee supplanted the 'morning draughts,' the fasting from which threw Savil Bradley, fellow of New College and Magdalene, 'into a sowne' at the Ordination in 1661, as A. Wood records. In 1822 'Breakfast-parties are usually composed of idlers. I have known—the fast broken, indeed, with a vengeance, but—the party not dispersed, when the bell has sounded for dinner[1]. "After dinner," cries *Eugenius,* "I will apply. This morning I must devote to back-gammon[2]."'

Lord Macaulay, in his essay on the *Constitutional History,* says, 'The reign of William the Third, as

---

[1] *Hints to Freshmen at the University of Cambridge,* ed. 4, p. 14.
[2] *Ibid.* p. 20.

Mr Hallam happily says, was the Nadir of the national prosperity. It was also the Nadir of the national character. [Macaulay repeats this expression
in his essay on the *Comic Dramatists of the Restoration.*] It was the time when the rank harvest of
vices, sown during thirty years of licentiousness and
confusion, was gathered in ; but it was also the seed-
time of great virtues.'

·To the last sentence it may be objected that the
king did not set a very good example, and that
bishop Gilbert Burnet was of a different opinion[1].
Sherlock, and Butler later, gave no more hopeful
account.

A Letter to the Heads of the University of Oxford,
on a Late very Remarkable Affair. 'The Head of
Argus, &c.' London: *Printed And Sold by* A. Dodd
without *Temple-Bar;* J. Robinson in Ludgate-street;
Mrs Amey at *Charing-Cross,* and at the Pamphlet
Shops at the *Royal Exchange,* 1747, pp. 32 [Bodl.
Godwin Pamphlets, 1858], signed 'Terrafilius,' relates
a scandalous instance of wanton heartlessness on the
part of some Oxonians, praises Dr *Cockman* of *University College* as a model Head, and expresses envy
at the discipline in those days kept up in the 'Universities of *Scotland,* particularly those of *Glasgow*
and *Aberdeen.*'

In December, 1751, while the *Associators* were agi-
tating for the right of appeal [see above, p. 75 *n.*],
some of the younger members of our university were

---

[1] See Palin's *History of the Church of England,* 105, 113.

alarming their neighbours by parading the streets with lighted torches or links[1].

Dr Whewell, in his *Principles of English University Education*, 1837, p. 121, quotes the following from the *Remains of the* Rev. Edward Griffin (of New York), II. 259: 'Much has been said of the indolence of Fellows; of their disposition to quarrel and petty intrigue; and of their fondness for guzzling ale, tippling port, and playing whist. Such things *were*. Nay, since such are the natural consequences of a want of ambition to be useful or distinguished, a want of occupation, and a want of that most practical stimulant dire necessity, such things *are*. The cases, however, are unfrequent. The Fellows to whom I had the honour to be introduced were men of a different stamp. They were gentlemen, in the highest sense of that high term, and bore about them no traces of their somewhat monastic system. Their conversation smelt a little of the shop;—was sometimes a little too mathematical, at least for me;—but was throughout the most thoroughly intellectual I ever enjoyed. Their *reunions*, after a plain but well-cooked dinner on the dais of their College-hall, either in the common sitting-room, or in the apartments of some individual members, left on my mind a delightful impression. It was such as literary society should be, composed only of men of real learning; of friends confiding in the mutual esteem entertained by all, undisturbed by ambitious quacks or impudent pretenders.'

[1] Cooper's *Annals*, IV. 285. See above, p. 75.

In May, 1716, Waterland, as vice-chancellor, had occasion to give notice that the statutes relating to the frequenting of taverns and public houses would be enforced against persons in *statu pupillari*[1].

In 1728 it was ordered upon Interpretation of part of the Statute *De modestia et urbanitate morum*, that if any scholar shall at any time resort to any Tavern or other publick house otherwise than the Statutes do allow, [an LL.B., M.B., Mus. B., M.A.; or a pupil accompanying his tutor, or invited to see a parent or friend, who has come into the town as a guest; but only to dinner or supper: or with the exception of the last-mentioned case (an undergraduate or B.A.) at other times with the leave of the master], he shall forfeit 1*s.* 8*d.* If after the statutable time of locking the gates [8 p.m.; or from Lady-day to Michaelmass 9], 3*s.* 4*d.* If at a more unseasonable hour, or disorder'd in liquor, he shall, besides the other penalties, be admonished by the vice-chancellor, which Admonition shall be entered in a book kept for that purpose; and after three admonitions be expelled. 'That if any number of Scholars, under pretence of being of the same year, School, or County, or otherwise, shall be found assembling together at any publick house, they shall, upon conviction thereof, beside the former penalty of 3*s.* 4*d.*, be suspended from taking any Degree 'til one whole year after the usual time of taking the same[2],' &c.

These, then known as 'SCHOOL-FEASTS celebrated

---

[1] Cooper's *Annals*, IV. 142.
[2] *Ibid.* IV. 204. Dyer's *Privileges of Camb.* I. 341, 342.

at the University *with any frequency*, are bad things. They tie a young man down to drink, on stated days, more than is good for him—and sometimes in the company of those of his school acquaintance, with whom it is least worth whiie to encourage a further intimacy[1].'

It was from one of these 'school-feasts' that the quarrels in 1750 arose (*see above*, pp. 71—75)[2].

In 1736—7, there was a contest between the University and certain vintners who had set up unlicensed houses for 'playing of Interludes[3].'

The *Regulations* of 1750 have been summarized already (p. 67).

In 1733, at Oxford, the new dean of Christ Church, Dr Conybeare, 'makes a great stir in the college, at present pretending to great matters, such as locking up the gates at 9 o'clock at night, having the keys brought up to him, turning out young women from being bedmakers, having the kitchen (which he visits) cleansed, and I know not what, aiming at a wonderful character, even to exceed that truly great man bishop Fell, to whom he is not in the least to be compared; as neither is he to dean Aldrich, nor dean Atterbury, nor even dean Smalridge[4].'

Dr Green mentions, in the *Academic* (1750, pp. 10, 19, 40), that the existence of the punishments in 1749, apparently for vicious practices, was appealed

[1] *Hints to Freshmen at the University of Cambridge*, ed. 4. 1822, p. 42.
[2] Cooper's *Annals*, IV. 227—9. [3] *Ibid.* IV. 279.
[4] *Reliqu. Hearn.* Bliss, III. 94.

to as evidence of the need of stricter discipline at Cambridge: 'upwards of twenty Persons, many of good Families and Fortunes,' had been expelled or rusticated 'for very heinous Violations of our Laws and Discipline.'

Dr Ri. Newton proposed in his scheme for Hart Hall [1747, *Rules and Statutes*, p. 42], that the Tutor should frequently visit his Pupils in their Rooms. Also (p. 76), that the College gate should be shut at 9 o'clock *p.m.*, and finally when the clock has struck 10, and the Key taken to the Principal by the Scholar in Waiting at the gate.

At St John's, Camb., 25 May, 1740, it was 'Ordered by the master and seniors, that if any scholar in *statu pupillari* shall, when the gates are shut by order of the master, break open any door, or by scaling of walls, leaping of ditches, or any other way, get out of the limits of the college, he shall be *ipso facto* expelled.' Also, 'that no scholars ever presume to loiter, or walk backwards and forwards in any of the courts or cloysters; and that when the names shall have been called over by order of the master, all depart quietly to their chambers, as they shall answer it at their peril[1].'

The rationale of College *punishments* has been excellently expounded by Dr Whewell, *Principles of English University Education*, 1837, p. 95, cp. 111. 'Its general character may be briefly stated: it is this:—*Every college punishment is an expression of*

---

[1] Mayor's *Baker's History of St John's*, p. 1036.

the disapprobation of the college; this disapprobation is increased by every successive offence; and, carried to a certain point, makes removal from the college necessary.'

In *Gradus ad Cantabrigiam,* 1803, under the word 'punishment,' reference is made to the tradition, that Milton was flogged at Christ college[1], to the *Student,* I. 80, *Fenn's Paston Letters* (quoted above, p. 93), T. Tusser's 'From *Paul's* I went to *Eton* sent,' &c.

'In the Statutes of Trinity College, An. 1556, the scholars of the foundation are ordered to be *whipp'd* even to the twentieth year. "Dr Potter," says Aubrey, "while Tutor of Trinity College (Oxford), *whipt* his pupil *with his sword by his side* when he came to take his leave of him to go to the inns of court." This was done to make him a smart fellow.'

To the list of instances of confession of offences in college halls given above, pp. 118, 119, may be added the notable one which has been supposed to refer to the poet when at Trinity College, Cambridge.

'July 19, 1652. Agreed that Dryden be put out of Commons, for a fortnight at least, and that he goe not out of the colledg during the time aforesaid, excepting to sermons, without express leave from the master or vice-master, and that at the end of that time he read a confession of his crime in the hall at the dinner time, at the three......fellowes table[2].'

---

[1] *Gent. Mag.* 1787, p. 947. Cf. Vol. XLIX. pp. 395, 493, 595. Fuller's *Worthies,* I. 506.

[2] *Life of Dryden,* by Sir Walter Scott, quoting the order from Malone.

At Peterhouse, in 1665, May 6, Mr Quarles was admonished. Likewise, 1667, June 20, 'sir Talbot;' and in 1669, April 3, Mr Witty was admonished by the master, according to the 33rd statute, for being *intolerabilis erga magistrum*. He appealed against Dr Jos. Beaumont accordingly.

June 14, 1771. Tho. Chapman was rusticated for three terms.

Jan. 8, 1776. [Ro.] Hopper, senior, was rusticated for disorderly behaviour in the hall, and for disrespectful conduct. He published (Jan. 20) a pamphlet entitled, *An Account of a late Rustication from* Peterhouse, *in the Univ. of* Camb.' 8vo. London, 1776. He had headed 'a Conspiracy to send Mr Christian [a relation of bp. E. Law the master] to *Coventry*,' and as 'President of the Pensioners' table,' had cut off Christian's 'commons,' and sent it to him 'seperately.' I have no reason to suppose that the Petreusians were more disorderly than members of other colleges, but I have given these instances as those to which I have easiest access. Sending a graduate to Coventry is put down by the late Prof. Sedgwick, in his *Four Letters in Reply to* R. M. Beverley, p. 8, as equivalent to the term *discommuning*. The latter is applied also to tradesmen, whose shops are put 'out of bounds,' under an interdict from the university authorities, for disregarding the statutes or *ordinationes* in their dealings with the students.

Discommonsing is prohibiting a scholar from taking his commons or allowance in the coll. hall for a period of days. This used to be the punishment at Trinity for those who neglected to say grace after dinner when 'in waiting.'

The following passages from Nevile's *Poor Scholar*, 1662, will illustrate the old custom of flogging at the butteries.

ii. 6. [The Watchmen have captured *Aphobos'* gown, as he scales the college walls.]

Demosth. The watch take it up? 'tis not worth taking up i' the highway; but if we knew the owner, we'd take him down to th' butteries, and give due correction.

Aphob. [*aside*]. Under correction, Sir, if you're for the butteries with me, I'le lie as close as *Diogenes* in *Dolio*, I'le creep in at the Bunghole before I'le mount a Barrel.

And a little later:

Aphob. I had need then have my wits about me, for had I been over to the ¡Butteries they'd have their rods about me. But *Pege*, let us, for joy that I'm escap'd, go to th' three Tuns, and drink a pint of wine and laugh away our cares.

Sings:

We'l carouse in Bacchus's *fountains, hang your Beer and muddy Ale;*
Tis only Sack infuses courage, when our spirits droop and fail;
Tis drinking at the Tuns that keeps us from ascending Buttery Barrels;
Tis this that safely brings us off, when we're engag'd in feuds and
        quarrels.

v. 4. My name too is cut out o' th' Colledge butteries [the 'boards']; and I have now no title to the honour of mounting a Barrel.

We will not fear an ill-look'd Dean nor mirth-disturbing Proctor,
We'l now carouze, and sing and bouze before the gravest Doctor.

The following definitions are taken mainly from *Gradus ad Cantabrigiam*, 1803:

'*Dean.*—Udorum tetricus censor et asper.   MART.

'The principal business of a *Dean* is to inflict *impositions* for irregularities, &c.   Old Holingshed, in his

Chronicle[1], describing Cambridge, speaks of "certeine censors, or deanes, appointed to looke to the behauiour, and maners of the Studentes there, whom they punish uerie severelie, if they make anie default, according to the quantitie and qualitie of their trespasses." When *flagellation* was enforced at the Universities, the Deans were *the Ministers of Vengeance.* Antony Wood tells us, that "Henry Stubbe, a Student of Christ Church, Oxford, afterwards a partizan of sir H. Vane, shewing himself too forward, pragmatic, and conceited, was publicly *whipp'd* by the Censor in the College-hall."'

The *Deans of Arts* of St John's, Oxon., are mentioned in the benefactions of Tobias Rustat (*Terrae Filius*, XLIX.) as well as the *moderator in arts*, the *dean of divinity*, and *dean of civil law.* Charles Simeon was *Dean of Arts* at King's coll., Cambridge, in 1788; 'the following year he was appointed to the important office of *Dean of Divinity*. He was afterwards *Senior Dean of Arts*.' (*Life* by Carus.)

In the Univ. Calendar for 1862, the title of office of 'Dean of Divinity' ceases to be recorded, and the two 'Deans of Arts' are called simply 'Deans.' There was a 'Divinity Lecturer' as well.

[At New College they have even a 'Dean' of Football!]

Dr Whewell's scale of penalties is:—'for the first offence let him forfeit one month's commons; for the second, three months;' for the third, let him be ex-

---

[1] 1587. I. p. 151, col. B. line 68.

pelled the College :—and the same kind of formula is used in almost every penal appointment. It will easily be seen, that in this manner, punishments, which are slight as inflictions, are serious as warnings. A small fine [e.g. *gate-fine*], the forfeiture of a college allowance [*discommonsing*], or some restraint on the pupil's motions [*gating*], or an exercise of the memory, or of the pen [an *imposition*], which in themselves might be thought lightly of, receive efficiency from the consideration of their possible consequences[1].'

By a *Decretum Praefectorum* of May 8, 1571, any B.A. caught bathing in Cambridge was to be set in the *stocks* in his college hall for a whole day, *in cippis, pedibus constrictis per unum diem integrum in aula communi eius collegii in quo commoratur plectatur;* and to pay a *sconce* or fine of 10s. And in 1606, any persons who were *not scholars* and were found to have taken part in the riots on Feb. 20, while the comedy was performing in King's coll., were to be punished by imprisonment, and sitting in the stocks at the Bull-ring in the market-place, so long as to Mr V.-Chan. shall seem good.

In *A Collection of English Words Not Generally used*, &c. By *John Ray*, Fellow of the Royal Society, *London*, 1674, among the North Country words (p. 44) occurs ' *A Stang:* a wooden bar; ab As. *staeng*, sudes, vectis, Teut. *stang*, pertica, contus, sparus, vectis. Datur & Camb. Br. *Ystang* Pertica, sed nostro fonte haustum. This word is still used in some Col-

---

[1] *Principles of English University Education*, p. 95.

leges in the University of *Cambridge;* to *Stang* Scholars in Christmas, being to cause them to ride on a
colt-staff or pole for missing of Chappel.' 'Captain'
Grose has transcribed this from Ray into his *Provincial Glossary*, ed. 2, 1790, without marks of quotation or the like: but I know of no reason to think
that it was not obsolete long before his time. Mr
Halliwell, in his *Archaic and Provincial Dictionary*,
shews that the *Stang* was a punishment used also in
the north of England for husbands who beat their
wives.

' *To Sconce;* " to impose a fine (*Academical Phrase*)."
Grose's *Dict. of the Vulgar Tongue.* This word is, I
believe, wholly confined to Oxford. " A young Fellow of *Baliol* college, having, upon some discontent,
cut his throat very dangerously, the MASTER of the
college sent his *servitor* to the *buttery-book* to *sconce*
(that is, *fine*) him *five shillings*, and, says the doctor,
tell him that *next time he cuts his throat*, I'll sconce
him TEN." (Amherst's *Terrae Filius*, XXXIX. A
Supplement to the *Oxford Toasts* or *feasts*.)

' But hark—the Bell summons—now must I sneak
away to Chappel like a parish Boy to sing Psalms—
no it may ting tang 'till Doomsday for me, I'll not
do it.

' *Gainlove.* Now, Heaven forbid.

' *Apeall.* No, no, my Dear, I understand more manners than to leave my Friends to go to Church—no,
tho' they Sconce me a Fortnight's Commons, I'll not
do it.'

[Jas. Miller's] *The Humours of* Oxford, I. 1, 1730.

In some of the smaller colleges still the President of both the high and lower tables has the power of fining any member who misbehaves at dinner-time or offends against etiquette. The penalty is generally either a bottle of wine or a claret or beer 'cup,' or *copus,* to be shared by the members of the table.

'*Convention;* a court *clerical,* consisting of the Master and Fellows, who sit in the *Combination Room* and pass sentence on any young offender.'

> When ye met all together of late
> In the room which we term *Combination,*
> To fix your petitioner's fate,
> Alas ! why did you choose *Rustication ?*
> *The Rusticated Cantab,* from the *Morning Herald.*

Cp. p. 69, *above.* Dec. 16, 1793, Best was rusticated from Peterhouse till Oct. 10, for admitting a member of another college by the back gate.

In 1803 *to cut gates* meant simply to be out after the gates were locked, not implying that the offender had previously been *gated,* or condemned to confine himself to the college precincts after a certain hour in the evening.

At the same period a *punishment* was equivalent to an *imposition.*

'*Imposition;* "an additional exercise given for a punishment. To *impose* that punishment—multam imponere. *Imposer cette peine.*" (Lovell's *Universe in Epitome,* 1679.) "Every pecuniary mulct whatever on young men *in statu pupillari* should be abolished. The proper punishment is employing their minds in some useful *Imposition.*" (Enormous Expence in

Education at *Cambridge*, 1788.) "Literary tasks, or frequent compulsive attendances on tedious and un-improving exercises in a College Hall." (*T. Warton.* See *Milton's* Minor Poems, by *T. W.*, p. 432.)'

In the *Laughing Philosopher* (1825), pp. 274, 275, the abbreviated form *Impos* also occurs, where the proctor sets 300 lines of Homer, and the dean 500 of Virgil to be learnt by heart.

'We have a company of formal old surly Fellows who take pleasure in making one act contrary to ones Conscience—and tho', for their own parts, they never see the Inside of a Chappel throughout the Year, yet if one of us miss but two Mornings in a Week, they'll set one a plaguy *Greek* Imposition to do—that ne'er a one of them can read when 'tis done. And so i'gad I write it in *French*, for they don't know one from t'other.' (*Jas. Miller's* Humours of *Oxford*, 1730, I. I.)

At Cambridge in 1803 'to *get the First Book of the Iliad by heart*, would be thought a severe "*punishment*."' The imposition by writing was not so effectual a method.

This will be understood from the following lines from an unpublished letter from Trin. Coll. Oxon in 1790:

> But the whole set, pray understand,
> Must walk full dress'd in cap and band:
> For should grave Proctor chance to meet
> A buck in boots along the street,
> He stops his course, and with permission
> Asking his name sets imposition;
> Which to get done if he's a ninny
> He gives his Barber half a guinea.

This useful go-between will share it
With servitor in College garret;
Who courts these labours sweet as honey
Which bring to purse some pocket-money.

At Cambridge our old friend *Maps* (pp. 378—385) was the great resource of the weak in this predicament. But there was another character, if less respectable, no less peculiar. The history of *Jemmy Gordon* is thus sketched in the sixth chapter of Gunning's *Reminiscences*.

It was at the election in the summer of 1790 that Jemmy Gordon (afterwards a well-known character in the University) made his first appearance in the Senate House. His father was Chapel Clerk at Trinity, and a man of some property; he gave his son a good classical education, and afterwards articled him to a respectable attorney by the name of Haggerstone. At the expiration of his articles, he commenced practice in Freeschool Lane, in the house which ought to have been occupied by the Master of the Perse School, but which was at that time (through the neglect of the Trustees) let to the highest bidder: here he led an expensive and profligate life, and placed at the head of his table a young woman of considerable beauty, who went by the *sobriquet* of "the Duchess of Gordon."

Soon after the election commenced, Gordon entered the crowded Senate and joined Mr Pitt; he was handsomely dressed in the Windsor Livery, a blue coat with red cuffs and collar; he congratulated the Premier upon the triumph he was about to obtain, and censured in strong terms Mr. Tharp, who had lately purchased the Chippenham estate, and was talked of as a candidate for the County—"his presumption in coming forward!"—and could not understand "what claim his large possessions in Jamaica gave him to disturb the peace of the county of Cambridge!" He added that his influence (which he hinted was pretty considerable) should be exerted in support of the old members. He continued walking backwards and forwards, conversing with Mr Pitt, for about half-an-hour; those who knew him were extremely indignant at his presumption, but no one liked to interfere. At length Beverley undertook to have him turned out, and walked up to him, attended by two constables, for that purpose. Jemmy, finding it vain to resist, made a hasty retreat. Mr Pitt was all astonishment to see his new friend, of whose loyalty and good sense he had formed a very favourable opinion, so unceremoniously treated. The crowd below the barrier hustled him out of the Senate House. Beverley, elated with his victory, followed, and urged the persons assembled outside to take him off and place him under the Conduit. Beverley's zeal carried him beyond the steps of the Senate House, where he soon found that Gordon had more friends than himself. Gordon was immediately rescued, and if the constables had not interfered, Beverley would probably have undergone the punishment he would so willingly have inflicted on another.

Jemmy had at that time a cousin of the name of Goode, who resided for a few terms at Trinity Hall; he had been well educated, and was a remarkably good-looking man, but his habits were low and profligate. I do not recollect ever to have met him in a party at Trinity Hall, or any other College; he had, however, his friends in the University, and to all those parties his cousin Jemmy was always a welcome guest, for he sang a good song, told a good story, had Horace at his fingers' ends, and was in the habit of quoting him with considerable effect.

Though Gordon realized but little by his profession, yet, as his father made him a handsome allowance, he used to give in his turn some very jovial entertainments at his own house; but his extravagance knew no bounds, and he was, after a time, under the necessity of going into cheap and obscure lodgings; for his means would not enable him to gratify his extraordinary fondness for wine and liquor. He was then at the service of any man who thought proper to send him an invitation to entertain his friends, and to get very drunk by way of recompense. Dressed in a huge cocked-hat, and the tarnished uniform of a general or an admiral, (for Jemmy was *not too proud* to accept any article of apparel that was occasionally given to him from an old-clothes shop,) he was to be heard about the streets, frequently until daylight, roaring out scraps of songs, or quoting fragments of poetry. A relation dying left him a guinea a-week, to be paid weekly, but it was soon deeply mortgaged. Spending every shilling he could get in liquor, he at length became so shabby and so dirty, that no one would suffer him to enter his rooms. As he was not ashamed to beg, he applied to every person he met, and raised money in that way; some giving because they believed him to be in distress; others because they were afraid of him; for if any person (no matter what his rank or position in Town or University might be) had been guilty of any indiscretion, Jemmy would be sure to proclaim it aloud whenever he met him. As he was known to have a very great objection to fighting, many men whom he insulted, preferred breaking his head to giving him half-a-crown, but these per-

sons Jemmy contrived to render ultimately his most profitable customers; so that it might be said of him, as of the Grecian orator, Ὁ γὰρ
ἄνθρωπος οὐ κεφαλὴν, ἀλλὰ πρόσοδον κέκτηται. Æschines in Ctesiph.
p. 447.

Passing through Trinity College one day, he saw the Bishop of
Bristol walking backwards and forwards in front of his Lodge. Gordon
accosted him in his usual strain, "I hope, my Lord, you will give me a
shilling!" To this his Lordship replied, "If you can find me a greater
scoundrel than yourself, I will give you half-a-crown." Jemmy made
his bow, and shortly after meeting Beverley, said "Have you seen a
messenger from the Bishop of Bristol, who is seeking you everywhere,
as his Lordship wishes to see you on particular business?" Beverley
thanked him for his information, and hastened to Trinity, Jemmy
following him at no great distance. "I understand you are wishing to
see me, my Lord," said Beverley, addressing the Bishop; to which the
latter replied, "You have been misinformed, Mr Beverley." At that
moment Jemmy joined them, and taking off his hat most respectfully,
said, "I think, my Lord, I am entitled to the half-crown!" The next
time the Bishop met Jemmy, he took an opportunity of proving to him
that there was *no great difference* of opinion between them respecting
Mr Beverley. [A similar story is told in Amherst's *Terrae Filius*,
No. XXXIX, 1721.]

For many years this extraordinary character infested the streets,
swearing and blaspheming in the most horrible manner; the magistrates not interfering, from a reluctance to expose themselves to his
violent and abusive language. At length the nuisance became intolerable, and Jemmy usually passed nine or ten weeks of every quarter
in the Town Gaol. It was during one of these incarcerations, that
John Taylor, the University Marshal, consulted me respecting a letter
he had received from a person formerly a member of the University,
in which he was asked to go to Maps (a well-known character), and
request him to procure for him short essays in Latin, on six subjects
which he sent him, all of a serious and religious nature. As Maps was
dead, Taylor was at a loss how to proceed, and wished to know who
was his successor. I told him I believed there was no one in that line
now; but added, jocularly, that I thought Jemmy Gordon would supply
him. Jemmy was then in gaol, and as he had been there for a long
time, was, of necessity, sober. The same evening Taylor called upon
me, and showed me an essay on one of the subjects; he asked my
opinion of it: (it occupied three sides of a sheet of foolscap:) I told
him there was no objection to it but its length, and that if Gordon
would reduce it to one-third of its size, and observe the same rule with

the other five, I thought they would answer his friend's purpose very well. They were finished in the course of that night and the following day, and Jemmy received half-a-guinea for each, which Taylor learned, from some quarter or other, was the price usually given for works of that description. But these opportunities of obtaining money during imprisonment seldom occurred, and by constant importunity he had wearied out those persons who, having known him in his better days, were unwilling that he should suffer from want. The instant he was released, and had begged a little money, he repeated that outrageous conduct which it was disgraceful to the magistracy to have so long tolerated, and which was loudly censured by all persons visiting the University. The fact was, that the characters of the magistrates at that time were not invulnerable: they possessed, at least, a proportionate share of the failings of their fellow-citizens, and were afraid that Jemmy (who was no respecter of persons) should proclaim, from the Huntingdon turnpike to Addenbrooke's Hospital, their frailties in his loudest tones. It was therefore arranged between the magistrates and Jemmy, that he should leave Cambridge, never to return.

He betook himself to London, and was to be seen daily waiting the arrival or departure of the Cambridge coaches: in this manner he earned a precarious subsistence; for even in London he became notorious, and is described at some length in one of Bulwer's early novels. [*Pelham*, Chapters 49, 50. 'This person wore a large cocked-hat, set rather jauntily on one side, and a black coat, which seemed an *omnium gather-um* of all abominations that had come in its way for the last ten years, and which appeared to advance equal claims (from the manner it was made and worn) to the several dignities of art, military and civic, the *arma* and the *toga*: from the neck of the wearer hung a blue riband of amazing breadth, and of a very surprising assumption of newness and splendour, by no means in harmony with the other parts of the *tout ensemble;* this was the guardian of an eye-glass of block tin, and of dimensions correspondent with the size of the ribbon. Stuck under the right arm, and shaped fearfully like a sword, peeped out the hilt of a very large and sturdy-looking stick, "in war a weapon, in peace a support." ' Hone, in the *Every-day Book* 1. col. 1295, says that Gordon left an autobiography which was in the hands of Mr W. Mason, picture-dealer of Cambridge (1826).] The London police, however, had no sympathy with Jemmy; when he offended against the laws he was taken to prison, where he had nothing to look to but the prison al-lowance. Jemmy sighed for liberty and his native air, and at last found his way back to Cambridge, where he lived in a state of the greatest destitution. For many months he slept in the grove belonging to Jesus

College, where he conveyed a bundle of straw which was but seldom changed. When winter set in, he was allowed to sleep in the straw-chamber belonging to the Hoop Hotel; still, on receiving a few shillings, he squandered them in the usual manner; offended and disgusted every one he met with; and when he became sober, often found himself in prison. In ascending his usual resting-place one night, when he was very drunk, he slipped off the ladder and broke his thigh; he called loudly for assistance; the ostler and postboys, not believing he had received any injury, took him up and threw him into an adjoining outhouse for the night: when in the morning he was found to be incapable of moving, he was taken on a shutter to the hospital; but was in so filthy a condition that he was refused admittance; he was then taken to the workhouse at Barnwell, where he died, after several weeks of suffering.

Mr E. Johnson, of Trinity-street, has a portrait of Gordon, 'Published Nov. 1817, by W. Mason, near the Hospital, Cambridge.'

'James Gordon of Cambridge,

> Who to save from *Rustication*
> *Crams* the Dunce with *Declamation*,'

is there represented in pantaloons, Wellington boots, the large tin eye-glass and ribbon mentioned in *Pelham*, with cocked-hat and feather on the back of his head, visiting cards peeping out of his waistcoat-pocket, left hand in bosom, and right hand holding a switch beneath his coat-tail. This was reduced in scale for the columns of the *Every-day Book* I. 693. (1826).

On p. 121 of the 2nd ed. of *Gradus ad Cantabrigiam*, 1824, is another head more rudely cut, the cocked-hat being set on properly, described on the title-page as 'a striking likeness of that celebrated character *Jemmy Gordon.*' It is certainly not prepossessing. It bears the same couplet. I have a

29—2

pair of small pictures of inferior art, but with the physiognomy. In the one he appears in his glory with hat on head and ring on finger, in the famous buckskin breeches mentioned in *Pelham*, sitting by a round table which bears a bottle and two liqueur glasses, an ink-glass and the paper on which he is writing from the book which he holds at left arm's length to the admiration of a brainless fellow-commoner who sits astride over the back of a chair. On the wall of the room, which has a staring stripe-patterned paper, hang cap and gown, fowling-piece, powder-horn, dog-whip and tandem-whip, spurs and a sporting picture. The companion shews him alone in adversity within a vaulted cell, but dressed as usual. He has amused himself by writing on the stone wall,

> 'The King by clapping of a sword on
> May make a Knight of Jemmy Gordon,
> Who to save from Rustication,
> Crams the Dunce with Declamation.'

The former distich of this quatrain is preserved also in the *Every-day Book* I. 693, with slight verbal difference: it is said to have been an *impromptu* spoken by Jemmy in the face of a new-made knight whom he met in the streets of Cambridge. The following *memorabilia* are preserved by Hone in the same place; 'At a late assize at Cambridge, a man named Pilgrim was convicted of horse-stealing, and sentenced to transportation. Gordon, seeing the prosecutor in the street, loudly vociferated to him, "You, sir, have done what the pope of Rome cannot do;

you have put a stop to *Pilgrim's Progress.*" ' ' Gordon was met one day by a person of rather indifferent character, who pitied Jemmy's forlorn condition (he being without shoes and stockings), and said "Gordon, if you will call at my house, I will give you a pair of shoes." Jemmy, assuming a contemptuous air, replied, "No, sir! excuse me, I would not stand in your shoes for all the world!"....No man's life is more calculated

> To adorn a moral, and to point a tale.
>
> N.'

A curious list follows (columns 699, 700), of above a hundred quaint or incongruous names of Cambridge tradesmen in 1825, e.g. ' A Bishop—a tailor, A Leech—a fruiterer, A Roe—an engraver, A Grief —a glazier, A Bacon—a tobacconist.' Gordon's mantle (but not his cocked-hat or vices) fell upon a well-known character called *Agamemnon.*

As I have mentioned portraits of Cambridge worthies in the possession of Mr Johnson (pp. 136, 138, 153, 384, Porter, Vaughan, Hobson, Gordon), though I have not always stated that he was the possessor, I may speak here of engravings of two other 'characters:' the first is a portrait of *D. Randall,* fruit-seller, of Cambridge; who appears with a good-natured full face; he is girt with an apron, and on each arm carries two baskets of fruit (T. Orde f. 1768). Two others depict the same worthy, *D. Randall* with *Mother Hammond.* The one of these pictures (T. Orde ft. 1768) shews her of very little stature, in a gipsey hat, and Randall in more tidy clothes and hat than in the above-mentioned portrait, where he is not in lady's society; apron apparently girt up, one basket of china on his right arm. In the other (T. Orde invt. et fecit 1768), the portraits are less flattering; the pair look older and out at elbows; each carries two baskets with fruit, but one of *Randall's* appears to hold old boots, gaiters, and lavender. He walks lame with a stick.

Mr Cooper (*Annals* IV. 417) records the death of 'the widow Hammond, aged 102,' at Spital House End, Dec. 19, 1785.

Before entering upon so important a subject as the dress of the last century, I will put before the reader a few notes relating in part to that matter in earlier generations. The two first are inventories of scholars' goods, one from either university in the 16th century.

'Decretum Saccarii de Bonis *Leonardi Metcalfe,* anno. 1541 (a scholar of St John's Coll. Camb., executed for the murder of a townsman, Will. Lamkyn):

	li.	*s.*	*d.*
' First, a great thinne Chest, with a hanging Locke and Key, at	o	1	8
Item, a long Gowne, with a Whood faced with Russels[1]	1	o	o
Item, a Jacket of tawny Chamblet, old	o	3	4
Item, an old Dublett of tawny Russels	o	1	2
Item, a Jacket of black Sage[2]	o	1	8
Item, a Doublet of Canvas	o	1	o
Item, a Pair of Hoose	o	1	8
Item, a Cloke	o	2	8
Item, a Sheet, old	o	o	8
Item, half an old Testure of darnix[3]	o	o	4

[1] '*Russel* a kind of satin.' Halliwell's *Dict. Archaic and Provincial.*

[2] qy. *Serge.* Possibly a misprint in *Dyer* for *Saye.*

[3] *Darnex.* A coarse sort of damask used for carpets, curtains, &c. originally manufactured at Tournay, called in Flemish *Dornick.* Spelt

	li.	*s.*	*d.*
Item, an old Hat	0	0	4
Item, a Chaire and a Meat Knyfe	0	0	5
Item, an old Lute	0	1	0
Item, a Callepine of the worst	0	1	8
Item, Vocabularius Juris et Gesta Romanorum . .	0	0	4
Item, Introductiones Fabri	0	0	3
Item, Horatius sine Commento	0	0	4
Item, Tartaretus super Summulas Petri Hispani . .	0	0	2
Item, The Shepheard's Kalender	0	0	2
Item, Moria Erasmi	0	0	6
Item, Compendium 4 Librorum Institutionum . .	0	0	3
Item, in the Bailiff's hand—A pair of Sheets . .	0	1	0
Item, a Coverlet	0	0	10
Item, a very old Blankett	0	0	2
Item, lent to the same Lamkyn	2	0	0
Summa . .	4	1	8

By me *John Edmondes,*
Vice-chan. of the University of Cambridge[1].'

' A trewe inventorye of all ye goods of Christopher Tilyard of ye vniversitie of Oxon. bachelor of arts, late deceased. [1598.]

	li.	*s.*	*d.*
'Imprimis Natalis comitis	0	2	6
Item, Tullis orations	0	2	6
Donet vpon ye Ethickes	0	0	10
Jules Apologie [Jewell]	0	0	10
Vallerius Maximus	0	0	8
Parkins vpon ye Lordes prayer [Perkins] . . .	0	0	8
Saunderson's lodgike [appeared in 1618!] . .	0	0	6
A testament in lattin	0	0	6
Tullie de oratore	0	0	4
Oved's metamorphoses	0	0	4
Osorius agaynst Haddon	0	0	6

darnep in Cunningham's *Revels Acc.* p. 215. It was composed of different kinds of material, sometimes of worsted, silk, wool, or thread. Perhaps *darnak* (a thick hedge-glove, *co.* Suffolk) is connected with this term. *Darnick*, linsey-wolsey, North. (Halliwell). ' *Dornex* inferior damask of Tournai.' Peacock's *Monuments of Superstition.*

[1] Dyer's *Privileges*, I. 109, 110.

	li.	s.	d.
Aristotle's Ethicks	o	o	10
2 Pallengenius	o	o	6
Aristotles's lodgicke	o	o	10
Cammerarious vpon tusculus qs'ti	o	o	8
An answer of ye bishop of Winchester	o	o	4
Silva sinonimorū	o	o	4
Apthonius and Clares gramer	o	o	6
Hiperius' phisickes and gouldin chayne . . .	o	o	8
Horrace uinutiosū epistols	o	o	6
Other ould bookes valued at	o	2	6
11 mappes and paper	o	1	8
5 singinge bookes	o	1	o
An ould cheste	o	1	4
2 dobletes 2 payre of hose & frise Jerkin . . .	o	10	o
An ould cloth gowne and a rugge gowne . . .	o	10	o
3 shirtes and a hatt	o	6	8
4 bandes	o	1	4
Showes and stockinges ould	o	2	6
A bachelor's hoode and cappe	o	5	o
In monye	vij	5	o
Somme .	xili.	2s.	4d[1].'

We may add to these, for the purpose of comparison, a few of the items from the college accounts of the earl of Essex when at Trin. coll. Cambridge, in 1577, given in Cooper's *Annals*, II. pp. 352—356.

'The parcells which my Lord of Essex bought at his entrance in his chamber at Cambridge.

'Inprimis, twenty yards of new greene brode sayes[2]. . lvjs.
Item, the frame of the South Window in the first Chamber vjs. 4d.
Item, for new glass in the same . . · . . . iiijs.
Item, for 40 foote of quarters[3] under the hangings . . ijs.
Item, payd to Mr Bird at my entrance for parcells which
    appear in his proper bill and acquittance . . xxjs.

[1] *A. Wood's Life*, Bliss, 64, *n.*
[2] '*Say.* A delicate serge or woollen cloth. "Saye clothe, *serge*," Palsgrave.' Halliwell.
[3] '*Quarters*, panels.' See Halliwell.

Item, two casements with hingells in the south window . ij*s.* vi*d.*
Item, new hangings in the study of painted cloth . xvj*s.* viij*d.*
Item, for paintinge both Chamber and study overhead . v*s.*
Item, shelves in the study . . . . . . xij*d.*
Item, a conveyance to the bedchamber out of the study . ij*s.* vj*d.*
Item, a place makinge for the trindle bed[1] to drawe through
   the waule . . . . xvj*s.*
Item, for bordinge a place for fewele and makinge a light
   into it . . . . vj*s.*
Item, a table in the study . . . . . . iij*s.* 4*d.*
Item, for the furniture in the litle study . . . . xviij*d.*
Item, little irons to hould open the casements with . viij*d.*
Item, my part of the dore betwixt Mr Forcett and me . iij*s.* vj*d.*
Item, a crest at the chimnay . . . . . 4*d.*
Item, for a footestoole at the window . . . . 4*d.*
Item, for two shelves mo in the frame of the study . xij*d.*
Item, a locke and three keys to the outward chamber dore iij*s.* 4*d.*
Item, a table in the bedchamber . . . . . ii*s.* vj*d.*

               Summa totalis,   7*li.* x*d.*'

His tutor sent besides, June 11, 1577, a list of farther necessaries without which 'he shall not onley be thrid bare but ragged.'

'Ther wants A faire gowne for my Lords holidaies, 2 Dublets. Three paire of Hose. Two paire of nether socks. A velvet Cap. A Hatte. A basen and Ewer. Potts or Goblets. Spones. Plats. A Salte. Candlestiks. Potts to be given to the Colledge. Hangings.'— As well as outfit for his servant 'Mungomery' of whom 'ther is consideration to be had...sith he is to be mayntayned as a gentleman and the place doth require the same.'

Among the earl's expenses from Midsummer 1577 are

'Item, for my lord v. pair of shoes, v*s.*
Item, for my Lord at the saltinge[2], according to the custome, vij*s.*
Item, for arrowes for my Lord, ij*s.* vi*d.*

  [1] Trindle-bed, or trundle-bed, the same as truckle-bed. See above, p. 89, and notes.
  [2] The *salting:* see above pp. 204—206. Cp. the old Eton custom of observing *Montem.* See notes.

Item, for iij. frames of wainscot for mapps for my Lord his use, iiij*s*. vj*d*.

Item, for rushes and dressinge of the chambers, iiij*s*.

Item, for horse-hire for those that attended on my Lord at severale tymes, xix*s*.·

Item, for my Lord his commens[1] for the quarter, liiij*s*.

Item, for his Lordship's cisinge[1], xxxv*s*.

Item, for his Lordship's breakefaste for the quarter xxiij*s*.

Item, for meate on fastinge nights and tymes extraordinarie, xxv*s*.

Item, for the Laundres for his Lordship's washinge, vj*s*. viij*d*.

Item, for my Lord to the chief reader[2], ij*s*.

Item, for Ramus' Logique, with a commentarie, xx*d*.

Item, for Ramus on Tullie's Orations, iiij*s*.

Item, for Sturmius De Elocutione, iiij*s*.

Item, for Questiones Besae theologicae, xx*d*.

Item, for Grimalius De optimo Senatore, ij*s*. iiij*d*.

Item, for Isocrates in Greeke, iiij*s*.

Item, for a standinge deske for my Lord his studie, vj*s*.

Item, for the barber for his Lordship's trimming, ij*s*.

Item, for a broad ridinge hatte, viij*s*.

Item, for Taffetta[3] and makinge of canions[4] for his Lordship's hose, vj*s*. viij*d*.

Item, for the carriadge of his Lordship's tronke with his apparell from London to Cambridge, ij*s*. iiij*d*.

Item, for ij dosen of trenchers, x*d*.

Item, for a board of wood and the cuttinge of the same, v*s*. x*d*.

Item, for a loade of coales, xviij*s*.

Item, for inke and quilles, vj*d*.'

The reverend Mackenzie E. C. Walcote, in his *William of Wykeham and his Colleges* (pp. 166—169), gives the accounts of a school-boy in the beginning of the seventeenth century.

[1] *Commons, Sizings:* see *Index.*

[2] *Chief reader*, the Praelector or Head Lecturer.

[3] '*Taffeta*, a sort of thin silk.' Halliwell.

[4] '*Canions*. Rolls at the bottom of the breeches just below the knee. They were sometimes indented like a screw; the common ones were called *straight canions*. See Planche, p. 266; Strutt II. 148; Webster III. 165; Middleton III. 573. "*Subligar*, a paire of breeches without *cannions*," Welde's *Janua Linguarum*, 1615.' Halliwell.

In 1342—3 'great complaint was made against the clergy and the students in the Universities, on account of their extravagance in dress, and the gay and unclerical appearance of their garments : disdaining the tonsure, the distinctive mark of their order, they wore their hair either hanging down on their shoulders in an effeminate manner, or curled and powdered : they had long beards, and their apparel more resembled that of soldiers than of priests ; they were attired in cloaks with furred edges, long hanging sleeves not covering their elbows, shoes chequered with red and green, and tippets of an unusual length ; their fingers were decorated with rings, and at their wrists they wore large and costly girdles, enamelled with figures and gilt : to these girdles hung knives and swords[1].' Archbishop Stratford and eleven of his suffragans decided to prohibit offenders from taking any ecclesiastical degree or honour till they should amend.

The following passage from the Elizabethan statutes of 1570 (*cap.* 46) relates to the non-academical dress of Cambridge students :

'We forbid also any scholar, of whatever condition he be, to wear a plumed cap (*galero utatur*), except he be unwell, either within any college or without it, on pain of incurring the same fine (6*s.* 8*d.*) as often as he shall herein have offended.

'We wish also that no one, dwelling in the University on pretence of study, shall presume to wear

---

[1] Cooper's *Annals*, I. 94, 95.

more than a yard and a half of cloth on the outside of his hose, or shall walk forth in reticulated, slashed, silk-sewn, in any way padded or stuffed hose, on pain of incurring a fine of 6s. 8d. as often as he shall have offended herein.

'We wish besides, that no one who is supported at the expence of any college, or who has been admitted to any ecclesiastical benefice, shall wear a *camisia*, a plaited ruff about his neck, or plaited ruffles at his wrists, on pain of incurring the fine aforesaid. It shall be allowable, nevertheless, to wear a moderate plaited ruff about the neck, provided no silk be interwoven therein : provided, nevertheless, that the above regulations about dress shall not bind in any way the sons of lords, or the heirs of knights.'

Mar. 25, 1571, it was decreed that no excuse of wearing hats should be allowed, either within the colleges, or abroad in the university, 'unless he that did wear any hatt within any college were non-commons ; and without the college within the university, did wear a kercher with his hatt; else to pay the mulct[1].' This was, I suppose, an interpretation of cap. 46 of the statutes of 1570:—*Prohibemus etiam, ne quis scholarium cuiuscunq. condicionis sit, galero utatur, aut in collegio aliquo, aut extra collegium, nisi aegrotauerit, sub eadem poena quotiens deliquerit.*

The following extract is from a MS. letter of the same date in the library of Corpus Christi C. C.

'As touching the statute of apparell, none in all the

---

[1] Dyer's *Privileges*, I. 306.

university do more offend against that statute than the two proctors who should give best ensample, and these other two regents, Nicolls and Browne, who doe not only go verye disorderlie in Cambridge, waring for the most part ther hatts and continually verye unsemly ruffles at their handes, and greate Galligaskens and Barreld hooese stuffed with horse Tayles, with skabilonians[1] and knitt netherstockes to fine for schollers: but also not disguysedlie theie goe abroade waringe such Apparell even at this time in London (although like hipocrites they come at this time outwardlie covered with the scholler's weed before your honours).'
Art. x. *exhibited against Mr* Beacon, Pureseye, Nicholls, Browne *and others.*

The 'disguised apparel' of Lakes, fellow of King's, who troubled provost Goad in 1577, has already been mentioned, p. 352. Dr Goad himself, when a fellow in 1566, had joined in an address[2] to certify that King's was free from the general quarrel *de re uestiaria.*

Nov. 5, 1585, Lord Burleigh, then chancellor of Cambridge, made orders for the apparel of Scholars.

They might walk in 'cloake and hatt to and fro the feildes.' Also 'within his colledge, hall, ostell or habitation' it was lawful for any student to wear a gowne or gaberdine[3] of playne Turkye fasshion with a round falling cap without garde, welte, lace, cutt, or silke, except one cutt in the sleeves thereof, to putt out his armes onelye: so that as well the saied gowne or gaberdyne, as also the lyning and facing be of sad

---

[1] '*Scavilones*, drawers; pantaloons, Strutt.' Halliwell.

[2] Strype's *Annals*, 483, 484.

[3] '*Gaberdine.* A coarse loose frock or mantle. "Mantyll a gaberdyne," Palsgrave. Still in use in Kent.' Halliwell. Cp. Shakespeare's *Tempest*, II. 2.

colour and playne stuffe, and such as is not prohibited to the wearer, by her majesties said proclamation and lawes.

'Also that everie graduate wearing the above gowne and gaberdyne within the Universitie or Towne, out of his chamber or lodging, doe weare withall in the day tyme a square cap and none other: no hatt to be worn, except for infirmities sake with a kerchiffe about his head, or in going to and fro the Feeldes, or in the streete or open ayre when it shall happen to rayne hayle or snowe; And then at all other tymes within the Universitie and without, the hatt which shal be worne to be blacke, and the band or lace of the hat to be of the same colour, playne and not excessive in bignes, without feather brooche or such like un-comelye for Studentes...And that as well the hatt as the band to be suche as the wearer may by law use and weare......Also that no Graduat remaining within any Colledge, Hall or Ostell, or clayming to enjoye the priviledg of a Scholler as aforesaid, doe weare within the Universitie nor without the same, if he have any living or sustentation of any Colledge or halle, any stuffe in upon or about his doublett, coates, Jerkyn, jackett, cassock or hose, of velvett or silke, or of any such stuffe as is forbidden by her majesties said proclamation and lawes. Nor any other stuffe not so forbidden that shal be embrodered, powdred[1], pynked[2], or welted, savinge at the handes, verge, showlder, or coller: or gathered, playted, garded, hacked, raced[3], laced or cutt, saving the cutt of the welt[4] and button holes, nor of any other redde, grene, and such other like colour. The offendour to be ordered, reformed and punished, from tyme to tyme, both for stuffe, fasshion and colour, by the Vicechauncelour, with such reasonable pecuniarie mulct as to hym shal be thought convenient......Finally, if hereafter any new forme of excesse in apparell, either other colour then blacke or such like sad colour, except that the doublett being close worne and not seene may be of other colour saving that it may be lawfull to Bachelers of law phisicke and musick, Masters of arts and other highe degree, to have two playne stitches or one small lace of silke of the colour of the garment about the edges thereof, and at the gorgett[5], and in the length of the doublett sleeves. Also having living or mayntenance of any colledge or Hall doe weare within the universitie or without, nor other graduate pensioner doe weare within the Universitie, in uppon or about his hose,

[1] *Powdered*, sprinkled (with fur, ermine, &c.).
[2] *Pinked*, ornamented with open work or eyelet-holes.
[3] *Raced*, pricked.
[4] *Welt*, a border, or hem.
[5] *Gorget*, the breast or neck piece.

any silke or other stuffe of like charge, saving onely stitching the clockes and setting on the upper stockes[1]. And that the upper stockes of the hose be of none other stuffe, but either of broad cloth, kersye, or mock-adowe[2] not above the measure of kersye. Nor to weare anye slop[3] but the playne small slop, such as is not to be lett downe beneathe the knee, not paned[4] and without gardes, cutt, pynke, welt, lace, stitche, or such like, and of none other colour but blacke, or of like sad colour, except Masters of Arts, Bachelers and Doctors of lawe, phisicke and musicke who may have in the length of their upper stockes or slop, two playne stitches or one small lace, so it be of like sad colour with the hose, and that the garters be of the colour of the hose, and playne without needlework, lace or twist: And that no deacon minister, graduate or not graduate, doe weare in his slop, stock or hose, any velvett, silke or tuft mockadowe, or other such like stuffe.

'Allso, that no Scholer or Student of what degree or calling soever he be, doe weare within the universitie or without anye shirt wrought with any kinde of sylke or other stuffe, in upon or about the same shirt, band or ruffe, but onelye a playne hemme of the small clothe, and one or two stitches at the most, and with white thred onelye, without cutt, purle, stringe, jagge, carving, lace, twiste, pynke, or any suche like[5], but playne as is aforesaid. The standing band of the shirt not to be

---

[1] '*Upper stocks*, Breeches.' Halliwell. As opposed to *nether socks* (or *nether-stocks*, K. Henry IV. Part I. Act II. Sc. 4), stockings.

[2] '*Mockado.* A kind of woollen stuff, made in imitation of velvet, and sometimes called mock-velvet. "My dream of being naked and my skyn all over-wrought with work like some kinde of tuft *mockado*, with crosses blew and red." Dr Dee's *Diary*, p. 6.' Halliwell.

[3] *Slop*, wide breeches: the word seems also to have been used for a smock frock or *robe de nuit*, and for a summer boot or buskin much worn in the 15th century.

[4] *Pane*, an ἐπίβλημα, *patch or stripe* of coloured cloth inserted in a garment of another hue. See Donne's *Poems*, p. 121, quoted by Halliwell s.v. *Pane* (2).

[5] *Petruchio.* Thy gown? why, ay.—Come, tailor, let us see't.
 O mercy, God! what masking stuff is here?
 What's this? a sleeve? 'tis like a demi-cannon:
 What! up and down, carved like an apple-tart?
 Here's snip and nip, and cut, and slish, and slash,
 Like to a censer in a barber's shop.'
        Taming of the Shrew, IV. 3.

above four ynches, and the ruffe in depth at the coller and handes not above one ynche and a quarter above the neckband or wrestband, and in thicknes or length not above four yardes at the coller, nor above two yardes at either hand. The falling band of the shirt not to be turned downe on the outsyde in any parte of it, above two ynches and a halfe, except the corners, which may have one ynche more. And this band to be without tassells, lace, stringe, twist, button, knott, or such like.

' Also that no graduate having living or stipend of any Colledge or Hall, doe weare any stuffe for the outside of his cloake, but woolen clothe, of blacke or the like sad colour, to be made with a standing coller of truncke fashion[1], or a round standing coller, or a round falling cap with sleeves, or a playne round casting cloke over the same without sleeves not lower than the midcalfe of the legge: and not to be faced with any silke but onelye in the coller: (all Provostes and Masters of Colledges and Halls and Principales of Ostells, the Oratours and Proctours of the Universitie in this poynt only excepted, for the lyninge of their cloakes onelye), and not to be gathered, paned, garded, or welted, saving with a small welt at the shoulders, coller and handes, not embrodered or layd with lace, nor wrought with silke, saving the button holes, and one or two single stitches, or one small lace about the verge, coller and sleeve bandes thereof, nor cutt but at the welt of the shoulder, coller, handes, and button holes, and in the sleeves to putt out the armes. And that no such graduate doe weare abroade without the Universitie, for his upper apparrell, any other garment then one of the saied fashioned cloakes, or one of the above named fasshioned gownes or gabberdynes.

' Also, that no Scholler doe wear out of his chamber and studdye, any pantaples[2] or pynsons[3], but in the tyme of his sicknes. And further it is ordered that everie Scholler being no graduate, doe not only re-

[1] ' *Tai.* "With a trunk sleeve."
   Gru. I confess two sleeves.
   Tai. "The sleeves curiously cut."
   Pet. Ay, there's the villany.' 	*Ibid.*
[2] ' *Pantables,* slippers. "To stand upon one's *pantables,*" to stand upon one's honour. Baret, 1580, spells it *pantapple.*
      Is now, forsooth, so proud, what else !
      And stands so on her *pantables.*
Cotton's *Works,* 1734, p. 85, &c.' Halliwell. Pantoffel (*German*).
[3] ' *Pinsons.* (1) A pair of pincers...(2) Thin-soled shoes. "*Calceolus,* pinsone," *Nominale* MS. Compare MS. Arundel 249, f. 88. "Pynson sho, *caffignon,*" Palsgrave. The copy of Palsgrave belonging to

frayne to weare such apparrell as is before in these orders forbidden hym to wear under the paynes hereafter following and sett downe, but also every such Scholler who hath living and stipend of any Colledge or Hall, doe also absteyne to weare in his apparrell, anye stuffe, colour or fasshion, that shall not be playne and schollerlike, and which shall be disallowed by the Provost or Master, or in his absence by hym that shall supplye his place, by the substraction of the weekelye commons and allowance of the offendours to the use of the Colledge, untill the fault be amended. And that none other such scholler being pensioner, doe weare abroade either in any Colledge, Hall or Ostell, or without, any apparell but comelye and agreeing to his calling and degree, not offending her said Majesties proclamacion, laws, injunctions and advertisements, especiallie in the upper apparrell, avoyding as much as may be the diversitie of fasshion and coloure : namelye, not to weare skarlett colour, crymsyne, yellowe or such like light colour, in stuffe, fasshion, or otherwise, as shal be devised and used, other then is here above appoynted, comelye for everye degree.......all Masters of Colledges and all Doctors of Divinity in the said Universitie, shall when they either ride or goe out of the Universitie, weare a blacke cloake with sleeves: nevertheles it shal be lawfull in theire jorney, to weare over the same a castinge cloake without sleeves[1].'

·In 1587, complaints were made by parents to the Vice-chancellor of Cambridge through Lord Burleigh, concerning the idleness, avarice and luxury of tutors and fellows: also their sons' tailor's bills. Fellows 'wearinge of Sattin Dublettes, silke and velvett overstocks and facynge of gownes with velvett and sattin to the grounde ; and in great fine ruffes, contrarye to lawe and order.[2]'

Two years later, archbishop Whitgift found fault with *Oxford* on the same score ; and especially with

the Cambridge public library has "or socke" written by a contemporary hand. "*Soccatus*, that weareth stertups or pinsons," Elyot, ed. 1559. See *Ord. and Reg.* p. 124.' Halliwell.

[1] Cooper's *Annals*, II. 411—414.

[2] *Ibid.* 448.

'Scholars and Graduates neglecting to use their habits according to their degrees, and attiring themselves like courtiers in silks contrary to their statutes and all good order.[1]'

In 1602, a detailed statement was sent to Dr Whitgift, archbishop of Canterbury, of *Disorders tending to the decaye of learning and other dissolute behaviour*: among other things, it was complained that the academical habit was disused, and the 'Scholars now goe in their Silkes and Velvets, liken to Courtiers then Schollers.[2]'

The *Seventy-fourth* of the *Constitutions and Canons Ecclesiastical*, 1603, Of *Decency in Apparel enjoined to Ministers*, after censuring the 'newfangleness of apparel in some factious persons,' proceeds to constitute and appoint as follows:

'That the Archbishops and Bishops shall not intermit to use the accustomed apparel of their degrees. Likewise all Deans, Masters of Colleges, Archdeacons, and Prebendaries in Cathedral and Collegiate Churches (being Priests or Deacons), Doctors in Divinity, Law, and Physic, Bachelors in Divinity, Masters of Arts, and Bachelors of Law, having any Ecclesiastical Living, shall usually wear Gowns with standing Collars, and sleeves strait at the hands, or wide Sleeves, as is used in the Universities, with Hoods or Tippets of silk or sarcenet, and square Caps. And that all other Ministers admitted or to be admitted into that function shall also usually wear the like apparel as is aforesaid, except Tippets only. We do further in like manner ordain, That all the said Ecclesiastical Persons above mentioned shall usually wear in their journeys Cloaks with Sleeves, commonly called Priest's Cloaks, without guards, welts, long buttons, or cuts. And no Ecclesiastical Persons shall wear any Coif or wrought Night-cap, but only plain Night-caps of black silk, satin, or velvet. In all which particulars con-

[1] Strype's *Whitgift*, 319.
[2] Peacock *On the Statutes*, p. 61, n. Cooper's *Annals*, II. 616.

cerning the apparel here prescribed, our meaning is not to attribute any holiness or special worthiness to the said garments, but for decency, gravity, and order, as is before specified. In private houses, and in their studies, the said Persons Ecclesiastical may use any comely and scholar-like apparel, provided that it be not cut or pinkt; and that in public they go not in their Doublet and Hose, without Coats or Cassocks; and that they wear not any light-coloured stockings. Likewise poor beneficed Men and Curates (not being able to provide themselves long Gowns) may go in short gowns of the fashion aforesaid.'

Sir Hugh Evans, in the *Merry Wives of Windsor*, III. 1, when waiting for the duel near Frogmore, as soon as master Shallow and Page come in sight, says to Simple, 'Pray you give me my gown; or else keep it in your arms.' Page, just afterwards, thus flouts him; 'And youthful still, in your doublet and hose, this raw rheumatic day?' The editions of 1602 and 1619 have not this gibe of master George Page; and in the former case they read, 'Then it is verie necessary *I* put vp my sword; pray give me my cowne too, marke you.'

There is a paper, endorsed by archbishop Laud, *Certain Disorders in* Cambridge *to be considered of in my visitation*, sent to him in 1636, probably by Dr Cosin, master of Peterhouse, or by his chaplain, Dr Sterne, master of Jesus college. 'Their other garments are light and gay, Some with bootes and Spurs, others with Stockings of diverse Colours reversed one upon another, and round rusti Caps theye weare (If they weare any at all) that they may be the sooner despised, though the fashion here of old time was altogether *Pileus quadratus*, as appears by reteining that custome and order still in King's Colledge, in

Trin. and at Caius whose Governours heretofore were more observant of old Orders than it seems others were. But in all places among Graduates, and Priests also, as well as the younger Students, we have fair Roses upon the Shoe, long frizled haire upon yᵉ head, broad spred Bands upon the Shoulders, and long large Merchants Ruffs about yᵉ neck, with fayre feminine Cuffs at yᵉ wrist. Nay, and although *Camisiae circa collum rugatae* be expressly forbidden by yᵉ statutes of the University, yet we use them without controule, Some of our Dʳˢ heads and all to the laudable example of others[1].'

In 1674 the D. of Monmouth, chancellor of the university, wrote from Newmarket, at the command of king Charles II., to reprehend the growing practice of *reading* sermons; and of the clergy wearing 'their hair and perukes of an unusual and unbecoming length.' Nine months later the heads sent satisfactory answers to the Quaeres received by them on that occasion[2].

At Oxford in 1694 'Dr Aldrich retook his place of vice-chancellor, which is the 3ᵈ year: in his speech he spoke against hatts turned up on one side, and after the speech, he dissolved the convocation; but Dr Jane went to him, and put him in mind of nominating the vice-chancellors ['Quaere if not *Pro Vice-Chancellors.* Sed sic MS.' *Warton* and *Hearne*], and swearing them, which was done. *O mirum*[3]!'

---

[1] MS. *Baker*, VI. 152, *ap.* Cooper's *Annals*, III. 280. Peacock *On the Statutes*, pp. 62, 63, n.

[2] Dyer's *Privileges*, I. 364, 367.

[3] *Life of A. Wood*, Bliss, p. 307.

In the reign of queen Anne, says Hone[1], 'French fashions were imported much to the satisfaction of the youthful and gay, though they were greatly disapproved by the aged and sedate.

'Gentlemen contracted the size of their wigs, and for undress tied up some of the most flowing of their curls. In this state they were called Ramillie wigs, and afterwards tie-wigs; but were never worn in full dress. The cravat had long ends, which fell on the breast; it was generally of point lace; but sometimes only bordered or fringed. The coat had no collar, was long, open at the bottom of the sleeves, and without cuffs, and edged with gold or silver from the top to the bottom, with clasps and buttons the whole length, and at the opening of the sleeve. Young gentlemen often had the sleeves only half way down the arm, and the short sleeve very full and deeply ruffled. An ornamented belt kept the coat tight at the bottom of the waist. The vest and lower part of the dress had little clasps, and was seldom seen. The roll-up stocking came into vogue at this period, and the sandal was much used by the young men; these were finely wrought. Elderly gentlemen had the shoe fastened with small buckles upon the instep; and raised, but not high, heels. Ladies and gentlemen had their gloves richly embroidered. Queen Anne would often notice the dress of the domestics of either sex.'

'There was not much variation in dress in the reign of George I., who was advanced in years, and did not

---

[1] *Table Book*, columns 475, 476.

see much of either his subjects or foreigners. There
was no Queen in England, and the ladies who accompanied his majesty were not of the character to set
modes[1].'

Compare Hogarth's picture of a fop in the french
mode, with his huge muff (*Taste in High Life*, 1742)
and wide skirts.

The 10th number of the *Guardian* contains a letter
dated *Oxford*, March 18, 1712—13, and signed *Simon
Sleek*, which mentions 'the sleeves turned up with
Green Velvet, which now flourish throughout the University.' The writer hints also that there was room
'to introduce several pretty Oddnesses in the taking
and tucking up of Gowns, to regulate the Dimensions
of Wigs, to vary the Tufts upon Caps, and to enlarge
or narrow the Hems of Bands.' He professes to have
'prepared a Treatise against the Cravat and Bardash.'
The editor introduces the letter by observing:—'As
to the men, I am very glad to hear, being myself a
Fellow of *Lincoln College*, that there is at last in one
of our Universities risen a happy Genius for little
things. It is extremely to be lamented, that hitherto
we come from the College as unable to put on our
own Clothes as we do from Nurse.'

Amherst, in the 33rd No. of his *Terrae Filius* (May
8, 1721), says that 'Raw, unthinking young men,
having been kept short of money at school, care not
how extravagant they are, whilst they can support
their extravagance upon trust [that foolish practice,

---

[1] *Table Book*, column 710.

so common at this time in the university, of *running upon tick*, as it is called], especially when they have numberless examples before their eyes, of Persons in as mean circumstances as themselves, who *cut a taring figure in silk-gowns*, and *bosh it about town in lace ruffles, and flaxen tye-wigs.'*

It is said of Dr Will. Richardson, master of Emmanuel, 1736—1775, a good-humoured tory, that he was so strict a disciplinarian 'as to punish the wearing of a neckcloth (which at that time was deemed unacademical) instead of a stock, with the same strictness as a deviation from moral rectitude[1].'

The 1st of the Orders and Regulations of 1750 (which have been mentioned, pp. 65, 68), provide that 'Every person in *statu pupillari* shall wear clothes of a grave colour in the judgment of the officers of the university, without lace fringe or embroidery; without capes or cuffs of a different colour from their coats.'

In 1751 a sizar is described[2] as wearing 'his own lank greasy hair:' and at the same period the university *Sloven* (the counterpart to the *Smart*) is thus sketched[3]. 'He never wore garters, greas'd his cloaths on purpose, tore his gown to make it ragged, broke the board of his cap, and very often had but one lappet to his band. He seldom allow'd his hair to be comb'd, or his shoes to be japann'd. He would put his shirt on at bed time, because he was asham'd to be caught in a clean one; and on Sundays he was

---

[1] Nichols, *Lit. Anecd.* II. 619. *n.*
[2] The *Student*, II. 189.
[3] *Ibid.* II. 106.

sure to be in a dishabille, because every body else was drest. Tho' it was not then the fashion (as it is now) to be blind, TOM constantly wore spectacles, star'd at every girl he met, and did a thousand strange things to appear particular; in all which he was protected by his *very singular modesty*, or (in other words) his invincible front of ever-durable brass. He was hail fellow well met with all the townsmen in general, would swig ale in a penny-pot-house with the lowest of the mob, and commit the most extravagant actions under the notion of humour. If he got drunk, broke windows, laugh'd at the mayor, ridicul'd the aldermen, humbug'd the proctors, 'twould be often pass'd over; 'twas his humour, and TOM was a well meaning, good natur'd fellow.' This is almost like a picture of Edmund Neale (Mun Smith), the *Handsome Sloven* of Ch. Ch., who was called also *Captain Rag*, and died in 1710. (See Johnson's *Lives of the Poets*.)

Three pages later we have a touch which may be compared with p. 134,—'his light frock and short bob were exchang'd for a grey coat and grizzle; the polite count was sunk in the grave divine.' See, on the othe hand, T. Warton's *Ode to a Grizzle Wig, by a Gentleman who had just left off his Bob.*

> 'Can thus *large wigs* our Reverence engage?
> Have *Barbers* thus the Pow'r to blind our Eyes?
> Is Science thus conferr'd on every Sage,
> By *Bayliss, Blenkinsop,* and lofty *Wise*[1]?
> But thou farewell, my *Bob!*...
> Safe in thy *Privilege*, near *Isis'* Brook,
> Whole Afternoons at *Wolvercote* I quaff't;

[1] Eminent Peruke-Makers in Oxford.

> At Eve my careless Round in *High-street* took,
> And call'd at *Jolly's* for the *casual* Draught.
>
> No more the *Wherry* feels my stroke so true;
> At *Skittles*, in a *Grizzle*, can I play?
> *Woodstock*, farewell! and *Wallingford*, adieu!
> Where many a *Scheme* reliev'd the lingering Day.' &c[1].

Sir John Trotley, an old-fashioned country gentle-man in Garrick's *Bon Ton*, 1775, complains of the abandoning the long cravats with ends twisted through the button-hole, while all grades of society tied up their own hair, instead of wearing bobs or tye-wigs.

It was about that period that *Porson* satirised his schoolfellow, *Charles Simeon*, at Eton, as a coxcomb in dress; as he afterwards called him 'a coxcomb in religion.'

Gradus, the awkward Brasenose scholar in Mrs Cowley's *Who's the Dupe* (1779), act i. sc. 3, when he first comes from Oxford, wears 'a grizzle wig curled as stiffly as Sir *Cloudesley Shovel's* in the Abbey—a dingy brown coat with vellum button-holes—and cambric enough in his ruffles to make his [grandson's] shirt.'

The following extracts are from the private accounts (1768—1775) of Francis Dawes, bursar of Peterhouse, and esquire bedell. (See Gunning's *Reminiscences*, ch. V.)

To altering the sleeves of yr Coat . .	0	1	0
To letting your Weastcoat out at the sides .	0	1	0
To putting a new holland body lining in Ditto	0	3	0
	£0	5	0

[1] *Oxford Sausage,* 1764.

The 5th, of Novr. 1774, Recvd. of Mrs Bosworth for Mr Dawes the full contents of this Bill. By me Thos. Hayes Thompson, for the use of my Father Thos. Thomson.

		£	s	d
1 End Superfine ¼ Ell Newfashd. Corderoy 15 yds. 3s. 6d.		£2	12	6
(Worrall and Key, Manchester.)				

		£	s	d
Making a pair of fusting Breeches		0	3	6
pockitts linings Buttons and trimings		0	6	0
2 yds. ¼ of Superfine (?) nunham Gray cloth		2	5	1
4 yds. of Superfine Shalloon		0	8	8
Buttons trimings and making a Mourning Coat		0	13	6
Seating a pair of Black Breeches		0	1	0
(Jno. Duckett.)				

		£	s	d
To altering the Cape of yr. Surtout Coat and furnishing a broad scarlet Velvet Coller		0	6	6
To letting oute at the Sides yr. Rateen weastcoat		0	0	6
(Thos. Thompson.)				

		£	s	d
4¼ yds. Barragon Jean		1	0	3
5 yds. Rattinet 2s. 8d.		0	13	4
2¼ yds. Corded Velverett		0	15	9
Captn. Stevenson { 3¾ yds. Superfine Scarlet Cloth		3	14	3
5 yds. Rattinet 3s. 8d.		0	18	4
2 dozn. Scarlet Dth hd. Ct. Buttons		0	3	0
2 doz. Breast do.		0	1	6

(Another bill from the same haberdasher Jas. Hatsell contains several items for 'Your Friend,' among them 1½ doz. death head Coat Buttons, 1s. 6d. The back of one of these bills is elaborately decorated with three Personages answering to the description of the six as described in the long stage-direction to Q. Katherine's dream: below the Public is advertised that '*James Hatsell* Mans Mercer and Draper, *At the Three Angels*, opposite the New Church, *Strand* Sells Superfine Cloths, Dutch Ratteens, Duffles, Frizes, Beaver Coatings, Kerseymeres, Forrest Cloths, German Serges, Wilton Stuffs, Sagathies, Nanquins, Silasia and Brown Cambricks—*Manchester Velvets*—Silk Grongrams, Double Allapeens, Silk and Hair Camblets, Barragons, Brussells, Camblets, Princes Stuffs, Worsted Damasks, *Worsted and Silk Knit Pieces*; Velvets, Corded Silks, Sattins, Shagg Velvets, Sergedesoys,

Shalloons, Allapeens, and all Sorts of new Fashionable Goods, made for Gentlemens Wear. *Livery Cloths, Thicksets, Plain Fustians, Flannels, Cloth, Serges, Hair Shaggs, Dimity, Everlastings, &c.*')

1772. Jany. 2d. To a pair of white Gloves for Sr. Jno.

Cotton's Ball	o	1	6
19. To Snuff	o	o	4
Augst. 2d. To Honey Water	o	1	o

(Eliza Elbonn.)

Mr Dawes Bill for washing.

from Midsummer to Mickilmus one Quarter	1	1	o
mending of Stockings . .	o	2	6

Rec^d. ye Contents in full of all Demarnds by me James Elbonn.

1 pr. of worsted gloves	o	1	4

12 yd. Vere poplin 1s. ½	o	12	6

1 pr. Coloured silk [stockings]	o	14	o

(Messrs. English, at their Nottingham Warehouse, the corner of Catherine Street, Strand.)

1771.

1 Fine Hatt	1	1	o
Girdle & Buckle	o	1	o

(Rich^d. Cordeux, No. 189 near Chancery Lane, Fleet Street.)

1768.

2 Pr. Brown Thr^d. Hose at 4s. 9d. 1 Pr. D°. w^t. at 5s. & a pr. Do. 4s.	o	18	6
Marking	o	o	3
a Hat clean'd, Silk Lining and Hooks and Eyes .	o	2	6
a Hat clean'd & Loop'd & Silk binding . .	o	2	o

1769.

a Gold Cord Band wth Gold Fringe Tassels . .	o	5	o

1770.

a Bever Hat & Girdle Band	3	15	3
a Hat clean'd & a wire	o	1	o

1771.

a Hunting hat	o	10	6
a hat clean'd & gimp Loope	o	1	o

(Geo. Brooks.)

A Boot toed	o	o	4
A pare of Shoes soled and heelpecd . . .	o	2	6

(Ed. Wilson.)

1774.	a pr. Boots	1	2	0
	2 pr. shoes	0	13	0
	a pr. shoes mend	0	2	0
	a pr. splaterdashes men'd	0	1	0
	(Ri. Fisher.)			
1775.	To pr. Call°. Pumps french heeles	0	5	0
	(for a pupil who was *rusticated*, to Sam. Saul.)			

A Plain and Friendly Address to the Undergraduates of the Univ. of *Camb.* in 1786, complains (p. 15) of the waste of money on fashionable buckles, coats, or waistcoats, through the 'artful civility of the accommodating shopkeeper.' .

The *Remarks on the Enormous Expence in the Education of Young men* in the Univ. of *Camb.* in 1788, proposes (p. 29) 'That the Dress of the Undergraduates be taken into most serious Consideration: Being in its present State, Indecent, Expensive, and Effeminate.' · · · ·

In 1799 'the Vice-Chancellor, Mansel, in his inaugural speech in the Senate-House, inveighed against the *togatum ocreatumque genus;* the dress of the time was so different from that of the present day. Shorts of any colour, and white stockings, were the only regular academical dress, gaiters were forbidden. It was usual for the undergraduates, or at least the more particular ones, to dress daily for the dinner in hall in white waistcoats and white silk stockings, and there were persons who washed them for us, as things too special for a common laundress. There were two or three undergraduates who wore powder. My namesake, Richard Prime of Trinity [afterwards M.P. for

West Sussex], was one of them. The rest of us wore our hair curled. It was thought very rustic and unfashionable not to have it so. Wigs were still worn by the Dons and Heads, with two or three exceptions. Cory, the master of Emmanuel, was, I have heard, the first to leave his off, complaining of headache. Dr Barnes of Peterhouse preserved his to the last.'

Prof. Geo. Pryme then proceeds to relate the anecdote of a practical joke played by Dan Sykes and others on the seniors of Trinity (see above, pp. 132, 133). He then continues; 'I have heard my uncle say that as a boy he wore a wig, and that it was common for boys to do so. [As it was also in the time of his great-great-uncle, Abraham de la Pryme, the antiquary, in 1692; *Surtees Soc.* 54, p. 25]. Footmen wore their hair tied up behind in a thick loop called *a club*. Gentlemen had theirs in a thin one, and it was named a pigtail. Dr Hubbersty, of Queens' College [B.A. 1781; M.D. 1796], was the last person I saw in one. In every well-ordered house there was a powdering room. Pitt's tax sent powder out of fashion. People paid it for a year or two, and then gave up wearing it. Pitt is not so much to be blamed for imposing this tax, for he was at his wits' end to supply means for the French war. Every common soldier was obliged to wear it, and, I believe, one cause of its disuse was the scarcity of '96 or '99, when the government forbad it, as flour was greatly employed for that purpose, and was then too dear to be wasted[1].'

[1] Pryme's *Autobiog. Recollections*, pp. 43—45.

'With regard to dress, I remember shortly after my going to reside in London [1804] the introduction of tight pantaloons, over which were worn a pair of black boots called Hessians. They came up in a point to within a few inches of the knee, and from this depended a tassel. But the most fashionable morning dress was pale-yellow leather breeches with top-boots, in which the men of distinction promenaded in Bond Street [see *Dighton's* caricatures of this date] from two till four o'clock. It was to be supposed that they had been riding, or were going to ride. [March 18, 1796. "No business in the House of Commons; but Popham, an old M.P., represented to me that I was disorderly in wearing my spurs in the House, as none but County Members were entitled to that privilege." *Lord Colchester's Diary*, L. 45.] Charles James Fox was frequently there, but dressed in the old-fashioned costume which we see in his portraits. His waistcoat had immense pockets with a flap over them. I saw him at an election in Covent Garden, when one of the crowd called out, "Holloa! you with the salt-box pockets," in allusion to Fox's large waistcoat. Such pockets and flaps were called by this name. Coltman, who stood next me, and I, thought it a clever hit.

'Beau Brummell was pointed out to me. He was then the reigning dandy. I remember my tailor saying, "Mr Brummell wears it so'." See Hone's *Table Book*, I. 666.

---

1 Pryme's *Autobiog. Recollections*, pp. 74, 75.

John Hookham Frere writes to his brother Bartle, July 11, 1802. 'Ted's intended spouse is Miss Green —we are all very well satisfied with what we hear of her—he has been in town too, and for some time wore his pantaloons over his half boots [a whig innovation] in spite of remonstrance and example[1].'

The gentlemen in Mr Gliddon's Cigar Divan, King Street, Covent Garden [Hone's *Table Book,* *col.* 673], in 1826, wear full trowsers reaching to the heel.

Wretch Wright, in *Alma Mater,* I. 9, 10, says that in 1815 he was sent for by Dr Mansel and threatened with being put out of sizings and commons, for appearing at hall time in trowsers instead of breeches and gaiters.

When Dr Goslin, of Gonville and Caius, was Vice-Chancellor in 1619, 'he made it a heavy fine for any under-graduate to appear in *boots.* A student undertook for a small bet to visit him in the prohibited articles, and actually did so, entreating the Vice-Chancellor's advice for a *numbness* in his legs, which he pleaded was hereditary; the Vice-Chancellor dismissed him, lamenting he could not do him any service; and the under-graduate won his wager[2].'

A passage has been quoted from *Ayliffe* on p. 301 of this compilation, whence we learn that the Doctors and Masters of the Act were obliged to wear '*Boots* and *Slop Shoes*' during the Comitia. It was necessary

---

[1] *The Works of* J. H. Frere, ed. 1. 1872. I. 48.
[2] *Facetiæ Cantabrigienses,* 1836, ed. 3. p. 133.

to pass a grace every year to allow them to leave them off at the close of the Act[1].

Mr G. V. Cox[2] records that when he was first in office as esquire bedel 'there was a dispensation annually passed after the Act Tuesday, for any farther use of the *ocreae* and other paraphernalia. *Supplicatio de ocreis et crepidis et soccatis exuendis.*

On the other hand, in 1633, it was 'ordered "that no person that wears a gown wear boots; if a graduate, he was to forfeit 2s. 6d. for the first offence,"' &c, for the custom of wearing boots and spurs had come up, and Masters of Arts preposterously assumed 'the part of the Doctor's formalities, which adviseth them to ryde *ad praedicandum Evangelium*, but in these days imply nothing else but *animum deserendi studium*[3].'

In a sketch[4] in the *Laughing Philosopher* (1825), p. 273, the Cambridge *varmint* ('fast') man is described as to be seen by day 'in a *jarvey* tile[5], or a low-crowned-broad-brim, a pair of white swell tops, *varmint* inexpressibles, a regular flash waistcoat, and his coat of a nameless cut; his "*cloth*" of the most

---

[1] Ayliffe's *Antient and Present State of the University of Oxford*, II. pp. 133, 146. *Stat. Acad. Oxon.* VII. II. 4.

[2] *Collections and Recollections*, p. 414.

[3] *Oxford and Cambridge Nuts to Crack*, p. 199. (1834.)

[4] (Reprinted from an appendix to ed. 2 of *Gradus ad Cantabrigiam*, 1824.)

[5] A roof or hat such as was fashionable with *Jarvies* or coachmen. There was a favourite song beginning—

'Ben was a hackney-coach-man rare
(Jarvey, jarvey! "Here I am your Honour"),' &c.

uncommon pattern, tied after his own way, and a short crookt-stick or bit o' plant in his hand; and thus he goes out riding.'

According to the Oxford Statutes (collected in 1633), xiv. § 1, all heads of colleges, fellows, scholars, and persons in holy orders, are to wear the clerical canonical dress; all others (excepting sons of Barons in the House of Lords, or with Scotch or Irish titles) are to wear black or at least dark clothes (*coloris nigri aut subfusci*) without pride or extravagance. *Insuper ab absurdo illo et fastuoso publice in ocreis ambulandi more abstinere compellantur. Etiam in capillitio modus esto; nec cincinnos, aut comam nimis promissam alant:* on pain, if graduates, of a fine; if undergraduates and not too old, of corporal punishment.

xiv. § 2, prohibits the making or buying of novel and strange-fashioned dresses.

In the section of the Oxford Statutes IX. iv. § 2. *De Materia Dispensabili, in qua Congregationi dispensare permissum est*, the 17th subsection stands as follows: *Ut Doctores Ocreas, et Magistri Crepidas et Socculos, quibus ex antiquo ritu uti tenentur, exuant.*

This afterwards became subsection 14, but it was not altered when the section was revised in 1801 and 1808.

The following is the section of the old Oxford Statute (Laudian Pandect 1633), Titulus xiv. *De Vestitu et Habitu Scholastico.*

§ 3. *Habitus Academici, singulis Gradibus et Facultatibus competentes.*

Statutum est, quod non Graduati, quotquot alicujus Collegii Socii,

Probationarii, Scholares, Capellani, Clerici, Choristae, denique quotquot de Fundatione Collegii cujusvis fuerint, Studentes insuper Aedis Christi, quoties in publicum in Universitate prodeunt, Togis laxe manicatis et Pileis quadratis induti incedent.

Quotquot vero Commensales, Communarii, Batellarii, Servientes; quotquot denique de Fundatione Collegii alicujus haud fuerint: quoties in publicum in Universitate prodeunt, Togis talaribus et Pileis rotundis induti incedent.

Graduati omnes, Togas Gradui et Facultati competentes, etiam Epomidas, et Pileos quadratos, aut rotundos (Juristae scilicet et Medici) gestabunt; praecipue in Contionibus Ordinariis, Praelectionibus, et Disputationibus publicis.

In Contionibus vero solennibus, et singulis diebus Dominicis intra Terminum ante meridiem in Templo B. V. Mariae; etiam in Aede Christi; et in XL^ma, et in Dominica Paschatis post meridiem, ad S. Petri in Oriente; Capis et Caputiis, sive e Serico sive e Minuto Vario, obversis, Contionibus intersint.

Contionatores itidem Habitu Gradui suo competente induti (pro ratione temporis, prout ceciderit intra vel extra Terminum) ad Ecclesiam accedant, et eodem induti Contiones suas habeant, sub poena 6s. 8d.

Lectores etiam et Professores publici, in Lectionibus suis ordinariis, Togis Gradui vel Facultati suae competentibus, Epomide et Pileo induti, ad Scholas accedant, et eodem Habitu induti legant, ac iterum a Scholis recedant. In solennibus autem Lectionibus in Vesperiis, Pileis, Capis et Caputiis, Gradui et Facultati suae competentibus, induti ad Scholas accedant, legant, ac iterum recedant.

Quoties vero ad Congregationes, Convocationes, Preces publicas, et Contiones ad Clerum, accedant, omnes, praeter Togas, etiam Capas, vel clausas vel apertas, et Caputia Gradui congrua adhibeant.

Doctores singulis Diebus Dominicis intra Terminum, ante meridiem, in Ecclesia B. Virginis Mariae; et in Quadragesima, et in Dominica Paschatis post meridiem, in Ecclesia S. Petri in Oriente, Capa et Caputio coccineo induti Contionibus intersint.

Si quis vero in praemissis delinquere deprehensus fuerit, si non Graduatus fuerit, pro arbitrio Vice-Cancellarii castigetur (corporaliter, si per aetatem congruat;) si Graduatus, Pro prima vice qua deliquerit, 20d. Pro secunda 3s. 4d. Pro tertia 5s. Pro quarta 6s. 8d. et sic toties quoties. Si quis vero ad Congregationem vel Convocationem accesserit, Habitu competente destitutus, praeter mulctam praedictam nullam omnino suffragandi potestatem habeat. Quas mulctas ad usum Universitatis exigendi non solum Vice-Cancellarius, sed et Procuratores potestatem habeant. Procuratores etiam ad poenas consimiles, si in exigendo negligentes fuerint, teneantur.

Ne vero, propter diu intermissum Habitus Gradui competentis usum, ignorantiam causari possit quis; aut, prae novandi libidine, ab antiquis Schematis desciscere, novosque Habitus introducere moliatur; Statutum est, quod Praefecti Collegiorum et Aularum in conventu suo hebdomadali, diligenti inquisitione habita de Toga, Capa (seu clausa, seu aperta) Caputio, Epomide, Pileo, cuique Gradui et Facultati (praesertim Medicis et Juristis) competentibus determinabunt. Ac, prout inter ipsos convenerit, singulorum instar aliquod (e vili quacunque materia) concinnandum, et, titulo affixo, in Praelum sive Abacum huic usui destinatum reponendum, curabunt; inde exemplar uniuscunque Habitus petere ut liceat, siquando circa haec controversia oriatur.

Si quis autem in forma Habitus praestituti aliquid novare conetur, puniatur pro arbitrio Vice-Cancellarii, ac insuper Sartoribus vestiariis interdicatur, ne a forma seu Schemate recepto Habitus, cuivis Gradui competentis, vel latum unguem recedant, sub poena pro arbitrio Vice-Cancellarii infligenda.

For this section the following was substituted by a decree of July 13, 1770.

§ 3. *De habitu Academico singulis Gradibus et Facultatibus competente.*

Statutum est, quod omnes Doctores cujuscunque Facultatis, Baccalaurei etiam in Sacra Theologia, Medicina, et Jure Civili, Magistri et Baccalaurei in Artibus, Baccalaurei itidem in Musica, togas Gradui et Facultati competentes, hodie usitatas, juxta exemplar in aere incidendum, et in abaco Domus Convocationis reponendum, gerant.

Ambo Procuratores, eorumque Deputati, et Collectores Quadragesimales, habitu hodie usitato, juxta exemplar, induti incedant.

Baronum filii in superiore Parliamenti Domo suffragii jus habentium necnon Baronum ex gente Scotica et Hibernica, toga talari deaurata, sive toga nigra laxe manicata serica cum epomide, et pileo quadrato cum apice deaurato, induti incedant. Baronetti autem toga talari nigra, deaurata, sive toga laxe manicata serica cum epomide, et pileo quadrato cum apice deaurato.

Superioris ordinis Commensales togam talarem sericam, sive ex quovis panno nigro confectam, cum ornamentis secundum exemplar, et pileum quadratum holosericum, Anglice *velvet*, cum apice ; Commensales vero sive Communarii togam talarem, ex quovis panno nigro, non serico, confectam, cum ornamentis secundum exemplar, et pileum quadratum panno obductum cum apice, gerant.

Quod non graduati, quotquot alicujus Collegii Socii, Probationarii, Scholares, Capellani, Clerici, et Choristae, si modo in matriculam Universitatis sint relati, denique quotquot de fundatione Collegis cujusvis fuerint, Studentes insuper Aedis Christi, quoties in publicum in Universitate prodeunt, togis laxe manicatis, ita ut manicae longitudo dimidiam partem longitudinis togae non excedat, et pileis quadratis cum apice, induti incedant.

Batellarii vero, et Servientes, togam talarem hodie usitatam juxta exemplar gerant, et pileum quadratum sine apice.

Studentes in Jure Civili, nondum graduati, qui sedecim Terminos a tempore matriculationis compleverint, (vel etiam antea, modo de fundatione alicujus Collegii fuerint, cujus Statuta id fieri requisiverint) togam talarem semimanicatam, juxta exemplar, gerant, et pileum quadratum cum apice.

Quod Artium Baccalaurei in omni actu Scholastico caputium fimbria pellita praetextum gerant ; in tempore vero Quadragesimali Determinantes tum in Scholis, tum in Choro Beatae Mariae Virginis, quoties ad celebrandas preces convenerint, pellem etiam lanatam, secundum exemplar, adhibeant.

Graduati omnes, togas Gradui et Facultati competentes, et pileos quadratos cum apice, aut rotundos (Juristae scilicet et Medici) gestabunt ; praecipue in contionibus ordinariis, praelectionibus, et disputationibus publicis.

In contionibus vero solemnibus, et singulis diebus Dominicis intra Terminum ante meridiem in Templo B. V. Mariae, etiam in Aede Christi ; et in Quadragesima, et in Dominica Paschatis post meridiem ad S. Petri in Oriente, caputiis, sive e serico, sive e minuto-vario, obversis, contionibus intersint.

Contionatores itidem habitu Gradui suo competente induti (pro ratione temporis, prout ceciderit intra vel extra Terminum) ad Ecclesiam accedant, et eodem induti contiones suas habeant, sub poena 6s. 8d.

Lectores etiam et Professores publici, in lectionibus suis ordinariis, togis Gradui vel Facultati suae competentibus, et pileo induti, ad Scholas accedant, et eodem habitu induti legant, ac iterum a Scholis recedant. In solennibus autem lectionibus in Vesperiis, pileis, et caputiis, Gradui et Facultati suae competentibus, induti ad Scholas accedant, legant, ac iterum recedant.

Quoties vero ad Congregationes, Convocationes, preces publicas et contiones ad Clerum accedant, omnes praeter togas, caputia Gradui congrua ; Doctores etiam capas, vel clausas vel apertas adhibeant.

Doctores singulis diebus Dominicis intra Terminum, ante meridiem, in Ecclesia B. Virginis Mariae ; et in Quadragesima, et in Dominica Paschatis post meridiem in Ecclesia S. Petri in Oriente, capa et caputio coccineo induti contionibus intersint.

Insuper statutum est, quod omnes Academici cujuscunque ordinis aut gradus fuerint, collari, vulgo vocato *Band*, juxta exemplar, tum in privato tum in publico se induant.

Si quis vero in praemissis delinquere deprehensus fuerit, si non Graduatus fuerit, pro arbitrio Vice-Cancellarii vel Procuratorum, penso aliquo literario puniatur. Si Graduatus, pro prima vice qua deliquerit, *20d*. pro secunda, *3s. 4d*. pro tertia, *5s*. pro quarta, *6s. 8d*. et sic toties quoties. Si quis vero ad Congregationem vel Convocationem accesserit, habitu competente destitutus, praeter mulctam praedictam, nullam omnino suffragandi potestatem ea vice habeat. Quas mulctas ad usum Universitatis exigendi Vice-Cancellarius vel Procuratores potestatem habeant.

Ne vero quis prae novandi libidine ab exemplaribus in hoc statuto descriptis desciscere, novosque habitus introducere moliatur, statutum est, quod Vice-Cancellarius et Procuratores singulorum habituum exemplar aliquod aere incidendum, et in abacum huic usui destinatum, reponendum curabunt.

In 1816 it was found necessary to enforce the statute for academical dress by a 'punishment' or *imposition* ('penso aliquo literario') for three offences: farther transgression being visited with inhibition from degrees, and stigma in the Proctors' *Black Book*.

To pass now to the topic of dress distinctively academical: the following extract is taken from Wood's *History of* Oxford, quoted in *Oxoniana*, I. 19—21. (J. Walker, 1808.)

'The Scholars are supposed in their dress to have imitated the Benedictine Monks, who were the chief restorers of Literature. Their gowns, at first, reached not much lower than their knees. The shoulders were but a little, or not at all gathered; neither were the sleeves much wider than an ordinary coat, but were afterwards much enlarged. When degrees became more frequent in the reigns of Richard I. and John, other fashions were invented for the sake of distinction, not only with respect to degrees but faculties. The wide sleeves are still worn by Bachelors, and by those undergraduates who are on the foundation at different colleges. The gowns were at first black, afterwards of different colours. In the Chancellorship of Archbishop Laud, all were confined to black, except the Sons of Noblemen, who were allowed to wear any colour. The gown used at present by Masters of Arts is not ancient, and never known to have been worn before the time of John Calvin, who, as it is said, was the first who wore it. The ancient gown had the slit longways and the facing lined with fur.

'With respect to caps, the square form with the upper part pointed is supposed to have been the most ancient; but on the introduction of the faculties of Divinity, Law, and Medicine, the doctors in them wore round caps. The two latter still retain them. Some years before the Reformation, the Theologists wore square caps, without any stiffening in them, which caused each corner to flag. They were such as the Judges now use. It was the custom for the Clergy to preach in caps, and for their auditors, if scholars, to sit in them; which continued till the troubles in the time of Charles I. On the Restoration of Charles II. the auditors sat bare, lest if covered, they should encourage the laity to put on their hats, as they did during the Rebellion.

'The most ancient form of the Hood was that which was sowed or tied to the upper part of the coat or gown, and brought over the head for a covering, in the same manner as a cowl: but when caps were introduced, the hoods became only an ornament for the shoulders and back; they were then enlarged and lined with skins.

'The Boots were introduced by the Benedictines. The ancient form or fashion of them was but small, and came up to the middle of the leg, with little or no tops to them. They were worn by Masters of Arts at their inception; which custom continued till the introduction of the Degree of Doctor, when they were used by them, and the Masters wore Pantables or Sandals.'

1414. At Cambridge, in 'a congregation of regents and non-regents, held on the 24th of May, a statute was made prohibiting (under penalty of suspension, disability, and excommunication) every bachelor in any faculty, to use in the schools, processions, or acts, a cloak, or fur, or facings of silk, satin, or other material of similar price or value, in his tabard, hood, or other scholastic habit, except lamb's wool or budge fur, on his hood. This statute does not extend to masters gremial, the sons of peers, beneficiaries having promotion to the value of 30 marks per annum of prebends or canonries, or otherwise of 40 marks; nor to persons upon whom the privilege was expressly conferred by the major part of the regents and non-regents. Bachelors in all faculties were also prohibited from using a bonnet, cap, coif, or other like ornament for the head at their lectures or scholastic acts. This statute appears to have been much complained of by the scholars in Canon and Civil Law. On the 17th of September, the King [Henry V.] by writ commanded Stephen le Scrope, Chancellor of the University, to appear upon this business, before the Archbishop of Canterbury and his brethren, in the convocation of the province at St Paul's, London, on the 1st of November, together with four persons named by the masters regent, and four named by the scholars in Canon and Civil Law. In the mean time the King had sent to Oxford to ascertain the practice of that University, which he found to be conformable to the statute in dispute, the observance of which he, on the 4th of December, enjoined, under the penalty of 1000 *li.*[1]

A few months later we read of the law students refusing to attend the *ordinaries* (lectures with full comments).

In 1429 and 1467 the privileges of the universities were respected in acts prohibiting the giving liveries (*liberaturae*) or signs[2]. *Livery money*, or an allowance for statutable dress, still continues to be an item in the stipend of members of college foundations.

In an act of parliament of 153⅞ '"for Reformacyon of Excesse in Apparayle," there is a clause permitting

[1] Cooper's *Annals*, I. 156, 157. See Dyer's *Privileges*, I. 53.
[2] *Ibid.* I. 182, 215.

" Doctours, or Bachelours in Divinitie, Doctors of the one Lawe or the other, and also Doctours of other Sciences, which have taken that degree, or be admitted in any Universitie, to weare sarcenett in the lynyng of their gownes, blacke saten, or blacke chamlett in their doublettes and sleveles Cotes, and blacke velvett or blacke sarcenett or blacke saten in their Tippitts and Ryding hoodes or Girdels, and also Clothe of the Colours of scarlett, murey or violett, and Furres called gray blacke boge[1] foynes[2] shankes[3] or menever[4] in their gownes and sleveles Cotes," and prohibiting the clergy under these degrees to "weare any manner of Furres other than blacke cony boge grey cony shankes calaber[5] gray fiche[6] foxe lambe otter and bever;" the clergy under those degrees (except Masters of Arts, or Bachelors of the one law or the other of the Universities, and such as could dispend 20*l. per annum*) were also prohibited from wearing sarcenet or silk in their tippets, and a *proviso* was inserted that the act should not be prejudicial "to any Graduates, Beadles, or Ministers to the Graduates in Universities and Scoles for wearing of their

---

[1] *Budge,* Lambskin with the wool dressed outwards. (*Halliwell.*)

[2] *Foins,* fur made of polecatts' skins. (*Piers Plowman.*)

[3] *Shanks,* fur from the legs of animals. "Schanke of bouge, *fourrure de cuissettes.*" Palsgrave, &c. (*Halliwell.*)

[4] *Menever* (probably the *minutum uarium* of the Oxford statutes), a kind of ermine mixed with the fur of a species of weasel called vair: see the ballad of *Alice Brand.* Vair, the heraldic fur tincture, is represented by small belts or shields in horizontal lines.

[5] *Calaber,* a kind of fur. See *Brit. Bibl.* II. 401: Strutt, II. 102. Cov. Myst. p. 242. (*Halliwell.*)

[6] *Fitch,* a polecat. (*co. Somerset.*)

habittes or hoodes with furre lynynges or otherwise, after such forme as heretofore they have been accustomed to doo[1]."[1]

In the complaint of *disorders at* Cambridge, sent to Whitgift in 1602 (*supra*, p. 466), it is said that 'It is required by the statute, that the scholars should have and wear gownes, cappes, and hoods, according to their degrees, and to this statute every graduate is sworn: but this statute is generally neglected.' Peacock, *on the Statutes*, p. 61, *n.*

In answer to the 11th *Quaere* sent to the V. Chanc. and Heads of Camb. in 1675, they replied that 'The Doctors in the several Faculties do generally resort to Congregations in the Regent house, and to sermons *Ad Clerum*, and supplications in St Mary's in the habits and ornaments appointed by Statute; and so do the University Officers, as Proctors, Taxors, and Scrutators; and those of the head, and some few others in theirs: but the Non-Regents and Regents are much failing herein; especially the Regents in their Habits at Congregation, and in their caps and hoods at English sermons, and abroad in the town.' Dyer's *Privileges*, I. 367, 370.

David Loggan's prints of *Habitus Academici* in his *Oxonia Illustrata* (1675), and *Cantabrigia Illustrata* (1690), we shall have occasion to mention by and by.

The much-contested '*Orders and Regulations* which passed the Senate on the 11th day of May, and the 26th day of June, 1750,' commence as follows:—

[1] Cooper's *Annals*, I. 355.

'I. Every person *in statu pupillari* shall wear clothes of a grave colour in the judgment of the officers of the university, without, lace, fringe, or embroidery; without cuffs or capes of a different colour from their coats.

'Fellowcommoners who take degrees, and such as enter into fellows' commons after they have taken any degree, shall wear the proper habit of such degree.

'Bachelors of arts shall provide themselves with gowns made of prunello, or princes stuff.

'The privilege of noblemen, or others, of wearing hats in the university, does not extend to wearing of them laced. The penalty for every offence against each of these particulars, is, and shall be, 6*s.* and 8*d.*

'II. Every fellowcommoner shall immediately provide himself with his proper gown, cap, and band, in which he shall constantly appear, under the penalty of 6*s.* 8*d.* for every offence.'

In *Remarks on the Enormous Expence* in the education of young men in the Univ. of *Cambridge,* with a Plan, &c., 1788, it is proposed (p. 28), that any undergraduate found without his academical dress after sunset, or in hall, should, for the first offence, be rusticated for a period of six months, for the second for one year, and if he again offended, he should be expelled.

In 1837 Dr Whewell, then a fellow and tutor of Trinity, wrote thus (*On the Principles of English University Education,* p. 89): 'It may be, too, that with an improvement in many respects, there is an increased laxity in the observance of rules on other points; for example, the constant use of the academic dress. But in most such cases, the fault is in those of superior position, who ought to enforce the observance of rules, and who are not sufficiently vigilant and earnest in this part of their duty. *Nos, nos consules desumus.* If, for instance, all persons in the Universities, who have pupils under their care, were persuaded that the academic dress is a valuable remembrance of the duties and obligations of the student's position, and were to enjoin its use on all occasions, and to rebuke its absence, there can be little doubt that omission in this respect might soon be rendered as rare as it ever was.'

But to come down to particulars: the HOOD (*caputium*[1]) of our University combines with the *hood* proper (as worn alone at Oxford) another garment, the *tippet* or exaggerated collar of the overgarment or gown falling square over the shoulders behind and fastened in a peak on the chest. From this peak springs the hood proper, being with us, as in its original form, merely an upper fold of the tippet, or ample collar, so shaped as to be conveniently drawn over the head as occasion should offer. Such has been the conservatism of Cambridge tailors, that a bachelor of arts hood, if drawn up close to the neck behind, neatly folded, and fastened where the fur begins in front, the slovenly modern string being abolished, will correspond minutely with the hood worn in the fourteenth century

---

[1] Caputium, *id quod* Capitium, *capitis tegumentum quod Caput assutum erat.* Du Cange.

by all classes, civil and military, and by monks and friars in all later times (*Cucullus*, cowl.) This is shewn, for instance, in the picture of 'the popish Spaniards .. carying Nic. Burton...after a most spitefull sort to the burning,' in the black-letter editions of Foxe's *Acts and Monuments*, and also in the 'liuely picture' which forms the tail-piece: also in the modern sculpture of Hugh de Balsham teaching the Cambridge Scholars, in the fellows' garden of Peterhouse, and in several 14th century pictures relating to the quintain, Strutt's *Sports and Pastimes*, figg. 31, 34, 35, 36, 38. At the same time it must be confessed that the fashion of wearing the hood slung loose from the collar in the ordinary way is at least as old as the effigies of the four chantry monks who kneel in the stone doorway of the 15th century screen of the Founders' chantry in the S.W. transept of Lincoln cathedral. The curious busts, one of which on the south represents a clerk flinging on his hood, were introduced into the arcade work in the choir aisles of that cathedral about the same time as the figures in the 'angel choir' and were largely restored in the present century. From the apex of the hood still hangs the *liripipe*[1], which was probably used as a purse or pocket, like the pen-

---

[1] *Liripoop*, n. s. [*liripion, liripipion*, Fr. "Chaperon des docteurs de Sorbonne, longue robe de docteur, suivant Rabelais." Roquefort. *Leri-ephippium*, a contraction of *cleri-ephippium*, the tippet or hood of a .clergyman, Littleton.] The hood of a graduate. *Cotgrave and Sherwood*. 'In this letter the good primate doth not trouble his clergy with recommending a single virtue, or reproving a single vice; but he charges them, with great solemnity, not to wear short *liripoops* of silk, nor gowns open before, nor swords, nor daggers, nor embroidered girdles.' Henry, *Hist. of Gr. Britain*, vol. 6 (*regn. H.* VII.). Todd's *additions*

dent sleeves of the master of arts and Trinity fellow-commoner's gowns. Du Cange (s. v. *caputium*) quotes from the Carthusian statutes of 1368 (II. i. § 2), *Caputia cucullorum sint quadrata, nec duorum palmorum mensuram in latum excedant, vel in longum. Caputia vero caparum sint aliquantulum longiora.*

The '*Caputium* or Cloak' (says Fosbroke, *Encycl. Antiqu.* 847 *a*), 'a hooded-cloak.. originated with the inferior classes, and succeeded the short mantle in the thirteenth century, also in the higher ranks. It covered the shoulders, and extended below the breast. The hood was thrown behind, or covered the head at option.' Laymen wore a hat over the hood in the 14th century (*ibid. p.* 856 *a*). In the 12th century to throw back the hood (which was then worn by both sexes) was a sign of mourning (*ibid.* 842).

Of the use of the hood in ceremonies at degrees in the middle of the 16th century, see the extracts from bedel Stokys' book, supra pp. 208, 209, 214, 245. The words of the Cambridge Elizabethan statute (*cap.* 46) of 1570, which relate to hoods are, *Statuimus, ut nemo ad aliquem in Universitate gradum euectus, nisi toga talari, caputioque ordini congruente, aut ad minimum insigni circa collum sacerdotali indutus collegio exeat: contra delinquentes sex solidi et octo denarii mulcta sit. Et si quispiam disputationi publicae in sua facultate, publicis in ecclesia beatae Mariae precibus, contioni ad Clerum, sepulturis, congregationibus, sine toga, habitu, et caputio gradui suo conuenientibus, iuxta antiquum*

to Johnson's *Dictionary.* Du Cange explains the word to mean *longa fascia, vel cauda caputii.*

Academiae morem, interfuerit, eandem mulctam in-
·urrat......Socii discipuli et pensionarii singulis domini-
:is et festis diebus in chorum honesto cum apparatu et
:uperpelliceis tecti ueniant; graduati autem cum caputiis
;radui suo conuenientibus sub poena duodecim denari-
·rum, &c.

Nov. 25, 1578. It was decreed 'by Mr. Jo. Young
Dr of Divinity, and V. Chan. of the University of
Cambridge, with the assent and consent of all the
Masters and Presidents of all the Colleges, in the
common Schools assembled; that no man, unless he
were a Dr, should wear a Hood lined with silk upon
his Gown as Doctors usually do, upon the forfeiture
of 6s. 8d. *toties quoties;* and if any shall refuse to
pay the said fine or mulct, then he to be inforced
by Mr V. Chancellor's Authority to shew why he
should not be punished for wilfull perjury[1].'

According to the Orders of Apparell made for
Cambridge by lord Burleigh in 1585, 'no Graduate
remayninge within any Colledge, Hostell or Hall, or
clayminge to enjoye the priviledge of a Scholler, doe
weare any stuffe in the outward part of his gowne,
but woollen cloth of blacke, puke, London Browne,
or other sad color: And the gowne to be made with
a standing coller, as the use hath bene, and not falling: And the hood that is worn with the same gowne,
to be of the same or like cloth or color that the
gowne is of. And that none as is aforesaid, doe weare
for the upper apparell of his bodye, in the daye tyme
out of his colledg, hostell, hall, or habitation, and pre-

[1] Dyer's *Privileges*, I. 308.

cinctes of the same, in any common streete of the
towne, that is to saye, in the high streete from the
greate bridge, as it leadeth right to Christes Colledge,
in the streete called the High Ward streete, from
St. John's Colledge as it leadeth right to Pembrook
Hall and Peter House, in anye of the Markett places,
in the streete called the Peticurie, or in the Court or
Quadrant of any other Colledge then that where he
remayneth, or within the comon Schooles, or at any
disputation, or any common lecture, or at any Sermon or common prayers, or being called and coming
to the Vicechancellor or Proctors, or any other then
the said gowne and hood or tippett, as to his degree
apperteyneth, except the habitt and hood be then required to be worne: And the gowne sleeves in all
these tymes and places to be worne over and uppon
his armes (except he walke in his cloake and hatt to
and fro the feildes).

'The facing of gownes for Bachelors of musick,
phisick and law, and for Masters of Art and upward,
at the onely half a yard downe ward by the brest, and
a quarter of a yard at the handes of a streight sleeve,
and no where else, unless the wearer be a doctour,
Provost or Master of a Colledge or Hall, or Principal
of an hostell, or Oratour of the Universitie, or Proctor
or Taxter of the same, or be or have one of the
Quenes Majesties Readers, and the ladye Margarettes
Reader, or have bene Proctour or Oratour of the Universitie, may be of playne Taffita, untuffed of sattyn,
silk, grograigne, sarcenett or such like, not forbidden
to the wearer by proclamation and lawes of the

realme. But no silke to be worne to the hood, except the wearer be a doctour, or be or have bene Provost &c. &c.

'Also that all Regentes hoods for Masters of Arte be of one sorte, faced, lyned, and edged, with myniver, and with no silke (the Oratours of the University onely excepted)[1].'

When queen Elizabeth visited Cambridge in 1564 'great inquisition was made, both at this time (Monday, Aug. 7.) and yesterdays sermon *ad clerum*, and some fault found as well by the Prince as by other of the nobility, why some Masters Regents went in white silk, and others in mynever? Also some Masters were noted by the Queens Majestie to be but Masters ; because their habits and hoods were torn and too much soiled. *Sed haec hactenus*[2].'

In the English *Constitutions and Canons Ecclesiastical* of 1603, the regulations (Nos. 17, 25) on this matter coincide with the Cambridge statute. *Eves*, however, are specified in addition to Sundays and holydays, when all students shall wear surplices, and graduates hoods: Heads of collegiate churches to wear them at all services.

For the use of the hood in ceremonies for degrees, see the extracts from bedel Buck's book above, pp. 249—251.

Among *Loggan's* University Habits (1670—1685), the most remarkable hoods are those of the doctors in each faculty, which pass across the chest in a broad,

[1] Cooper's *Annals*, II. 410, 411.
[2] *Ibid.* II. 195.

almost horizontal line. With the exception of that of the M.A., the Oxford hoods are almost as full as ours: the B.A.'s in each are 'flourished.' And the Cambridge LL.D. or M.D. in Congregation or Supplication and Contiones ad Clerum has a fur-edged tippet to his hood reaching nearly to his heels. The Oxonian proctor wears a hood of *miniver* or striped fur. Our non-regent's hood was little better than a square black tippet hanging to the middle of the back. The taxor wears his hood 'squared,' the Proctor his ordinary white regent's hood.

The B.A. hood used to be made of lambskin, as are those now worn in Jesus College, *Cambridge* (made, I believe, after a pattern of Pugin's, which corresponds with one depicted in Speede's map of 1610, and revived there by Mr Gilbert Scott the younger, as I have heard). James Howell, in a letter written from Venice to Dr Fr. Mansell in 1621, where he remarks, that his hair has quite changed colour since he has changed his diet, compares the time when he carried a Calf-Leather Satchil to School in *Hereford*, with that when he 'wore a Lambskin Hood in *Oxford*' at Jesus college. *Epist. Ho-elianae*, I. xxxi.

The B.A. hood at Cambridge is usually worn '*flourished*,' i.e., with an inch or two of the fur lining turned over outward at the back.

The hood *squared* is now worn by the proctors, and in past years was also a badge of taxors and scrutators. It is so folded that the neck, instead of being under the string, is yoked by the part which joins tippet and hood, and which would ordinarily hang over the back veiled by the folds of the hood. The result produced is a large loose square collar or tippet, none of the white lining being visible.

Before the days when the 'Council' took the place of the *Caput* at Cambridge, masters of arts wore white linings to their hoods only as long as they were 'regents.' As soon as they should be removed to the 'black-hood, or non-regent house,' they wore plain black hoods; by which arrangement the white lining had a shorter time to get soiled than at present.

According to the Oxford Statute, XVI. § 4, De Contionibus quibusdam extraordinariis ad Ecclesiam B. Mariae, those who were about to 'determine' as bachelors were to attend the Latin sermon on Ash-Wednesday in *caputia obverso Rhenone*[1], *seu pelle agnina.*

With regard to the academical CAP (*pileus quadratus*): a distinction has been drawn between the *quadratum* or B.A.'s square cap and the *birrettum* or Doctor's cap in the mediaeval universities. (J. Helfenstein, *Contemp. Review*, IV. 237—264, *Feb.* 1867.) And it has been stated that the former, the square trencher-cap is identical with the head-dress of the

---

[1] *Rheno, reno,* pellicium, vestis ex pellibus conficta, quae humeros et latera tegebat...usque ad umbilicum. *Iso magister in glessis*: 'Vocamus etiam mastragas Renones quae rustice Crotina vocatur,' Vide *Crusina. Ioannes de Garlandia in Synonymis.*

> "Vestes quae fiunt de solis pellibus hae sunt:
> Pellicium, Rheno, quibus Andromeda sociatur."

Du Cange, glossar.

ancient Chinese kings[1]. The varieties in caps have been considerable.

Dean Colet (Magd. coll. Oxon.) is painted in a mediaeval birretta without 'combs'. He died in 1519.

Cardinal Wolsey (Holbein) wears a round cardinal's cap, the top falling in quadrants from its central button.

Archbishop Will. Warham of Canterbury (Holbein) died in 1532. He wears a loose skull-cap, the hinder part falling behind the ears, like the skull-piece of our modern academical cap.

Cardinal Beatoun of St Andrews and Paris (portrait at Holyrood, engraved in Lodge's *Portraits of Illustrious Personages*), who died in 1546, wears a zucchetto, band and cassock.

In the wood-cuts to Foxe's *Actes and Monuments* ('Book of Martyrs'):—

The preacher at Paul's cross, before whom John Bainham is doing penance (anno 1532), wears no birretta. He has on an albe with a stole embroidered with several crosses.

In 1549 an Injunction was sent to Cambridge— *Sociorum et discipulorum uestitus et cultus corporis honestus sit et decorus: pilei autem scholastici et quadrati.*

In the picture of the execution of Ro. King and the others who destroyed the Rood at Dovercourt in 1532, the ecclesiastic in the foreground wears a birretta with diagonal seams on the top: otherwise

---

[1] *Clarence Hopper*, ap. N. and Q. S. I., Vol. VI. p. 579 a.

hardly distinguishable from our college cap. He has also a gown with an upright collar, and a doctor's scarf, which hangs at the back about four inches below the seam of his gown-collar.

Bonner (Pemb. coll. Oxon.) and the four other doctors in the picture, where he is represented as burning Thomas Tomkin's hand (1555), wear scarves not drawn close to the nape of the neck. Their caps, which they wear in the room, seem to have had a square top originally; but it has been pinched with the finger and thumb in four places, so as to take the shape (roughly) of a star with four points, that over the nose projecting more than that at the back of the head, where the cap is of course pulled lower, so as to look something like the back of our cap.

In the common frontispiece to the two volumes the protestant on the dexter side wears, in the pulpit inside the church, a furred gown, and a close skull-cap. The papist on the sinister side wears a loose-sleeved surplice, a stole embroidered with crosses, and a low ill-shaped birretta, rather less regularly pinched than those just described.

'Certaine Bishops talking with Master Bradford in prison' wear (albes or) rochets, one with an embroidered collar, and over it a chimere or gown, with a broad D.D.'s scarf flowing loosely over the shoulders. It reaches about six inches below the knee: caps, as above, the skull-piece being better defined.

In the astonishing caricature entitled 'the right picture and counterfeit of Boner, and his crueltie, in scourging of God's saints, in his Orchard at Fulham,'

the dress of the attendant Doctors of divinity is like
that already described, except that for gowns, they
seem to have full-sleeved long cassocks.

John Bradford wears an M.A. gown and a round
cap, with a skull-piece such as ours.

The doctor looking on at the racking of Cutbert
Simson wears also a round cap with cross seams at
the top, and a skull-piece.

The portrait of Luther by Lucas Cranach 1543 (in
the possession of Carl Haag, esq., and exhibited in
the Old Masters' Exhibition of 1872—3), displays a
round cap with a skull-piece.

Among Lodge's *Portraits* :—

Nic. Ridley (*ob.* 1555) wears long pointed collars
and a gown.

Tho. Cranmer (*ob.* 1556) has a cap rather square
than round.

In this period the caps of laymen seem to have
projected farther than those of the clergy.   That of
John Russell, earl of Bedford, in Lodge's 2nd vol. is
well worth noticing.

Matt. Parker (*ob.* 1575) has a cap like that of Cranmer, but it projects farther (like some in Foxe).

Cardinal Allen (of Oriel, S. Mary hall, and Louvain, *ob.* 1594) has a mediaeval birretta, and a collar
less pointed than Ridley's.

Geo. Abbott (of Balliol, and Univ. coll. Oxon., *ob.*
1633) has a cap rather round than square, with a
large button at the top, and a well-defined skull-
piece.

Will. Laud (*ob.* 1645) returns to the squarer top,

but more projecting, a skuil-piece, but no button apparent.

John Tillotson (*ob.* 1694) wears his own hair, band-like collars, his cap which lies on the table is only a little less stiff than our own, with a button or tuft: the back of the skull-piece crumpled on the table.

Gilbert Burnet (by Kneller) in his court dress, wears a low-crowned wideawake, less ample than bishop lord keeper John Williams.

Fr. Atterbury (*ob.* 1732) is painted by Kneller in bands and a wig.

In the frontispiece to ΕΙΚΩΝ ΑΛΗΘΙΝΗ *The Pourtraiture of Truths most sacred Majesty truly suffering, though not solely. Wherein the false colours are washed off, wherewith the Painter-steiner hath bedaubed Truth, the late King and the Parliament in his counterfeit Piece entituled εἰκὼν βασιλική*, &c., &c., 1649, where

> 'The Author...hath conceiv'd it meet
> The Doctour should doe pennance in this sheet.

He introduces us to him in spite of his clutching at the curtain, so far as to disclose a gown, through the sleeve of which the fore-arm appears as through that of an M.A. He has plain white cuffs, and a narrow turn-over collar without band. The skull-piece of the cap is just indicated, the penthouse of it is rectangular at the base, but rises to a pyramid of perhaps three inches altitude.

In the frontispiece of ΕΙΚΩΝ Η ΠΙΣΤΗ *or The faithfull Pourtraicture of a Loyall Subject, in Vindication of εἰκὼν βασιλική*, &c., &c., 1649, where the tables are turned, the author of *Eikôn hê pistê*, who is being crowned with a foolscap and coxcomb for his pains, while he has his left hand on the King's crown, holds in his right a doctor's cap, whether triangular or four-corner'd, it is not easy to say.

It has no skull-piece;—which suggests the conjecture that the skull-piece of the last named picture also may be worn beneath the cap not covering the forehead but separate, as we have already mentioned the hood being worn under a hat, and like the cap seen in portraits of Jer. Taylor, bishop Launcelot Andrewes (*ob.* 1626), and others.

If this be so, the modern cap may be called a combination of the papist and the protestant head-dress mentioned already, as pourtrayed on the frontispiece of Foxe. Or more properly speaking, it will be a union of the *zucchetto* or skull-cap with the *birretta*[1] or small stiff slightly overhanging cap, sewn together for convenience in removing, at the proper moments, in sermons, &c. The custom of handing the birretta to the server before mounting to place the Chalice on the Altar has still a curious parallel in the practice at Westminster Abbey of handing the college cap to the virger at the reading of the lessons on Sundays.

The regulation in our 46th statute of 1570 prescribes that fellows and resident graduates should wear *superiore pileo scholastico et quadrato*, and that none of any sort or condition should wear a hat (*galero*), except in case of ill-health. We might infer

---

[1] *Birrus* and *Birrettus*, a pointed cap, hood, or bonnet (see *Fosbrokt*).

rom this that undergraduates in old times wore no covering on their heads (as at Winchester school, and Christ's hospital).

Dr Ashton, of Jesus, in his *collectanea* on cap. 42, defined (about the year 1703) the word *pileatorum* as equivalent to *Doctorum.*

In 1585 lord Burleigh ordered for Cambridge, 'that everie graduate wearing the above gowne and gaberdyne [which might be worn within the precincts of his college, and in bye-streets: see a few pages below;] within the Universitie or Towne, out of his chamber or lodging, doe weare withall in the day tyme a square cap and none other; no hatt to be worne except for infirmities sake, with a kerchiff about his head, or in going to and fro the Feeldes, or in the streete or open ayre, when it shall happen to rayne, hayle, or snowe; And then at all other tymes within the Universitie and without, the hatt whiche shall be worne to be blacke, and the band or lace of the hatt to be of the same colour, playne and not excessive in bignes, without feather, brooche, or such like uncomelye, for Studentes. And that, as well the hatt as the band, to be suche as the wearer may by law use and weare[1].' And again, 'it is provided that all Masters of Colledges and Doctors of Divinity of the saied Universitie of Cambridge, shall weare openly within the saied Universitie, a truncke gowne and a hood, or a truncke gowne and a tippett, according to their degrees: and that they shall therewith weare a scholler's cap being square: And when he or they shal be out

---

[1] Cooper's *Annals,* II. 411.

of the Universitie in Citie by the space of three dayes, and at such tymes as they shall preache elsewhere, they shall weare a truncke gowne, tippett, and square cap, according to the Quenes Majesties and Injunction and advertisementes, under the payne of forfecting xx⁴. to be devided in three partes and imployed as is aforesaid[1].' In process of time, at any rate, undergraduates came to wear round caps.

The statement of 'common disorders' at Cambridge sent to Laud, probably by Dr Cosin, of Peterhouse, in 1636, complains that 'the Clericall Habit appointed for students here is generally neglected, unles it be in King's College only, where they reteine yᵉ antient manner, both for color and fashion, with yᵉ use of square Caps from the first entrance. At Trinitie, and otherwhiles at Caius, they keep their order for their wide-Sleeve Gowns, and for their Caps too when they list to put any on...and round rusti Caps they weare (If they weare any at all), that they may be the sooner despised, though the fashion here of old time was altogether *pileus quadratus*, as appears by reteining that custome still in King's Colledge, in Trin., and at Caius, whose Governours heretofore were [Roger Goade, Fogg Newton, W. Smith;—J. Richardson Leonard Mawe, S. Brooke, T. Combe;—and T. Legge, W. Branthwaite, J. Gostlin, T. Batchcroft] more observant of old Orders than it seems others were[2].'

The *Oxford University Statutes* were revised and

---

[1] Cooper's *Annals*, II. 414.

[2] MS. Baker VI. 152. Cp. Peacock *on the Statutes*: also Cooper's *Annals*, III. 280.

digested in 1633 under Laud, then bishop of London, the chief persons employed being Dr Pink, warden of New college, Dr James, fellow of that society, and Keeper of Bodley's library, Dr Zouch, who had also been fellow of New college, and was principal of Alban Hall, Brian Twyne, of Corpus Christi, who transcribed the Statutes, and was afterwards appointed keeper of the archives, and Peter Turner, of Merton, Savilian professor. The following extracts are taken from the Oxford Statutes.

VII. ii. § 4. *Habitus Vesperiales et Comitiales Inceptorum in Artibus.*

Cum ex frequentia Inceptorum Habitu sollenni indutorum cohonestatur Academia, singuli Inceptores in Artibus, in Vesperiis, Facultatis suae; Togis laxe manicatis, Capis ac Capitiis ex Serico, et Crepidis et Soccutis induti, nudis Capitibus interesse, sub poena 3*s.* 4*d.* ibique quoad exercitia peracta fuerint permanere, teneantur. Etiam in die Comitiorum, eodem modo sub poena eadem intersint; praeterquam quod pro Caputiis Sericis, Caputiis ex minuto-vario (Anglice *Miniver*) induti incedant.

§ 5. *Habitus Inceptorum in aliis Facultatibus.*

Inceptores in Musica, in Vesperiis et Comitiis, Togis manicatis, cum Capis albis Damascenis undulatis, Pileisque rotundis holosericis utantur.

Inceptores in Medicina et Jurisprudentia Capas coccineas cum Caputiis itidem coccineis, serico cujusvis intermedii coloris subsutis, et Pileos ex holoserico[1] rotundos gestent.

Inceptores in Theologia Capas itidem coccineas cum Caputiis similibus, serico tamen nigri coloris subsutis, et Pileos Quadratos habeant.

Singuli Inceptores, donec solenniter creati fuerint, capitibus aperti in publico sedeant, et incedant, sub poena 13*s.* 4*d.*

By Stat. VIII. § 6, it was ordered that respondents and opponents in the Ordinary Disputations should appear in the dress of their faculty and degree; 'id

_____
[1] *Holosericum*, velvet.

est, Pileo, Capis et Caputiis induti.' And, according
to IX. vi. § 1, after the oaths have been administered
to the persons to be presented as inceptors, &c. in
Congregation, the proctor is to admonish them to
procure proper habits within five days, to be worn at
Acts and in university processions. The eighth 'title'
of the statutes was abrogated May 7, 1819, when the
Ordinary Disputations were abolished as obsolete and
unprofitable.

In Loggan's plate of *Habitus Academici in Univer-*
sitate Oxoniensi (1672), the servitor, battellar, undergraduate commoner, and the *commensalis superioris*
ordinis (gentleman-commoner) wear limp round caps,
the crown falling down close on the brim, and being
of the same diameter, of a radius about two inches
greater than that of the head. Doctors in Music,
Medicine, and Law, noblemen, sons of peers, &c.
Superior and inferior Bedells (Esquire and Yeomen
Bedells), and the Virger of the University, wear similar caps but of velvet, higher in the crown, and more
deeply pleted. Wigs seem then to have been worn
chiefly by persons of rank or position.

An undergraduate on the foundation wore a *square*
cap without tassel or tuft; a student of Civil Law
who had completed four years (like the Cambridge
harry-soph), a Mus. B., B.A., B.A. about to determine
in Quadragesima, L.B., M.A., M.B., Proctor, B.D.,
D.D., and the Vice-chancellor, wore stiff square caps
with tufts, the edges of the cap, or at least the covering, being slightly turned downwards over the top.

The Cambridge habits drawn about ten years later

shew *square* caps (with tufts, but otherwise similar to those now worn, unless it be that the skull-piece was rather longer and squarer at the back), worn by scholars of King's, Trinity, and some other colleges, B.A., L.B., M.B., M.A., Taxor, Proctor, D.D., and Vice-Chancellor. There is no representation of a B.D.

Undergraduates wore ill-shaped narrow wide-awakes; Fellow-commoners the ordinary broad-brimmed low-crowned billy-cock hat of the period subsequent to the Restoration, not much unlike what was then worn also by bull-dogs, taxor's and vice-chancellor's servants: the Noblemen and the Yeoman Bedell (*Bedellus inferior*) wear like hats, only cocked in front. The D.C.L., Mus. D., M.D., Commissary and Esquire Bedells (*Bedelli Armigeri*) wore *round* caps as at Oxford. The M.A. in a mourning gown at Cambridge wears the square *mourning-cap* with diagonal bands and rosette, and bows at the back: at Oxford he wears the ordinary square tufted cap.

Here is the description of caps in *Academia:* or, the Humours of the University of *Oxford* in Burlesque Verse. *By Mrs* Alicia D'Anvers. *London,* Printed and sold by *Randal Taylor* near *Stationers Hall,* 1691 [4to pp. 68; Bodl. c. 2, 14; MS. Linc.] p. 34.

> Some Trenchers on their Heads have got
> As black as yonder Porridge Pot;
> And some have things, exactly such
> As my Old Gammers mumbles' Pouch,
> Which fits upon his Head as neat
> As 'twere sew'd to't by e'ry Pleat.

Compare this with the description of the servitor's cap in 1709 given above, p. 102.

In 1737 Hogarth published his engraving of the *Publick Lecture* on *datur uacuum*, for which Mr Fisher of Jesus, Oxon., the registrar of that university, sat as the lecturer. Among the audience who are depicted as specimens of stolidity and empty-headedness, the older men wear little square-caps with tufts, and the undergraduates round caps.

The foreground of *a Prospect of* Cambridge, drawn and engraved by *Sam.* and *Nat. Buck*, 1743, of which there is one copy in Peterhouse library, and another in the reading-room of the Cambridge Town Free Library, shews groups of men and ladies sauntering in the unenclosed meadows skirting the S. Neot's road; those that are in academical costume wear square caps with tassells; those in three-corner'd hats wear no gowns.

It is mentioned in the *Gentleman's Magazine* of 1754, that undergraduates at Oxford then wore square caps, those at Cambridge 'frightful things.'

Professor Pryme recollected that when he first went to Cambridge in 1799, his uncle Dinsdale, who had not been there since 1782, and who had resided in 1762, 'was scandalised at seeing the M.A.'s wearing round hats. Cocked hats had formerly been universals among those of them who did not wear a cap. He remarked, too, that, in his time, the streets were not paved, and that the run of water had been in the *middle* of them[1]', as in the town of Berne.

[1] *Autobiog. Recoll. of G. Pryme, p.* 37.

Until 1769 the undergraduates at Cambridge continued to wear 'round caps or bonnets of black cloth, lined with black silk or canvass, with a brim of black velvet for the pensioner, and of prunella or silk for the sizars.' Farish, in his *Toleration of Marriage in the Universities*, recommended to the attention of the Heads of Houses, p. 44, [see above, p. 356] records incidentally the method by which this 'change of dress, which the Heads of Houses obligingly condescended to patronize,' was brought about. 'Notice was sent to every College, for the friends of that minute change to meet together, and a letter was prepared to the Chancellor of the University, requesting that he would obtain the consent of Government. It was urged that the Heads of Houses were not unwilling that the change should take place, and that they wished to attend his Grace's "approaching installation in a dress more decent and becoming." The Duke of Grafton mentioned the matter to the council-board, and intimated to the University that the new habit might be adopted. In this quiet way was a change made in a trifling matter, which if it had happened in the days of Whitgift and Cartwright, would have set the whole University in an uproar.'

This seems to have been a popular precedent, for it had already been quoted by 'Camillus' in an impudent Letter to Dr Powell, which he published in the *London Chronicle* of Jan. 25, 1772, complaining that the Petition of undergraduates for the removal of Subscription had not been favourably received. There it is mentioned that the petition was offered for an alteration of their statutable dress *by Under-graduates* 'in the month of *June*, 1769[1].'

Cooper (*Annals* IV. 356) refers also to Hartshorne, *Book Rarities of Univ. of Cambridge*, 447 *n.*, and quotes from the *Cambridge Chronicle* of 1 July, 1769, the contemporary *jeu d'esprit :—*

> '*Mutantque rotunda*
> *Quadratis.*
>
> Ye learn'd of every age and climate yield,
> And to illustrious Cambridge quit the field.
> What sage Professors never yet could teach,
> Nor Archimedes nor our Newton reach ;
> What ancients, and what moderns, vainly sought,
> Cambridge, with ease, hath both attain'd and taught:
> This truth even envy must herself allow,
> For *all* her Scholars *Square the Circle* now.'

The leaders were Jas. Mead of Emmanuel, Alex. Cleeve of C. C. C., and Nedham Dymoke of St John's. (MS. Cole XLI. 397, 398, ap. Prof. Mayor's *Baker's St John's*, p. 1047, *cp.* 1057).

We have had instances of the vice-chancellor, fathers, and proctors, wearing caps garnished with gold lace at commencement in the sixteenth century. (*See above*, pp. 249, 250.)

We are now living to see the cap distinctive of their faculty left off by the doctors of law and medicine, as they have been already by the esquire bedells.

The graduate's GOWN (*toga*) is prescribed by the 46th statute of 1570 as *talaris*, reaching to the ancles: a regulation which seems to have been regarded for at least a century, to judge from Loggan's pictures.

---

[1] Nichols, *Lit. Anecd.* I. 574.

For lord Burleigh's regulations with respect to gowns in 1585, see above, pp. 461, 496, 505.

There are several representations of black and of scarlet gowns in the picture of the vice-chancellor's court and university officers presented by Matt. Stokys in 1590, and now preserved in the university registrary's office.

The same paper which told Laud in 1636 'that at Trinitie and otherwhiles at Caius,' his order for wide-Sleeved gowns was kept, informed him also that 'others, all that are undergraduates, wear ye new fashioned gowns of any colour whatever, blue or green, or red or mixt, without any Uniformity but in hanging sleeves[1].'

'In 1659 there was a great outcry against the universities and learning, and after the removal of Richard Cromwell, it seems to have been intended to remodel the universities after the Dutch fashion, and to reduce the Colleges to three in each University, namely, one for each of the faculties of divinity, law, and physic, each to have a professor, and all students to go in cloaks[2].' Mat. Poole, of Emmanuel, published his scheme for an university in 1658[3], with the approbation of Baxter, Bathurst, Reinolds, Calamy, Clarke, Robert lord Titchburne, Whichcot, Cudworth, &c.

It seems that at one period puritans were no less jealous of the gown than of the surplice, for it is said

[1] MS. Baker, VI. 152, ap. Cooper's *Annals*, III. 280.

[2] Cooper's *Annals*, III. 47, referring to Wood-Gutch *Hist.* Oxon. II. 695.

[3] '1648' being an error of the press in the title-page of the revised edition. See Mayor's Appendix to the *Life of M. Robinson* (1856), p. 158.

of them in a volume not unlike [Eachard's] *Speculum Crape-gownorum*, 'their ordinary Cant is, *Beloved, we read in the Word, that the Apostles went up together, one did not go before the other; there was no Precedency amongst them, Beloved; and therefore it's clear, that there was no Prelacy in those days: And again we read, that honest* Paul, (they never call him St. *Paul*, because he never swore the Solemn League and Covenant) *left his Cloak at* Troas: *Why, Sirs, you see plainly from this Text, that* Paul *had not a Gown but a Cloak, for says the Text, he left his Cloak, it does not say that he left his Gown, never a Gown had that precious Man to leave, Beloved, and therefore you may be sure he was no Prelate; for, they false Lowns, have no Cloaks but Gowns.'* (*The Scotch Presbyterian Eloquence; or, the Foolishness of their Teaching discovered, &c.*, 2nd ed. with additions, London, 4to. 1693, pp. 60, 61, and 16mo. 1786, p. 80.)

June 3, 1681. 'Whereas severall under-Graduates, and Batchelers of Arts, have of late neglected to wear such gowns, as by Order and Custom are proper for their rank and standing in the Universitie, whereby the comon distinction of Degrees is taken away, uppon which have followed manye and great in-conveniences: It was this day in Consistorie resolv'd, order'd, and decreed, by the V. Chan., with the consent of the Heads of Colleges, whose names are underwritten, that none residing in the University, under the Degree of Master of Arts, shall hereafter, upon any pretence whatsoever, be allowed to appear publickly, either in or out of Colleges, in mourning gowns, or gowns made after that fashion, or any other, but what by order and custom of the Universitie belongs to their Degree and standing : And that if any shall presume after the feast day of St. Barnabas, next following the date of this Decree, to act contrary to the tenor of it, he shall be proceeded against, and punished with all the severitie, that such disobedience and contumacie will deserve.

Dr Gower, V. Chan.

Sr Tho. Page.	Dr Blythe.
Dr Beaumont.	Dr Peachell.
Dr Spencer.	Dr Saywell.
Dr Eachard.	Dr Brady.
Dr James.	Mr Balderston[1].'

To one of these heads, Dr John Eachard[2], of Katherine-hall, was ascribed a pamphlet printed in 1682, the title of which points to some clerical fashion of the tory clergy of the day. ' *Speculum Crape-Gownorum*, or a Looking-Glass for the Young Academicks, new Foyl'd, *with Reflections on Some of the late Highflown Sermons.* To which is added, *An Essay towards a Sermon of the Newest Fashion.* By a Guide to the Inferiour Clergie.—*Ridentem dicere Verum Quis Vetat?*—Loudon [*sic*], *Printed for* E. Rydal, 1682,' 4to. pp. 34, in the library of Queens' coll., Camb., ' P. 35. (15).' The bulk of this pamphlet is little else but

---

[1] Dyer's *Privileges*, I. 336, 337, where there is a misprint 'morning gowns.'

[2] Dr R. Watt, however, in *Biog. Brit.*, ascribes the pamphlet (which he calls '*Speculum*... or an Old Looking-glass new foyl'd,' &c.) to Milton's nephew, *John Phillips.*

a reproduction of the anecdotes and satirical hits in Eachard's '*Grounds and Occasion for the Contempt of the Clergy and of Religion considered,*' which he printed in 1670. A specimen of one of the parallel passages common to the two will be found in the notes at the end of the present compilation.

It had been customary, a few years earlier, for persons who had taken no degree to wear a mourning-gown (or else a fellow-commoner's gown) on the occasion of their admission *ad practicandum in Medicina uel Chirurgia. Bedel* Buck's *Book* ap. *Senate-house Ceremonies*, Wall-Gunning, 1828, p. 199 *n.*

The *mourning-gown* worn at both universities by Masters of Arts (and at Cambridge with the mourning cap) is represented by Loggan (1670—85) as having long full pudding-sleeves pleted round the wrist.

The following passages in Eachard's pamphlet relate to the clerical fashion of *Crape* gowns :—

SPECULUM CRAPE-GOWNORUM. *Part* I., 1682. *P.* 1.—'The Nation is so overstocked with *Crape Gowns*, that 'tis impossible but that in such a number there must be failings among them, subject to great Remark and Observation : An ill Omen of sick Divinity when it comes to be mantled in the shrouds appropriated for the dead. Now these men in Crape, as they are generally young, so they are generally very highly conceited.' *Pp.* 22—23.—'However they will get into Orders, come what will of it, though perhaps they understand neither their message nor their business. For some are hugely in love with the new Title of a Priest, or Minister; others fancy that a long Crape Gown, and Cassock is a handsome garment, though it be in the Winter, and never paid for. But if they get but a Scarf about their necks, by virtue of a Chaplainship in some Noble Family, then how big they look in an English Bookseller's Shop! for the Latin ones they seldom haunt, as being out of their sphear. From thence they cluster to the Coffee-House, there to order the Government, and rail against the

Dissenters, men of far more understanding than themselves, and shew an equal composition of discretion, learning, and charity, of each two drams; their discretion in medling with those things that nothing [p. 22] concern them, their learning in the management of their Arguments, and their charity in the continual invectives against they know not who themselves, and of whom they know no more by due proof, but that they are their fellow Christians. 'Twas a happy invention for the Crape Gown Men this setting up of Coffee-Houses; For to drink in Taverns was scandalous, to be seen in an Alehouse more unbeseeming; but to sit idling away their time in a Coffee-House, like the Disciples of *Italy and Mahomet*, till it be time to go to farthing *Lantra-ton*[1] with a young Gentlewoman, that's employment without the verge of reprehension: Especially if they can be heard to rail loud enough, like the Popes white Boys[2], against Heresie, Schism, and Fanaticism. But what's become of *Rome*, and the so much exclaim'd against *Babylon?* Those are Airy motions now, *Fanaticism* and *Dissenterism* is the mode now, and as they are modish in their Habits, they think it more convenient to be modish in their Sermons. Besides the Papists are a sort of cunning Fellows, they argue shrewdly, they dispute Philosophically and Metaphysically. And there be many knotty points in controversie between them and the Church of *England*, which cost King *James*, Archbishop *Laud*, and several others, much pains and labour in those days to refute, and of late have put Bp. *Gunning*, Bp. *Barlow*, and Dr *Stillingfleet* to look to their Hits: And therefore our *Crape Gown* men think it more convenient to let them alone, than to betray their folly and their ignorance. But for the *Fanaticks*, they are more easily dealt with: 'Tis but going into a Pulpit and calling a man *Fanatick*, and he's presently confuted with a jerk; 'tis but calling a *Dissenter Schismatick;* 'tis but calling *Religion Division*, and there's an end of the business. The *Observator's* learn'd half Sheets come easily at a penny a piece; but *Grotius's* Works will cost Four [p. 23] Pounds odd mony, and that

---

[1] *Lanterloo* is a game at cards mentioned says Strutt (*Sports and Pastimes*, p. 335) in *the Complete Gamester* (1734). In the inventory of a Lady's property, the *Tatler*, n°. 245 (Nov. 2. 1710), Steele mentions 'an old nine-pence bent both ways by *Lilly* the almanack maker for luck at langterloo." *Lanturlu* (fr.) nonsense. Perhaps the word before us is the name of a game formed from *l'entretien*, conversation.

[2] 'Could he have done as the damsel that we read of in Acts 16. did, to wit, fill his master's purse with his badness, he had certainly been his *white-boy*.' Bunyan's *Life and Death of Mr Badman*. 1680. (ed. *Offor*, ch. IV. Works III. 615. *b.*)

will go far in a new *Crape Gown*, and a narrow brim'd Hat, with a Perriwig to boot.   And therefore who would not chuse a lazie Coffee-drinking Life with the pleasure of good Company, and suffer themselves to be deluded back to the vomit of Popery, though to their own destruction, than undergo the labour of a studious Life, and improving themselves in the soundness of that Doctrine which they outwardly profess.'

'SPECULUM CRAPE-GOWNORUM, The Second Part.   Or a Continuation of *Observations* and *Reflections* Upon the Late *Sermons* Of some that would be thought *Goliah's* for the *Church* of *England*.   By the same *Author*.   London: *Printed for* R. Baldwin, 1682,' pp. 1—40.   In a Dialogue between *Priestlove* and *Meryweather*.   P. 3.—'In so saying, you dishonour the whole Society of the *Crape-Gown* Order of D.D's and B.D's, and the more inferior sort of Rectors and Vicars, who have now undertaken to be the State Physitians themselves.   And do you think that Applications of *Bow Church* Sermons, *Guild-hall* Sermons, Assize Sermons, and Anniversary Sermons are not much more wholesome for the present distempers of the State than the *Euphorbicum* and *Cantharides* of the *Observator* and *Heraclitus?* [p. 4] *Priestl.* Both Applications may be good in their kinds.

Mery. Oh Sir, but the *Levites* pretend their Licences from Heaven, which th' other can never lay claim to: So that the other are meer Intruders; and whether the *Levites* do not practice beyond their Skill and Commission is much to be question'd.'

Priestlove complains (p. 11) how in the meeting-houses 'while the Minister is in the Pulpit, there you shall see a company of People, Young and Old, Rich and Poor,...their Hats pull'd over their Eyebrows, with their Pens, and their Books, and their Blotting-Papers all so busily employed, as if they were so many men copying of News-Letters, and this in such a strange Ethiopic Character, that no-body can tell what they Write; They may be setting down their last Weeks Gains and Expences for ought I know.   Nay, I saw one so wedded to his Hat, that after the Minister was in his last Prayer, he would not stir it from his Head, til he had concluded what he had to Write, wiped his Pen, screw'd his Inkhorn, fix'd his Blotting-Paper, clasp'd his Book, and put it in his Pocket: and by that time the Minister had almost done.'

Meryweather, the dissenter, while admitting the impropriety of the posture in question retaliates (p. 12) upon the Churchman by telling 'ye of another Indecency which I take to surpass yours, from which, I can except no Parish-Church within the Lines of Communication; and which I look upon to be the mischief of Pews, not us'd in other Reformed Churches; and that is the hideous noise and clatter in the time of

Divine Service. For it behoves Mr *Sexton*, or Mrs *Sextoness*, to have a vigilant eye that day, knowing that *Christmas* will come: And the greater the reputation of the Minister that Preaches that day, the worse it fares with mortal Ear and disturb'd Devotion. At one end of the Church come in Two or Three Women, and then perhaps in the midst of the *Absolution, slap-slap-slap;* by and by come in Three or four men together, and then 'tis, *Our Father which art in Heaven, slap-slap-slap:* and if the lock be a little refractory, then three or four *slaps* more into the bargain. By and by comes a whole shole of Slugabeds, and then 'tis, *We beseech ye to hear us good Lord; slap here, and slap there, slap there, and slap here; slap* a that side, and *slap* a this side ; *slap-slap-slap.* Anon come in two or three gay Peticoats, then upstarts Mrs *Ginglekey* from her Hasock, opens this Pew, that Pew, and then 'tis *Lord encline our hearts, &c.* Slap here, and slap there: And there is no end of *Slapping* all the whole Prayer-time; as if the Pew dores had been ordain'd to supply the place of Organ Responsories; a confusion that would not be endur'd at a common Musick-meeting.

Priest. This is so customary, that no-body minds it; and besides it may be very advantageous to keep people from falling asleep.

Mery. Then keep your Dores open while Prayers are done, and *slap* 'em in Sermon-time.

Priest. But how will you help it?

Mery. Nay, look you to that: I am sure 'tis a very great Indecorum. Go to the *Observator* and *Heraclitus*, they are wise men, perhaps they'l advise you to Oil your Locks every *Saturday* night, and line your Pew-dore with Cony-skin-Fur [p. 13]. But I'le tell you of a greater inconvenience than this, and that is the Translation of *Hopkins* and *Sternhold*. I may call it a Common Nuisance to the Service of the Church; a Translation (to use Mr *Abraham Cowley's* expression) that hath *revil'd* David *worse than* Shimei.'

This is certainly much in the vein of Eachard's *Contempt of the Clergy.* In the latter part of the pamphlet is a critique by *Meryweather* on certain quotations from the then Authorized Version of the 'singing psalms,' and from some assize sermons, panegyrics, &c.

Priestlove rejoins (p. 14) 'All this is nothing, the people will sing; and should you bring in new ones, they will say we are bringing in Popery.

Mery. This, indeed, is the common *Crape-Gown* excuse: Much like what was alleadg'd in the Council of *Trent*, that no alteration in Divine-worship was to be made, tho' for the better, for fear of intimating a fallibility before. But I hope our young *Crape-Gowners* are better taught at *Sam's Coffee-house* than so; or else they keep their *Sanhe-*

drims there to little purpose. But there is another reason, these Gentlemen are so addicted to Haranguing, that they have no time to spend in
mending *Psalms;* as if the *gingling* of an Alamode Sermon were the
only Musick that *pierced* Heaven.........another thing is this too, your
Crape-Gown men sit musing i' th' Vestry over the Churchwarden's
Half-pint (p. 15) till the beginning of the last Stave of all; and so never
hearing the Old, what should they concern themselves with a New-
Translation?'

Another abuse mentioned is the '*Church-Huzzaing*, or Hum-hum-
ming in the Church as a mark of approbation from the congregation at
'a Sembrief rest' after a brilliant point in the sermon, 'in so much that
you would even admire the Bells don't ring backward of themselves.'

I have not room to quote further: but these pamphlets deserve to
be reprinted with J. Eachard's works.

In answer to the latter part of the *Speculum* appeared

'CONCAVUM CAPPO-CLOACORUM; or, A View in Little of the Great
Wit and *Honesty* contain'd under a Brace of *Caps*, and wrap'd up in the
Querpo-Cloak of a *Phanatick*. In some Reflections on the Second
Part of a late *Pamphlet*, intituled, *Speculum Crape-Gownorum*, being *A
Dialogue* between *True-man* and *Cappo-cloak-man*. By an *Honest Gent.*
and a *true Lover* of all such. London: Printed for *Benj. Tooke*, at the
Ship in St *Paul's* Churchyard, 1682,' pp. 1—70.

This pamphlet contains *inter alia* an account (p. 34) of the slovenly
and irreverent manner among 'the Saints' of sitting round with their
elbows on the Lord's Table. 'The Minister after he hath drank gives
it to the next, and he to the next, and so it goes round the Table, and
when it is drank off, he that is to drink fills it again.'

There are several references to the 'Phanatical Habit' of the time,
the long close (or *querpo*) cloak fastened in front with small buttons, and
the skull-cap such as is seen in S. Clark's *English Martyrologie;* the
Lives of English Divines (1652; ed. 3, 1677, which is ridiculed by
Eachard, *Contempt of the Clergy*, 1670, p. 87, and the parallel passage of
Speculum Crape-Gownorum, I. 20, where [1682] the ridicule is softened
down).

Thus *True-man* says, 'Consider them, say you; I will put on twice
as many Caps as the famous Night-cap-Brother *T. Goodwin* ever wore,
but I will surely consider them.'

'*True-man.* Well met, Neighbour, What in *Querpo?* I cannot
but admire how well those *Caps* and the pretty *Apes-cloak* becomes you,
upon my Reputation, I cannot but look on you, you'r so spruce to day.

Cappo-cloak-man. Why? what ail you to stare so? did you never
see one in such a Dress before?

True-man. No truly, not very often : For that Dress was out of fashion (I thank God) before I was capable of taking notice of it.

Cappo-cloak-man. I should thank God that it was as much in fashion as ever it was. For I cannot but honour the precious remains of those glorious times, when the Saints enjoyed their Priviledges to the height ; (*i. e.*) *When they bound their Kings in chains, and their Nobles in Fetters of Iron,* even according to the very Letter : when we kept *Sabbaths* to the Lord, but no *Holy-Days:* and when our holy *Fasts and Prayers* were always answered with the next days *Feast upon the good things of the Wicked,* which the Lord was pleased to send us, by those precious wayes and methods of his own chusing, (as one of our Brethren did then well call them) *viz.* those which the Profane call *Sequestration, Confiscation, Plundering,* and *Decimation.*

True-man. Well, I cannot but think that a Gown and Cassock, and a Canonical-Girdle, is a much more grave, solemn, decent, and honourable Habit for a Clergy-man.

Cappo-cloak-man. I cannot help your thoughts, but to tell you the truth (which is not our common method) I have not heartily loved *Gowns, &c.* since Dr. *J. O.* [John Owen] then Vice-chancellor of *Oxford,* did so zealously and learnedly declaim against them, as *rags of Popery.* Oh, that precious man, whose very name is enough to sanctifie the Prophane Title of *Dean!* Had you but seen with what earnestness he *paid off the Whore of Babylon,* how he laid himself forth with all his might upon her, and stript her from all her rags, you could not but have been willing, not only to have put off your *Gown,* but *your Breeches too,* rather than have complied with those *Sons of that Whore, the Papists,* in any Garment that they wear. Oh, I can never forget that most precious Speech as long as I have a day to live !

True-man. Hold, Neighbour, hold. Don't be too much transported with the remembrance of that glorious Dispensation. How can any man but be abundantly satisfied with such an eloquent Oration, *that the Gown, &c. is the mark of the Beast?* But you seem not only to have a dislike to the *Gown* in general, but to the *Crape-Gown* in particular. Now several of those Gentlemen you have a fling at in your Book (I believe) never wore a Crape-Gown in all their Lives ; and I never read that *Crape-Gowns* were the particular fashion amongst Papists ; and therefore you would do very well, either to get the Learned Doctor to make another Speech, (which if you can get him to be *Dean of Christ-Church* again, I doubt not but he will readily do) particularly against *Crape-Gowns;* or else to give us in short your particular Reasons against them.

Cap-cloak-man. Why—now I think on't—It hath always been the privilege of our Party, to do things for which we can give no reason. Ask me for Reason? Don't you know that we have nothing to do with Reason, nor ever had, nor ever will have? therefore reason me no more reason, for if you do, I'll be gone.

True-man. Not so hasty, Neighbour, stay a little, I pray you. I beg your Pardon, that I was not so well acquainted with the priviledges of you *Army-Saints, and your Chaplains;* and do assure you, that it was not in any derogation to your dear Priviledges, but for my own satisfaction, that I gave you this trouble.

Cap-cloak-man. Well, well, if it be for your own Instruction, do you see, I shall give you some satisfaction in this weighty matter.

Why—first, your *Crape-Gown* is too light, and that (you know) though it may do well enough for a Sister, yet is not to be endured in a substantial-grave-brother. For (mark ye me) Lightness and Gravity do no more agree than Light and Darkness.

Then, Secondly, your *Crape-Gown* may be seen thorough; and of all things in the world, we Saints hate the Wicked should see thorough us: for as it is well hinted, *Crape-Gown. part* 2. *p.* 26. since neither the Piety of *David,* nor the Prudence of *Solomon,* could keep them from falling so fouly as they did with Women, how do we know but it may be any of our Cases, and that we may not come off so sound as they did? Now then, what a great Folly, yea, I say, what a Madness is it for us to wear such a Garment through which our Imperfections may be utterly laid open to the Female Saints, and so our Persons be rejected as well as our precious Doctrines? yea, I say, our precious Persons be rejected! would not this be a very great madness—yea—and no small folly?

Thirdly, The main cause why *our Sober party* do not love *Crape-Gowns,* may be this, that to wear them would be an intrenchment upon our Christian Liberty; for you know the Fashion came up in obedience to the late Act for the Improvement of Woollen-Manufactures, there being no other Woollen-stuff so cool and fit for Summer as Crape[1].'

[1] In the fly-leaf of a copy of W. Warner's Albion's England, 1612, is a fragment of the draft of some dedicatory verses or the like:

'his name
Now yours cant die as long as Balshams stone
Shall stand on ground or Peters Chaire be knowne.
　　　　　　　my wit
Is meane and yet my meanes is lesse than it.
Great Sir. If't be yr. will I shall be glad
To weare his Mourning-vest; If not, be sad.'
In the first instance *gowne* stood for *vest.*

The *gowns* in Loggan do not differ much from those now worn at the universities, except in length, being truly and statutably *talares*. Those of the Commissary, of graduates in law and medicine, and of the esquire Bedells, have apparels (*paruras*) of fur on the sleeves and hem, the noblemen's and fellow-commoners' of lace.

About 1720 the tory clergy only wore the M.A. gown away from the university; others wore pudding-sleeves. See p. 36.

The first of the *Orders and Regulations* of 1750 provided that 'Fellow-commoners who take degrees, and such as enter into fellows' commons after they have taken any degree, shall wear the proper habit of such degree.

'Bachelors of arts shall provide themselves with gowns made of prunello, or princes stuff.

'II. Every fellow-commoner shall immediately provide himself with his proper gown,' &c.

It appears from the *Portrait of the Founder* in the Fitzwilliam Museum (*North Gallery*, No. 17), painted by Wright of Derby, that lord Fitzwilliam, when a fellow-commoner of Trinity-hall in 1764, wore over his blue coat, with gold buttons, a *pink gown* with pink strings, trimmed and the sleeves laden with *gold lace*. When the regulations were made 'they were not aware,' as the author of *Strictures on Discipline* in 1792 observes (p. 28), 'that...a coxcomb may flutter in a black coat as well as a red one.'

The following note is borrowed from *Notes and Queries*, 2nd S., VIII. 75.

'The slit in the sleeve of the Cambridge B.A. gown was by sufferance, and for the convenience of dining.... No B. A. would, in days of yore (had the Proctor been of his college), have appeared without gown looped at the elbow either in hall or at chapel. The person to whom I have alluded was the originator of a move which permitted all undergraduates to wear the square cap as at present. Up to that date (probably about 1770 [1769, see above, p. 511]), some of the colleges used "the Monmouth cap" [in shape such as the round cap of LL.D or M.D.] till the undergraduate took his B.A. degree. This explains the allusion in the *Gradus ad Cantabrigiam,*

> "My head with ample *square cap* crown,
> And deck with hood my shoulders." '

(From a Paraphrase of Horace, *Carm.* III. 30, by *Kit Smart*, about 1745, quoted in the article *B. A.*).

A sleeveless gown, called a *curtain* and other opprobrious names, was worn by the undergraduates of St John's, Pembroke, Christ's, Gonville and Caius, Corpus Christi (Bene't), S. Mary Magdalene, Emmanuel, and Sidney Sussex, until the year 1834, or 1835[1].

If the Cambridge undergraduates' caps in old times were 'frightful things,' the Oxford commoners' gowns still merit some such appellation, though they have scarce better title to that of 'gowns' than the Paris gown, which may be seen depending from the shoulders of many a Belgian *curé*.

An undergraduate wrote thus in 1790 from Trinity college, Oxon. :

[1] See the Note on this passage.

> Behind our gowns (black bombazeen)
> Are seen two *leading strings*, I ween,
> To teach young Students in their course,
> They still have need of Learning's Nurse
> To stay their steps.

Mr G. V. Cox has recorded in his *Recollections*, p. 413, an attempt made at Oxford in 1857, when a statute was moved, unsuccessfully, to alter the commoners' gowns. He says that 'such a fuss about dress has not probably occurred since the olden days, when the new-made masters of Arts, while keeping (as it was called) their Regency at the Act, were fined if they did not present themselves in a sort of half-boots, *ocreae.*'

Among the laity, old fashions in male apparel have been preserved by livery-servants, who were wearing their masters' cast-off suits of a fashion last past at the time when the style of servants' dress was fixed. Among the clergy, the bishops have done the same, as being unwilling to sanction a departure from decorum. Though with them the priest's coat or CASSOCK has shrunk into a gremial or apron, it has never been entirely disused by the English clergy[1]. At the universities and with masters of public schools, as well as with the scholars of Christ's hospital, it has continually been worn; and among the parish clergy it was only disused for a few years. The occasions of its use at Cambridge may be seen in *Senate-house Ceremonies* (Wall-Gunning, 1828), pp. 175, 177, 179, 182. Dr Eachard writes of the poor clergy in 1670

---

[1] See *Canon* 74 of 1603, as above p. 467.

as considering it part of their ordinary dress. The 'curates,' in Fielding's novels about 1750, constantly wear it; and of late years it is becoming again more usually worn. The portraits of· *Dr Syntax* [by W. Coombe, 1741, †1823] with which we are familiar, shew that in his time, 1810, it was not always worn by clergymen travelling.

In the reign of George III. we find some signs of reviving attention to the particulars of clerical dress. The writer of one pamphlet, *An Admonition to the Younger Clergy*, &c. London : Printed for *John Rivington*, at the *Bible and Crown* in *St. Paul's Church-Yard*, 1764, enforces (pp. 15—17) the duty of circumspection in the matter. Another is more explicit in *A Letter of Free Advice to A Young Clergyman:* Ipswich, *Printed by* E. Craighton *and* W. Jackson,' &c. 1765 : on pp. 15, 16; 'See that your Church, Books, and Vestments be kept clean, and in order : A dirty Church, a filthy Surplice, and a tattered Hood, are the great marks of Indifference and Disrespect to that Being, whom we meet to worship,—Do no Office in the Church upon any Occasion without a *Band*, nor on Sundays, without a *Gown* and *Cassock*, if your Distance, and the Weather will permit; nor think it a trifling Correctness to keep a *Beaver-Hat* and *Rose* to wear with your Habit. In all Ages of the World, and in more than one Profession, certain Vestments have been constantly used in Office, an awful Ensign of the Dignity and Importance of it.

'In your Undress, let me advise you to keep to

that *Colour*, which Custom and good Men have appointed, as most suitable to your Station, and not run into *motley Mixtures*. A dangling Crape Hat-band from a Gold-laced Hat makes not a more ridiculous Appearance, than *white Waistcoat* and *white Stockings* on a Clergyman: and after all, for want of Ruffles you will not be taken for a Man of a higher, if of so high a Rank as you really are, of yourself. So that you may lose and certainly can gain nothing by affecting the Lay-man.—Wear always a *full Wigg*, as well out as in your Habit; and not *one* that *scarce covers your ears:* the latter looks, at best, as if it had been in a Fray, and came off with no inconsiderable Loss. And if this suggests such ludicrous Ideas, how ridiculous must the Owner himself appear! Neither wear your own Hair, till Age has made it venerable; or if you do, let Cleanliness alone be your Hair-dresser: For the modern *Frisures* are but preternatural Excrescencies, for want of a due Circulation of the Understanding; and can at best but make us *Petit-Maitres;* a Character composed of the Affectation of both Sexes so blended together, that we see not the distinctive Qualities of either.—Neither come into that *Jewish* Fashion of wearing a skirting of Beard round the Face; in *them* it may be proper enough, but with us, Openess of Countenance is the Characteristic of an ingenuous Mind.'

'*An Essay towards Pointing Out In a Short and Plain Method* the *Eloquence* and *Action Proper for the* Pulpit ; *Under which Subject is considered The* Miseries *and* Hardships *of the* Inferiour Clergy *of*

England *in General, and* London *in particular, Together with a Variety of* Remarks *and* Anecdotes *incident to the* Subject : *And upon such of our* City-Divines
as have made Themselves Popular (or *truly* Admired)
by their Abilities in Pulpit-Oratory. *By* Philagoretes,
&c. &c. *London :* Printed for J. Fletcher...Mr. Merrill
in *Cambridge ;* and Mr Fletcher in *Oxford.* 1765.'

The writer censures ' the *Boyish* and *Absurd* DRESS
of the YOUNGER CLERGY, as to CURLED HAIR, or
SCRATCH WIGS, WHITE STOCKINGS and LEATHER
BREECHES, with a long Train of ET CETERAS[1],'—
having previously written more at length on the topic.
(pp. 39—42).

' What Notion or Opinion can a Congregation possibly have of a
CLERGYMAN, who is quite careless in the Week-Time, even in his
DRESS, (as to CURLED HAIR, and CLOATHS and STOCKINGS of an
improper colour,) how very much unlike one he affects to appear! and
on a *Sunday*, instead of a *grave* and *decent* Grizzle Wig handsomely
combed out, comes in a short *Shock*, (or sometimes *shocking*) Head of
Hair consisting of *one round Curl* only, and *that* so *plaistered* and
powdered out, (not a single Hair of which must be touched by the filthy
Hands of *good Mr. Philipps* or the *Surplice*) that he looks more as if he
was going to a *Ball* than to the *sacred Place* of GOD's *Worship*, to
teach the great, aweful, and important Duties of Religion, whereby his
Congregation may be enabled to become better Men, and better Christians.   The Author is really very sorry to be, or even to be thought,
ludicrous on this serious and solemn SUBJECT.   But—RIDICULUM *acri*,
Fortius & melius, &c.—

The CLERGY of the ESTABLISHED CHURCH would do well to
observe the DISSENTING MINISTERS as to this Point, how little
culpable, even the *younger* Part of them are, comparatively with the
younger Part of ours ; and no doubt, the Reason is, of it's being given
to them in such *strict* Charge by their ELDERS or PASTORS at the
Time of their *Ordination*.—That an *Impropriety* and *Indecency* of DRESS

[1] p. 93.

abounds too much amongst the *former*, especially the *younger* Part, is too plain by daily Experience, in *Country* as well as *Town;* but much more in the *last.*—How strict and careful the *Canons* of our CHURCH are in this Point is well known, tho' not so well practiced : But if the *short Cassock* and *Rose* are looked upon as too stiff and formal for this *polite* and *delicate* Age ; is there no *Medium* between them for our *younger* CLERGY, especially, and their *present* DRESS ? Whose Province it is more particularly to take Cognizance of and correct this Error (for an Error most certainly it is, as indeed every Thing is so, even such seemingly minute Circumstances, which tend to discredit RELIGION and the CLERGY) does not become the Author to say : But this he is very sure of, that if the BISHOPS would be pleased to take this Matter into Consideration at their *Visitations*, and to exhort earnestly the ARCHDEACONS to do so too at theirs, and to appoint *Rural* DEANS throughout their respective *Dioceses* to inspect the Lives of the CLERGY, as well in Regard to their DRESS, as their *Moral Behaviour*, we should soon see a very sensible Difference ; no less to their own Honour and Satisfaction, than to the Credit and Ornament of RELIGION and the CLERGY in general. The Story of the late Dean PRIDEAUX upon this Point is perhaps not so well known as it should be, and therefore the Author begs leave to lay it before the Reader : The DEAN'S great Learning is sufficiently known : As to his Natural Temper and Disposition, he was honest, blunt and warm. " As he was upon an ARCHI-DIACONAL Visitation in his Diocese, he had had a previous Hint or two given him by the superior CLERGY in Age as well as Preferment, of this *Impropriety* and *Indecency* of DRESS, which had crept in among some of them, and accordingly they being pointed out to him, the worthy *Disciplinarian* was determined, if possible, to crush it at once. He called for a Glass of Wine at Table, and drank to one of them as he sat at the Bottom opposite to him, saying, " Mr. CHURCH-WARDEN your Health!" upon which a *Doctor* that sat next to him, pretended as tho' the DEAN knew nothing of what had passed before, said "Mr. DEAN I beg pardon for interrupting you going to drink, for that Gentleman is not a CHURCH-WARDEN, but a CLERGY-MAN."—"A CLERGYMAN! impossible, *Doctor!* I should have hoped that no one would have presumed to come before me in a DRESS so unsuitable to the SACRED CHARACTER."—"The DEAN took no further Notice at present ; but before he went away, made an handsome Apology to the *Gentleman*, for his seeming Warmth ; which had so good and happy Effect upon him, and the Rest, that they forthwith put the DEAN'S Admonitions and Advice into Practice." Thus, as *Solomon* finely and justly observes, " Words fitly spoken

L. B. E.   34

(and seasonably apply'd) are like Apples of Gold in Pictures of Silver."—The Author now returns to his main SUBJECT again, by asking a few more Questions. Are the *Turns* which are given away at ST. PAUL'S, the TEMPLE CHURCH, the FOUNDLING-HOSPITAL, and MERCERS CHAPELS, calculated to promote *true* PULPIT ORATORY?'

Scarlet gowns were worn on 'scarlet days' by doctors in all faculties (excepting those of divinity for such times as they were bound to wear scarlet copes, as will be seen below) on Nov. 5, Christmas-day, Easter-day, May 29, Trinity Sunday, at the proclamation of Barnwell (or Midsummer) fair, and of Sturbridge fair, on Commencement Sunday, Commencement day, and the anniversary of the Sovereign's Accession[1].

The *Scarlet days* at present are Easter-day, Holy Thursday, Whitsun-day, Trinity Sunday, Commencement Sunday, Commencement-day, Michaelmas-day, Commemoration of Benefactors, Christmas-day.

On Ash-Wednesday, being a *Litany-day*, doctors and noblemen wear their robes, and the proctors their congregation ruffs.

The Oxford Statute, IX. iv. § 2, provides that Congregation may dispense *ut Magister Cumulatus, pro Habitu coccineo, nigro et solito, post peracta praesentationis solennia, uti possit.*

That the SURPLICE (*superpelliceum*, the robe worn over the garment of skins *pelliceum, pelisse*) was put on over the head, and open only for a few inches at the chest, may be seen from Loggan's University Costumes of the latter part of the 17th century. After-

[1] *Senate-House Ceremonies*, Wall-Gunning. 1828, pp. 60, 68, 80, 101, 108, 109, 118—121, 129.

wards the surplice, like the Cambridge doctor's 'cope,' was split down the front out of slovenliness, or else for the sake of the wearers' wigs.

The STOLE was discontinued after the Reformation, and, unfortunately, was never restored until the revival of doctrine, under the 'tractarians,' had produced cravings for a revival of external ornaments. I have heard it said, that about the year 1838 there was only one shop in England where Anglican stoles could be had,—French's at Leicester.

In most instances *black* stoles have been introduced, probably because people were accustomed to the broad doctor's or chaplain's scarf. (See pp. 500, 501, 516.)

One of the medallions on the title-page of '*S.* Austin *imitated: or Retractations and Repentings in Reference unto the late* Civil *and* Ecclesiastical Changes *in this* Nation. *In II Books By* John Ellis.' 1662, with the imprimatur of the chaplain of *Gul.* [i. e. Gilbert Sheldon] Ep. *Lond.* July, 1661, displays a bishop in cassock, rochet (with ruffles at neck and wrists, and a limp square cap on his head), giving absolution to a boy kneeling before him in a black gown. The bishop sits in a highbackt chair, and lays his right hand on the boy's zuchetto. He wears a doctor's scarf, which seems to shew that the *scarf took the place of the stole.* The reference to 'I Peter 3' below the picture relates probably to some interpretation of the 'harrowing of hell' bearing upon penal satisfaction, or spirits in prison. The other pictures represent the pardon of Shimei and of the Prodigal.

34—2

The *Spectator* of Oct. 20, 1714, No. 609, thus discourses on this topic. 'As I was the other Day walking with an honest Country Gentleman, he very often was expressing his Astonishment to see the Town so mightily crowded with Doctors of Divinity: Upon which I told him he was very much mistaken if he took all those Gentlemen he saw in Scarves to be Persons of that Dignity; for that a young Divine, after his first Degree in the University, usually comes hither only to show himself; and on that Occasion, is apt to think he is but half equipp'd with a Gown and Cassock for his publick Appearance, if he hath not the additional Ornament of a Scarf of the first Magnitude to intitle him to the Appellation of Doctor from his Landlady, and the Boy at *Child's*. Now since I know that this Piece of Garniture is looked upon as a Mark of Vanity or Affectation, as it is made use of among some of the little spruce Adventurers of the Town, I shou'd be glad if you would give it a Place among those Extravagancies you have justly exposed in several of your Papers: being very well assured that the main Body of the Clergy, both in the Country and the Universities, who are almost to a man untainted with it, would be very well pleased to see this venerable Foppery well exposed. When my Patron did me the Honour to take me into his Family (for I must own myself of this Order) he was pleased to say he took me as a Friend and Companion; and whether he looked upon the Scarf like the Lace and Shoulder-knot of a Footman, as a Badge of Servitude and Dependence, I do not know, but he was so kind as to leave my wearing of it to my own Discretion ; and not having any just Title to it from my Degrees, I am content to be without the Ornament.'

The frontispice of Symon Patrick's *Devout Christian Instructed*, &c., ed. 16, *London:* Printed for *J. Walthoe, Ja.* and *Jo. Knapton, R. Knaplock, R. Wilkin, D. Midwinter,* and *A. Ward, R. Bettesworth, J. Downing, R.* and *J. Bonwicke, R. Robinson, W. Mears, R. Gosling, W. Innys, B. Motte, T. Ward, S. Birt, D. Brown, M. Wyat,* and *C. Bowyer,* 1730, displays a remarkable interior of a church, looking eastward. Over the Altar, which is vested in a large white cloth, are the tables of the decalogue, surmounted by a cherub's head; on each side is an oblong slab similarly over-topped, and bearing, no doubt, the Lord's Prayer and the Apostles' Creed. The people all kneel on the marble pavement with no desks, (a few with books,) *extensis manibus.* The celebrant wears wig, bands, and chaplain's scarf, but appears *not to have changed his black gown after preaching.* While communicating the people he extends his left hand in benediction. The assistant while ministering the Chalice lays his right hand upon the head of the communicant. He wears wig, bands, surplice, and scarf. The Flagon does not stand upon the Altar. The Altar in many books of devotion of this and the earlier period stands either under a canopy or in a recess inaccessible from the ends, and deeper than Dr Bentley's *baldacchino* in Trinity Chapel. It usually has a super-frontal. That in an older picture, in Foxe's *Actes and Monuments*, of a Protestant service just at the time of the Reformation, has also two orphreys. Two immense Flagons stand on the ground near it. A Chalice and Paten on the Table itself. The frontispice of *Liturgia: seu Liber Precum Communium, et Administrationis Sacramentorum... Epistolae, Evangelia, et Psalmi inseruntur juxta* Sebastiani Castellionis *Versionem.* Editio septima, prioribus longe emendatior. *Londini,* Impensis *J. Bonwicke, C. Hitch* et *L. Hawes, E. Wicksted, Joan. Rivington, Jac. Rivington* et *J. Fletcher, W. Johnson, J. Richardson, S. Crowder* Soc. et *P. Davey* et *B. Law, T. Longman, T. Calson,* et *C. Ware,* 1759, bears the motto *Agite veneremur supplices, flexis ante Dominum Creatorem nostrum genibus.* PSAL. xcv. 6, and shews the interior of a church. In the foreground, on the north side is the Font; the congregation kneels on the pavement: no desks or seats. One gentleman of quality kneels on a round hassock, and has a book in his hand. One minister with gown, band, and skull-cap, kneels in the western pew of a 'three-decker.' Another in surplice and band above him. The pulpit has a sounding-board, a pendent cloth, and a plump cushion. The Holy Table is railed-in, no room being left, at least on the south side, for any one to stand. On it are placed two Flagons, a Chalice, and an Almsbason leaning against the wall. The words of the rubrics in this Latin version of our Common prayer, which relate to the position of the Celebrant are *Presbyter autem stans ad septentrionalem partem Mensae,* and *Quum Presbyter stans ante Mensam Domini*

*Panem et Vinum ita disposuerit, ut expeditius ac de-
:entius possit Panem frangere coram Populo, et Cali-
:em in manus sumere, dicit formulam Consecrandi
'rout sequitur.*

A frontispice to another of bishop Symon Patrick
of Ely's books, *A Book for Beginners: or, an Help to
Young Communicants,* ed. 13, 1695, depicts communicants kneeling at the Altar-rails. On the Altar stand
two Flagons and Chalices *with covers* and the Paten
veiled. The priest in surplice and hood stands *extensis manibus* diagonally at the north-west corner,
the book supported on a desk or cushion placed accordingly to his position. That it was thought in 1640
that the placing of the Table altar-wise was incompa-
tible with their last rubric before the Communion Office
(the North-side) is clear from the articles of the trial
of Dr Matthew Wren, bishop of Norwich and Ely
(Cobbett's *State Trials,* § 153. IV. col. 29). However,
bishop Andrewes and Laud seem not to have stood
at the side, but at the end, to judge from the position
of the cushions in the plan of their chapels; (Prynne's
Canterburies Doome, 1646, p. 122) at least for the
beginning of the service. Possibly up to the Prayer
of Consecration they may have taken the view of the
Privy Council in *Hebbert* v. *Purchas,* as bishop Cosin
said he did, (in reply to Rouse's *Article of Impeachment,* No. 2. *anno* 1640, *ap.* Cobbett's *State Trials,*
§ 152, Vol. IV. col. 23. The decision of the Privy
Council in *Martin* v. *Mackonochie,* as Mr Phillimore
reminds me, had nothing to do with the 'North-side'
rubric, but only with that immediately preceding the

Prayer of Consecration, and seemed to apply the words *standing before the Table* to the whole of that prayer). On the other hand, if we may judge from a sermon of prebendary Smart, for which he was pilloried as inveighing against his bishop, the puritan party would not have been much pleased with bishop Cosin if he had stood at the north *end* of the Altar. Thus he descanted in *A Sermon preached in the cathedrall chvrch of Dvrham, July* 7, 1628, *by* Peter Smart. *Psal.* 31. 7 *v.* 'I hate them that hold of superstitious vanities.' *Printed in the yeare* 1640. [Camb. Univ. Lib. 47. 5. 93.] *p.* 33, 'Our Communion table must stand as it had wont to doe in the midst of the quire: not at the east end, as farre as is possible fro the people, where no part at all of evening prayer is ever said, and but a peece of the morning, and that never till of late. Neither must the table be placed along from north to south, as the Altar is set, but from East to West as the Custom is of all reformed Churches: otherwise, the Minister cannot stand at the north side, there being neither side toward the North. And I trow there are but two sides of a long table, and two ends: making it square and then it will have foure sides, and no end, or foure ends, and no side at which any Minister can stand to celebrate.'

p. 36. 'The Lords table I say eleven years agoe was turned into an altar, and so placed, that the Minister cannot stand to do his office on the north side, as the law expressly chargeth him to doe, because there is no side of the table standing *Northward.*'

[Dr *John Cosin* was in 1624 prebendary of Durham.
—1628 joined in the prosecution of Peter Smart.—
1634 succeeded bishop Matt. Wren as master of
Peterhouse.—1640, Nov. 7, instituted dean of Peterborough ; Nov. 10, on Smart's petition is sequestrated
by the house of Commons for superstitious practices.
—16$\frac{40}{41}$, Mar. 15, is acquitted by the house of Lords,
Smart's counsel being 'ashamed' of his client.—1643
being among the deprived royalists he retires to Paris
and ministers to the protestant part of Q. Henrietta
Maria's household.—1660 dean, and then bishop, of
Durham, having been restored to Peterhouse for a
short time.]

It has been stated by correspondents to the *Guardian* newspaper in July 1873, that in 1814 bishop Law
of Chester consecrated standing before the midst of
the Altar ; and that bishop Maltby of Durham and
Chichester began the Liturgy at the north *side* (not
end) and afterwards passed to the midst.

In an illustrated Book of Common Prayer,—(of
which the standing title-page is ' *London,* printed by
John Bill, Christopher Barker, Thomas Newcomb, and
Henry Hills, Printers to the King's most Excellent
Majesty, *Anno Dom.* 1678. *Cum Privilegio*', but with
prayers for William and Mary), containing a portrait
of K. William, pictures of Guido Fawkes, of the
martyrdom of K. Charles I. and the Restoration of
his son, besides historical illustrations of the proper
offices, about sixty in all,—is a curious cut of a
clergyman in long cassock, short surplice ornamented
with lace at the sleeves and hem, and with a skull-

cap on his head, saying the litany at the foot of the Altar. He kneels *extensis manibus* on a cushion at the bottom of the two steps on which it is raised (in the body of the church, for all that one can see to the contrary), the people too kneel on the pavement behind him: a few also at the south end, looking with their faces towards the Altar, at a respectful distance. The Altar is vested with a fringed short frontal (or long super-frontal). On the middle of the Altar lies an open book at which the priest seems to be looking, but it is turned away from him, though at too great a distance and at a most inconvenient angle if to be used by one standing at the end of the Holy Table, or indeed anywhere except behind it at the north-east corner, or in front at the midst. There are no rails.

For a description of other engravings see notes at the end of this book.

The university COPE (*cappa, capa, pluviale*) is more full than the circular choral cope; more full, that is, even than the medieval cope which (like the medieval chasuble) was not so scanty as those of the modern Roman pattern. The Cambridge scarlet cope has an ermine hood, likewise somewhat full: there is also a narrow edging of ermine from the neck downwards rather lower than the height of the elbow. The history of this is clearly to be gathered from the costumes in the margin of Speed's map of Cambridge and Cambridgeshire early in the 17th century, and from Loggan's *habitus* towards its close. The doctors there do not wear copes fastened with a morse, nor open in front except so far as to allow the hands and forearm to be thrust out. This may also be seen in the portraits of 16th century doctors, now being removed into the hall of Peterhouse, and which in Fuller's time (*Hist. Camb.* 1655, p. 32), and till the present century, were panels in the parlour (*locutorium*) or Combination-room. Thus the strip of ermine (which is shown in all the pictures aforesaid) was the edging of the opening in front; and though the copes have been split down the front (with better excuse than that which we may allow to the rending of surplice-fronts) this has been preserved at its original length: another instance of the conservatism of the Cambridge tailors. The occasions when the university cope was worn may be gathered from the pages of *Senatehouse Ceremonies* (Wall-Gunning, 1828), pages 2, 3, 39, 59, 80-82, 115, 121, 175, 181, 183, 209, 215. These were as follows: By the regius professor and doctors of divinity at the *clerum* before the beginning of Michaelmas term; also by the preacher if a B.D. and candidate for the doctor's degree. By the vice-chancellor at the *magna congregatio* or 'black assembly'; on the Friday before SS. Simon and Jude (Oct. 28), when the aldermen, burgesses, and parishioners took oaths before him and the mayor in the chancel of S. Mary's church: also at the speech on the afternoon of Nov. 5 (Papists' Conspiracy). By D.D. on Nov. 5, at the sermon, and on the Accession, at the litany and sermon on Jan. 30 (Charles K. & M.) till after service, when they put on their scarlet gowns: and at the *clerum* on Ash Wednesday. By the regius professor at the graduation of bachelors in divinity on S. Barnabas (June 11), also when moderating the acts for the degree of B.D. At Commencement by commencing D.D. By B.D. or nobleman when presented to the vice-chancellor for the degree of D.D. It was also put on in the ceremony of admitting any person to that degree by mandate. According to bedel Buck's *Book*, 1665 (quoted above, p. 249), the vice-chancellor was to wear his cope, provided that he were a 'father' on the vepers or vespers of the commencement (*in uesperiis comitiorum*).

When queen Elizabeth visited Cambridge in 1564, she was received by the provost of King's 'with all his company standing in copes': afterwards in 'the King's College Church' (where 'the communion table ...stood north and south'), 'Mr Doctor Baker with all his company was in copyes,' and 'the Provost revested in a rich cope of needle-work,' and after they had gone into the Quire 'the Queen following, and going into her travys, under the canopy; and marvellously revising at the beauty of the chappel, greatly praised it, above all other in her realme. This song [a song of gladness in English] ended, the Provost began the *Te Deum* in English in his cope: which was solemnly sung in prick-song, and the organs playing. After that, he began even-song, which also was solemnly sung: every man standing in his cope.' On the Sunday 'when mattens were ended, every man repaired unto the Court gate to wait upon the Queen. All the Doctors, saving the Physicians, in their gowns of scarlet, as they went continually as long as the

Queen tarried.' They then went to the church *ad clerum.* 'Incontinently began the Letany. And after that, Mr. Andrew Perne D.D. [master of Peterhouse 1553—89] ready in his Doctors cope, was by the Bedells, brought to the pulpit, which stood over against her travis, which her Highness caused to be drawn open. And so, at the end of the stoole did sit downe, and was seene of all the people all the time of the sermon.

'The Preacher, after he had done his duty, in craving leave by his three curtesys, and so kneeling, stood up, and began his matter, having for his theme *Omnis anima subdita sit potestatibus supereminentibus.* About the midst of his sermon, her Majesty sent the Lord Hunsdon to will him to put on his cap: which he did unto the end. At which time, or he could get out of the pulpit, by the Lord Chamberlayn, she sent him word, that it was the first sermon that ever she heard in Latin; and she thought she should never hear a better. And then the quire sung in prick-song a song[1].'

It appears from the articles of impeachment of Dr Cosin (of Peterhouse) and his answers in 1640 that there were copes in use in Durham cathedral immediately before his consecration to that throne: one with the story of the Passion embroidered on it (on the 'hood' no doubt). He himself wore one of white satin without embroidery 'when at any time he attended the Communion-service[2].'

---

[1] Cooper's *Annals*, II. 182, 186, 167, 190—192.

[2] *Biog. Brit.* Kippis.

'Copes or vestments,' *i.e.* chasubles, are ordered for bishops and priests celebrants in the rubric of 1549, which is continued by the existing rubric. This was interpreted as applicable to all cases by the dean of arches (Sir Ro. Phillimore), but the privy council have since discovered that this is restricted by the 24th canon of 1603 to the use of a cope (not a vestment) on the chief festivals in cathedral and collegiate churches. Copes were used in Durham cathedral till 1779, when Warburton (then prebendary) complained of the heat. He is said to have thrown the cope off in a pet because it ruffled his full-bottomed wig. They continued to be worn on festivals a few years later[1]. Also at coronations. Since the judgment in the appeal Hebbert *v.* Purchas, copes have been restored in some cathedrals: but not (so far as I am aware) in any collegiate church. It is almost incredible that in the first instance the word *cope* should have been used strictly as the only vestment admissible for the celebrant (see J. H. Blunt and W. G. F. Phillimore's *Book of Church Law*, 1872, p. 95 *n.*). It appears from the use of the word in our university that the term was not restricted to the *pluuiale;* and it is also noteworthy that one name of the *cope* was '*casula* processoria[2].' Is it possible that permission was given by the rubric for poor parishes to use the red cope, which was left them if they could not afford a new chasuble (*casula, planeta,* or 'principal vestment')? It is evi-

---

[1] *Quarterly Review,* XXXII. 273, *Traditions and Custom of Cathedrals.* Mackenzie, E. C. Walcott, *ed.* 2. p. 47.

[2] See Scudamore's *Notit. Eucharistica.*

dent, from inventories of ornaments left in parish-churches by the reformation commissioners in 1566[1], that a red cope was frequently left, and in some cases converted into an altar frontal or *antependium :* a fact which in some measure accounts for the prevalence of red in Altar-cloths : crimson being at once a good wearing colour and the colour seasonable for the greatest number of Sundays in the English custom.

In the margin of Speed's maps of Cambridge (1610, &c.), one of the personages wears a vestment shaped like an unshorn chasuble, and a birretta.

The *congregation habit* of the proctors (according to *Wall-Gunning,* 1828, p. 15), is RUFFS (*camisiae*) with white hoods, to be worn on 'litany days.'

According to bedel Stokys' Book, in the middle of the sixteenth century, the bedells were to wear QUOIFS, and hoods, at the time of the oration at the examination of questionists in quinquagesima, when they were to bring heads and doctors 'through the Prese with their Staffs turned', *i.e.* with maces reversed to make way through the crowd.

---

[1] *English Church Furniture,* by E. Peacock, Esq. F.S.A. 1866. pp. 42, 47, 48, 49, 52 *bis,* 68, 75, 81, 92, 106, 114, 117, 130. It is mentioned p. 42 that we 'haue a cope in the churche, the wch wee are admitted [by the iniunc]tions to kepe for o͞r. mi'ster.' A *vestment* remained in one instance, p. 112. *Copes* were also made into pulpit cloths, pp. 89, 97 : *albes* were converted generally into surplices, also into Altar cloths, 29, 43 ; as sometimes were *vestments,* 65, 73.

APPENDICES.

A.   On a New Project for *Riding the Great Horse*.   [1700.]

B.   *Prideaux's University Reform*.   1715.

C.   *Serjeant Edmond Miller's Account* of *Cambridge* and *Trinity* College.   1717.

D.   *Whiston's Emendanda in Academia*.   1717.

E.   Lord *Macclesfield's* Memorial relating to the Universities. 1718.

F.   *Ri. Newton's Expence* of the University Education *Reduced*: and *Statutes of Hart Hall* (Hertford College).   1727–1747.

G.   *Diary of a Student at Trinity* College, *Cambridge*. 1793–1801.

APPENDIX A.

On a ·

New Project

for Riding

the

GREAT HORSE:

and other Exercises Physical and Mental
to be practised

in the

NEW 'ACCADEMY.'

[1700.]

Gutch, *Collectanea Curiosa*, Oxford, 1781. Vol. 2, pp. 24—35. No. VI. 'A Letter from a Friend of the *Universities* in reference to the new *Project* for riding the *Great Horse.*' MS., the greater part in Dr J. Wallis' hand, and probably composed by him on the threshold of the 18th century.

It appears that our present pronunciation of the word Academy was a French innovation on the more correct Académy.... Riding the Great Horse, singing, dancing, instrumental musick, mathematics, &c.... 'In our College (as larger Societies) every Tutor with his pupils is such a private College as what they complain for want of; whose business is (beside lectures and other publick exercises in the College at large) to instruct his pupils (in one or more classes as there is occasion) in his private chamber or other convenient place in the several parts of directing them what books to read for the purpose; explaining these authors to them; and taking account of their proficiency therein; inspecting their manners and conversation from time to time, and otherwise taking the care and oversight of them... Dancing, singing, playing on musick &c. (which be rather an hindrance than a promotion of other studies, as taking up the time which might otherwise be better employed) there is no cause to complain for want of teachers in the Universities, for there are dancing-masters, singing-masters, musick-masters &c. enough to be had to teach those who are desirous to learn; or if not in the Universities, at least in *London* ..

'I could give many instances in our Universities of a like nature with what they call private Colleges, or Clubs by voluntary agreements for particular parts of knowledge; and that there is no cause to complain for want of such. It is now almost fifty years ago that Mr *Staal* (a skilfull Chymist) made it his business in *Oxford* to instruct such as did desire it in the practise of Chymistry. That is, when six, eight or more persons (of the better quality amongst us) have agreed together for that purpose;

he would with them in a convenient place go through a whole course of Chymistry, and so with one company to another from time to time. And the like hath been continued ever since by Dr *Plot*, Mr *White* and others to this time. And a convenient Laboratory built for that purpose by the University, well furnished with furnaces and Utensils for that purpose. The like hath been done as to Anatomy by Dr *Musgrave* (while he was in *Oxford*) and others amongst us; who at the request of some persons agreeing to that purpose hath gone through a course of Anatomy for their particular information. And there seldom happens a publick execution of condemned persons but one or more bodies are privately dissected for that use. And at other times the like is performed on the bodies of other animals.

'The like was done as to Botanicks by Dr *Morrison* in the Physick Garden for the instruction of such as desire it in the nature of difference of herbs and other plants.......

'That Mathematicks are a good accomplishment for gentlemen or others is very true: But I wonder with what face it can be pretended (unless from great ignorance therein) that they are not to be learned in our Universities? When it is well known that within fifty or threescore years last past Mathematicks have been more improved in our Universities than for five hundred years before. 'Tis above fifty year since (upon the asswaging of our civil wars in England, and re-settling the University) Dr *Wallis* and Dr *Ward* (Professor of Mathematics in Oxford) beside other public lectures, have (in their private lodging) instructed Gentlemen and others therein (who have desired it) from time to time; some of whom have since been publick Professors therein. And the like hath been done by others (his successors) since Dr *Ward* was advanced to higher preferment. Beside which, Mr *Caswell* hath now for many years last past made it his business (and a good part of his livelyhood) to teach Mathematicks to such Gentlemen or others singly or by companies. And the like hath been done by some others; and will be so as there is occasion. And I think it not amiss here to set down Dr David *Gregory's* method therein who is at present the Savilian Professor of Astronomy in *Oxford*. [Gutch does not transcribe the Method, if it be given in the MS. 'Ex archivis Univ. Oxon. in Turre Scholar.'].......His Great Horse we had

rather want in our University than be troubled with it: which
would have more spectators than riders to the misspending of
time which might be better employed....I do not think it proper
that the publick should be charged with erecting Acáddemies
for each of these [Hunting, Hawking, and more useful manual
employments]; no more than for teaching to drink wine, ale,
and coffee...which rather stand in need of laws for restraint and
regulation than for encouragement. [The MS. concludes in
another hand.] The Universities are not enemies to exercises
of the body no more than of the mind; and in particular they
have a good esteem of riding the Great Horse as contributing to
a sure seat and graceful air on horseback....But &c.'

APPENDIX B.

Dean PRIDEAUX'S

LVIII Articles

for REFORMATION of the
UNIVERSITIES.

1715.

Dean *Humphrey Prideaux* of *Norwich* (author of
the *Connexion* of the Old and New Testament) wrote,
Nov. 26, 1715, to *Charles* viscount *Townshend*, principal secretary of state, certain Articles for the Reformation of the Universities.

He had lived seventeen years at Oxford [at Christ Church,
having been a pupil of *Busby*] but (he says) knew of Cambridge
'only by enquiry and hear-say.'

He regrets the neglect of episcopal visitations and also of
visitation of the universities. One was proposed in the time of
king *William* 'and the Lord Chancellor *Sommers* was for it;
but, the Lord Chief Justice *Holt* giving his opinion to the contrary, the King answered, That if they could not agree it to be a
clear case, he would not meddle with it; and so this matter
dropped. And therefore, to put the thing beyond doubt, an Act
of Parliament now seems necessary; and indeed without that
authority the Articles I now offer cannot be put in execution.'
(Prideaux's *Life*, 1748, pp. 189—193.)

The substance of the ARTICLES (pp. 199—237) is as follows.

1.   Prayers on week-days at 6 *a.m.* and at 9 *p.m.*

2.   The university bell to be tolled for half an hour before
evensong.

3.   The college gates to be locked while prayers are going
on, and the keys to be delivered to the head after they are over,
and to be kept by him till after prayers next morning.

4.   The porter must apply to him in the meanwhile if necessary. The person so let in to 'give an account to the Government of the said College or Hall next morning.'

5.   Any one missing evening and morning prayer running to
be considered to have been out all night. For which last offence

the punishment is public admonition for the first, the loss of a year for the second, and expulsion for the third time.

6. Persons to be turned out of common-fire-rooms or combination-rooms at 10 *p.m.* and the keys to be taken to the heads.

7. Any person so locked in, or any climbing over the college walls or the like, to be finally expelled.

8. *Stourbridge* Fair to be abolished or removed 10 miles from *Cambridge.*

9. Fasting Nights to be abolished, and suppers to be provided in hall: and persons to fast at their own discretion.

10. For resorting to Taverns or Alehouses (1) admonition; (2) admonition, a public declamation, and the loss of a year; (3) public expulsion: the tavern-keeper to be fined (1) 5*l.*, (2) 10*l.*, (3) 20*l.* and perpetually discommuned.

11. Female servants and lodgers in the town to give certificates of good character. Lewd women to be carted out of the university town, and if they return before they are 50 years old to be publicly whipped. Six persons to be appointed annually to inspect certificates.

12. There shall be an act of parliament to make it felony without benefit of clergy for any to be accessory to the clandestine marriage of a minor.

13. To prevent fellows living a 'dronish slothful life' they shall vacate their fellowships when they are of 20 years standing from matriculation: excepting a Public Professor, or Lecturer, or Upper or Under Library-Keeper, or Keeper of the Archives, or Register of the Convocation, or Judge of the V. C.'s Court or a Minister in the town or its suburbs.

14. 'That, for the maintenance and support of such superannuated Fellows or Students, who, in 20 years time, shall not have qualified themselves for any public service, there shall be an Hospital built, in each of the said Universities;.. which shall be called *Drone Hall.*' Their late colleges to provide 20*l. per annum* for each inmate, it being fitting that 'this burthen should be laid upon them, as a just mulct for their having bred up the said superannuated person to be good for nothing.'

15. After 10 years from matriculation the rule of residence should be relaxed so as to allow a fellow to become chaplain to a bishop or nobleman, or for any employment approved by the Government of his college.

16. Fellowships to be vacated by acceptance of a preferment above 80*l. per annum, secundùm uerum ualorem*, after a year of grace.

17. A 'Beadle' to vacate his Fellowship, &c.

18. Pre-elections, by which a new fellow makes a payment to the out-goer, to be abolished.

19. Dividends to be equalised, saving that each superior degree shall receive $\frac{1}{4}$ more than that next below it. B.A.:— M.A., LL.B., M.B. :—B.D., LL.D., M.D.:—D.D.

20. The number of fellows in each college to be proportioned to its income : none receiving above 60*l. per annum.*

21. Elections with regard to merit only.

22. Claim of Founder's kin disallowed.

23. No treats to be given but in the College Hall.

24. The abuse of taking degrees by forfeiting bonds given for the future performance of statutable exercises abolished.

25. All persons of standing to take M.A. degree must perform the exercises even if they do not choose to proceed, or have their names struck out of the Buttery-book.

26. The privilege of non-residence at cures on pretence of study, under 21 Hen. VIII. *cap.* 13 and 28 Hen. VIII. *cap.* 12, disallowed.

27. Popish statutes to be reformed.

28. Members of the foundation to communicate in their College Chapel at least once a month. The members to preach in rotation.

29. Meeting of the heads and proctors every Monday at 1 *p.m.* to prepare for Convocation.

30. A standing commission of 20 Curators of the universities to be appointed at the beginning of a new parliament by King, Lords and Commons.

The archbishops and lord chancellor to be *ex officio* members of the board.

31. To prepare statutes for such societies as have them not.

32. Three Commissioners may be delegated to visit.

33. 'Whereas Fellows of Colleges often spend a great part of their time, as well as of their revenue, in quarrels among themselves, or with their Head;' a select senate of all the resident doctors of the three faculties with the bachelors of Divinity shall arbitrate, with appeal to the Visitor of the college.

34. This senate shall dispose all university preferment, since 'the junior Masters of Arts often give their votes rashly and partially, without that due consideration, which they ought to have towards the merits of the Candidates.'

35. Heads not to be out of residence more than two months consecutively, or three months altogether in a year.

36. The income of the Head to be made up to the value of 3 of the best fellowships.

37. Bishops and Deans must be D.D.; Archdeacons B.D., LL.D., or D C.L.; Prebendaries or beneficiaries of 100*l.* M.A., LL.B., or B.C.L., &c. &c.

38. In the Schools the O. T. must be quoted in the Hebrew, and N. T. in the Greek.

39. All tutors must be allowed and appointed by the Master and Seniors and licensed by the V. C.

40. Tutors to find a deputy or read constantly to their pupils till their degree of B.A., except for 3 weeks at Christmas, 1 week at Easter and Whitsuntide, and during the Act or Commencement.

41. Tutors constantly on all Sundays and holidays (except as under § 40) to read and expound 'the Articles of the Church of England or such other books or tracts of divine institution as shall be judged best.'

42. No person to be licensed by the V. C. as tutor till he has sworn to observe § 41, as well as all such Oaths, Declarations and Subscriptions as the keeper of a public Grammar School is bound to take.

43. Penalties for neglectful Tutors.

44. Removal of ill-conducted Tutors.

45. Tutors to have proctorial authority over their pupils, with power of search in houses.

46. Undergraduates to pay ready money to tradesmen.

47. Heads to examine students quarterly, and to enquire into the causes of deficiency.

48. Any undergraduate found non-proficient three times together to be removed from the university.

49. For the checking of illiterate curates, none is to be admitted B.A., till he has passed an examination in the Christian Religion as taught and professed in the Church of *England.*

50. The Church Catechism and XXXIX. Articles to suffice till the Professors have fixed upon an uniform system for the Divinity Examination.

51. Four resident divines of B.D. standing to be chosen examiners by the V. C. and Heads.

52. The examination to be held in the Schools.

53. Two examiners at a time to examine classes of six for two hours at least.

54. The examiners to be paid from the stipend of the useless lectures of Grammar, Rhetoric, Logic [the *Trivium*] and Metaphysics, at *Oxford;* and at *Cambridge* by a similar method. [Perhaps by the abolition of the *Barnaby* ordinaries.]

55. No person to be ordained till he have taken his B.A. degree, or have gone through an equivalent course in a foreign university.

56. No Players or Actors of Interludes to come within the university notwithstanding any grant or licence whatsoever. which they may bring.

57. 'That, whereas the Lawyer's Gown...is often made an *Asylum* for the idle and the ignorant [*harry sophs*] such as have not, by their proficiency in their studies, qualified themselves for the Degree of B.A., it be ordained, that no person for the future, shall be allowed in either of the said Universities, to put on the Lawyer's Gown, till he hath first taken the Degree of B.A., or till three years after that, be admitted to take the Degree of Batchelor of Law.'

58. *Cambridge* to follow the practice of *Oxford* for the degree in Physic both for times and exercises, that there may be uniformity.

Dean *Prideaux* mentions that about the year 1675, '40*l. per annum* for a Commoner (or *Pensioner*, as the term is in *Cambridge*) and 80*l. per annum* for a Fellow Commoner, was looked on as a sufficient maintenance; and, when I was a Tutor in *Oxford* (M.A. and tutor of Christ Church, 1675), I never desired more for such of my Pupils, as were of either of these orders, and always found it amply to suffice for both. But now, (1715,) scarce 60*l. per annum* for the former and 120*l. per annum* for the latter, will serve for a compleat maintenance. And in proportion hereto, are increased the expences of all other orders and members of these two bodies.' (pp. 196, 197.)

'*Atheists, Deists, Socinians, Arians, Presbyterians, Independents, Anabaptists,* and other Adversaries and Sectaries, surround us on every side, and are set, as in battle array, against us: and if we do not come armed and provided with equal knowledge and learning to the conflict, how shall we be able to support our Cause against them?' (p. 198.)

APPENDIX C.

An Account of

CAMBRIDGE:

Together with a few Natural
and Easie Methods

propos'd

to both Houses of Parliament

by

Edmond Miller, Serjeant at Law.

1717.

'An *Account* of the University of *Cambridge*, and the *Colleges* there. *Being* A Plain Relation of many of their Oaths, Statutes and Charters. By which will appear, The Necessity the present Members lie under, of endeavouring to obtain such ·Alterations, as may render 'em practicable, and more suitable to the present Times. *Together with* A Few Natural, and Easie Methods, how the Legislature, may for the future fix That, and the other great Nursery of Learning, in the true Interest of the Nation, and Protestant Succession. Most humbly propos'd to both Houses of *Parliament.* By *Edmond Miller,* Serjeant at Law.

> Sincerum est nisi vas, quodcunque infundis,
> acescit.

London: Printed and Sold by *J. Baker,* at the *Black Boy* in *Pater-noster Row.* 1717.' (8vo. pp. 200.)

Serjt. Miller mentions (p. 45) the answer to the 12th Query of K. Charles II. in 1675. 'The Coffee-houses are daily frequented, and in great Numbers of all sorts (the Heads of Houses and other Doctors excepted) at all Hours; especially Morning and Evening.'

But the most interesting part of his pamphlet is the attack upon his enemy *Ri. Bentley,* Master of Trinity. Like Sam. Cobb in his Tripos Speech, Miller reaches '*Aristarchus*' by a boomerang shot. He takes the Statutes of Trinity College as a typical instance of the obsolescence which prevailed in the collegiate Statute books—and then the attack on Bentley is inevitable. Thus Miller apologizes (p. 98):—

' Neither cou'd any thing have induc'd me seemingly to act
so ungenteel a Part as (unless upon Proof in a Court of Justice)
to say such ill things of any Person living, except Doctor
Bentley : But verily believing That there is no History of any
one in such a Station, who ever before acted so vile a Part ; and
has committed such Rapine and Plunder, upon a College; and
so impudently insulted their Properties, Persons and Priveleges
for about sixteen Years together, as he has done; of all which
he has been accused many Years since in a legal Method; and
his Accusers still desire nothing [P. 99] more than an Opportunity of proving the same things before the proper Judges.

' These circumstances I hope will take off the Imputation of
Scurrility from anything which has been or can be said of such
a Person, especially since the necessity of the case almost
requires That these matters should be made Publick; because
this Wretch, by what Means is very wonderful, has found some
Friends in three successive Ministries, who it seems have thought
it worth exercising their Powers in skreening him hitherto from
this most just Prosecution.

' 'Tis suppos'd that by his vain Boastings of himself and
insolent contempt of others (a pretty Collection of his Expressions
of which sort may be seen in Mr *Johnson's Aristarchus*) he has
created a Belief in some considerable Persons who are better
employ'd than to search into those Matters That he is a Prodigy
for Learning, grounded upon his Corrections or rather Alterations of some Words, Syllables and Letters in *Horace;* which
wou'd have been an irreparable Loss to the Nation, if they had not
been retrieved by this great Genius ; Whereas among the many
good Editions, and various [P. 100] Lections, that are to be found
as well of *Horace* as other Classicks, who is there that has a
tollerable understanding of 'em but can steal or invent several
Alterations which shall with some colour of Reason please a
Majority of Readers ; there being very few, who will think it
worth their while to examine into the Reason and Authority of
'em. But the Doctor has had the ill Fortune to fall into the
Hands of Mr *Johnson* who (by giving himself the trouble of
examining, only into the first Book of this applauded Performance) has in his *Aristarchus* above mention'd, discover'd
so much want of Judgment, so many Absurdities, Inconsistencies,

silly affected Alterations; together with so much Carelessness even to the writing not only improper but false Latin in many Instances; besides a knavish Arrogance of assuming other Peoples Discoveries to himself; That he has made it plain (in much better Latin than his own) that the Doctor in this Edition as well as in his other Actions had his chief View upon the Profit; And next (by the help of Favourers of Learning falsely so call'd) to gain an Impunity for what he is accus'd of; tho' it may be truly said as to whatever he has publish'd within these last seven Years (if there has been any Merit) it has been more owing to his Prosecutors than to himself; who if he had been suffer'd quietly to go on in all Probability wou'd have contented himself in his Projects of sharping upon the College. Surely no sort of learned Men are so scarce now-a-days that 'tis needful for the Publick to encourage to tollerate 'em to Plunder and rob honest Men who are more scarce; if they have nothing to plead in their Defence but the Benefit of Clerks: much less should this Clerk be so tolerated who has robb'd some more learned than himself; since he is discover'd to be so defective in the only part of Learning of which he cou'd pretend to boast.' pp. 98—101.

Miller proposes the repeal of certain Statutes for which scheme he gives, among other recommendations, the hope of weakening the 'Nonsensical as well as Destructive High Church Principles.' p. 170.

APPENDIX D.

EMENDANDA

in

ACADEMIA

by *W. Whiston*
Sometime of *Clare-Hall.*

1717.

William Whiston, of *Clare-Hall*,

Resided 1686—1694, 1703—1710. In his *Memoirs* (ed. 1749, p. 45), he says, 'While I was Resident at *Cambridge*, which I was in all about 17 years, I observed great Defects and Disorders in the Constitution of our College of *Clare-Hall;* as also in that of the University in general. And I accordingly drew up two Papers, the one under the Title of *Emendanda in Collegio*, the other of *Emendanda in Academia;* the former Paper, which was of less consequence, I have not preserved, but the latter of greater consequence I have by me, and, as improved a little afterward, [it] stood thus *Verbatim.*

EMENDANDA IN ACADEMIA.

(See *Parson's* Advice to a *Roman* Catholick King of England.)

1. All Old Statutes to be repealed: yet so that their useful Parts be taken into the New Statutes; and the Designs of the Founders preserved, as much as may be.

The New Statutes to be,

        Few in Number:
        Plain in Words:
        Practicable in Quality:
        Known by all.

2. No more than one Civil Oath, that of Allegiance, to be imposed.

3. Penalties and not Oaths to be Securities in all other Cases.

4. No more than one Ecclesiastical Subscription to be imposed; that to the original Baptismal Profession; with the owning the sacred Authority of the Books of the Old and New Testament; and this only on Students in Divinity.

36—2

5. Civil Authority and Courts to be put into the Hands of proper Persons, distinct from the University: with one Appeal to the Judges, and all to be governed by the Common Law.

6. Visitors to be appointed where there are none; but still with one Appeal to the Judges.

7. Expences to be limited within certain Bounds.

8. Particular Tutors in Colleges to be appointed by the Master; and to unite in common for the teaching that particular Science they are best acquainted with.

9. Publick Professors to consent to the Master's Appointment; and to be Overseers to all those Tutors and Pupils in t.icir own Faculties; and to examine the Scholars every year, to see what Proficiency they have made the foregoing year.

10. Rewards or Privileges to be allotted to the best Scholars upon such Examination, and the grossly idle, ignorant, and vicious not to advance in standing, till they have made some competent Proficiency.

11. All Elections into Scholarships and Fellowships to be after open Examination and Trial, as to Learning; as well as full Testimony as to Morals. And the Times for such Election to be known long beforehand, and fixed in the Statutes.

12. Visitors may openly examine again upon Complaints; and in notorious Cases may alter the Election.

13. *Desert* for Learning and Morals; *Fitness* for the Duty; and, *caeteris paribus, Want*, the only Qualifications for free Elections, *viz.* in all such Cases as are without Propriety [i.e. *close appropriation*, in the gift of one family, or the like].

14. No Persons to interpose to hinder the Freedom of Elections. And the Procurers of Letters from great men to be incapable.

15. No present Possessor to be displac'd; [upon a Visitation, of the University:] Otherwise than according to their former Statutes, or those of the Realm.

16. Fellowships to be annually diminished, if not vacated, after a certain Number of Years; excepting [Heads of Colleges]

Tutors, and Professors. And this for the Advantage of sending men into the World while they may be useful, and the procuring a quicker Succession.

17. Heads of Colleges and Professors to be chosen as now; but from any College or Place whatsoever, and to be approved by the Bishop of the Diocese where the Founder lived. And in all Royal Foundations by the King.

18. Discipline to be strict, but not rigorous, Prayers not to be too long, nor too early; Short Prayers at nine at Night in Winter, and ten in Summer, for all to be present at.

19. Scholars to be encouraged to do their Duty rather than forced, especially in the case of the Communion, which should at least be monthly.

20. Fellows to be obliged to frequent the publick Worship as well as the Scholars.

21. The College Servants to be instructed and catechized, either in their several Parishes, or Colleges, and to frequent the Prayers.

22. Scholastick Disputations about modern Controversies in Divinity, to be changed into Lectures on the Scriptures, or most primitive Writers, &c.

23. Preachers not to meddle with State Affairs farther than the Gospel directly requires or allows.

24. No modern Systems of Divinity to be followed; but the original Languages of the Bible, and the most ancient Authors, with such later Helps as are necessary to the Understanding of them, to be recommended.

25. Admissions into Colleges to be better taken Care of.

26. No uncertain Systems of Philosophy to be recommended ; but Mathematicks and Experiments to be prefer'd.

27. None in Holy Orders, nor Undergraduates to go to Taverns or publick Houses at all, without particular Business with Strangers there, and at early Hours. Others to be restrained from much frequenting the same.

28.   All Undergraduates to be in their several Colleges by nine at Night in Winter, and ten in Summer: and all Graduates within an Hour after.

29.   New Galleries to be built at St *Mary*'s to hold all the Scholars, [This was done by the legacy of *William Worts*], and the Colleges to go thither on Lord's-Days in Order, as they do now to *Clerums*.

30.   None to have Testimonials for Orders till they have studied the Scriptures and Antiquity for three years.

31.   No Treats for Degrees to exceed a certain small sum, to be fixed for them.

32.   All pecuniary Punishments to go to the Charity-Schools, or Poor of the Parishes in *Cambridge*.

WILL. WHISTON.

April 15, 1717.

APPENDIX E.

. —————

QUESTIONS

for

UNIVERSITY REFORM,

considered by

Lord Chancellor *Macclesfield.*

1718.

Ld. Chancellor *Macclesfield's* Scheme for University Reform cir. 1718 (see above, p. 53). Extracted from Gutch, *Collectanea Curiosa*. Oxford, 1781, II. pp. 53—75, No. IX. ' A Memorial relating to the Universities.'

Three Questions are discussed.

QUESTION I. By what method learning and industry may be promoted in the Universities, setting aside all party considerations?

The suggestions are

(1) All Heads to be chosen by a body of State Officers, Archbishops, Bishops and the Visitor.

(2) Fellowships limited to twenty years; limit to number of College Livings; augmentation of poor Vicarages; two Tutors in each College, after fifteen years' service, to hold Fellowships for life.

All Fellows to take office in turn. Non-residence of not more than six months at a time, and not more than ten times; and that not till after five years' residence.

Faculty Fellowships (Law and Physic) to be allowed.

Others not taking Orders at once to vacate in ten years.

(3) Foundation of a Professor of the Law of Nature and Nations.

(4) Lectures in Divinity, Law of Nature and Nations, Anatomy, Chymistry, Mathematics, Experiments in Natural Philosophy.

QUESTION II. What force may be necessary to ease the present disaffection of the Universities?

Vest the right of electing to Scholarships, Exhibitions, Fellowships, &c., in a Commission: but ' much wiser heads are employed in digesting for an Act of Parliament whatever is proper on this head.'

QUESTION III. What gentle methods may be of service to win them over to the Government?

1. By I. §§ 3, 4.

2. Tutors should encourage Noblemen and Gentlemen-Commoners to go through a course of Law of Nature and Nations.

3. And English Law and Constitution.

4. Pensions of £20 or £30 to about twenty Fellows to encourage them to serve Government.

5. Let the Crown or Great Seals give yearly two or three Preferments to well-affected Persons.

6. Let well-affected Patrons prefer well-affected Persons.

7. Exhibitions of £10 or £20 to poor Scholars till they gain Fellowships.

8. Government should pay for the education of needy students in different branches of study.

9. Government to return persons to recommend fit objects for bounty.

(a) Establish a Court of Appeal from the dominant power in Universities.

(β) Government to favour loyal Colleges, also to bestow a few livings on discontented persons.

We learn also incidentally that £20 or £30 per annum at the University with a Fellowship made a pretty easy subsistence. There was an entire change of all that were not on the Foundation, in less than seven years, and more than a third of those on the Foundation were dead or gone in seven years.

Courses of Classick Learning and Philosophy were provided by Tutors. Bishops complained of gross ignorance in the Scripture and Divinity of the Candidates. The Nobility and Gentry and other Laymen that came from the Universities proved as generally disaffected to the present Government as those in Holy Orders.

Marriage of a Fellow was often concealed for many years, or till after death. Resident Fellows as they advanced in years were overrun with spleen, or took to sottishness. Unworthy men chosen Heads of Houses by their winking at a youth who might have a vote in a future election.

APPENDIX F.

The

EXPENCE of

University Education Reduced,

by *Richard Newton.*

1727.

====

Rules and *Statutes*

for

HERTFORD COLLEGE

in the University of *Oxford,*

by the same Hand.

1747.

The Expence of University Education Reduced. In a Letter to a Fellow of a College in *Oxford.*

Matri utilis *Almae*
Si das hoc, Parvis quoque rebus magna juvavi.

The Fourth Edition, *London:* Printed for *G. Strahan,* in *Cornhill; C. Rivington,* in *St Paul's Church-yard; J. Osborn* in *Paternoster Row;* and *R. Clements,* and *J. Fletcher,* in *Oxford,* 1741 (dated 27 May, 1727): pp. 47. [By Dr *Ri. Newton,* Principal of *Hart Hall.*]

Expensiveness is not inherent in the university system, but is only the work of individual humour, vanity and luxury.

It should be a rule (p. 6) 'that nothing be allow'd to be dress'd in the *Common Kitchen* for any member of the Society, but *Commons:* And that every Scholar affecting to make *Entertainments,* at his *private Chamber,* for Strangers visiting him in his Studious Retirement, be obliged to defray the Entire Charge thereof out of his *Own Purse.*'

(pp. 8, 9.) 'The largest Endowments in any Society of the UNIVERSITY are but barely sufficient for *Maintenance* in the Manner intended, for Decent *Apparel,* and for a few Useful *Books...*There are Stated Times for *Devotion,* for *Study* and *Improvement,* for *Private Lectures,* for *Public Exercises,* for the Refreshments of *Eating, Walking, Conversing* (p. 10). Each Scholar hath his Separate Apartment. The Furniture of it is suppos'd to be no other, than that of a Lodger in a private Family who never eats at Home...What Sort of *Strangers,* now, are those who expect to be Invited to an *Elegant Entertainment* in this *Chamber?*...Hath he so much as a *Servant* to attend him upon this Occasion, but who, at the same time, is the *Common* Servant of *Twenty* Scholars more?...(p. 11.) And what a *Consumption* of the Common Fuel will this Entertainment, at a Later Hour, occasion, at the *equal* Expense of *Others* of the

Community, whose prudence, as well as Circumstances, will not permit them to give in to this *Affected* and *Impertinent* Hospitality?'

If the Stranger wishes to see Students' life, he should dine at the ordinary hall.   If he only wants their conversation in private rooms, let him refresh himself in his Inn.   It is monstrous to allow your time and money to be frittered away 'in Absurd and Conceited Entertainments for every trifling Acquaintance, who has a mind to take *Oxford* and *Blenheim* in his Way to the *Bath*.   I say trifling Acquaintance; for no Man living, that is well bred and understands what is proper, will ever *Accept* of an Entertainment at a Scholar's Chamber.' (p. 13.)   'A *Fellowship* in a College of 40*l.* a-year, which may instantly become Void by Misbehaviour, Cession, Death or Marriage, and which, 'till any of these Accidents shall happen, will not yield 20*l.* a-year clear to a Sequestrator, will give the Scholar Credit for 500*l.*' (p. 17.) Even the richer students are often in arrears when they have left a College beyond their caution money (p. 21); and even they ought to live in the same style as their less wealthy companions, and not to waste their time.   It is preposterous that 'Scholars may have what Entertainments they please dress'd in the Common Kitchen and the Charge thereof inserted in their *Note* of Battels at the End of the Quarter.' (p. 23.)

'Another source of expence and inconvenience is the having notable *Ale* in the College Cellars.   In plain Terms I would not advise Young Men to use it in a *Morning* or at their *Meals*; if in the *Evening*, when they mix in Conversation with each other or with Scholars of other Societies in their respective Rooms, they would, in a sober manner, recruit the Spirits, which by hard Study have been exhausted, with this Liquor, the most abstinent Person in the World would not be so morose as to think it might not innocently be done.' (pp. 30, 31.)   'Ale and Wine are *already* introduc'd into the Private Cellars of Scholars.'   Bishop *Fell*, Dean of Ch. Ch. prohibited *Ale* being supplied from the Butteries, and it did *not* result in the Scholars introducing 'not only *Ale*, but *Wine* into their Private Cellars either in *his* time or in his *Successor's*' [dean *Massey*, 1686—9]. (p. 35.)

Nothing should 'be put upon the Scholar's Name in the Book of Battels for either *Bye-Services* or *Charities*.' (p. 38.)

Some of the undergraduates 'find as much employment for a Common Servant as Ten other Scholars of the same Society.' (p. 39.)

As to the *Charities*, the practice of keeping a Note or Sub-scription list hanging in the public Refectory to be transferred to the Action of Battels is reprehensible: 'A Multitude of Appli-cations are made at the University for Collections of this Sort, and what incredible Success they meet with. Young men are often *Vain* and desirous to be thought liberal…Whoever pre-tends to *Give*, must Give of his *Own;* and must call that only his *Own* which he can save out of his Founder's or his Parent's Provision for his maintenance.' (pp. 41—43.)

RICHARD NEWTON when he had been a member of the university of Oxon. above 31 years wrote Nov. 8, 1725, a pamphlet which was printed in pp. 207, 8vo., by G. Strahan at the *Golden-Ball* over against the Royal Exchange, 1726. Its title is *Uni-versity Education* or, an Explication *and* Amendment of the Statute which, under a Penalty *Insufficient* and *Eluded*, pro-hibits the Admission of Scholars going from One Society to another without the Leave of their respective Governors, or of the Chancellor, &c. &c. In a word it is the pamphlet criticized by *Amherst* in the Appendix to *Terrae Filius*, ed. 1726, in 'a Letter to the Reverend Dr *Newton*, Principal of *Hart-Hall;* occasion'd by his Book entitled, *University Education*, &c.' The case in ques-tion was that of *Will. Seaman* or *Sayman* mentioned above, p. 60.

Newton was elected principal of *Hart-Hall* in 1710 and was succeeded by W. Sharp in 1753.

Hart-Hall had been the nursery, both of Exeter and New College in the 14th century, and numbered among its students Tyndale, sir W. Waller, Selden, Clarendon, [bp. Ken], Hobbes, Swift and Fox[1]. Dr Newton was discontented with the title Hart *Hall*, and after many struggles procured, Sep. 8, 1740, its incorporation as Hertford *College* (chiefly for persons intending for holy orders): thus taking a less picturesque name as several of our societies in Cambridge have been led to do by the sug-gestion of a late procrustean Commission.

Newton's Statutes were so forbidding that the dissolution of his College was hastened in 1816, on the death of Bernard Hodg-son, by the refusal of every one to administer them.

---

[1] Moore's *Handbook to Oxford*, 1871.

Rules and *Statutes* for the Government of *Hertford College* in the University of *Oxford*, with *Observations* on particular Parts of them shewing the *Reasonableness* thereof by *R. Newton*, D.D., Principal of *Hertford*-College. London: Printed for John Osborn, in Pater-noster-Row, 1747. (pp. 162.)

The Principal may hold his office for life: the four senior Fellows, *Vice-Principal, Catechist, Chaplain* and *Moderator* may be Tutors till eighteen years after their matriculation: the eight junior B.A. Fellows may continue in the position of Assistants for three years. There shall be but thirty-two Students, and four Scholars.

One of the four Seniors is to be principal Tutor for a year in rotation; he is to receive the fees and to lecture once a week to all students. Each Tutor to have a class of eight Students and one Scholar who are to continue under his special care for their career of sixteen terms.

The Revenue of the Principal to be 281*l.* 6*s.* 8*d.*
  „   „ each Tutor or Senior 93*l.* 11*s.* 8*d.*
  „   „ each Junior Fellow 26*l.* 13*s.* 4*d.*
  „   „ each Student 13*l.* 6*s.* 8*d.*
  „   „ each Probationer Student 6*l.* 13*s.* 4*d.*
  „   „ each Scholar 4*l.* 3*s.* 4*d.*

These stipends are only to be augmented by an allowance of 6*d. per diem* for Commons, for 31 weeks, making an addition of 5*l.* 8*s.* 6*d. per annum* for each member of the foundation.

Any Person of Superior Condition to pay double fees, &c., and to be 'distinguish'd tho' not by a different *Gown* yet by a *Tuft* upon his *Cap*, varying according to the different Rank in which he is Admitted.'

One Tutor is to lodge in the middle Room of the middle Stair-case in each Angle of the College Court. [Hence, according to Nic. Amherst (Appendix to *Terrae Filius*, 1726, p. 295, *n.*), they were nicknamed *Anglers*]. Each compartment shall contain an outward Room, a Bed-place, and a Study. One Bedmaker (a Man or elderly Woman), assisted by a Son or Servant, who shall lodge in the tutor's suite and serve him out of the hours of their common service, to have care of each Angle, i.e. of 15 sets of rooms apiece.

§ 2. *Morning* Prayers, on *Common* Days at 6.30 or 7.30 according to the time of year. On Litany Days the Second Service at 9. Fines of 2*d.* for absence or bad behaviour in chapel.

Evening Prayer at 6.30 *p.m.*

Immediately after *First* Service on *Sundays* and *Holidays* in *Term*, shall follow a very short *Explication* of some Part of the *Church Catechism*, or *Instruction* in some *Moral Duty*, in a manner Useful to the *Servants*. On Sundays at 8 or 9 *p.m.* a *Catechetical* or *Theological* Lecture for undergraduates. All to communicate on Xmas Day, Easter Day, Whitsunday, the first Sunday in every Term, and at the Admission of a new Principal. Undergraduates to read in course in Chapel on surplice days; and on other days the 2nd lesson for the morning before dinner, and the 2nd lesson for the evening before supper, in Hall, when all shall be present. None to rise from table without leave till the second grace is said. The college officers may examine the reader as to his comprehension of the chapter. He shall write explanations of the difficulties in the lessons instead of his weekly theme, disputation or translation.

§ 3. Oaths on admission. § 4. The Principal to be chosen from the Westminster students of Ch. Ch. by the Chancellor of Oxford.

§ 5. There shall be *Lectures* (1) by the Principal to all Undergraduates on Thursdays; (2) by the Tutors to their respective classes on M. Tuesdays, W. F.; (3) by the Officers or their Assistants at 9 *p. m.* on Tu. Th. Sat. and on Sundays at 8 *p.m.* in winter, 9 *p.m.* in summer.

Disputations 4 to 5 *p.m.*: of Undergraduates (beginning from Easter term in their second year) on M. W. in Philosophy (Logic, Ethics, Physics and Metaphysics): of B.A. on Fridays in Divinity. All persons to take their turn in seniority of being Respondents and Prior Opponents. Notice to be given, a term in advance, of the subjects and persons required in the disputations. And in order to give interest to the proceedings the college moderator is to order the same questions to be disputed in college, as any of the society are intending to take up in their public exercises in the Schools. On these occasions only those of B.A. degree may take part in *philosophical* disputations.

'The *Respondent* and *Opponent* shall each of them, by way of Introduction to the Disputation, premise something relating to them in certain *Speeches* commonly called *Supposition* and *Opposition* Speeches, which shall not be bare *Transcripts* out of Philosophical or Theological Books ; but the *Former* a short state of the Question, shewing in what respect the Question is true, in what false, with the Application of such Distinctions as are to be met with in those Books which treat of the Questions to be Disputed upon ; the *Latter* an Elusive Speech, treating plausibly of the Other Side of the Question, the known Part of a Declaimant who holds the Wrong Side of the Thesis ; unless the Question may be such as may be well supported by good Arguments on *both* Sides.' [This was probably the original function of the *Terrae Filius* at Oxford, and the *Praevaricator* at Cambridge.]

Undergraduates (even when not in residence) to make a *Theme* or a *Declamation* or a *Translation* every week in full term. Declamations in English during their 2nd and 3rd, and Latin during their 4th year. Translations from Latin into English, or English into Latin, or by advanced students into Greek, to be looked over by the Tutors on Saturday at 4 *p. m.,* and corrected in the following week, so as to be ready for reading or recitation the following Saturday morning. Permission may be given to any that has a genius that way, to write English verse instead.

'*Batchelors of Arts* for the 1st *six* Terms which they aim to keep towards their *Master's* Degree, shall read in the *College* as an Exercise of the House the *Six Solemn Lectures* (One every Term) which are afterwards to be read, by those in the Schools as an Exercise of the University for the said Degree ; and in every of the Other Terms to be kept for the said Degree, they shall make and publickly Speak or Read a short *Sermon* upon a Text of Scripture assigned them by the *Principal.* Without the Performance of this Exercise they shall neither keep the *Term* nor receive a *Testimonium* for Orders, nor an Instrument of

Leave to go to another House.' [A *licet migrare:* still less a *bene discessit.*]

Two Undergraduates a week to deliver *Narration* [cp. p. 119, above. These 'collections' are common-place Beauties, Difficulties, and other noteworthy references, from four classic authors chosen for each student by his tutor, in the way of *Elegant Extracts* to be recited] instead of their Theme or Translation.

§ 6. The *Principal* is to have the sole nomination of servants, assistants; also of the tutors, only they may not be his own or his wife's relations 'even to the Fourth Remove inclusive,' except at the Visitor's recommendation; he shall be present at all Exercises; shall visit Students in their rooms, reprimand them when necessary, preside over a *Tutors' meeting* fortnightly in his own Lodgings, as *Bursar* shall hold two audits a year. He may take one private pupil only, and that in excess of the statutable number of students (32). If a tutor's place fall vacant within the first year of his Principalship he may take the duties and stipend himself. The Principal shall be removed if he accept any other lectureship, professorship, care of souls, dignity requiring him to break the statutable residence, &c. &c.

§ 7. The *Tutors* shall instruct their classes 1 hour *per diem:* for the first year in classics (composition and translation) and Theology: for the three next 'in *University Learning,* not Exclusive of *Other:* For the Three several Weeks immediately preceding *Christmas*-day, *Easter*-day, and *Whitsunday,* in Divinity *Proper* to that Season: For two several Vacations of the Year, in Whatsoever the *Tutor* shall think *useful* to them.' But as few probably will then stay up, two of the tutors may be absent for either half of each vacation, and only one of the two then in residence need lecture each day. Tutors shall criticize their pupils' themes, &c., see that they do them in good time; shall always commence a lecture by examining them in the last: they shall frequently visit pupils in their Chambers; shall with the Principal's sanction appoint them 'what *Traders* they shall deal with for *Necessaries*...shall insist upon it that no *Pupil*...do contract any *Intimacies* with Tradesmen or their Families; nor accept of *Invitations* to their Houses, nor introduce them to *Entertainments* at his Chamber.'

'The *Quarterly Allowance* to Scholars' is to be paid back.

L. B. E. 37

into the tutor's hand, who shall deduct money to pay tradesmen's bills, and shall return the remainder or part of it for the Scholars' pocket-money. They shall have no debt above the value of 5s. with any person keeping a coffee-house, cook's-shop, or any other public house whatsoever.

§ 8. The *Vice-Principal* acts as *Dean* and *Praelector* of the Society.

The *Chaplain* to pray for any sick member of the house, though he be not dangerously ill, to lecture to the servants, &c.

. The *Catechist* to instruct undergraduates at 8 p.m. on Sundays, to recommend books, answer cases of conscience, &c.

The *Subordinate Governour* shall examine the rooms and furniture and punish disorders committed in rooms of the angle over which he presides.

§ 9. A Register of *exit* and *redit* to be kept. Any undergraduate or fellow shall be fined 1s. for each day's absence in Term Time.

§ 10. Three years' notice to be given of intention to apply for Holy Orders, before the *testimonium* is granted. Such intention will not be registered before the candidate is 20 years of age. .

[Minute rules follow against encouraging idleness in one's neighbours and the like.]

No one is to give an entertainment on the occasion of taking his degree; nor to ' *Treat* any Examining Master, or Collector, or Other Officer of the University; or *Present* any of them with any thing more than their precise *Fees*...or accept of any Entertainment from any Proctor, or Collector, or Other Officer of the University as such.'

Persons in *statu pupillari* to apply to the Principal for any favour, redress, &c. by written English letters only.

No dogs in college.

No disturbance in *Studying Hours* (6.30 or 7.30 *a.m.* to *noon*, and from 2 to 6 *p.m.*) or *Sleeping Hours* (9 *p.m.* to 6.15 *a.m.* in summer or 7.15 *a.m.* in winter).

§ 11. *Caution Money* for a Student 8*l.*, for a Scholar 4*l.*

. The Principal to take his *Commons* with the Tutors[1]. No

---

[1] When his family was not with him, which was often for two or three weeks together, Newton says that he generally supped ' in the common

Student accepting the Indowment, shall exceed the sum of 6*s.* a Week for *Commons* and *Battels,* nor any *Scholar* 4*s.* 6*d.* The excess of one week to be deducted from the ordinary allowance of the next.

Exceedings of 1*s.* 6*d.* apiece to be allowed on the noon of Christmas-day, Easter-day, Whitsunday, and the commemoration of the Incorporation, at the expence of non-residents as well.

The President is the proper entertainer of Students' relatives. He alone may have food cooked in the kitchen in addition to the regular commons.

The gate to be shut during dinner and supper time.

[The rules for Commons have been given already and will be found on pp. 124, 125, 128, 129 in this essay.]

§ 12. Room-rent to vary from 6 to 3*L per annum.* The outgoing tenant to receive for furniture two-thirds of his original outlay, or after six years' tenure one-half: according to the common system of 'Hirings' (called *at Thirds,* p. 73). He is to pay *detriments* to the college as landlords if required.

§ 13. Each of the four *Scholars* is in his course to summon the Society to *Prayers,* to *Meals,* to *Disputations,* to Public and Private *Lectures,* to note absentees, and to be *Officer* of the *Gate.* Any one coming into College between 9 and 10 *p.m.* to be reported to the Principal. At 10 o'clock the key is to be taken to the Principal for the night : Newton thinking it proper that any one who was out of College at that late hour should lodge at an inn, or walk about all night; and if his behaviour was not good, be shut up in the Round-house by the Proctor. He should be subject to a fine of 1*s.* The like fine to be exacted for each stranger kept by a student in his rooms after that hour. Half the fines and a capitation of 1*d. per* week to be paid to the Scholar.

refectory,' that he neither varied the meat nor exceeded the proportion which was set before the *lowest* commoner; that 10*d.* a day paid for his breakfast, dinner, and supper, even when there *was Ale* in the society, which then there *was not.* Amherst, in his letter or Appendix to *Terrae Filius,* remarks that one of these statements 'is liable to dispute; I will only put you in mind of the late instance of PEASE and BACON. You remember what you said upon that occasion, *viz. Is such* diet *as this to descend to the* populace?'

'There is not a greater Slave in *Turkey* than a College *Porter;* and I pronounce that *He,* or his *Deputy,* shall die a Death immature.' (p. 131.)

§ 14. The *Butler* to attend at his Office between 8 and 9 *a.m.,* and 12 to 2 *p.m.,* and 6 to 8 *p.m.* No *By-Services, Charities,* or *Liberalities* to be entered to Students' accounts. *Bedmakers* to be in college from 5.30 or 6.30 to 9 *a.m.,* 10 *a.m.* to 2 *p.m.,* 6 to 9 *p.m.* To receive 4*d.* a week from a Scholar, and 7*d.* from other persons. One shall attend in turn for a week near the gate within call; so as also to receive parcels, direct strangers, 'to keep out all *Beggars, Fruiterers, Pamphlet* Sellers, and other Idle and Vagrant Persons ;' to keep the Chapel, and the *Greens, Borders,* and *Flowers* neat, for which a payment of 4*d.* a day shall be provided from the common public stock.

[§ 15. Of the College *Stock* and of the *Disposal* thereof. § 16. Of *Penalties.* § 17. The *Statutes.* § 18. The *Visitor.*]

p. 138. Condemning the gay clothes of some of the clergy Dr Newton says, that by it a clergyman cannot "*be known to be a Clergyman,*" whilst the *Graver* Men of the Order still wear *Black,* and whilst a *Blue* Coat, Waistcoat, Breeches, and Stockings, often worn by Others of the Clergy, is a Dress so near a Common *Livery,* that it doth not distinguish them from *Footmen.* The Statutable exception in favour of a less sombre raiment for the sons of Barons having a vote in the House of Lords does not prove, he thinks, 'that they are therefore at liberty to Expose themselves in a *Green* Gold-lac'd Waistcoat, and *Red* Breeches, and in a *Black* Wig one Day, and a *White* One another.'

p. 146. 'I would not Advise a young Man, in order to shew his *Breeding,* to pull off his *Hat* to every well-dress'd Person he meets in the Streets of *London*...there is a *Crowd* to be gotten through, and the *Calls* of *Chairmen* to be attended to, and *Room* to be made for them, and the *Porters'* Burdens to be evaded. The Difficulty of passing safely makes it necessary for him to look *wholly* to his Own Way.

' But I would Advise the same young Man to pull off his *Cap,* and give the honourable Place, to all well-dress'd Persons he meets in the *Colleges* or *Streets* of *Oxford,* tho' he be certain he never saw any of them in his Life....

'But if the well-dress'd *Stranger* should happen to be a *Pickpocket*, and the young Scholar, if he had known it, would have been far from paying him the Respect due to a *Gentleman;* yet, since he did *not* know it, let him not be over-much concerned.'

p. 150. Scholars not upon the Foundation 'are Admitted under the Title of *Commoners*, and must stand to *Commons* of a certain Value at their *Own* Expence....It hath already been observed, that *Putting out of Commons* is a Penalty in *All* Colleges, and, in *Many*, for almost all *Faults*. But of this Sort of Penalty they could not be capable, if they were not to *stand* to Commons during their Residence.'

There be 'Masters of Publick-Houses in *Oxford*, who, as it is well known, in their Inquiries after Maid-Servants,' have insisted that they should be somewhat Pretty.

'In the History of the Chancellorship of Archbishop *Laud*, upon a Representation that there were at that time *Three* Hundred Alehouses in *Oxford*, He is said to have reduced them to *One* Hundred at first, and afterwards to *Fewer*.'

p. 152. To the *Coffee-Houses* 'all the irregular and extravagant Youth resort, as it should seem, to read the *News*, after which an Inquiry is natural, and may be useful; and to drink a Dish of *Coffee* or *Tea*, Liquors neither Intoxicating nor Expensive[1]; but, in Deed and in Truth, to Dine, at much *Later* than the College *Hours*, upon costly Varieties before bespoken, and ordered to be sent thither from the *Cooks'-Shops;* and to regale themselves, afterwards, with *Punch*, or *Wine*[2], till they find

---

[1] 'I firmly believe that a lad may *thrive* full as well, and *chop logick* as glibly in a college, where they *eat* and *drink like Christians*, as in any SMALL-BEER HALL whatsoever.

'I wonder that you did not, under this head, acquaint us with that wise injunction, which you have caused to be promulgated within your dominions, against the consumption of *Tea* and *Coffee;* a fashionable vice, which tends only to squandring away money, and mispending the *morning;* since (as you once ingeniously express'd it) nothing more can be expected from those JENTACULAR CONFABULATIONS.' Amherst's *Letter to Dr Newton*, in the Appendix to *Terrae Filius*, ed. 1726, p. 330.

[2] It is not proper, says *Amherst*, in the colleges, 'to indulge upon

themselves in a Humour for childish, mischievous, or cruel En-
terprizes.'

There is not 'a more piteous Creature anywhere to be found,
than a young Scholar, who, having been *Hunting* and *Shooting*
for four or five Months in the Country, can think of nothing but
Hunting and *Shooting* from the Moment he returns to his College.' And that not under the care of an experienced gamekeeper, but in large Troops, whereby 'sad *Accidents*...happen
every year.' Not to mention that much of this Sport is
poaching.

Billiards are forbidden by the spirit of the statute against
Cards, Dice, &c. The *Gladiators'* Entertainments condemned by
Statute have long been discontinued at Oxford. Stage Players
are admitted only at *the Act,* and then they are not necessary,
and licence has sometimes been refused. 'It is enough that our
Young *Gentlemen* do at that Time speak fine *Verses,* upon well-
chosen Subjects, in a handsome manner; and that the *Proceed-
ers* to their Degrees in the several Faculties do perform their
Exercises to the Satisfaction of Learned Men, who shall come
to hear them; and that those who shall then complete their
Degrees in *Musick,* do agreeably Entertain the Ladies of the
worthy Families in the Neighbourhood of the Place, who shall
then honour us with their Presence, with *Harmony* Vocal and
Instrumental. To *Rope-dancers,* it seems, there is not the same
Exception as to *Players:* These are still said to give *Innocent,*
and not *Expensive* Entertainment.' The book ends with a
reference to what was a sore point with the writer, the migration
of students to another society. This topic was discussed at
length by him in another pamphlet, entitled *University Education.* See above, p. 60. It was to ridicule that book that
N. Amherst wrote his 'Letter to the Reverend Dr *Newton,* Principal of *Hart-Hall;* occasion'd by his Book, entitled, *University*

venison and *salmon,* upon *burgundy, champaigne,* and *rack-punch* on
one hand; so I think there ought to be something allow'd, besides
small-beer and *apple-dumplings,* on the other. Nay, the *niceties* before
mentioned, if taken in a moderate degree, tend to *inspire* the genius,
and *enliven* the imagination; whereas nothing can be expected from
only *rot-gut small beer,* and heavy *apple-dumplings,* but *stupidity, sleepi-
ness,* and *indolence.*'

Education, etc.,' which formed the appendix to the reprint of *Terrae Filius*, pp. 289—337, in 1726. *William Seaman* was admitted from Hart-Hall to *Oriel* by Mr *Bowles* the senior fellow, in the absence of provost *Carter*, on the request of Mr *Brooke* the tutor. Amherst makes fun of the Friday's diet at 'a certain *hall* in Oxford,' which was '*small beer* and APPLE-DUMPLINGS... with their *concomitants*, as they are call'd; *viz. a farthing* brown sugar, *and a farthing* butter.' He refers also to the case of *Joseph Somaster*, who applied for a *bene discessit* to go to *Baliol*, where he had the promise of a tutor for nothing, a scholarship, and cheaper living in the Mastership of Dr *Hunt.* The precedent on which Ri. Newton relied was that of *Thomas Wysse*, who was *restored* from *St. Mary College* to *Whitehall* in 1548, by order of the V. C. (*Terrae Filius*, p. 310.)

p. 317. 'By those who would obstruct your *charity*, I suppose you mean the *Rector* and fellows of *Exeter College*, who gave you that *grievous opposition*, so often complained of, to the *incorporation of your hall.*'

p. 322. 'Speaking of one of your Scholar's Reasons for leaving your *Hall* and going to *Trinity College*, because they had a *fine garden* there, which he hoped would be of advantage to his *health*, you make this curious reflection (p. 82), "I do acknowledge it is a very *fine garden.* I question whether there are finer *evergreens* in any garden in *Europe*, than in that of *Trinity-College*: But I would have him consider, that the proper use of that *fine garden* is not to create in *philosophers* an appetite for *elegance*, but to set forth to young men the advantage of *education*: For those *fine eughs* could not have been so beautifully formed, if they had not been *obedient to the bender's will*,"' &c., &c.

APPENDIX G.

DIARY, &c.

at *Trin.* Coll. · *Cambridge.*

Oct. 1793—*Mar.* 1801.

Extracts from the DIARY, &c. of a Student of *Trin.* coll. Cambridge. (Oct. 1793—March 1801.)

[CHRISTOPHER WORDSWORTH (youngest brother of the Poet) was born at Cockermouth co. Cumberland in 1774, June 9. —He was educated at Hawkshead and at Trin. coll. Camb.— 10th Wrangler, 1796.—Fellow of Trinity.—M.A. 1799.—S.T.P. per litt. regias, 1810.—Chaplain to Dr Manners Sutton (abp. of Canterb.), Dean of Bocking co. Essex, 1807.—Rector of Lambeth and of Sundridge co. Kent, 1816.—Master of Trinity 1820— 1841.—Had (says Dr Whewell) 'a principal share in the establishment of the classical tripos, which was adopted by the univ. in 1822.'—Rector of Buxted-cum-Uckfield co. Sussex.—Died at Buxted, Feb. 2, 1846. Portrait in Trinity Lodge by Mr Joseph.

He married Priscilla daughter of Charles Lloyd, banker of Birmingham. Their children were,

1. *John,* born 1st July, 1805, educated at Winchester 1819 and Trin. coll. Cant. 1824.—Bell's scholar, 1825.—Schol. Trin. and Porson prizeman 1826.—Fellow of Trin. 1830.—Philol. Museum 1822.—Assistant-tutor and classical lecturer, 1834.— Ordained deacon and priest 1837.—Died Dec. 31, 1839, aet. 35. He is buried at the foot of Newton's statue in the coll. chapel. A bust by Mr Weekes, under the superintendence of Sir F. Chantrey, stands in the ante-chapel, its position having been moved in the present alteration.

2. *Charles,* educated at Harrow (captain of cricket) and Christchurch (4 univ. boat, and eleven, 1829).—Chancellor's Prize for Latin verse, 1827.—Latin essay, 1831.—First class in *Litt. humanioribus,* 1830.—Senior Student and Assistant-tutor. Among his private pupils were the late D. of Newcastle, Mr Gladstone, and Dr Manning.—Second Master (Hostiarius) of Winchester, 1835.—1st Warden of Trin. coll. Glenalmond, 1846. —Bishop of St Andrews, 1852.—D. C. L. *honoris causa,* 1853.— Subwarden of Winchester, 1870.

3. *Christopher,* educated at Winchester. (Senior commoner

praefect, and captain of cricket), scholar and fellow of Trin. coll. Cant. Gained many prizes. Senior Classic, having been 14th Senior Optime in the Math. Tripos, 1830.—Public Orator.— Head-master of Harrow, 1836—44.—Married Susanna Hatley Frere, daughter of Geo. Frere of Twyford House co. Herts, and 45 (46) Bedford Square; niece of Rt. Hon. J. Hookham Frere, 1838.—Hulsean Lecturer, 1847—8.—Canon in 1844 (and Arch- deacon) of Westminster, Vicar of Stanford in the Vale of White Horse, co. Berks. Consecrated Bishop of Lincoln, on feast of S. Matthias, 1869.

Dr Chr. Wordsworth, the elder, was the author of

'Six Letters to Granville Sharp' on the use of the Definite Article in the Greek Testament, 1802.

'Ecclesiastical Biography,' 6 vols. 1809 (reprinted 1818; ed. 3, 4 vols. 1839; ed. 4, 1853).

Two Pamphlets on '.the Bible Society,' 1810.

Sermons, 2 vols., 1814.

'Who wrote ΕΙΚΩΝ ΒΑΣΙΛΙΚΗ?' Six Letters to the abp. of Canterbury, 1824.

'King Charles I. the Author of *Icòn Basilikè* further Proved,' 1828.

Concio ad Clerum, 1831.

'Sacred Edifices,' a Sermon at the Consecration of St Mark's Chapel, Buxted, 1836.

'Christian Institutes,' 4 vols. 1837 (ed. 2, 1841).

'The Ecclesiastical Commission and the Universities; a Letter to a Friend.' Ed. 2, 1837.]

Extracts from the Diary of Chris. Wordsworth, [afterward Master of] Trin. coll. Camb. Oct. 9, 1793 —Mar. 8, 1801.

When a Junior Soph.
' *Wednesday*, Oct͏ᵗ. 9, 1793. Arrived at C[ambridge]. Breakfasted with Satterthwaite—sized with Young. Drank wine with Satterthwaite...

Tuesday, 15. Rose at eight. Breakfasted—read Math[ematics] till half-past 11. Walked—lounged in library. Drank wine with Reynolds; same party as yesterday [Satterthwaite and Malcolm]. Tea at home commenced, and intend to pursue this plan, at least while in town [Cambridge]. Mathematics an hour. Began Milton's Paradise Lost. To-day Satterthwaite gave us an account of a Mr Brown an Oxon., nephew of Mr Brown of Sallentire, who has undertaken an expedition in Abyssinia. Letters had been received, purporting that he had discovered the temple of Juppiter Ammon. Mr Beaufoy, on the part of the African Association, called upon Mr B. when in London, to inquire if he knew how any communication might be had with his nephew: he did not. Mr Beaufoy told Mr B., who had not then heard it, that a report had reached Rome that Mr B. had been· cut off near the cataract of the Nile and that a man of the name of Grave (they supposed a young artist at Rome) had written, saying that Mr B. had entrusted to him all his papers and drawings, &c. and that his intention was as soon as possible to prepare them for the press. Mr Beaufoy on going made Mr Brown a present of the Transactions of the African Society.

Wednesday, 16. Rose to chapel. Drank wine with Satterthwaite. Present: Young, Malcolm, Reynolds, Benson, &c. Drank tea at home. Drank a beaker with Young. Present: Richmond, Tate, Hoyle, Satterthwaite. Went to bed at eleven.

Thursday, 17. Rose to chapel. Read till one Trigonometry

(plane). In the afternoon lounged in the library. Walked with Reynolds. Drank tea at home. Read Tweddell's Panegyric on Locke. Proceeded in my syllabus of Trigonometry. Read part of Aeschylus' Seven against Thebes...Bilsborrow saw the Letter in which Johnson offers Dr Darwin £1000 for his Ζωονομια, without having ever seen it. Dr D. confesses it in his Botanic Garden, &c.; he propounds many opinions which he does not himself believe. Hayley, Bilsborrow says, is employed on a life of Milton...

Wednesday, 23. Chapel. A Latin declamation brought me. All morning spent in chusing a subject, finding my opponent, going to the Dean, procuring books, &c.

Thursday, 24. Went to the library to consult some books on my Declamation subject. Met Bilsborrow there, and went with him to his lodgings. Tells me Dr Darwin got more knowledge in that way from Kaim's [Kames'] *Essay on Criticism* than from any book he ever read. He has seen a Letter from Dr Priestly much to the same purport. Dr Darwin and a few friends meet every evening. Whatever be the subject of their conversation they divide half and half; each gives his sentiments on the side allotted; and when all have so done, they change again, each having to defend the side he before condemned.

Dr Darwin's receipt for Poetry which he recommended to B. To take some beautiful picture and turn it into verse. An instance of this is Dr D's rape of Proserpine, of which B. says he very well remembers the picture.

Saturday, 26. Nearly finished my declamation. The subject *Utrum Attici vitae ratio bonum civem deceat:* I have to support the negative.

Tuesday, 29. Chapel...Chapel. Holden had to repeat his declamation of last Saturday. After proceeding a very short way in it he began to look on, and soon after to read straight forwards. Upon this the Dean (Basketh, newly elected) called out, apparently very angry (N. They had already been before the Master and Seniors), *Descendas, descendas;* he was seconded by the Vice-Master's *descendas;* Collier, Jones, Ramsden, &c. were present. Upon this H., with a very high air immediately came down, and throwing his declamation indignantly from him, which fell into the hands of a man (Salter) on the opposite side the Chapel, he stalked along the chapel, throwing his gown from off his shoulders.

Wednesday, 30. Chapel. Carried my declamation to Cautley for his revision, and sat about an hour with him. Drank wine with Walton. Present : Tweddell, Malcolm, and Ryley my antagonist, all Trin. C. Chapel. Satterthwaite declaimed against Browne. Drank tea afterwards with him.

Thursday, 31. Employed the evening in getting my declamation by heart. [Reading from MS. has been permitted since 1867.]

Tuesday, Nov. 5. Roused about nine o'clock by Bilsborrow and Le Grice with a proposal to become member of a literary society: the members they mentioned as having already come into the plan, [S. T.] Coleridge, *Yes.*, Satterthwaite, Rough, and themselves, *Trin. C.*, and Franklin, *Pembroke.* Heard Allen's dissertation on K. William ; was to have gone to Coleridge's to wine, to consult on the plan, had I not been engaged at home with the Howeses and Strickland. Went with them to the coffee-house. On my going out met Bilsborrow : returned back with him. Soon after came in Le Grice, Coleridge, and Rough. Got all into a box and (having met with the Monthly Review of my Brother's Poems), entered into a good deal of literary and critical conversation on Dr Darwin, Miss Seward, Mrs Smith, Bowles, and my Brother. Coleridge spoke of the esteem in which my Brother was holden by a society at Exeter, of which Downman and Hole were members, as did Bilsborrow (which he had before told me) of his repute with Dr Darwin, Miss Seward, &c., &c., at Derby. Coleridge talked Greek, Max. Tyrius he told us, and spouted out of Bowles. At nine o'clock called on Satterthwaite, and sat awhile with him.

Thursday, 7. Rose at half-past eight. Lectures began, went to them at nine. Breakfasted with Rough. Met with Vaughan. Coleridge called on Rough: we sat in criticism on some of his poems. In one of these he wished he were a Woodbine bower, a Myrtle, the Zephyr to fan the folds of her garment, neck, hair, &c.; a Dream ; and finally he wished

> to be the Heaven that he aloft "might rise
> And gaze upon her with unnumber'd eyes,"

which, by the bye, is borrowed from an epigram of Plato. Vid. Brunck.

There was one idea, however, in its application to me new, which may compensate for the above. Somehow thus:

The waving poplar " sleeps upon the stream "
(" How sweet the moonlight *sleeps* upon this bank," &c.).—*Merch. Ven.*
...Vaughan...is become a member of the Society.

Friday, 8. Chapel. Lectures. Considered of a subject for my essay on Wednesday se'nnight. Drank Wine with Coleridge. Present, *the Society.* Chapel. Read *Morning Chronicle.* Found in it an ode to Fortune, by Coleridge, which I had seen at Rough's yesterday. Read *Ratios* and *Variable Quantities,* and Burton's *Anatomy of Melancholy.*

Saturday, 9. Chapel. Lectures. Took out a dormiat....No author ought, I think, without he enters the world with considerable advantages, to begin with publishing a very elaborate work; however, not a work upon which tastes may very considerably vary, e.g. my Br[other]'s Poems. If *he* had had his reputation raised by some less important and more *popular* poem, it would have ensured from petty critics a different reception to his *Descriptive Sketches* and *Evening Walk.*—Chapel.

Monday, 11. Rose at eight. Lectures nine. Borrowed Howes' *Syllabus of Mechanics* to transcribe, in doing which spent the remainder of the morning.

Wednesday, 13. Satterthwaite and Malcolm, Trin., drunk Wine with me. The Society, this evening, met at my rooms for the first time. Time before supper was spent in hearing Coleridge repeat some original poetry (he having neglected to write his essay, which therefore is to be produced next week), and other men each his voluntary contribution. After supper, in debating and adjusting the Rules of the Society.

Mem. Began to read Mathematics, January, 1794.

Sunday Evening, March 9, 1794. Have lately been reading Boswell's *Johnson;* to which, perhaps, I may impute the resumption of my plan of keeping a Diary.

Monday, March 10. Rose at eight. Till ten read some of the definitions at the beginning of Astronomy. At ten went for the first time to lectures to Mr Tavel, beginning with the 11th Book of Euclid... [After Evening Chapel and tea] read Lowth *de Sac. Poesi* and the *Hippolytus* of Euripides till quarter past eight. After supper read Locke.

· *Tuesday*, March 11. Rose to Chapel. Read Euclid. Went to St Mary's at eleven, to-day being the Assize Day, and heard a Sermon by Mr Owen, a Fellow of Bennet. The text, "Judge righteous judgement." We are told that their Massacres are without Murder. At twelve called upon Greenwood, who is unwell.

Wednesday [March 12.] Rose to Chapel. Till ten read Euclid. Went to lectures: found we had none to-day on account of the assizes. Went to the library. Called on Rough. About eleven returned home and began Astronomy. Read till dinner. After dinner till a quarter past four read a little of Locke. Walked alone till Chapel time. After Chapel read Lowth and Euripides. After supper a little of Astronomy. At ten went to bed.

Friday, March 14, till half-past twelve, read Astronomy. Walked till dressing-time with Satterthwaite. After dinner sat with Howes till a quarter before four. Present: Hayes, Bollond, Gleed, Trin. Went with them to Wollaston's lectures. Chapel. Drank coffee with Reynolds. Till eight wrote to my Brother William. Read a little in Hippolytus and Astronomy. Exceedingly drowzy and languid. Went to bed at half-past nine.

Saturday, March 15. Rose to Chapel. Read Euclid 11th Book and Sphaerical Trigonometry till ten. Lectures till one. Read Astronomy. Walked till ten minutes before two. Dressed for Dinner. [Cp. pp. 134, 476, 479.]

Owen spoke of the assuming and arrogant part which the Johnians always act; and that they are disliked, as a body, by nine-tenths of the University.

Monday, 17. At ten called on Greenwood. Got from him a note for Ferguson's Astronomy out of the library. After dinner drew out a Manuscript of Mr Tavel's lecture on Saturday on Spherical Trigonometry. At five walked till Chapel time. Afterwards read *Œd. Colon.*, Lowth and Locke till half-past ten. Went to bed.

Tuesday, 18. Do not intend reading any more Greek till Scholarships, except perhaps Xenophon.

Wednesday. ...Till half-past ten read Astronomy. Walked with Tweddell till half-past eleven. Read Astronomy till one. After Dinner went to Merrills [publishers]: bought Mr Owen's

Sermon. Drank wine with Reynolds. Present: Le Grice, Richmond, Satterthwaite, Trin.; Mr Lombe the Ink Man came in. He entertained us with Hamlet and Ghost, dressed in Reynolds' surplice, and with part of Alexander Stephens' lecture on heads[1].

Saturday, 22....[forenoon] played at Shuttlecock with Vaughan...Quarter past ten [*p.m.*]. Began Millot's History; read till eleven; bed.

Monday, 24...half-past twelve. Called on Satterthwaite. Played with him at Shuttlecock till dinner time. [At this period he was revising the early books of Euclid, reading Grecian History, Trigonometry, Astronomy, Lowth, and 'lounging' in Byshe's *Art of Poetry*, and Vol. I. of the *Literary Magazine*, borrowed from Rough.]

Tuesday, 25. After supper drank a beaker with Rough, by appointment to meet Tilt, to consult for the first time on a projected periodical publication. On mentioning a slight hint for it, they requested me to take the first paper, and all more which may have any relation to the character of the author[2]. It is in-

---

[1] 'A Lecture on Heads, by *Geo. Alex. Stevens*, with Additions, by Mr *Pilon*, as delivered by Mr *Charles Lee Lewes*. To which is added an Essay on Satire. With 47 Heads by *Nesbit*, from Designs by *Thurston*.' London: &c. 1812.

[2] In the University Library [Z. 23. 11], bound up with other tracts, is the *University Magazine*, i—v, 1—136 being numbers for January and February 1795. It contains, among a variety of other matter, Euclid I. 1 'poetically rendered.' Among the poetry is a 'Monody on the Death of *Chatterton*. By *S. T. Coleridge*, Jesus College. [From the Cambridge edition of Rowley's Poems.]' It is also announced that '*Mr Coleridge* of Jesus College, will shortly publish some Sonnets.'

In the same volume is bound up an Advertisement to the following effect :—

'*Stolen* or *Strayed*, this day, between *Magdalen Bridge* and the *Petty Cury*, on its road to the *Press*,

the

University Magazine,

Had on when it disappeared a *Strait Waistcoat*.

Whoever will give information thereof to its distressed owners shall receive a reward of *Eighteen Pence*, or 3000 copies printed on very soft paper.'

nded to begin publishing it early next October. Sat till near
·elve. Went to bed.

Thursday, 27. Afternoon...After Chapel walked with Rough
· Maps'. [see p. 379.] Called with [? R.] on Tilt the first time.

Saturday, 29. Rose to Chapel. Till nine read Astronomy
·r lectures, and a paper of Spectator at breakfast. In the after-
oon sat at home, examined Hale on the primary origin of man-
ind; found nothing very interesting in him.

Monday 31...In the evening lounged in Lity. Mag. Frend's[1]
·ial, &c.

Tuesday, April 1st..,Rodwell, St John's...told us a curious
·ircumstance which he said he had from Vince respecting a
·ong account which Bruce in his travels gives of an eclipse, &c.,
·hat no such eclipse did take place where Bruce was, and that
·iis whole account was copied almost literally from a French
·ilmanack which Vince had seen. Chapel. Met Tilt. Lounged
·vith him till half-past six at Lunn's and Merrill's...In the Evening
·read the British Critic for March...

Thursday 3rd....with Rough into ye library, and lounged
·there at Lunn's and at home about a name for paper till dinner...

Friday 4...read Vince's Conic Sections at the beginning...
At 5 went to Harwood's [? anatomical] lectures...Began Paradise
Lost at breakfast, intend continuing him.

Monday [7]...10 till 11 Roman Antiquities.

Tuesday 8...read Dryden's preface to his fables and two
books of Palamon and Arcite...G. Antiquities.

Thursday [April] 10...Finished lectures for this term...Supped
with Reynolds. A lion from Oxford. At 12 came home.'

About this time he used to translate passages of the Spectator, and read Xenophon.

'N.B. Messrs *Wit, Common Sense*, and *Grammar*, are totally un-
suspected of knowing any thing about it.

Sydney College, March 1st, 1795.'

With the above is bound a pamphlet of eight pages, dated 1795,
and called '*A Strait Waistcoat for Lunatics*,' wherein the several papers
are hardly criticised.

[1] Mr Frend's Appeal forms the staple of University Intelligence in
the *University Magazine*, January 1795, p. 65.

'*Monday* 14...Read Vince till supper. Afterwards drank Milkpunch with Walton. Present Ryley and Owen.

Friday [18]...Chapel before dinner, being a fast day...Went to the coffee-houses. [? 7 p. m.] Walked half an hour with Rough.

Sunday [20]...Chapel at 9, sacrament.

Monday [21] rose at half-past eight. Read Astronomy half-an-hour. Till twelve looked over Plane Trigonometry...From eight till half-past nine, translated Adventurer into Latin. Till eleven looked over Paley.'

(April 21, 1794.)

A small notebook contains entries of 'Miscellaneous questions relating to Arithmetic and the first part of Algebra' (e.g. 'What is that property of the No. 9 by which the fundam. rules of Arith. may be proved?')

A list of Subjects read from December to April probably in a later year (including the Psalms of the day in Horne, Gk. Test. &c.)

A scheme of Classical Reading.

A List of curious English books, the Class-marks of some library apparently being prefixed.

A list of Authors and Editions to be read for the degree.

'Mechanicalia' (formulae, &c.).

'Fluxions, Nov. 5, 1794' (about 50 examples).

'Fluxional Problems, &c.' above 60.

From Vince and Simpson.

On sheets of paper pinned together are summaries of the time employed on each subject every day from 'Monday, Sept. 7, 1795' to 'Saturday,' January 2, 1796, with a holiday on Thursday, Dec. 17, Commemoration Day.

On an average he appears to have read nine hours and three quarters per diem between his act and examination.

'Saturd., Sep. 12, eleven to twelve, bathed, &c.'

At the time of the Fellowship Election, October 1st, he allowed himself time to take part in the rejoicings of the success ful candidates, and dined out three times in the following week, once 'at Ditton with Richmond.' About the 29th he reads Cotes, Newton, Optics, &c., and reads 'for Thesis,' with Demosthenes for a change.

'Monday 9 [Nov. 1795]...Drank tea with Barnes. 1st oppt.

Wednesday...Drank tea at Dealtry's secd. oppt. F[rom] 7 to $\frac{1}{2}$ p. 9 Thes[is].

Friday [Nov. 13] kept act.'

The following are the records of his shortest and of one of his two longest days of work in the twelve weeks following that time.

'Wednesday [Nov. 25, 1795].

F[rom] $\frac{1}{4}$ p. 9 to 11. Alg. H[ours] = $1\frac{3}{4}$.

Went to County meeting.

F. $\frac{1}{4}$ p. 5 to $\frac{3}{4}$ p. 7. Hyd. H[ours] = $2\frac{1}{2}$.

F. 10 to 12. Argts.

F. 12 to 1. Euclid.

$\therefore$ H[ours] T[otal] = $4\frac{3}{4}$.'

'Thursday [Dec. 17] Commemoration Day.'

'Friday [Dec. 18] F[rom] $\frac{1}{2}$ p. 10 to 3.

Newt. H[ours] = $4\frac{1}{2}$.

F. $\frac{1}{4}$ p. 5 to $\frac{1}{2}$ p. 10. Mechs. with Malc. H. = 5.

F. $\frac{1}{2}$ p. 10 to $\frac{1}{2}$ p. 1. Probs. H. = 3.

$\therefore$ H[ours] T[otal] = $12\frac{1}{2}$.'

'Saturday [Dec. 19] at 10 went to Sheepshanks to be examined.

F[rom] 1 to $\frac{1}{2}$ p. 2. Newt. H = $1\frac{1}{2}$.

F. 5 to $\frac{1}{4}$7 read Mechs. and Ast. with Malcolm. H. = $2\frac{1}{4}$.'

In the Notebook.

Hints for turning a tour to account.

List of Views of the Lakes.

- Scheme for Mathematical reading.

Including Composition Decr. 5th (1796).

38—2

Summary of Arithmetic and Algebra.
Plane Trigonometry (27 Sections).
Spherical Trigonometry.
Geometry.
24 Problems.
Newton.

[At the other end of the book. Brief Botanical Notes Febr. and March, 1797.]

[In another note-book. Notes on Roman and Grecian Antiquities, Feb. and March, 1797.]

List of Classical authors. History, Antiquities, Geography, Moral Science, Philology and Grammar. Questions on Euclid.

List of books read in October and November, 1797. Feb., March, April, May, 1798. Select passages of Cicero.

Brief Diary ('Dates, Memorandums, &c.', beginning Nov. 14, 1797, ending March 8, 1801.

'Cambridge, Nov'. 14, 1797, Tuesday. This Evening introduced by Dealtry to the Speculative Society the members of wch at present are Dealtry B.A. Trin. Fell d^o. Broadley 'd^o. Hey Mag. Grant d^o. Grant d^o. Braisier Sidney.

The five first were present.

The subject of the Essay (Hey's) was Whether Charles 1 was justifiable in consenting to the execution of Strafford. All spoke except Hey, who is also a new member. Dealtry and Fell spoke *twice*. Among the rest I tried my hand. I kept going, wth a good deal of hesitation, for I suppose, six or eight minutes.

Ordered Flower's Paper Saturday Nov' 18th 1797.

Xtmas day went to Birmingham with Lloyd. Returned Feb' 5th [1799]...May 12th 1799. Whitsunday ordained Deacon by the B^p of Norwich at the Chapel Royal St James's. May 15th. Resolved to read the lessons of ye day in the Septuagint & New Test. daily...

Camb. May 22nd began Italian.

Returned to Camb. Oct. 20th.

Sunday Dec' 22nd. Ordained Priest by the B^p of Nor. at Norwich.'

1800.

[The Diary is recommenced regularly March 6, 1800.]...

'At 9 my pupil Doyne came. My other pupil Brandreth comes at 11. From ten my plan is to shave, take a turn in the walks &c. Library &c. I breakfast before 9. At half-past 12 walked with Lloyd till time for dressing for Dinner (at ¼ past 2, first bell ringing at 2). Sat at home after dinner. Began Shakespeare...Walked a little before 5. Chapel half-past 5. Vaughan drank tea with me, and staid till near 8. Supped in Hall (¼ before 9).

Contrived however in the course of the Evening to read the (4) lessons of the Day. Consulted Newton on the Prophecies on the 28th ch. of Deuteronomy, &c.

Bed at 11.

Saturday, 8. Got up to Chapel (7 o'clock)...

(Coveney near Ely). Among the people in the fens he says there is a maxim which is proverbial with them that

> "it is fair and no sin
> to cheat the priest and the king."

In reading the lessons of the Day, to be a day before the Calendar.

Saturday [March] 15...read the last (3d) section of Cave's Apparatus, and two Acts of Coleridge's Tragedy (Osorio).

Monday 16...Half-past 5 an hour at Hebrew (learning the letters).

Wednesday 18...Lucretius at breakfast. Fm. ¼ bef. 10 to 11 Hebrew (Grammar)...At 11 went to read prayers at the Hospital for Brown.

Tuesday, 24th June...Afternoon Combination-room. Home at ¼ p. 5. Duct: Dub: Chap. 1. of *Law's Xtn. Perfectn.*

[Beside Shakespeare and the daily Lessons he was reading several of Jer. Taylor's works, Hooker, Barrow, Hey, Buddeus, and the earliest Greek and Roman authors.]

Thursday, June 26th...Went to St Mary's to hear Sheepshanks' Sermon [for Addenbrooke's hospital]. After Dinner at the Divinity Schools. Mr (Dr) Bayley's Act.

Tuesday, July 1...Fm. ½ p. 10 in the Senate-House—heard the Odes, &c. Kipling's Speech, severely censuring the conduct of the Regent Masters of Arts about Mitchell. In the afternoon in the Combination-room. Evening read the *Monthly Review* and *British Critic.*

Friday, July 4...To-day the dinner-hour changed to 3 (first bell).

Wednesday, July 9...In the afternoon on the bowling green. [He sometimes went to take service in the country; he was reading divinity for a projected 'Syllabus.' Pearson, Barrow and Hey on the Creed, Horsley, St Paul's Epistles, &c. Justin Martyr, Ogden, Balguy, Waterland, Secker, &c., on the Sacrament. Warburton, Newton's and Johnson's lives of Milton, Wilkins on Preaching, Mrs Sheridan's Nourjahad.]

Tuesday, July 22...At five o'clock went with Carr, Tell and Brown to Chesterton to play at Bowls: returned at 9.

Saturday, Aug. 16...Idea occurred to me of a Chronologia Librorum. Thus under each successive year (1600, 1601, &c.) note down the most important works first published in that year. Mention also the year of the Author's death, and the *No.* of the edition first published *after* his death. For reference—an index of Authors' names should be added at the end. Make a trial of this plan for my own use, beginning A.D. 1600. [Very considerable ms. collections now in my Father's possession testify to the ardour with which this scheme was prosecuted.]

Monday 25. Employed about [Granville] Sharp's Pamphlet in the Library, &c.

[1801, Jan. 15] *Thursday*. Went to consult Jesus Library.

Saturday...at 11, Mr Burke came to me. In the Evening finished Travis. Very unsatisfactory.

Hastily read through Marsh's Letters to Travis (except the Appendix). He is very satisfactory. Laborious and really superabundant. He sometimes falls into repetitions.

Monday 19...read Porson.

Thursday. Began Horsley's Tracts, read Chrysostom, &c.

Friday. The Day of Taking Degrees in the Senate House from ten till half-past twelve. On the Caput.

Friday, Jan. 30. Fast-day...hurried through the first volume of a novel, Memoirs of Modern Philosophers, the first book which has yet come round to me in our newly established College Fellows' Circulating Library.

Monday [Feb. 2]. Procured the second volume of Lyrical Ballads.

Friday, Feb. 6. Lardner, a good man, cruelly slighted by the Dissenters : he complained that the rich Dissenters never bought his books, and through his whole life he never received any mark of favour from the Dissenters "not" said he "so much as a trust," p. 82.

Friday 13. Fast-Day.

Wednesday, Feb. 18. Fast-Day. Ash-Wednesday.

Sunday [22nd]...Went to Simeon's Church in the Evening. S. preached. Text, Job 31, 14.

Thursday, Feb. 26, 1801. Sacrament Day for Term. Ramsden preached [John 14, 16].'

NOTES, ADDITIONS AND EMENDATIONS.

.˙. *The information conveyed in the remarks signed with an* M *is due to Professor J. E. B. Mayor of S. John's.*

Page 11. Bishops, Turner of Ely, Lake of Chichester, and White of Peterborough, were also members of St John's College, Cambridge. *M.*

p. 15. Those non-jurors who were already bachelors of divinity before William's time were allowed to retain their fellowships at St John's. *M.*

The following fuller list of *The Names of y⁻ Clergy, Fellows of Colledges, and Schoolmasters who have not taken y⁻ Oaths to y⁻ Government,* 1699, is extracted from Howell's *Collections for* Cambridge. Bodl. Rawlinson MS. B. 281.—I have omitted the names of such beneficed Clergy in the dioceses of Ely and Oxon. as are not distinguished in the list by the name of their College.

'Fol. 476. Diocese, Ely.

Mr [Hen.] Scrivener	fellow of Pembr. Hall [1687; M.B. f. of *Caius*, 1686].	
Mr Ephraim Howard	,, ,,	Queens' [A.M. 1690; A.B. *St John's*, 1685-6].
Buddle	,, ,,	Kath. Hall [? Adam, A.B. 1681-2, A.M. 1685].
Mr [John] Worthington	,, ,,	St Peter's coll. [1688, A.B. *Jesus*, 1684-5].
[John] Woodward	,, ,,	,, ,, [1683, A.B. 1679-80, S.T.P. 1707].
Maleverer	,, ,,	Magd. coll. [John Maulyverer, A.B. 1666-7, A.M. 1670].
Tho. Boteler	,, ,,	Trin. coll. [1666, A.B. 1662-3].
[Peter] Redmayne	,, ,,	,, ,, [1684, A.B. 1680-1].
[Tho.] Browne	,, ,,	St Johns Howse [A.B. 1673-4].
[Charles] Ottway LD.	,,	,, ,, [A.B. 1674-5, A.M. 1678, LL.D. 1688].
Tomkinson	,, ,,	
[Robert] Appleford B.D. ,,	,, ,,	[A.B. 1671-2, B.D. 1682].
[John] Naylor B.D. ,, ,,	,, ,,	[A.B. 1675-6, B.D. 1686].
[Will.] Lake ,, ,,	,, ,,	[A.B. 1686-7].
[John] Billers (univ. orator 1681—8) , ,, ,,	,, ,,	[A.B. 1669-70, A.M. 1673, S.T.B. 1680].
[Alex.] Horton ,, ,,	,, ,,	[A.M. 1681].
[John] Hope ,, ,,	,, ,,	[A.B. 1685-6].
Hobson ,, ,,		

[Edw.] Kenyen   ,, ,,   ,,   ,,   [A.B. 1684-5, A.M. 1688].

[Hilkiah] Bedford   ,, ,,   ,,   ,,   [A.B. 1683-4, A.M. 1687].

[? Tho.] Davison   ,, ,,   ,,   ,,   [A.B. 1684-5, A.M. 1688].

[Ri.] Headlam   ,, ,,   ,,   ,,   [A.B. 1685-6, A.M. 1696].

[Tho.] Johnson   ,, ,,   ,,   ,,   [A.B. 1677-8, A.M. 1681].

[? Jos.] Cook   ,, ,,   ,,   ,,   [A.B. 1683-4].

[? Tho.] Alleyn, B.D.   ,, ,,   ,,   ,,   [A.B. 1672-3, A.M. 1676].

[Tho.] Baker   ,, ,,   ,,   ,,   [A.B. 1677-8, A.M. 1681, S.T.B. 1688].

Barth. Wortley   ,, ,,   Cais. [A.B. 1675-6, A.M. 1679].

Sanderson, A.B. Schol. of S. Joh.

ffr. Roper, B.D. Preb. [of Ely] f. of St Jn. [A.B. 1662-3, A.M. 1666, S.T.B. 1673].

Wm. Phillips, f. of Kath. Hal. [A.B. 1684-5, A.M. 1688].

Stephen Phillips, Schol. Trin. coll.

Nath. Pearson, A.B. f. of St Jn. [? Matt. P., A.B. 1686-7, S.T.P. litt. regg. 1703].

Arth. Perl, A.M. f. of Qu. coll.

Tho. Leach, B.D. R. of Textor, f. of St Jn.

Joshua Hopson, A.M. f. of St Jn. [Hobson, A.B. 1678-9, A.M. 1682].

Mr Heron, Jn. f. of St Jn. A.B. [1687-8] Ap.[1] Ch(ap)la^n (to) Ld Preston.

Mr Arth. Heron Do. [A.B. 1683-4, A.M. 1687].

Wm. Emerson, A.B. Schol. of St Jn. [A.B. 1686].

Mr [Chris.] Armitage, f. of Peterhouse [A.M. com. regiis, 1682, A.B. St John's, 1680-1].

Mr Bold, f. of K. Hall.

Mr Jno. Beaufort, Schol. of Trin. Coll. [A.B. 1686-7, Beauford, M.D. comitiis regiis, 1728].

Among the *London* clergy Ambrose Bonwicke senior appears as 'Mr Bunwick M^r of Merch^t Tayl^r Scho.'

'Fol. 479. Dio. *Oxon.*

...Mr Henry Dodwell, Hist. Profess^r. [from Dublin, 1688].

     Robt. Plott, LLD. [Magd. Hall, M.A. 1664, DCL. 1671].

Mr Cha. King, Student of Ch. Ch. [M.A. 1677].

Mr Bishop, Fell. of Baliol Coll.

Mr [? John] Hughes   Do.   [M.A. 1673, B.D. 1684].

Mr Strachan   Do.   [M.A. from Edinb. 1692, DCL. 1709].

Mr Theoph. Downes   Do.   [M.A. 1679].

Dr Tho. Smith, fell. of Magd. Coll. [DD. 1683, B.D. 1674, M.A. Queens' 1663].

Dr Crostwayt fell. of Qu. Coll. Preb. of Exon. [DD. 1684, M.A. 1664].

[1] As I am informed by Mr Coxe 'Ap.' is the non-jurors' mark for 'apostatized.' It occurs against several of the names of the beneficed clergy of these and other dioceses which I have not transcribed.

Mr Edw. Hopkins, fell. of Lincoln Coll. [M.A. 1676, B.D. 1687].
Mr [? John] Gandy sen^r. fell. of Oriel Coll. [DD. 1661].
Dr [Hugh] Wynne, Fell. of All Souls [BCL. 1667, DCL. 1672].
Dr [Bernard] Gardiner   Do.   [BCL. 1693, DCL. 1698].
Mr [Chris] Wase, Eq^r. Beadle [Ch. Ch. M.A. 1684, B.D. 1694].
Mr [Tho.] Hart, f. of Pembroke [M.A. 1681].
Mr Weybergh C^l. of Qu. Coll.
    Wm. Pyne, St^{dt} Xt Ch.
    Wm. Pinock, Senr. f. of br. Nose.
    Jn. Nutting of Pembr.
Mr [Will.] Morgan, A.M. Stu. of Xt. Ch. [M.A. 1674].
    Tho. Lewis, Scho. of Magd. Hall.
Mr Leigh, F. of St Jno. Coll.
    Jn. Lewis, A.B. of Jesus Coll.
    Jo. Urry, Stu. of Xt Ch.
    Tho. Smith, DD. F. of Magd. Coll. [1682; M.A. Queen's, 1663].
    Stephen Seagar, F. of Bras-nose Coll.

---

p. 25. In 1712 (see Swift's *Journal to Stella*, Aug. 7) loose PAM-
PHLETS were made a source of revenue. 'Do you know that *Grub
Street* is dead and gone last week? No more ghosts and murders now
for love or money. I plied it pretty close the last fortnight, and published at least seven penny papers of my own, besides some other
people's: but now every single sheet pays a halfpenny to the queen.
The *Observator* is fallen; the *Medleys* are jumbled together with the
Flying Post; the *Examiner* is deadly sick; the *Spectator* keeps up and
doubles its price; I know not how long it will hold. Have you seen
the red stamp the papers are marked with? Methinks the stamping is
worth a halfpenny.' [The *Spectator* doubled its price from 1d. to 2d.
(see No. 445, July 31, 1712). The original series survived only till the
beginning of the following December. An interval of a year and a half
elapsed between the appearance of No. 555 and the following paper.
Swift, who had given the name and some other assistance to the *Tatler*,
had already written bitterly against *Steele.* He contributed only one
paper to the *Spectator* (No. 50). He had also discontinued his writings
in the *Examiner* above a year.]

    p. 30, line 8 from top. ERRATUM: *for* second *read* sound.

    pp. 32, 33. The Professor seems to have been a *Janus bifrons* in
politics, having for a short period passed for a Whig. 'He was a
strenuous maintainer of the divine right of kings during the reign of
Charles II.: and drew up the famous *Oxford Decree.* Upon his subsequently taking the *oath of allegiance* to William, the following epigram
was written:—

"Cum fronti sit nulla fides, ut carmina dicunt,
Cur tibi bifronti, Jane, sit ulla fides?"'
(*Lusus Alteri Westmonasterienses*, pars 2, p. 341 a.)

p. 36. LOYAL ADDRESSES. Hearne mentions the Loyal Address of the *Oxford* Whigs in the early years of the Hanoverian dynasty (*Diary*, May 2, 1710), and this can hardly have been the expression of the real feelings of that University which received Sacheverell with open arms in the same year. See also the proposal rejected in 1716, and later notices in the volumes of *Silvanus Urban*. The following list of Addresses taken to the Throne from *Cambridge* University is gathered from the Fourth volume of Cooper's *Annals*.

1697. On the peace of Ryswick.

1701. On the occasion of Louis XIV. acknowledging the Pretender. Presented at Hampton Court by the D. of Somerset (chancellor), the V. C. Dr J. Richardson, of Peterhouse, who had succeeded Bentley two days before.

170¼. On the accession of Q. Anne.

1704. On the queen's liberality to the poor clergy, and on the victory of Blenheim.

1707. On the Union with Scotland. D. of Somerset; Dr J. Balderston (Emman.) V. C.; abp. of Canterbury; bps. of Norwich, Peterboro', &c.

170⅚. Against the devices of the Pretender. Dr Edward Lany, *Pemb.* V. C.

1710. Styan Thirlby published '*The Univ. of* Camb. *vindicated from the* Imputation *of* Disloyalty *it lies under on account of not* addressing; *as also from the malicious and foul Aspersions of Dr* Bentley, *late Master of* Trinity *College, and of* a certain Officer *and* pretended Reformer *in the said University.* London, 1710,' (8vo. pp. 1—35). Mr Cole says, his copy is subscribed in MS., '*Saint* Thirlby of Jesus college, since editor of *Saint* Chrysostom.' Nichols' *Lit. Anecd.* IV. 265, and *note*.

1712. On the Truce between England and France, opening of the Congress of Utrecht. At Kensington, by Bentley (*in absence of V. C.* Dr Gabriel Quadring, *Magd.*).

1713. On the Peace of Utrecht. Dr Adams of *King's*, V. C. introduced like Bentley by the E. of Oxford Ld. High Treasurer.

1714. K. George I. on his Accession. Dr Thomas Green of *Corpus*, V. C.; D. of Somerset, Chancr.; E. of Manchester, High Steward; Abp. of York; E. of Anglesea and of Nottingham; Bp. of St Asaph; M.P.'s; Heads of Houses and Doctors; Senr. Proctor;

M.A.'s and others   The book of Verses mentioned below was then presented.

171;. On the anticipated invasion by the Pretender. Dr T. Sherlock of *Cath. Lcil*, V. C. [after riotous demonstrations in the university].

1715. Thanks for the royal benefaction to the public Library. (Sherlock, V. C.)

1716. After the defeat of the Pretender at Preston Pans and the death of Louis XIV. This was drawn up by Bentley, and after some opposition presented to the Prince of Wales at Hampton Court by Daniel Waterland, B.D. *Magd.* V. C.

171$\frac{8}{9}$. A demonstration against the Pretender, a few weeks after the ejection of the non-jurors from *S. John's*. Will. Grigg, M.A. *Clare*, V. C.

1719. On the king's return to England.

1720. On a similar occasion.

1724. On the Modern History Professorship.

172$\frac{5}{6}$. A year after the exiled bp. Atterbury had been fomenting the jacobitism of Scotland, Dr Thomas Gooch of *Caius* (who had been V. C. 1717—9) as deputy-vice-chancellor for Dr John Davies of *Queens'*, presents a declaration of loyalty to George I.

1727. Accession of George II. Dr Joseph Craven, *Sidney*, V. C. (The Chancellor, six bishops, and others accompany the address.)

173$\frac{3}{4}$. On the marriage of the Princess Royal. Dr Roger Long, *Pemb.* V. C.

1736. Marriage of Fred. Prince of Wales. Dr John Adams, *Sid.* V. C.

1737. Birth of his daughter Augusta, mother of Q. Caroline II. Dr John Wilcox, *Clare*, V. C.; D. of Newcastle, newly elected High Steward.

1738. On the Birth of the Prince of Wales.

174$\frac{3}{4}$. [After the victory of Dettingen] a loyal protestant address. Dr W. George of *King's*, V. C.

1745. On the rebellion.

1746. Victory of Culloden. Dr Geo. Hen. Rooke, *Chr.* V. C.

1748. On the King's safe return. Dr Tho. Chapman, *Magd.* V. C. 'On a late *gratulating* occasion our very worthy the Vice-Chancellor deign'd to tag a rhyme, and our learned Professors play'd at crambo in *Hebrew, Arabic*, and—WELCH.' *The Student*, 1751, II. 225.

1756. Grateful and loyal address from the Chancellor (D. of Newcastle), Masters, and Scholars, sent to the Chancellor through the

'Beadle,' and the answer returned by the Chanc. to the V. C. Dr Edmund Law, *Peterhouse.*

... On the victories of Cape Breton, Louisbourg, Crevelt, &c.

1758. American successes in the ministry of W. Pitt (Ld. Chatham). Dr John Green of *Corpus*, V. C.

1759. On the battle of Minden and reduction of Quebec. Jas. Borrough, M.A. *Sid.* V. C.

1760. Accession of K. George III. Dr G. Sandby, *Magd.* V. C.

... Address to the Princess Dowager of Wales the royal mother.

1761. Marriage of the king with Q. Charlotte. Sandby, V. C.

1762. Birth of the Prince of Wales. Dr Ro. Plumptre, *Queens'*, V.C.

1763. On the Peace of Fontainbleau. Dr Peter Stephen Goddard, *Clare*, V. C.

1769. Camb., as in former years, expresses her intention of educating her progeny in loyalty. Dr John Hinchcliffe, *Trin.* V. C.: Jebb of Peterhouse, and Tyson of Bene't opposed the grace.

1775. Protest against the 'unnatural rebellion' in America, D^r Ri. Farmer, *Emman.* V. C. (the address carried by 46 to 21 in Non-Regent Ho: and 38 to 25 in Regent).

[1780. Petition to the *House of Commons* for constitutional redress of grievances sent by a general meeting in the Senate-House yard. It was written by D^r Ri. Watson, *Trin.* Regius Prof. of Div^y. (who in 1782 drew up an address to the King from a county meeting to congratulate him on the occasion of L^d. Rockingham—who died very soon after —succeeding L^d. North in the ministry). The Dukes of Rutland and Manchester—and John Wilkes, were present. A fortnight later another meeting resolved upon a vote of thanks to the majority of 233 M.P.'s who voted to diminish the increasing influence of the crown.]

1786. Addresses to King George on the attempt of Marg^t. Nicholson upon his life, presented by Dr Joseph Turner, *Pemb.* V. C.; E. of Euston, and W. Pitt, M.P.'s for the Univ.; Hon. E. J. Eliot, and G. Pretyman, D.D. (Pitt's tutor).

[1788. The Senate votes a Petition to the Commons against the Slave Trade. Dr Farmer, V.C.]

1789. An Address to the King and Queen on his recovery, presented by the D. of Grafton, Chanc^r.; Dr Francis Barnes, *Pet.* V.C.; Pitt, and E. Euston; the Caput; Esquire Bedels; Prince Will. Fred^k., the Rev. Mr Walesby his preceptor.

1792. Expression of Conservatism by the Univ. M.P.'s (Pitt and E. Euston) and other representatives. Dr Tho. Postlethwaite, *Trin.* V. C.

1795. Marriage of the Pr. of Wales with Princess Caroline, D. of Grafton, Chanc[r]. ; Dr Lowther Yates, *Cath.*, V. C.; Pitt and E. Euston, M.P.'s; D. of Rutland; 6 Bps.; cet.

1795. On an attempt on the King's life. Dr Philip Douglas, *Bene't*, V. C.; Pitt (then High Steward) and others.

1796. On the birth of the Princess Charlotte of Wales, presented by Pitt, as High Steward, and a distinguished company.

1797. On the marriage of the Princess Royal. D[r] Ri. Belward, *Caius*, V.C.; the Caput; Proctors; Registrary; Senior Esq. Bedell; Noblemen; Bishops, &c.

1798. On the occasion of the victory of the Nile. D[r] Ro. Towerson Cory, *Emman.* V. C.

1800. On Hadfield's attack upon the king.

ROYAL VISITS, &c.

1689. K. William at Cambridge.
1695. The King expected.
1698. The University visit him at Newmarket.
1699. Again at Newmarket.
1705. Q. Anne at Cambridge.
1717. George I. at Cambridge.
1728. George II. at Cambridge.
1763, 1771, 1785. George III. expected.

VERSES of Congratulation and Condolence.

168$\frac{8}{9}$. Accession of William and Mary.
169$\frac{4}{5}$. Death of Q. Mary.
1697. Peace of Ryswick.
1700. Death of D. of Gloster.
170$\frac{1}{2}$. Accession of Q. Anne.
1708. Death of Prince George of Denmark.
1713. Peace of Utrecht.
1714. Accession of George I.
1727. Accession of George II.
173$\frac{3}{4}$. Marriage of Prince of Orange and Princess Royal.
1736. Marriage of the Prince of Wales.
1748. On Peace.
1751. Death of Frederick, Prince of Wales.
1755. On the visit of D. of Newcastle, Chancellor.

1760. Accession of George III. *Academiae* Cantabrigiensis *Luctus et Gratulationes*, not recorded by Cooper.—*M.*

1762. Birth of Prince of Wales.

1763. The Peace.

---

p. 37. *Final* COMPLIANCE *of non-jurors.*

T. Hearne (*Reliqu. Bliss* I. 314), Jan. 23, 171$\frac{4}{5}$, mentions the death of *Rob. Nelson*, late a fellow-commoner of *Trin. Coll.* Cant. 'a very learned, religious and pious gentleman and a non-juror,' author of the History of the *Fasts and Festivals* of the Church. Although a friend of Tillotson's he continued a non-juror until the death of Bp. William Lloyd of Norwich in the year 1717, when with Dodwell (of T. C. Dublin, and on refusing to take holy orders, a resident at Oxford) and others he became a '*Complyer*' (ibid. III. 117).

BP. Wm LLOYD of S. Joh. *Camb.* bp. of Landaff, Peterboro', and (in 1685) Norwich, *must not be confused with the other bp.* Wm Lloyd, Oriel and Jesu, *Oxon,* bp. of St Asaph (one of 'the Seven' at least in will), Lichfield, Coventry, and Worcester (also a friend of H. Dodwell—see *Biog. Brit.* Kippis, art. *Dodwell*), who died in 1717. Some notices of each will be found in Mr Mayor's *Baker*. For a testimony to the character of the bp. of St Asaph, see *W. Whiston's* memoir of himself, *ed.* 1749, p. 31.

p. 38. The Tory WHITE ROSE.

> 'Of all the days that's in the year
> The tenth of June I love most dear,
> When our white roses will appear,
>   For sake of *Jamie* the Rover.
> In tartans braw our lads are drest,
> White roses glancing on their breast;
> For amang them a' we love him best
>   Young *Jamie* they call the Rover.'

> 'And here's the flower that I lo'e best
> The rose that's like the snaw.'
>   (Kenmure's *On and Awa,* 1715, edited by BURNS.)

> 'See the white rose in his bonnet!
> See his banner o'er the *Tay;*
> His good sword he now has drawn it,
> And has flung the sheath away.'
>   (*Gathering of* Athol.)

> 'There grows a bonnie brier bush in our kail yard,
> And white are the blossoms o't in our kail yard,
> Like wee bit cockauds, to deck our hieland lads,
> And the lasses lo'e the bonnie bush in our kail yard.'
>   (By LADY NAIRNE.)

The *white cockades* also are mentioned in '*Come ye by* Athol.' *The White Cockade*, '*To your Arms.*' '*Though* Geordie *reigns in* Jamie's *stead*,' &c. See *the* Jacobite *Songs of* Scotland *chronologically arranged.* Maurice Ogle, 1871.

p. 38. Apud Oxonienses *convocatio est* 'magna congregatio' magistrorum *regentium* et *non-regentium* qui 'per fidem' a bedellis conuocantur. *Congregatio* autem est conuentus magistrorum tantum *regentium* qui ad magnae campanae pulsationem, utpote pauciores numero, sponte sua congregantur.

The REGENT MASTERS or Actual Teachers at Oxford kept all power over scholastic matters, especially the right of conferring the Degree. This is the Oxford House of CONGREGATION—of which the members are so ready to do their duty that they 'flock together' of their own accord. The 'Great Congregation'—like the Greater Chapter of our old capitular bodies—or CONVOCATION, was the general assembly of Regents and Non-Regents who waited to be 'summon'd to meet together.'

This constitution was developed from the XIIIth to the XVth century. See *English Universities*, by Prof. *V. A. Huber*, translated and edited by *F. W. Newman*, Vol. II. pt. I. p. 99, ed. 1843.

At Cambridge *all* matters passed first through the Non-Regent House.

In this university *magna congregatio* was a totally different thing (Cooper's *Annals*, I. 176, 442), it was the *Black Assembly* or meeting between town and university in the chancel of Great S. Mary's on the Friday before SS. Simon and Jude, when the oaths of aldermen, burgesses, and parishioners were taken by the V. C. and Mayor. (*Senate-House Ceremonies*, Wall-Gunning, 1828, pp. 39—41.)

p. 39. 'I remember when a VICE-CHANCELLOR suspended the proudest Doctor in the University from all his Degrees without a Hearing.' [In Oct. 1718, when 'the late great Dʳ B. was reduc'd to be a bare Harry-Soph' in the Vice-Chancellorship of 'the empty *Gotch* of Caius.' *Diary* of *E. Rud*, edited by Mʳ *Luard*, 1860, and Monk's *Life of Bentley*, II. 48.] 'I remember when another Vice-Chancellor punished in the same manner a saucy member of the *Caput* for giving a Vote which he did not approve.' *Friendly and Honest Advice of an Old Tory*, 1751, p. 1. The latter case was that of 1725 when Dʳ Wᵐ S[avag]e of *Emman.* V.C. suspended William C[ampbe]ll of *King's*, Senior Regent, for contumacy in stopping several times, and without any reason assigned, divers graces and supplicats of candidates for degrees. The sentence was reversed on appeal to University Delegates, and the V. C. had to pay costs and damages. See [Chapman's] *Inquiry into the Right of Appeal*, p. 39, and *A Letter to the Author of a Further Inquiry into the Right of Appeal*, p. 4.

p. 41. The XXIXth of MAY.

> 'I asked a man what meant the fray!
> "Good sir," said he, "you seem a stranger:
> This is the *twenty-ninth of May;*
> Far better had you shun the danger."'

(The ballad of *Lochmaben gate*, 1714, from the *Jacobite* Songs of *Scotland* chronologically arranged, *Maurice Ogle*, 1871, p. 26.)

p. 42. As to the political character of Colleges—C. Wesley, writing in 1734 to his eldest brother Sam., uses the names *Wadham, Merton, Exeter,* and *Christchurch* as the types of the opponents of Jacobitism in Oxford. See Southey's *Life of Wesley* (1846), I. 19.

Amherst boasts in Terrae-Filius, No. 50, that 'it was known to the whole university that a marquis, several noblemen's sons, two or three baronets, besides a great number of clergymen, and others of the best rank and quality, were members of the *Constitution Club*.' It was probably an irregular dining club.

p. 43. 'TERRAE-FILIUS: Or, the Secret History of the University of Oxford in several Essays,' which appeared on Wednesdays and Saturdays from January to July, 1721, and was printed in two vols. London: Printed for R. Francklin, under Tom's Coffee-House, in Russel-Street, Covent-Garden, 1726, pp. 354, including an Appendix on D[r] Newton of Hart Hall's 'University Education.' The frontispice by Hogarth seems to represent the unwigging and unfrocking of the Author and the tearing of his paper in the presence of the Vice-Chancellor, proctor, and other members of the University in the Sheldonian Theatre, by the Dons and the 'Toasts' whose character he had aspersed. The writer and in great part the *inventor* (if we may believe the late M[r] Ri. Robinson of Queen's) of this scurrilous attack upon Oxford was NICHOLAS AMHURST (1701—1742). Like Ambrose Bonwicke he had been educated at the Merchant Taylors'. He was expelled from St John's Coll. under D[r] Delaune, Oxon, June 29, 1719. Though he himself gives an ironical description (in n°. 1) of the causes of his removal, it appears that the charges brought against him were for immoral conduct and libertine principles (see Kippis, *Biogr. Britann.* ed. 2). Amhurst revenged himself by satirizing the University in a poem called *Oculus Britanniae* (1724) and in the Terrae-Filius Essays above mentioned. He joined Pulteney and Ld. Bolingbroke in conducting the *Craftsman,* a periodical written against Sir R. Walpole's ministry, but died in 1742, having become disliked or neglected by them. He appears to have led a discontented life at Oxford, grumbling at the loss of the genial town life, and of the smiles of his Laura. Southey says, 'the preface of Amhurst's poems is written with the spirit of a man who thinks himself injured, without waiting to consider whether the world would be of his opinion' (*Specimens of later English Poets,* 1807, I. 394). See also pp. 23—26 of '*Law and Arguments in Vindication of the University of Oxford,*' including a detection of the main primary author of the Imputation of Jacobitism. [*Camb. Univ. Lib.* XXIX. 8. 88 (2)].

p. 44. Dr *Charlett's* name was struck out of the list of King's chaplains, March, 1717 (Dr Rawlinson's MSS. in the Bodleian Library. *Letters from the Bodleian and Ashmole,* 1813, I. p. 31, *n.*).

p. 47. This SERMON (preached at a crisis when there was an attempt to place a Roman Catholic upon the throne) is as well worth perusal as anything BENTLEY ever wrote for accurate criticism and crushing argument. We are familiar with the minute criticism of the text, with which he begins: Οὐ γὰρ ἐσμεν ὡς οἱ πολλοί, καπηλεύοντες τὸν λόγον τοῦ Θεοῦ. 2 Cor. ii. 17.

It is hardly necessary to add that the occasion was the anniversary of the Landing of the Prince of Orange, as well as of the Gunpowder Plot. This day was sometimes, as in later times, made the occasion of party incivilities—as at Oxford in 1723 (Hearne)—at Cambridge all the more, we may suppose, as it followed the election of the Vice-Chancellor, which took place upon Nov. 4 (Sundays not excepted, save in 1716).

p. 50. OXFORD LOYALTY.

Mr A. J. Horwood, in the third Report of the *Historical MSS. Commission,* 1872, p. 194, mentions a folio volume of 76 leaves among *Matt. Prior's* MSS. (1693—1721) in the collection belonging to the Marquis of Bath at Longleat, *co.* Wilts, beginning, 'The present design of vindicating the University of Oxford from the odious and unjust charge of disloyalty to His Majesty King George — .' Prior played an important part in the political world, especially at the time of the peace of Utrecht (1713). He was a Cambridge man, of St John's, 1682—6, in the library of which College he recited a set of verses to lady *H. C. H. Harley,* Nov. 9, 1719. (*Harl. Misc.* II.)

p. 51. The punishment for the first offence mentioned in the Vice-Chancellor's notice against the disturbances at *Cambridge* (*vide supra,* p. 48) was one year's suspension or retention from the first degree. At Cambridge the riot seems to have been confined to undergraduates and bachelors.

I cannot resist quoting from the account of the CALVES'-HEAD CLUB in 1734, 1735, referred to above, as it is highly illustrative of the disturbances in the universities. 'On the 30th of January, 1735, certain young noblemen and gentlemen met at a French tavern in Suffolk-street (Charing Cross) under the denomination of the "Calves'-head Club." They had an entertainment of calves' heads, some of which they showed to the mob outside, whom they treated with strong beer. In the evening they caused a bonfire to be made before the door, and threw into it with loud huzzas a calf's-head dressed up in a napkin. They also dipped their napkins in red wine, and waved them from the windows, at the same time drinking toasts publicly. The mob huzzaed as well as "their betters"—but at length broke the windows, and became so mischievous that the guards were called in to prevent further outrage [*Gent. Mag. and Brit. Chron.*]...There is a print entitled "The true Effigies of the Members of the Calves'-head Club, held on the 30th of January, 1734, in Suffolk-street in the County of Middlesex." This date is the year before that of the disturbance related, and as regards the company, the health drinking, huzzaing, a calf's head in a napkin, a bonfire, and the mob, the scene is the same ; with this addition, that there is a person in a mask with an axe in his hand...' Hone's *Every-Day Book*, II. 158—160, where an engraving from the print is given. The toasts ranged from 'the pious memory of Oliver Cromwell' to 'The man in the mask' (i. e. the Executioner).

p. 52. In 1718 proceedings were taken in the Vice-Chancellor's Court against the Library Keeper at *Cambridge, Philip Brooke,* B.D., Fellow of S. John's, for disaffection to the king. Dr Gooch dropped the proceedings upon Brooke's resignation, and was consequently accused of Jacobitism by the Whigs. See Monk's *Life of Bentley,* II. 45.

p. 53. *footnotes* 2, 3, *for* Appendix (A. I.) *read* Appendix C. *and for* (Appendix A. II.) read Appendix E.

p. 54. The other Lives contained in the vol. of *De Quincey's* NORTHERN WORTHIES are those of *Andrew Marvell,* Tho. Ld. *Fairfax, James* 7th E. of *Derby,* Lady *Anne Clifford, Roger Ascham, John Fisher,* Rev. *Will. Mason,* Sir *Ri. Arkwright, Will. Roscoe,* Capt. *Cook, Will. Congreve,* Dr *John Fothergill.* (Univ. Lib. Oo. 35, 23.)

p. 55. The protest of ten Junior Fellows in 1787 (Cooper's *Annals,* IV. 424) rather approves the general fairness of the ELECTIONS, though the system of examining had been occasionally set aside, and the seniors had sometimes voted as electors without having been present at the examination. 'From the date of this memorable appeal (1787) TRINITY College assumed that high character in the University which it has ever since maintained. The system of favouritism which had so long prevailed...received its death blow.' Gunning, *Reminisc.* II. 109.

p. 60. When Dr Matthias Mawson, Master of C. C. C. C. was Vice-Chancellor in 173⅞, he procured the augmentation of the fine at Camb. for a *bene discessit*, from 40*s.* to £10, since capricious migration had become common. Masters' *Hist. of C. C. C. C.* p. 196, *original ed.*

p. 61.

The Conduct of ——— College Considered; with some Reflections upon a late Pamphlet, entitled, A Defence of the Rector and Fellows of Exeter College. In a Letter from a *Cambridge Soph.* to a Gentleman in Hampshire... London: Printed for C. Corbett, opposite St Dunstan's Church in Fleet Street, price sixpence,

pp. 16 (dated Cambridge, December 15th, 1754). In the Bodleian, *Gough Add^{s.}. Oxfordshire*, 4°. 31, which vol. contains many other pamphlets and squibs relating to the question of Exeter Coll. 1754—5.

An amusing instance of impetuous zeal for the Government is related of 'Gaby,' Dr Tho. Shaw, F.R.S. (author of *Travels in Barbary and the Levant*, see below, Part 2), by Herbert Beaver of Corpus, in the *Oxford Sausage.* The doctor, who had been fellow of Queen's, on succeeding Dr Felton in 1740 as President of Edmund Hall, picked out the initials of Jemmet Raymond, a benefactor from the cushion he had presented, mistaking it for a remnant of Jacobitism. In 'A Key to the Fragment,' 1751, p. v. an anecdote similarly characteristic of the political suspicion rife in 1745 is given; the initials of the words *Civis Ejus Coloniae* in an inscription being mistaken for 'Charles Edward, Come!'

p. 61. At Cambridge Gray complains (in a Letter, No. LXI. ed. 1819, dated Feb. 3, 1746) two weeks after the battle of Falkirk and two months before Culloden, of the apathy of the students. 'I heard these people, sensible middle-aged men (when the Scotch were said to be at Stamford and actually were at Derby) talking of hiring a chaise to go to Caxton (a place in the high-road) to see the Pretender and the highlanders as they passed.' A Cambridge *coffee-house jest* of the Revolution tells how 'Some scholars were sitting at a coffee-house together, and one asking what news there were, one replied that 40,000 men had risen the day before; which made them all stare about, and ask him to what end they rose, and on what side. "Faith," says the informant, "for nothing I know of but to go to bed again."'

p. 62. 'The advice given in 1748 to a young Jacobite by Dr Bentham, Fellow and Tutor of Oriel, sums up, I believe, the views predominant in the minds of the majority of resident Oxonians through the previous sixty years.' (M[r] *Ri. Robinson*, Oxf. Undergr. Journal, May 4, 1867.)

p. 65. We may be inclined to question the sincerity of Mason's eulogium upon the D. of Newcastle when we find in the *MS. letter*, quoted below, that he had the credit of writing one of the squibs of which we shall speak presently.

pp. 65—76. The ORDERS and REGULATIONS of 1750.

No. 2. See pp. 491, 523 of this Essay.

No. 6. Compare the *King's Letter*, 1616.

It appears from *The Academic*, p. 44 *n.* that this Regulation was not put in force in 1750; but the writer of *Considerations on the...Regulations*, p. 58, rejoins that it was only delayed while arrangements were being made with the Trustees 'to make a proper Disposition of seats in the galleries and a convenient allotment of Places for the several Colleges.'

No. 13. Cf. a decretum Praefectorum, 1606.

No. 17. By Stat. Univ. Eliz. XLVII. dice were never to be used; cards only for 12 days after Christmas Day, and that only with moderation and at the proper time openly in the Coll. hall. Cf. College Statutes.

p. 70. JAMES BROWN of *Pembroke Hall.*

He is called 'Obadiah Fusk' in the *Key to the Fragment.* In *Another Fragment* he is called *Dun*, 'universally hated among the Boys because he us'd to carry a great stick in his Hand to frighten them Home from their play making them come in by Daylight to go to Bed, or read good Books, for which Reason whenever his Back was turn'd they would make Faces at him and us'd to beryme him calling out *hoo! Doctor Proctor!—hoo! Doctor Proctor*, and so on; for which however whenever he catch'd them he *down'd* with their *apple carts* and made them smart for it.' He was particularly severe upon the noted '*Free School* which was founded by one *Lady Betty...*' and so on. 'One of them with a Gentle Look and *Savage* Name carrying the staff of office' (*Fragmentum est pars*, p. 28) refers to F(orreste)r who accompanied the Sen[r]. Proctor (*Authentic Narrative*).

Before leaving Oxford I had not seen M[r] Cooper's list of pamphlets relating to the Regulations, Westminster Club and Appeal, 1750—1751, accordingly I had not discovered 3 of the 23 documents mentioned by him (*Annals*, IV. 280, 281), viz. '*A Tale.*' *London Evening Post*, 25 Dec. 1750—An Expostulatory Address of the Undergraduates of the University of Cambridge, to the Doctor and 36 Masters of Arts met together at the Tuns Tavern and adjourn'd to the eleventh of January, sent by post to the gentlemen of the several Colleges, 4 January, 1750-1.—'*Free Thoughts upon University Education; occasioned by the present debates at* Cambridge, *and calculated for the advance ment of religion and learning. By a sincere well wisher to our Univer-sities.'* London, 8vo. 1751. Besides these I omit, as uninteresting, '*The Metamorphosis of C(ambridg)e,'* a cutting from the Evening Post, Nov. 10, 1750; it is to be found in Bodley, in one of the vols. of pamphlets mentioned in the following notes. '*David's Prophecy; relating to C—b—ge (found among the Papers of a certain Rabbi, famous for a Collection of all the Prophecies from the Beginning of the World to this Day), with an Account of its Accomplishment in that U——y. By Isaac Van-Sampson, a learned Dutch Commentator. Dedicated to the V—C—r, H—ds, and M^r B— the P—r.'* London, 8vo. 1751, is in the Bodleian. Mr Cooper tells us that it was written by Will. Waller, an undergra-duate of Trinity College, who in 1752, being then B.A., was expelled the University for publishing it. A MS. note on the Queens' college copy [*Ii.* 3—31.] [pp. I—XXV, 26—53, 'price One Shilling'] adds that 'he was a Westminster Schollar.' According to the *index actorum curiae* in the registrary's office he made his confession before being expelled. The note in Queens' says merely that he was 'degraded by y⁰ Senate.'

PAMPHLETS, &c. relating to the ORDERS and REGULATIONS.

'A Letter to Lord Eg[mo]nt on the Dangerous Ambition, and overgrown Power of a certain M(in)is(ter)r. Contra publicos Hostes et Majestatis reos, omnis Homo Miles est. *Tertull.* Printed at London and Sold at all the Pamph-let Shops in *Great Britain*' (8vo. pp. 18. 1750).

This is referred to in *Considerations on the Expediency*, &c., *of the late Regulations,* p. 1. *n.* It is a violent pamphlet accusing the D. of Newcastle of Tyranny and Corruption. (In the Bodleian, *Gough Camb.* 56.) It is ascribed by Cooper to *Peter Chester*, M.A., Fellow of Ca-therine Hall.

'An Occasional Letter to the Rev. Dr Keen, Master of Peter House and Vice Chancellor of the University of *Cam-bridge.*

Cave, Cave, namque in malos asperrimus
Parata tollo cornua.

London: Printed for Sam. Johnson, at Charing-Cross; and William Smith, near the Royal Exchange' (pp. 24. 8vo. 1750).

This is a full statement of a previous accusation (? the Letter to Ld. Egmont) of Dr Keene against which that gentleman had protested. The facts related coincide with those figured forth in the 'Fragment.'

The Chancellor is (p. 14) civilly alluded to as a 'senseless Idol' and the Bishops are 'Priests of Baal.' The letter (in Bodley, *Gough Cambr.* vols. 11, 36, 47, 56) is signed, 'Your generous Adversary, Cantabrigiensis —Richmond October 19, 1750.'

This also (says Mr Cooper) is attributed to Chester of S. Catherine Hall.

EDMUND KÉENE (1713—1781) educated at the Charterhouse, whence he went to Caius Coll. Camb., and in 1739 was elected fellow of Peterhouse. Here he succeeded Dr Whalley as master. A few days after he was elected Vice-Chancellor of Cambridge the meeting of the Westminster New Regulation Club took place: he is nicknamed *Mun 'Sharp'* and *'Acutus'* in the pamphlets and Squibs on that matter —Bishop of Chester, 1752.—Resigns his mastership of Peterhouse, 1754.—On Dr Mawson's death is translated to Ely, 1770.—Procures an Act to enable him to part with Ely-place, Holborn, and to build Ely-house in Dover-street, Piccadilly.—Dies 1781.

'*London—The Capitade, a Poem.*

"Manners with Fortunes, Humours change with Climes:
Tenets with Books, and Principles with Times."

POPE.'

Originally printed in the London *Evening Post,* Nov. 1, 1750, and reprinted with notes by the Rev. John Duncombe in the *Gentleman's Magazine* for 1781, p. 580 (530 Nichols), attributed to Thomas Nevile (of Lincolnshire), M.A. (1749), fellow of Jesus College [see Cole quoted in] Nichols' *Lit. Anecd.* IX. 783, also to James Devie, M.A. 1748, fellow of Emmanuel College, Cooper's *Annals,* IV. 280. If Nevile was the author it is to his credit that the only person he commends in the wholesale abuse of the *Heads* is honest old Dr Ashton, by whose decision he had once been obliged to sojourn for a time in Emmanuel in order to take his M.B. degree (which is not mentioned in the *Graduati Cantab.* 1823. See also Nichols' *Lit. Anecd.* II. 306 n.). Nevile and Devie were very nearly of the same standing when at Emmanuel, and one of them may have assisted the other in this somewhat discreditable performance. Nevile died in 1781, Sept. 9; was this before the reprint of the Capitade?

The copy in the Bodleian (*Gough Camb.* 56) is much cut away— it is, I suppose, the *Evening Post* edition.

'The Academic: or a Disputation of the State of the University of Cambridge and the Propriety of the Regulations made in it, on the 11th Day of May and the 26th Day of June, 1750.

"Neque nostrae disputationes quicquam aliud agunt nisi ut in utramque partem dicendo et audiendo eliciant et quasi exprimant quod aut verum sit aut ad id quam maxime accedat." TULLY.

London: Printed for C. Say, in *Newgate Street*, near the *Gate*, 1750' (8vo. pp. 59).

In the Bodleian Catalogue ascribed to Dr John Green, bp. of Lincoln, *Gough Camb.* 11, 36, 47, 56, 69. A MS. note in the Vol. *Gough Camb.* 56, tells us that it was 'Said to be wrote by Dr John Greene.' In Nichols' *Lit. Anecd.* VI. 472, it is attributed to Ri. Hurd, of Emmanuel (afterwards bp. of Worcester), and this, Cooper says, is the general opinion—but in the Additions to Nichols' (IX. 668) ' An Old Cantab.' considers that Hurd can have had no part in it, and that the quotation from Terence in [Green's] ' *Considerations*' points to Alex. *Davie*, a Master Commoner of Sidney Sussex College, as one of the joint authors. However, the author of *Remarks on the Academic* chooses to consider that the pamphlet in question was the work of a single person. Cole ascribed it to Green on the authority of *Gent. Mag.* 1779, p. 235. Lamb (*Hist. C. C. C. C.*, p. 241), is in favour of the authorship of Mr Phil. *Allen*, fellow of St John's. (Mayor, *Baker's Hist.* p. 711). This agrees with the statement of the letter quoted in the text. Powel mentioned there is no doubt Will. Sam. *Powell*, master in 1765. Thos. *Balguy* of St John's took his M.A. degree in 1741; his name is in connexion with Powell and Hurd in Mr Mayor's *Baker*, p. 1061. '*Mason* of Pembrook' is Gray's friend, author of ' Isis' and the Inaugural Ode, supra, pp. 63, 72, 616.

'The Academic' is meant to appear impartial and tentative, though the conclusion intended to be left upon the reader's mind is one unfavourable to the ' Regulations.' If it had appeared now-a-days it might have been taken for the work of an uninterested person anxious to display his skill in sceptical discussion. Such a writer would not have found readers in Cambridge in the 18th century, and all contemporaries who speak of the tract are at one upon its destructive intention.

Other publications (in addition to those already mentioned in this note) which relate to the Cambridge squabbles of 1750—52 are :—

'Remarks on the Academic—

Mihi viderim facere idem quod seditiosi cives solent...

London: Printed for T. Trye, near *Gray's-Inn-Gate, Holborn*, 1751, price sixpence.'

(pp. 19, 8vo. dated '*Cambridge*, Dec. 16, 1750,' delayed in the publication. Bodleian *Pamphlets*, 350, *Gough Cambr.* 36, 56.) In defence of the members of the *Senate* who on the second occasion (June 26, 1750) voted with the majority for passing the 'Regulations' of the Caput. The author charges the writer of 'the Academic' with a design to bring the Reformers in the Senate into ill-odour as unskilful busybodies; and secondly, to gain himself preferment like *Chremylus* in the Plutus of Aristophanes.

For the behaviour of *Thomas Ansell*, Fellow of Trinity Hall, LL.B., 1744, see the references on pp. 621, 628, infra.

Dr WILL. GEORGE, Provost of King's (Nichols' *Lit. Anecd.* II. 193, IV. 342, V. 339, VI. 237, VIII. 433, 436, IX. 251, 289, 575, 581, 701, 743, 808). He had been Provost of Eton, and noted for his severity. Nicknamed *Dionysius* the Tyrant.

> " Big with himself stern Dionysius view
> A slave to P—lh—m but t's own Int'rest true.
> Stern Dyonisius ! who unmov'd con'd hear
> The cries of Youth nor feel the falling Tear :
> He at whose Name Thames trembles as he flows,
> And dreads, as Ocean did mad Xerxes' Blows :
> He at whose Name (what they deny to God)
> Beaus, Soldiers, Senators with Rev'rence nod,
> And why ? why still they fear the Lashes of his Rod."
> *The Capitade,* 1751.

If we may believe the *Authentic Narrative*, p. 33 *n.* he behaved uncourteously to Prof. Francklin in the V.-Chancellor's Court. He also commented on Ansell's want of modesty and respect (*ibid.*), and afterwards answered him when he asked to know why he was to be deprived of his degrees—'Sir, it was not what you said, but the manner of it; Sir, you know *you elevated your Voice.*'

Authentic Narrative of Proceedings against the W —— r Club, p. 61 *n.* Cf. *Another Fragment*, p. 26. In *Fragmentum est pars rei fractae*, p. 31, he is described thus—'looking as surly *as the Devil looked over* LINCOLN......This was a blunt man named *Dionysius*, not descended from the *Areopagite*, but from one of that Name at Syracuse. The *Sicilian* to attone for the Tyrrany of his youth in his advanced years turned his *Iron Sceptre* into a *Birchen* one; but *our Dionysius* changed the *Ferule* and *Rod* for *two* small *Sceptres* tipped with *Silver* which are carried daily before him by the Posterity of *Vergerius*......Notwithstanding Dionysius behaved in this strange manner he is certainly a good-natured Man and loves his Wife and Children, and a Game at Cards as well as any Body; but 'tis supposed he fancied himself *administering Justice* with the same *heavy Hand* he used formerly among his *young* subjects; or believed that he was only *whipping* in some of his own *Hounds*.'

'An Authentic Narrative of the Late Extraordinary Proceedings at Cambridge against the W——r Club.'

The Public in these cases have a Right to demand that all circumstances be produced to Examination. .*Dr Keene's Sermon* at London, Printed for M. Cooper, at the Globe in Pater-noster Row, 1751. Price one Shilling (8vo. pp. 62. edd. 1, 2. Bodleian, *Gough Camb.* 56. *Pamph.* 350), dated '*Cam. Dec.* 16. 1750.'

By Thomas Ansell, LL.B. Fellow of Trinity Hall, written in defence of the Westminster Club—giving an account of the offence, trial before the Vice-Chancellor, and intended appeal of the author.

'A Fragment. London: Printed for M. Cooper at the Globe in Paternoster-Row.' (pp. 28, 8vo. edd. 1, 2. 1750, Bodl. *Gough Cambr.* 36, 56.)

Attributed to Hen. *Stebbing*, D.D., Fellow of Catherine Hall, royal chaplain, author of *A Caution against Religious Delusion* (a sermon against Wesley), 6 editions in 1739, opponent of Warburton. (So Mr Cooper, *Annals*, IV. 280, and a MS. note in the Bodleian, *Gough Camb.* 56, where the claims of one C —— r, are dismissed.) Attributed also to Jas. Bickham, of Emmanuel, see p. 76. Cole, however (in the *Athenae Cantab.* quoted in Nichols' *Lit. Anecd.* IX. 801), refers the squib to Francis Coventry (? of Magdalen). It is very much in the style of a modern *jeu d'esprit* called 'Dame Europa's School,' with much of the coarseness of Swift's *Tale of a Tub.* The contents are an allegorical description of the progress of the Chancellorship of the D. of Newcastle—who figures as 'a sprightly volatile fellow,' one *Tom Standish,* who was Clerk (Sec. of State) to an old Justice of the Peace in the neighbourhood—from his

Installation (marriage to an ' old Lady' *Alma Mater Cantabr.*) till the rejection and final swallowing of the new Regulations (20 Pills pre-scribed by the learned Doctors—the Bishops—for the poor old Lady who had been upset by her'wedding, at the request of her truant Lord). *Tom* and *Mun*—Dr T. Chapman, of Magdalen, ex-Vice-Chancellor, and Dr Edmund Keene, of Peterhouse, V.C.,—who went to consult their Step-Father—the Chancellor—not without looking forward to a Jaunt in Town and to *seeing Westminster and St Paul's*—approved of the smell of the Pills, but found that the largest had been supplied by *Standish's* own Apothecary, Dr *Squirt*—Squire, Chaplain to the Duke, Cooper's *Annals*, IV. 271—in order to ' *heighten* the medicine; they threw that into the fire. ' During the Bustle the Old Gentlewoman rang her Bell and her Sons went up to enquire how she did '—the pills are produced and ' the Old Gentlewoman having smelt to them and not seeming to like, they were handed about the Room.' Some thought that it had been unnecessary to trouble the London Doctors when there was such an excellent Book of Recipes at home (the Statutes), and other objections were whispered — ' For all this *Mun* advanc'd up to the Old Gentlewoman's Chair with a large Mace-Cup and *forc'd* her to take them: she did so, and in taking them she made a wry Face and said in her comical Way—*They have pass'd the Caput, but how they will agree with the Body* (the Senate) *the Lord knows.*' In a word the Senate rejected several of the proposed Regulations (May 11, 1750), and the others were distasteful. The old lady asked for her favourite sons. *Roger* (Dr Roger Long, of Pembroke Hall, V. C. 1733, Prof. of Astronomy), was said by *Mun* to be at home mending his Kitchen Jack which had been out of repair ever since the wedding. As to *Richard* (Dr Will. Richardson of Emmanuel, V. C. 1737) ' he did not know what to make of him, and he thought she would do very well without him.' [' Many of those who had before opposed you were gone out of the University, and it is well known that several others, suspecting they should be overpowered by your hireling Troops, ab-sented themselves that day from the Senate.' *Occasional Letter to Dr Edmund Keen*, p. 21 *n.* Cf. *Academic*, p. 2.] Their eldest brother ' is so much taken up with his Books that he's not *fit to be consulted* on this Occasion; he's *not acquainted with Things of this Nature*, and in all Probability would contradict what we are about.' [The venerable Dr CHARLES ASHTON, Master of Jesus, V. C. 1702. ' One of the most learned men of the age; his great knowledge in Ecclesiastical Antiquities was excelled by none,' Nichols' *Lit. Anecd.* IV. 226 *n.* His *Collectanea* manifest a diligence in the study of University History very remarkable. It speaks very highly indeed for his character as an honest man and a gentleman that he is always mentioned with respect by those who were not even decently reverent to the Heads of other Colleges; e.g. in the *Capitade*, where all his colleagues are accused of servility, he is celebrated as

> 'Asht—n the wise, the learn'd, the ag'd, the good,
> Whose soul unmov'd Temptation hath withstood
>
> . . . . .
>
> He rests a C—llege Monarch—yet a worthy man.'

See the note to *Bentley's Correspondence*, p. 824.]

'*Harry*, (who stands up much for the strength of his Mother's natural constitution) he assured her, had not withheld his sanction.' Henry *Hubbard* of Catherine Hall *and Emmanuel*, Registrary, 1758—not to be confounded with D[r] *Edward* Hubbard, Master of Catherine Hall, V. C. 1739—was accused of having been bribed by Keene to forward the Regulations, cp. *Occasional Letter*, p. 18; 'he had for many years gloried in being Defender of the Liberties and Privileges of the Senate.' *Key to Fragment*, pp. 31, 32. See below, p. 627,—also the *Capitade*.

> 'And thou too Patriot H—bb—d wilt comply,
> Led by the sav'ry odours of Plum-Pye.'

HENRY HUBBARD had been tutor to Hurd and to Prof. Thomas Martyn at Emman. The Prof., writing to Nichols, says, 'I could have wished a fairer account of our most respectable tutor and D[r] Farmer's firm friend M[r] Hubbard. He was a Tory, but not the least of a Jacobite; nor was D[r] Richardson. They were both disciplinarians, and considered *minutiae*, perhaps with some reason, as the outworks of discipline. We see *now* [this was written in 1813] the consequence of their having been given up; the citadel has been stormed.' *Gorham's Martyns*, p. 97. Born at Ipswich, 1708. Educated at Cath. Hall, removed to Emman. 1732.

Elected Registrary of the Univ. 1758.

Unanimously elected to succeed D[r] Richardson as Master of Emman. 1775; 'but on account of his age and infirmities, with his wonted moderation and disinterestedness, he declined that honour.' See MS. Cole, Brit. Mus. XLVI. p. 355, ap. *Gorham's Martyns*, p. 96. n.

His portrait hangs in the registrary's office.

Upon this she resigned herself, though not without a struggle, and *Mun* gained his end by silencing and offering to do their errand to their Father for his brothers. Cp. *Occasional Letter*, p. 19. [Having used the Chancellor's name to summon 'People from every Part of the Country, nay from distant Parts of England by the usual complaint that a wicked opposition had been made to the Minister, the Royal Family and the present Constitution in Church and State,' the Vice-Ch. procured the passing of the late rejected Regulations against the Inclination of the Resident Part of the University. *Occasional Letter to Dr Keen*, pp. 20—22 (the author of which says he was himself 'an eye-witness...upon the Day when these Laws were the second Time offered'—June 26, 1750.—p. 22); cf. the *Academic*, pp. 47, 48.

'Considerations on the Expediency of Making and the Manner of Conducting the late Regulations at Cambridge. London, Printed for J. Payne and J. Bouquet in *Paternoster-Row*, 1751.'

(8vo. pp. 60. Bodleian *Gough Cambr.* 47; the owner of that copy seems to have attributed it to Dr John Green.) Nichols, *Lit. Anecd.* IX. 668, says that this was 'avowedly by Dr John Green, King's Divinity Professor, Master of Bene't College, afterwards Bishop of Lincoln.' The tract is published by the same firm as [Chapman's] *Inquiry into the Right of Appeal*. It may possibly be worth mentioning that when the present writer first read this pamphlet and the *Academic*, and had as yet no further knowledge of the controversy, he supposed that *Considerations* were written by the same author as the *Academic*, in order to pull down the 'man of straw' which he had set up for the purpose in the latter pamphlet. It will be remembered that each tract has been ascribed by some to Dr Green. The *Considerations* are a cool and elaborate defence of the Senate and of the Regulations (some of which had by that time come into operation) against arguments raised in the Academic. It purports to be by 'one who had no share in projecting, nor much in promoting these Laws.' p. 2.

Dr *John Green*, bp. Lincoln 1761 (dean of Lincoln, 1756), one of the reputed authors of the *Academic*, 1750; author of *Considerations on the...new Regulations*, 1751. Died at Bath, 1779. Preached the morning sermon at St Mary's *Camb.* at the *Commencement* in 1749, when the D. of Newcastle was installed Chancellor. Cooper, IV. 271. At that time he was Regius Professor of Divinity and Fellow of S. John's. He had a suit in Chancery (Cooper, IV. 277) for the rectory of Barrow, co. Suffolk, which was decided in his favour by Ld. Hardwicke against Dr Tho. Rutherforth (who succeeded him as Divinity Professor on his nomination to the Deanery of Lincoln in 1756) and their college in the interval between the rejection and reception of the 'Regulations' by the Senate in the summer of 1750. Cooper's *Annals*, IV. 277.

A week after the final passing of the Regulations he was elected Master of C. C. C. C. on the recommendation of Archbp. Herring, whence the electors received the nickname *Cappadocians* for surrendering their freedom of choice (Mʳ *Mayor's Baker*, 712, where reference is made to Nichols' *Lit. Illustr.* VI. 794. Lamb, 240—243).

Cp. The *Capitade*—

> ' Rise, rise ye cringing servile Souls to sight,
> Ye Foes to Freedom Cappadocians' height; [*sic.*]
> Hold, hold in Slav'ry G——n the abject Race,
> Make them serve thee as thou dost L—eth's Grace.'

A note on the word *Cappadocians* is cut away in the copy in Bodley, but the allusion will be understood by reference to the earlier Letter to Ld. E(gmon)t, pp. 13, 15, in p. 12 of which tract Bene't Coll. is denominated '*alias* Coll. *Lambethinium*.' Vice-Chancellor, 1757. ' He belonged to the "liberal" party...In 1772 Green alone of the bishops voted in favour of a repeal of the corporation and test acts. This was not forgotten by the king, who is reported to have rejected "a suggestion for Green's promotion in the words, *Green Green, he shall never be translated*"......He was strongly in favour of legalising marriage with a deceased wife's sister.' *Baker-Mayor*, 712, where a full account is given of this member of St John's and Corpus Colleges. Bp. *John Green* of Lincoln *must be carefully distinguished* from another master of C. C. C. C. Bp. *Thomas Greene*, of Norwich and Ely.

Dʳ *Thomas Greene* (bp. Norwich 1721, Ely 1723, Master of C. C. C. C. 1698). Soon afterwards ' he introduced the use of Publick Prayers in the Chapel immediately after locking up the Gates that he might know what Scholars were abroad, and if need were visit their Chambers ; an Institution so wise and good, that it has been thought worthy of being continued ever since.' (Masters' *Corpus*, 1753, p. 178.) Vice-Chancellor 1699, 1713. He was nicknamed *Miss* Greene. Nichols' *Lit. Anecd.* VI. 640 (while his successor, Dʳ *John Green*, some 40 years later, was called Gamwell, ibid. VIII. 581, 622) like the poets Milton and Gray. In 1734, when Bp. of Ely, as Visitor of Trin. Coll. he pronounced sentence of deprivation on *Bentley* some quarter of a century after the proceedings had been first instituted against him for dilapidating the goods of the college and violating the statutes (Monk's *Bentley*, II. 344), and after all the Doctor died in possession of his mastership, July 14, 1742. Bentley had been associated with Dʳ Tho. Greene (then V. C.) on a very different occasion in 1700, when they joined in writing poems for the *Threnodia*, in which Cambridge condoled with Q. (then Princess) Anne on the death of her son Will. D. of Gloucester.

L. B. E.   40

Dr THOMAS CHAPMAN, master of Magd. 1746—1760. He is indicated by asterisks in Gray's works (ed. 1835—47) II. 170, III. 67, 253.

D^r SAM. SQUIRE, of St John's, afterwards dean of Bristol and bp. of St Davids : died 1766.   Gray says in his character of himself (1761),

> 'A post or a pension he did not desire,
> But left church and state to Charles Townshend and Squire.'

Bishop Warburton said to dean Tucker of Gloster, that never bishoprick was so *bedeaned*, for that his predecessor, Dr *Squire*, had made *religion his trade*, and that he, Dr Tucker, made *trade his religion*. (See *Cradock* quoted in *Gray's* Works, I. 156 n.).   Dean Squire's 'dark complexion procured him in college conversation, and in the squibs of the time, the nick-name of "the Man of *Angola*." (Nichols' *Lit. Anecd.* II. 348.) Squire and Green preached before the Chancellor, July 2, 1749. (*Gent. Mag.*)

' A Key to the Fragment by *Amias Riddinge*, B.D., with a preface [pp. I—VIII.] by *Peregrine Smyth*, Esq....London, Printed for W. Webb, and sold by the Booksellers of *London, Oxford* and *Cambridge*, 1751.'

(8vo. pp. 46 ; Bodleian, *Gough Camb.* 56.)   In this Key (a hoax written by Dr Will. King, Principal of St Mary's Hall in Oxford, writer of the *Toast, the London Evening Post*, cet., whom Cole had often seen 'at St Mary's Church, Cambridge, when he used to be on a visit to Mr Mackenzie who married Mr Chambers the town-clerk's daughter,' Nichols' *Lit. Anecd.* II. 608) it is pretended that the 'Fragment' was a reprint of one (a non-entity of course) first published in October, 1658 relating to the troubles. ['*Amias Riddinge, Cambr.*' admitted fellow of St John's, 22 Mar. 161⅝. 'Ridding,' ejected in accordance with a writ of the E. of Manchester, 16 Sept. 1644. 'A writ from the king's bench, 7 Jul. an. reg. 12, for restoring Amias Readinge to his fellowship; received and executed 1 Aug. 1660.' Mayor's *Baker's Hist. of St John's*, p. 298, l. 25. cf. 293, l. 15. 296. ll. 9, 14.   The name is spelt also ' Amias' (or 'Amyas) Ridding.'] The Key lets us into the secret of the purport of the names in the *Fragments* by giving others no less fictitious but approaching the real ones.   Thus in the Key *Tom Standish* is explained '*Sir Thomas Duke*' (the Chancellor Newcastle)—*Mun* as '*Edmund Sharp*' (Edm. Keen), '*Acutus*' in the *Capitade—Tom*, ' *Thomas Forward*' (Dr Chapman of Magdalen)—Dr *Rock*, '*George Crow*' (G. H. Rooke, D.D. of Christ's), who took a prominent part in the composition of the 'Regulations.' In the *Capitade* he is addressed,

> 'Hail *Gobrias*, hail thou doughty Chief whose Nod
> Makes Ch——ians tremble and deny their God,
> In whose dark Realms nor Wit nor Learning spread,
> Nor Merit sprouts, nor Honour rears her Head,
> Where 'midst a gen'ral Pravity of Spirit
> Poor Robin only suffers—for his Merit.'

Again he is associated with ' *Tom*,'

> 'As *Gobrias* honest and as C—p—n fair.'

Like Dr J. Green and Hon. Philip and Chas. Yorke wrote in *Athenian Letters*, 1741. Nichols' *Lit. Anecd.* III. 222.

'*Dr Squirt, Samuel Squib*' (Dr Squire, the Duke's Chaplain, who preached one of the sermons at his Installation).

Roger, '*Roger Newton*' (Dr Roger Long of Pembroke, V.C. 1733). 'Jolly *Roger* Twangdillo.' Fragmentum est pars...p. 28.

Richard, '*Will. Fitzrichards*' (Dr W. Richardson of Emmanuel, V.C. 1737).

The Elder Brother, '*Charles Goodman*' (Dr C. Ashton of Jesus, V.C. 1702).

Harry, '*Mr Henry Hobbes*' (H. Hubbard of Emmanuel. There is a curious character of him in Nichols' *Lit. Anecd.* II. 619. n.).

Dun (Another Fragment), '*Obadiah Fusk*' (J. Brown of Pembroke, Proctor).

'*John Comus*' or *Belshazzar*, Dr J. Newcome, Master of St John's.

'*Broomstick*,' bp. Gooch.

In the Preface to the Key (p. v.) Dr King tells a remarkable story; 'I remember in the year 1745 an old acquaintance came into my Chamber just as I had transcribed an Inscription out of *Gruter*, in which were these three Letters C. E. C.'...(signifying *Cives Ejus Coloniae*). 'My Friend having cast his eye on the Paper which lay wet on my Table, shook his Head and said that he wondered I would venture to write a treasonable Song at such a critical Juncture. For although, added he, you have disguised the rest in *Latin*, yet those three Capital Letters, which I suppose are the Burden of the Song, must be understood by the meanest capacity, and can only signify *Charles Edward Come!*'

'Another Fragment. London Printed for A. Pope, near the *Royal Exchange*, and sold by all Booksellers in

London, Oxford and Cambridge.' (8vo. pp. i—iv, 1—26. Bodleian, *Gough Cam.* 36, 56.)

This closely illustrates the *Narrative of the Late Extraordinary Proceedings against the W*(estminste)*r Club*—continuing the account of the disturbances from the adoption of the Regulations as described in the original Fragment down to the trial of Members of the Club, who are represented as boys of the Free School founded by Lady Betty, whose birthday they were celebrating 'at a little alehouse hard by their Mother's House, where they us'd to have *Wigs* and *Ale* ['The bakers metamorphose their trade from one shape to another, his round, half-penny loaves are transformed into square wigs, (which wigs, like drunk-ards, are drowned in their ale),' Taylor (the waterpoet's) *Jack a'Lent.* 1619: *Wigs* a sort of north-country bun, with a *double entendre*], when they were interrupted by *Dun* (Jas. Brown the Senr Proctor, and 'one with a Gentle Look and *Savage* Name carrying the staff of office,' as Forrester of Pembroke is described in *Fragmentum est Pars* at p. 28, here called *Fetch*. There is a burlesque account of *Dun's* discomfiture and their sly ridicule of him, also of their applause of *Snap*, their chair-man (Prof. Franklein). Dun makes a series of ingenious charges against them, Snap and *Catch* (Ansell) in particular. The latter intends to lay his case before the Learned Bench in 'the great Hall that stands by Lady *Betty's* School' (Westminster).

'"Fragmentum est pars rei fractae" *Ulpian*, London, printed for M. Cooper in *Pater-Noster Row*, 1751. price 6*d*.' (8vo. pp. 34. Bodleian, *Gough Camb.* 36, 47, 56.)

Attributed to Zachary Grey (editor of *Hudibras*), of Trinity Hall, 'said to be by Dr Grey and Dr Tathwell,' Bodleian new Catalogue. (Cornewall Tathwall corresponded with Z. Grey, see Nichols' *Lit. Anecd.* II. 534, VI. 114, IX. 556. He was fellow of St John's Oxon., M.A. 1748, M.D. 1755, vicar of Hitchin.) Like 'Another Fragment' it is a conti-nuation of the original 'Fragment.' The writer or writers give a not very refined diagnosis of the disorders of Alma Mater. 'Dr Rock' (G. H. Rooke of Christ Coll.) is called in. He sends the company to sleep by a long plausible discourse after some fine speeches (for you must know he had been reading over *The Academy of Compliments, Cupid's Garland*, and *The Flowers of Parnassus*, having just then began his addresses to his sweet *Dulcinea*), p. 15. An allegorical account of the Westminster Club question is given pp. 27 *fol.* A MS. note in Bodleian, *Gough Camb.* 56, says 'One of ye Fragments by Dr Grey.'

'An Epistle to a Fellow Commoner at Cambridge occasioned by the present Disputes there. London, printed for Charles Corbett in Fleet-Street (price Sixpence).'

(A poem of 183 lines, folio, 1751. Bodleian, *Gough Cambr.* 36, 103, addressed to *Lollius,* a sober and industrious Fellow-Commoner, who is set up as an example of peaceableness and attentiveness to the duties of the University.

> 'Leave to the Bowl its Jokes, its Jibs and Puns,
> Its *Profs., Clubs, Standish's,* its *Toms and Muns.*
> Such ill become the Mouth of Learned Sense,
> And such from Wisdom are a weak Defence.'

i. e. the innuendos by which Professor Francklin, the Westminster Club, the Chancellor, Dr T. Chapman and Edmund Keene V.C. were indicated in the 'Fragment,' and such like trash which was inflaming the parties at Cambridge.

We may here quote an extract from a Letter dated Jan. 17, 175¾ (i. e. after Ansell's notice of Appeal from Dr Keene's sentence) in the Bodleian, *Gough Cambr.* 36.

'There came down lately An Epistle to a Fellow-Commoner on the Vice-chancellor's side, and which was very horridly treated by some of the younger people, for they took the print of the Bellman off his Town verses and sticking it upon the Epistle to a Fellow-Commoner wrote under it by way of Motto, "Good Morrow, Mr Vice-chancellor—Good Morrow, Good Morrow, Mr Pelham." As the Epistle speaks very honourably of Pelham, and is supposed to be inscribed to him under the name of Lollius, that Gentleman goes by the name of *Lolly Pelham.*' [qu. was he related to the D. of Newcastle?]

'The Friendly and Honest Advice of an Old Tory to the Vice-Chancellor of Cambridge.

Idem hoc tute ipse melius quanto invenisses. *Terent.*

London, Printed for S. Johnson at *Charing Cross.* 1751.'

[*Written,* however, Nov. 20, 1750. The dramatic date lies in the middle of the week between the Proctor's visit to the Westminster Club and the holding of Vice-Chancellor's Court.]

8vo. pp. 35, Bodleian, *Gough Camb.* 36, 47. The tract is an ironical expression of advice pretending to come after delay from an old Tory to Dr Keene, encouraging to a course of arbitrary conduct similar, if not identical, with that which he was known already to have pursued.

'An Inquiry into the Right of Appeal from the Chancellor or Vice-Chancellor of the University of Cambridge in matters of Discipline : Addressed to a Fellow of a College. To which is added an Appendix Containing some Observations on the Authentic Narrative,' &c.

"Est genus hominum qui esse priores se omnium rerum volunt nec sunt." *Terent.*

London : Printed for J. Payne and J. Bouquet in Paternoster Row. 1751.

(8vo. pp. 79, Bodleian, *Gough Camb.* 47, 56, by T. Chapman, Master of *Magd.* See Index to pamphlets in Gough Camb. 56.)
The writer quotes legal opinions of W. N—— and R. W—— [qu. Noel and Wilbraham], stating that Ansell had no right of appeal from Dr Keene's sentence.

'The Opinion of an Eminent Lawyer concerning The Right of Appeal from the Vice-Chancellor of *Cambridge* to the Senate ; supported by a short historical account of the Jurisdiction of the University.   In answer to a late Pamphlet entitled an Inquiry into the Right of Appeal...

Isne erret, mones, et desinat lacessere.

By a Fellow of a College.   London, Printed and Sold by M. Cooper at the Globe in Paternoster Row, 1751.   Price one Shilling.'   (8vo. pp. 65.   Bodl. *Gough Camb.* 36, 56.)

This answer to [Chapman's] *Inquiry into Right of Appeal* is rather uncourteous at the commencement, attributed to M^r Ri. Hurd (bp. of Worcester, 1781.) Nichols' *Lit. Anecd.* II. 230.—Cooper *Annals,* IV. 281, mentions the claim of John Smith, M.A. Fellow of King's. The Eminent Lawyer was Philip Yorke, first E. of Hardwicke (Nichols' *Lit. Anecd.* II. 230, VI. 473). Mr Cooper says 'Mr Charles Yorke,' *Annals,* IV. 281.

'Some Considerations on the Necessity of an Appeal in the University of Cambridge.

> Erat in more apud Athenienses...
>
> Lord Bacon, *de Augm. Scient.*

London: Printed for J. Roberts in *Warwick Lane,* 1752.' (8vo pp. 27. Bodl. *Gough Camb.* 47, 56.)

Urges the desirability of a Right of Appeal from common sense backed by the practice of other nations.

'A further Inquiry into the Right of Appeal from the Chancellor or Vice-Chancellor of the University of Cambridge in matters of Discipline, in which the objections of the author of a late pamphlet intitled "The Opinion of an Eminent Lawyer..." are fully obviated.

> Faciunt nae intelligendo...

London: Printed for J. Payne and J. Bouquet in Paternoster Row; and for T. Merrill, Bookseller in Cambridge, 1752.'

(8vo. pp. 84, Bodl. *Gough Camb.* 47, 56.) By Dʳ T. Chapman of *Magd.* (cf. Nichols' *Lit. Anecd.* II. 230 n.), who maintains, as Middleton did in 1725, that the appeal lay only in *civil* causes. The meaning of the words '*causa forensis,*' Univ. Stat. 48, was in dispute (see *Opinion of Eminent Lawyer*, p. 14). There was an appeal to dictionaries and to Cicero; compare the curious arguments in Wrangham's Appeal given in Gunning's Reminiscences, II. 20—26.

'A Letter to the Author of A Farther Inquiry into the Right of Appeal from the Chancellor or Vice-chancellor of the University of Cambridge in Matters of Discipline. London, Printed and Sold by M. Cooper, at the *Globe,* in Pater-noster Row, 1752.'

8vo. pp. 84. Bodl. *Gough Camb.* 36, 47, 56. By John Smith M.A. Fellow of King's. See the *Capitade.*

> 'Next S——th, supremely blest with ev'ry Charm
> In Virtue's Cause e'en Royal Youth to warm;

> With deep-designing P[a]r[i]s's Grimace,
> And good, tho' gloomy W[il]c[o]x must have Place ;
> Poor tim'rous S—dw—k and that Crowd of Slaves
> Who cringe for Promises to Fools and Knaves.'

The Author of the Letter insinuates that when his name is known he will be recognized as 'one of the earliest Adherents to the Duke of *Newcastle* ..one of the firmest *Whiggs* in the University of *Cambridge.* You too well know that the greatest Number of Assertors of Appeals are to be found in each of these Lists,' pp. 80, 81. These were called '*Associators*,' a body who met at the Tuns tavern some 30 or 40 strong to support the right of appeal. Cooper's *Annals*, IV. 283.

The writer adds in a P.S. that a Grace had just passed unanimously, 'Mat (i.e. March) 13, 1752, in the fullest congregation that had been seen since the Dissensions began to petition the Chancellor, Thomas Hollis, Duke of Newcastle, Philip Ld. Hardwicke, High Steward of the Univ., Thomas, Bp. of London, Chief Justice Sir W. Lee, Hon. Geo. Lee, Knt. LLD., to hear the question of appeal argued by three lawyers on each side. The V. C. (D' J. Wilcox of *Clare*), D' J. Green, *Bene't* Coll., and D' Chapman, *Magd.*, and M' Bickham [*Eman.*], M' Smith of *King's* and M' Balguy nominated as syndics.'

'A Letter to the University of Cambridge on a Late Resignation by a Gentleman of Oxford.

Sunt verba et voces quibus hunc lenire dolorem possis.

London: Printed for M. Cooper at the *Globe* in Paternoster Row. 1756.

(8vo. pp. 28, dated 'Oxford Nov. 15, 1756,' Bodl. *Gough Camb.* 36.) Taunts the University with not expressing sympathy with their Chancellor, the D. of Newcastle, who resigned the place of First Ld. of the Treasury for this year. This is merely made the occasion for abusing 'the two celebrated Heroes of the *Fragment* [D' Chapman and Keene], the author of a dissertation on the book of *Job* [Garnet], dedicated to his Grace; the Secretary for University affairs who has devellop'd the whole mystery of Anglo-Saxon policy [Sam. Squire]; the author of a sermon preached at the consecration of the Lord Bishop of Chester and his successor in the Divinity Chair [? J. Whalley, Pet., and J. Greene, St John's], who has written so *much* and so *well* on all subjects that one is really at a loss which of his works to distinguish him by. Amongst such as his Grace has prudently overlooked, are the Editor of *Demosthenes* [John Taylor], the Editor of the Epistle to the *Pisos* [Ri. Hurd.], the Maker of the Churchyard Essay [T. Gray], and the author of Elfrida [W. Mason],' pp. 13, 14, n.

Such an Address as the author said he desired to see was sent by the Univ. of Cambridge to the D. of Newcastle on his retiring from office in 1766. Cooper's *Annals*, IV. 343, 344.

p. 70. Among Swift's *Tracts Historical and Political* (Works edited by Sir W. Scott, v. 399—416, *ed.* 2. 1824), is '*a True Relation* of the several Facts and Circumstances of the intended *Riot* and *Tumult* on QVEEN ELIZABETH'S BIRTHDAY:...first printed in *November*, 1711.' Scott records that 'in 1682 the ceremony was celebrated with peculiar splendour under the auspices of no less a person than the renowned *Elkanah Settle*,' Dryden's rival, who spent some years at Trin. Coll. *Oxon*. 'The Whigs of Queen Anne's time had, it seems, formed a resolution to revive the splendour of this grand ceremony. Several of the leaders, members of the Kit-Cat Club, are said to have subscribed a considerable sum for this purpose :' 1000*l*. says Swift to Stella on the 17th; a fortnight later he had seen them and they were 'not worth 40*l*.; so I stretched a little when I said 1000*l*.' *Garth* subscribed 5*l*. Beside the pope, cardinals &c., an effigy of the Chevalier St George was seized in an empty house in Drury-lane; the Romanists who were put into the Magdalen fellowships were to be represented; as were Treasurer Harley, Mr Secretary St John, Mrs Masham, Dr Sacheverell, &c. The pamphlet, which seems to have been written by 'an understrapper,' under Swift's direction, refers to the *Spectator* (Steele), who was to have been an assistant in the procession: also the author of 'a certain *lillibullero* song' [Thomas Warton, earl of Wharton, who had been lord-lieutenant of Ireland, 1708—10], which was to have been sung. The portraits of the Seven Bishops were to have been carried in triumph on banners.

S. HUGH'S DAY, Nov. 17, the anniversary of the ACCESSION of Q. ELIZ. (10 days after her *birthday*), was made the occasion of provoking the popular protestantism against the D. of York in the reign of Charles II. In Scott's edition of *Dryden's* Works, vol. VI. opposite p. 222 (edd. 1808, 1821) is an impression of a curious print representing '*The Solemn Mock Procession of the Pope, Cardinals, Jesuits, Friars, &c. through the City of London, November 17th*, 1679.' The contemporary description of this print is given also in Hone's *Every-Day Book*, I. 1488—1490. The chief features of the procession are six whifflers with pioneers' caps and torches, the bell-man, a jesuit riding with an effigy of justice Godfrey before him, priests, friars, jesuits with bloody daggers, trumpeters, bishops, cardinals, the pope's doctor (sir Geo. Wakeman, the queen's physician), with jesuit's powders and the emblem of his profession, acoluths with banners displaying daggers, &c., on a platform the pope to whom 'the degraded seraphim' is whispering advice. Another part of the plate shews his holiness being precipitated into a bonfire within view of Temple-bar, 'over against the Inner Temple Gate.' His ghostly counsellor has by some quaint device or other flown into the air. Near the eaves of the houses is a curious apparatus for fireworks.

p. 75. The SENATE's VETO. Another instance of this strange symptom of Constitutional sulkiness will be found in the next year. Writers of the time were fond of applying the Fable of *Menenius Agrippa* to the Caput and Body of the Senate (Occasional Letter to Dr Keene, p. 15, cp. *A Fragment*, p. 23). How apt was the parallel when the Habit of Disease had penetrated to such an Unoffending Member as a poor Questionist waiting for his Degree!

p. 76. JAS. BICKHAM (a Tory and classical tutor to Dr Farmer, Nichols' *Lit. Anecd.* II. 619) was one of the persons to whom the *Fragment* (see p. 621) was attributed; see the following extract 'from a Letter dated Feb. 22, 175⁰/₁' in the Bodleian, *Gough Camb.* 47. 'Some characters in our university are very cleverly displayed in the last ch^r. of Pompey the Little [or the Adventures of a Lap-dog, 1751, discovered by Gray to be the hasty composition of Francis Coventry of *Magd.* Camb. B.A. 1748, Nichols' *Lit. Anecd.* v. 569. *n.*], certainly by some Cambridge man. We have every now and then some sorry imitations of The Fragment, which is now said to be wrote by B—k—m of Emanuel.'

Tho. Martyn writing to Nichols says, 'Bickham the junior tutor was a bold man, and had been a bruiser when young. I do not think he was of any party. It is inaccurate to call him the *classical* tutor; for he gave us Lectures in Euclid. He did not want parts, but he was idle.' *Gorham's Martyns*, p. 98.

p. 77. Smith's Prizes commenced 1768 by the M^r of Trinity.
Chancellor's Medals ,, 1752 ,, D. of Newcastle.
Seatonian Prize ,, 1750 ,, legacy in 1741.
4 Members' Prizes ,, 1752 ,, Finch and Townshend.
Browne's Medals ,, 1774 ,, Sir W. B.'s legacy.

p. 77. The Late M^r Ri. Robinson of Queen's remarked that Smollett gives a widely different character of the D. of Newcastle (as 'Fikikaka') in the *Adventures of an Atom*, from that which he paints in his *History* (*Oxf. Undergrad. Journal*, No. 18).

p. 88. CHUMS. The 34th Statute of St John's college, Cambridge, *De cubiculorum dispositione* (Bp. Fisher's code, 1530: *distributione*, K. Hen. VIII. 1545) is interesting. The chambers are to be assigned by the Master (with regard had to the learning and character of each, 1545): only doctors of Divinity and preachers to have one to themselves, fellows and scholars above 14 years of age to sleep singly, or not more than two in a bed : the seniors to teach their younger chums. (Compare [Eachard's] *Speculum Crape-Gownorum*, 1680, p. 3, quoted in a note to p. 105 of this book.) The royal statutes (1545) provided farther that not more than two fellows should be obliged to occupy the same chamber, also that scholars should resign the studies (*musea*) and other furniture, if a fellow were put into their chamber. The bishop's statutes (1530) had specified that in the upper and lower chambers there should be two beds *quorum unum sit altius, alterum humile aut rotale pro arbitrio magistri; in altiori cubet socius scholaris si uelit, in altero duo discipuli aut saltem unus semper.*

Such a TRUCKLE BED was commonly used at the universities.

At *New College* (Stat. rubr. LII. 1385—1400) every one was to have a bed to himself, there was to be a fellow in each chamber to keep order and to report offenders for punishment. Care was to be taken not to slop water, beer, wine, &c. on the floor of the chambers upstairs. The warden was to mix canonists and civilists as *chums* with students of other faculties.

At Magdalen coll. Oxon. (Stat. 1459) it was ordered '*quod in singulis cameris superioribus nostri collegii, turri ac cameris praesidentis una cum cameris inferius reseruatis exceptis, sint duo lecti principales et duo lecti rotales,* Trookyll beddys *uulgariter appellati; et quod in inferioribus cameris, omnibus et singulis, infra quadratum eiusdem collegii, camera subtus librariam contigua portae et pro praesidente reseruata, ac camera pro computo inferius reseruata, exceptis, sint duo lecti principales et unus lectus rotalis, si latitudo et longitudo camerarum inferiorum id admittant, quod iudicio praesidentis committimus; ac quod, in illis et aliis quibuscunque cameris nostri collegii, socii, scholares, capellani,* Demyes, *clerici, choristae, comminarii, et quaecumque personae nostri collegii et eidem pertinentes locentur et ponantur......Itaque omnes socii, et scholares in anno probationis existentes, ac* Demyes, *aetatem xv annorum completam habentes, soli in singulis lectis, in cameris infra quadratum uel extra, distinctos lectos habere et solos infra collegium iacere praecipimus. Cameram angularem superiorem......et aliam cameram......pro filiis dominorum et aliis personis, secundum discretionem praesidentis.*'

Cap. 36 of the Statutes (bp. Fox, 1517) of Corpus Christi, Oxon, corresponds with *cap.* 34 of the episcopal and royal codes of St John's,

Camb. (1530, 1545) already quoted. This was adopted in *cap.* 39 of those of St John's, Oxon, 1555.

In the *Return from* Parnassus, *or Scourge for Simony*, II. 6, acted at Cambridge in 1602, *Amoretto* says 'Sirrah, this predicable, this saucy groom, because when I was in *Cambridge*, and lay in a trundlebed under my tutor, I was content in discreet humility to give him some place at the table; and because I invited this hungry slave sometimes to my chamber, to the canvassing of a turkey-pie or a piece of venison, which my lady grandmother sent me...'

So in the inventory of furniture in the earl of Essex' rooms when student at Trinity, Cambridge, in 1577 (Cooper's *Annals*, II. 353) is

' Item a place makinge for the trindle bed to drawe through the waule, xvjd.'

Compare Hall's description of an obsequious tutor—

> 'He lieth in a truckle-bed
> While his young master lieth o'er his head.' *Satires*, II. 6. 5.

See *Singer's* note, vol. XII. p. 185, Warton's *Hist. Eng. Poets*, Hazlitt, IV. 378.

The bed (Mr Mayor reminds me) was thrust in the day time under the high bed of the tutor. In the court of King's, which was sold to the University when the new buildings were erected, and in the unused garrets of Caius (only lately pulled down) the *studiola* or *musea* (branching off from the *camera*) were plainly to be seen.

The following extract from the archives of *King's Hall* (Trinity college) is given in the 1st Report of the *Historical MSS. Commission*, 1870, p. 84, where Mr Riley says 'In 1342 the building, consisting apparently of a former edifice, with new chambers added, was ready, probably for the first time, for the reception of the Fellows. The rooms were allotted to them mostly in pairs, as *consocii* or *camerarii* chums or chamber-fellows, p. 131 :—" Dispositio Camerariorum facta per Magistrum, et per Sex, et per Comitivam. Imprimis ordinantur Magister Walterus Milemete et Magister Johannes Sawtry in solario juxta gardinum; et in solario sub eis Radulphus de Stonham, Nicolaus Hersle et Johannes Sturtone. Item in garito Johannes Plumtone. Item in solario novo juxta gardinum Magister Johannes Glastone et Magister Symon Stratford, et in selario [sic] sub eiis Thomas Pyribroke et Thomas Priour. Item in alio novo solario proximo praedicto Magister Richardus Bytrynge et Richardus Ficling; et in selario sub eis Magister Robertus Byght et Johannes Pultone. Item in solario proximo Dominus Thomas Berkynge et Philippus Weylland, et sub eis Johannes Perers et Thomas Copham. Item in alio solario proximo, Magister

Adam Werlyngwort et Johannes Multone ; et sub eis Ricardus Hales et Alanus Mareschal. Item in solario proximo......Magister Thomas Paxtone et Magister Johannes Yekeswort ; et sub eiis Dominus Robertus Senky et Jacobus Beverley. Item in camera parva juxta coquinam Thomas Springhet, Alexander Sawmford. Item in camera juxta Annable Pyke [a maltster in the employ of the Society,] Dominus Rogerus Harlistone, et cum eo Willelmus Hoktone. Item in solario sub Custode, Willelmus Bridport, Baudet, Rumseye, Yimwort, et Ward.'

p. 88. ' To keep '—to live. "Where do you *keep?*" Where are your rooms?—"In the way to my friend's, having quite forgotten the direction to his Chambers in his College, I asked a Bed-maker, who was perambulating one of the courts, where Mr ——'s Chambers were, as I understood he lived in that court. The fellow stared me in the face, with an insipid vacant look, gradually improving into a grin. I repeated my demand in a more impatient tone of voice, and added, 'I came to dine with Mr ——.' The man scientifically shrugged up his shoulders, and walked away protesting he could not tell. I luckily espied my friend at the other end of the quadrangle and went to him. Upon my mentioning the recent embarrassing circumstance, he said with a smile, 'I ought to have asked for his rooms or enquired where he KEPT.' The word in this sense is often used by old writers." (*Gent. Mag.*).—Dr Johnson, in his Dictionary, cites a very apposite passage from Shakespere : "Knock at the study where they say he *keeps.*" [*Titus Andron.* Act V. Sc. 2.] Sir Thomas More, in a letter to Dean Colet, says " Yff the discommodities of the cittie doe, as they may very well, displease you, yet may the countrie about your parish of Stepney afforde you the like delights which that affordes you wherein now you KEEPE." (More's *Life and Death of Sir Thomas More.*)

p. 92. MEN. I do not know that any one was so bold as to use the word ' lad ' of a gentleman of the University towards the end of the 18th century, much less would a student deign to use it of himself or of one in his own rank, as Bonwicke did in 1711. The following extract from the *Gradus ad Cantabrigiam*, 1802, is curious. ' MEN.— Vix sunt HOMINES hoc nomine digni.' Ovid *de Trist.*

'At Cambridge, and, eke at Oxford, every stripling is accounted a *Man* from the moment of his putting on the gown and cap. Consequently there are many MEN in our two Universities whose chins are out of all dread of a *lathering!*'

A CHILD = a *Scholar* (absolutely). See Ken's *Manual for Winchester Scholars.*

p. 93. SMOKING. See the 10th of the regulations which the Vice-chancellor and Caput thought necessary to put forth in Cambridge before the visit of the royal Author of *A Counter-blaste to Tobacco*, when in 1614—15 he was about to have the pleasure of witnessing Ruggle's Comedy of *Ignoramus* in Clare Hall before the hobby-horse was quite forgot. See Nichols' *Progresses of James the First*, 1828, III. 44.

p. 94. 'MENNE NOT WERYE OF THEYR PAYNES.' See Sermons by Thomas Lever, M.A., p. 122, in Arber's *English Reprints*, 1870. The context of this passage, which George Dyer and others are fond of quoting, is extremely interesting and amusing as a description of Cambridge life in the middle of the 16th century. It is beside my purpose to quote it here in full, but owing to the exertions of Mr Arber any one may now procure for eighteen-pence an exact reprint of the truly original sermons in which the passage occurs. The discourse in question was delivered at Paule's crosse, Dec. 14, 1550, i.e. in the same year that *Lever* had been ordained by the new Bp. of London, Nic. *Ridley*, which was also the year when Roger *Ascham* (who with Ridley has just been mentioned as a learned man who did not neglect wholesome recreation) found the Ladye Jane Grey reading her Phaedon Platonis in Greek. On the accession of Q. Mary in 1553, Lever (who was Senior Fellow and Preacher of St John's, Camb.) resigned with 24 fellows and left the country.

p. 94. ERRATUM. *l.* 15 from top. *For* 'in 1667' *read* about 1677.

p. 94. At *Cambridge* the *scholars' oath* was postponed till they were 14 years old.

p. 95. TUTORS. By K. Henry VIIIth's Statutes for St John's Camb. (1545) Cap. XVI. no fellow was to have more than *one* pupil; and the master not more than *four*.

In 1727. Hearne is surprised that the mother of a commoner of Trin. Coll. has never been to Oxford to see after her son: whence he concludes that the lad and his brother of Magd. hall have 'some particular directions as to their entrance and conduct.' Hearne-Bliss, III. 5.

p. 95. AGE OF ADMISSION. In 1713, 'Jack Lizard' was about *Fifteen* when he was first entered in the University. *Guardian*, No. 24.

A passage in 'the *Student*,' II. 203, seems to imply that *seventeen* was not an uncommon age for matriculation about 1750.

We learn from [Eachard's] 'Grounds and Occasions of the Contempt of the Clergy,' p. 18, that *sixteen* was the ordinary age for lads to come up in 1670, so that they would be eligible for Holy Orders ' after seven years being at the University.'

p. 97. PENSIONER. One who *pays* a *pensio* or rent for lodging in College. On the word SIZAR see below, note to p. 121.

p. 98. The following statistics of the NUMBERS of different classes of Undergraduates at the several Colleges in Cambridge, from the third Calendar for 1801, 1802, may be thought interesting :

	Noblemen	Fellow-Commoners	Scholars	Pensioners	Sizars	Four-and-Twenty, or Ten-year
Peterhouse......	1	3	...	17	3	...
1802	1	4	...	20	2	...
Clare	...	1	...	14	5	...
1802	...	2	...	14	2	4 ten-year men
Pembroke	...	2	...	22	8	
1802	1	4	...	16	8	
Caius	...	7	...	24	2	2 four-and-twenty men
1802	...	9	...	24	2	2 four-and-twenty men
Trinity Hall ...	...	11	11	16	1	...
1802	...	9	11	15	1	...
Corpus	...	2	...	13	3	...
1802	...	1	...	11	2	1 four-and-twenty man
King's		[21 graduate fellow-commoners]	18	[3 undergraduate fellows]		
1802	...	1	13	[4 undergraduate fellows]		2 four-and-twenty men
Queens'	...	2	...	16	3	...
1802	...	3	...	16	9	2 four-and-twenty men
Catharine Hall	...	2	...	7	...	...
1802	...	2	...	2	1	

	Noblemen	Fellow-Commoners	Scholars	Pensioners	Sizars	Four-and-Twenty, or Ten-Year
Jesus	...	8	...	22	4	...
1802	1	8	...	27	3	...
Christ's	...	3	...	18	4	...
1802	...	5	...	16	8	...
S. John's	1	17	39	38	17	5 ten-year men
1802	2	22	38	42	22	3 ten-year men
Magdalen	...	...	...	3	13	...
1802	...	...	...	4	10	...
Trinity	6	22	24	69	23	14 four-and-twenty men
1802	5	27	20	69	19	13 four-and-twenty men
Emmanuel	...	14	4	13	10	6 four-and-twenty men
1802	...	12	6	8	10	6 four-and-twenty men
Sidney	...	2	...	9	2	1 four-and-twenty man
1802	..	1	...	8	2	1 four-and-twenty man
Total for two Years	18	209	184	593	198	59
Annual Average	9	105	92	297	99	30

Annual Total number of Undergraduates in 1801, 1802—632.

The total NUMBER ON THE BOARDS (including Graduates) in certain years is gathered from Cooper's *Annals*, II. 206, 269, 315, III. 148, 553; and the Camb. *Univ. Calendar*.

At Trinity and King's *servants are counted* as members of the College. This is the case in all Colleges throughout the census of 1672.

	Master & Fellows	Fellow-Commoners	Scholars	Bible Clerks	Pensioners	Sizars or Poor Scholars	Total (*see p.* 643)
Peterhouse							
in 1564	11	17	...	2	24	7	61
1573	16	...	...	5	60	8	89
1672	23	...	45	...	&c.	...	86
1796	22	2	15	...	17	9	83
Clare Hall							
in 1564	9	17	17	...	34	9	86
1573	13	...	40	...	60	12	125
1672	19	...	41	...	&c.	20	100
1796	21	8	23	...	13	8	95
Pembroke Hall							
in 1564	18	4	8	...	18	...	48
1573	25	...	6	...	36	13	87
1672	...	...	...	...	...	about	100
1796	17	8	23	...	22	7	107
Caius							
in 1564	9	11	10	...	18	...	48
1573	11	...	10	...	33	3	57
1672	27	...	75	...	&c.	...	140
1796	27	5	51	...	...	1	104
Trinity Hall							
in 1564	...	...	...	...	...	...	51
1573	11	...	9	...	33	...	53
1672	13	...	14	...	&c.	...	68
1796	13	6	14	...	48	1	85
Bene't (Corpus Christi)							
in 1564	9	6	...	3	8	6	32
1573	13	...	20	4	54	...	91
1672	13	...	37	...	&c.	...	145
1796	11	4	14	...	8	20	68
King's							
in 1564	71	9 conducts	...	16 choristers	9	13 servants	118
1573	71	9 conducts	...	16 choristers	13	13 sizars	122
1672	71	&c.	...	&c.	...	...	113
1796	58	1	11	...	...	...	96
Queens'							
in 1564	16	6	...	23	14	6	65

L. B. E.

41

	Master & Fellows	Fellow-Commoners	Scholars	Bible Clerks	Pensioners	Sizars or Poor Scholars *(see next p.)*	Total *(see next p.)*
1573	20	...	17	8	77	...	122
1672	20	...	27	12	...	about	120
1796	20	17	30	...	...	4	91
Catharine Hall							
in 1564	14	...	7	...	...	...	21
1573	7	...	...	1	21	...	29
1672	7	...	18	9	&c.	...	150
1796	18	2	26	...	2	2	51
Jesus							
in 1564	26	...	85	...	...	...	111
1573	11	...	17	...	90	...	118
1672	17	...	26	...	&c.	...	112
1796	17	4	5	...	34	...	108
Christ's							
in 1564	12	8	42	...	51	23	136
1573	14	...	53	...	58	39	157
1672	14	...	55	...	&c.	...	206
1796	16	12	...	...	41	11	116
St John's							
in 1564	44	11	62 sub-sizars 15		43	9	184
1573	52	...	78	...	89	46	265
1672	53	...	92	...	&c.	...	372
1796	62	36	73	...	70	20	303
Trinity							
in 1564	48	23	&c.	&c.	55	13	306
1573	61	...	71	&c.	138	110	393
1672	61	...	67	&c.	...	13	400
1796	67	44	61	...	146	23	558
Magdalene							
in 1573	6	...	...	...	23	17	46
1672	16	...	31	...	&c.	...	118
1796	14	...	...	...	27	16	62
Emmanuel							
in 1672	15	...	50	...	&c.	10	170
1796	14	16	19	...	34	18	152
Sidney							
in 1672	...	...	...	...	...	...	122
1756	11	5	...	...	18	9	58

In 1564 the total number in Cambridge was 1267.
... 1570 ... .-. ... ... 1630.
... 1573 ... ... 1813.
... 1618 ... ... 2998.
... 1622 ... ... 3050.
... 1672 ... ... 2522.
... 1796 ... ... 2137.
... 1873 ... ... 9655.

It will be noticed that the last column does not correspond with the sum of all the columns to the left hand. In *them* no account of Masters of Arts or other persons not *in statu pupillari* is taken, except so many as were fellows.

Four-and-twenty-men, Ten-men (or *ten-year-men*), *Sixteen-men, harry-sophs,* and Bachelor of Arts '*not-scholars*' are reckoned with the *pensioners*. Owing to my temporary ignorance in this matter no account is taken of the *non-entes* at Trinity or St John's.

In 1796 there were seven SIXTEEN-MEN at Peterhouse. TEN-YEAR MEN (TEN-MEN at Magdalene in 1796), or FOUR-AND-TWENTY MEN were the nondum graduati who were qualifying for a B.D. degree under *Stat. Acad. Cantab. Eliz.* Cap. IX. (1570), *qui ad academiam xxiv annos nati accedunt, et se in studio Theologiae totos tradunt, si omnes huiusmodi exercitationes coluerint, quae ad magistros artium ad Theologiam conuersos spectant, post decennium, ad gradum baccalaureatus Theologiae accedere poterunt sine ullo in artibus gradu suscepto: Ita tamen ut officiariis pro inferioribus gradibus, more ab academia recepto satisfaciant.* 'Mr *Chilcot* perform'd this exercise *ad assignationem D̄ni Procan.*' Grace Book, 13 June, 1734. Dr Ashton of Jesus framed the Grace for J. Proudman of that College to take his degree of B.D. under this statute in 1719. He adds that this was the first instance. (Ashton's *Collectanea,* 3 fol. 9.) The Cambridge *Calendar* for 1812 adds (p. 13) that such students, being graduates, but neither members of the senate nor in *statu pupillari,* are bound during the last two years of their decade to reside the greater part of those several terms. They must be in priests' orders at the time of their admission.

'HARRY-SOPH,' or, *Henry Sophister;* students who have kept all the terms required for a law act, and hence are ranked as Bachelors of Law by courtesy. They wear a plain, black, full-sleeved gown. Many conjectures have been offered respecting the origin of this term, but none of which are satisfactory. First: That "King Henry the Eighth, on visiting Cambridge, staid all the Sophisters a year, who expected a year of grace should have been given them." Secondly: "Henry the Eighth being commonly conceived of great strength and stature, these *Sophistae*

Henriciani were elder, and bigger than others." Thirdly: "In his reign, learning was at a loss, and the University stood at a gaze what would become of her. Hereupon many students staid themselves two, three, some four years, as who would see had their degrees before they took them would be rewarded and maintained." (See Fuller's *Worthies*, and Ray's *Proverbs*.)—A writer in the *Gent. Mag.* thinks "*Harry* quasi *Apa utique nempe*—a *Soph* INDEED!" He had better have said, an *arrant* 'Soph.' *Gradus ad Cantabrigiam*, ed. 1803. The editors of the *second* edition (1824), while retaining the above paragraph, prefixed to the definition the words, 'in reality Harisophs, a corruption of Erisophs (ἐρίσοφος, *ualde eruditus*).' This is now the favourite etymology, and was adopted in a note in some of the old University Calendars.

'Soon after this the usual time came of this student's taking his first degree of bachelor of art. He performed his acts and disputations in the public schools...and he sat in the schools to be posed by all or any master of arts that would examine him, and his grace was passed in the house...but when the day came that he should actually commence...he...returned no more until Ash-Wednesday (the day of commencement) was past: so that he continued Harry Sophister (so-called), it being five years before he would have his cap put on.' *Life of* Fairclough, in Clarke's *Lives of Eminent Persons* (1683), p. 158. 'So the late great Dr B. was reduc'd to a bare Harry-Soph [i. e. ἐρίσοφος, a person who has kept all his terms, but who is without a degree], being not able to gain above 50 votes in the whole University:' when Bentley was deprived of his degrees in October, 1718. Rudd's *Diary*, ed. Luard, 1860, pp. 23, 32.

A manuscript note in a copy of Grose's *Local Proverbs*, gives ' *haeret sophos;* because he remains a Soph, and does not proceed to his degree.'

'NON ENS; a Freshman in *Embryo!* one who has not been *matriculated*, though he has resided some time at the University, consequently is not considered as having any *being!*' *Gradus ad Cantab.* 1803, 1824. In our own time a youth who resides in Cambridge reading with a university 'coach' before coming into residence in a college is called a *beast*, as distinguished from a '*man*.' I have heard that about forty years ago an incepting M.A. was called a *beast* while passing through the few weeks which elapse between taking that degree and becoming a member of the senate.

> Constantinople! Hear it, all ye penmen!
> Who thirst to get, and will attempt the Prize,
> Whether ye be the merest of "non en' men,"
> Still ye shall know where this Byzantium lies.

And eke I will astonish the "year ten-men"
And ope their sapient and learned eyes."
Cambridge Odes by Peter Persius. [1830.]

p. 98. A QVIP for an VPSTART SIR IOHN.

The Return from Parnassus, *or the Scourge of Simony,* III. 2, acted at Cambridge in 1602.

'*Recorder*......your proud university princox[1] thinks he is a man of such merit the world cannot sufficiently endow him with preferment, an unthankful viper, an unthankful viper, that will sting the man that revived him.

> Why, is't not strange to see a ragged clerk
> Some stamel[2] weaver, or some butcher's son,
> That scrub'd alate within a sleeveless gown,
> When the commencement, like a morris-dance
> Hath put a bell or two about his legs,
> Created him a sweet clean gentleman;
> How then he 'gins to follow fashions:
> He whose thin fire dwells in a smoky roof,
> Must take tobacco and must wear a lock;
> His thirsty dad drinks in a wooden bowl,
> But his sweet self is serv'd in silver plate.
> His hungrye sire will scrape you twentye legs
> From one good christmas meal on christmas day,
> But his maw must be capon cram'd each day;
> He must ere long be triple beneficed,
> Else with his tongue he'll thunderbolt the world,
> And shake each peasant by his deafman's ear.
> But had the world no wiser men than I,
> We'd pen the prating parates in a cage;
> A chair, a cradle, and a tinder-box,
> A thacked chamber, and a ragged gown,
> Should be their lands and whole possessions;
> Knights, lords, and lawyers, should be lodg'd and dwell
> Within those over stately heaps of stone,
> Which doting sires in old age did erect.

'Well, it were to be wished that never a scholar in *England* might have above forty pounds a year.

'*Sir Roderick.* 'Faith, master *Recorder,* if it went by wishing, there should never an one of them all have above twenty a year; a good stipend, a good stipend, master *Recorder.*'

p. 99. *Strictures upon the Discipline of the University of* Cambridge *Addressed to the Senate* [Motto from *Dion. Halic. de Numa*], London.

---

[1] *princock.* A pert forward youth. '*Ephebus, puer praecox,*' Cambr. dict. 1693. *Romeo and Juliet,* i. 5. (Nares.)

[2] *Stamel.* A kind of fine worsted. (*Halliwell.*)

Printed by C. Stafford, *for* Shepperson *and* Reynolds, Oxford-Street;
and sold by W. H. Lunn, Cambridge, 1792. (8vo. pp. 53, Bodleian,
Gough Camb. 65.)

p. 99. TUTORS OF ST JOHN's. There is a more satisfactory account
of the tutors (Turner and Fog) in St John's, Camb., about 1656 in the
life of *Isaac Milles*, rector of *Highcleer*, 1721, pp. 12, 13. Also pp. 17,
18, among his contemporaries is mentioned 'D' *Humphry Gower*, afterward the worthy Master of St *John's* College. This Gentleman was
pretty near of the same standing, I believe of the same Year, with M'
Milles. He was a most clean and comely Youth, and look'd on as
one of the best scholars of his year. M' *Milles* and he happened to be
under the same Tutors, who used to propose *Gower* to all the rest, as a
Pattern. His Exercises were always commended, and sometimes shewn
about, and in the Disputations in the Tutors' Chambers, as the Custom
then was, he used to be styled *Eruditus Juvenis*. This Applause and
Commendation, or the natural bent of his Temper, or, perhaps, both
together created in this young Man, as M' *Milles* used to say, such a
Pride and Stateliness of Deportment, as render'd him very distasteful to
and hated by all, as well as despis'd by some of his Contemporaries.
He was, however, afterwards advanced to the Government of the College of St *John's*, and is said to have been one of the best Governors the
College ever had.'

p. 100. Though *Gentleman-Commoners* at *Oxford* seem not unfrequently to have been called FELLOW-COMMONERS in the seventeenth
and eighteenth century, we find in the middle of the latter however the
distinction of the Oxonian and Cantabrigian orders insisted upon in
1750 in [*Fr. Coventry's*] Pompey *the Little* [See above p. 634], Part II.
ch. x.

A *fellow-commoner*, 'according to the definition given by a member
of the university in a court of justice, is one who sits at the same
table, and *enjoys the conversation* of the fellows. It differs from what is
called a gentleman-commoner at *Oxford*, not only in the name but also
in the greater privileges and licences indulged to the members of this
order; who do not only *enjoy the conversation of the fellows*, but likewise
a full liberty of following their own imaginations in everything. For as
tutors and governors of colleges have usually pretty sagacious noses
after preferment, they think it impolitic to cross the inclinations of
young gentlemen, who are heirs to great estates, and from whom they
expect benefices and dignities hereafter, as rewards for *their want of
care of them*, while they were under their protection. From hence it
comes to pass, that pupils of this rank are excused from all public

exercises, and allowed to absent themselves at pleasure from the private lectures in their tutors' rooms, as often as they have made a party for hunting, or an engagement at the tennis-court, or are not well recovered from their evening's debauch. And whilst a poor unhappy soph, of no fortune, is often expelled for the most trivial offences, or merely to humour the capricious resentment of his tutor, who happens to dislike his face; young noblemen, and heirs of great estates, may commit any illegalities, and, if they please, overturn a college with impunity.'

The *Gradus ad Cantabrigiam* of 1803 and 1824 has the following article.

'FELLOW COMMONERS. *Students* (A NON *studendo!*) who are, in *appearance*, the most SHINING men in the University, their gowns are richly trimmed with gold or silver lace—their caps are covered with velvet, the tassels to which are of gold or silver. ["These *gold threads* have almost as much influence in the University as a red or blue ribband at court." (*See the Connoisseur*, *No.* 97.)] These gentlemen enjoy the privilege of cracking their bottle, and their *joke*, if they have one, in the public parlour, or *Combination Room*, where they are literally "Hail FELLOW, well met." It were almost endless to enumerate the privileges which these gentlemen enjoy by virtue of *hereditary talents*, instilled into their *breeches' pockets*. Those privileges however have raised the envy of their inferiors in point of fortune, who in describing them seem to have racked their invention to find terms sufficiently indignant, *e. g.*

'FELLOW-COMMONERS have been nick-named "Empty Bottles!" They have been called likewise "*Useless* Members!" "The licensed Sons of Ignorance!" "The order of *Fellow-Commoner*," says one writer, "has by immemorial usage a kind of prescriptive right to idleness; and fashion has inspired it with an habitual contempt of discipline!" It is even recorded as the saying of Dr Watson, the present Bishop of Llandaff, that "a Fellow Commoner is of no use but to the Bed-maker, *Tutor*, and Shoe-black!!!"

> "O, mighty Jove, what have I liv'd to see!
> *Bed-makers* and *shoe-blacks* class'd with *me!*"

"That Dr Watson was *Tutor* of a College is known of a surety. Who can doubt then but that his Lordship spoke from experience?" It is, likewise, well known, that in the year 1786 a gentleman who had been a *pupil* of his Lordship, Mr Luther of Essex, left him by will the USE-FUL sum of 20,000*l.* !!!'

In the service an empty bottle was called a *marine*. The D. of York when presiding at a public dinner happening to say to a waiter

'Take away that marine,' discovered that he had offended one of that order who was sitting within ear-shot. Bowing he made his apology. 'I meant no offence; only a gentleman who has done his duty, and is ready to do it again.'

Mar. 15, 1743—4, it was ordered at Peterhouse that all fellow-commoners and by-fellows should have the master or one of the fellows of the old foundation as a *sponsor.*

p. 102. *rusty round cap*, see pp. 499—512.

Ibid. 'BROWN-SHILLERS.—Ripe nuts, more particularly applied to wood nuts.' *Brogden's* Lincolnshire Words.

p. 103. 'TO CAP. (1.) To touch the cap, *en passant*, in token of dutiful submission, whether it be to the Vice-Chancellor as supreme; or, unto Proctors, as unto them that are sent by him for the punishment of evil doers. (2.) To pull off the cap, and make obeisance *aperto capite*, in the academic phrase. (See BORE.)—*Capping* appears to have b:en carried to its highest, or rather LOWEST, pitch of perfection, in old Catholic times. Thus in a work entitled *Sacrarum Ceremoniarum se t Rituum Ecclesiasticorum.* S. ROMAE *ecclesiae Libri tres...Romae* MDLX. [*Venetiis*, 1506, &c.] one part treats 'of the reverence which a Cardinal is enjoined to pay the Pope.' 'To transcribe the whole would require no small portion of that *Cardinal* virtue PATIENCE.' *Gradus ad Cantabrigiam*, 1803, 1824. The passage however clearly refers to the *cope.*

The following is a Cambridge *Coffee-house Jest* of the 17th century, reprinted by M' Halliwell. 'A poor but witty youth, brought up in one of the colleges, could not afford the price of a pair of shoes, but when his old ones were worn out at the toes, had them capped with leather; whereupon his companions began to jeer him for so doing: "Why," said he "don't you see they must be *cappd.* Are they not *fellows?*"'

p. 103. China is still called CHANY by some old fashioned persons; and, locally, in Berkshire.

p. 105. *too much vain philosophy*. After transcribing almost verbatim the passage from his *Grounds and Occasions of the Contempt of the Clergy*, &c., D' Eachard, Master of Catharine hall, adds to it in 1682 in his Speculum Crape-gownorum [see above, p. 516], p. 3, the following sketch of the fate of a Sizar. 'However the *Fellow* whom he serves cannot but in pitie, if not for Concience sake, let him glean some small morsels of his knowledge, which costs him no more than only the expence of that time while the young Sizar is pulling off his Master's Stockins, or warming his Nightcap : From thence he learns,

Quid est Logica? Quae sunt Virtutes morales? and to number the
Predicaments in their order. This being done he takes his leave of
the University, and by the first Carrier, upon a Pack, away he goes
by slow Marches into his own Country, with a common place Book
and a *Medulla Theologiae,* and then have at a Parsonage,' &c.

p. 106. Alicia D'Anvers in 'Academia : or *the Humours* of Oxford,'
1691, p. 7, says,

> A SERVITOR to serve ye,
> Brings Bread and Beer, or what is call'd for,
> Eating what's left, Trencher and all (Sir).

p. 106. *George Whitefield's* early occupation at the BELL INN,
Glo'ster, in the days when he wore his '*drawer's Swabbers,*' is referred
to in Coventry's *Pompey the¦ Little* and in Fielding's *Tom Jones,*
VIII. 8.

p. 121. TANSY (*tanacetum*), a herb from which puddings were
made. Hence any pudding of the kind. Selden (*Table Talk*) says
' Our tansies at Easter have reference to the bitter herbs.'

In '*Adam's* Luxury and *Eve's* Cookery ; or, the Kitchen-Garden
display'd,' &c. *London, R. Dodsley,* &c. 1744, 12mo, are given the
following recipes.

' An *Apple Tansey.* Take three or four Pippins or other Apples,
pare them, and slice them in thin Slices, and fry them with Butter.
Then take four Eggs; six Spoonfuls of Cream, a little Rose-Water,
Nutmeg and Sugar; beat all together, and pour it over the Apples.
Let it fry a little till brown, and then turn it and let it fry till brown on
that Side. Garnish with Lemon, and strew Sugar over it.' (p. 106.)

' To make *Bean Tansey,* both savoury and sweet.—Blanch your
Beans, and beat them in a Mortar ; for the savoury Way season them
with Pepper, Salt, Cloves, and Mace ; then put in the Yolks of six
Eggs, and a Quartern of Butter. Butter your Pan and bake it, as
you'd do a Tansey, and stick slices of fryed Bacon a-top. The sweet
Way is with Beans, Biskets, Sugar, Sack, and Cream, and eight Yolks
of Eggs ; so bake it, and stick on the Top Orange and Lemon peel
candy'd.' (*Ibid.* p. 118.)

' *Goosberry Tanzey.*—Pick a Quart of green Goosberries, and boil
them in half a Pound of Butter, till they are well coddled. Then pour
into them the Yolks of sixteen Eggs well beaten with half a Point
[sic] of Cream. Sweeten to your Taste with Sugar, then boil [sic]
it as you would a Tanzey ; and when baked, strew over it Rose-
water and Sugar.' (*Ibid.* p. 138.)

p. 120. Sir T. More means, We will beg, like good Catholics,
in the name of our Lady : singing the *antiphona.*

'SALVE REGINA, mater misericordiae, vita, dulcedo, et spes nostra salue. Ad te clamamus exules filii Euae. Ad te suspiramus gementes et flentes in hac lacrimarum valle, Eia ergo aduocata nostra illos tuos misericordes oculos ad nos conuerte Et Iesum benedictum fructum ventris tui, nobis post hoc exilium ostende. O clemens, ô pia, ô dulcis virgo Maria. Ʋ O. P. N., S. Dei genetrix, ℟ Vt digni efficiamur promissionibus Christi.

Let vs pray

Omnipotens sempiterne, &c.'

According to the *Office* of the Blessed *Virgin Marie,* &c. By *John le Covstvrier.* Permissu Superiorum, 1633. This was appointed as the Antiphon to *Benedictus* or *Nunc Dimittis* to close Lauds and Compline *from the Compline on Trinitie Eue, vntil* [nones on the Saturday before] *Aduent.* From the Purification to Easter Eve was used ' Ave Regina caelorum.' From Easter to Trinity ' Regina caeli laetare,' as also to *Magnificat* at Evensong. No mention is there made of *Alma Redemptoris Mater,* though we know from Chaucer's *Prioresses Tale* that it had been in the pre-reformational *antiphonere.*

pp. 121, &c. CIZA, SICE, SIZE—SIZINGS—SIZAR—CUES and CEES. I am unable at present to offer any account of the etymology of one or all of these words, satisfactory even to myself. I prefer therefore to follow my common practice of putting before the reader materials whence he may construct a theory for himself.

With regard to the word *size* we are at once met by two possible roots. One of *cutting,* with the idea of partition : the other of *setting,* with the notion of position. The Glossary of *Du Cange* supplies the following list of words, some of which may have a connexion with those before us.

assessor ferculorum,...*asseour'* (escuyer, asseoir, *sewer*).

assidere est censum describere...peraequare.

assisa, and *Assisia,* Littletoni, sect. 234. est *nomen aequivocum:*... Comitia publica...Quidquid in Assisis definiebatur inter litigantes... Quod in Assisiis, &c. a Bailliuis et Justiariis definitum est super rerum venalium qualitate quantitate pondere mensura et pretio...Interdum pro ipso tributo (*Sissa* pro tributo in Foris Aragonensibus : *Sisa* Hispanis ; *Sissarii,* Sissarum exactores), &c. &c.

Assisi in Ecclesiis Cathedralibus Beneficiati, minores tamen ordine Canonicis, in Ecclesiis Cypriis, qui videntur functi officio Canonicorum, quos *Vicarios* dicimus : vel quibus assignata est *assisia* seu pensio annualis, quasi *Pensionarii* [references given to constitutions *ann.* 1248,

1 320 cet. concil. Nicosiens]. *Assisia* munus Vicarii (Stat. Nicos. an. 1 350).

If connected with *asseoir* the parallel with the Oxford *Servitor* will be more close. The spelling with a *c* is found in the letter of Strype, quoted pp. 121, 122 (*ciza, cize*). The form *cizing* is given in Cooper's *Annals of Cambridge,* II. 354, from a document of the year 1577. The following is taken from *Gradus ad Cantabrig.* 1803, the quotations being corrected by the originals. 'SIZE—*in academiis,* from *Assize*— Fr. *Asseoir,* to set down, sc. *sumptus qui in tabulas referuntur.* Ray derives it from *scindo.* Minshew has inserted the word in his Guide into the Tongues, second Ed. 1626 [? 1627], and with it the following. "A 𝕾𝖎𝖟𝖊 is a portion of bread or drinke ; it is a *farthing,* which Scholl- lers in *Cambridge* have at the Buttery; it is noted with the latter S. as in *Oxford* with letter Q. for halfe a *farthing,* and q⁴ for a *farthing;* and whereas they say in *Oxford,* to *Battle* in the Buttery-booke, i.e. to set downe on their names what they take in Bread, Drinke, Butter, Cheese, &c., so in *Cambridge* they say to SIZE, i. to set downe their *quantum,* i. how much they take on their names in the Buttery-booke. Vi. to 𝕭𝖆𝖙𝖙𝖑𝖊." This word, as was observed of EXHIBITION, was not confined to the University. King Lear, in Shakspear's inimitable Tragedy, is made to address one of his daughters ;

> 'Tis not in thee
> To grudge my pleasure, to cut off my train,
> To bandy hasty words, to scant my SIZES.'

'To SIZE, "at dinner, is to order yourself any little luxury that may chance to tempt you, in addition to your general fare ; for which you are expected to pay the cook at the end of the term." This is often done when *commons* are scanty, or indifferent. As a College term, it is of very considerable antiquity. In the Comedy called The Return from Parnassus, 1606, one of the character says (*act.* ix. *sc.* 2),

"You that are one of the Devil's *fellow commoners;* one that SIZETH the devil's *butteries,* sins and perjuries very lavishly, one, that are so dear to *Lucifer,* that he never puts you out of *commons* for non-pay-ment, &c."

'Again in the same, act v. sc. 2, Amoretto's Page personating his master says—

'"Fidlers, I use to *size* my musick, or go on the *score* for it : I'll pay it at the quarter's end."'

In act IV. scene 2 of the same play, *The return from* Parnassus, or *Scourge of Simony. Publiquely acted by the Students in Saint John's Colledge,* Cambridge [in 1602] 1606, there is a corrupt passage where one of the scholars in a sort of interlude addresses the famous comedian of the time, the hero of the *Nine Days' Wonder* (reprinted by the Camden Society) :

'*Philomusus.* Indeed, master *Kempe*, you are very famous: but that is as well for workes in print, as you[r] part in kne (cue)—

'*Kempe.* You are at *Cambridge* still with sice kne (size cue) and be lusty humorous poets.'

According to Grose, in his *Classical Dictionary of the Vulgar Tongue,* ed. 3, 1796, A *Size of Ale* is 'Half a pint. Size of bread and cheese; a certain quantity. Sizings; Cambridge term for the college allowance from the buttery, called at Oxford battles.'

In his *Provincial Glossary,* ed. 2, 1790, he gives 'SIZE OF BREAD, AND CUE OF BREAD. Cambridge. The one signifying half the other; one fourth part of a half-penny loaf; cue being Q, the abbreviation of [quadrans, or] a quarter, a size, comes from scindo, I cut.' This proves to be a mere transcription from Ray's *Glossary of South and East Country Words,* ed. 1737.

Archdeacon *Ro. Nares,* in his Shakesperian Glossary, defines *size* as 'A small portion of bread, or other food, still used at Cambridge; whence the term *sizer*, &c.' A more important article is 'CUE. A small portion of bread or beer; a term formerly current in both the English universities, the letter q being the mark in the buttery books to denote such a piece. Q should seem to stand for *quadrans,* a farthing; but Minshew, who finished his first edition in Oxford, says it was only half that sum, and thus explains it : "Because they set down in the battling or butterie bookes in Oxford and Cambridge, the letter q for half a farthing ; and in Oxford when they make the cue or q a farthing, they say, *cap my q,* and make it a farthing, thus ♉. But in Cambridge they use this letter, a little s ; thus ſ, or thus s, for a farthing." He translates it in Latin *calculus panis.* Coles has "A *cue* [half a farthing] minutum."

'*Cues* and *cees* are generally mentioned together, the *cee* meaning a small measure of beer ; but why, is not equally explained.

> Hast thou worn
> Gowns in the university, tost logick,
> Suckt philosophy, eat *cues,* drank *cees,* and cannot give
> A letter the right courtier's crest?"
>
> 1st part of *Jeronimo.*

That he, poor thing, had no acquaintance with above a muse and a half; and that he never drank above *sis-q* of Helicon.—*Contempt of the Clergy,* p. 26, 1670, by J. Eachard, master of Katherine hall.

Bishop Earle [of Merton] also has *cues* and *cees*. *An old colledge Butler*...domineers over freshmen, when they first come to the hatch, and puzzles them with strange language of *cues* and *cees*, and some broken latin, which he has learnt at his bin.

Earle's *Microcosmographie*, 1628. *character* 17.

So strict
A niggard to your commons, that you're fain
To size your belly out with shoulder fees,
With kidneys, rumps, and *cues* of single beer.
Beaum [Oxon] and Fletcher [Camb.] *Wit at Several Weapons*, act ii. sc. 4.

Cues there stand for *cees*, which proves that the terms were not well defined.'

Again Nares writes—

'Q, formerly the mark for half a farthing, in the college accounts at Oxford. See CUE. This will enable us to explain the following :

'*R.* What gave you the boy that had found your pen-knife ?

L. I gave him a *quu cee*, and some walnuts.' Hoole's *Corderius*, 1657, p. 157.

The boy means that he gave him a small portion of bread or drink (for *cee* may mean either) value a *q*. The Latin is " Dedi sextantem," etc.

'Rather pray there be no fall of money, for thou wilt then go for a *q*.' Lyly's [Magd. Coll. Oxon, migrated to Camb.] *Mother Bombie*, iv. 2.

This is said to a boy whose name is *Halfpenny*.'

In the passages above quoted we find there combinations of these words; '*cues* and *cees*,' '*q c*,' '*size q*.' Two at least of the terms are still in partial use at Cambridge. In Peterhouse a *size* is the name for a small silver tumbler or cup holding rather more than half a pint (half the contents of a *stoup*). In King's college a *cue* is the name for a similar measure of beer, called in Trinity a *plate* (see above p. 291, and below the *note* on that passage) ; and at Trinity-hall a *tun*, from the shape of the vessel.

It seems probable that the letter *q* stood for the price. *c* may have been a symbol of quantity. But whereas prices have become altered, the capacity of silver cups is constant, and the name *cue* may have become attached to that which once cost a mite. Either *cee* or *size* may have experienced a similar process. I see no reason to doubt that *q* originally stood for *quadrans*, a farthing, i. e. when a student ordered a cup of beer the butler scored him up a *q* though he only owed ¼ of a penny, feeling sure that he would soon have an opportunity of scoring up the other half-farthing by *capping his cue*, or completing the entry with a little *a* or circumflex superscribed, so that the second draught should make up, with the first, a debt of a current coin of the realm. The letter *c* may have stood for some such word as *cyathus*. We have noticed that 'a *quu cee*' was the rendering of *sextans;* this may perhaps account for the use of the little *s* at Cambridge, where the *⁏* was employed at Oxford. According to the Roman liquid and dry measures, the *sextans* contained 2 *cyathi*, and the *quadrans* held 3: the *sextarius* or ξέστης held 12, and was nearly equal to an English pint. We need not suppose that the English *cyathus* was so small as the Roman. We have seen also that the *cee* was a measure of *beer* as well as of *bread*. It may have been used even as a symbol of *price* at one time. There is a corresponding variety of use in the Latin words just mentioned, which relate to a duodecimal system of liquid and dry measure, while *sextans* and *quadrans* occur also in the money table as well. Is it possible that the word *size* or *sice* also may have been once a measure of capacity connected with the word *six*, the French form of which is sometimes pronounced *size* (Spanish *seis*) in scoring at backgammon? It would then be parallel to *sextans*, and possibly equivalent with *cee*, and with *cue:* the combinations of them having been formed when *cue* alone stood for *price*, and the others for *measure*. Grose explains *sice* to mean *sixpence.* He also mentions 'a bale of flat sice aces' in a list of false *Dice.*

If the word *sizar* is thus traceable to the fact of receiving an allowance *pro pane aut potu*, it may be compared with its synonym *quadrantarius*, Ashton's *Collectanea in Stat. Acad. Cantab.* folio 70.

Swift's burlesque phonetic etymology will be remembered.

Another peculiar use of the word *size* is mentioned in Edmund Carter's *History of the county of Cambridge*, 15. *ap.* Cooper's *Annals*, IV. 272. 'The chief market-place called Market Hill...is on Saturdays well supplied with the best butter (made up into pounds and half-pounds, each being a yard long, for the convenience of the college butlers cutting it into what they call *sizes.*' The *Gradus ad Cantabrigiam*, 1803, defines 'A BUTTER, 'a *size* or part of butters (see *Size.*) "Send me a roll and two *Butters.*"' Grose, in his *Classical Dictionary of the Vulgar Tongue*, had the same example, ed. 3, 1796, explaining it, 'an inch of butter, that commodity being sold at Cambridge by the yard, in rolls of about an inch in diameter.'

p. 122. Vincent Bourne speaks of *sparrows* feeding in a COLLEGE HALL. Mrs A. D'Anvers in 'Academia : or *the Humours of* Oxford,' 1691, p. 9 says, in what she calls Burlesque Verse,

> De'e think then 'twould not make the *Young Lad*
> At a *Three half pence* Meat become *sad,*

Which at the *College*, you must know, Man's
No more, nor less; than one *Boy's* Commons.
And then, they make a hideous chatter
For a *Farth'n Drink, Bread, Cheese* or *Butter;*
And would that pay, now, in your thinking,
For washing of the *Pot* they drink in?

p. 123. From the junior bursar's book : Peterhouse, 1751 :—

Qr 3d. to Midsr. Week 10th.	Mr Nourse, Mr Stuart, Mr Nicholson, Mr Smith, Mr Osborne, Mr Longmire, Mr Oldham, Ds Hirst, Mr Gray, Mr Hedges, Mr Price, Mr Cavendish, *Mr Bennet*, Mr Williams.

			s.	d.	q.
Sat.	Pane	x = o			
	Potu	v = o	1	4	o
Prand.	Poc[ulum] Gr[atiac] . . .	r = o			
Sol.	Pane	viij = o			
	Potu	iiij = o	2	2	o
Prand.	Poc. Gr.	j — ij = o			

And so on. Presently follows :—

					s.	d.	q.
Sat. Dinner	3 Mess 2 pts	Veal	v⁵. x P. Sch. viij	. . .	5	10	o
Wit Sunday	Mackrill				5	6	o
	Chickens				5	o	o
	a Sparagrass				2	o	o
	Lemon puding				3	o	o
	Green Goos				3	6	o
	Salit, Cucumbers, Egs & Oile . . .				2	o	o
	Lobsters				3	6	o
	Loine of Beef				11	o	o
Supper	2 Mess 2 pts	Lamb	iij⁵. iv P. Sch. viij.	.	3	4	o
Mund. Dinner	2 Mess 2 pts	Mutton	iv⁵. ij P. Sch.	. .	4	2	o
Supper	2 Mess 2 pts.	Veal cutlets	iij⁵. iv P. Sch. viij.	.	3	4	o
Tuesd. Dinner	2 Mess 2 pts	Beef	Ex. Mr Bennet, iv⁵. ij. P. Sch. vj.	. .	4	2	o

				s.	d.	q.
Supper	2 Mess / 2 pts {Pidgeons}	iij*. iv. P. Sch.	. .	3	4	0
Wedn. Dinner	2 Mess / 1 pt { Mutton }	iij*. ix. P. Sch.	. .	3	9	0
Thursd. Dinner	2 Mess / 1 pt { Mutton }	iij*. ix. P. Sch.	. .	3	9	0
Supper	2 Mess / 1 pt { Veal Collops }	iij*. =0, P. Sch.	. .	3	0	0
Frid. Dinner	2 Mess / 1 pt { Mutton }	iij*. ix. P. Sch.	. .	3	9	0
		P. Sch.	. .	2	6	0

£3 13s. 11d.

Here is an entry in 1779.

1779. Nov. 30, St. Andrew—[bp. *Cosin's* commem. feast].

	£.	s.	d.
Cod. Head—Lobster Sauce	1	6	6
a Quart of Oyster	0	4	0
Mock Turtle	0	7	6
Crimp Cod	0	18	0
3 fowles	0	6	0
Greens, &c.	0	0	8
Chicking Pie	0	7	6
hunting puding	0	3	0
Coller. Brawn			
Leamon puding	0	3	6
a Ham	1	0	0
3 fowles	0	6	0
Greens, &c.	0	0	6
Scholings pottato	0	0	8
Sallad	0	1	6
36—Sir Loyn Beef	0	16	6
Mock Turtle	0	7	6
Soales, &c.	0	15	6
Side Table:			
Soales, &c.	0	15	0
Pease Soop	0	3	0
Turkey and Oyster	0	8	6
Brawn			
Mince pies	0	3	6

2d Course.

	£.	s.	d.
Qr Lamb	0	9	6
Sallad	0	1	4
Cag and Sturgeon	1	1	6
Snipes	0	8	6
Cranberry pie	0	3	6
Trifile	0	3	6
Mince pie	0	3	6
Turkey and Sauceagues	0	6	6
6 Lobster	0	9	0
Rost Tongue Uder	0	5	6
Current Jelley	0	1	0
Leamons	0	0	6
Oyle and Suger	0	1	0
Durrum Lad	0	10	0

Supr.

	£.	s.	d.
Chine pork	0	8	6
3 fowles	0	6	0
Apricot puffs	0	3	6
Cold Beef, &c.	0	2	0
paid Carr^e. for fish	0	5	8
Baskett and Booking	0	2	6
	14	7	x

Receva the Contents in full by me Richd. Thrig.

p. 124. PANCAKE BELL. J. Brady in his *Clauis Calendaria*, ed. 2. 1813. I. 207, says that this was originally the *shriving* bell rung in the morning to summon persons to confession. The bell rung before service was (he says) still called the pancake-bell in some country places. Shrove Tuesday was known as *Confession Tuesday.*

p. 125. In Huddesford's *Wiccamical Chaplet*, 1804, p. 31, we find ' the Monckes Complaynte to Alma Mater. Touching dyverse newe Matters wrought in Oxenforde Cytie,' in affected archaic style :

> At wonted noone thie trenchermenne unseene,
>   At eve unheard thy chawnte of godlie tonge
> More godlie far soch holie chawnte I weene
>   Than mottryng clerke with messe ne said ne songe,
> Staie, holie Modher, staie soch vanitee
> Albe so trymm, this nought beseemeth thee.

The note explains that 'Twelve, the usual HOUR OF DINNER,' was in 1792 'changed to three ;' and 'chaunting the service abolished in the choirs.'

L. B. E.   42

On page 212 of the same collection is 'An early view of the [American] Question, 1776. In a Dialogue between some Boilers and Chafing-dishes:'

> Each morn the Chafing-dishes round
> The College quadrangle are found;
> And, as the Coals begin to glisten
> You'll hear the Boiler, if you listen,
> Running his treble notes up high,
> To Chafing-dish beneath him cry:
> Wee, wee, wee, we, wehee, wee, we! [2 Octaves *Da Capo.*]
> Shall both of us exhausted be,
> Between this Fire and you and me,
> About a Dish or two of Tea?

This looks as if men hadn't fires in their rooms at breakfast time. Perhaps it was only in the summer. The illustrations of the *Oxford Sausage*, some 20 or 30 years earlier, represent the grates in undergraduates' rooms as black and empty; but in some instances with a pair of bellows or tongs lying near.

p. 128. 'A poem of Sam. Wesley the elder;' viz. *A King Turned Thresher*, given in Southey's Specimens of Later English Poets. 1807. I. 328.

p. 130. BEAKER. See page 592. The *recipe* for *sherry-beaker* was as follows. Take a bottle of good sherry; scald, and mix with calves-foot jelly. Pour into three glasses with a slice of lemon.

Ib. 'Oct. 1812. Orders were published in Trinity and St John's that students appearing in hall or chapel *in pantaloons or trousers* be considered absent.' Cooper's *Annals*, IV. 503.

p. 132. *Elbonn.* See p. 475.

p. 133. SHAVING ON SUNDAY. In 1727—8 Betson was fined 5*s.* in the Vicechancellor's court at Cambridge for this offence.

Ib. Among the *Ordinances* of *Oliver Cromwell* is 'An Act for the Better Observation of the *Lord's day.* At the Parliament begun at *Westminster* the 17th day of *September, An. Dom.* 1656. *London:* Printed by *Hen. Hills* and *John Field*, Printers to His Highness the Lord *Protector.* 1657.'

The act provides against any 'Waggoner, Carrier, Butcher, Higler, Drover, or any of their servants travelling or coming by Land or Water' into an Inn, House or Lodging, betwixt 12 P.M. on Saturday, and 12 P.M. on Sunday, to be punished with the owner of such Inn, &c. 'Every person using or imploying any Boat, Wherry, Lighter, Barge, Horse, Coach or Sedan, or travelling or laboring with any of them upon the Day aforesaid (except it be to and from some place for the Service of God, or except in case of necessity, to be alowed by some Justice of the Peace). Every person being in any Tavern, Inn, Ale-house, Victualling-house, Strongwater-house, Tobacco-house, Cellar or Shop, (not lodging there, nor upon urgent necessity, to be allowed by a Justice of Peace), or fetching or sending for any Wine, Ale, or Beer, Tobacco, Strong-water, or other strong Liquor unnecessarily, and to Tipple within any other House or Shop: and the Keepers or Owners......; every person Dancing or prophanely Singing or Playing upon Musical Instruments, or Tipling in any such Houses, Cellars or Shops, or else-where......, or Harbouring or entertaining the persons so offending; Every person Grinding or causing to be Ground any Corn or Grain in any Miln, or causing any Fulling or other Mills to work upon the Day aforesaid; And every person working in the Washing, Whiting or Drying of Clothes, Threed or Yarn, or causing such Work to be done......; Every person setting up, burning or branding Beet, Turf of Earth......; gathering of Rates, Loans, Taxations or other Pay-ments...... (except to the use of the Poor in the Publique Collections); Every Chandler Melting or causing to be melted, Tallow or Wax belonging to his Calling. And every common Brewer and Baker, Brewing, &c. And every Butcher killing any Cattel, and every Butcher, Costermonger, Poulterer, Herb-seller, Cordwayner, Shoo-maker or other persons Selling, exposing or offering to sell any their wares or Commodities, and the persons buying......; All Taylors and other Tradesmen fitting or going to fit, or carry any wearing Apparel or other things; And Barbers Trimming upon the Day aforesaid; All persons keeping, using or being present...... at any Fairs, Markets, Wakes, Revels, Wrestlings, Shootings, Leaping, Bowling, Ringing of Bells for pleasure, or upon any other occasion (saving for calling people together for the Publique Worship), Feasts, Church-ale, May-poles, Gaming, Bear-baiting, Bull-baiting or any other Sports and Pastimes: All persons unnecessarily walking in the Church or Church-yards, or elsewhere in the time of Publique worship; And all persons vainly and prophanely walking on the Day aforesaid; And all persons Travelling, carrying Burthens, or doing any worldly labors or work of their ordi-nary Calling on the Day aforesaid, shall be guilty of prophaning the Lord's Day.'

Offenders of the age of 14 years and upwards to be fined 10*s.* and wares forfeited. 'Nothing in this Act contained, shall extend to the prohibiting the Dressing of Meat in private Families, or the Dressing or Sale of Victuals in a moderate waye in Inns, Victualing Houses or Cooks Shops, for the use of such as cannot otherwise be provided for, or to the crying or selling of Milk before Nine of the clock in the morning, or after Four of the clock in the afternoon' in summer, and an hour later in winter. Persons attending markets on Saturday or Monday must be careful not to transgress the statute.

'And it is enacted by the Authority aforesaid, That if any children or servants under the Age of Fourteen years, offending in any the offences within this Act mentioned, and thereof convicted before any Mayor, Head-Officer, or any one or more Justices of the Peace as aforesaid, the Parents, Guardians, Masters, Mistresses or Tutors of all such children and servants, shall forfeit the Sum of One shilling for every such servant or childe so offending and thereof convicted as aforesaid, unless such Parent, &c....... shall in the presence of the Church-wardens, Overseers for the Poor, or other Officer, or one of them, give or cause to be given unto such childe or servant so offending, due correction...... That all and every person and persons shall......upon every Lord's-Day diligently resort to some Church or Chappel where the true Worship and Service of God is exercised, or shall be present at some other convenient Meeting-place of Christians, not differing in matters of Faith from the publique Profession of the Nation, as it is expressed in the Humble Petition and Advice of the Parliament to His Highness the Lord Protector, where the Lord's-Day shall be duly sanctified,' under a penalty of 2s. 6d. No Minister or Publique Preacher to be molested.

'That all persons Contriving, Printing or Publishing any Papers, Books or Pamphlets for Allowance of Sports and Pastimes upon the Lord's-Day, or against the Morality thereof, shall forfeit the Sum of Five pounds, or be committed to the House of Correction.'

This bill was enacted in the same parliament which produced those appalling debates on Naylor the mad 'Quaker' (as Quakers then were); which prove that, with few exceptions, the educated parliamentarians of England were as pitiless in executions as Laud had been when in power. The progress of the Lord's-Day Bill is sketched in the Diary of T. Burton, then M.P. for Westmoreland, Rutt's edition, 1828, I. pp. 295, 310; II. 260—268. A clause prohibiting 'profane and idle sitting' (II. p. 264) was negatived; one objection (by Major General *Whalley*) being that 'as at Nottingham, many people that have houses in the rock, and have no air, live most part of their time without doors.' It was a long debate, 'One gentleman speaking low Mr Speaker was called upon to report.' Being strengthened by the opinion of the Master of the Rolls, he refused, and complained of the loud talking of hon. members. Finally '*Colonel Winthorpe* stood up again, and spoke against the Bill, or to adjourn the debate, but was taken down by the noise of calling for the question. *Colonel Purefoy* cried "Give him the Bill," meaning Mr Speaker. The clerk said, "if such words had been spoken in some Parliaments, he would have been called to the bar".

The debate held so late that *a candle was called in* [i. e. on a special motion, as until the year 1717. The Speaker at this time took the chair at 8 A.M. and the House generally rose at noon. Committees sat very early in the morning, and in the afternoon and evening], and, after a while, the Bill was agreed to pass, and ordered to be ingrossed.

The House rose at almost ten (P.M. Saturday, June 20, 1657), and adjourned till Monday morning, eight o'clock.

There had been a similar Act passed in April, 1650, and in this same parliament on *Christmas* Day, 1656, this curious debate arose in the House :

'*Col. Mathews.* The House is thin ; much, I believe, occasioned by the observation of this day. I have a short Bill to prevent the super-stition for the future. I desire it to be read.'

'*Mr Robinson.* I could get no rest all night for the preparation of this foolish day's solemnity. This renders us in the eyes of the people to be profane. We are, I doubt, returning to Popery....'

'*Sir Chr. Pack.* I am as much for this Bill as any man, but I would not have us, under the notion of taking away festivals, take away the Lord's-day, for in the Bill the festival of Easter and Pentecost are abolished.' (*Ibid.* I. 229, 230).

p. 141. *Master of Arts' Coffee House.* See Mayor's edition of 'A Pattern for Young Students' (Life of *Ambrose Bonwicke,*) p. 198.

p. 145. *Horseman's Coffee House.* See above p. 131.

p. 151. Warton's *Companion to the Guide,* &c. See pp. 388—390.

p. 152. ANTIQUITY HALL, WHITTINGTON AND HIS CAT, or THE HOLE IN THE WALL. For the story of *Hearne* and the supposed tesselated Roman pavement of sheeps' 'trotters' at 'an antique Pot-house known by the Historical Sign of *Whittington and his Cat,*' see T. Warton's *Companion to the Guide,* &c., pp. 20, 21. In Skelton's *Oxonia Antiqua,* 1823, vol. II. is *The Plan of the Hall, with the Tesel-lated Floor.* There is an accompanying sketch of Tom Hearne, Humphry Wanley, and Mr Whiteside (keeper of the Ashmolean Museum), and also Hearne's printer at Oxford waiting for company. There is depicted '*The Manner of Entring,*' '*Propylaeum, or hole in ye Wall, the Entrance to* Antiquity Hall.'

p. 157. THE ZODIACK. This club was founded in 1725. *Gray* in a letter to *Wharton,* '*Cambr. March* [1747]. *Tuesday* Night,' mentions that *Kit Smart* of Pembroke intends to perform his comedy [*A Trip to* Cambridge, *or The Grateful Fair;* see p. 195,] publickly, borrowing the ZODIACK ROOM for the purpose. In another letter to *Wharton,* '*March* 9th [1748-9] *Thursday, Cambridge,*' he speaks bombastically of the master of Pembroke hall as 'the high and mighty Prince *Roger* surnamed the *Long,* Lord of the great ZODIAC, the Glass Uranium, and the Chariot that goes without horses.' This refers, not of course to the Club, but to the great sphere constructed by Dr Roger Long and Jonathan Munns the tin-plate worker. It was taken down and pulled to pieces at the time of the alterations in 1871—2. The Observatory which held it used to stand at the north eastern corner of the inner court of Pembroke. The sphere itself, illustrating the motions of the heavenly bodies, measured 18 feet in diameter. The '*coach*' or '*chariot*' mentioned by Gray was probably the water-velocipede constructed by Dr Long, for his amusement on the water in Pembroke-basin. See Carter's *History of the Univ. of Cambridge,* p. 77.

The sphere is described in Britton and Brayley's *Beauties of England and Wales,* 1801. II. 39, 40. It is said to be rusty and much damaged; 'but the disgrace must heighten into ignominy, if the *report* is true, that the interest of 200*l. Bank Annuities* was bequeathed by the Doctor [R. Long,] to keep the "Instrument and Place" in good order.' A description of this mechanical curiosity may be found in Long's *Astronomy,* vol. II.

p. 158. THE HYSON CLUB. See pp. 334, 335.

p. 160. A. D'Anvers in her 'Academia: or *the Humours of Oxford,*' p. 50, 1691, speaks of undergraduates condescending in defect of Tobacco to smoke the straws, &c. of mats. Compare with this the macaronic lines quoted in the notes to some editions of Percy's *Reliques* (Ballad of *St George*):

> at si
> *Mundungus* desit: tum non *fumcare* recusant
> *Brown-Paper* tostâ, uel quod fit arundine *bed-mat.*

p. 161. When Combe's Dr *Syntax* (in Search of the Picturesque, *canto* VI.) dines with the provost at *Oxford,* at the College feast,

> They eat and drank, they SMOK'D, they talk'd,
> And round the College-garden walk'd.

Ib. Dr Farmer's silver *tobacco pipe* is still preserved in Emmanuel College. Porson's own japanned *snuff-box* at Trinity. The portrait of Dr Parr, which hangs at the end of the combination room in S. John's, faithfully represented that worthy with a 'yard of clay' betwixt hand and mouth. For some reason or other this was subsequently painted out.

p. 162. The COMBINATION-ROOM, COMMON-ROOM, COMMON-FIRE-ROOM, or COMMON-PARLOUR, represented the *stone parlour* or *locutorium*, where strangers could speak or *parley* with regulars in the old monastic houses. *Du Cange* gives 'PARLATORIUM locus colloquiis destinatus in Monasteriis vulgo *Parloir*. Bernardus Mon. in Consuetud. Cluniacensibus MSS. *c.* 4, &c.' That of the hospital de Penitentia Jesu stood between the old court and the Gisborne Court of Peterhouse. In the *computus* of that society the Combination-room fire and Combination-room servant are still entered as *Parlour fire* and *servant*. The stone *halls* and tiled halls were (says M' Perry, in his life of Ro. Grosseteste), the more solid hostels built at Oxford after the fire there, *anno* 1190.

p. 163. 'A SCHEME, A party of pleasure.' Grose, *Classical Dictionary of the Vulgar Tongue*, ed. 3. 1796. This word seems to have been most common in the time of Tom Warton. In his *Companion to the Guide and Guide to the Companion* (see p. 388), he says 'the *Axis in Peritrochio* is admirably illustrated by a *Scheme* in a Phaeton.' Again, in the *Student or Oxford and Cambridge Miscellany*, 1751, II. 107, a parasite is said to 'take schemes or do anything with my Lord.' In the *Oxford Sausage*, which he edited, it is found several times.

> 'Your *Schemes* make work for *Gloss* and *Nourse*' [Oxford Surgeons.]
> (*The Phaeton and the One Horse Chair.*)

> 'Cans't thou to *schemes* invite the GOWN?' (*Ibid.*)

> 'No more the wherry feels my stroke so true;
> At skittles in a grizzle can I play?
> *Woodstock*, farewell! and *Wallingford*, adieu!
> Where many a *scheme* relieved the lingering day.'
> *Ode to a Grizzle Wig by a Gentleman who had just left off his Bob.* (Ibid.)

'The young *Cantab......*had come up to *London upon a scheme* as it is called, to treat himself to a masquerade and other diversions of the town.' Fr. Coventry's *Pompey the Little*, II. X. 1750. '*Schemes on the Water*' are mentioned in a Cambridge farce of 1786.

p. 168. Old *Terms of Horsemanship*. The following are gathered from the First Part of the *Gentleman's Dictionary* (from the French of the Sieur *Guillet*), 1705, viz.: The *Art of Riding the Great Horse:* the *Manage*. 'CURVETS are Leaps of an indifferent heighth, which a Horse makes in raising first his two Fore-legs in the Air, and making the two hinder Feet follow with an equal Cadence; so the Haunches go down together, after the Fore-feet have touch'd the Earth in continual and regular Reprizes.' (Some curious examples of the use of the term follow.) 'CAPRIOLES or Leaps of *firma a firma*, are Leaps that a Horse makes in one and the same place, without advancing forwards, and that in such a manner, that when he's in the Air and at the height of his Leap, he yerks or strikes out with his Hinder-legs even and near. A Capriole is the most difficult of all the high Manage, or rais'd Airs. It differs from a Croupade in this, that in a Croupade the Horse do's not shew his shoes; and from a Balstade in this, that in a Balstade he do's not yerk out. Your Horse will never work well at Caprioles unless you put him between two Pillars,' &c.

'TERRA A TERRA, is a Series of low Leaps, which a Horse makes forwards, bearing side-ways, and working upon two Treads. In this Motion the Horse lifts both his Fore-legs at once; and when these are upon the point of descending to the Ground, the Hinder-legs accompany 'em with a short and quick cadence, always bearing and staying upon his *Haunches;* so that the Motions of the Hinder-quarters are short and quick; and the Horse being always well prest and coupled, he lifts his Fore-legs pretty high, and his Hinder-legs keeps always low and near the ground. This Manage call'd *Terra à Terra,* because in this Motion the Horse does not lift his Legs so high as in *Corvets.'*

'CARACOL is an oblique Piste or Tread traced out in Semi rounds, changing from one hand to another without observing a regular ground. When Horse advance to charge in Battel, they sometimes ride up in *Caracols,* to perplex the Enemy, and make 'em doubtful whether they are about to take 'em in the Front, or in the Flank. *Caracol* is a Spanish word, and in that Language signifies the Motion that a Squadron of Horse makes, when upon an Engagement the first Rank has no sooner fired their Pistols, than they divide and open into two Half-Ranks, the one wheeling to the right, and the other to the left, along the Wings of the Body to the Rear. Every Rank observes the same Order after firing; and the Turning or Wheeling from the front to the rear is call'd a *Caracol.'*

'SERPEGER, a *French* Word us'd in the Academies, to Signify the Riding of a Horse in a Serpentine way, or in a Tread with wav'd Turnings, like the Posture of a Serpent's Body. This word is now obsolete.' [1705.]

'CAREER; This Word signifies both the Ground that's proper for the Manage, and the Course or Race of a Horse that do's not go beyond two Hundred Paces.' Among the examples is 'This *English* Horse do's not furnish his Career; that is, he does not finish his Course with the same Swiftness, and does not move so short and swift at the middle and end, as at the beginning.'

p. 170. SIMEON on WALKING EXERCISE. Mᵣ Abner W. Brown gives the following note of a Friday evening conversation party of *Charles*

Simeon in his *Recollections*, 1863, p. 126. May 15, 1829, ' *The duty of students.*—It is your duty to God to work hard at the studies which belong to the University. Hard regular study is the best discipline which your minds can have, and the most likely to fit your characters to usefulness in the ministry, if you are called to that office. But act wisely. Remember to give your hearts to God in the way of this duty. Use common wisdom also. I always say to my young friends, Your success in the senate-house depends much on the care you take of the three-mile stone out of Cambridge. If you go every day and see that nobody has taken it away, and go quite round it to watch lest any one has damaged its farthest side, you will be best able to read steadily all the time you are at Cambridge. If you neglect it, woe betide your degree. Yes,—Exercise, constant, and regular and ample, is absolutely essential to a reading man's success.'

p. 172. Watt mentions in his *Bibliotheca Britannica*, The LAKERS, a comic opera [? by Jas Plumptre, B.D.] 1798; Grose in his *Provincial Glossary*, 1790, gives ' LAKE. To play. From the Saxon, laikan.' Quaere our modern slang *lark* ?

p. 175. BOATING. In Skinner's fifth unpublished letter from Trin. Coll. Oxon. June 15, 1793, he speaks of sailing, rowing, or towing the ' Hobby-horse' by ' Foley's bridge' (qu. Folly bridge) to Ifley and Sandford where

> *Beckly* provides accustomed fare
> Of eels and perch and Brown Beefsteak,
> Dainties we oft taste twice a week
> Whilst *Hebe*-like his daughter waits,
> Froths our full bumpers, changes plates.
> The pretty handmaid's anxious toils
> Meanwhile our mutual praise beguiles ;
> While she delighted, blushing sees
> The bill o'erpaid and pockets fees
> Supplied for ribbon and for lace
> To deck her bonnet or her Face !
> A game of Quoits will oft our stay
> A while at *Sandford* Inn delay,
> Or rustic ninepins :—then once more
> We hoist our Sail and ply the Oar
> To *Newnham* bound.

In the sixth letter, October 1793, he describes their taking their ' gay yacht the *Hobby-horse*' at the river,

> 'where a Dame,
> *Hooper* yclept, at station waits
> For gownsmen whom she aptly freights
> In various vessels moored in view,
> Skiff gig and cutter or canoe.

'Election made, each in a trice
Becomes transformed with trowsers nice,
Jacket and catskin cap supplied,
Black gowns and trenchers laid aside.'

p. 175. V. L. = *Charles V. Le Grice* of Trinity.

p. 177. Some persons used to refer the proverbial saying of CAM-BRIDGESHIRE CAMELS to the practice of walking on STILTS in the fens. *Grose* mentions this explanation, but Ray discarded it as improbable.

p. 178. TENNIS-COURT. W. Chambers of *S. Joh.*, H. Tedstill, *Corpus*, and J. Hawes, *Pet.*, who took their first degree in 1719, with G. Ball, made their recantation in the Vice-chancellor's court and were suspended for being at the Tennis Court. Chambers and Hawes took their second degree in 1723.

In Loggan's *Cantabrigia illustrata*, cir. 1690, a sphaeristerium or racquet-court is shewn in Christs, in Emmanuel, and in St John's (where there is also a 'Bowlin green'). The second view of that college (No. 27) gives a bird's-eye view into the court. Bowls are being played at New College. *Oxonia illustrata*, 1675.

In Loggan's *Oxonia Illustr.* 1675, a game of fives is represented as going on at Merton, and there seems to be a fives-court at University.

p. 178. Dr Charles Wordsworth (bishop of S. Andrews, &c.) has in his possession an old engraving 'CRICKET. *F. Hayman pinx. C. Grignon sculp.*' The paper used in framing the picture in the first instance bears a reference to the '[Rep]resentatives of the Rt. Hon. George Grenvile, late Treasurer of the [Navy]' whence it may be inferred that the picture was engraved about the year 1755: it is clearly earlier than the introduction of the third stump. (See *The Cricket Field*, and vol. I. of Lillywhite's *History of Cricket*.) I have seen two pictures on other subjects, bearing the names of the same artist and engraver, of the dates 1752 and 1758.

In the foreground the *scorers* are lying upon a heap of coats and are engaged in *notching* sticks. The score appears to have reached 17. There are *two stumps* at each end, the *ball* is large, and the bowler is taking deliberate aim as about to toss it cunningly. There is *no return-crease* visible nor the *hole* between the stumps.

The *umpires* are in the ordinary morning dress of the period; both stand close up to the wickets; not one at short leg's place. They and the batsmen hold *bats* curved at the bottom of the blade something like an old-fashioned knife: the handle extremely long, stringed, and without any shoulder tapering upwards so as to follow the lines of the blade.

The players mostly wear hunting caps, hair cropped as for wigs; some have long waistcoats, and the wicket-keeper has loosened his breeches at the knee. The *field* is set for underhand bowling, but with *longstop; no short-leg nor short slip; mid wicket* on either side, *point* slightly behind the wicket, *cover-point* quite square; *'hit-on* and *'hit-off* covering mid-wickets on either side.

In Huddersford's *Wiccamical Chaplet*, 1804, p. 131, is printed a '*Cricket Song for the* Hambledon *Club* [the earliest cricket-club established], Hants, 1767.' The players are said to be 'array'd all in white;' and the *crease* is called 'the scratch.'

Mr Lillywhite speaks of bishop Tho. Ken (author of the Morning and Evening Hymns, &c.) when at Winchester, as the first cricketer upon record. I am afraid this must be only a pleasant conjecture of the imagination, for we have, I believe, no authority beyond the passage quoted by Mr Timbs, in *Schooldays of Eminent Men*, from a fanciful picture of what may have been Ken's schoolday life.

p. 180. BILLIARDS. The keepers of a billiard-table were fined 40*s*. and costs in 1727, and the scholars playing admonished in the vice-chancellor's court at Cambridge. The game is mentioned in Warton's *Companion to the Guide*, &c., p. 11; see *Oxoniana*, I. 237.

p. 184. In an Account of the Life and Conversation of the Reverend and Worthy Mr *Isaac Milles*, Late Rector of *Highcleer* in *Hampshire*, pp. 25—28. 1721, there is a curious story about a duel with swords forced upon *Thos. Smoult*, Knightbridge professor, a clergyman.

p. 187. LORD TAP. Nares quotes in his Glossary from *Lingua*, 'He may be *my lord Tappes* for his large titles,' adding, 'who this personage was remains to be discovered.' I would suggest in answer, the mock grandee of *Stirbridge Fair*.

p. 188. PLAYS AT CHRISTMAS. So the Statutes (1545) of St John's, Camb. *cap.* XXVI. (differing here from those of bishop *Fisher*, 1530), provide 'ut in festo Nativitatis Domini singulus quisque socius ordine suo Dominum agat, quo tempus illud honesta animi remissione et litterariis exercitationibus cum laetitia et hilaritate transigatur. Eum autem volumus ad festum Omnium Sanctorum designari ad id et pronuntiari, post quod tempus nullo modo licebit ut hoc munere se abdicet atque ad alium transferat. Et quo alacrior ad hoc munus conficiendum et idonee transigendum sit, viginti solidos a collegio ad sumptus suos levandos habeat, sic ut statuta eius ad formam Atticae aut Romanae aut alterius cuiusvis reipublicae vel Graecis vel Latinis versibus faciat et sex ad minus dialogos aut festiva aut litteraria spectacula totidem duodecim dierum noctibus exhibeat. Nam ceteras comoedias et tragoedias quae inter Epiphaniam et Quadragesimam aguntur lectores singuli et singuli examinatores accurabunt, ut aliqua litteraria contactione omnes exerceantur. Pro unoquoque vero dialogo aut festivo spectaculo omisso et non exhibito dominus viginti denariorum mulcta punietur. Lectorum quoque singulorum et examinatorum, si illi quoque nihil in publicum exhibuerint, ea mulcta esto quam magister et seniores iustam designaverint. Nolumus autem omnino ut quisquam e sociis cursum suum in agendo domino praetereat aut omittat, sub poena amissionis aliorum viginti solidorum collegio intra mensem post lapsum tempus Nativitatis Domini solvendorum; quod nisi fecerit, communis interea careat, donec plene praedictam summam et fideliter persolverit.'

On these plays see a paper (qu. by Hartshorne?) in the *Retrospective Review.*—M.

THE CHRISTMAS PRINCE was a later form of the ceremony of the Boy Bishop. A play, or rather a series of interludes, under that name acted at S. John's, Oxon, in·1607, on All hallows' e'en, was printed in 1816, in *Miscellanea Antiqua Anglicana;* where a similar performance at Gray's Inn, in 1598, printed in 1688, is mentioned.

p. 189. ACTING ON SUNDAY. It seems that after the Reformation it was not unusual to act plays on Sunday. In a comedy called *Wily Beguiled* (of which there was an edition printed in 1623, a reprint in the third vol. of Hawkins' *English Drama*, 1773) the *Clerk* says to *Will Cricket*, who desires to have his banns put up and to be 'axed up' (as we say in Lincolnshire) as soon as possible: 'Faith you may be ask'd i' the church on sunday at morning prayer; but *Sir John* cannot tend to do it at evening prayer: for there comes a company of players to the town on sunday i' the afternoon; and *Sir John* is so good a fellow, that I know he'll scarce leave their company to say evening prayer. For, though I say it, he's a very painful man, and takes so great delight in that faculty, that he'll take as great pains about building of a stage, or so, as the basest fellow among them.

Will Cricket. Nay, if he have so lawful an excuse, I am content to defer it one day the longer.'

p. 189. '*Richard* III.' by Legge. See a paper by Mr. C. H. Cooper communicated to the Cambridge Antiquarian Society. '*Pedantius*,' by T. Beard. Printed in 1631.

p. 191. Ruggle's *Ignoramus* was acted frequently at *Westminster* School in the place of a play of Plautus or Terence. Sir J. Hawkins (in his edition 1787, p. lxxxvii, *n.*) gives the names of the actors there in 1730 and in 1747. In 1731 it was acted at King Edward's School;

Bury St. Edmund's; and, abridged into two acts, at the *Merchant Taylors',* in 1763. As to the first performance see Nichols' *Royal Progresses of James I.,* the ballad in Bp. Corbet's works, &c.

p. 191. In 1611 was printed *Sicelides,* a dramatic piece by Phineas Fletcher, the poet, which was intended for representation before K. James.

Albumazar, a comedy, was revived at Drury Lane with alterations in 1773.

Melanthe.

Piscatory. Some poems called Piscatory Eclogues; and the Poetical Miscellanies by Phineas Fletcher, were printed at Camb., 4to, 1633. A new edition, London, 1771.

. *Work for Cutlers,* and

Exchange Ware...Band, Ruffe, and Cuffe, reprinted in the *Old Book Collector's Miscellany* for Messrs. Reeves and Turner in 1872.

Loyola. Comoedia Loiola data, per Ioh. Hacket episc. Litchf. Lond. 1648. 8vo,

Paria, by T. Vincent. Printed, Lond., 1648. 8vo.

Senile Odium, by Peter Hausted. Printed, Camb., 1633. 12mo. See *Historical MSS. Commission Report,* III. p. 200. col. b.

1634. *Jealous Lovers,* a Comedy by T. Randolph. Printed at Camb. in 4to.

1642. Sept. 2 was made an *Ordinance against Stage Plays.*

p. 193. The TYRING ROOM reached from bay-window to bay-window in *Trinity Lodge.* See Monk's *Life of Bentley,* I. 175.

p. 195. Smart's TRIP TO CAMBRIDGE. See above note on p. 157. ('Zodiack,' *sub fine.*)

p. 197. Cp. 'NEW COLLEGE STUDENTS. Golden scholars, silver bachelors, and leaden masters.' Grose, *Classical Dict. of the Vulgar Tongue,* 1796. I think I have seen this expression in *Epistolae* Ho-Elianae.

p. 198. (Bishop) *Tho. Ken* of *Hart Hall* and *New College,* 'a junior would sometimes sing his part' in *A. Wood's* concerts about the year 1656.

p. 204. *All hallow e'en,* October 31st. See note on p. 188, the *Christmas Prince.*

p. 205. PENNILESS BENCH is mentioned also in *Statut. Acad. Oxon.,* XV. 2.

p. 208.　For this use of FRENCH and LATIN FORMULAE compare the summons to dinner at New College, which existed till a generation back; when two *quiristers* walked slowly from the chapel-door to the garden-gate, '*backing up*' (crying out) one prolonged *peal* (or ejaculation) *Tempus est uocandi, mangez tous seigneurs.* (M. E. C. Walcott's *W. Wykeham and his Colleges*, p. 317. G. V. Cox, *Collections and Recollections.*) So in Gray's Inn the *pannier man* (see Grose's *Vulgar Tongue*) proclaimed *Manger* in the three courts.

p. 211.　RESPONSAL SEAT in the Schools. Compare Cooper's *Annals of Camb.*, II. 195.

p. 215.　OYSTERS used to be provided by the proctors for the company present at the proclamation of Stirbridge Fair in September, in the Tiled Booth. See *Senate-house Ceremonies*, Wall-Gunning, 1828, p. 130. Cp. p. 284.

p. 216.　The University, or Schools, BELL was in old times the bell of S. Benet's Church at Cambridge.

p. 217.　COLLECTORS, see p. 317.

p. 222.　*Tyring-room*, see note on p. 193.

p. 223.　'*Hills.*—GOGMAGOG HILLS, near Cambridge; a common morning's ride.' *Gradus ad Cantabrigium*, 1803. See Speed's map in 1610, and Buck's in 1743. In Loggan (about 1680) '*Hogmagog.*' It is stated in Britton and Brayley's *Beauties of England and Wales*, 1801, II, 130, that Mr Layer remembered having seen an enormous figure of a giant which the scholars had cut in the turf, but which had ceased to be repaired in his time. They are now often called absolutely 'the Hills,' and the road, 'the Hills Road.'

p. 223.　The HIP, a common complaint like the Spleen. 'HYP. The hypochondriac; low spirits. He is hypped; he has got the blue devils, &c.' Grose *Classical Dict. of the Vulgar Tongue*, 1796. Ailing ἐν τοῖς ὑποχονδρίοις, in the parts below the cartilage of the breast-bone.

p. 224.　JACKISH.—*Jacobite.*—HUMANITY; '*in literis humanioribus.*'

p. 226, *line* 3.　ERRATUM. *For* street, *read* sheet.

P. 229.　UMBRA COMITIORUM.
[*Cir.* 1650.]

The following is reprinted from a copy of a small 4to tract in the Cambridge Free Town Library [B. 14. 45], inscribed *Suum cuiq. Tho. Hearne* 1719. *Ex dono Richardi Dyer, A.M. coll. Orielensis socii.*

Page 1 begins:

UMBRA COMITIORUM,
OR
CAMBRIDGE COMMENCEMENT.
In Types.

A *Commencement*[1] now-a-dayes is the *Synods Adjournall-House;* A Visitation of all the *Empirick Divines:* It differs from the Old, as the Parochiall *Bason* from the Parish *Font;* Indeed it is the *Font* turn'd into the *Bason* for the baptising of all (within the *Pale* of the *Vniversity*) into the Church of *Adoniram.* The *God-fathers* are of the same Religion with the *Fathers,* nurtur'd in the *Christ-Crosse-Directory;* and the *Synods* little principall *Catechisme* will answer for none, but such as deny *John Goodwin*[2] and all his *Works.* These are the Babes of this new *Jerusalem,* still in their non-age, like *Cows-tails,* or their Father's *Beard* growing longer and lower. But yet how do they lift up their *Crests,* and budge with the *Horns* of Salvation on their Fore-heads! And because Master *Lazarus*[3] ha's none of his own, they say he exalteth others.

But round with the *Morice-Dance.* And since the greatest Head ha's the least wit, enter first (with reverence to your *Antlets*) the Preacher at *Trinity*[4], a Silenced-Minister in the times of the Gospel, even since illumination, and the gifts of the Spirit came into fashion. This Prodigy of faith, to shew the virtue of regeneration (which they term a Creation) would seem to be a *Scholar:* A man against *Reason* (by the moving of his eye-brows) to be made a *Logician.* He kept a fluttering with an Argument, but prov'd *Haggard*[5] in disputing. An old third-bare Saint new-cloth'd with a long-wasted Conscience in the fashion, to be a pattern to others, ha's shewn the good work of Conversion upon his own soul first, in setting up the *States Arms* in his Colledge. And its reported too, that (according to the *Solemn League*

---

[1] The Public Commencement was dispensed with in the summer of 1643 on account of the troublous time, and again in 1644. Also in 1649 on the plea of expence.

[2] J. Goodwin. *Thomas* was the Christian name of the celebrated nonconformist fellow of S. Catharine hall and lecturer (and afterwards vicar) at Holy Trinity Church Cambridge, 1628—34. He was an Independent, and in 1649 made by Cromwell President of Magdalen Coll. Oxon.

[3] Lazarus (Seaman) put in as master of Peterhouse in 1644. His diary is in the custody of the head of that society.

[4] *Trinity.* Thomas Hill, master 1645—53.

[5] Haggard. *A wild hawk; one that has preyed for herself before being taken.*

and *Covenenant*) he intends to saddle his *Asses*, and ride[1] in triumph
with *Christ Jesus* from Colledge to Colledge, upon the next Thanksgiving Day.   But oh for some *Oculist* to help me in the sight of the
next; that spiritual *Hocas Pocas:* he must be drawn like *Janus* with
two faces or rather vizards; when turns up the White of one eye, and
looks upon the *Old Covenant*, and with the Green of the other beholds
[*Page* 2] the *New*, he contracts the *Species* of both, and sayes, that the
New is but the fulfilling of the *Old.*   The dark Vail of *Presbytery* being
now withdrawn, the clear Lights of *Independency* shine upon him.
There is not a murder'd Fellow of his Colledge, but bleeds at the touch
of this Malefactour; nor a *Bastard* one begotten, but he is the Parent.
Unmask him but well, and his inside as ill as his outside is sophisticate.
This Man shews but a *blinde* commencement.

The next *Puppit* in this Fools-Play, is the little pretty *Immanuelist*[2],
who likewise should be a Brat of the whore, did he but speak the
Language of the *Beast* a little truer.   This is a Lisper in Learning, and
a Lisper too in Religion; he never speaks plain but when he scolds at
his Wife; or threatens M. *Goodwin* for denying Election, and Reproba-
tion of Women.

Just such another Linguist is *Christ's Colledge Samuel*[3]; he under-
stands nothing but *Hebrew*, and in this too he must be read backwards.
There's more Monsters retain to him, then to all the Limbs in *Anatomy*;
Death it self cannot quit scores with this same Fellow, for hee'l rise
with his *Guts* full at the *Resurrection*.   But by the way, after he had
disgorg'd his Brains here, he takes such a Surfet in his giblets at
Dinner, that (as if he meant to do death a curtesie) he sate upon the
Close-stool of *Repentance* for seven Days after, praying with Groans and
Grunts unutterable against all *Compurgatours*.   And how can the Grave
entertain such a Skull and Carkass, as being not Meat but Poyson for
Worms?   This is the *Summum genus*[4] of *Non sense*, beyond which
there is *Terra incognita:* So curious a *Logician* is He, that he never
makes a *Syllogisme* but invents a new *Figure*.   Hee's like a *cock* of the
Game, striking at anothers, knocks out his own Brains : But had he
ever any?   Surely no; for he comes of the Lineage of *Peter Harrison*,
the same begat him both *Master* and *Scholar*.   As a dark Shop then is
to commend its Wares, such was the use of this Man here.   These
purblinde fancies show the Commencement but in *Duskie Types*.

[1] *A Phrase of his own.*

[2] *Immanuelist.* Anthony Tuckney was master in 1644, and was succeeded by
Will. Dillingham in 1653.

[3] *Samuel* Bolton, put in as master of Christ's in 1645, was succeeded by Cudworth
in 1654.

[4] *His own Phrase.*

: Next appears in a Vision the young *Husband* of *Queens;* when he looks upon his Sweeting, he lifts up the eyes of his minde, and blesseth all his *Fellows.* Who observed his Syllogismes? they were all corrected: and indeed the common Example which *Logicians*[1] give to the *Rule,* may be applied to him; though so careful a Man of his *Wife,* that when he goes forth, he locks up the *Chamber-door,* (I wish he would lock up her mouth too) and carries the Key in his Pocket with him; so it is not for us to lodge here.

[*Page* 3.] *Room* for the *Antichrist* of *Peter-house,* that by virtue of S. *Peters* Key locks and opens all. A Mummer in Religion, that thinks to out-brave us with his Name, though himself be fowler. Un-ravell the *Creature,* and every limb is *Heteroclite.* This *Pelagian*[2] fights always against *Orthodox* men, and Opinions; onely the purity of his own remains untouch'd in all Times and Ages. If *Pythagoras* were now alive, he might confirm his Opinion by seeing this Soul pass so many *Transformations;* It would puzzle the *Catholike Church* to give him a Name, were he a Member thereof: Certainly, he is *Universal Superfoetation, Transcendent* beyond *Ens.* Its a drawn match between him and *Hill,* which is the worst Pulpit man; the one *weeps* out his Sermon, the other *howls* it out; And indeed this man (Crocodile-like) weeps and devours. But how did he lift up the tufts of his Beard, and snivell with his *Negative Voice*[3] against rendering any future account of his evil Actions; as if the Man with the long Beard could give him a Dispensation to truck mischief against M. *Hotham*[4] with everlasting impunity!

Thus have ye the Combat of the *Spiritual Host* against the Arm of *flesh,* and his Shoulder-bone M. *Vice-chancellour.* These are so much for *Reason,* and the others for *Faith,* that its a burden to their Spirits, they have any thing to do with them.

They be six of our seven *Planets,* whose Motions are so Eccentrical; *Icosaëdra's* of divers sides, and faces; like *Cats,* toss them which way you will, and they shall still light upon their leggs. Surely Nature varied her course in their composition, for though (according to their

---

[1] *Syllogismus cornutus.* The dilemma. Cp. 'Beginning with a most confound-ing disjunctive *Syllogism,* called by the wicked and hard-hearted, a *Dilemma,* or *Cornute.*' Eachard's *Observations upon the Answer to the Contempt of the Clergy.*

[2] *Pelagian.* Lazarus *Seaman* was put in as master of Peterhouse by warrant of the E. of Manchester, in March, 1643—4, and continued in that place till Dr Cosin was restored in 1660.

[3] *Quæst. Disp. Dantur rationes boni et mali indispensabiles.*

[4] See the accounts of his *Case* published by Mr Hotham in 12mo.

plain capacities) Earth[1] is most predominant in them, yet take them in their Politick, and three shall be an equality of the rest, in that they live so alike in all Elements. And yet these equivocal *Priests* stand clothed (forsooth) with *Christ's Robes* girt about their Consciences with a double Pack-thrid of the *Covenant* and *Engagement*[2]: Thus Evil Spirits appear to some in Silks and Sattins. But what a prudential *Religion* is theirs, that expects Salvation by *Imputed* Righteousness, since the Professours be such changeable creatures, as its not possible there should be any *Inherent* in them! Is the Divinity of the very little *Orthodox Assembly* infallible, whenas as now we see their *Regenerated Brethren* of the *Covenant* can *fall totally* and *finally* from *Presbyterian Grace?*

But the *Saints* are not so valiant at disputing, as at Preaching. They can throw off their Caps in the Pulpit, and the Spirit comes fresh again to the nineteenth *Doctrine* and *Application;* but here they are glad to hold them [*Page* 4.] on, and now and then to refresh them with their *Holy-water'd Handkircheifs*, to keep in the scantling of their Wits, least they stand in their Robes like those *Statues* among the Tombs at *Westminster.* Indeed they are *Masters* and *Scholars* much of a size; empty Bladders of *Manchesters* blowing onely with a few Peas, and Beans in them, to rattle to the Fraternity of Noddies on *Sunday mornings*[3] at *Michaels*, and in the *Afternoon* at *S. Trinity;* The veryest dry *Nurses*, that ever our *Mother* the *University* had.

Their Teeth here are sharper set than their Tongues, and everywhere their Guts are too large for their Brains: wherefore now they must have *Cordials*, and *Custards*, and D. *Hill* a sup of his *Asses-Milk* to strengthen his brains, and lengthen his ears. But let the *first course* pass.

A *Voyder* with the *Second* for the M. *Proctours* jests, that *Scrap* and *Fragment* of wit; His anger-quodled brain did so boyle against M. *Goodwin*, and the zeal of his tongue spat so much fire and faggot, as if the flat-pated Heads had appointed him Executioner for the

---

[1] *Earth is most predominant:* according to the medico-astrological theory of *humours*, which has been succeeded by *vapours, spleen, nerves*, and *electrobiology.*

[2] The Committee for reformation of the Universities was ordered by Parliament, June 21, 1650, to enquire who had not taken the *engagements*, and proceedings were instituted later in the year.

[3] Aug. 17, 1657, 'the Corporation voted the Mayor the yearly allowance of 20 marks "for and towards the entertainment of Ministers such as he should think fitt to invite to dynner upon the lecture days holden at Trinity Church on Wednesday in every weeke, for and during the continuance of the said Wednesday Lecture there."' Cooper's *Annals*, III. 467, 468.

burning of his *Book* (which their illiterate Noddles are not able to answer) as being blasphemous against the totality and finality of their *Graces*. This is *Moses made angry* the second time; because the *Father* cannot beat him the young *Boy* takes his part: Wonderfull Swordsmen of the Spirit, that can pierce through the *Heart* of Reason, with but ranching of the *Skin*, like those Artists that cut off the Head without removing it.

But room for M. *Umbra* of *Wit*, as fit for the Function, as if the *Synod* had *ordained* him with the Imposition of D. *Burgesses* Brains. And have we any thing more than Shadows here? The shadow of a Commencement, the shadow of a University, the shadows of Masters, Fellows, and Scholars? The *Body* has been dead, ever since *Manchester* set new *Heads* upon it. But the mischief was, his profane intermixture spoil'd the Fabricks of the holy Brotherhood; who because he spoke in Sir *Empiricks* tone, and quackt Doctrination, like an *Ordained Brother*, was accounted forsooth (according to the thirteenth Article in the *Synods Doctrine of Faith*) all over blasphemous against their hallowed Reverences. Its an emblem of the *Golden-Age* (and such indeed their new Masterships make it) when so tame a *Pigeon* may commerce with *Vultures*. But how often was this sorry Fellow executed alive? First knocks him dead that *Sampson Presbyter*, and with the same engine too, the Jaw-bone of an *Ass?* Why did he quarrell with *Illumination*, when his *black Hue darkned* the place? This *Brother* is squeamish in Conscience, as he is in his Countenance; *Astrology* must begin her Alphabet again to discover a [page 5] more ugly *Planet* then *Saturn* to be Lord of his *Ascendent:* The fairest *Representation* of *Croyden* that can be; even so like, that his *Wife* ha's taken him for her *Husband;* and thus he supplies all Offices in M. *Proctours* absence. Next out-kills him by a pound and an half in false Weights his *gude Christian Brother.* Then (with a mouth-full of grave simplicity) comes his *Father*, like to that *Beast*, that destroys her first Breed. But he is no better at killing of Women, for his *Mistris* at *S. Iv:s* never was love-sick for him yet, though he made it a Case of Conscience to her, that she ought to die for him. But for all these *Bombals* of the *Gospel*, the *Law* is not yet dead; like *Caius Colledge Fox*, that has been often times hunted down, but, as they say, not yet laid: Thus some grow rich by breaking; *Vipers* thus being slain, do more increase.

Next come the *Philosophers;* such mean Scholars, that its courtesie to call them so; but let them be cast into the Scales to make downweight a *Sir John's Commencement.*

The *Quack-salvers* (according to their Office) peep in the Rear; more doubly gifted for the *Soul* and the *Body*; whilest one hand is spreading of *Treacle*, the other is thumping of the *Pulpit*. *Times Hermaphrodites*, *Jacks of all Trades*, but good at none; like *Stage-Players*, they would make us believe they are not the same Persons, when they have changed the *Classick Cloak* into a *Plush Jump*. But let us turn over these *Jack-tumblers*.

Thus are all this dayes He-goats milkt; let us see what the morrow affords: And now we sit in as much *Darkness* and *Shadow* of Learning, as in the *Vespers*[1] before.

First enters, as a Whiffler before the Shew, that precious Jewell of the *Lady Margaret*, who can hollow here, but whispers to the *engagement*. This good man is mightily troubled with the Palsie in his *Head*; Oh! it shakes in *Religion* like an empty Bottle.

Next comes to the *Stake* a most *Orthodox Cub* of *Immanuel*, with *everlasting*[2] grace to their new-born *Masters Life*. Amongst the rest of the *Bayters* roars out a *blatant beast* of *Presbytery*, predestinated champion by SMEC against *John Goodwin*, hanging forth in his very countenance the red flag of defyance against him. This pulpit *Fire-man* was a *shining light* in a *dark* Commencement.

As an elder to that *Presbyter* serves the *Prevaricatour*, dubb'd at adventure Sir *Jack* of wit; with wonderfull sagacity hunt his jests dry foot; before they are conceiv'd, here are *Boy-Midwives* that bring them [page 6] forth: How did the Rampant *Brotherhood* play their prizes, and caterwaul one another! The *Bel-weather* goes before, and all the simple *Sheep* follow after. Thus whilst the *Brethren* feed on a Woodcock, it is (*Thyestes-like*) on their own breed: Those stomachs that spew'd him out at a *Lent Act*, come hungry now and lick up the *Vomit*. Is not wit grown strait-lac'd, when such a squibber of an inch and an half can compasse it? like thunder within the cloud, he onely rumbled, the clap was made below: Thus they crack nut shels; these Artificers of wit forge it in their own fancies; Surely, we mistake either him, or ourselves, if we think his Brain-pan sounds so much Musick, as to make us dance after it. Wit the last year *chew'd* the *Cud*, this year it *starves*: between two *Wooden* stools it falls now to the ground: Two whole *Prevaricatours*[3] are not able to make half a jest. And had

---

[1] *In Vesperiis Comitiorum*, see pp. 244, 245.

[2] Quæst. ejus disp. *Renati non possunt totaliter, et finaliter excidere à gratia.*

[3] It would seem that the *Prevaricator* at the *Commencement* or *Comitia Maiora* had a stool, as the *Tripos* or 'Bachelor of the Stool' had at the disputations *in Quadragesima* (see p. 227).

the case been alter'd, especially with the *Law*, our thick-skull'd *Heads*, fellow-feelers of their *Members* infirmities, might have voted it a breach of their *Gospel-Reformation;* as Mr *Harrison* (of blessed memory) out of the *Chaldee Paraphrase* in *English*, prov'd *Christs-Colledge-Diurnall-maker* to be against *Scripture.* Wit (in this State of grace) looks with the *excommunicated* Face of the *Assembly;* its of the same *Ordination, Institution,* and *Induction* with the *Directory, Catechisme, Doctrine of Faith,* and the rest of that still-born Breed.

But with *Sir-reverence* the *Father* should have gone before the *Sonne:* (yet remember *Tuesdayes* mode) Be it spoken now (without profaning of his sanctified Cap) to the tender conscienc'd *Intruder* at S. *Ives:* He's such a *Jade* for wit, that he was fain to be *spurr'd* [1] by his Son to bleed it; and then comes a pittifull Use and Application of *Will Lillies* Accidence. Its as disputable whether this grave Coxcomb was witty, as whether *Peter Harrisons* two *Tables of Stone* were made of *Shittim-wood.* He fetch'd a course in his speech over the *Arts,* as he does in his sermons over Bishop *Andrews;* but like a *Hare* over the *Snow,* leaves a foul impression all the way; you may track him from *Cambridge* to S. *Ives* and then take him close-sitting in a *Sisters* Lap, with his black Cap turn'd into a white one; and then how like is the *Brothers* to a *Calves Head* bound up in a clout!

But I am all in a sweat with the reakings of the *Parsons Caps,* and can endure no longer.

These then are the *Ingredients* of a *Commencement,* the *Simples* of this precious *Compound; Metalls,* that brought to the *Touch-stone* (like *Chymists* tinctures) prov'd all *adulterate;* the more they are *tried,* the more *drosse* comes from them; no fire is able to *refine* them; O may that [page 7] come which will consume them! I am sure they have not the rarity of *Phœnixes,* that we should fear their *Ashes* may engender the like.

Our *Apollo* now wears midnight; this new-fashion'd day is beetle-brow'd; Links and torches to set off this Mask of learning, where the *Muses* act all in vizards! I can hold open mine eyes no longer; they even shrink within their pent-house at this vile disguise. Good night to learning! One word more, before I go to rest.

A *Commencement* is a *Crack* of *Powder,* shot to gratulate the empty *Worships* of the *Assembly;* A *Bell* and a *Rattle* to sound to the leather ears of the *Country-Hobby-Horses:* This is *Manchesters* second Triumph in the *Muses* warfare without a victory: And may all his *Sonnes* follow

---

[1] *Tantus ingenii cessator, ut calcaribus indigeat.*

their *Fathers* Fate ; after a pastime of glory, live and die in shame and obscurity !

Amen.

Reprinted at *Oxford* for the famous
University of *Cambridge.*
Anno secundo libertatis ignorantiæ Academicæ.'

p. 230. In his *Grounds and Occasions of the Contempt of the Clergy and Religion*, 1670, Dr Eachard of S. Catharine Hall, speaking of Wits who have won reputation without being beholding to Puns and Quibbles, remarks that ' There is the prodigious *Lucian*, the Great *Don* of *Mancha*, and there are many now living Wits of our own, who never certainly were at all inspired from a TRIPUS'S, TERRAE-FILIUS'S, or PRAEVARICATOR'S speech.'

ERRATA. p. 232, *line* 16, *for* optima, *read* optime.

p. 233, *line* 9, *for* Idem, *read* Idea.

p. 233. Such papers for Divinity, Law, and Philosophy Acts are, I find, not very uncommon. Among TRIPOS VERSES should have been mentioned those of *Gray* and *Vincent Bourne* (e.g. 1731, *Luna est habitabilis*) ; several of the latter were collected in an edition of his works, published at Cambridge, by Mr. W. P. Grant.

1747—8. It was customary for verses by the lads to be hung in the hall of Bene't, near the Fellows' table, on Nov. 5, &c. Nichols, *Lit. Illustr.* VI. 793.

p. 256. REMEDYES are mentioned in the old statutes of S. Paul's school. They are *res mediae* between holidays and ' whole-school-days.'

p. 257. BACCALAVREVS. See also *Notes and Queries*, 4th S. IV. 334, 466, 548 ; XI. 257.

p. 261. *L. Eusden* wrote some verses on the occasion. The latin speeches, &c. at the Act in 1714 and 1730 are bound in a volume in the Camb. Univ. Library, R. 17. 64.

p. 275, note. HARRY HILLS, cp. p. 102, line 1, also p. 537.

p. 277. There is a grotesque print, illustrating an incident at POT FAIR, (Mr *Bunbury* delt. Published 25th June, 1777), in the Custodian's room at the Free Town Library, Cambridge.

p. 278. SVIS. There is a similar opprobrious allusion in the name given to the piece of land to the west of Trinity Library—the *Isthmus of Suez.* See ' Oxford and Cambridge *Nuts to Crack*,' 1834, pp. 201, 202. Compare ' HOGS ; JONIAN HOGS ; an appellation given to the members of St John's College. Cambridge.' Grose, *Classical Dict. of the Vulgar Tongue*, 1796:

> 'Nor shall one *Iohnian* Doctor save his Bacon.'
>
> S. Cobb's *Tripos Speech*, 1701.

'JOHNIAN HOGS; an appellation bestowed on the members of St John's College. Whence it arose has not been rightly, or with any degree of probability, ascertained. A variety of conjectures are offered in the *Gent. Mag.* for 1795, with the following *jeu d'esprit*. A genius espying a Coffee-house waiter carrying a mess to a Johnian in another box, asked, if it was a dish of *grains*. The Johnian instantly wrote on the window:

> 'Says —— the Johns eat grains; suppose it true,
> They pay for what they eat; does he so too?'

Another writer, whom I should suspect to be *Maysterre* Ireland, the pseudo-Shakspeare, has, or pretends to have, discovered the following, in a very scarce little book of Epigrams, written by one Master James Johnson, Clerk, printed in 1613:

> '*To the Schollers of Sainct John his College.*
> Ye Johnishe men, that have no other care,
> Save onelie for such foode as ye prepare,
> To gorge your foule polluted trunks withall;
> Meere SWINE ye bee, and such your actyons all;
> Like themme ye runne, such be youre leaden pace,
> Nor soule, nor reasonne, shynethe in your face.'

Edmond Malone, Esquire, of Black-Letter sagacity, would discover, with half-an-eye, that the above was not the orthography of 1613: *Sainct—themme—reasonne—shynethe*, &c. *Gradus ad Cantabrigiam*, 1803. See also the notes to the *Cambridge Tart*, 1810. The author of the *Gradus* quoting the expression 'stake-stuck *Clarians*' from Kit Smart's Ballad of *The Pretty Bar-keeper of the Mitre*, 1741, adds that 'The *men* of Clare-Hall are called likewise, *Greyhounds*. But I am equally at a loss to account for this, as I am for *Johnian Hogs*, and *Trinity Bulldogs*; and wonder what pleasure men can find in *making* BEASTS *of themselves!*' Smart says in the same poem:

> 'Her snuff-box if the nymph pull'd out
> Each *Johnian* in responsive airs,
> Fed with the tickling dust his snout
> With all the politesse of bears.'

In 1691 Mrs Alicia D'Anvers mentions in 'Academia: *or the Humours of the University of Oxford, in Burlesque Verse*, the *Christians, Jesuits,* and the *Jonians*' [members of Colleges]:

Will. Broome of Eton and St John's, Camb., writing to a friend in the spring of 1709 says:

'Hic Johannensi latitans suilli
grunnio scribens sitiente labro
aut graues haustus inimica musis
pocula duco.'

'*Johnians* have been famed for ages as the *best punsters* in the University [*Spectator*, No. 396]. Let them enjoy the distinction un-rivalled.' *Hints to Freshmen at the Univ. of Camb.* ed. 4. 1812, p. 39.

'JONIAN HOGS, jô-ne-an-hogz, *s. pl. cant.* Ekelname der Mitglieder am *St John's* Collegium in *Cambridge.*' J. G. Flügel's *English-German Dictionary.* Leipsic, 1830. This curious article has been withdrawn in later editions of Flügel's *Lexicon.* The name *Johnian* occurs in Barham's *Ingoldsby Legends,* 1840 (*A Lay of St Dunstan*), and in W. M. Praed's poem *the Vicar.*

p. 283. OBADIAH WALKER. See above, pp. 8, 9, and Mr Wilkin-son's *History of Worsborough,* (1872. London and Barnsley), chapter XXIX.

p. 291. A PLATE OF ALE, PLATEMONEY, see p. 653. In the 17th cent. a fellow-commoner on his departure would bequeath to the Col-lege the silver tankard which he had bought for his own use.

pp. 297, 298. TERRAE FILII. An incomplete list is given by *Ricardus Frederici* in *Notes and Queries,* 3rd S. XII. 242. I am in-debted to his paper for the following additions to my list:

1659. *Ro. South.*
1661. Field's christian name was *Robert.*
1664. See Wood's *modius salium.*
1671. ? *Wm. Rotheram.* Ch. Ch.
1693. *H. Alworth,* Ch. Ch. *H. Smith,* Ch. Ch.
1703. R[*obert*]s of Magd. and *Ro. Turner,* Wadh.
1713. *Ro. Robery,* Ch. Ch.

p. 303. ERRATUM. *line 6, for* speed, *read* speech.

p. 304. HODMAN, a nickname for a canon of "the House", Christ-church. See Halliwell's *Archaic and Provincial Dictionary.* Ray in his *Glossary* (ed. 3, 1737) gives '*A Dodman;* a Shell-snail or *Hodman-dod,* co. *Norfolk.*' (Dodman=slug. *Nat. Fairfax,* Bulk and Selvidge of the World, p. 130. =snail *ib.* p. 125. Cp. [Mansel's] Phrontisterion.

And the hodmandod crawls in its shell confined
A symbol exalted of slumbering mind.—*M.*)

p. 321. In the Bodleian Catalogue of 1738, a copy is marked 'C. 16. 18, Linc.' The notice of the archbishop of Philippopolis in Michael Le Quien's *Oriens Christianus,* I. col. 1162, to which Mr

Williams refers, is as follows : ' *Diocesis Thracica Provincia Thraciae.*]
No. XXVI. NEOPHYTVS. Alexander Helladius juvenis Graecus, libro
quem Lipsiae, anno 1714, Latine edidit *De praesenti statu ecclesiae
·Graecae*, his meminit *Neophyti* nostra aetate Philippopolis metropolitae,
cujus nonnullas epistolas apud se servari ait. p. 327, huncque in
Angliam profectum, orationem Oxonii in Theatro Sheldoniano habuisse.
Is nimirum ille ipse est Philippopolis Metropolita, qui anno 1701,
Lutetiam quoque venit Christianissimi Regis Ludovici XIV. videndi
salutandique causa, a quo humanissime acceptus auditusque fuit, quum
Italica ad eum usus dialecto esset, quam Rex apprime callebat.'

p. 324. *For* Lucas *read* Lucar. 1703. The Greek youths are
mentioned in *Notes and Queries*, 2nd S. IX. 457.

p. 346. *Ralph Aynsworth*, master of Peterhouse, was *deprived* in
the 1st year of Q. Mary, 1553—4, for having been married. He was
succeeded by Andrew Perne. Proceedings had been instituted against
him in 1545, by J. Fanne, a burgess, and removed to the V.-C.'s court.
See Univ. *Registrary*, Index II.

p. 349. For Sir J. Harrington's anecdote of Q. Eliz. and Mrs
PARKER (*Nugae Antt.* II. 16), see Dr Hook's remarks in his *Life of
Abp. Parker*, ch. xvi. pp. 553—4, 1872. The dean is of opinion that
Her Majesty spoke in merry guise.

p. 350. The WIFE OF P. MARTYR was buried also at Oxford, the
protestants taking the precaution of mingling her bones with those of
S. Friedeswyde, thereby precluding the veneration of the one, and
securing the rest of the other, in case of a future revolution.

p. 358. The LOCKING OF PEWS seems to have come in with Puritanism, though the hint seems to have been taken by some Roman
Catholic old maids for their chairs, and in our own country by the
designers of church furniture, devotional hat-boxes and foot-warmers,
and the like. Earle's *Shee precise Hypocrite* [Microcosmographie, § 43,
1628, Arber's reprint] 'doubts of the Virgin Marie's Saluation, and
dare not Saint her, but knowes her own place in heaven as perfectly, as
the Pew shee ha's a key to.'

On the other hand, in Charles II.'s reign, *locked pews* were peculiar
to the Established Church of England, as appears from a passage in
the *Second Part* of *Speculum Crape Gownorum*, which is already quoted
in p. 519 of this essay. One of the unworthy tricks, to which the
parishioners of Holy Trinity in Cambridge had recourse, when in 1782
Simeon was instituted incumbent, was to lock up their pews so that
his followers could not get seats. They did not appoint him to the
'lectureship' until 1794.

p. 372. STREPHON'S REVENGE is also advertised among books
.lately printed for *R. Francklin,* under *Tom's* Coffee-House in *Russel-*
street, Covent Garden, at the end of *Terrae Filius,* 1726.

p. 377. BOOK STRINGS. When it was customary to have large
books with metal clasps, they were put in the shelves with the clasps
and edges outward. There was no lettering on the back, but the titles
were written on the edges, as will be seen in some old books which
have not been cut down. Such an arrangement of books may be seen
in the portrait of Sir I. Newton over the high-table in the hall of Trin.
Coll., in some old monuments, in the frontispiece to old editions of
Ruggle's Ignoramus, where the books have strings instead of clasps.
The clasps have been torn off most of the old books in Peterhouse
library, but on the edges of many remain the titles and the class-marks
written. Slight traces are still left of the contents of each shelf having
been catalogued in ink on the oak uprights of the bookcases.

p. 389. For Prideaux's DRONE HALL, see p. 553.

p. 396. 'ADMIRABLE STUCCO.'
The following sentence relating to the crumbling nature of the
Oxford stone, from (Britton, Brayley and Bower's) *Beauties of England
and Wales,* 1813, vol. XII. part ii. p. 217, does not, I think, coincide
with the prevalent taste of our own generation :—

'Although the circumstances may not seriously affect the durability
of the splendid architectural assemblage, it conveys an idea of decay
productive of unpleasing sensations in the beholder.'

p. 400. A MEERE SCHOLLER.
Return from Parnassus, *or the Scourge of Simony,* acted at *Cambridge* in 1602, act ii. sc. 6.

'*Amoretto's Page.* Nay, master, let me define a mere scholar : I
heard a courtier once define a mere scholar to be *animal scabiosum,*
that is, a living creature that is troubled with the itch; or a mere
scholar is a creature that can strike fire in the morning at his tinder-
box, put on a pair of lined slippers, sit reasoning till dinner, and then
go to his meat when the bell rings, one that hath a peculiar gift in a
cough, and a licence to spit : or if you will have him defined by nega-
tives, he is one that cannot make a good leg; one that cannot eat a
mess of broth cleanly; one that cannot ride a horse without spur-
galling; one that cannot salute a woman, and look on her directly......
Had you invited him to dinner, at your table, and have put the carving
of a capon upon him, you should have seen him handle the knife so
foolishly, then run through a jury of faces, then wagging his head, and
showing his teeth in familiarity, venture upon it with the same method

that he was wont to untruss an apple-pie, or tyrannize an egg and butter: then would I have applied him all dinner-time with clean trenchers, clean trenchers; and still when he got a good bit of meat, I would have taken it from him, by giving him a clean trencher, and so have served him in kindness.'

p. 405. THOMAS HOBSON, of Cambridge, carrier; and OLD HOB-SON the merrie *Londoner.*

In the Aldermen's Parlour, in the Guildhall at Cambridge, is an equestrian painting of Hobson in riding-cloak and ruff, 'Mr Hobson, 1620.' Mr Elijah Johnson, of Trinity-street, has an old engraving, 'Mr Hobson obijt ano 1630 vixit annos 86.

> 'Laugh not to see so plaine a Man in print,
> The Shadow's homley yet ther's something in't,
> Witnes the Bagg he wear's (though seeming poore)
> The fertile Mother of a thousand more:
> He was a thriueing Man through lawfull gaine,
> And wealthy grew by warrantable paine ;
> Than laugh at them that spend not them that gather,
> Like thrueing sonnes of such a thrifty Father.'
> Published by W. Richardson, Castle Street, Leicester Fields.

Thomas (not Tobias) Hobson was born about 1544, probably in Herts. His father (who bequeathed to him 8 horses and a nag) settled in Cambridge in 1561, purchasing the freedom of the town. In 1604 T. H. contributed 50*l.*, a considerable sum, to the loan to the king. He was well known in 1617 when a 4to. tract was published with the title 'Hobson's *Horse Load of Letters or President for Epistles of Busi-ness.*' In 1623 he was summoned for contempt of orders of the Lords of the Council relative to thatched houses and the number of inmates. In 1626 he gave a large Bible to S. Benet's church, where he was after-wards buried. In 1628 he gave land for the Spinning-House, or 'Hobson's *Workhouse.*'

He had considerable property in land, and one of his daughters was married to Sir Symon Clarke, Knt. and Bart. He left a trust for the perpetual maintenance of the *conduit* which bears his name. His saddle and bridle were shewn in the town hall in this century.

Till the close of the 18th there was a sign of the *Old Hobson* to-wards the N. W. of Mill-lane. His house and stables are said to have been in the S. W. of Peas Hill. The portrait mentioned in the *Spec-tator* was removed from his London inn to Cambridge, when it passed into the hands of Mr Swann in Hobson *street.* (Cooper's *Annals,* III. 230—237.)

Milton's two grim sonnets on this worthy are well known.

' *On the University Carrier, who sickened in the time of vacancy, being forbid to go to London, by reason of the plague,* [1630].

Here lies old *Hobson.* Death hath broke his girt,
And here alas! hath laid him in the dirt;
Or else the ways being foul, twenty to one,
He is here stuck in a slough, and overthrown.
'Twas such a shifter, that, if truth was known
Death was half glad when he had got him down;
For he had any time this ten year full
Dodged with him betwixt *Cambridge* and the *Bull.*
And surely Death could never have prevailed,
Had not his weekly course of carriage failed;
But lately finding him so long at home,
And thinking now his journey's end was come,
And that he had ta'en up his latest inn,
In the kind office of a chamberlin
Shewed him his room where he must lodge that night,
Pulled off his boots and took away the light.
If any ask for him, it shall be said
Hobson has supped, and is newly gone to bed.'

' *Another on the same.*

Here lieth one, who did most clearly prove
That he could never die while he could move;
So hung his destiny, never to rot
While he might still jog on and keep his trot;
Made of sphere-metal, never to decay
Until his revolution was at stay.
Time numbers motion,—yet without a crime
'Gainst old Truth—motion numbered out his time;
And, like an engine moved with wheel and weight,
His principles being ceased, he ended straight.
Rest, that gives all men life, gave him his death,
And too much breathing put him out of breath;
Nor were it contradiction to affirm
Too long vacation hastened on his term.
Merely to drive the time away he sickened,
Fainted and died, nor would with all be quickened.
"Nay," quoth he, on his swooning bed outstretched,
"If I mayn't carry, sure I'll ne'er be fetched,
But vow, though the cross doctors all stood hearers,
For one carrier put down to make six bearers."
Ease was his chief disease, and, to judge right,
He died for heaviness that his cart went light.
His leisure told him that his time was come,
And lack of load made his life burdensome,
That even to his last breath—there be that say't—
As he were prest to death, he cried: more weight!

But, had his doings lasted as they were,
He had been an immortal carrier.
Obedient to the moon he spent his date
In course reciprocal, and had his fate
Linked to the mutual flowing of the seas,
Yet—strange to think!—his wain was his increase.
His letters are delivered all and gone,
Only remains this superscription.'

We may compare with this the character of a *A Carryer* in Earle's *Microcosmographi* (§ 15, as reprinted by Mr Arber) which was published about two years before Hobson's death, '*A Carryer* Is his own Hackneyman, for hee lets himself out to trauell as well as his horses. Hee is the ordinarie Embassador betweene Friend and Friend, and brings rich Presents to the one but neuer returnes anye backe againe. He is no vnletter'd man, though in shew simple; for questionlesse, hee has much in his Budget which hee can vtter too in fit time and place; Hee is the Vault in Gloster Church, that conueyes Whispers at a distance; for hee takes the sound out of your mouth at Yorke, and makes it bee heard as farre as London. Hee is the young Students ioy and expectation, and the most accepted guest, to whom they lend a willing hand to discharge him of his burthen. His first greeting is, Your Friends are well; then in a piece of Gold deliuers their Blessing. You would thinke him a Churlish blunt fellow, but they find in him manye tokens of humanitie. He is a great afflicter of the High-way, and beates them out of mesure, which iniury is somtimes reuenged by the Purse-taker; and then the Voyage miscaries. No man domineers more in his Inne, nor cals his Host vnreuerently with more presumption, and this arrogance proceeds out of the strength of his Horses. He forgets not his load when he takes his ease, for he is drunke commonly before he goes to bed. He is like the Prodigall child, still packing away, and still returning againe. But let him passe.'

The origin of the saying 'Hobson's *Choice*,' which (like '*cassianum illud cui bono* fuerit?') has somewhat lost in the application, is thus clearly defined by *Vincent Bourne* and by *Steele* in the *Spectator*.

'*Hobsoni Lex.*

Complures (ita, Granta, refers) Hobsonus alebat
    In stabulo longo, quos locitaret, equos;
Hac lege, ut foribus staret qui proximus, ille
    Susciperet primas, solus et ille, uices.
Aut hunc, aut nullum—sua pars sit cuique laboris;
    Aut hunc, aut nullum—sit sua cuique quies.
Condicio obtinuit, nulli uiolanda togato;
    Proximus hic foribus, proximus esto uiae.

Optio tam prudens cur non huc usque retenta est?
Tam bona cur umquam lex abolenda fuit?
Hobsoni ueterem normam reuocare memento;
Tuque iterum Hobsoni, Granta, uidebis equos.'

V. B.

The conclusion of the *Spectator* for *Tuesday, October* 14, 1712, No. 509, runs as follows :

'I shall conclude this discourse with an explanation of a proverb, which by vulgar error is taken and used when a man is reduced to an extremity, whereas the propriety of the maxim is to use it when you would say there is plenty, but you must make such a choice as not to hurt another who is to come after you.

'Mr Tobias[1] Hobson, from whom we have the expression, was a very honourable man, for I shall ever call the man so who gets an estate honestly. Mr Tobias Hobson was a carrier ; and, being a man of great abilities and invention, and one who saw where there might good profit arise, though the duller men overlooked it ; this ingenious man was the first in this island who let out hackney horses. He lived in Cambridge ; and observing that the scholars rid hard, his manner was to keep a large stable of horses, with boots, bridles, and whips, to furnish the gentlemen at once, without going from college to college to borrow, as they have done since the death of this worthy man. I say, Mr Hobson kept a stable of forty good cattle, always ready and fit for travelling ; but when a man came for a horse, he was led into the stable, where there was always great choice, but he obliged him to take the horse which stood next to the stable-door ; so that every customer was alike well served according to his chance, and every horse ridden with the same justice : from whence it became a proverb, when what ought to be your election was forced upon you, to say, "Hobson's choice." This memorable man stands drawn in fresco at an inn (which he used) in Bishopsgate Street, with an hundred-pound bag under his arm, with this inscription upon the said bag :

"The fruitful mother of a hundred more."

'Whatever tradesmen will try the experiment, and begin the day after you publish this my discourse, to treat all his customers all alike, and all reasonably and honestly, I will ensure him the same success.

'I am, Sir, your loving friend,

'HEZEKIAH THRIFTY.

T.'

---

[1] This should have been *Thomas.*

The following anecdote has been reprinted by Mr Halliwell from *England's Witty and Ingenious Jester.* 12mo. London, 1692, p. 11.

'A young maiden coming from Cambridge to *London* to seek for a service along with old *Hobson* the carrier, being upon the road, he, among other questions, ask'd her name ; she made answer it was *Joan.* "Oh dear, *Joan,*" says he "you'll never get a place in *London* with such a coarse name. Your name must be *Precilla,* for that's a fine name."'

'Of plainest household-stuff
Must homely *Joan* be fashioned.'

says Charles Lamb.

Hobson is among the *dramatis personae* of the second part of '*If You Know Not Me, You Know Nobody, or The Troubles of Queene Elizabeth,*' a Comedy, by T. Heywood of Peterhouse, 4to. 1632.

It is said that *Hobson* used to tell the *Cambridge* scholars that they would get to *London* in time if they did not ride too fast. This is like the dry humour of his *namesake* 'OLD HOBSON, the merry Londoner.' who died in 1581, and was buried in St Mildred's Church in the Poultry, and whose '*Pleasant Conceits,* full of humorous discourses, and wittie *merriments, whereat the quickest wits* may laugh, and the wiser sort take pleasure,' were published by *Richard Johnson,* author of *The Nine Worthies of London,* early in the 17th century. He *must not* of course *be confounded* with our carrier ; but I reprint here two anecdotes relating to our neighbourhood from an imperfect copy of a unique black-letter edition in my own possession. Leaf c 2 *b,* line 8, § 22, '*Of Master Hobson's riding to Sturbridge Faire.* Master *Hobson* on a time in companie of one of his neighbours, rode from *London* towards *Sturbridge* faire, so the first night of their iourney they lodged at *Ware,* in an Inne where great store of company was, and in the morning when euery man made him ready to ride, and some were on horsebacke setting forward, the Citizen, his neighbour, found him sitting at the Inne gate booted and spurd, in a browne studie, to whom hee said, for shame, *M. Hobson,* why sit you heere, why doe you not make your selfe ready to horsbacke, that we may set forward with company? *M. Hobson* replied in this manner, I tarry (quoth he) for a good cause : for what cause, quoth [p. c 3] his neighbour : marry, quoth *M. Hobson,* here be so many horses, that I cannot tell which is mine owne, and I know well, when euery man is ridden and gone, the horse that remaineth behind, must needs be mine.'

23. '*How Master Hobson found a Farmer's purse.*—There was a Farmer that lost fortie pounds betwixt *Cambridge* and *London,* and

being so great a summe, hee made a proclamation in all market townes thereabout, that whosoeuer had found forty and fiue pounds, should haue the fiue pounds for his labour for finding it, and therefore he put in the fiue pound more than was lost: it was *M. Hobson's* fortune to finde the same summe of forty pounds, and brought the same to the Bayliffe of *Ware* and required the 5 pounds for his pains, as it was proclaimed: when the country Farmer vnderstood this, and that he must needs pay fiue pounds for the finding, hee said, that there was in the purse fiue and forty pounds, and so would he haue his mony and fiue pounds [p. c 3 (*b*)] ouer: so long they stroue, that the matter was brought before a Justice of peace, which was then one *M. Fleetwood,* who after was the Recorder of London: but when *M. Fleetwood* vnderstood by the Bailiff, that the Proclamation was made for a purse of fiue and forty pound, hee demanded where it was, here quoth the Baily, and gaue it him: It is iust fortie pound said *M. Fleetwood;* yes truly (quoth the Bailiffe): here *M. Hobson,*. said *M. Fleetwood,* take you this mony for it is your owne, and if you chance to finde a purse of fiue and forty pound, bring it to this honest Farmer. That is mine, quoth the Farmer, for I lost iust forty pound: you speake too late (quoth *M. Fleetwood*). Thus the Farmer lost the money, and *M. Hobson* had it according to iustice.'

p. 405. It was not uncommon to premise 'God willing' in advertisements of stage-coaches or waggons. Grose in his *Classical Dictionary of the Vulgar Tongue,* ed. 3. 1796, gives '*God Permit*' as the cant name for a stage-coach. This pious formula became a mere equivalent for 'unless any circumstance prevents.' So that we hear of one Scotch coach which was advertised to run six times a week with that provision, but twice *whether or no.*

p. 408. Professor Mayor reminds me that oil-lamps are still used in the old courts of St John's, where, amid all the woodwork, gas on the staircases would be dangerous. Tapers have only lately been abandoned in the chapel of Trinity College, and are still used at Peterhouse.

p. 409. Frances Dawes, bursar of Peterhouse, used to pay 18*s.* half-yearly to Tho. Froggatt for lighting the LAMP on his staircase in 1771.

p. 410. The STEWARD, *seneschallus,* was regularly a *senior fellow.* —M.

p. 412. It is recorded that when Gray was at Pembroke, his 'chamber windows were ever ornamented with mignonette or other sweet-scented herbs and flowers, elegantly planted in china vases, as were other parts of his room, in which the utmost neatness and delicacy prevailed, as well as in his person.' Appendix on Gray's Works from the copy of the 4to ed. of Mason's *Memoirs*, which belonged to G. Steevens and S. Rogers, IV. 133. It was perhaps to gratify his taste for flowers that iron bars were fixed outside his windows at Peterhouse to support Ἀδώνιδος κῆπους. Another note of III. 148 tells how the noisy fellow-commoners on his staircase 'knowing Mr Gray had a dread of fire, had rope-ladders in his chamber; [His letter to Wharton ordering one of a certain length is extant;] they alarmed him in the middle of the night with the cry of fire, in hope of seeing him make use of them from his window in the middle story of the new building.' The tradition which tells how they prepared a tub of water to receive him at the foot of the ladder, says that he lodged on the *second* floor. This corresponds best also with the length of his ladder. *T. Gray* was born in 1716; 1734 entered pensioner at Peterhouse; 1742 returns to Cambridge; 1756 migrates to Pembroke-hall; 1768 Prof. of Modern History; 1769 Installation Ode to Duke of Grafton. Dies July 30, 1770.

p. 432. 'A racketty scholar calling for a glass of CLARET was told by his physician that it was not good for his gout. "What, my old friend claret? Nay, give it me; for in spite of every doctor in the land, it shall never be said that I forsook my friend for my enemy."' Cambridge *Coffee-house Jest* of the 17th century. In '*Some Observations* upon the *Answer* to an enquiry into the grounds and occasion of the *Contempt of the Clergy*' (cir. 1671, ed. 7, 1705), by J. Echard, *claret* is mentioned (p. 124), and '*Florence, Champagne, Frontiniack, Burdeaux, Languedoc, Flascon de vin, vin de Bourgongne, vin de Pressorage, vin Pare, vin de Parole* and *Taffalette.*' (p. 127.)

p. 442. Dec. 1556. ' James the carpenter's boy for stealinge owte of the Vicechancellor's [Dr A. Perne's] stodye, was BEATEN in the hall at Peterhouse, by Mr Bronsted the butler, Robert the Vicechancellor's man, and the scholers of the house.' Cooper's *Annals*, II. 3.

p. 452. On taking these portraits of *J. Gordon* out of their frames, the titles TERM TIME and NON TERM appeared, *Wm. Mason, del.* JEMMY died Sept. 16, 1815. See Hone's *Every-Day Book*, I. col. 1294. The pictures are now in the Camb. Free Library; where also in vol. B. 13. 52, a piece of high-flown abuse of his composition, in a fly-sheet without date, entitled *Description of an Attorney's Office, by James Gordon.*

p. 454. *Saccarii.* I should suppose that this is a misprint for SCACCARII or *Exchequer;* from the Persian word for *king*, which appears in the term of chess, *check-mate*, which means literally *le roy est mort.* See Du Cange.

L. B. E. **44**

p. 456. Prof. Mayor refers to similar bills of the Bacons, pupils of Whitgift, printed by Dr Maitland in *Brit. Mag.*, reprinted by *Spedding.*

p. 485. ACADEMICAL DRESS.

John Foxe in his account of Tho. Garret (*Actes and Monuments*, s. anno 1540,) relates how a clerk flying from the hue and cry cast off his *hood* and his *gown*, and borrowed 'a *sleeved coat* of fine clothe in graine,' but could find no *cap* 'but priestlike such as his own was.'

p. 491. The 10th of the *Regulations of Discipline, &c. for the Students at* Durham (C. Thorp, Warden) is, that 'The Academical Dress is always to be worn in public, except

1. On the River; and then the Cap and Gown must be worn down to the boat-house. In the boat, either the Academical Cap, or a boating cap may be used, but no hat.

2. In going to a gentleman's house more than two miles distant from *Durham;* and of this notice must always be given beforehand, by entry in the Butler's Book.' &c.

p. 498. A Table of Academical HOODS, by J. W. G. Gutch, M. R. C. S. L., is given in *Notes and Queries*, 2nd S. VI. 211, and Supplement, VI. 258, 337; VII. 74, 384; VIII. 75a.; cp. also IV. 36. 3rd S. VI. 481, 542. See also an interesting paper by H. P. D., 3rd S. X. 129—131.

In S. Clark's *Martyrologie* (Lives of 32 English Divines, ed. 3, 1677, p. 125) Dr Tho. Taylor is represented with a lace-edged skullcap, small ruff, and over his M.A. gown a HOOD SQUARED as it has been said. However I feel some doubt as to this last statement. Dr Taylor was of Christ Coll. Camb., and died in 1632. The portraits of Aquinas, Zuinglius, J. Rainold, A. Willet in S. Clark's *Marrow of Ecclesiastical History* (pp. 108, 147, 436, 448 ed. 2), exhibit some remarkable types of *hoods:—caps* passim.

In the Chapter Library at Durham is an oil-painting of the Reverend Sir *Geo. Wheler,* knight, 1714. He is depicted in a gown and hood; the latter coming down full to a peak in front and being edged with red. My friend, to whom I am indebted for the notice of this picture, describes the hood as being like that of an Oxford M.A. Sir G. Wheler (the famous traveller, who was a prebendary of Durham) had been a commoner of Lincoln, Oxon.; presented a collection of MSS. to that University; was created M.A. Mar. 26, 1683; and D.D. by diploma May 18, 1702. Died Feb. 18, 1723—4.

p. 501. Foxe in his *Actes and Monuments*, writing of some transactions in the year 1177, speaks of a bishop wearing *casule, chimer* and *rochet* together. The word CHIMERE is connected with the Italian *simarra.* The *doctor's cope* was in shape like the old English *cappa nigra.*

p. 516.

| *The Grounds and Occasions of the* Contempt *of the* Clergy *and* Religion, 1670. | *Speculum Crape-Gownorum:* or a *Looking-Glass* for the *Young Academicks,* 1682. |

[p. 20]. 'And as some think, two or three years continuance in the University, to be time sufficient for being very great Instruments in the Church, so others we have so moderate, as to count that a solemn admission and a formal paying of Colledge-Detriments, without the trouble of Philosophical Discourses, Disputations, and the like, are Virtues that will influence as far as *Newcastle,* and improve, though at never such a distance.

'So strangely possessed are People in general, with the easiness and small Preparations that are requisite to the Undertaking of the Ministry, that, whereas in other Professions they plainly see what considerate time is spent, before they have any hope of arriving to skill enough to practice, with any confidence, what they have design'd, yet to preach to ordinary People, and [p. 21] govern a Country-Parish, is usually judg'd such an easie performance, that any body counts himself fit for the Employment. We find very few so unreasonably confident of their parts, as to profess either *Law,* or *Physick,* without either a considerable continuance in some of the *Inns of Courts,* or

[p. 4]. 'Now as there are some who think that Two or Three years continuance at the University, to be time sufficient to fit a young man for being a great Instrument in the Church, so others we have so moderate, as to believe, that a solemn admission, and the paying Colledge-Duties (without the trouble of Philosophical Discourses and Disputations and the like) are virtues that will influence as far as *Cumberland,* and improve though it be as far as St *Michael's* Mount. So strangely are some People possessed, with the easiness and the small preparations required for the undertaking of the Ministry, that though in other Professions they plainly see what considerable time is spent by young Students, before they have any hopes of attaining to experience and knowledge enough to practice; yet to preach to ordinary People, and govern a Country Flock, is usually deem'd such an easie Task, that every one thinks himself fit for the employment;

an industrious search in Herbs, Anatomy, Chymistry, and the like, unless it be only to make a Bond ; or give a Glyster. But as for the knack of Preaching, as they call it, that is such a very easie attain-ment, that he is counted dull to purpose that is not able at a very small warning, to fasten upon any Text of Scripture; and to tear and tumble it till the Glass be out. Many I know very well are forced to discontinue, having neither stock of their own, nor Friends to main-tain them in the University. But, whereas a Man's Profession and Employment in this World, is very much in his own, or in the Choice of such who are most nearly concern'd for him : He therefore that foresees that he is not likely to have the advantage of a continued education, he had much better commit himself to an approved-of Cobbler or Tinker, wherein he may be duly respected according to [p. 22] his Office and condition of Life, than to be only a dises-teemed *Pettifogger* or *Empyrick* in Divinity.'

'and that as for the knack of Preaching, as they call it, it is a perfection so easily at-tained, that he is esteemed a Dunce indeed, that is not able at a very small Warning, to fasten upon any Text of Scripture, and to teize and tumble it for an hour, till the Glass be fairly run out, without the Clerks jogging.

' Though indeed a man had better commit himself to the Instruction and Teaching of an approved Cob-ler or Tinker, whereby he may be duly respected according to his Art and condition of Life, than to live only a disesteem'd Emperick in Divinity.'

p. 518. LEVITES. Eachard in *Some Observations upon the Answer to an Enquiry into the Grounds and Occasion of the Contempt of the Clergy* (about 1671) ed. 7, 1705, p. 135, speaking of the attempts at humour at the expense of the clergy, remarks, ' But if a *Clergy-man* chance to meet an *Old Testament Wit*, and that he sets into his *Tricks* and *Drollery's ;* then he must expect to be called *Levite*. And that you may not think his Fancy to be stinted, sometimes he calls him *Tribe*, some-times *Leviticus*, and for variety sake, at other times *Numbers*.' Foxe calls Vincent of Saragossa a *Levite*, meaning a *Deacon*.

pp. 520, 521. Dr JOHN OWEN, Cromwell's Vicechancellor of Oxford, used to go (says A. Wood in his *Athenae Oxon.*) ' in quirpo like a young scholar with powdered hair, snake bone band-strings, with very large tassels, a large set of ribbons at his knees, and Spanish leather boots, with large lawn tops, and his hat mostly cocked.' (See Hudibras in Johnson, and Howell's Letters, I. 4. 28, p. 180.—M.)

> *Host.* CUERPO! what's that?
> *Tip.* Light skipping hose and doublet,
> The horse-boy's garb! poor blank and half-blank.
>   B. JONSON, *New Inn*, II. 5.

p. 524. It was, I suppose, by inadvertency that the author of *Gradus ad Cantabrigiam* did not enumerate *Clare Hall, Trin. Hall, S. Cath. Hall*, and *Jesus Coll.*, among the societies which then wore the ugly UNDERGRADUATE'S GOWN. Mr Richard Shilleto thus writes to me : 'July 24, 1873... When I first knew *Cambridge*, the "curtain" was worn by Undergraduate Scholars, Pensioners and Sizars of all Colleges, with the exception of *Trinity, King's, Peterhouse, Queens'*, and scholars on certain foundations at *S. John's* and *Jesus*. Whether these scholars wear now the ordinary college gown or retain the older gown—like the King's, made of cloth—I know not. The four colleges have still the same as they had before. *Downing* had no pensioner's gown, the society till comparatively late times admitting only Fellow-commoners.

'*Pet.* and *Qu.* wore the B.A. gown less the strings. You have heard, I dare say, the tailor's intentional or accidental joke, who to an aspiring freshman of our college (or *Queens'*) asking for the ornamental appendage, replied, "strings, Sir, come by degrees." It was attributed to *Law*, father of *Law*, senior wrangler, 1826, whose shop was in *Trin.* Street, near to *Foster's* Bank. He togged me when I assumed the *libera toga.*

'*Corpus* men (or as we, not to their entire satisfaction, still continued to dub them, *Benet Hall* men) on a petition to the governing body of their Society, impetrated their present gown, I think—but am not certain—in the year 1834. The universal adoption of a distinctive gown for each of all other colleges which had hitherto sported the "curtain," dates from October, 1835. I can state this positively.'

I have a printed copy of rhymes on *The New* Caius *Undergraduate's Gown.*

p. 535. POSITION OF THE CELEBRANT. There are in Durham Cathedral two faldstools, placed inside the Sanctuary, for the Deacon and Subdeacon in their old ritual position in front of the Altar and facing east. If not actually given by bishop Cosin, they are of that date, and are still used.

Mr T. M. Fallow of St John's, to whom I am obliged for the above statement, has put before me the following extracts from two attempts made in the last century at Arianizing the Book of Common Prayer. They are curious as exhibiting the sense put upon our rubric by some nonconformists of the time. The first is from *The Liturgy of the Church of England Reduc'd nearer to the Primitive Standard. Humbly Propos'd to Publick Consideration.* By William Whiston, *M.A.* (see above, p. 563), 1713. [Reprinted in Hall's *Fragmenta Liturgica,* Vol. III.] Instead of our rubrics before *the Collect* for Purity, Whiston (whose father had been a non-juror, cp. p. 696) proposes the following :

'¶ *The Altar at the Communion-time having a fair white linen cloth upon it, shall stand in the body of the Church, or in the Chancel, where Morning and Evening Prayer are appointed to be said. And the Priest standing humbly before the same, shall say the Collect following, the People also kneeling.*

Note. *That no part of this Service is ever to be used but when there is a Communion.*'

Whiston keeps the rubric immediately before the Prayer of Consecration, *verbatim,* exactly as it stands in the Book of Common Prayer.

The other rubric is from *The Book of Common Prayer, compiled for the use of the* English *Church, at* Dunkirk, *printed by* Van Schelle, *and Compagn.,* Soubisse-street, No. 202. 1791 [Reprinted in Hall's *Fragmenta Liturgica,* Vol. VII.], in which the rubrics generally are abbreviated from our authorized form. That before the (altered) Prayer of Consecration runs as follows :

'¶ *Then the Minister, standing before the Table, shall say the Prayer following.*'

p. 538. RITUAL TESTIMONY OF PICTURES. The frontispiece of a copy of Wheatly's *Rational Illustration of the Book of Common Prayer,* ed. 3, folio, 1720, depicts a congregation kneeling on the pavement with their faces toward the Holy Table, which stands against the wall, and is railed in. Upon it are two flagons, two chalices, a paten containing bread in diagonal cubes, apparently not quite severed. The alms-dish, containing money, stands at the south, and the other vessels (with the exception of the paten with bread) are towards that end of the table, which has not even a cloth to cover it. The priest, before whom the book lies open, stands at the north end facing southward. He wears surplice and hood. Above his head, among clouds and seraphim, stands the Great High Priest before the *sublime in caelis Altare.* He stands immediately above the earthly minister, and looks in the same direction, but the Altar is turned so as to have its *length or side*, not the end, before Him. Charles Wheatly's own view was that as 'Bishop *Beveridge* has shewn [*Pandect.* II. 76, § 15], wherever in the antient Liturgies, the Minister is directed to stand before the Altar, the Northside of it is always meant.' *Rational Illustration*, ch. VI. § 1. And *Northside* Wheatly seems to have identified with *north end*.

At the beginning of bishop Ant. Sparrow's *Rationale of the Book of Common Prayer*, 1684, reprinted by Parker in 1839, the saying of the litany is shewn in a view similar to that in my prayer-book mentioned above (p. 537), excepting that the view is taken from the S. E. of the Altar, so as to shew the faces and not the backs of priest and people. Also the priest kneels at a regular fald-stool, and wears a very long plain surplice: the book lies open in the midst of the altar for the use of one standing before it. There is another book for the litany. The altar stands apparently on three steps, near the west end of the chancel foot pace. This frontispiece is evidently a reproduction of that to the editions of 1668, 1676, 1704, which contain also (beside portraits of Hooker, Andrews and Overall) a curious representation of the delivery of a sermon; the preacher wears a surplice with a stole or scarf, but in 1704 he has a black gown and bands.

In *Hierurgia Anglicana* is a lithograph taken from an illustration of *Domus Carthusiana*, 1677; this corresponds very nearly with the picture in the Prayer-book of the same period (p. 537), excepting that in the former instead of a hassock there is a litany-desk and cushion, the altar stands on five steps instead of two, and the book is at the end and upon an inclined plane or desk. There is a copy of Sam. Herne's *Domus Carth.* in the Univ. Library, Ll. (58) 8. 21.

In our University Library [G. (46) 1. 13] is a Prayer Book, *London*, printed by *Charles Bill* and the Executors of *Tho. Newcomb*, 1693, with a frontispiece (*R. White, sculp.*) of what it calls a *Domus Orationis*, with the door open, exhibiting within an Altar with a large dish in the centre, and a flagon on either side, the office-book resting on a cushion, open and almost entirely eastwards, as arranged for a priest standing in front, three parts to the east. It is quite at the north part of the side.

'A New Exposition On the Book of Common Prayer, &c., by *John Veneer*, Rector of St Andrew's in *Chichester*, London, C. Rivington, 1727,' has a frontispiece with a congregation kneeling before the altar-rails. A priest in band, cassock, and gown, reads from the Prayer-book in a desk to the west of the congregation. On the midst of the Altar stands a handsomely bound book, upright on a cushion before the middle of the altar-piece, no doubt the Bible and Prayer-book bound together, which used to be thus placed in St John's College Chapel, according to Laud's injunction. Engraved by G. Vdr. Gucht.

In editions of Burnet's *Abridgement of the History of the Reforma-tion*, London, Ric. Chiswell, 1782 and 1783, in one compartment of the first plate, king (? Edward) kneels at the Altar-rails, a bishop at the north end. On it are two chalices, a large alms-dish leaning against the wall, no paten visible, a small square book (or a pall) leans against the flagon ; but quite out of the king's reach, and in the middle of the western part.

Since the greater part of this and the preceding note were sent to the press, the Bishop of Lincoln has drawn attention, in the sixth of his *Twelve Addresses* delivered at his Visitation of the Cathedral and Diocese of *Lincoln* in the year 1873, *Rivingtons*, and *Williamson*, Lincoln, p. 110, to another rubric, that of the *Nonjurors' Prayer Book*, 1718. (Hall's *Fragmenta Liturgica*, Vol. v.)

'Note, *that whenever in this office the Priest is directed* to turn to the *Altar*,' [as he is in the Prayer of Consecration] '*or to stand or kneel* before it *or* with his face towards it, *it is always meant that he should stand or kneel* on the North side thereof.'

If however this be taken strictly, it would seem to imply that the nonjurors stood at the North side to order the Bread and Wine.

The evidence which has been given in the foregoing pages is neither exhaustive nor conclusive : and if it is of any interest to the antiquarian, it does not immediately affect the question of obedience.

INDEX.

Goad, Roger (King's), 351, 352, 362, 461, 506
— , Mrs, 352
'Gobrias,' 627
Goddard, P. S. (Clare), 608
Godfrey, Sir Edmundbury, 633
Godfrey, T. (waggoner), 405
Godstow, 172
'God-willing,' 688
Gogmagog hills, 168, 181, 223, 260, 402, 670
Goldsmith, O. (T. C. D.), 'Double Transformation,' 399
'*Golgotha*,' 43, 309
'gomers,' 310
Gooch, T. (Cai.), 44, 607, 611, 614, 627
Goode, W. (Tr. H.), 448
'Goodman,' 627
Goodwin, J., 670, 674
Goodwin, T., 520, 571 n.
Goose, mother, 153
Gordon, Jemmy, 447—453, 689
Gordon, J. (Emm.), 335
gorget, 462
Gosnal, ? Lionel (Pet.), 118
Gostlin, J. (Cai.), 410, 479
gotch (beer-jug), 611
gothick, 234, 391, 396, 412
Gough, R. (Corpus), 171
Gower, Hum. (Joh.), 19, ?229, 646
gowns, 36, 67, 68, 102, 273, 275, 310, 375, 377, 426, 454, 456, 482—485, 512—530, 693
grace-cup, 655
'Gradus' (Who's the Dupe?), 307, 404, 473
'Gradus ad Cantabrigiam,' 378, 439, 441—446, 647, 648, 651
Grafton, duke of (Pet.), 65, 77
grammar, curious ceremony of incepting, 248
Grant or Cham, see 'Cham'
Grant, C. (Magd.), 596
Grant, R. (Magd.), 173, 176
Grantchester, 173, 176
Gray, T. (Pet. and Pemb.), 63, 64, 78, 127, 187, 390, 633, 655, 689
—— parodied, 134, 159
great horse, 163, 167, 547—550
Great Tom, 310

Grecian coffee-house, 139
Greeks visit the University, 319—325
Greek's coffee-house, 141, 199
Green, J., bp of Linc. (Joh. and Corpus), 72, 429, 437, 606, 608, 619, 624, 625, 627, 632
Greene, Man. (Mus. D.), 269, 276
Greene, T. (Corpus), 40, 73, 224, 625
Greenwood, R. H. (Trin.), 591
Gregory, Dav. (Ch. Ch.), 549
Gregory, H. (Ch. Ch.), 312
Grenville, G., lord Lansdowne (Trin.), 94
Grey, Zech. (Tr. H.), 628
'greyhounds,' 679
Grief (glazier), 453
Griffin, E. (U. S. A.), 435
griffin's head, 119
Grigg, W. (Clare), 52, 607
Grizzle-wig, 472, 473, 528
groats, 248, 253
Grose, 'capt.' F., 444
groves, 364, 368, 394
Grubb, J. (Ch. Ch.), 308
'Guardian' (a play), 192
Guardian (essays), 194, 298, 401
Guibbons, see 'Gibbons'
'*Guide to the Companion*,' 387
Gunning, H. (Chr.), 409
Gunning, Pet. (Clare), 246
Gutch's 'Collectanea,' 167, 548, 568
Gwynne, Nell, 11
gymnastics, 166
Gynewell, J., bp of Lincoln, 423

Hacket, J. (Joh.), 669
hackney-coaches, 279, 406
Hadley's coffee-house, 389
'haggard,' 671
Hailstone, J. (Trin.), 85
Hale, sir Matt. (Magd. H.), 19
Hall, A. (mayor), 427
Hall, N. (Wadh.), 297
Hallifax, S. (Jes.), 335
halls, 151, 388
Halywell Mill, 192
Hambledon cricket club, 667
Hamilton's coffee-house, 375
Hamlet, ghost, 592

f

ERRATA.

page	line	from	for	read
30	8	top	second	sour'd
40	15	...	Lang	Long
94	15	...	in 1667	about 1677
133	5	bottom		*add* loose and untied
232	16	top	optima	optimè
233	9	...	Idem	Idea
242	11	bottom	Gaudy	Gandy, of King's
247	15	top		[I have not succeeded in discovering this piece of Duport's]
309	10	bottom	*St Mary's Golgotha*	*St Mary's, Golgotha*
313	10	...	Crackenode	Clayton Cracherode
317	10	...	Van der Hwyden	Van der Heyden
324	6	...	Lucas	Lucar
444	11	...	*feasts*	*Feasts*
457	note 2		See notes	See *Hone's* Year Book, 597—608
458	12	...	Walcote	Walcott
573	5	top	Action	Account
588	7	bottom	Basketh	Baskett
591	17	top	Bollond	Bolland
598	15	...	Tell	Fell
606	4	bottom	Thomas Green	John Green

ADDITIONAL NOTE.

(P. 538.)

Mr Wright, who was elected fellow of *Balliol* in 1784, has left on record that the Master of his college, Dr *Theophilus Leigh*, not only bowed to the Altar on entering and leaving the college chapel; but at his country living of Huntspill (1767—1785), dio. Bath and Wells, he always wore *a distinctive vestment* at Holy Communion, for he was a constant resident at his rectory in vacation time.

CAMBRIDGE: PRINTED BY C. J. CLAY, M.A. AT THE UNIVERSITY PRESS.

To avoid fine, this book should be returned on
or before the date last stamped below

Ingram Content Group UK Ltd.
Milton Keynes UK
UKHW022047250523
422376UK00005B/79

9 781019 151723